Fodor's

THE BEST OF ITALY

D1559345

Welcome to Italy

Rome, Florence, and Venice are home to awe-inspiring art and architecture, iconic museums, and stunning historical ruins—as well as some of the world's best food, wine, and shopping. Also beckoning are the sun-kissed olive groves and vineyards, charming hill towns, and atmospheric castles, monasteries, and farmhouses of the Tuscan and Umbrian countryside. As you plan your travels to Italy, please confirm that places are still open and let us know when we need to make updates by writing to us at: editors@fodors.com.

TOP REASONS TO GO

★ **Food:** Italy is a pasta lover's paradise, but don't forget the pizza and the gelato.

★ **Romance:** Whether you're strolling atmospheric Venice or sipping wine, Italy enchants.

★ **History:** The ruins of ancient Rome and the leaning tower of Pisa breathe antiquity.

★ **Art:** The big hitters—Botticelli, Michelangelo, Raphael, Caravaggio, and more.

★ **Shopping:** Few things say quality or style like "made in Italy."

★ **Stunning landscapes:** Tuscany, Umbria, the Cinque Terre, to name just a few.

Contents

1 **EXPERIENCE THE BEST OF ITALY** ... 6
   14 Ultimate Experiences............ 8
   What's Where 14
   Italy Today....................... 16
   Best Ancient Sites in Rome........ 18
   Best Museums in Rome 20
   Architectural
   Wonders in Venice................ 22
   10 Best Museums in Florence....... 24
   Best Hilltop Villages in
   Tuscany and Umbria 26
   What to Watch and Read.......... 28
   Making the Most of Your Euros 30

2 **TRAVEL SMART** 31
   Know Before You Go 32
   Getting Here and Around 34
   Essentials 38
   Great Itineraries 41
   On the Calendar................... 44
   Helpful Italian Phrases 46
   Contacts.......................... 48

3 **ROME** 49
   Welcome to Rome................. 50
   Eat Like a Local in Rome........... 52
   Planning.......................... 54
   Ancient Rome with
   Monti and Celio 58
   The Vatican with Borgo and Prati ... 69
   Piazza Navona, Campo de' Fiori,
   and the Jewish Ghetto 84
   Piazza di Spagna................. 101
   Repubblica and the Quirinale 113
   Villa Borghese and Environs 120
   Trastevere....................... 126
   Aventino and Testaccio........... 132
   Esquilino and Via Appia Antica..... 138

4 **VENICE**......................... 141
   Welcome to Venice 142
   Eating and Drinking
   Well in Venice 144
   Planning......................... 146
   San Marco 151
   Dorsoduro 168
   San Polo and Santa Croce........ 178
   Cannaregio 185
   Castello 193

San Giorgio Maggiore
and Giudecca..................... 201
Islands of the Lagoon 204

5 **NORTHERN ITALY**............... 209
   Welcome to Northern Italy........ 210
   Eating and Drinking Well in the
   Veneto and Friuli–Venezia Giulia ... 212
   Eating and Drinking
   Well in Emilia-Romagna 214
   Planning......................... 216
   Padua 218
   Verona 225
   Vicenza.......................... 231
   Milan............................ 235
   Riomaggiore 267
   Manarola......................... 269
   Corniglia......................... 275
   Vernazza 275
   Monterosso al Mare 277
   Bologna 278
   Ferrara 286
   Ravenna......................... 290

6 **FLORENCE**...................... 295
   Welcome to Florence............. 296
   Planning......................... 299
   Around the Duomo 302
   San Lorenzo 316
   Santa Maria Novella 323
   Santa Croce 331
   The Oltrarno 342
   A Side Trip from Florence......... 348

7 **TUSCANY AND UMBRIA**........ 351
   Welcome to Tuscany and Umbria .. 352
   Eating and Drinking
   Well in Tuscany.................. 354
   Eating and Drinking
   Well in Umbria and the Marches... 356
   Planning......................... 358
   Lucca 360
   Pisa 365
   Chianti 368
   Volterra 375
   San Gimignano................... 377
   Siena............................ 380
   Arezzo........................... 386
   Cortona.......................... 388

Perugia...........................390
Assisi 394
Spoleto..........................401
Orvieto 405

INDEX.........................408

ABOUT OUR WRITERS........416

MAPS

Travel Times by
Train and Ferry.................. 36–37
Rome Metro and
Suburban Railway.................. 62
Ancient Rome with
Monti and Celio 64–65
The Vatican with
Borgo and Prati 70–71
Piazza Navona, Campo de' Fiori,
and the Jewish Ghetto 88–89
Palazzo di Spagna............ 104–105
Repubblica and
the Quirinale................. 116–117
Villa Borghese and Environs .. 122–123
Trastevere.................... 128–129
Aventino and Testaccio....... 134–135
Esquilino and Via Appia Antica..... 139
San Marco 162–163
Dorsoduro 172–173
San Polo and Santa Croce.... 180–181
Cannaregio 188–189
Castello, San Giorgio
Maggiore, and Giudecca 196–197
Islands of the Lagoon 205
Padua........................... 220
Verona 227
Vicenza.......................... 232
Duomo 240–241
Castello, Sempione, Brera,
Sant'Ambrogio,
Fiera and San Siro 246
Quadrilatero 254
Porta Garibaldi and Repubblica 260
Cinque Giornate, Palestro,
Porta Venezia, Buenos Aires,
Loreto, and Bicocca.............. 264

Fodor's Features

Heavens Above:
The Sistine Ceiling 74
Cruising the Grand Canal...............153
Hiking the Cinque Terre..................271
The Duomo.......................................308
Who's Who in Renaissance Art.....335
Assisi's Basilica
di San Francesco 397

Porta Romana, Ticinese,
Navigli, and Tortona............... 268
Bologna 280
Ravenna.......................... 292
Around the Duomo 304–305
San Lorenzo 320–321
Santa Maria Novella 326–327
Santa Croce 332–333
The Oltrarno 344–345
Lucca 362
Pisa............................. 366
Chianti 370
Volterra 375
San Gimignano................... 378
Siena........................... 382
Arezzo.......................... 387
Cortona......................... 389
Perugia.......................... 391
Assisi 395
Spoleto......................... 402

Chapter 1

EXPERIENCE THE BEST OF ITALY

14 ULTIMATE EXPERIENCES

Italy offers terrific experiences that should be on every traveler's list. Here are Fodor's top picks for a memorable trip.

1 Hike the Cinque Terre

Walk the scenic footpaths that connect the five former fishing villages that make up the Cinque Terre; each one appears to hang off the cliffs, allowing for absolutely stunning views of the vineyards above and blue waters below. *(Ch. 5)*

2 People-Watch in Venice

Venice's Piazza San Marco (St. Mark's Square), flanked by the gorgeous Basilica di San Marco, is certainly one of the world's loveliest squares for people-watching. *(Ch. 4)*

3 Shop in Milan

In Italy's fashion capital of Milan, you'll find the highest of high-end designers in the Quadrilatero della Moda district, north of the Duomo. *(Ch. 5)*

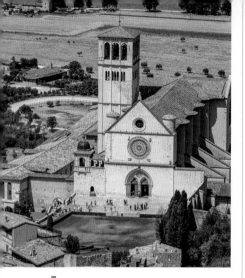

4 See Assisi's Frescos

The peaceful medieval town of Assisi is home to enormous Basilica di San Francesco, which includes 28 frescoes showing the life of St. Francis. *(Ch. 7)*

5 Marvel at Mosaics

Some of the greatest Byzantine mosaics can be found in the unassuming city of Ravenna. You can view the most elaborate ones in the 5th-century Mausoleo di Galla Placidia. *(Ch. 5)*

6 Ponder *The Last Supper*

Restoration work has returned *The Last Supper* to its original glory, so the painting is amazingly clear and luminous. *(Ch. 5)*

7 See a Medieval City

Perhaps Italy's best-preserved medieval city, Siena's narrow streets are fun to explore. The Piazza del Campo is one of the most beautiful squares in the country. *(Ch. 7)*

8 Toss a Coin in Trevi

The can't-miss-Instagramming Trevi Fountain, in Rome, is a Baroque fantasy of sea beasts, seashells, and mermaids in front of a triumphal arch. *(Ch. 3)*

9 Rent a Villa in Tuscany

One of the supreme pleasures of a visit to the countryside of Tuscany is the chance to stay in a villa—preferably one with a swimming pool and vineyard views. *(Ch. 7)*

10 The Vatican Museums

As the home base for the Catholic Church and the papacy, the Vatican sees millions of visitors each year, who come to explore its museums and Michelangelo's Sistine Chapel. *(Ch. 3)*

11 Taste Wine in Chianti

With 17,000 acres of vineyards, sipping your way through Chianti is a fine way to spend a day. *(Ch. 7)*

12 Walk Along Lucca's Walls

This elevated walkway is the site of what for some is a daily ritual of *passeggiata delle mura* (walk along the walls). *(Ch. 7)*

13 See Michelangelo's *David*

David, 17 feet of Carrara marble carved by Michelangelo in the 1500s, could be the most famous man in the world. *(Ch. 6)*

14 Stand in Awe

Dominating Florence's skyline, the magnificent Duomo is an architectural marvel that took almost 600 years to complete. *(Ch. 6)*

WHAT'S WHERE

1 Rome. Italy's capital is one of the greatest cities in Europe. It's a large, busy metropolis that lives in the here and now, yet there's no other place on earth where you'll encounter such powerful evocations of a storied and spectacular past, from the Colosseum to St. Peter's.

2 Venice. One of the world's most unusual cities, Venice has canals instead of streets, along with an atmosphere of faded splendor. It's also a major international cultural center.

3 Northern Italy. In the Veneto region of Italy, the green plains stretching west of Venice hold three of northern Italy's most artistically significant midsize cities: Padua, Vicenza, and Verona. To the west is Milan, Italy's second-largest city and its business capital. It holds Italy's most renowned opera house, and as the hub of Italian fashion and design, it's a shopper's paradise. Northern Italy's attractive coastline runs along the Italian Riviera and includes Cinque Terre and its famous hiking trails and villages. Many of Italy's signature foods come from

the Emilia-Romagna region, where Bologna is a significant cultural center and the mosaics of Ravenna are glittering Byzantine treasures.

4 Florence. In the 15th century, Florence was at the center of an artistic revolution, later labeled the Renaissance, which changed the way people saw the world. Five hundred years later the Renaissance remains the reason people visit Florence.

5 Tuscany and Umbria. Outside Florence, the town of Lucca is laid-back yet elegant while Pisa is still famous for its leaning tower. The hills spreading south of Florence make up Chianti, a region of sublime wine. South of Chianti, hillside towns like Arezzo and Cortona offer gorgeous views of the countryside. In Tuscany, Siena remains one of Italy's most appealing medieval towns. Umbria, north of Rome, is a region of beautiful rolling hills topped by towns full of history, like Orvieto, Spoleto, Perugia, and Assisi, the birthplace of Saint Francis.

Italy Today

ENDURING CUISINE

The old joke goes that three-quarters of the food and wine served in Italy is good—and the rest is amazing. In some sense, that's still true, and the "good" 75% has gotten even better. Those pundits would claim that ingredients that in the past were available only to the wealthy can now be found even in the remotest parts of the country at reasonable prices. Dishes originally conceived to make the most of inferior cuts of meat or the least flavorful part of vegetables are now made with the best.

But many Italians would say that the food in Italy is getting worse. There's a proliferation of fast-food establishments, and increasing tourism has allowed many restaurants to lower their standards while raising their prices. This is true not only in Rome, but in most other tourist centers as well. The good news is Italy is home to one of the world's greatest cuisines, and its traditional favorites still put meat on bones and smiles on faces. Italian restaurateurs seem determined to make the most of the country's reputation for good food. Although quaint, family-run trattorias with checkered tablecloths, traditional dishes, and an informal atmosphere are still common if on the decline, nearly every town has a newer eatery with matching flatware, a proper wine list, and an innovative menu.

This also holds for Italian wine. Today, through investment and experimentation, Italy's winemakers are figuring out how to get the most from their gorgeous vineyards. It's fair to say that Italy now produces more types of high-quality wine from more different grape varieties than any other country in the world.

SOCCER RULES

Soccer (or, as the Italians say, *calcio*—which means "kick") stands without rival as the national sport of Italy, though some complain that big-money influence and loose financial regulations are polluting the beautiful game. That aside, Italy did win its fourth World Cup in 2006, giving the country more world titles than any other this side of Brazil. More recently, Italy won the prestigious UEFA Euro 2020 championship (though due to COVID-19 it was played in 2021). Italy's major clubs have fared better in Europe in 2022, but the predominance of foreign players means a smaller pool of talent to pick at national level. More games in the schedule and a dwindling fan base mean fewer people are seen at the stadium. Still, fans can't stop watching the game on television. Indeed the allure of its famed teams like Juventus, Inter, and Napoli and their *ultras* (vociferous fans) means the top league, Serie A, has a worldwide following.

AN AGING POPULATION

Italy's population is the oldest in Europe (as percentage of population)—the result of its low birth rate and one of the highest life-expectancy rates in the world. The median age of an Italian in 2020 was 46; projections for 2050 exceed 50. Underfunding of the public health-care system has left older Italians vulnerable.

Italy's famously stable population is now aging and set to contract according to recent estimates, putting a strain on the country's pension system and on families because elderly family members are likely to live with their children or grandchildren as retirement homes are rare.

The trend also has an impact in other areas, including politics (where older politicians are eager to promote policies aimed at older voters), the popular culture (where everything from fashion to television programming takes older consumers into consideration), and a kind of far-reaching nostalgia. Thanks to a long collective memory, it's common to hear even younger Italians celebrate or rue something that happened 50 or 60 years earlier as if it had just taken place.

THE BLACK-MARKET ECONOMY

Nobody knows how big Italy's black-market economy is, though experts all agree it's massive. The presence of the black market isn't obvious to the casual observer, but whenever a customer isn't given a printed receipt in a store or restaurant, tobacco without a tax seal is bought from a street seller, or a product or service is exchanged for another product or service, that means the transaction goes unrecorded, unreported, and untaxed. But that's all penny-ante stuff compared to what many professionals evade by neglecting to declare all they earn.

Austerity measures imposed in 2012 have led to much disgruntlement among the population; now most shopkeepers insist that you take a receipt. If you don't, you could be fined, as could the shopkeeper. These measures remain in place, but the country still struggles to meet the 3% limit to its budget deficit as mandated by European Union (EU) agreements, and it is pretty certain that Italy will continue to struggle to meet it in coming years.

A GROWING PARKS SYSTEM

Italy has 25 national parks covering a total of around 1½ million hectares (5,800 square miles), or about 6% of the entire surface area of the country—more than twice as much as 25 years ago.

Part of the reason for the expansion has been a growing environmental movement in Italy, which has lobbied the government to annex undeveloped land for parks, thus protecting against development. But the trend is a boon for visitors and nature lovers, who can enjoy huge expanses of unspoiled territory.

STAYING HOME IN AUGUST

Italy used to be the best example of Europe's famous August exodus, when city dwellers would spend most of the month at the seaside or in the mountains, leaving the cities nearly deserted. Today the phenomenon is less prevalent, as economic pressures have forced companies to keep operating through August.

The loss of shared vacation time for Italian workers means good things for visitors: in August there's a little more room on beaches and mountains; in addition, cities promote events for nonvacationing natives. Summers in Italy now offer a plethora of outdoor concerts and theatrical events, extended museum hours, and local festivals.

MUSEI DIFFUSI

In recent years the idea of promoting tourism away from Italy's increasingly clogged destinations has spurred the idea of *Musei Diffusi* or "Scattered Museums." The result of COVID regulations and social-distancing measures have accelerated the need to support local communities and encourage visitors to seek out art in overlooked hilltop *borghi* (villages) instead of queuing to glimpse Botticelli's *Venus*. The trend has evolved from *Strade dei Vini* (Wine Roads) and theme itineraries: now grand collections like the Uffizi are launching curator-led online exhibition tours and dusting off artworks in storage destined for display in municipal collections.

Best Ancient Sites in Rome

COLOSSEUM

Perhaps the monument most symbolic of ancient Rome, the Colosseum is one of the city's most fascinating—and popular—tourist attractions. It officially opened in AD 80 with 100 days of games, including wild-animal fights and gladiatorial combat.

ROMAN FORUM

One of the Eternal City's most emblematic sites, the Roman Forum stretches out between the Capitoline and Palatine hills. This vast area filled with crumbling columns and the ruins of temples, palaces, and shops was once the hub of the ancient world and the center of political, commercial, and religious life in the city.

CIRCUS MAXIMUS

It might be hard to imagine now, but the grassy area between the Palatine and Aventine hills was once the site of the largest hippodrome in the Roman Empire. The huge oval course was rebuilt under Julius Caesar and later enlarged by subsequent emperors. During its heyday, it hosted epic chariot races and competitions that sometimes lasted for up to 15 days.

BOCCA DELLA VERITÀ

Legend has it the mouth in this ancient stone face will bite off the hand of a liar, and tourists line up to stick their hand inside the mouth and put it to the test. (Gregory Peck's character tricks Audrey Hepburn's Princess Ann into thinking he lost a hand inside it in a scene from *Roman Holiday*.) You'll find the enigmatic face in the portico of the Church of Santa Maria in Cosmedin, near the Circus Maximus.

FORO DI TRAIANO

Trajan's Forum was the last of imperial Rome's forums—and the grandest. Comprising a basilica, two libraries, and a colonnade surrounding a piazza, it's connected to a market that once bustled with commercial activity.

PANTHEON

Built as a pagan temple, the Pantheon is Rome's best-preserved ancient site, perhaps because it was later consecrated as a church. Step inside, and you'll be amazed at its perfect proportions and the sunlight streaming in from the 30-foot-wide oculus. It's truly a wonder of ancient engineering.

The Roman Forum

TEATRO MARCELLO
What looks a bit like a smaller version of the Colosseum was once ancient Rome's largest and most important theater. Julius Caesar ordered the land for the theater to be cleared, but he was murdered before it was built. It was inaugurated in AD 12 by Augustus and hosted performances of drama and song. It's kept that purpose even today, at least during the summer, when it hosts concerts.

APPIA ANTICA
Head to the southeastern edge of the city to Appia Antica Park and you can walk on the stones—which are incredibly well-preserved—that ancient Roman soldiers and citizens once trod. This thoroughfare once stretched all the way to Brindisi, some 300 miles away on the Adriatic Coast. Today, the first 10 miles are part of a regional park, and it's a perfect spot for bike rides and picnics in the grass under the shadow of Rome's emblematic umbrella pines.

ARA PACIS AUGUSTAE
Now housed in a modern glass-and-travertine building designed by renowned American architect Richard Meier, the Ara Pacis Augustae has some of the most incredible reliefs you'll see on any ancient monument. It was commissioned to celebrate the Emperor Augustus's victories in battle and the Pax Romana, a peaceful period that followed. It's definitely worth a visit and is centrally located on the Tiber River in the Piazza di Spagna district.

TERMI DI CARACALLA
A testament to ancient Rome's bathing culture, this site on the Aventine Hill was essentially a massive spa, with saunas, baths, what would be an Olympic-size pool, and two gymnasiums for boxing, weight lifting, and wrestling.

Best Museums in Rome

MACRO
The former Peroni brewery in the Repubblica district houses this museum with a focus on Italian art from the 1960s through the present. The building, with its striking red structure and glass walkways, was designed by French architect Odile Decq and is worth a visit in and of itself.

MUSEI CAPITOLINI
Second in size only to the Vatican Museums, the Capitoline Museums were the world's first public art museums. Two buildings on Michelangelo's Piazza del Campidoglio house a collection spanning from ancient Rome to the Baroque era, with masterpieces that include Caravaggio's *St. John the Baptist*.

GALLERIA NAZIONALE D'ARTE MODERNA E CONTEMPORANEA
A huge, white, Beaux-Arts building in Villa Borghese has one of Italy's most important collections of 19th- and 20th-century art. You'll find works by Degas, Monet, Courbet, Cézanne, and Van Gogh, but there's also an emphasis on Italian Modernism.

GALLERIA BORGHESE
It would be hard to find a more beautiful villa filled with a must-see collection of masterpieces by Bernini, Caravaggio, Raphael, Rubens, and Titian. Cardinal Scipione Borghese had the gorgeous Renaissance villa built in 1612 to display his collection, though it has undergone many changes since.

MUSEO NAZIONALE ETRUSCO DI VILLA GIULIA
The pre-Roman Etruscans appeared in Italy around 2,000 BC, though no one knows exactly where they originated. To learn more about them, plan a visit to this museum in Villa Giulia, which was built for Pope Julius III in the mid-1500s.

PALAZZO DORIA PAMPHILJ
For a look at aristocratic Rome, visit this museum in the 15th-century palazzo of the Doria Pamphilj family just south of the Piazza di Spagna. Wander through the Hall of Mirrors—fashioned after the one at Versailles—but don't miss the Old Master paintings.

MUSEI VATICANI

One of the largest museum complexes in the world, the Vatican palaces and museums comprise some 1,400 rooms, galleries, and chapels. By far the most famous attraction is the Sistine Chapel painted by Michelangelo and a team of others, but the Raphael Rooms come in a close second when it comes to must-see works.

MAXXI

Tucked away in the quiet Flaminio neighborhood, the Museo Nazionale delle Arti del XXI Secolo (National Museum of 21st Century Arts)—or MAXXI, for short—proves that there's more to Rome than ancient and Baroque art.

CENTRALE MONTEMARTINI

Nowhere else is the theme of gods and machines more apparent than at this museum. Situated in the Testaccio district, Rome's first power plant now houses the overflow from collections at the Capitoline Museums; the sculptures of men in togas and women in dresses form a poignant contrast to the machinery.

Architectural Wonders in Venice

PONTE DI RIALTO
The iconic Ponte di Rialto was completed in 1591. Its generous arch, central portal, and Renaissance arcade make it appear so beautifully balanced that Palladio himself would surely have approved.

SAN FRANCESCO DELLA VIGNA
The harmonious combination of architectural designs by two Renaissance maestri and the tranquil neighborhood setting make this church a wonderful place to escape the crowds.

MOLINO STUCKY
This behemoth, neo-Gothic warehouselike building, formerly a flour mill and pasta factory, on the western end of the Giudecca certainly stands out on the Venetian skyline.

SANTA MARIA DELLA SALUTE
One of the city's most beloved and iconic churches, La Salute was built to mark the end of the 1630 plague that took almost 50,000 Venetian lives.

PUNTA DELLA DOGANA
There has been a Punta della Dogana (Sea Customs House) situated between the Grand and Giudecca Canals since the 15th century, although the building you see today was designed in the 1860s. Above the entrance tower, two Atlases lift a bronze sphere topped by the figure of Fortune.

ARSENALE
For centuries, the colossal Arsenale complex of shipyards, warehouses, and armories was Europe's largest military-industrial compound. Although many areas are still cordoned off as military zones, the southern side is open to the public during the Biennale Arte.

JEWISH GHETTO
Originally the site of a foundry (*geto* in the local dialect), both the atmosphere and the architecture set the Jewish Ghetto apart: palazzi and *case* are taller here than elsewhere, with story upon story piled on high in an effort to make the best use of limited space.

PALAZZO DUCALE

Adorned with a series of soaring Gothic arches topped by an ornately columned arcade, the labyrinthine Doge's Palace has a wedding-cake-like delicacy when viewed from the Piazza San Marco or the waterside Bacino di San Marco. A palace has been here since the 9th century: its present palatial pink Verona marble and Istrian limestone splendor was the vision of architect Filippo Calendario (1315–1355).

MADONNA DELL'ORTO

An alluring, redbrick Gothic church with ornate marble decoration, it was dedicated to St. Christopher, the patron saint of travelers, until a Madonna statue was found in a nearby *orto* (kitchen vegetable garden). Tintoretto's local church is where he learned his craft as a young man. Seek out the powerful *Martyrdom of St. Paul*, which captures the tension between the violent sword act of a Roman soldier and Paul's saintly calmness below rays of holy light.

CA' DA MOSTO

As you drift along the Grand Canal, you'll see palazzi far more eye-catching than the Ca' da Mosto, but none more enduring—the crumbling Byzantine-style palace has been here since the 13th century. The ground and first floors are an example of a *casa-fondaco* (a house-warehouse). A 2019–21 restoration and renovation has transformed the palace into a luxury hotel filled with innovative design and interesting artworks.

10 Best Museums in Florence

PALAZZO PITTI

Florence's rich and powerful all walked down the halls of Palazzo Pitti. Today, its gallery rooms and royal apartments are lavishly decorated as a palace should be and contain more than 500 paintings (mostly Renaissance-era) including works by Raphael and Titian.

BARGELLO

The fortress-like Bargello has had many incarnations—family palace, government building, prison, and execution site (on its patio). As a nod to its conflicted past, it also houses a collection of weapons, armor, and medals from the powerful Medici family. The real draws, though, are Donatello's bronze *David*, standing victorious over the head of Goliath, and Michelangelo's marble *Bacchus*, as well as works by other major Renaissance sculptors.

GALLERIA DEGLI UFFIZI

It's one of the most visited museums in Florence, Italy, and the world for a reason. Head to the former offices of Florentine magistrates to see a wow-worthy collection of art. In one room, gaze at Sandro Botticelli's *Birth of Venus* and *Primavera*, and in another, Leonardo da Vinci's *Annunciation*. Works by Michelangelo, Raphael, Giotto, and Caravaggio are also here. Avoid the lines by booking tickets in advance on the Uffizi Gallery website.

GALLERIA DELL'ACCADEMIA

Come for *David*, stay to see everything else. There's no doubt that the line running down Via Ricasoli to enter a seemingly nondescript building is for Michelangelo's most famous man in the world—*Il Davide*. There is something marvelous about seeing his 17 feet of artfully carved Carrara marble "in the flesh," poised before his battle with Goliath. After you've caught your breath, check out the museum's early- to late-Renaissance works by Sandro Botticelli, and Andrea del Sarto; Florentine Gothic paintings; and collection of musical instruments.

MUSEO DELL'OPERA DEL DUOMO

When Santa Maria del Fiore—also known as Florence cathedral, or Il Duomo—and its baptistery and bell tower were completed in the 1400s, it was the largest church in Europe, and it was decorated by some of Italy's most celebrated artists. Today, however, some of its master works, like Lorenzo Ghiberti's famous bronze doors, or *Gates of Paradise*, which took him 27 years to finish, are fake. To save them from the elements, the doors and other decorative items and sculptures are now housed in the Museo dell'Opera del Duomo.

MUSEO SALVATORE FERRAGAMO

You may think that you've died and gone to shoe heaven at this museum in a palazzo featuring the work of southern Italian–born shoe designer, Salvatore Ferragamo (1898–1960). The permanent collection from the brand's archives includes a wedge sandal in gold and Technicolor rainbow colors that was designed for Judy Garland in 1938 and a cross-strap ballet flat that was created for Audrey Hepburn's slim feet in the 1950s and is still one of the label's signature styles. Because of Ferragamo's reputation as a "creator to the stars," the museum's temporary exhibits often merge film, art, and culture with fashion history.

PALAZZO STROZZI

Unlike Galleria degli Uffizi and other city-run museums, Palazzo Strozzi is an independent foundation. Hence, its exhibits are often eclectic, featuring, say, a retrospective of cinquecento Florentine art while at the same time showcasing avant-garde works such as a 65-foot spiral tunnel called *The Florence Experiment* or performance artist Marina Abramovic's *The Cleaner* (controversial for its use of nude actors). The permanent collection highlights the history of the palace, which was built for prominent Florentine banker, Filippo Strozzi, who died before it was completed.

PALAZZO VECCHIO

Also called Palazzo della Signoria, the monumental building surrounded by one of Italy's most famous piazzas has been home to Florence's city government since the Renaissance. Walk past a copy of Michelangelo's *David* at the entrance and up opulent marble staircases to see expansive gold-highlighted and frescoed ceilings and walls. The Salone dei Cinquecento is one of the grandest spaces, designed and painted by celebrated art historian (and artist in his own right), Giorgio Vasari.

SANTA CROCE

In Florence, churches are museums, too. At Santa Croce—considered the largest Franciscan church in the world (and said to be founded by St. Francis of Assisi)—you'll find 16 chapels that were once frequented by significant Florentine families who funded their decoration. There are frescoes by Renaissance master Giotto in the Bardi and Peruzzi chapels, and a terra-cotta altarpiece by another quattrocento heavy hitter, Andrea della Robbia. If the art isn't enough of a draw to visit, note that the basilica also contains the tombs of Michelangelo, Galileo, and Machiavelli.

Santa Croce

SANTA MARIA NOVELLA

Dominican monks founded the basilica of Santa Maria Novella in the 13th century, making it one of the most religiously significant churches in Florence—both then and now. The facade is a beauty, with green and white marble inlay work by Genoa-born Leon Battista Alberti. Inside are some of the world's finest examples of Renaissance art. On the main altar is Masaccio's *Trinita* fresco, which was painted in the 1400s, was covered and rediscovered in the 1800s, and is considered one of the earliest examples of perspective from the Renaissance period. Giotto's *Crucifix* is another master work that was likely painted in the late 1200s. In the basilica's largest chapel, Tornabuoni, Ghirlandaio painted frescoes about the life of the Virgin Mary, to whom the church is dedicated, in the late 1400s.

Best Hilltop Villages in Tuscany and Umbria

ORVIETO, UMBRIA

Although medieval architectural wonders adorn Orvieto, the labyrinth of subterranean tunnels beneath the town is even more fascinating. Orvieto is also recognized for its white and red wines, its olive oils, and its culinary classics—from boar and dove to pastas and pastries.

PITIGLIANO, TUSCANY

Although most Italian villages are overflowing with impressive churches, Pitigliano may be most famous for its synagogue, drawing attention to its rich history of Jewish settlement and giving the old town its nickname of Little Jerusalem. Of course, countless churches dot the rest of this Tuscan village. There's also a smattering of museums and other historic gems like the Palazzo Orsini, a Renaissance palace built on the ruins of medieval fortresses and containing both art and archaeological museums of its own.

SAN GIMIGNANO, TUSCANY

Most medieval towers have given way to war and erosion through the centuries, but San Gimignano retains so many that it has been dubbed the Town of Fine Towers and its historic center is a UNESCO World Heritage site. Although it's packed with immaculate examples of medieval architecture, this village is among the more tourist-minded, with contemporary events like music festivals and art exhibitions and plenty of modern conveniences and services for travelers. San Gimignano even has its own app.

VOLTERRA, TUSCANY

Twenty kilometers (12 miles) from the better-known village of San Gimignano is the less visited (less crowded) Volterra. Although there are some serious medieval remnants in this village, especially its narrow streets in the town center, it's much more famous for the historical periods before and after. Some of its ancient Etruscan fortification walls still surround Roman ruins, including an impressive amphitheater worth exploring (there are also remains of ancient Roman baths and a forum). The Florentine influence of the Medici family left behind some dazzling Renaissance art and architecture throughout the once bustling mercantile village. The alabaster trade remains strong today and provides beautiful souvenirs of this Tuscan treasure.

SORANO, TUSCANY

Ham it up in Sorano, where the local prosciutto is so revered that the town holds a festival for it every August. If you don't eat pork, don't worry; there are plenty of other local specialties, particularly dairy products, including sheep's milk ricotta cheese, as well as oranges and other fruits and the ever-popular Italian liqueur, *limoncello*. Don't miss the Masso Leopoldina (sometimes called the Rocca Vecchia). It was once central to the defense of the town but is now a fabulous terrace that's a good place to enjoy panoramic views of Tuscany—and, perhaps, yet another limoncello.

VINCI, TUSCANY

Yes, *that* Vinci. Established in the early Middle Ages among the rolling hills of Montalbano and with Arno Valley views, Vinci's claim to fame is Leonardo da Vinci ("Leonardo from Vinci"). The town is filled with tributes to him—like the imposing wooden sculpture, *Vitruvian Man,* by Mario Ceroli; the Biblioteca Leonardiana, an archive of his manuscripts and drawings; Santa Croce, the church where he was baptized; and the Museo Leonardiano Vinci, which houses his inventions and anatomical research, including drawings, studies, and replicas, in two buildings. You can also visit the birth home of this true Renaissance man in the nearby village of Anchiano. It's accessible via a 3-km (1.8-mile) walk up the *strade verde* (a dirt path with valley views) or by car or bus.

TODI, UMBRIA

Compact and ancient Todi is a hilltop citadel town with a beautiful patch-work of architecture that includes three sturdy walls, begun by the 3rd-century-BC Etruscans followed by Roman and medieval dynasties. Starting at the café-community hub Piazza del Popolo, with an impos-ing 12th-century Roman-esque-Gothic Duomo built upon a Roman temple, a maze of cobbled lanes and steep staircases fans out, inviting leisurely explora-tion. For grandstand views over roofs and the Umbrian hills beyond, climb the campanile of San Fortu-nato. Leafy walks abound in the Parco della Rocca, the city-wall park.

ASSISI, UMBRIA

Assisi claims history as ancient as 1000 BC and is probably best known for its most famous resident, St. Francis, whose 13th-century basilica is now a UNESCO World Heritage site, as is the entire village itself. Plenty of other impressive churches, Roman ruins, and not one but two castles top the extensive list of the town's architectural offerings. From ceramics to medieval weaponry, Assisi's artisan history is also strong. Cured meats and chocolate are popular here, so grab a snack between sword fights, and refuel on the Assisi ribbon-type pasta *stringozzi,* often served with Norcia black truffles, asparagus, or *piccante* (spicy) tomato sauce.

What to Watch and Read

ITALIAN FOLKTALES BY ITALO CALVINO

In 1956 the celebrated, Cuban-born and Liguria-raised, magical realist published this fabulous collection of some 200 traditional folktales from across the archipelago. The prose in the 800-page *Fiabe italiane* tome is simple yet evocative, and the stories appeal to young and old alike. They're largely fantastical morality tales involving love, loss, revenge, and adventure on the part of kings, princesses, saints, and peasants. The book is a fabulous bedtime or beach read.

AMARCORD, DIRECTED BY FEDERICO FELLINI

Amarcord ("I remember," in the Romagnol dialect) is filled with comic archetypes and dreamlike excursions inspired by Fellini's 1930s adolescence in Rimini. The rosy-cheeked protagonist, Titta, and his pals have humorous encounters with authority figures—pompous schoolteachers, frustrated fathers, cruel Fascist officials—as well as with the buxom hairdresser, Gradisca. The 1973 movie, which won the Oscar for Best Foreign Language Film, offers poignant, entertaining, and often bonkers insight into the Italian psyche, family dynamics, and interwar society. Nino Rota's wistful soundtrack adds to the feeling of nostalgia.

THE ITALIANS BY JOHN HOOPER

In this 2015 book, longtime Rome correspondent John Hooper addresses the complexities of contemporary Italy, attempting to reveal "what makes the Italian tick." Here you'll learn the lexicon needed to negotiate and understand Italian culture. Of course, food, sex, and the weather—among other things—are heartily embraced in everyday life, but there is also an *amaro* (bitter) side. Hooper illustrates how the power of the *famiglia* (family) and the *chiesa* (church) has produced a society in which *furbizia* (cunning) is rewarded and meritocracy is replaced with *raccomandazioni* (favors) to get ahead in the world.

THE LEOPARD BY GIUSEPPE TOMASI DI LAMPEDUSA

Il gattopardo, an Italian literary classic, chronicles the tumultuous, revolutionary years of the Risorgimento (1860s–early 20th century). Lampedusa was the last in a line of minor princes, and the novel, born of a lengthy depression, was published in 1958, a year after his death. Set in Sicily, the epic story of decay amid a changing society centers on the ebbing influence and power of Don Fabrizio, Prince of Salina, and his family, and hints at the emergence of the Mafia. One particularly insightful quote in the book—spoken by the prince's young nephew, Tancredi—sheds light on how Italy adapts to shifting political forces and class struggle: "For everything to stay the same, everything must change."

COSA NOSTRA BY JOHN DICKIE

Journalist and academic John Dickie packs a lot of gruesome detail into this fast-paced history of the Mafia. He traces the Cosa Nostra's origins during the Risorgimento years, its infiltration and corruption of the First Republic, and the curious and notorious role of the town of Corleone in its development. Dickie also recounts the organization's birth and rise in America, the Mafia Wars, and the recent crises and tragedies connected to Italy's corrupt political system.

THE CONFORMIST, DIRECTED BY BERNARDO BERTOLUCCI

Il conformista, Bertolucci's stylish psychological thriller set in 1930s Fascist Italy, is considered a postwar cinematic classic. As its name suggests, the 1970 film tackles the issue of conformity through the lens of the cruel, febrile political atmosphere created by Mussolini and his followers. Despite its dark themes, the movie is beautifully lit and shot, filled with vibrant colors, exquisite costuming, and atmospheric locations. It has inspired many directors of the American New Wave and beyond, including Martin Scorsese, Francis Ford Coppola, and the Coen brothers.

DELIZIA! BY JOHN DICKIE

If you think you know all there is to know about Italian food, you'll think again after reading this book. Dickie's gastronomic journey across the regions of Italy through the ages covers everything from *pastasciutta* in 12th-century Palermo to today's Slow Food movement in Turin. Carry this book with you as you travel, so you can compare your menu to, say, that for a 1529 Ferrara banquet, which featured "105 soused sea bream" and "15 large salted eels" for starters, followed by "104 roasted capon livers" and "sweet pastry tarts deep-filled with the spleens of sea bass, trout, pike and other fish." *Che delizia!*

THE GREAT BEAUTY, DIRECTED BY PAOLO SORRENTINO

Although directed by a Neapolitan, this Oscar-winning 2013 film is set in Rome and serves as a kind of contemporary *La Dolce Vita.* The lead character in *La grande bellezza,* Jep Gambardella (Toni Servillo), is an aging hedonistic journalist, who, while pining for his glory days, comes to realize the superficiality of his bourgeois lifestyle. Beset by Roman ennui after his raucous rooftop 65th-birthday bash, Jep goes in search of beauty beyond the vanity of his milieu.

THE NEAPOLITAN NOVELS

Elena Ferrante's novels (2012–15) and the HBO TV series bring multilayered postwar Naples to life, going beyond postcard beauty to portray the grim, savage reality of growing up in a rough *rione* (district). The four books explore the complexities of friendship and Italian society. With vivid depictions—mixing the palatial and the squalid—the pseudonymous author details the lifetime bond and inner lives of Elena and Lila and their interactions with a cast of characters across Italy as well as in Naples.

1992, 1993, AND 1994

The 10-episode television series *1992* and its follow-ups, *1993* and *1994,* (originally aired in 2015, 2017, and 2019, respectively) are political dramas that follow the intertwined lives of six people amid the tumult of early-1990s Italy. Massive cracks appear in the postwar political compromise, with the Mani Pulite (Clean Hands) investigation led by prosecutor Antonio Di Pietro initiating the fall of the First Republic. As the country is rocked by the so-called Tangentopoli (Bribesville) scandal, marketing man Stefano Accorsi sees an opportunity for an outside figure to seize power. And so up steps media tycoon Silvio Berlusconi and his populist Forza Italia party. Sound familiar?

STANLEY TUCCI: SEARCHING FOR ITALY (2021–22)

Italian-American actor Stanley Tucci goes on a culinary and cultural adventure around the Italian regions in this CNN TV production. In the first series he visits six regions, their urban centers, and fecund hinterlands. In Naples and the Amalfi Coast he visits a San Marzano tomato farm on the shadows of Vesuvius and discovers the art of mozzarella making. In Rome he samples imaginative *quinto-quarto* offal creations and Roman classics rigatoni *all'amatriciana* and *guanciale*-laden *carbonara.* Trips to Tuscany, Bologna, and Milan yield engaging encounters and mouthfuls of *bistecca alla Fiorentina,* the most sought-after Parmigiana-Reggiano cheese, and a cool hangout for an *aperitivo Milanese.* Tucci rounds off the series meeting young female vintner Arianna Occhipinti in Sicily.

Making the Most of Your Euros

TRANSPORTATION

Italy's state-sponsored train system has been given a run for its money by a private company. Sadly, the competitor (Italo) only operates major, high-speed connections (such as Rome to Naples, Florence to Venice, Milan to Bologna) and not local routes. Because of the competition, Trenitalia and Italo engage in price wars, which only plays to the consumer's advantage; depending on time of day and how far in advance you purchase the tickets, great bargains can be had.

No such good news exists for the *regionali* trains. These are trains connecting cities, highly frequented by commuters and used often by visitors who want to get to less visible towns. These trains are habitually late and almost always crowded. Patience is a virtue, and much needed when taking them, particularly during high season.

FOOD AND DRINK

Always remember, when you enter a bar, that there is almost always a two-tier pricing system: one if you stand and one if you sit. It's always cheaper to stand, but sometimes sitting is not only necessary but fun: you can relax and watch the world go by.

Italians love a good sandwich for lunch. Seek out popular sandwich shops (long lines signify that the place is worth visiting) or go to a *salumeria* (delicatessen) and have them make a sandwich for you. It will be simple—cheese and/or cold cuts with bread, no trimmings—but it will be made while you wait, fresh, delicious, and inexpensive.

SIGHTS

There are plenty of free wonderful things to see. Visit the Musei Vaticani, the Uffizi, and the Accademia in Florence (book ahead whenever possible), but don't forget that many artistic gems are found in churches, most of which can be visited with no charge (some of Caravaggio's best work can be found in various churches in Rome). Also, consider renting audio guides if you want direction to any specific place; if you find the idea of joining an organized tour daunting, most museums sell official guidebooks that can help you target what to see. Walking in *centri storici* (historic centers) is also a joy, and free. Seek out piazzas, climb towers, and look for views.

LODGING

High season in Italy runs from Easter to mid-October. If you want to have Florence practically to yourself, come in November or February (most Italian cities are very crowded during the Christmas holidays, which begin around Christmas and finish on January 6). Many hotels in cities offer bargain rates in July and August because most people are off to the beach or the mountains. Remember to factor in great heat and massive crowds, along with the money you'll save. If you decide to travel then, ensure that you have access to a pool and/or air-conditioning.

A great budget-conscious way to travel is via Airbnb (⊕ *airbnb.com*), although prices have soared in recent years, making pads in popular places pricier than many hotels. You can sleep on someone's couch, rent a private room in an apartment (sometimes with en suite bathroom), or spread out in an entire apartment or house. One of the best things about Airbnb is that many of these accommodations come with refrigerators and kitchens, which means you don't have to spend all your money eating out.

In general, whatever your lodging choice, book sooner rather than later. You'll often find better deals that way.

Chapter 2

TRAVEL SMART

Updated by
Nick Bruno

★ **CAPITAL:**
Rome

♙ **POPULATION:**
58,850,717

💬 **LANGUAGE:**
Italian

$ **CURRENCY:**
Euro

☏ **COUNTRY CODE:**
39

⚠ **EMERGENCIES:**
112

🚗 **DRIVING:**
On the right

⚡ **ELECTRICITY:**
220v/50 cycles; electrical
plugs have two round prongs

🕐 **TIME:**
6 hours ahead of New York

🌐 **WEB RESOURCES:**
www.italia.it
www.beniculturali.it

Know Before You Go

A TALE OF TWO COUNTRIES

Italy as we know it is just over 160 years old, united by Giuseppe Garibaldi in 1861, and traditions and customs die hard. Differences and rivalries between the wealthier north and the more relaxed south abound, but you will need to spend time in both for the full Italian experience.

DRINK YOUR FILL

Bottled water is available everywhere but often at an inflated price. Carry a refillable bottle and fill up for free at the strategically placed water fountains in cities. In restaurants you can ask for tap water (*acqua del rubinetto*), although you may have to insist.

GO FOOTBALL CRAZY

Soccer—*calcio*—is taken very seriously in Italy, with rivalries running deep. A little knowledge of a local team's performance makes for great conversation. Just avoid wearing your Juventus shirt in Naples if you want to make new friends. To get a taste for the football fervor, its songs and excitement, visit the *stadio* of the local *squadra* (team) and join the *tifosi* (fans) on the *curve* (in the stands).

BOOK IN ADVANCE

Avoid waiting in line for hours by buying museum tickets online before your visit. Also, the earlier you buy train tickets, the less expensive they're likely to be. Trenitalia and Italo offer substantial first-come-first-served discounts on high-speed services; check their websites, and prepare to be flexible with your travel times. Discounts aren't offered on regional trains, and neither is seat reservation. Unless bought online, tickets for regional trains must be stamped before boarding.

TAKE THE BACK ROADS

So you've rented a car. Why stick to the highways? Much of Italy's beauty is along winding mountain roads or coastal secondary routes, so take your time and wander a little. Not only will you save on tolls, but you'll save on fuel, too, as gas prices are generally lower than on the *autostrade*. Also, if you're renting a car between November 15 and April 15, remember to ask for snow chains (obligatory on many roads).

EAT FOR (NEARLY) NOTHING

The *aperitivo* is a staple of many areas of the north, where, for little more than the price of a drink, you can partake of a vast buffet to substitute for your evening meal. Bars vie with each other to provide the best array of pasta dishes, *pizzette*, and panini , so check out a few of them before sitting down. Look out for signs like "Aperitivo Happy Hour" and "Stuzzichini": there are bite-size snacks like *patatine* (potato chips), olives, and *grissini* (breadsticks) either served with your drink at the table, or else in a buffet-style spread replete with pasta, rice, and other dishes.

PLAN YOUR DAY

Although breakfast (*la colazione*) is generally served from 7 to 10:30, other mealtimes vary by region. In the north, lunch (*il pranzo*) is noon to 2, whereas restaurants in the south often serve it until 3. You may have difficulty finding dinner (*la cena*) in the north after 9 pm, when most southerners are just sitting down to eat (restaurants there tend not to open until 7:30). And shoppers take note: many stores close from 1 to 4:30.

LACE UP YOUR WALKING SHOES

The best—and often the only—way to see a city is on foot. Public transport works well (albeit generally better in the north), and in recent years many city and town centers have been pedestrianized. Parking costs and fines can add up (avoid ZTL or limited traffic zones), so when possible don your most comfortable shoes and prepare to pound the pavement. Fall in with a weekend afternoon *passeggiata* in smaller towns, where Italians stroll the main street dressed in their Sunday best.

DRINK LOCAL
Italy offers a vast array of fine wines, with each region boasting its own appellation. While you may see Chianti on a wine list in Catania, it will probably be no different to what you find at home; for a more authentic taste of the area, try a local Sicilian wine instead.

YOU GET A COFFEE IN A BAR
Coffee culture is different here. Italians take their single-shot espresso standing at a bar—where snacks and alcoholic drinks are also served, and which usually closes in the evening. Pay the cashier, then set your receipt on the counter and place your order. If you choose to sit, there is usually a surcharge, whether there is table service or not. Also, if you order a latte you'll get a glass of milk.

NEVER PASS A RESTROOM
Public restrooms in train stations usually cost €1, and bars frown on the use of theirs without making a purchase, so before you leave the hotel, restaurant, or museum, use the facilities.

DAY-TRIPPER
Lodging in tourist hot spots is at a premium during high season, but deals can be found a little farther from the action. Consider booking outside town and taking a local train or bus to see the sights—you might miss the evening atmosphere, but you'll have more to spend on lunch.

TAKE YOUR TIME
The Italian experience differs from region to region. Try to plan an itinerary that leaves time to explore each destination at leisure. Sure, quick in-and-out visits to cities will allow you to see the major sights, but rushing things means missing out on each area's unique atmosphere.

BE ITALIAN
Food is one of Italy's defining features, and locals continue to be horrified by the idea of pineapple on pizza or (heaven forbid!) ketchup on pasta. You don't need a knife to eat spaghetti (although using a spoon to help wind the pasta around a fork is allowed), and it's fine to pick your pizza up. Most restaurants set a per-person fee for *pane e coperto* (bread and cover charge), although waiters also appreciate a tip—which is standard (around 10%) in the south.

BEWARE OF SCAMS
Larger train stations are notorious for porters insisting on carrying your bags, then charging a fee, so be firm if you're not interested. Also, be careful where you store your wallet and valuables and avoid purchasing from illegal street vendors.

LOOK INTO SIGHT PASSES
Many cities and towns sell multiday passes for access to different museums and sights. These offer great savings if you plan to visit several attractions; some include deals on public transport.

LEARN THE LINGO
Most Italians have some command of English, although this isn't a fail-safe rule, particularly in the south. You can get by on hand gestures and pointing, but a *grazie* or *buongiorno* here and there can't hurt.

SPECIAL SUNDAYS FOR CULTURE
A fabulous Ministero della Cultura initiative, "Domenica al Museo," allows free entry to state-run museums, galleries, and archaeological sites throughout Italy on the first Sunday of the month. For the latest upcoming "Sunday at the Museum" details consult the list of participating institutions at ⊕ *cultura.gov.it/domenicalmuseo* and look out for the hashtag #DomenicaAlMuseo. Naturally, there are lots of crowds and families on these days.

FOOD-SHOP SAVVY
Save money on restaurant and hotel food, and pricey drinks bills, by seeking out stores to stock up. Head to the *alimentari*, the local food and general store, to buy groceries, cheese, cold cuts, and essential refreshments for hot days out, such as water in bottles. The *supermercato* has a wider selection and may stock interesting housewares and other items that make fab gifts to take home. For picnic supplies the *panificio* or *fornaio* is essential for bakery goods such as *pane* (bread) and *panini* (rolls).

Getting Here and Around

Air

Most nonstop flights between North America and Italy serve Rome's Aeroporto Internazionale Leonardo da Vinci (FCO), better known as Fiumicino, and Milan's Aeroporto Malpensa (MXP), though the airports in Venice, Pisa, and Naples also accommodate nonstop flights from the United States. Flying time to Milan or Rome is approximately 8–8½ hours from New York, 10–11 hours from Chicago, and 11½ hours from Los Angeles.

Alitalia has direct flights from London to Milan and Rome, while British Airways and smaller budget carriers provide services between Great Britain and other locations in Italy. EasyJet connects London's Gatwick and Stansted airports with a dozen or so Italian destinations. Ryanair flies from Stansted to even more airports. Since tickets are frequently sold at discounted prices, investigate the cost of flights within Italy (even one-way) where you're faced with a long, multichange train journey—a potentially time-saving alternative (although less green) way to travel.

You can take the Ferrovie dello Stato Italiane (FS) airport train or bus to Rome's Termini station or to Cadorna or Centrale in Milan; from the latter you can then catch a train to any other location in Italy. It will take about 40 minutes to get from Fiumicino to Roma Termini, less than an hour from Malpensa to Milano Centrale.

A helpful website for information (location, phone numbers, local transportation, etc.) about all the airports in Italy is ⊕ *www.italianairportguide.com*.

Bus

Italy's far-reaching regional bus network, often operated by private companies, isn't as attractive an option as in other European countries, partly due to convenient train travel. Schedules are often drawn up with commuters and students in mind and can be sketchy on weekends. But, car travel aside, regional bus companies often provide the only means of getting to out-of-the-way places. Even when this isn't the case, buses can be faster and more direct than local trains, so it's worth taking time to compare bus and train schedules. Busitalia–Sita Nord covers Tuscany, Umbria, Campania, and the Veneto. Sita Sud caters to travelers in Puglia, Basilicata, and Campania. FlixBus offers a low-cost long-distance service.

All buses, even those on long-distance routes, offer a single class of service. Cleanliness and comfort levels are high on private motor coaches, which have plenty of legroom, sizable seats, luggage storage, and usually toilets. Smoking isn't permitted on buses. Private lines usually have a ticket office in town or allow you to pay when you board.

Major Italian cities have inexpensive urban bus service. Although some city buses have ticket machines on board, generally you buy tickets from newsstands or tobacconists while cities like Rome, Naples, and Milan allow smartphone app and Tap & Go contactless travel. Remember to get your ticket validated on board. Buses can get packed during busy travel periods, school commutes, and rush hours.

Car

Italy has an extensive network of *auto-stradas* (toll highways), complemented by equally well-maintained but free *super-stradas* (expressways). You'll need your autostrada ticket from entry to pay the toll when you exit; on some shorter auto-stradas, you pay the toll when you enter. The condition of provincial roads varies, but maintenance is generally good.

Most gas stations have self-service options. Those on autostradas are open 24 hours; others are generally open Monday through Saturday 7–7, with a break at lunchtime. Automobile Club Italiano offers 24-hour road service. To call the police in an emergency, dial ☎ *112*. Auto-grill provides decent highway catering across the country.

PARKING
Curbside spaces are marked by blue lines; pay at a nearby *parcometro* machine, and leave the printed ticket on your dashboard. Fines for violations are high, and towing is common. You often need a permit to enter historic centers with a vehicle—violating this strictly enforced rule can also result in hefty fines. It's best to park in designated (preferably attended) lots; even small towns often have them just outside their historic centers.

RULES OF THE ROAD
You can rent a car with a U.S. driver's license, but Italy also requires non-Europeans to carry an International Driver's Permit (IDP), available for a nominal fee via the AAA website (⊕ *www.aaa.com*). Speed limits are generally 130 kph (80 mph) on autostradas, 90 kph (55 mph) on state roads, and 50 kph (30 mph) in towns; this can drop to 10 kph (6 mph) in congested areas. Exceed the speed limit by more than 60 kph (37 mph), and your license could be confiscated.

Right turns on red lights are forbidden. Headlights must be kept on outside municipalities, and you must wear seat belts. Fines for using mobile phones while driving can exceed €1,000. The blood alcohol limit is 0.05% (stricter than in the United States).

Train

The fastest trains on the Ferrovie dello Stato Italiane (FS), or Italian State Railways, are the Frecciarossa. Their privately owned competitor, Nuovo Trasporto Viaggiatori (NTV), or Italo, also runs high-speed service between all major northern cities and as far as Reggio Calabria in the south. Seat reservations are mandatory for these bullet trains, just as they are for the Eurostar and slower Intercity (IC) trains; tickets for the latter are about half the price of those for the faster trains.

You can buy your tickets at machines in the station or on ⊕ *www.trenitalia.com*—consider downloading the Trenitalia app. Reservations are not available on Regionale and Espresso trains, which are slower, make more stops, and are less expensive. For these trains, you must validate your ticket before boarding by punching it at a wall- or pillar-mounted yellow or green box—if you forget to do this, find a conductor immediately. Fines for attempting to ride a train without a ticket are €50–€200.

TRAIN PASSES
A rail pass can save you money on train travel. Generally, the more often you plan to travel long distances on high-speed trains, the more sense a pass makes. Keep in mind that even with a pass you still need to reserve seats on the trains that require them.

Travel Times
by Train and Ferry

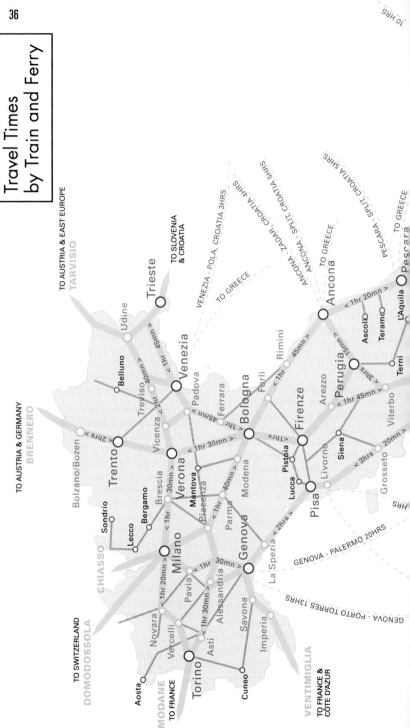

TO AUSTRIA & EAST EUROPE
TARVISIO

TO SLOVENIA
& CROATIA

Trieste

TO AUSTRIA & GERMANY
BRENNERO

Udine

Belluno

Treviso

< 40mn >

< 1hr 45mn >

Venezia

Padova

Ferrara

VENEZIA - POLA, CROATIA 3HRS

TO GREECE

ANCONA - SPLIT, CROATIA 4HRS

ANCONA - ZADAR, CROATIA 6HRS

PESCARA - SPLIT, CROATIA 5HRS

TO GREECE

Ancona

< 1hr 20mn >

L'Aquila

Ascoli

Teramo

Pescara

TO GREECE

Bolzano/Bozen

< 2hrs >

Trento

Vicenza

< 2hr >

< 1hr 45mn >

< 1hr >

Bologna

Rimini

Forlì

< 1hr 45mn >

Firenze

Arezzo

Perugia

< 15mn >

< 3hrs >

Terni

Viterbo

< 20mn >

< 1hr 45mn >

Sondrio

Bergamo

Brescia

< 1hr 30mn >

Verona

Mantova

< 1hr >

Modena

< 40mn >

Pistoia

Lucca

Siena

< 3hrs >

Grosseto

HRS

Lecco

< 1hr 20mn >

Milano

< 1hr >

Piacenza

Parma

< 1hr >

Pisa

Livorno

CHIASSO

Novara

Pavia

< 1hr 30mn >

Alessandria

< 30mn >

Genova

La Spezia

< 2hrs >

GENOVA - PALERMO 20HRS

TO SWITZERLAND
DOMODOSSOLA

Aosta

Vercelli

Asti

Savona

Imperia

GENOVA - PORTO TORRES 13HRS

MODANE
TO FRANCE

Torino

Cuneo

VENTIMIGLIA

TO FRANCE &
CÔTE D'AZUR

TO GREECE
TO GREECE
BARI - DUBROVNIK, CROATIA

Brindisi
Lecce
Taranto
Crotone
Catanzaro
Bari
Potenza
Reggio Calabria
Foggia
Campobasso
Benevento
Avellino
Salerno
< 5hrs 30mn >
Messina
Siracusa
Catania

< 3hrs 20mn >
< 4hrs 45mn >
Sulmona
< 5hrs >
Isernia
Caserta
Napoli
< 1hr 15mn >
< 3hrs 30mn >

NAPOLI - CATANIA 11HRS
NAPOLI - PALERMO 8HRS
< 3hrs >
Enna
Palermo
Agrigento

Roma
CIVITAVECCHIA - PALERMO 13HRS
Trapani

Civitavecchia
CIVITAVECCHIA - OLBIA 5HRS
NAPOLI - OLBIA 12HRS
LIVORNO - OLBIA
CIVITAVECCHIA - CAGLIARI 15HRS
CAGLIARI - PALERMO 14HRS

Olbia
Sassari
< 4hrs >
Oristano
Cagliari

KEY

◯ Major train stations
National train service
Regional train service
------ Ferry service
MODANE Border stations
<time> Eurostar (shortest) travel time between stations.

38

Essentials

🍴 Dining

Italian cuisine is still largely regional, so try spaghetti *alla carbonara* (with cured pork jowl and egg yoke) in Rome, pizza in Naples, *cinghiale* (wild boar) in Tuscany, or *tartufi* (truffles) in Piedmont. Nowadays, vegetarian and gluten-free options are widely available. Still, if you have dietary restrictions, ask about ingredients; not everything is listed in menu descriptions.

The restaurants we list are the finest in each price category. Unless otherwise noted, they're open for lunch and dinner, closing one or two days a week.

MEALS

Although the distinction has blurred, *ristoranti* tend to be more elegant and expensive than trattorias or *osterie,* which serve traditional, home-style fare. Meals generally consist of an *antipasto* (starter) followed by a *primo* (first course), a *secondo* (main course) or *contorno* (vegetable side dish), and *dolce* (dessert). You can, of course, eat less (perhaps just a primo or secondo and a dolce). Single dishes are more the norm at an enoteca or pizzeria, and you can grab affordable snacks at bars, cafés, and spots for pizza *al taglio* (by the slice).

WINES, BEER, AND SPIRITS

The grape has been cultivated here since the time of the Etruscans, with Tuscany, Piedmont, the Veneto, Puglia, Calabria, Sicily, Le Marche, and Umbria among the renowned areas. Beer is readily available, and Italy has some excellent microbreweries, so ask about local brews. In addition, Italians are imaginative with their cocktails, so consider trying the *aperitivo della casa* (house aperitif). The minimum drinking age in Italy is 16.

⇨ *Restaurant reviews throughout this guide have been shortened. For full*

information, visit Fodors.com. Restaurant prices are the average cost of a main course at dinner or, if dinner is not served, at lunch.

What It Costs in Euros			
$	$$	$$$	$$$$
AT DINNER			
under €15	€15–€24	€25–€35	over €35

➕ Health/Safety

EMERGENCIES

No matter where you are in Italy, dial ☎ 112 for all emergencies. Key words to remember for emergency situations are *aiuto* for "help" (pronounced aye-you-toh) and *pronto soccorso,* which means "first aid." When confronted with a health emergency, head straight for the Pronto Soccorso department of the nearest hospital or dial ☎ 118. To call a Red Cross *ambulanza* (ambulance), dial ☎ 800/065510. If you just need a doctor, ask for *un medico.* Ask the physician for *una fattura* (an invoice) to present to your insurance company for reimbursement.

HEALTH

Smoking is banned inside all public places, so sit indoors (where there's also often air-conditioning) if the smoke in outdoor seating areas bothers you.

It's always best to travel with your own trusted medications. Should you need prescription medication while in Italy, speak with a physician to ensure it's the proper kind. Aspirin (*l'aspirina*) can be purchased at any pharmacy, as can over-the-counter medicines such as ibuprofen or acetaminophen.

COVID-19

COVID-19 brought travel to a virtual standstill for most of 2020 and into 2021, but vaccinations have made travel possible and more safe. However, each destination (and each business within that destination) may have its own requirements and regulations. Consider protecting yourself by purchasing a travel insurance policy that will reimburse you for cancellation costs related to COVID-19. Not all travel insurance policies protect against pandemic-related cancellations, so always read the fine print.

🛏 Lodging

Many Italian lodgings, some quite luxurious, are in palazzi, villas, monasteries, and smaller historic buildings that have been restored to blend modern comforts with original atmosphere. Another option is renting a vacation property—although, in addition to budget, you should keep in mind location (street noise and neighborhood ambience in cities and towns, degree of isolation in the countryside), the availability of an elevator or the number of stairs, the utility costs, and what's supplied (furnishings, including pots and linens, as well as sundries like dish detergent).

If you're intrigued by the "locavore" movement, ask local tourism offices about *agriturismo* accommodations. Rural farm-stay properties range from luxury villas to farmhouses with basic facilities.

The lodgings we list are the cream of the crop in each price category. Properties are assigned price categories based on the rate for two people sharing a standard double room in high season, including tax and service.

Item	Average Cost
Cup of coffee	€1–€1.60
Soft drink (glass/can/bottle)	€1.80–€3.25
Glass of beer	€3.50–€7
Sandwich	€3–€5.50
2-km (1-mile) taxi ride in Rome	€9

⇨ *Hotel reviews throughout this guide have been shortened. For full information, visit Fodors.com. Hotel prices are for a standard double room in high season.*

What It Costs in Euros			
$	$$	$$$	$$$$
LODGING FOR TWO			
under €125	€125–€200	€201–€300	over €300

💲 Money

Of Italy's major cities—where, as in other countries, prices are higher than in the countryside—Milan is by far the most expensive. Resort areas like Capri, Portofino, and Cortina d'Ampezzo cater to wealthy vacationers and also charge top prices. Good value can be found in the scenic Trentino–Alto Adige region of the Dolomites and in Umbria and Le Marche. With a few exceptions, southern Italy and Sicily also offer bargains for those who do their homework before they leave home.

Essentials

 ## Passport

A U.S. passport is relatively simple to obtain and is valid for 10 years. You must apply in person if you're getting a passport for the first time; if your previous passport was lost, stolen, or damaged; or if it has expired and was issued more than 15 years ago or when you were under 16. The cost of a new passport is $165 for adults, $135 for children under 16; renewals are $130. Allow 10 to 13 weeks for processing.

 ## Tipping

In restaurants a service charge of 10%–15% may appear on your check, but it's not a given that your server will receive this; consider leaving a tip of 5%–10% (in cash) for good service. At a hotel bar, tip €1 and up for a round or two of drinks. Taxi drivers also appreciate a euro or two, particularly if they help with luggage.

In hotels, give the *portiere* (concierge) about 10% of the bill for services or €3–€5 for help with dinner reservations and such. In moderately priced hotels, leave chambermaids about €1 per day, and tip a minimum of €1 for valet or room service. In expensive hotels, double these amounts. Sightseeing guides should receive €1.50 at least per person for a half-day group tour, more if the tour is longer and/or they're especially knowledgeable.

 ## U.S. Embassy/Consulate

In addition to the embassy in Rome, the United States has consulates general in Florence, Milan, and Naples. If you're arrested or detained, ask Italian officials to notify the embassy or nearest consulate immediately. Consider participating in the U.S. Department of State's Smart Traveler Enrollment Program (STEP) (⊕ *step.state.gov/step*) to receive alerts and make it easier to locate you in an emergency.

 ## Visa

From 2024, entry for visa-exempt nationals from 60 countries including the U.S. and Canada will require travel authorization from ETIAS (European Travel Information and Authorization System). It is linked to your current passport and valid for three years, allowing stays up to 90 days in any 180-day period. Most applications should be approved in a few minutes via the website (⊕ *etias.com*) and costs €7 (free for those under 18 and over 70) but do allow at least 30 days should further evidence and an interview be required.

When to Go

High Season: June through September is expensive and busy. In August, most Italians take their own summer holidays; cities are less crowded, but many shops and restaurants close. July and August can be uncomfortably hot.

Low Season: Unless you're skiing, winter offers the least appealing weather, although it's the best time for airfare and hotel deals and to escape the crowds. Temperatures in the south can be mild.

Value Season: By late September, temperate weather and saner airfares can make for a happier trip. October is also great, but November is often rainy. March and early April weather is changeable. From late April to early May, the masses have not yet arrived.

Great Itineraries

Rome in 3 Days

Rome wasn't built in a day—so don't try to see it all in a day. Three days is a doable, if jam-packed, amount of time to visit the ancient city's major attractions.

Logistics: Much of the city shuts down on Sunday (including the Vatican Museums, except for the last Sunday of the month), and many restaurants and state museums are closed on Monday. To skip lines and better enjoy your experiences, reservations are a good idea at the Colosseum and the Vatican Museums; they're required for the Galleria Borghese.

DAY 1: ANCIENT ROME
Spend your first day in Rome exploring the likes of the **Roman Forum, Musei Capitolini,** and the **Colosseum.** This area is pretty compact, but you can easily spend a full morning and afternoon exploring its treasures. It's best to try and beat the crowds at the Colosseum by getting there right when it opens at 8:30 am (advance tickets help, too). A guided tour of the Forum is also a good way to make the most out of your afternoon. After your day of sightseeing, stop for a classic Roman dinner in nearby Monti.

DAY 2: THE VATICAN AND PIAZZA NAVONA
Another full day of sightseeing awaits when you make your way to the city-state known as the **Vatican.** You'll once again want to try and avoid the biggest crowds here, especially for a glimpse of the Sistine Chapel (the best way to do this is to make online reservations ahead of time). Booking a tour of the **Vatican Museums** is a good way to take full advantage of the site; most tours last two hours. Be sure to stop in and marvel at **St. Peter's Basilica,** too. Stop for lunch in nearby Prati, but after you're done with the Vatican, cross the river to **Piazza Navona.**

Spend some time exploring this glorious piazza and its sculptures, but make sure to stop by the **Pantheon** before heading to Campo de' Fiori for dinner at an outdoor restaurant. Afterward, there are plenty of nearby bars to keep you occupied.

DAY 3: PIAZZA DI SPAGNA, VILLA BORGHESE, AND TRASTEVERE
Start your morning with breakfast near the **Trevi Fountain** before doing some window-shopping up Via Condotti and along the many surrounding backstreets as you make your way to the **Spanish Steps.** Pose for some postcard-worthy photos there before heading to nearby **Villa Borghese.** If you're sick of museums, feel free to explore Rome's main park and enjoy the great views; if you're up for some more art, the **Galleria Borghese** is one of the city's best art museums. Afterward, head to trendy Trastevere for dinner, and soak up the cobblestone streets and charming medieval houses as you barhop your last night in town.

IF YOU HAVE MORE TIME
If you want to make the most of your time in the city itself, take your time exploring the many churches and cathedrals, like **Sant'Ignazio** or **San Clemente.** You can also stop by to explore gorgeous palaces, like the **Palazzo Doria Pamphilij,** and check out lesser known but just as impressive museums, like the MAXXI or the MACRO. Visiting the ancient Roman road known as the Via Appia Antica and its spooky yet mesmerizing catacombs is a great way to spend an afternoon immersed in Roman history. Make time for some shopping: early evenings are a good time to saunter around the big-label boutiques of Piazza di Spagna and historic independents of Piazza Navona. For flea market bargains check out the Mercato di Porta Portese.

Great Itineraries

Venice, Florence, Rome, and Highlights in Between

Think of this itinerary as a rough draft for you to revise according to your interests and time constraints.

DAY 1: VENICE

Arrive in Venice's Marco Polo Airport, and hop on the bus to the city's main bus station. Check into your hotel, get out, and get lost along the canals for a couple of hours before dinner.

Logistics: At the main bus station, you can immediately transfer to the most delightful "bus" in the world: the vaporetto. Enjoy your first ride up the Grand Canal, and make sure you're paying attention to the *fermata* (stop) where you need to get off.

DAY 2: VENICE

If you like photography, rise before dawn to catch a vaporetto to Giudecca and walk along the long Fondamenta, observing the golden hour hues bathe Palladio's Redentore and the stunning canal views. Grab a coffee at a real Italian coffee bar before taking in the top sights, including the **Basilica di San Marco, Palazzo Ducale,** and **Galleria dell'Accademia.** Don't forget **Piazza San Marco**: the intense anticipation as you near the giant square climaxes in a stunning view of the piazza. Stop for lunch, sampling the traditional Venetian specialty *sarde in saor* (sardines in a mouthwatering sweet-and-sour preparation with onions and raisins), and check out the fish market at the foot of the **Rialto Bridge**; then see the sunset at the **Zattere** before dinner. Later, stop at a bar on the **Campo San Luca** or **Campo Santa Margherita,** where you can mingle with the students and families enjoying the open space, and toast to being free of automobiles.

Logistics: Venice is best seen on foot, with the occasional vaporetto ride. Always carry a city map: it's very easy to get totally lost here.

DAY 3: FERRARA/BOLOGNA

The ride to **Ferrara,** your first stop in Emilia-Romagna, is about 90 minutes. Visit the **Castello Estense** and **Duomo** before grabbing lunch. Wander Ferrara's cobblestone streets, then hop on the train to **Bologna** (less than an hour away). Check into your hotel, and walk around **Piazza Maggiore** before dinner, soaking up the bustle and architectural gems including the **Fontana del Nettuno.** Later check out some of Italy's best nightlife.

Logistics: The train station lies a bit outside the center of Ferrara, so you may want to take a taxi or a less expensive city bus into town.

DAY 4: BOLOGNA/FLORENCE

After breakfast, visit some of Bologna's churches and piazzas, and climb the leaning **Torre degli Asinelli** for a red-rooftop-studded panorama. After lunch, take the short train ride to **Florence.** You'll arrive in time for an afternoon siesta and an evening passeggiata.

DAY 5: FLORENCE

Start with the **Uffizi Gallery,** where you'll see Botticelli's *Primavera* and *Birth of Venus,* the *Madonna of the Goldfinch* by Raphael, and *Bacchus* by Caravaggio, among other works. Next, walk to **Piazza del Duomo,** site of Brunelleschi's spectacular dome, which you can climb for an equally spectacular view. After a simple trattoria lunch, either devote the afternoon to art or hike up to **Piazzale Michelangelo,** which overlooks the city. Finish the evening in style with a traditional *bistecca alla fiorentina* (grilled T-bone steak with olive oil).

Logistics: It's best to reserve Uffizi Gallery tickets in advance; you *must* reserve in advance to climb Brunelleschi's dome.

DAY 6: LUCCA/PISA

After breakfast, board a train for a 90-minute ride to the walled medieval city of **Lucca.** Don't miss the Romanesque **Duomo** or a walk along the city's ramparts. Have lunch at a trattoria before continuing on to **Pisa** (30 minutes away) and its **Campo dei Miracoli,** where you'll spend an afternoon seeing the **Leaning Tower,** along with the **Duomo** and **Battistero.** Walk down to the banks of the Arno River and dine at one of the inexpensive local restaurants in the real city center.

Logistics: Lucca's train station is conveniently situated just outside the walled city. Although across town from the Leaning Tower, Pisa's train station isn't far from the city center.

DAY 7: ROME

Take a high-speed train bound for **Rome,** a 90-minute trip from Florence, or three hours from Pisa. Although the Eternal City took millennia to build, on this whirlwind trip you'll have just two days to tour it. Make your way to your hotel and relax for a bit before heading to the **Piazza Navona, Campo de' Fiori,** and **Trevi Fountain**—it's best in the evening—and have a stand-up aperitivo (Campari and soda is a classic) at an unpretentious local bar. For dinner, you can't go wrong at any of Rome's popular local pizzerias.

DAY 8: ROME

In the morning, head to the **Vatican Museums** to see Michelangelo's glorious frescoes at the **Sistine Chapel.** Visit **St. Peter's Basilica and Square** before heading for lunch near the Pantheon. Next, visit the magnificent **Pantheon,** and then the **Colosseum,** stopping along Via dei Fori Imperiali to check out the **Roman Forum** from above. From the Colosseum, walk or take a taxi to **Piazza di Spagna,** a good place to shop at stylish boutiques.

Logistics: Avoid lines and waits by buying tickets online.

DAY 9: ROME/DEPARTURE

Head by taxi to Termini station and catch the train to Fiumicino airport.

Logistics: For most people, the train from Termini station is preferable to a taxi ride.

On the Calendar

Spring

Carnevale. Venice earned its international reputation as the "city of Carnevale" in the 18th century, when partying would begin several months before Lent and the city seemed to be one continuous masquerade. The celebration was revived for good in the 1970s, and each year over the 15- to 17-day Carnevale period (ending on the Tuesday before Ash Wednesday), more than a half-million people attend concerts, theater and street performances, masquerade balls, historical processions, fashion shows, and contests.

If you're not planning on joining in the revelry, you'd be wise to choose another time to visit Venice. Crowds throng the streets (which become one-way, with police directing foot traffic), bridges are designated "no-stopping" zones to avoid gridlock, and prices skyrocket. ⊕ *www. carnevale.venezia.it*

Scoppio del Carro (Explosion of the Cart). On Easter Sunday, Florentines and foreigners alike flock to the Piazza del Duomo to watch as the Scoppio del Carro, a monstrosity of a carriage pulled by two huge oxen decorated for the occasion, makes its way through the city center and ends up in the piazza. Through an elaborate wiring system, an object representing a dove is sent from inside the cathedral to the baptistery across the way. The dove sets off an explosion of fireworks that come streaming from the carriage. You have to see it to believe it. ⊕ *www. visittuscany.com*

Vinitaly. This widely attended international wine and spirits event in Verona takes place for a few days in April. Recent gatherings have attracted more than 4,000 exhibitors from two dozen countries. The festivities kick off with Opera Wine,

a showcase for the top 100 Italian wines as chosen by *Wine Spectator* magazine, which takes place in the Palazzo della Gran Guardia, in Piazza Bra. ⊕ *www. vinitaly.com*

Biennale di Venezia. Come springtime every two years (the even-numbered) the contemporary art world and the curious descend on Venice's Giardini pavilions, Arsenale dockside warehouses, and scattered palazzi. In odd years it's the turn of the world's leading architects to display their creations. ⊕ *www.labiennale.org*

Milan Design Week. For a week in April Italy's northern powerhouse city hosts the biggest gathering of the design world. Pride of place in the calendar is the Salone di Mobile, a furniture fair like no other, staged in the cavernous Fiera Milano exhibition center and in dozens of venues across this design-mad city. ⊕ *www.salonemilano.it*

Summer

Arena di Verona Opera Festival. Milan's La Scala and Naples's San Carlo offer performances more likely to attract serious opera fans, but neither offers a greater spectacle than the Arena di Verona. During the venue's summer season (June to August), as many as 16,000 attendees sit on the original stone terraces or in modern cushioned stalls. Most of the operas presented are big and splashy, like *Aida* or *Turandot*, demanding huge choruses, lots of color and movement, and, if possible, camels, horses, or elephants. Order tickets by phone or through the arena website: if you book a spot on the cheaper terraces, be sure to take or rent a cushion—four hours on a 2,000-year-old stone bench can be an ordeal (from €28 for general admission). ⊕ *www.arena.it*

Festa del Redentore. On the third Sunday in July, crowds cross the Canale della Giudecca by means of a pontoon bridge, built every year to commemorate the doge's annual visit to Palladio's Chiesa del Santissimo Redentore to offer thanks for the end of a 16th-century plague. The evening before, Venetians—accompanied each year by an increasing number of tourists—set up tables and chairs along the canals. As evening falls, practically the whole city takes to the streets and tables, and thousands more take to the water. Boats decorated with colored lanterns (and well provisioned with traditional Redentore meals) jockey for position to watch the grand event. Half an hour before midnight, Venice kicks off a fireworks display over the Bacino, with brilliant reflections on its waters. You'll find good viewing anywhere along the Riva degli Schiavoni; you could also try Zattere, as close to Punta Dogana as you can get, or on the Zitelle end of the Giudecca. ⊕ *www.redentorevenezia.it*

Festa di San Giovanni (Feast of St. John the Baptist). On June 24 Florence mostly grinds to a halt to celebrate the Festa di San Giovanni in honor of its patron saint. Many shops and bars close, and at night a fireworks display lights up the Arno and attracts thousands. ⊕ *www.visit-tuscany.com/en/ideas/june-24th-in-flor-ence-san-giovannis-celebrations*

Festival dei Due Mondi. Each summer Umbria hosts one of Italy's biggest arts festivals: Spoleto's Festival of the Two Worlds. Starting out as a classical music festival, it has now evolved into one of Italy's brightest gatherings of arts aficionados. Running from late June through mid-July, it features modern and classical music, theater, dance, and opera. Increasingly there are also a number of small cinema producers and their films. ⊕ *www.festivaldispoleto.com*

Luminaria. Pisa is at its best during the Luminaria feast day, on June 16. The day honors St. Ranieri, the city's patron saint. Palaces along the Arno are lit with white lights, and there are plenty of fireworks. ⊕ *www.turismo.pisa.it/en/events*

Ravenna Festival. Orchestras from all over the world perform in city churches and theaters during this renowned music festival, which takes place in June and July, as well as during a few days at the beginning of November. ⊕ *www.raven-nafestival.org*

Umbria Jazz Festival. Perugia is hopping for 10 days in July, when more than a million people flock to see famous names in contemporary music perform at the Umbria Jazz Festival. In recent years the stars have included Wynton Marsalis, Sting, Eric Clapton, Lady Gaga, Tony Bennett, and Elton John. There's also a shorter Umbria Jazz Winter Festival from late December to early January. ⊕ *www.umbriajazz.com*

Fall

Eurochocolate Festival. If you've got a sweet tooth and are visiting in fall, book early and head to Perugia for the Eurochocolate Festival. This is one of the biggest chocolate festivals in the world, with a million visitors, and is held over a week in late October. From 2021 there's a new International Chocolate Exhibition event in late March–early April. ⊕ *www.eurochocolate.com*

Sagra Musicale Umbra. Held mid-September, the Sagra Musicale Umbra celebrates sacred music in Perugia and in several towns throughout the region. ⊕ *www.perugiamusicaclassica.com*

Helpful Italian Phrases

BASICS

Yes/no	Sí/No	see/no
Please	Per favore	pear fa-**vo**-ray
Thank you	Grazie	**grah**-tsee-ay
You're welcome	Prego	**pray**-go
I'm sorry (apology)	Mi dispiace	mee dis-pee-**atch**-ay
Excuse me, sorry	Scusi	**skoo**-zee
Good morning/ afternoon	Buongiorno	bwohn-**jor**-no
Good evening	Buona sera	**bwoh**-na **say**-ra
Good-bye	Arrivederci	a-ree-vah-**dare**-chee
Mr. (Sir)	Signore	see-**nyo**-ray
Mrs. (Ma'am)	Signora	see-**nyo**-ra
Miss	Signorina	see-nyo-**ree**-na
Pleased to meet you	Piacere	pee-ah-**chair**-ray
How are you?	Come sta?	**ko**-may-**stah**
Hello (phone)	Pronto?	**proan**-to

NUMBERS

one-half	mezzo	**mets**-zoh
one	uno	**oo**-no
two	due	**doo**-ay
three	tre	Tray
four	quattro	**kwah**-tro
five	cinque	**cheen**-kway
six	sei	Say
seven	sette	**set**-ay
eight	otto	**oh**-to
nine	nove	**no**-vay
ten	dieci	dee-**eh**-chee
eleven	undici	**oon**-dee-chee
twelve	dodici	**doh**-dee-chee
thirteen	tredici	**trey**-dee-chee
fourteen	quattordici	kwah-**tor**-dee-chee
fifteen	quindici	**kwin**-dee-chee
sixteen	sedici	**say**-dee-chee
seventeen	dicissette	dee-chah-**set**-ay
eighteen	diciotto	dee-chee-**oh**-to
nineteen	diciannove	dee-chee-ahn-**no**-vay
twenty	venti	**vain**-tee
twenty-one	ventuno	**vent**-oo-no
thirty	trenta	**train**-ta
forty	quaranta	kwa-**rahn**-ta
fifty	cinquanta	cheen-**kwahn**-ta
sixty	sessanta	seh-**sahn**-ta
seventy	settanta	seh-**tahn**-ta
eighty	ottanta	o-**tahn**-ta
ninety	novanta	no-**vahn**-ta
one hundred	cento	**chen**-to
one thousand	mille	**mee**-lay
one million	un milione	oon **mill**-oo-nay

COLORS

black	Nero	**nair**-ro
blue	Blu	bloo
brown	Marrone	ma-**rohn**-nay
green	Verde	**ver**-day
orange	Arancione	ah-rahn-**cho**-nay
red	Rosso	**rose**-so
white	Bianco	bee-**ahn**-koh
yellow	Giallo	**jaw**-low

DAYS OF THE WEEK

Sunday	Domenica	do-**meh**-nee-ka
Monday	Lunedi	loo-ne-**dee**
Tuesday	Martedi	mar-te-**dee**
Wednesday	Mercoledi	**mer**-ko-le-**dee**
Thursday	Giovedi	jo-ve-**dee**
Friday	Venerdì	ve-ner-**dee**
Saturday	Sabato	**sa**-ba-toh

MONTHS

January	Gennaio	jen-**ay**-o
February	Febbraio	feb-**rah**-yo
March	Marzo	**mart**-so
April	Aprile	a-**pril**-ay
May	Maggio	**mahd**-joe
June	Giugno	**joon**-yo
July	Luglio	**lool**-yo
August	Agosto	a-**gus**-to
September	Settembre	se-**tem**-bre
October	Ottobre	o-**toh**-bre
November	Novembre	no-**vem**-bre
December	Dicembre	di-**chem**-bre

USEFUL WORDS AND PHRASES

Do you speak English?	Parla Inglese?	**par**-la een-**glay**-zay
I don't speak Italian	Non parlo italiano	non **par**-lo ee-tal-**yah**-no
I don't understand	Non capisco	non ka-**peess**-ko
I don't know	Non lo so	non lo **so**
I understand	Capisco	ka-**peess**-ko
I'm American	Sono Americano(a)	**so**-no a-may-ree-**kah**-no(a)
I'm British	Sono inglese	so-no een-**glay**-zay
What's your name?	Come si chiama?	**ko**-may see kee-**ah**-ma
My name is ...	Mi chiamo...	mee kee-**ah**-mo
What time is it?	Che ore sono?	kay **o**-ray **so**-no
How?	Come?	**ko**-may
When?	Quando?	**kwan**-doe
Yesterday/today/ tomorrow	Ieri/oggi/domani	**yer**-ee/ **o**-jee/ do-**mah**-nee

This morning	Stamattina/Oggi	sta-ma-**tee**-na/ **o**-jee
Afternoon	Pomeriggio	po-mer-**ee**-jo
Tonight	Stasera	sta-**ser**-a
What?	Che cosa?	kay **ko**-za
What is it?	Che cos'è?	kay ko-**zey**
Why?	Perchè?	pear-**kay**
Who?	Chi?	**Kee**
Where is …	Dov'è…	doe-**veh**
the train station?	la stazione?	la sta-tsee-**oh**-nay
the subway?	la metropolitana?	la may-tro-po-lee-**tah**-na
the bus stop?	la fermata dell'autobus?	la fer-**mah**-ta del-ow-tor-**booss**
the airport	l'aeroporto	la-er-roh-**por**-toh
the post office?	l'ufficio postale	loo-**fee**-cho po-**stah**-lay
the bank?	la banca?	la **bahn**-ka
the hotel?	l'hotel…?	lo-**tel**
the museum?	Il museo	eel moo-**zay**-o
the hospital?	l'ospedale?	lo-spay-**dah**-lay
the elevator?	l'ascensore	la-shen-**so**-ray
the restrooms?	…il bagno	eel **bahn**-yo
Here/there	Qui/là	kwee/la
Left/right	A sinistra/a destra	a see-**neess**-tra/a **des**-tra
Is it near/far?	È vicino/lontano?	ay vee-**chee**-no/ lon-**tah**-no
I'd like …	Vorrei…	vo-**ray**
a room	una camera	**oo**-na **kah**-may-ra
the key	la chiave	la kee-**ah**-vay
a newspaper	un giornale	oon jore-**nah**-vay
a stamp	un francobollo	oon frahn-ko-**bo**-lo
I'd like to buy …	Vorrei comprare…	vo-**ray** kom-**prah**-ray
a city map	una mappa della città	**oo**-na **mah**-pa **day**-la chee-**tah**
a road map	una carta stradale	**oo**-na **car**-tah stra-**dahl**-lay
a magazine	una revista	**oo**-na ray-**vees**-tah
envelopes	buste	**boos**-tay
writing paper	carta de lettera	**car**-tah dah **leyt**-ter-rah
a postcard	una cartolina	**oo**-na car-tog-**leen**-ah
a ticket	un biglietto	oon bee-**yet**-toh
How much is it?	Quanto costa?	**kwahn**-toe **coast**-a
It's expensive/cheap	È caro/economico	ay **car**-o/ ay-ko-**no**-mee-ko
A little/a lot	Poco/tanto	**po**-ko/**tahn**-to
More/less	Più/meno	pee-**oo/may**-no

Enough/too (much)	Abbastanza/troppo	a-bas-**tahn**-sa/tro-po
I am sick	Sto male	sto **mah**-lay
Call a doctor	Chiama un dottore	kee-**ah**-mah-oondoe-**toe**-ray
Help!	Aiuto!	a-**yoo**-to
Stop!	Alt!	ahlt

DINING OUT

A bottle of …	Una bottiglia di…	**oo**-na bo-**tee**-lee-ah dee
A cup of …	Una tazza di…	**oo**-na **tah**-tsa dee
A glass of …	Un bicchiere di…	oon bee-key-**air**-ay dee
Beer	La birra	la **beer**-rah
Bill/check	Il conto	eel **cone**-toe
Bread	Il pane	eel **pah**-nay
Breakfast	La prima colazione	la **pree**-ma ko-la-**tsee**-oh-nay
Butter	Il burro	eel **boor**-roh
Cocktail/aperitif	L'aperitivo	la-pay-ree-**tee**-vo
Dinner	La cena	la **chen**-a
Fixed-price menu	Menù a prezzo fisso	may-**noo** a **pret**-so **fee**-so
Fork	La forchetta	la for-**ket**-a
I am vegetarian	Sono vegetariano(a)	**so**-no vay-jay-ta-ree-**ah**-no/a
I cannot eat …	Non posso mangiare	non **pose**-so mahn-gee-**are**-ay
I'd like to order	Vorrei ordinare	vo-**ray** or-dee-**nah**-ray
Is service included?	Il servizio è incluso?	eel ser-**vee**-tzee-o ay een-**kloo**-zo
I'm hungry/thirsty	Ho fame/sede	oh **fah**-meh/**sehd**-ed
It's good/bad	È buono/cattivo	ay **bwo**-bo/ka-**tee**-vo
It's hot/cold	È caldo/freddo	ay **kahl**-doe/**fred**-o
Knife	Il coltello	eel kol-**tel**-o
Lunch	Il pranzo	eel **prahnt**-so
Menu	Il menu	eel may-**noo**
Napkin	Il tovagliolo	eel toe-va-lee-**oh**-lo
Pepper	Il pepe	eel **pep**-peh
Plate	Il piatto	eel pee-**aht**-toe
Please give me …	Mi dia…	mee **dee**-a
Salt	Il sale	eel **sah**-lay
Spoon	Il cucchiaio	eel koo-kee-ah-yo
Tea	tè	tay
Water	acqua	**awk**-wah
Wine	vino	**vee**-noh

Contacts

Air

**AIRLINE SECURITY
ISSUES Transportation
Security Administration.**
(*TSA*). ☎ *866/289–9673*
⊕ *www.tsa.gov.*

**AIRPORT INFORMATION
Aeroporto di Bologna.**
(*BLQ, aka Guglielmo
Marconi*). ✉ *6 km (4
miles) northwest of
Bologna* ☎ *051/6479615*
⊕ *www.bologna-airport.it.*
Aeroporto di Caglari. (*CAG,
aka Elmas*). ✉ *7 km (4½
miles) from Cagliari, Via
dei Trasvolatori, Elmas,
Cagliari* ☎ *070/211211*
⊕ *www.sogaer.it.* **Aeroporto di Catania.** (*CTA, aka
Fontanarossa*). ✉ *7 km
(4½ miles) southwest of
Catania* ☎ *095/7239111*
⊕ *www.aeroporto.catania.
it.* **Aeroporto di Firenze.** (*FLR, aka Amerigo
Vespucci or Peretola*). ✉ *6
km (4 miles) northwest of
Florence* ☎ *055/3061830*
⊕ *www.aeroporto.firenze.
it.* **Aeroporto di Milan
Linate.** (*LIN*). ✉ *8 km (5
miles) southeast of Milan*
☎ *02/232323* ⊕ *www.
milanolinate-airport.
com.* **Aeroporto di Milano
Malpensa.** (*MXP*). ✉ *45 km
(28 miles) north of Milan*
☎ *02/232323* ⊕ *www.
milanomalpensa-airport.
com.* **Aeroporto di Palermo.**
(*PMO, aka Falcone e
Borsellino or Punta
Raisi*). ✉ *32 km (19 miles)
northwest of Palermo*
☎ *091/7020273* ⊕ *www.*

aeroportodipalermo.it.
Aeroporto di Pisa. (*PSA,
aka Aeroporto Galileo
Galilei*). ✉ *2 km (1 mile)
south of Pisa, 80 km (50
miles) west of Florence*
☎ *050/849111* ⊕ *www.
pisa-airport.com.* **Aeroporto
di Roma Ciampino.** (*CIA*).
✉ *15 km (9 miles) south-
west of Rome* ☎ *06/65951*
⊕ *www.adr.it/wcb/aero-
porti-di-roma-en/pax-cia-ci-
ampino.* **Aeroporto di Roma
Fiumicino.** (*FCO, aka Leonardo da Vinci*). ✉ *35 km (20
miles) southwest of Rome*
☎ *06/65951* ⊕ *www.adr.it.*
Aeroporto di Venezia. (*VCE,
aka Marco Polo*). ✉ *6 km
(4 miles) north of Venice*
☎ *041/2609260* ⊕ *www.
veneziaairport.it.* **Aeroporto
Internazionale di Napoli.**
(*NAP, aka Capodichino*).
✉ *5 km (3 miles) northeast
of Naples* ☎ *081/7896111*
⊕ *www.aeroportodi-
napoli.it.* **Aeroporto Orio al
Serio–Milan Bergamo (BGY).**
✉ *Via Orio al Serio 49/51,
24050 Grassobbio (BG)*
☎ *035/326323.*

Bus

ACTV Venezia. ✉ *Venice*
☎ *041/041 call center*
⊕ *actv.avmspa.it.* **ANM
Napoli.** ✉ *Via G. Marino 1,
Naples* ☎ *800/639525 toll-
free in Italy* ⊕ *www.anm.
it.* **ATAC Roma.** ☎ *06/0606*
⊕ *www.atac.roma.
it.* **ATM Milano.** ✉ *Milan*
☎ *02/48607607* ⊕ *www.*

atm.it. **Autolinee Toscane.**
✉ *Biglietteria Firenze, Via
Santa Caterina da Siena
17, Florence* ☎ *800/142424*
⊕ *www.at-bus.it.* **Busitalia.**
✉ *Viale Fratelli Rosselli 80,
Florence* ☎ *075/9637001
Umbria, 089/9847299
Campania, 049/8206811
Veneto* ⊕ *www.fsbusita-
lia.it.* **Dolomiti Bus.** ✉ *Via
Col da Ren 14, Belluno*
☎ *0437/217111* ⊕ *www.
dolomitibus.it.* **FlixBus.**
⊕ *www.flixbus.com.* **Marino Bus.** ☎ *080/3112335*
⊕ *www.marinobus.it.* **Sita
Sud.** ✉ *Via S. Francesco
d'Assisi 1, Putignano*
☎ *080/5790111* ⊕ *www.
sitasudtrasporti.it.*

🚆 Train

**TRAIN INFORMA-
TION FS-Trenitalia.**
☎ *06/68475475 from
outside Italy (English),
892021 in Italy* ⊕ *www.
trenitalia.com.* **NTV Italo.**
☎ *892020 Call Center*
⊕ *www.italotreno.it.*

CONTACTS Eurail. ⊕ *www.
eurail.com.* **Italia Rail.**
☎ *877/375–7245 in U.S.,
06/97632451 in Italy*
⊕ *www.italiarail.com.*
Rail Europe. ⊕ *www.
raileurope.com.* **RailPass.**
☎ *877/3757245 toll-free
from U.S.* ⊕ *www.railpass.
com.*

Chapter 3

ROME

Updated by
Laura Itzkowitz
and Natalie Kennedy

◉ Sights	🍴 Restaurants	🛏 Hotels	🛍 Shopping	🍸 Nightlife
★★★★★	★★★☆☆	★★★★★	★★★★☆	★★★★☆

WELCOME TO ROME

TOP REASONS TO GO

★ **The Vatican:** Although its population numbers only in the hundreds, the Vatican makes up for it with the millions who visit each year. Marvel at Michelangelo's Sistine Chapel and St. Peter's Basilica.

★ **The Colosseum:** The largest amphitheater of the Roman world was begun by Emperor Vespasian and inaugurated by his son Titus in AD 80.

★ **Piazza Navona:** You couldn't concoct a more Roman street scene: crowded café tables at street level, wrought-iron balconies above, and, at the center, Bernini's Fountain of the Four Rivers and Borromini's Sant'Agnese.

★ **Roman Forum:** This fabled labyrinth of ruins variously served as a political playground, a center of commerce, and a place where justice was dispensed during the Roman Republic and Empire.

★ **Trastevere:** This neighborhood is a maze of jumbled alleyways, traditional Roman trattorias, cobblestone streets, and medieval houses.

1 **Ancient Rome with Monti and Celio.** The Forum and Palatine Hill were once the hub of Western civilization.

2 **The Vatican with Borgo and Prati.** St. Peter's Basilica and the Sistine Chapel draw millions.

3 **Piazza Navona, Campo de' Fiori, and the Jewish Ghetto.** This is the heart of the historic quarter. The Ghetto still preserves the flavor of Old Rome.

4 **Piazza di Spagna.** Travel back to the days of the Grand Tour in this area.

5 **Repubblica and the Quirinale.** These areas house government offices, churches, and sights.

6 **Villa Borghese and Environs.** Rome's most famous park is home to the Galleria Borghese.

7 **Trastevere.** Rome's left bank has kept its authentic roots.

8 **Aventino and Testaccio.** Aventino is a posh residential area, and Testaccio is more working class.

9 **Esquilino and Via Appia Antica.** These neighborhoods have plenty of ancient sights and churches.

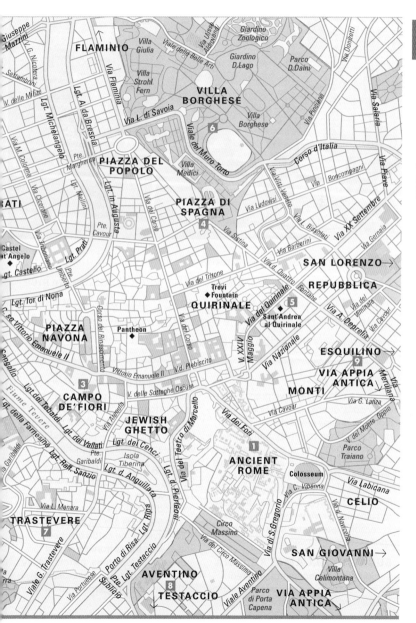

EAT LIKE A LOCAL IN ROME

A local salumeria or cured meat shop

In Rome, tradition is the dominant feature of the cuisine, with a focus on freshness and simplicity, so when Romans continue ordering the standbys, it's easy to understand why. That said, the influx of residents to the capital from other regions has yielded many variations on the staples.

ARTICHOKES

There are two well-known preparations of *carciofo*, or artichoke, in Rome. Carciofi *alla romana* are stuffed with wild mint, garlic, and pecorino, then braised in olive oil, white wine, and water. Carciofi *alla giudia* (Jewish-style) are whole artichokes, deep-fried twice, so that they open like a flower, the outer leaves crisp and golden brown, while the heart remains tender. When artichokes are in season—late winter through the spring—they're served everywhere.

BUCATINI ALL'AMATRICIANA

It might look like spaghetti with red sauce, but there's much more to *bucatini all'amatriciana*. It's a spicy, rich, and complex dish that owes its flavor to *guanciale*, or cured pork jowl, as well as tomatoes and crushed red pepper flakes. It's often served over bucatini, a hollow, spaghetti-like pasta, and topped with grated pecorino Romano.

CODA ALLA VACCINARA

Rome's largest slaughterhouse in the 1800s was in the Testaccio neighborhood, and that's where you'll find dishes like *coda alla vaccinara*, or "oxtail in the style of the cattle butcher." This dish is made from ox or veal tails stewed with tomatoes, carrots, celery, and wine, and it's usually seasoned with cinnamon. It's simmered for hours and then finished with raisins and pine nuts or bittersweet chocolate.

GELATO
Its consistency is often said to be a cross between regular American ice cream and soft-serve. The best versions of gelato are extremely flavorful, and almost always made fresh daily. When choosing a *gelateria*, watch for signs that say *gelato artigianale* (artisan- or homemade); otherwise, keep an eye out for the real deal by avoiding gelato that looks too bright or fluffy.

Artichokes

PIZZA
There are two kinds of Roman pizza: *al taglio* (by the slice) and *tonda* (round pizza). The former has a thicker, focaccia-like crust and is cut into squares; these are sold by weight and generally available all day. The typical Roman pizza tonda has a very thin crust and is served almost charred. Because they're so hot, the ovens are usually fired up only in the evening, which is why Roman *pizzerie* tend to open for dinner only.

CACIO E PEPE
The name means "cheese and pepper," and this is a simple pasta dish from the *cucina povera*, or rustic cooking, tradition. It's a favorite Roman primo, usually made with *tonnarelli* (fresh egg pasta a bit thicker than spaghetti),

Gelato

which is coated with a pecorino-cheese sauce and lots of freshly ground black pepper. Some restaurants serve the dish in an edible bowl of paper-thin baked cheese.

FRITTI
The classic Roman starter in a trattoria and especially at the pizzeria, is *fritti*: an assortment of fried treats, usually crumbed or in batter. Often, before selecting a pizza, locals will order their fritti: *filetti di baccalà* (salt cod in batter), *fiori di zucca* (zucchini flowers, usually stuffed with anchovy and mozzarella), *supplì* (rice balls stuffed with mozzarella and other ingredients), or *olive ascolane* (stuffed olives).

LA GRICIA
This dish is often referred to as a "white amatriciana" because it's precisely that: pasta (usually spaghetti or rigatoni) served with pecorino cheese and guanciale—thus amatriciana without the tomato sauce. It's a lighter alternative to carbonara in that it doesn't contain egg, and its origins date back further than the amatriciana.

The timeless city to which all roads lead, Mamma Roma enthralls visitors today as she has since time immemorial. Here the ancient Romans made us heirs-in-law to what we call Western Civilization; where centuries later Michelangelo painted the Sistine Chapel; and where Gian Lorenzo Bernini's Baroque nymphs and naiads still dance in their marble fountains.

Today the city remains a veritable Grand Canyon of culture. Ancient Rome rubs shoulders with the medieval, the modern runs into the Renaissance, and the result is like nothing so much as an open-air museum.

But always remember: *"Quando a Roma vai, fai come vedrai"* (When in Rome, do as the Romans do). Don't feel intimidated by the press of art and culture. Instead, contemplate the grandeur from a table at a sun-drenched café on Piazza della Rotonda; let Rome's colorful life flow around you without feeling guilty because you haven't seen everything. It can't be done, anyway. There's just so much here that you'll have to come back, so be sure to throw a coin in the Trevi Fountain.

Planning

Getting Around

Although most of Rome's sights are in a relatively circumscribed area, the city is too large to be seen solely on foot. Try to avoid rush hour when taking the Metro (subway) or a bus, as public transport can

be extremely crowded. Midmorning or midday through early afternoon tends to be less busy. Otherwise, it's best to take a taxi to the area you plan to visit if it is across town. You should always expect to do a lot of walking in Rome, especially considering how little ground the subway actually covers, so plan on wearing a pair of comfortable, sturdy shoes to cushion the impact of the *sampietrini* (cobblestones). You can get free city and transit maps at municipal information booths.

METRO

Rome's integrated transportation system includes buses and trams (ATAC), the Metropolitana (the subway, or Metro), suburban trains and buses (COTRAL), and the commuter rail run by the state railway (Trenitalia). A ticket (BIT), valid for 100 minutes on any combination of buses and trams and one entrance to the Metro, costs €1.50. Tickets are sold at tobacco shops, newsstands, some coffee bars, automatic ticket machines in Metro stations, some bus stops, in machines on some buses, and at ATAC ticket booths. You can purchase individual or multiple tickets. It's always a good idea to have a few tickets handy so you don't have to hunt for a vendor when you need one. All tickets must be validated by time-stamping in the yellow meter boxes aboard buses and in Metro stations, immediately prior to boarding. Failure to validate your ticket will result in a fine of €54.90. You can now pay for fines on the ATAC website. Pay immediately, or the fine will increase to €104.90 if you pay after five days. You can also pay fines in post offices, authorized shops, or by wire transfer. Do not pay the ticket inspectors in cash; some may be equipped for payment by mobile POS.

A Roma24H ticket, or *biglietto integrato giornaliero* (integrated daily ticket), is valid for 24 hours (from the moment you stamp it) on all public transit and costs €7. You can also purchase a Roma48H (€12.50), a Roma72H (€18), and a CIS (Carta Integrata Settimanale), which is valid for one week (€24). Each option gives you unlimited travel on ATAC buses, COTRAL urban bus services, trains for the Lido and Viterbo, and Metro. There's an ATAC kiosk at the bus terminal in front of Termini station. If you're going farther afield, or planning to spend more than a week in Rome, think about getting a BIRG (daily regional ticket) or a CIRS (weekly regional ticket) from the railway station. These give you unlimited travel on all state transport throughout the region of Lazio. This can take you as far as the Etruscan city of Tarquinia or medieval Viterbo.

BUS AND TRAM

Although not as fast as the Metro, bus and tram travel is more scenic. With reserved bus lanes and numerous tram lines, surface transportation is surprisingly efficient, given the volume of Roman traffic. At peak times, however, buses can be very crowded. If the distance you have to travel is not too great, walking can be a more comfortable alternative. ATAC city buses are red or gray; trams are green. Remember to board at the rear and to exit at the middle: some bus drivers may refuse to let you out the front door, leaving you to scramble through the crowd to exit the middle or rear doors. Don't forget that you must buy your ticket before boarding, and be sure to stamp it in a machine as soon as you enter. The ticket is good for a transfer and one Metro trip within the next 100 minutes. Buses and trams run 5:30 am–midnight, after which time there's an extensive network of night buses with service throughout the city.

The bus system is a bit complicated to navigate due to the number of lines, but ATAC has a website (⊕ *www.atac. roma.it*) that will help you calculate the number of stops and bus route needed, and even give you a map directing you to the appropriate stops. To navigate the site, look for the British flag in the upper right-hand corner to change the website into English. Or do as the locals do and use the Moovit app.

When to Go

Spring and fall are the best times to visit, with mild temperatures and many sunny days. Summers are often sweltering, so come in July and August if you like, but we advise doing as the Romans do—get up and out early, seek refuge from the afternoon heat, resume activities in early evening, and stay up late to enjoy the nighttime breeze.

Most attractions are closed on major holidays. Come August, many shops and restaurants shutter as locals head out for vacation. Remember that air-conditioning is still a relatively rare phenomenon in this city, so carrying a small paper fan in your bag can work wonders. Roman winters are relatively mild, with persistent rainy spells.

Addresses

In the *centro storico* (old town/historic center), most street names are posted on ceramic-like plaques on the sides of buildings, which can make them hard to see. Addresses are fairly straightforward: the street name is followed by the street number, but it's worth noting that Roman street numbering, even in the newer outskirts of town, can be erratic. Usually numbers are even on one side of the street and odd on the other, but sometimes numbers are in ascending consecutive order on one side of the street and descending order on the other side.

Etiquette

Although you may find Rome much more informal then many other European cities, Romans will nevertheless appreciate attempts to abide by local etiquette. When entering an establishment, the key words to know are: *buongiorno* (good morning), *buona sera* (good evening), and *buon pomeriggio* (good afternoon). These words can also double as a goodbye upon exit. Italians greet friends with a kiss, usually first on the right cheek, and then on the left. When you meet a new person, shake hands and say *piacere* (*pee*-ah *-chair*-ay).

Restaurants

In Rome, simple yet traditional cuisine reigns supreme. Most chefs prefer to follow the mantra of freshness over fuss, and simplicity of flavor and preparation over complex cooking techniques. Rome has been known since antiquity for its grand feasts and banquets, and dining out has always been a favorite Roman pastime. Until recently, the city's *buongustaii* (gourmands) would have been the first to tell you that Rome is distinguished more by its enthusiasm for eating out than for a multitude of world-class restaurants—but this is changing. There is an ever-growing promotion of slow-food practices, a focus on sustainably and locally sourced produce. The economic crisis forced the food industry in Rome to adopt innovative ways to maintain a clientele who were increasingly looking to dine out but wanting to spend less; the result has been the rise of "street food" restaurants, selling everything from inexpensive and novel takes on the classic *supplì* (Roman fried-rice balls) to sandwich shops that use a variety of organic ingredients.

Generally speaking, Romans like Roman food, and that's what you'll find in many of the city's trattorias and wine bars. For the most part, today's chefs cling to the traditional and excel at what has taken hundreds, sometimes thousands, of years to perfect. This is why the basic trattoria menu is more or less the same wherever you go. And it's why even the top Roman chefs feature their versions of simple trattoria classics like carbonara, sometimes in a "deconstructed" or slightly varied way. To a great extent, Rome is still a town where the Italian equivalent of "What are you in the mood for?" still gets the answer, "Pizza or pasta."

Nevertheless, Rome is the capital of Italy, and because people move here from every corner of the Italian peninsula, there are more variations on the Italian theme in Rome than you'd find elsewhere in Italy: Sicilian, Tuscan, Pugliese, Bolognese, Marchegiano, Sardinian, and northern Italian regional cuisines are all represented. And reflecting the increasingly cosmopolitan nature of the city, you'll find a growing number of good-quality international foods here as well—particularly Japanese, Indian, and Ethiopian.

Oddly enough, though, for a nation that prides itself on *la bella figura* ("looking good"), most Romans don't fuss about music, personal space, lighting, or decor.

After all, who needs flashy interior design when so much of Roman life takes place outdoors, when dining alfresco in Rome can take place in the middle of a glorious ancient site or a centuries-old piazza?

Hotels

When it comes to accommodations, Rome offers a wide selection of high-end hotels, bed-and-breakfasts, and designer boutique hotels—options that run the gamut from whimsical to luxurious. Whether you want a simple place to rest your head or a complete cache of exclusive amenities, you have plenty to choose from.

Luxury hotels are justly renowned for sybaritic comfort: postcard views over Roman rooftops, silver flatware on white linen atop a groaning breakfast-buffet table, and the fluffiest towels. But in more modest categories, very often Rome's hotels are not up to the standards of space, comfort, quiet, and service taken for granted in the United States: you'll still find places with tiny rooms, lumpy beds, and anemic air-conditioning. The good news: if you're flexible, there are happy mediums aplenty.

One thing to figure out before you arrive is which neighborhood you want to stay in. There are obvious advantages to staying in a hotel within easy walking distance of the main sights. If a picturesque location is your main concern, stay in one of the small hotels around Piazza Navona or Campo de' Fiori. If luxury is a high priority, head for Piazza di Spagna or beyond the city center, where quality/price ratios are higher and some hotels have swimming pools.

⇨ *Hotel and restaurant reviews have been shortened. For full information, visit Fodors.com. Prices in the lodging reviews are the lowest cost of a standard double room in high season. Prices in the dining reviews are the average cost of a main course at dinner, or, if dinner is not served, at lunch.*

What It Costs in Euros			
$	$$	$$$	$$$$
HOTELS			
under €125	€125–€200	€201–€300	over €300
RESTAURANTS			
under €15	€15–€24	€25–€35	over €35

Roman Hours

In Italy, almost nothing starts on time except for (sometimes) a theater, opera, or movie showing. Italians even joke about a "15-minute window" before actually being late somewhere. In addition, the day starts a little later than normal here, with many shops not opening until 10 am, lunch never happens before 1 pm, and dinner rarely starts before 8 pm. On Sunday, Rome virtually shuts down, and on Monday, most state museums and exhibition halls, plus many restaurants, are closed. Daily food shop hours generally run 10 am–1 pm and 4 pm–7:30 pm or 8 pm; but other stores in the center usually observe continuous opening hours. Pharmacies tend to close for a lunch break and keep night hours (*ora rio notturno*) in rotation. As for churches, most open at 8 or 9 in the morning, close noon–3 or 4, then reopen until 6:30 or 7. St. Peter's, however, has continuous hours 7 am–7 pm (until 6 pm in the fall and winter); and the Vatican Museums are open Monday but closed Sunday (except for the last Sunday of the month).

Roma Pass

In addition to single- and multiday transit passes, a three-day Roma Pass (🚌 €52) covers unlimited use of buses, trams, and the Metro, plus free admission to two museums or archaeological sites of your choice and discounted entrance to others. A two-day pass is €32 and includes one museum. The pass also allows you to skip the line at the Colosseum and Castel Sant'Angelo. Purchase the pass at either of Rome's airports, at tourist information offices, or at any of the participating attractions.

Tours

Some might consider them kitsch, but guided bus tours can prove a blissfully easy way to enjoy a quick introduction to the city's top sights—if you don't feel like being on your feet all day. Sitting in a bus, with friendly tour-guide commentary (and even friendlier fellow sightseers from every country under the sun), can make for a fun experience—so give one a whirl even if you're an old Rome hand. Of course, you'll want to savor these incredible sights at your own leisure later on.

The least expensive organized sightseeing tour of Rome is the one run by **CitySightseeing Roma** (🌐 www.city-sightseeing.it/rome). Double-decker buses leave from Via Marsala, beside Termini station, but you can pick them up at any of their nine stopping points. A day ticket costs €30 and allows you to get off and on as often as you like. The price includes an audio guide system in six languages. The total tour takes about two hours and covers the Colosseum, Piazza Navona, St. Peter's, the Trevi Fountain, and Via Veneto. Tickets can be bought on board. Two- and three-day tickets are also available. Tours leave from Termini station every 20 minutes 9–7:30.

All operators can provide a luxury car for up to three people, a limousine for up to seven, or a minibus for up to nine, all with an English-speaking driver, but guide service is extra. Almost all operators offer "Rome by Night" tours, with or without dinner and entertainment. You can book tours through travel agents.

Visitor Information

The Department of Tourism in Rome, called Roma Capitale, staffs green information kiosks (with multilingual personnel) near important sights, as well as at Termini station and Leonardo da Vinci Airport.

Ancient Rome with Monti and Celio

Time has reduced ancient Rome to fields of silent ruins, but the powerful impact of what happened here, of the genius and power that made Rome the center of the Western world, echoes across the millennia. In this one compact area of the city, you can step back into the Rome of Cicero, Julius Caesar, and Virgil. You can walk along the streets they knew, cool off in the shade of the Colosseum that loomed over the city, and see the sculptures poised over their piazzas. Today, this part of Rome, more than any other, is a perfect example of the layering of historic eras, the overlapping of ages, of religions, of a past that is very much a part of the present.

Outside the actual ancient sites, you'll find neighborhoods like Monti and Celio, *riones* (districts) that are just as much part of Rome's history as its ruins. These are the city's oldest neighborhoods, and today they are a charming mix of the city's past and present. Once you're done exploring ancient Rome, these are the easiest places to head for a bite to eat or some shopping.

GETTING HERE AND AROUND

The Colosseo Metro station is right across from the Colosseum and a short walk from both the Roman and the Imperial Forums, as well as the Palatine Hill. Walking from the very heart of the historic center will take about 20 minutes, much of it along the wide Via dei Fori Imperiali. The little electric Bus No. 117 from the center or No. 85 from Termini will also deliver you to the Colosseum's doorstep. Any of the following buses will take you to or near the Roman Forum: Nos. 60, 75, 85, and 170.

Sights

Arco di Costantino (*Arch of Constantine*)
RUINS | This majestic arch was erected in AD 315 to commemorate Constantine's victory over Maxentius at the Milvian Bridge. It was just before this battle, in AD 312, that Constantine—the emperor who converted Rome to Christianity—legendarily had a vision of a cross and heard the words, "In this sign thou shalt conquer." Many of the costly marble decorations for the arch were scavenged from earlier monuments, both saving money and placing Constantine in line with the great emperors of the past. It is easy to picture ranks of Roman centurions marching under the great barrel vault. ⊠ *Piazza del Colosseo, Monti* Ⓜ *Colosseo.*

Basilica di Santa Maria in Aracoeli

CHURCH | Perched atop 124 steps, on the north slope of the Capitoline Hill, Santa Maria in Aracoeli occupies the site of the temple of Juno Moneta (Admonishing Juno), which also housed the Roman mint. According to legend, it was here that the Sibyl, a prophetess, predicted to Augustus the coming of a Redeemer. Augustus responded by erecting an altar, the Ara Coeli (Altar of Heaven). This was eventually replaced by a Benedictine

monastery and then by a church, which was passed in 1250 to the Franciscans, who restored and enlarged it in Romanesque-Gothic style.

Today, the Aracoeli is best known for the Santo Bambino, a much-revered olive-wood figure of the Christ Child (a copy of the 15th-century original, which was stolen in 1994). At Christmas, everyone pays homage to the "Bambinello" as children recite poems from a miniature pulpit. In true Roman style, the church interior is a historical hodgepodge, with classical columns and large marble fragments from pagan buildings, as well as a 13th-century cosmatesque pavement. The richly gilded Renaissance ceiling commemorates the naval victory at Lepanto in 1571 over the Turks. The first chapel on the right is noteworthy for Pinturicchio's frescoes of St. Bernardino of Siena (1486). ⊠ *Via del Teatro di Marcello, Piazza Venezia* ☎ *06/69763839* Ⓜ *Colosseo.*

★ The Campidoglio

PLAZA/SQUARE | Your first taste of ancient Rome should start from a point that embodies some of Rome's earliest and greatest moments: the Campidoglio. Here, on the Capitoline Hill (which towers over the traffic hub of Piazza Venezia), a meditative Edward Gibbon was inspired to write his 1764 tome, *The History of the Decline and Fall of the Roman Empire.* Of Rome's famous seven hills, the Capitoline is the smallest and the most sacred. It has always been the seat of Rome's government, and its Latin name echoes in the designation of the national and state capitol buildings of every country in the world. While there are great views of the Roman Forum from the terrace balconies to either side of the Palazzo Senatorio, the best view is from the 1st-century BC Tabularium, now part of the Musei Capitolini. The museum café on the Terrazza Caffarelli, with a magical view toward Trastevere and St. Peter's, and is accessible without a museum ticket. ⊠ *Piazza* del Campidoglio, including the Palazzo Senatorio and the Musei Capitolini, the Palazzo Nuovo, and the Palazzo dei Conservatori, Piazza Venezia Ⓜ Colosseo.

Circo Massimo (*Circus Maximus*)
RUINS | From the belvedere of the Domus Flavia on the Palatine Hill, you can see the Circus Maximus; there's also a great free view from Piazzale Ugo La Malfa on the Aventine Hill side. The giant space where 300,000 spectators once watched chariot races while the emperor looked on is ancient Rome's oldest and largest racetrack; it lies in a natural hollow between the two hills. The oval course stretches about 650 yards from end to end; on certain occasions, there were as many as 24 chariot races a day, and competitions could last for 15 days. The charioteers could amass fortunes rather like the sports stars of today. (The Portuguese Diocles is said to have totted up winnings of 35 million *sestertii*.)

The noise and the excitement of the crowd must have reached astonishing levels as the charioteers competed in teams, each with their own colors—the Reds, the Blues, etc. Betting also provided Rome's majority of unemployed with a potentially lucrative occupation. The central ridge was the site of two Egyptian obelisks (now in Piazza del Popolo and Piazza San Giovanni in Laterano). Picture the great chariot race scene from MGM's *Ben-Hur*, and you have an inkling of what this was like. ⊠ *Between Palatine and Aventine Hills, Aventino* ☎ *06/0608* 💷 *€5* 🕙 *Closed Mon.* Ⓜ *Circo Massimo.*

★ **Colosseum** (*Colosseo*)
RUINS | The most spectacular extant edifice of ancient Rome, the Colosseum has a history that is half gore, half glory. Once able to house 50,000 spectators, it was built to impress Romans with its spectacles involving wild animals and fearsome gladiators from the farthest reaches of the empire. Senators had marble seats up front, the vestal virgins took the ringside position, the plebs sat

in wooden tiers at the back, and the masses watched from the top tier. Looming over all was the amazing velarium, an ingenious system of sail-like awnings rigged on ropes and maneuvered by sailors from the imperial fleet, who would unfurl them to protect the arena's occupants from sun or rain.

⬛ TIP➔ **To enter, you must book a combination ticket (with the Roman Forum and Palatine Hill) in advance online, though if you have a Roma Pass, you can use it.**

Tickets cost €16 plus a €2 online booking surcharge. Aim for early or late slots to minimize lines, as even the preferential lanes get busy in the middle of the day. Alternatively, you can book a tour online with a company (do your research to make sure it's reputable) that lets you skip the line. Avoid the tours sold on the spot around the Colosseum; although you can skip the lines, the tour guides tend to be dry, the tour groups huge, and the tour itself rushed. To see the arena or the underground, you must purchase a special timed-entry ticket with those features, though they do not cost extra if you buy the Roman Forum–Palatine complex €22 two-day Full Experience ticket. ⊠ *Piazza del Colosseo, Colosseo* ☎ *06/39967700* ⊕ *www.coopculture. it* 💷 *Requires either the €16 24-hour ticket or the €22 Full Experience ticket (can include the arena and underground areas for no additional fee, but they must be specified during the purchase)* Ⓜ *Colosseo.*

Domus Aurea (*Golden House of Nero*)
RUINS | Legend has it that Nero fiddled while Rome burned. Fancying himself a great actor and poet, he played, as it turns out, his harp to accompany his recital of "The Destruction of Troy" while gazing at the flames of Rome's catastrophic fire of AD 64. Anti-Neronian historians propagandized that Nero, in fact, had set the Great Fire to clear out a vast tract of the city center to build his new palace. Today's historians discount

this as historical folderol (going so far as to point to the fact that there was a full moon on the evening of July 19, hardly the propitious occasion to commit arson).

Regardless, Nero did get to build his new palace, the extravagant Domus Aurea (Golden House)—a vast "suburban villa" that was inspired by the emperor's pleasure palace at Baia on the Bay of Naples. His new digs were huge and sumptuous, with a facade of pure gold; seawater piped into the baths; decorations of mother-of-pearl, fretted ivory, and other precious materials; and vast gardens. It was said that after completing this gigantic house, Nero exclaimed, "Now I can live like a human being!" Note that access to the site is exclusively via guided tours that use virtual reality headsets for part of the presentation. Booking ahead is essential. ⊠ *Viale della Domus Aurea 1, Monti* ☎ *06/39967700 booking information* ⊕ *www.coopculture.it* ⊠ *€15 including booking fee and guided visit* ⊘ *Closed Mon.–Thurs.* ⚐ *Reservations essential* Ⓜ *Colosseo.*

Fori Imperiali

RUINS | A compound of five grandly conceived complexes flanked with colonnades, the Fori Imperiali contain monuments of triumph, law courts, and temples. The complexes were tacked on to the Roman Forum, from the time of Julius Caesar in the 1st century BC until Trajan in the very early 2nd century AD, to accommodate the ever-growing need for administrative buildings as well as grand monuments.

From Piazza del Colosseo, head northwest on Via dei Fori Imperiali toward Piazza Venezia. Now that the road has been closed to private traffic, it's more pleasant for pedestrians (it's closed to all traffic on Sunday). On the walls to your left, maps in marble and bronze, put up by Benito Mussolini, show the extent of the Roman Republic and Empire. The dictator's own dreams of empire led him to construct this avenue, cutting brutally

through the Fori Imperiali and the medieval and Renaissance buildings that had grown upon the ruins, so that he would have a suitable venue for parades celebrating his expected military triumphs. Among the Fori Imperiali along the avenue, you can see the Foro di Cesare (Forum of Caesar) and the Foro di Augusto (Forum of Augustus). The grandest was the Foro di Traiano (Forum of Trajan), with its huge semicircular Mercati di Traiano and the Colonna Traiana (Trajan's Column). You can walk through part of Trajan's Markets on the Via Alessandrina and visit the Museo dei Fori Imperiali, which presents the Imperial Forums and shows how they would have been used through ancient fragments, artifacts, and modern multimedia. ⊠ *Via dei Fori Imperiali, Monti* ☎ *06/0608* ⊕ *www.mercatiditraiano.it* ⊠ *Museum €11.50* Ⓜ *Colosseo.*

Foro di Traiano (*Forum of Trajan*)

RUINS | Of all the Fori Imperiali, Trajan's was the grandest and most imposing, a veritable city unto itself. Designed by architect Apollodorus of Damascus, it comprised a vast basilica, two libraries, and a colonnade laid out around the square—all at one time covered with rich marble ornamentation. Adjoining the forum were the Mercati di Traiano (Trajan's Markets), a huge, multilevel, brick complex of shops, taverns, walkways, and terraces, as well as administrative offices involved in the mammoth task of feeding the city.

The Museo dei Fori Imperiali (Imperial Forums Museum) takes advantage of the Forum's soaring vaulted spaces to showcase archaeological fragments and sculptures while presenting a video re-creation of the original complex. In addition, the series of terraced rooms offers an impressive overview of the entire forum. A pedestrian walkway, the Via Alessandrina, also allows for an excellent (and free) view of Trajan's Forum.

To build a complex of this magnitude, Apollodorus and his patrons clearly had

Rome Metro and Suburban Railway

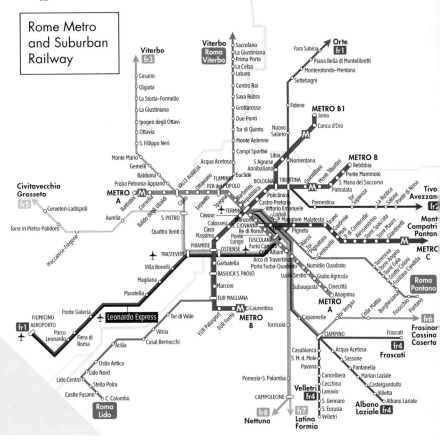

Tickets

A ticket (BIT) valid for 100 minutes on any combination of buses and trams and one entrance to the metro costs €1.50. Tickets are sold at newsstands, some coffee bars, ticket machines in metro stations, and ATAC and COTRAL ticket booths. Time-stamp your ticket when boarding the first vehicle, and stamp it again when boarding for the last time within 75 minutes. You stamp the ticket at Metro sliding electronic doors, and in the little yellow machines on buses and trams.

Fare fees	Price
Single fare	€1.50
Biglietto integrato giornaliero (Integrated Daily Ticket) BIG	€7
Biglietto turistico integrato (Three-Day Pass) BTI	€18
Weekly pass	€24
Monthly unlimited pass	€35

great confidence, not to mention almost unlimited means and cheap labor at their disposal (readily provided by slaves captured in Trajan's Dacian Wars). The complex also contained two semicircular lecture halls, one at either end, which are thought to have been associated with the libraries in Trajan's Forum. The markets' architectural centerpiece is the enormous curved wall, or *exedra*, that shores up the side of the Quirinal Hill excavated by Apollodorus's gangs of laborers. Covered galleries and streets were constructed at various levels, following the exedra's curves and giving the complex a strikingly modern appearance.

As you enter the markets, a large, vaulted hall stands in front of you. Two stories of shops and offices rise up on either side. Head for the flight of steps at the far end that leads down to Via Biberatica. (*Bibere* is Latin for "to drink," and the shops that open onto the street are believed to have been taverns.) Then head back to the three retail and administrative tiers that line the upper levels of the great exedra and look out over the remains of the Forum. Empty and bare today, the cubicles were once ancient Rome's busiest market stalls. Though it seems to be part of the market, the Torre delle Milizie (Tower of the Militia), the tall brick tower that is a prominent feature of Rome's skyline, was actually built in the early 1200s. ⊠ *Via IV Novembre 94, Monti* ☎ *06/0608* ⊕ *www.mercatiditraiano.it* ⊠ *€11.50 (€13 with exhibits)* Ⓜ *Cavour.*

★ Musei Capitolini

ART MUSEUM | Surpassed in size and richness only by the Musei Vaticani, the world's first public museum—with the greatest hits of Roman art through the ages, from the ancients to the Baroque—is housed in the Palazzo dei Conservatori and the Palazzo Nuovo, which mirror one another across Michelangelo's famous piazza. The collection was begun by Pope Sixtus IV (the man who built the Sistine Chapel) in 1473, when he donated a

room of ancient statuary to the people of the city. This core of the collection includes the She Wolf, which is the symbol of Rome, and the piercing gaze of the Capitoline Brutus. Buy your ticket and enter the Palazzo dei Conservatori where, in the first courtyard, you'll see the giant head, foot, elbow, and imperially raised finger of the fabled seated statue of Constantine, which once dominated the Basilica of Maxentius in the Forum. As you walk between the two halves of the museum, be sure to take the staircase to the Tabularium gallery and its unparalleled view over the Forum. ⊠ *Piazza del Campidoglio 1, Piazza Venezia* ☎ *06/0608* ⊕ *www.museicapitolini.org* ⊠ *€11.50 (€16 with exhibitions); €18 with access to Centrale Montemartini; €7 audio guide* Ⓜ *Colosseo.*

★ Palatine Hill

RUINS | Just beyond the Arch of Titus, the Clivus Palatinus gently rises to the heights of the Colle Palatino (Palatine Hill)—the oldest inhabited site in Rome. Despite its location overlooking the Forum's traffic and attendant noise, the Palatine was the most coveted address for ancient Rome's rich and famous. Augustus was born on the hill, and the Houses of Livia and Augustus are today the hill's best-preserved structures, replete with fabulous frescoes. Later emperors built even bigger, and much of what we see today dates from the reign of Domitian, in the late 1st century AD. ⊠ *Entrances at Piazza del Colosseo and Via di San Gregorio 30, Monti* ☎ *06/39967700* ⊕ *www.coopculture.it* ⊠ *€18 combined ticket, includes single entry to Palatine Hill–Forum site and single entry to Colosseum (if used within 24 hours); S.U.P.E.R. ticket €22 (€24 with online reservation) includes access to the Houses of Augustus and Livia, the Palatine Museum, Aula Isiaca, Santa Maria Antiqua, and Temple of Romulus* Ⓜ *Colosseo.*

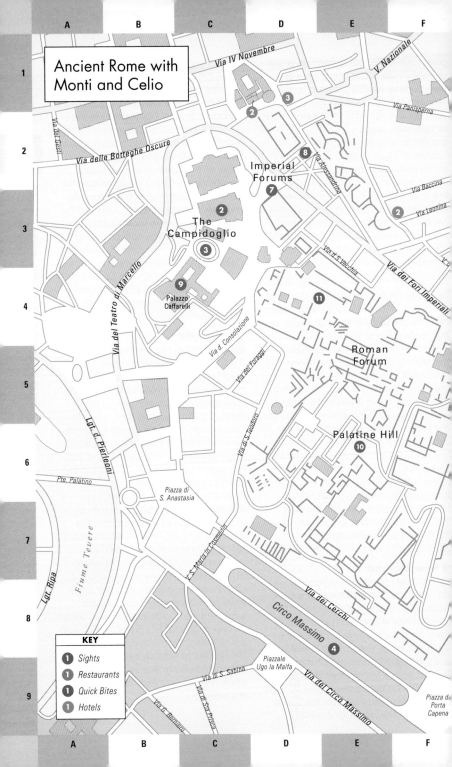

Sights ▼

1 Arco di Costantino................. **G6**
2 Basilica di
  Santa Maria in Aracoeli **C3**
3 The Campidoglio....................**C3**
4 Circo Massimo.....................**E8**
5 Colosseum.........................**H5**
6 Domus Aurea.......................**J4**
7 Fori Imperiali **D2**
8 Foro di Traiano **D2**
9 Musei Capitolini....................**C4**
10 Palatine Hill.........................**E6**
11 The Roman Forum **E4**
12 San Clemente **J6**
13 Santa Maria Maggiore............**J2**

Restaurants ▼

1 Li Rioni **J6**
2 Terra e Domus della
  Provincia di Roma **D1**

Quick Bites ▼

1 Fatamorgana Monti **I2**

Hotels ▼

1 Hotel Celio..........................**J6**
2 Hotel Forum **F3**
3 NH Collection
  Roma Fori Imperiali...............**D1**
4 Palazzo Manfredi **J5**

3

Rome ANCIENT ROME WITH MONTI AND CELIO

★ The Roman Forum

RUINS | Whether it's from the main entrance on Via dei Fori Imperiali or by the entrance at the Arch of Titus, descend into the extraordinary archaeological complex that is the Foro Romano and the Palatine Hill, once the very heart of the Roman world. The Forum began life as a marshy valley between the Capitoline and Palatine Hills—a valley crossed by a mud track and used as a cemetery by Iron Age settlers. Over the years, a market center and some huts were established here, and after the land was drained in the 6th century BC, the site eventually became a political, religious, and commercial center: the Forum.

Hundreds of years of plunder reduced the Forum to its current desolate state. But this enormous area was once Rome's pulsating hub, filled with stately and extravagant temples, palaces, and shops and crowded with people from all corners of the empire. Adding to today's confusion is the fact that the Forum developed over many centuries; what you see today are not the ruins from just one period but from a span of almost 900 years, from about 500 BC to AD 400. Nonetheless, the enduring romance of the place, with its lonely columns and great broken fragments of sculpted marble and stone, makes for a quintessential Roman experience.

There is always a line at the Colosseum ticket office for the combined Colosseum/Palatine/Forum ticket, but in high season, lines sometimes also form at the Forum and Palatine entrances. Those who don't want to risk waiting in line can book their tickets online in advance, for a €2 surcharge. Choose the print-at-home option (a PDF on a smartphone works, too) and avoid the line to pick up tickets. Your ticket is valid for one entrance to the Roman Forum and the Palatine Hill, which are part of a single continuous complex. Certain sites within the Forum require a S.U.P.E.R. ticket.

✉ *Entrance at Via dei Fori Imperiali, Monti* ☎ *06/39967700* ⊕ *www.coopculture.it* ▣ *€18 combined ticket, includes single entry to Palatine Hill–Forum site and single entry to Colosseum (if used within 24 hours); S.U.P.E.R. ticket €22 (€24 with online reservation) includes access to the Houses of Augustus and Livia, the Palatine Museum, Aula Isiaca, Santa Maria Antiqua, and Temple of Romulus; audio guide €5* Ⓜ *Colosseo.*

★ San Clemente

CHURCH | One of the most impressive archaeological sites in Rome, San Clemente is a historical triple-decker. A 12th-century church was built on top of a 4th-century church, which had been built over a 2nd-century pagan temple to the god Mithras and 1st-century Roman apartments. The layers were uncovered in 1857, when a curious prior, Friar Joseph Mullooly, started excavations beneath the present basilica. Today, you can descend to explore all three.

The upper church (at street level) is a gem in its own right. In the apse, a glittering 12th-century mosaic shows Jesus on a cross that turns into a living tree. Green acanthus leaves swirl and teem with small scenes of everyday life. Early Christian symbols, including doves, vines, and fish, decorate the 4th-century marble choir screens. To the right of the sacristy (and bookshop), descend the stairs to the 4th-century church, used until 1084, when it was damaged beyond repair during a siege of the area by the Norman prince Robert Guiscard. Still intact are some vibrant 11th-century frescoes depicting stories from the life of St. Clement.

Descend an additional set of stairs to the Mithraeum, a shrine dedicated to the god Mithras. His cult spread from Persia and gained a foothold in Rome during the 2nd and 3rd centuries AD. Mithras was believed to have been born in a cave and was thus worshipped in cavernous, underground chambers, where initiates into the all-male cult would share a meal while reclining on stone couches, some visible here along with the altar block. ✉ *Via Labicana 95, Celio* ☎ *06/7740021* 🌐 *basilicasanclemente.com/eng* 🎫 *Archaeological area €10* [M] *Colosseo.*

★ **Santa Maria Maggiore**

CHURCH | Despite its florid 18th-century facade, Santa Maria Maggiore is one of the city's oldest churches, built around 440 by Pope Sixtus III. One Rome's four great pilgrimage churches, it's also the city center's best example of an early Christian basilica—one of the immense, hall-like structures derived from ancient Roman civic buildings and divided into thirds by two great rows of columns marching up the nave. The other three major basilicas in Rome (San Giovanni in Laterano, St. Peter's, and St. Paul Outside the Walls) have been largely rebuilt. Paradoxically, the major reason why this church is such a striking example of early Christian design is that the same man who built the undulating exteriors circa 1740, Ferdinando Fuga, also conscientiously restored the interior, throwing out later additions and, crucially, replacing a number of the great columns.

The Cappella Sistina (Sistine Chapel), in the right-hand transept, was created by architect Domenico Fontana for Pope Sixtus V in 1585. Elaborately decorated with precious marbles "liberated" from the monuments of ancient Rome, the chapel includes a lower-level museum with some 13th-century sculptures by Arnolfo da Cambio that survived the Sack of Rome in 1527. Borgia popes Paul V and Clement VIII are buried here, as is Gian Lorenzo Bernini, under a simple engraved slab as humble as the tombs of his patrons are grand. The outside mosaic of Christ raising his hand in blessing is one of Rome's most beautiful sights, especially when lighted at night. ✉ *Piazza di Santa Maria Maggiore, Monti* ☎ *06/69886802* 🎫 *Free* [M] *Termini.*

🍴 Restaurants

Li Rioni

$ | **PIZZA** | **FAMILY** | This busy spot conveniently close to the Colosseum has been serving real-deal Roman-style pizza (super thin and cooked to a crisp) since the mid-1980s. The interiors—designed to resemble the exterior of a house—are kitschy, and the kitchen has made some concessions to tourists with items like a Greek salad, but it's a solid choice for pizza in this neighborhood. **Known for:** olive ascolane (fried, breaded olives stuffed with sausage); pizza margherita; homemade tiramisu. [$] *Average main: €10* ✉ *Via dei Santi Quattro 24, Celio* ☎ *06/70450605* 🌐 *lirioni.it* 🕒 *Closed Tues. and 2 wks in Aug. No lunch* [M] *Colosseo.*

Terre e Domus della Provincia di Roma

$ | **ITALIAN** | **FAMILY** | It's hard to find genuinely good food in the Campidoglio area, but this wine bar next to Trajan's Column is an exception. Ideal for coffee, a late lunch, early supper, or just an *aperitivo* (aperitif), it's run by the Province of Rome to showcase local produce and is a great spot to rest after wandering amid the ruins. **Known for:** local wines; tourist-friendly Roman classics; daily specials. [$] *Average main: €14* ✉ *Foro Traiano 82, Monti* ☎ *06/69940273, 366/1070358 WhatsApp* 🌐 *www.palazzovalentini.it/terre-domus* 🕒 *Closed Mon.* [M] *Cavour, Colosseo.*

☕ Coffee and Quick Bites

★ **Fatamorgana Monti**

$ | **ICE CREAM** | **FAMILY** | The emphasis is on all-natural ingredients at this woman-owned gelateria, which has several locations in Rome, including one near Campo de' Fiori and another in Trastevere. Flavors change often but might include favorites like stracciatella (with chocolate shavings) and hazelnut as well as more unusual flavors like matcha or carrot cake. **Known for:** all natural ingredients; unusual flavors; gluten-free with many vegan options. $ *Average main: €3* ✉ *Piazza degli Zingari 5, Monti* ☎ *06/48906955* ⊕ *www.gelateriafatamorgana.com* Ⓜ *Cavour.*

Hotels

Hotel Celio
$$ | HOTEL | At this hotel near the Colosseum, each of the small guest rooms is named after a famous Italian painter (Tiziano, Cellini, Michelangelo) and features decor that evokes the work of its namesake. **Pros:** beautiful rooftop garden; nice decor; comfortable beds. **Cons:** very small bathrooms; service can be iffy; breakfast not that substantial. $ *Rooms from: €180* ✉ *Via dei Santissimi Quattro 35/c, Celio* ☎ *06/70495333* ⊕ *www.hotelcelio.com* ➤ *22 rooms* ⦿ *Free Breakfast* Ⓜ *Colosseo.*

Hotel Forum
$$ | HOTEL | A longtime favorite, this hotel in a converted 18th-century convent has a truly unique setting on one side of the Fori Imperiali, with cinematic views of ancient Rome across the avenue so impressive that it has drawn celebrities and socialites. **Pros:** bird's-eye view of ancient Rome; "American" bar on rooftop terrace; discounted rates can be found from time to time. **Cons:** small rooms; outdated decor; food and drinks are expensive. $ *Rooms from: €180* ✉ *Via Tor de' Conti 25–30, Monti* ☎ *06/6792446* ⊕ *www.hotelforum.com* ➤ *80 rooms* ⦿ *No Meals* Ⓜ *Cavour, Colosseo.*

NH Collection Roma Fori Imperiali
$$ | HOTEL | It would be hard to find a modern hotel closer to the Roman Forum—the ancient ruins are practically right outside the door. **Pros:** incredible views of ancient Rome; rooftop serves a great aperitivo and refined dinners; restaurant Oro Bistrot by renowned chef Natale Giunta. **Cons:** breakfast foods are pre-packaged; not much public space; no spa or gym. $ *Rooms from: €200* ✉ *Via di Santa Eufemia 19, Piazza Venezia* ☎ *06/697689911* ⊕ *www.nh-collection.com/it/hotel/nh-collection-roma-fori-imperiali* ➤ *42 rooms* ⦿ *No Meals* Ⓜ *Cavour.*

Palazzo Manfredi
$$$$ | HOTEL | If you dream of waking up to head-on views of the Colosseum, book into this boutique hotel, which is set in a 17th-century palazzo built over the ruins of the Ludus Magnus, the gymnasium used by Roman gladiators, and offers refined luxury. **Pros:** incredible views; unparalleled location; excellent restaurant and cocktail bar. **Cons:** not all rooms have Colosseum views; some guests complain about noise; no spa. $ *Rooms from: €550* ✉ *Via Labicana 125, Colosseo* ☎ *06/77591380* ⊕ *www.manfredihotels.com* ➤ *20 rooms* ⦿ *No Meals* Ⓜ *Colosseo.*

Nightlife

★ Ai Tre Scalini
WINE BARS | An ivy-covered wine bar in the center of Monti, Rome's trendiest 'hood, Ai Tre Scalini has a warm and cozy menu of delicious antipasti and light entrées to go along with its enticing wine list. After about 8 pm, if you haven't booked, be prepared to wait—this is one extremely popular spot with locals. ✉ *Via Panisperna 251, Monti* ☎ *06/48907495* ⊕ *www.aitrescalini.org* Ⓜ *Cavour.*

★ The Court
COCKTAIL LOUNGES | For a winning combination of creative cocktails and incredible views of the Colosseum, this bar in Palazzo Manfredi can't be beat. Bar manager Matteo "Zed" Zamberlan cut his teeth in New York's top drinking establishments, and here his creativity is on full display. The cocktails are pricey, but they come with a bounty of snacks from the hotel's acclaimed restaurant. ✉ *Via Labicana 125, Colosseo* ☎ *06/69354581* ⊕ *www.manfredihotels.com* Ⓜ *Colosseo.*

🛍 Shopping

★ Sacripante

WOMEN'S CLOTHING | This tiny Monti art gallery/boutique/bar has some of the most sophisticated, retro-inspired garments in Rome. Its owner, Carlotta Cerulli, sells clothes by her mother, Wilma Silvestri, who cleverly combines vintage and contemporary fabrics for her label Le Gallinelle, creating stylish fashions with a modern edge made for everyday wear. ⊠ *Via Panisperna 59, Monti* ☎ *06/48903495* ⊕ *www.facebook. com/sacripantegallery* Ⓜ *Cavour.*

The Vatican with Borgo and Prati

Climbing the steps to St. Peter's Basilica feels monumental, like a journey that has reached its climactic end. Suddenly, all is cool and dark … and you are dwarfed by the gargantuan nave and its magnificence. Above is a ceiling so high it must lead to heaven itself. Great, shining marble figures of saints frozen mid-whirl loom from niches and corners. And at the end, a throne for an unseen king whose greatness, it is implied, must mirror the greatness of his palace. For this basilica is a palace, the dazzling center of power for a king and a place of supplication for his subjects. Whether his kingdom is earthly or otherwise may lie in the eye of the beholder.

For good Catholics and sinners alike, the Vatican is an exercise in spirituality, requiring patience but delivering joy. Some come here for a transcendent glimpse of a heavenly Michelangelo fresco; others come in search of a direct connection with the divine. But what all visitors share, for a few hours, is an awe-inspiring landscape that offers a famous sight for every taste: rooms decorated by Raphael, antique sculptures like the Apollo Belvedere, famous paintings by Giotto and Bellini, and, perhaps most of all, the Sistine Chapel—for the lover of beauty, few places are as historically important as this epitome of faith and grandeur.

The Borgo and Prati are the neighborhoods immediately surrounding the Vatican, and it's worth noting that, while the Vatican may well be a priority, these neighborhoods are not the best places to choose a hotel, as they're quite far from other top sights in the city.

GETTING HERE AND AROUND
Metro stop Cipro or Ottaviano will get you within about a 10-minute walk of the entrance to the Musei Vaticani. Or, from Termini station, Bus No. 40 Express or the famously crowded No. 64 will take you to Piazza San Pietro. Both routes swing past Largo Argentina, where you can also get Bus No. 46.

A leisurely meander from the centro storico, across the exquisite Ponte Sant'Angelo, will take about a half hour.

👁 Sights

★ Basilica di San Pietro
CHURCH | The world's largest church, built over the tomb of St. Peter, is the most imposing and breathtaking architectural achievement of the Renaissance (although much of the lavish interior dates to the Baroque period). No fewer than five of Italy's greatest artists—Bramante, Raphael, Peruzzi, Antonio da Sangallo the Younger, and Michelangelo—died while striving to erect this new St. Peter's.

The history of the original St. Peter's goes back to AD 326, when the emperor Constantine completed a basilica over the site of the tomb of St. Peter, the Church's first pope. The original church stood for more than 1,000 years, undergoing a number of restorations and alterations, until, toward the middle of the 15th century, it was on the verge of collapse. In

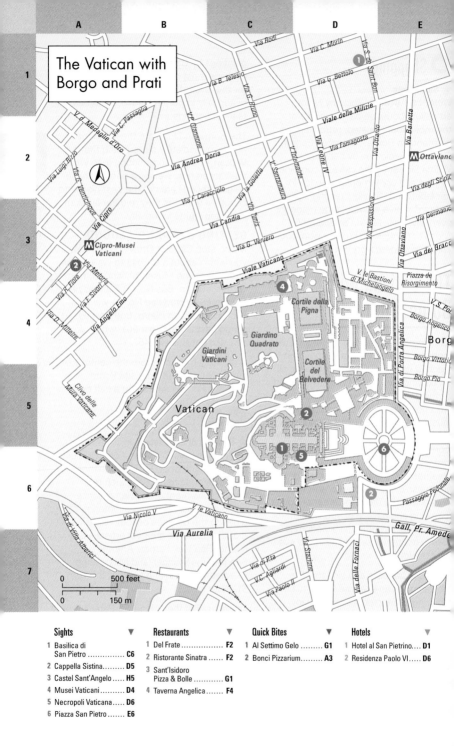

The Vatican with Borgo and Prati

Sights ▼

1 Basilica di
San Pietro **C6**
2 Cappella Sistina **D5**
3 Castel Sant'Angelo **H5**
4 Musei Vaticani **D4**
5 Necropoli Vaticana **D6**
6 Piazza San Pietro **E6**

Restaurants ▼

1 Del Frate **F2**
2 Ristorante Sinatra **F2**
3 Sant'Isidoro
Pizza & Bolle **G1**
4 Taverna Angelica **F4**

Quick Bites ▼

1 Al Settimo Gelo **G1**
2 Bonci Pizzarium **A3**

Hotels ▼

1 Hotel al San Pietrino **D1**
2 Residenza Paolo VI **D6**

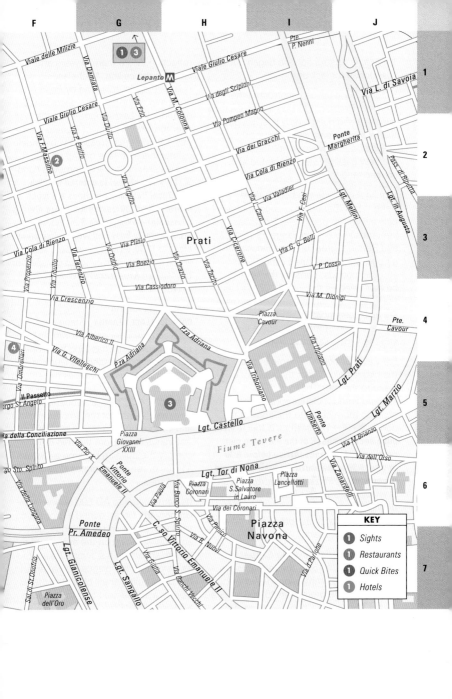

1452, a reconstruction job began but was abandoned for lack of money.

In 1503, Pope Julius II instructed the architect Bramante to raze all the existing buildings and build a new basilica, one that would surpass even Constantine's for grandeur. It wasn't until 1626 that the new basilica was completed and consecrated.

Highlights include the Loggia delle Benedizioni (Benediction Loggia), the balcony where newly elected popes are proclaimed; Michelangelo's *Pietà*; and Bernini's great bronze baldacchino, a huge, spiral-columncd canopy—at 100,000 pounds, perhaps the largest bronze object in the world—as well as many other Bernini masterpieces. There are also collections of Vatican treasures in the Museo Storico-Artistico e Tesoro and the Grotte Vaticane crypt.

For views of both the dome above and the piazza below, take the elevator or stairs to the roof. Those with more stamina (and without claustrophobia) can then head up more stairs to the apex of the dome. ■ TIP➔ **The basilica is free to visit, but a security check at the entrance can create very long lines. Arrive before 8:30 or after 5:30 to minimize the wait and avoid the crowds.** ⊠ *Piazza San Pietro, Vatican* ⊕ *www.vatican.va* ✉ *Free* ⊙ *Closed during Papal General Audience (Wed. until 1 pm) and during other ceremonies in piazza* Ⓜ *Ottaviano.*

★ **Cappella Sistina** (*Sistine Chapel*)
ART MUSEUM | In 1508, the redoubtable Pope Julius II commissioned Michelangelo to fresco the more than 10,000 square feet of the Sistine Chapel's ceiling. The task took four years, and it's said that for many years afterward Michelangelo couldn't read anything without holding it over his head. The result, however, was the greatest artwork of the Renaissance. A pair of binoculars helps greatly, as does a small mirror—hold the mirror facing the ceiling and look down to study the reflection. More than 20 years after his work on the ceiling, Michelangelo was called on again, this time by Pope Paul III, to add to the chapel's decoration by painting the *Last Judgment* on the wall over the altar. By way of signature on this, his late great fresco, Michelangelo painted his own face on the flayed-off human skin in St. Bartholomew's hand. ■ TIP➔ **The chapel is entered through the Musei Vaticani, and lines are much shorter after 2:30 (reservations are always advisable)—except free Sundays, which are extremely busy and when admissions close at 12:30.** ⊠ *Musei Vaticani, Vatican* ⊕ *www.museivaticani.va* ✉ *€17 (part of the Vatican Museums)* ⊙ *Closed Sun.* Ⓜ *Ottaviano.*

Castel Sant'Angelo
CASTLE/PALACE | **FAMILY** | Standing between the Tiber and the Vatican, this circular castle has long been one of Rome's most distinctive landmarks. Opera lovers know it well as the setting for the final scene of Puccini's *Tosca*. Started in AD 135, the structure began as a mausoleum for the emperor Hadrian and was completed by his successor, Antoninus Pius. From the mid-6th century the building became a fortress, a place of refuge for popes during wars and sieges.

Its name dates to AD 590, when Pope Gregory the Great, during a procession to plead for the end of a plague, saw an angel standing on the summit of the castle, sheathing his sword. Taking this as a sign that the plague was at an end, the pope built a small chapel at the top, placing a statue next to it to celebrate his vision—thus the name, Castel Sant'Angelo.

In the rooms off the Cortile dell'Angelo, look for the Cappella di Papa Leone X (Chapel of Pope Leo X), with a facade by Michelangelo. In the Pope Alexander VI courtyard, a wellhead bears the Borgia coat of arms. The stairs at the far end of the courtyard lead to the open terrace for a view of the Passetto, the fortified corridor connecting Castel Sant'Angelo with the Vatican. In the *appartamento papale* (papal apartment), the Sala Paolina (Pauline Room) was decorated in the 16th century by Perino del Vaga and assistants with lavish frescoes of scenes from the Old Testament and the lives of St. Paul and Alexander the Great. ✉ *Lungotevere Castello 50, Prati* ☎ *06/6819111 central line, 06/6896003 tickets* 🌐 *www.castelsantangelo.beniculturali.it* 🎫 *€13* ⏲ *Closed Mon.* Ⓜ *Lepanto.*

★ **Musei Vaticani** (*Vatican Museums*)
ART MUSEUM | Other than the pope and his papal court, the occupants of the Vatican are some of the most famous artworks in the world. The Vatican Palace, residence of the popes since 1377, consists of an estimated 1,400 rooms, chapels, and galleries. The pope and his household occupy only a small part; most of the rest is given over to the Vatican Library and Museums.

Beyond the glories of the Sistine Chapel, the collection is extraordinarily rich: highlights include the great antique sculptures (including the celebrated *Apollo Belvedere* in the Octagonal Courtyard and the *Belvedere Torso* in the Hall of the Muses); the Stanze di Raffaello (Raphael Rooms), with their famous gorgeous frescoes; and the Old Master paintings, such as Leonardo da Vinci's beautiful (though unfinished) *St. Jerome in the Wilderness*, some of Raphael's greatest creations, and Caravaggio's gigantic *Deposition in the Pinacoteca* ("Picture Gallery").

For those interested in guided visits to the Vatican Museums, tours start at €35, including entrance tickets, and can also be booked online. Other offerings include a regular two-hour guided tour of the Vatican gardens; call or check online to confirm. For more information, call ☎ *06/69884676* or go to 🌐 *www.museivaticani.va.* For information on tours, call ☎ *06/69883145* or ☎ *06/69884676;* visually impaired visitors can arrange tactile tours by calling ☎ *06/69884947.* ✉ *Viale Vaticano, near intersection with Via Leone IV, Vatican* ☎ *06/69883145* 🌐 *www.museivaticani.va* 🎫 *€17* ⏲ *Closed Sun. and church holidays* Ⓜ *Cipro–Musei Vaticani or Ottaviano–San Pietro.*

Necropoli Vaticana (*Vatican Necropolis*)
CEMETERY | With advance notice you can take a 1½-hour guided tour in English of the Vatican Necropolis, under the Basilica di San Pietro, which gives a rare glimpse of early Christian Roman burial customs and a closer look at the tomb of St. Peter. Apply via the contact form online, by fax, or in person (the entrance to the office is on the left of the Bernini colonnade), specifying the number of people in the group (all must be age 15 or older), preferred language, preferred time, available dates, and your contact information in Rome. Each group will have about 12 participants. Visits are not recommended for those with mobility issues or who are claustrophobic. ✉ *Ufficio Scavi, Vatican* ☎ *06/69873017 reservations, 06/69885318* 🌐 *www.scavi.va* 🎫 *€13* ⏲ *Closed Sun. and Roman Catholic holidays* ✍ *Reservations required* Ⓜ *Ottaviano.*

★ **Piazza San Pietro**
PLAZA/SQUARE | Mostly enclosed within high walls that recall the papacy's stormy history, the Vatican opens the spectacular arms of Bernini's colonnade to embrace the world only at St. Peter's Square, scene of the pope's public appearances and another of Bernini's masterpieces. The elliptical Piazza di San Pietro was completed in 1667 and holds about 100,000 people. It's surrounded by a pair of quadruple colonnades and is gloriously studded with 140 statues of saints and martyrs. At its center is the 85-foot-high Egyptian obelisk, which was brought to Rome by Caligula in AD 37 and moved

Continued on page 82

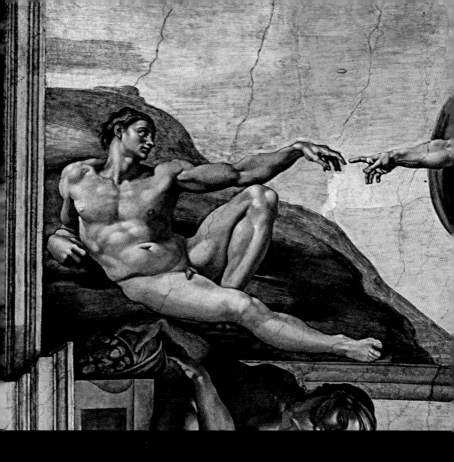

HEAVENS ABOVE:
THE SISTINE CEILING

Forming lines that are probably longer than those waiting to pass through the Pearly Gates, hordes of visitors arrive at the Sistine Chapel daily to view what may be the world's most sublime example of artistry:

Michelangelo: *The Creation of Adam*, Sistine Chapel, The Vatican, circa 1511.

Michelangelo's Sistine Ceiling. To paint this 12,000-square-foot barrel vault, it took four years, 343 frescoed figures, and a titanic battle of wits between the artist and Pope Julius II. While in its typical fashion, Hollywood focused on the element of agony, not ecstasy, involved in the saga of creation, a restoration of the ceiling, completed in 1994, and the installation of LEDs for better illumination, completed in 2018, have revolutionized our appreciation of the masterpiece of masterpieces.

By Martin Bennett

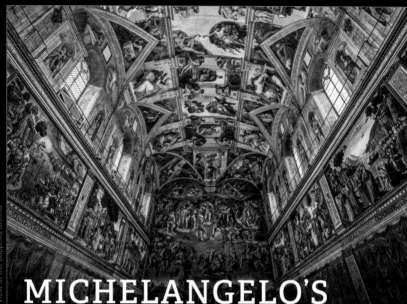

View of the Cappella Sistina

MICHELANGELO'S
MISSION IMPOSSIBLE

Designed to match the proportions of Solomon's Temple described in the Old Testament, the Sistine Chapel is named after Pope Sixtus VI, who commissioned it as a place of worship for himself and as the venue where new popes could be elected. Before Michelangelo, the barrel-vaulted ceiling was an expanse of azure fretted with golden stars. Then, in 1504, an ugly crack appeared. Bramante, the architect, managed do some patchwork using iron rods, but when signs of a fissure remained, the new Pope Julius II summoned Michelangelo to cover it with a fresco 135 feet long and 44 feet wide.

Taking in the entire span of the ceiling, the theme connecting the various scenes in this painted universe is seemingly mankind's need for redemption. The majestic panel depicting the Creation of Adam leads through the stages of the Fall and the expulsion from Eden to the tragedy of Noah found naked and mocked by his own sons. Witnessing all from the side and end walls, a chorus of ancient Prophets and Sibyls peers anxiously forward, awaiting the Redeemer who will come to save both the Jews and the Gentiles.

APOCALYPSE NOW

The sweetness and pathos of his *Pietà*, carved by Michelangelo only ten years earlier, have been left behind. The new work foretells an apocalypse, its congregation of doomed sinners facing the wrath of heaven through hanging, beheading, crucifixion, flood, and plague. Michelangelo, by nature a misanthrope, was already filled with visions of doom thanks to the fiery orations of Savonarola, whose thunderous preachments he had heard before leaving his hometown of Florence. Vasari, the 16th-century art historian, coined the word "terribilità" to describe Michelangelo's tension-ridden style, a rare case of a single word being worth a thousand pictures.

Michelangelo wound up using a *Reader's Digest* condensed version of the stories from Genesis, with the dramatis personae overseen by a punitive and terrifying God. In real life, poor Michelangelo answered to a flesh-and-blood taskmaster who was almost as vengeful: Pope Julius II. Less vicar of Christ than latter-day Caesar, he was intent on uniting Italy under the power of the Vatican and was eager to do so by any means, including riding into pitched battle. Yet this "warrior pope" considered his most formidable adversary to be Michelangelo. Applying a form of blackmail, Julius threatened to wage war on Michelangelo's Florence, to which the artist had fled after Julius canceled a commission for a grand papal tomb unless Michelangelo agreed to return to Rome and take up the task of painting the Sistine Chapel ceiling.

MICHELANGELO, SCULPTOR

A sculptor first and foremost, however, Michelangelo considered painting an inferior genre—"for rascals and sissies" as he put it. Second, there was the sheer scope of the task, leading Michelangelo to suspect he'd been set up by a rival, Bramante, chief architect of the new St. Peter's Basilica. As Michelangelo was also a master architect, he regarded this fresco commission as a Renaissance mission-impossible. Pope Julius's powerful will prevailed—and six years later the work of the Sistine Ceiling was complete. Irving Stone's famous novel *The Agony and the Ecstasy*—and the granitic 1965 film that followed—chart this epic battle between artist and pope.

THINGS ARE LOOKING UP

To better view the ceiling, bring binoculars or even just a mirror (to prevent your neck from becoming bent like Michelangelo's). Note that photos are not permitted. Admission and entry to the Sistine Chapel is only through the Musei Vaticani (Vatican Museums). To avoid crowds, visit at lunchtime or during the papal blessings and public audiences held in St. Peter's Square. Alternatively, book the Prime Experience Tour, which starts one hour before the museums open, or purchase the Extra Hours–Sistine Chapel ticket, which allows time in the chapel after the museums close.

SCHEMATIC OF THE SISTINE CEILING

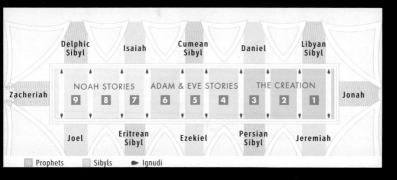

PAINTING
THE BIBLE

The ceiling's biblical symbols were ideated by three Vatican theologians, Cardinal Alidosi, Egidio da Viterbo, and Giovanni Rafanelli, along with Michelangelo. As for the ceiling's painted "framework," this quadratura alludes to Roman triumphal arches because Pope Julius II was fond of mounting "triumphal entries" into his conquered cities (in imitation of Christ's procession into Jerusalem on Palm Sunday).

THE CENTER PANELS

Prophet turned art-critic or, perhaps doubling as ourselves, the ideal viewer, Jonah the prophet (painted at the altar end) gazes up at the Creation, or Michelangelo's version of it.

1 The first of three scenes taken from the Book of Genesis: God separates Light from Darkness.

2 God creates the sun and a craterless pre-Galilean moon while the panel's other half offers an unprecedented rear view of the Almighty creating the vegetable world.

3 In the panel showing God separating the Waters from the Heavens, the Creator tumbles towards us as in a self-made whirlwind.

4 Pausing for breath, next admire probably Western Art's most famous image—God giving life to Adam.

The Creation of Eve from Adam's rib leads to the sixth panel.

6 In a sort of diptych divided by the trunk of the Tree of Knowledge of Good and Evil, Michelangelo retells the Temptation and the Fall.

Illustrating Man's fallen nature, the last three panels narrate, in un-chronological order, the Flood. In the first Noah offers a pre-Flood sacrifice of thanks.

8 Damaged by an explosion in 1794, next comes Michelangelo's version of Flood itself.

Finally, above the monumental Jonah, you can just make out the small, wretched figure of Noah, lying drunk— in pose, the shrunken anti-type of the majestic Adam five panels down the wall.

THE CREATION OF ADAM

Michelangelo's Adam was partly inspired by the Creation scenes Michelangelo had studied in the sculpted doors of Jacopo della Quercia in Bologna and Lorenzo Ghiberti's Doors of Paradise in Florence. Yet in Michelangelo's version Adam's hand hangs limp, waiting God's touch to impart the spark of life. Facing his Creation, the Creator—looking a bit like the pagan god Jupiter—is for the first time ever depicted as horizontal, mirroring the Biblical "in his own likeness." Decades after its completion, a crack began to appear, amputating Adam's fingertips. Believe it or not, the most famous fingers in Western art are the handiwork, at least in part, of one Domenico Carnevale.

In Focus | HEAVENS ABOVE: THE SISTINE CEILING

here in 1586 by Pope Sixtus V. The Vatican post offices can be found on both sides of the square and inside the Vatican Museums complex. **■ TIP→ The main information office is just left of the basilica as you face it.** ✉ *Piazza di San Pietro, Vatican* 🌐 *www.vaticanstate.va* [M] *Ottaviano.*

🍴 Restaurants

Del Frate

$$ | MODERN ITALIAN | This impressive wine bar pairs sleek, modern decor with creative cuisine and three dozen wines available by the glass. Marinated meat and fish are specialties, but you can also get cheeses, smoked meats, and composed salads. **Known for:** adjacent to one of Rome's noted wine shops; daily aperitivo with a nice selection of wines by the glass; wide selection of after-dinner drinks, including mezcal and amari (bitter cordial). [$] *Average main: €24* ✉ *Via degli Scipioni 118, Prati* ☎ *06/3236437* 🌐 *www.enotecadelfrate.it* 🕑 *Closed Sun. and Aug.* [M] *Ottaviano.*

Ristorante Sinatra

$$ | MODERN ITALIAN | Named in homage to the Italian-American crooner, this intimate restaurant has a refined yet casual atmosphere, with wine bottles lining the walls, black-and-white photographs of jazz musicians, and vintage touches like rotary telephones. Although the menu emphasizes Italian classics, there are a few surprises, including focaccia with Spanish pata negra ham, lime and raw shrimp in the *cacio e pepe* (pasta prepared with a pecorino-cheese sauce and black pepper), and a selection of sushi rolls. **Known for:** charming vintage setting; eclectic menu; live music. [$] *Average main: €18* ✉ *Via Fabio Massimo 68, Prati* ☎ *06/3219657* 🌐 *ristorante-sinatra.business.site* 🕑 *Closed Sun.* [M] *Lepanto.*

Sant'Isidoro Pizza & Bolle

$ | PIZZA | FAMILY | More upscale than a typical pizzeria but casual enough for a weeknight, this establishment pairs its pies with sparkling wines instead of beer. Opt for a classic pizza, or go with an innovative option, like one topped with stracciatella, raw shrimp, lemon peel, and mint. **Known for:** wide selection of sparkling wines; creative pizzas; chic modern design. [$] *Average main: €12* ✉ *Via Oslavia 41, Prati* ☎ *06/89822607* 🌐 *www.pizzaebolle.it* 🕑 *No lunch Sat.* [M] *Lepanto.*

Taverna Angelica

$$ | MODERN ITALIAN | The Borgo area near St. Peter's Basilica hasn't been known for culinary excellence, but this is starting to change, and Taverna Angelica was one of the first refined restaurants in this part of town. The dining room is small, which allows the chef to create a menu that's inventive without being pretentious. **Known for:** eclectic Italian dishes; high-quality cuisine; ravioli with salt cod in arrabbiata oil spiced with red chili. [$] *Average main: €23* ✉ *Piazza Amerigo Capponi 6, Borgo* ☎ *06/6874514* 🌐 *tavernaangelica.com* 🕑 *Closed Mon.* [M] *Ottaviano.*

☕ Coffee and Quick Bites

Al Settimo Gelo

$ | ICE CREAM | FAMILY | The unusual flavors of gelato scooped up here include cinnamon and ginger and fig with cardamom and walnut, but the classics also get rave reviews. Ask for a taste of the *passito* flavor, if it's available; it's inspired by the popular sweet Italian dessert wine. **Known for:** organic Sicilian lemon sorbetto; homemade whipped cream; completely gluten-free shop. [$] *Average main: €5* ✉ *Via Vodice 21/a, Prati* ☎ *06/3725567* 🌐 *www.alsettimogelo.it* 🕑 *Closed Mon. and 1 wk in Aug.* [M] *Lepanto.*

★ Bonci Pizzarium

$ | PIZZA | FAMILY | This tiny storefront by famed pizzaiolo Gabriele Bonci is the city's most famous place for pizza al taglio (by the slice). It serves more than a dozen versions, from the standard margherita to slices piled high with prosciutto and other tasty ingredients. **Known for:** Rome's best pizza al taglio; over a dozen flavors; long lines. $ *Average main: €5* ⊠ *Via della Meloria 43, Prati* ☎ *06/39745416* ⊕ *www.bonci.it* ☾ *Closed Mon.* Ⓜ *Cipro.*

 ## Hotels

Hotel al San Pietrino

$ | HOTEL | This simple budget hotel on the third floor of a 19th-century palazzo offers rock-bottom rates and is just a five-minute walk from the Vatican. **Pros:** heavenly rates near the Vatican; air-conditioning and Wi-Fi; free parking nearby. **Cons:** a couple of Metro stops from the centro storico; flat pillows and basic bedding; no bar. $ *Rooms from: €98* ⊠ *Via Giovanni Bettolo 43, Prati* ☎ *06/3700132, 328/3416714 WhatsApp* ⊕ *www.hotelsanpietrino.it* ⇥ *11 rooms* ⦿ *Free Breakfast* Ⓜ *Ottaviano.*

Residenza Paolo VI

$$ | HOTEL | Set in a former monastery—still an extraterritorial part of the Vatican—magnificently abutting Bernini's colonnade of St. Peter's Square, the Paolo VI (pronounced "Sesto," a reference to Pope Paul VI) is unbeatably close to St. Peter's, with comfortable and amazingly quiet guest rooms. **Pros:** direct views of St. Peter's from the rooftop terrace; quiet rooms; lovely staff and service. **Cons:** some rooms are really small; bathrooms are a tight space; far away from Rome's historical attractions. $ *Rooms from: €139* ⊠ *Via Paolo VI 29, Borgo* ☎ *06/684870* ⊕ *www.residenzapaolovi. com* ⇥ *35 rooms* ⦿ *Free Breakfast* Ⓜ *Ottaviano.*

 ## Nightlife

Emerald's Bar

COCKTAIL LOUNGES | This classy cocktail bar a few blocks from the Vatican makes you feel transported to a cozy salon in New York or London. In addition to some original creations, the bartenders make reliably good classics, including excellent dirty martinis. The kitchen stays open until midnight, so it's also a good spot for a late bite. ⊠ *Via Crescenzio 91C, Prati* ☎ *06/88654275* ⊕ *www.emeraldsbar.it* Ⓜ *Ottaviano.*

 ## Shopping

★ Castroni

FOOD | Opening its flagship shop near the Vatican in 1932, this gastronomic paradise has long been Rome's port of call for decadent delicacies from around the globe; there are now 13 locations throughout the city. Jonesing expats and study-abroad students pop in for local sweets, 300 types of tea, and even some good old-fashioned Kraft macaroni & cheese. If you need a pick-me-up, try the house-roasted espresso, which is some of the best coffee in Rome. ⊠ *Via Cola di Rienzo 196/198, Prati* ☎ *06/6874383* ⊕ *www.castronicoladirienzo.com* Ⓜ *Lepanto.*

Savelli Arte e Tradizione

SOUVENIRS | Here you'll find a fully stocked selection of religious gifts: everything from rosaries and crosses to religious artwork and Pope Francis memorabilia. Founded in 1898, this family business provides a place for pilgrims to pick up a souvenir from the Holy See and also specializes in mosaics. The store has another location at the Self-Service Restaurant in Piazza del Sant'Uffizio 6/7. It's closed on Sunday afternoon. ⊠ *Via Paolo VI 27–29, Borgo* ☎ *06/68307017* ⊕ *savellireligious.com* Ⓜ *Ottaviano.*

Piazza Navona, Campo de' Fiori, and the Jewish Ghetto

Set between Via del Corso and the Tiber bend, these time-burnished districts are some of the city's most beautiful. They're filled with airy piazzas, half-hidden courtyards, and narrow streets bearing curious names. Some of Rome's most coveted residential addresses are nestled here. So, too, are the ancient Pantheon and the Renaissance square of Campo de' Fiori, but the spectacular, over-the-top Baroque monuments of the 16th and 17th centuries predominate.

The hub of the district is the queen of squares, Piazza Navona—a cityscape adorned with the most jaw-dropping fountain by Gian Lorenzo Bernini, father of the Baroque. Streets running off the square lead to many historic must-sees, including noble churches by Borromini and Caravaggio's greatest paintings at San Luigi dei Francesi. This district has been an integral part of the city since ancient times, and its position between the Vatican and Lateran palaces, both seats of papal rule, put it in the mainstream of Rome's development from the Middle Ages onward. Craftsmen, shopkeepers, and famed artists toiled in the shadow of the huge palaces built to consolidate the power of leading figures in the papal court. Artisans and artists still live here, but their numbers are diminishing as the district becomes increasingly posh and—so critics say—"Disneyfied." But three of the liveliest piazzas in Rome—Piazza Navona, Piazza della Rotonda (home to the Pantheon), and Campo de' Fiori—are lodestars in a constellation of some of the city's finest cafés, stores, and wine bars.

Although today most of Rome's Jews live outside the Ghetto, the area remains the spiritual and cultural home of Jewish Rome, and that heritage permeates its small commercial area of Judaica shops, kosher bakeries, and restaurants. The Jewish Ghetto was established by papal decree in the 16th century. It was by definition a closed community, where Roman Jews lived under lock and key until Italian unification in 1870. In 1943–44, the already small Jewish population there was decimated by deportations. Today there are a few Judaica shops and kosher groceries, bakeries, and restaurants (especially on Via di Portico d'Ottavia), but the neighborhood mansions are now being renovated and much coveted by rich and stylish expats.

GETTING HERE AND AROUND

The Piazza Navona and Campo de' Fiori are an easy walk from the Vatican or Trastevere, or a half-hour stroll from the Spanish Steps. From Termini or the Vatican, take Bus No. 40 Express or the No. 64 to Largo Torre Argentina; then walk 10 minutes to either piazza. Bus No. 62 winds from Piazza Barberini past the Trevi Fountain to Campo de' Fiori.

From the Vatican or the Spanish Steps, it's a 30-minute walk to the Jewish Ghetto, or take the No. 40 Express or the No. 64 bus from Termini station to Largo Torre Argentina.

 Sights

Chiesa del Gesù

CHURCH | With an overall design by Vignola and a facade and dome by Della Porta, the first Jesuit church in Rome influenced the city's ecclesiastical architecture for more than a century. Consecrated in 1584—after the Council of Trent (1545–63) solidified the determination of the Roman Catholic Church to push back against northern Europe's Reformed Protestants—Il Gesù also became the prototype for Counter-Reformation churches throughout not only Italy but also Europe and the Americas.

Although low lighting underplays the brilliance of everything, the inside of the church drips with gold and lapis lazuli, gold and precious marbles, and gold and more gold. The interior was initially left plain to the point of austerity; when it was finally fully embellished 100 years later, no expense was spared to inspire believers with pomp and majesty. The most striking element is the ceiling, where frescoes swirl down from on high and merge with painted stucco figures at the base. The artist Baciccia achieved extraordinary effects, especially over the nave in the *Triumph of the Holy Name of Jesus*. Here, the figures representing evil who are being cast out of heaven seem to hurtle down onto the observer.

The founder of the Jesuit order himself is buried in the Chapel of St. Ignatius, in the left-hand transept. This is surely one of the most sumptuous altars in Rome, though as is typical of Baroque decoration, which is renowned for its illusions, the enormous globe of lapis lazuli that crowns the alter is really only a shell of lapis over a stucco base. Note, too, architect Carlo Fontana's heavy, bronze altar rail, which is in keeping with the surrounding opulence. ✉ *Via degli Astalli 16, Campo de' Fiori* ☎ *06/697001* ⊕ *www.chiesadelgesu.org.*

Crypta Balbi

RUINS | The fourth component of the magnificent collections of the Museo Nazionale Romano, this museum is unusual because it represents several periods of Roman history. The crypt is part of the Balbus Theater complex (13 BC), and other parts of the complex are from the medieval period, up through the 20th century. Though the interior lacks the lingering opulence of some other Roman sites, the written explanations accompanying the well-lit exhibits are excellent, and this museum is a popular field trip for teachers and school groups. Note that recent restoration works have resulted in closures here; check for updates before

visiting. ✉ *Via delle Botteghe Oscure 31, Jewish Ghetto* ☎ *06/39967701* ⊕ *www.coopculture.it* 🎫 *€10 Crypta Balbi only; €14 includes three other Museo Nazionale Romano sites over a 1-wk period (Palazzo Altemps, Palazzo Massimo, Museo Diocleziano)* ⊘ *Closed Mon.* Ⓜ *Bus Nos. 64 and 40, Tram No. 8.*

Fontana delle Tartarughe

FOUNTAIN | FAMILY | Designed by Giacomo della Porta in 1581 and sculpted by Taddeo Landini, this fountain, set in pretty Piazza Mattei, is one of Rome's most charming. Its focal point consists of four bronze boys, each grasping a dolphin spouting water into a marble shell. Bronze turtles held in the boys' hands drink from the upper basin. The turtles were added in the 17th century by Bernini. ✉ *Piazza Mattei, Jewish Ghetto.*

Galleria Spada

ART MUSEUM | In this neighborhood of huge, austere palaces, Palazzo Spada strikes an almost frivolous note, with its pretty ornament-encrusted courtyard and its upper stories covered with stuccoes and statues. Although the palazzo houses an impressive collection of Old Master paintings, it's most famous for its trompe-l'oeil garden gallery, a delightful example of the sort of architectural games that rich Romans of the 17th century found irresistible.

Even if you don't go into the gallery, step into the courtyard and look through the glass window of the library to the colonnaded corridor in the adjacent courtyard. You'll see—or seem to see—a statue at the end of a 26-foot-long gallery, seemingly quadrupled in depth in a sort of optical telescope that takes Renaissance's art of perspective to another level. In fact the distance is an illusion: the corridor grows progressively narrower and the columns progressively smaller as they near a statue, which is just 2 feet tall. The Baroque period is known for its special effects, and this is rightly one of the most famous. It was long thought that

Borromini was responsible for the ruse; it's now known that it was designed by an Augustinian priest, Giovanni Maria da Bitonto.

Upstairs is a seignorial picture gallery with the paintings shown as they would have been, hung one over the next clear to the ceiling. Outstanding works include Brueghel's *Landscape with Windmills*, Titian's *Musician,* and Andrea del Sarto's *Visitation.* Look for the fact sheets that have descriptive notes about the objects in each room. ⊠ *Piazza Capo di Ferro 13, Campo de' Fiori* ☏ *06/6874896* ⊕ *galleriaspada.cultura gov.it* ✉ *€5* ⊙ *Closed Tues.*

★ Palazzo Altemps

CASTLE/PALACE | Containing some of the world's finest ancient Roman statues, Palazzo Altemps is part of the Museo Nazionale Romano. The palace's sober exterior belies a magnificence that appears as soon as you walk into the majestic courtyard, studded with statues and covered in part by a retractable awning. The restored interior hints at the Roman lifestyle of the 16th–18th centuries while showcasing the most illustrious pieces from the Museo Nazionale, including the collection of the Ludovisi noble family.

In the frescoed salons you can see the *Galata Suicida,* a poignant sculptural work portraying a barbarian warrior who chooses death for himself and his wife, rather than humiliation by the enemy. Another highlight is the large Ludovisi sarcophagus, magnificently carved from marble. In a place of honor is the *Ludovisi Throne,* which shows a goddess emerging from the sea and being helped by her acolytes. For centuries this was heralded as one of the most sublime Greek sculptures, but, today, at least one authoritative art historian considers it a colossally overrated fake. Look for the framed explanations of the exhibits that detail (in English) how and exactly where Renaissance sculptors, Bernini among

them, added missing pieces to the classical works.

In the lavishly frescoed loggia stand busts of the Caesars. In the wing once occupied by early-20th-century poet Gabriele d'Annunzio (who married into the Altemps family), three rooms host the museum's Egyptian collection. ⊠ *Piazza di Sant'Apollinare 46, Piazza Navona* ☏ *06/684851* ⊕ *museonazionaleromano. beniculturali.it* ✉ *€8; €12 combined ticket includes three other Museo Nazionale Romano sites over one week (Crypta Balbi, Palazzo Massimo alle Terme, and Museo delle Terme di Diocleziano)* ⊙ *Closed Mon.*

★ Palazzo Farnese

CASTLE/PALACE | Rome's most beautiful Renaissance palace is fabled for its Galleria Carracci, whose ceiling is to the Baroque age what the Sistine Chapel ceiling is to the Renaissance. The Farnese family rose to great power and wealth during the Renaissance, in part because of the favor Pope Alexander VI showed to the beautiful Giulia Farnese. The massive palace was begun when, with Alexander's aid, Giulia's brother became cardinal; it was further enlarged on his election as Pope Paul III in 1534.

The uppermost frieze decorations and main window overlooking the piazza are the work of Michelangelo, who also designed part of the courtyard, as well as the graceful arch over Via Giulia at the back. The facade on Piazza Farnese has geometrical brick configurations that have long been thought to hold some occult meaning. When looking up at the palace, try to catch a glimpse of the splendid frescoed ceilings, including the Galleria Carracci vault painted by Annibale Carracci between 1597 and 1604.

The Carracci gallery depicts the loves of the gods, a supremely pagan theme that the artist painted in a swirling style that announced the birth of the Baroque. Other opulent salons are among the largest in Rome, including the Salon of Hercules, which has an impressive replica of the ancient *Farnese Hercules*. The French Embassy, which occupies the palace, offers tours (in English) on Monday, Wednesday, and Friday; book at least a few weeks (and up to eight months) in advance through the website, and bring a photo ID. ⊠ *French Embassy, Servizio Culturale, Piazza Farnese 67, Campo de' Fiori* ☎ *06/686011* ⊕ *www.visite-palazzo-farnese.it* 🎫 *€12* ⊘ *Closed Tues., Thurs., Sat., and Sun.*

★ **Pantheon**

RELIGIOUS BUILDING | The city's best-preserved ancient building, this former Roman temple is a marvel of architectural harmony and proportion. It was entirely rebuilt by the emperor Hadrian around AD 120 on the site of a Pantheon (from the Greek: *pan,* all, and *theon,* gods) erected in 27 BC by Augustus's right-hand man and son-in-law, Agrippa.

The most striking thing about the Pantheon is not its size, immense though it is, nor even the phenomenal technical difficulties posed by so massive a construction; rather, it's the remarkable unity of the building. The diameter described by the dome is exactly equal to its height. It's the use of such simple mathematical balance that gives classical architecture its characteristic sense of proportion and its nobility. The opening at the apex of the dome, the *oculus,* is nearly 30 feet in diameter and was intended to symbolize the "all-seeing eye of the heavens." On a practical note, this means when it rains, it rains inside: look out for the drainage holes in the floor.

Although little is known for sure about the Pantheon's origins or purpose, it's worth noting that the five levels of trapezoidal coffers (sunken panels in the ceiling) represent the course of the five then-known planets and their concentric spheres. Ruling over them is the sun, represented symbolically and literally by the 30-foot-wide eye at the top. The heavenly symmetry is further paralleled by the coffers: 28 to each row, the number of lunar cycles. In the center of each would have shone a small bronze star. Down below, the seven large niches were occupied not by saints, but, it's thought, by statues of Mars, Venus, the deified Caesar, and the other "astral deities," including the moon and sun, the "sol invictus." (Academics still argue, however, about which gods were most probably worshipped here.)

One of the reasons the Pantheon is so well preserved is that it was consecrated as a church in AD 608. (It's still a working church today.) No building, church or not, though, escaped some degree of plundering through the turbulent centuries of Rome's history after the fall of the empire. In 655, for example, the gilded bronze covering the dome was stripped. The Pantheon is also one of the city's important burial places. Its most famous tomb is that of Raphael (between the second and third chapels on the left as you enter). Mass takes place on Sunday and on religious holidays at 10:30; it's open to the public, but you are expected to arrive before the beginning and stay until the end. General access usually resumes at about 11:30. You can buy tickets at the site, but it's better to purchase them online in advance. ⊠ *Piazza della Rotonda, Piazza Navona* ☎ *06/68300230* ⊕ *www.pantheonroma.com* 🎫 *€5; audio guide €8.50.*

Piazza Campo de' Fiori

MARKET | **FAMILY** | A bustling marketplace in the morning (Monday through Saturday from 8 to 2) and a trendy meeting place the rest of the day and night, this piazza has plenty of down-to-earth charm. After lunch, it becomes a circus of bars particularly favored by study-abroad students, tourists, and young expats. Brooding over the piazza is a hooded statue of the philosopher Giordano Bruno, who was burned at the stake here in 1600 for heresy. ⊠ *Intersection of Via dei Baullari, Via*

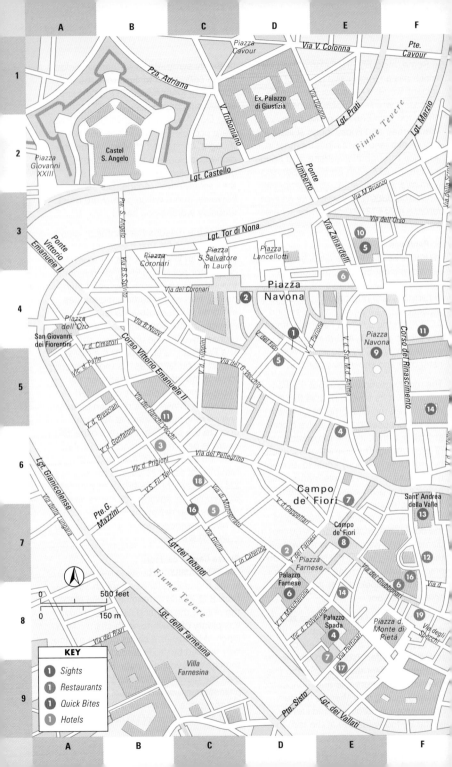

Piazza Navona, Campo de' Fiori, and the Jewish Ghetto

Sights ▼

1 Chiesa del Gesù..................... **I7**
2 Crypta Balbi **H7**
3 Fontana delle Tartarughe **H8**
4 Galleria Spada **E8**
5 Palazzo Altemps **E3**
6 Palazzo Farnese **D8**
7 Pantheon **G5**
8 Piazza Campo de' Fiori **E7**
9 Piazza Navona **E5**
10 Portico d'Ottavia **H9**
11 San Luigi dei Francesi............. **F4**
12 Santa Maria sopra Minerva **H5**
13 Sant'Andrea della Valle............ **F7**
14 Sant'Ivo alla Sapienza **F5**
15 Sinagoga.......................... **H9**
16 Via Giulia.......................... **C7**

Restaurants ▼

1 Armando al Pantheon............. **G5**
2 Ba'Ghetto **J3**
3 BellaCarne......................... **H9**
4 Cul de Sac **E6**
5 Da Fransceso **D5**
6 Dar Filettaro a Santa Barbara..... **F8**
7 Ditirambo **E6**
8 Emma **G7**
9 Enoteca Corsi **H6**
10 Il Convivio Troiani.................. **E3**
11 Il Pagliaccio **B5**
12 Il Sanlorenzo **F7**
13 La Ciambella **G6**
14 L'Angolo Divino.................... **E8**
15 Osteria dell'Ingegno............... **I4**
16 Pesci Fritti **F7**
17 Pianostrada **E9**
18 Pierluigi **C6**
19 Roscioli Salumeria con Cucina ... **F8**

Quick Bites ▼

1 Bar del Fico........................ **D5**
2 Gelateria Del Teatro **D4**
3 Giolitti **H3**
4 Pasticceria Boccione **G8**
5 Sant'Eustachio il Caffè........... **G5**

Hotels ▼

1 Albergo Santa Chiara **G6**
2 Casa di Santa Brigida **D7**
3 D.O.M. Hotel Roma **B6**
4 Hotel Chapter Roma............... **G9**
5 Hotel de' Ricci..................... **C7**
6 Hotel Genio **E4**
7 Hotel Ponte Sisto **E9**
8 The Pantheon Iconic Rome Hotel, Autograph Collection.............. **G5**

Giubbonari, Via del Pellegrino, and Piazza della Cancelleria, Campo de' Fiori.

★ Piazza Navona

PLAZA/SQUARE | Always camera-ready, this beautiful plaza has Bernini sculptures, three gorgeous fountains, and a magnificently Baroque church (Sant'Agnese in Agone), all built atop the remains of a Roman athletics track. Pieces of the arena are still visible near the adjacent Piazza Sant'Apollinare, and the ancient spirit of entertainment lives on in the buskers and artists who populate the piazza today.

The piazza took on its current look during the 17th century, after Pope Innocent X of the Pamphilj family decided to make over his family palace (now the Brazilian embassy and an ultra-luxe hotel) and its surroundings. Center stage is the Fontana dei Quattro Fiumi, created for Innocent by Bernini in 1651. Bernini's powerful figures of the four rivers represent the longest rivers of the four known continents at the time: the Nile (his head covered because the source was unknown); the Ganges; the Danube; and the Plata (the length of the Amazon was then unknown). Popular legend has it that the figure of the Plata—the figure closest to Sant'Agnese in Agone—raises his hand before his eyes because he can't bear to look upon the church's "inferior" facade designed by Francesco Borromini, Bernini's rival.

If you want a café with one of the most beautiful, if pricey, views in Rome, grab a seat at Piazza Navona. Just be aware that all the restaurants here are heavily geared toward tourists, so while it's a beautiful place for a coffee, you can find cheaper, more authentic, and far better meals elsewhere. ⊠ *Piazza Navona.*

Portico d'Ottavia

RUINS | Looming over the Jewish Ghetto, this huge portico, with a few surviving columns, is one of the area's most picturesque set pieces, with the church of Sant'Angelo in Pescheria built right into its ruins. Named by Augustus in honor of his sister Octavia, it was originally 390 feet wide and 433 feet long; encompassed two temples, a meeting hall, and a library; and served as a kind of grandiose entrance foyer for the adjacent Teatro di Marcello.

In the Middle Ages, the cool marble ruins of the portico became Rome's *pescheria* (fish market). A stone plaque on a pillar (it's a copy as the original is in the Musei Capitolini) states in Latin that the head of any fish surpassing the length of the plaque was to be cut off "up to the first fin" and given to the city fathers or else the vendor was to pay a fine of 10 gold florins. The heads, which were used to make fish soup, were considered a great delicacy. ⊠ *Via Portico d'Ottavia 29, Jewish Ghetto* ☎ *06/0608.*

★ San Luigi dei Francesi

CHURCH | San Luigi's Contarelli Chapel (the fifth and last chapel on the left, toward the main altar) is adorned with three stunningly dramatic works by Caravaggio (1571–1610), the Baroque master of the heightened approach to light and dark. They were commissioned for the tomb of Mattheiu Cointerel in one of Rome's French churches (San Luigi is St. Louis, patron saint of France). The inevitable coin machine will light up his *Calling of Saint Matthew, Saint Matthew and the Angel,* and *Martyrdom of Saint Matthew* (seen from left to right), and Caravaggio's mastery of light takes it from there.

When painted, they caused considerable consternation among the clergy of San Luigi, who thought the artist's dramatically realistic approach was scandalously disrespectful. A first version of the altarpiece was rejected; the priests were not particularly happy with the other two, either. Time has fully vindicated Caravaggio's patron, Cardinal Francesco del Monte, who secured the commission for these works and staunchly defended them. ⊠ *Piazza di San Luigi dei Francesi, Piazza Navona* ☎ *06/688271* ⊕ *saintlouis-rome.net.*

★ Santa Maria sopra Minerva

CHURCH | The name of the church reveals that it was built *sopra* (over) the ruins of a temple of Minerva, the ancient goddess of wisdom. Erected in 1280 by Dominicans along severe Italian Gothic lines, it has undergone a number of more or less happy interior restorations. Certainly, as the city's major Gothic church, it provides a refreshing contrast to Baroque flamboyance. Have a €1 coin handy to illuminate the Cappella Carafa in the right transept; the small investment is worth it to better see Filippino Lippi's (1457–1504) glowing frescoes featuring a deep azure expanse of sky and musical angels hovering around the Virgin.

Under the main altar is the tomb of St. Catherine of Siena, one of Italy's patron saints. Left of the altar you'll find Michelangelo's *Risen Christ* and the tomb of the gentle artist Fra Angelico. Bernini's unusual and little-known monument to the Blessed Maria Raggi is on the fifth pier of the left-hand aisle.

In front of the church, Bernini's *Elephant and Obelisk* is perhaps the city's most charming sculpture. An inscription on the base references the church's ancient patroness, reading something to the effect that it takes a strong mind to sustain solid wisdom. The church has been undergoing recent restorations to maintain the glorious interior, so be sure to check the back entrance on Via Beato Angelico if the main doors are closed during regular hours. ⊠ *Piazza della Minerva, Piazza Navona* ☎ *06/792257* ⊕ *www.santamariasopraminerva.it.*

Sant'Andrea della Valle

CHURCH | Topped by the highest dome in Rome after St. Peter's (designed by Maderno), this imposing 17th-century church is remarkably balanced in design. Fortunately, its facade, which had turned a sooty gray from pollution, has been cleaned to a near-sparkling white. Use one of the handy mirrors to examine the early-17th-century frescoes by Domenichino in the choir vault and those by Lanfranco in the dome. One of the earliest ceilings done in full Baroque style, its upward vortex was influenced by Correggio's dome in Parma, of which Lanfranco was also a citizen. (Bring a few coins to light the paintings, which can be very dim.) The three massive paintings of St. Andrew's martyrdom are by Mattia Preti (1650–51). Richly marbled and decorated chapels flank the nave, and in such a space, Puccini set the first act of *Tosca.* ⊠ *Piazza Vidoni 6, Corso Vittorio Emanuele II, Campo de' Fiori* ☎ *06/6861339* ⊕ *santandrea.teatinos.org.*

Sant'Ivo alla Sapienza

CHURCH | This eccentric Baroque church, probably Borromini's best, has one of Rome's most delightful "domes"—a dizzying spiral said to have been inspired by a bee's stinger. The apian symbol is a reminder that the church was commissioned by the Barberini pope Urban VIII (a swarm of bees figure on the Barberini family crest), although it was completed by Alexander VII. The interior, open only for three hours on Sunday morning, is worth a look, especially if you share Borromini's taste for complex mathematical architectural idiosyncrasies. "I didn't take up architecture solely to be a copyist," he once said. Sant'Ivo is certainly the proof. ⊠ *Corso del Rinascimento 40, Piazza Navona* ☎ *06/6864987* ⊕ *www.sivoallasapienza.eu* ⊗ *Closed Mon.–Sat., July and Aug.*

Sinagoga

RELIGIOUS BUILDING | This synagogue has been the city's largest Jewish temple, and a Roman landmark with its aluminum dome, since its construction in 1904. The building also houses the Jewish Museum, with displays of precious ritual objects and exhibits that document the uninterrupted presence of a Jewish community in the city for nearly 22 centuries. Until the 16th century, Jews were esteemed citizens of Rome. Among them were bankers and physicians to the popes, who had themselves given permission for the construction of synagogues. But, in 1555, during the Counter-Reformation, Pope Paul IV decreed the building of the walls of the Ghetto, confining the Jews to this small area and imposing restrictions, some of which continued to be enforced until 1870. For security reasons, entrance is via guided visit only, and tours in English are available twice a day but should be booked online ahead of time. Entrance to the synagogue is through the museum on Via Catalana. ⊠ *Lungotevere de' Cenci 15, Jewish Ghetto* ☎ *06/68400661* ⊕ *www.museoebraico.roma.it* ☎ *€11* ⊗ *Museum closed Sat. and Jewish holidays.*

★ **Via Giulia**

STREET | Straight as a die and still something of a Renaissance-era diorama, Via Giulia was the first street in Rome since ancient times to be deliberately planned. It was named for Pope Julius II (of Sistine Chapel fame), who commissioned it in the early 1500s as part of a scheme to open up a grandiose approach to St. Peter's Basilica. Although the pope's plans were only partially completed, Via Giulia became an important thoroughfare in Renaissance Rome. It's still, after more than four centuries, the address of choice for Roman aristocrats, despite a recent, controversial addition: a large parking lot along one side of the street (creating it meant steamrolling through ancient and medieval ruins underneath).

A stroll around and along Via Giulia reveals elegant palaces and churches, including one, **San Eligio**, on the little side street Via di Sant'Eligio, that was designed by Raphael himself. Note also the **Palazzo Sacchetti** (⊠ *Via Giulia 66*), with an imposing stone portal and an interior containing some of Rome's grandest staterooms; it remains, after 300 years, the private quarters of the Marchesi Sacchetti. The forbidding brick building that housed the **Carceri Nuove** (New Prison ⊠ *Via Giulia 52*), Rome's

prison for more than two centuries, now contains the offices of the Direzione Nazionale Antimafia. Near the bridge that arches over Via Giulia's southern end is the church of **Santa Maria dell'Orazione e Morte** (Holy Mary of Prayer and Death), with stone skulls on its door. These are a symbol of a confraternity that was charged with burying the bodies of the unidentified dead found in the city streets.

Designed by Borromini and home, since 1927, to the Hungarian Academy, the **Palazzo Falconieri** (⊠ *Via Giulia 1* ☎ *06/68896700*) has Borromini-designed salons and loggia that are sporadically open as part of guided tours; call for information. The falcon statues atop its belvedere are best viewed from around the block, along the Tiber embankment. Remnant of a master plan by Michelangelo, the arch over the street was meant to link massive **Palazzo Farnese,** on the east side of Via Giulia, with the building across the street and a bridge to the Villa Farnesina, directly across the river. Finally, on the right and rather green with age, dribbles that star of many a postcard, the **Fontana del Mascherone.** ⊠ *Via Giulia, between Piazza dell'Oro and Piazza San Vincenzo Palloti, Campo de' Fiori.*

🍴 Restaurants

★ **Armando al Pantheon**

$$ | **ROMAN** | In the shadow of the Pantheon, this small family-run trattoria, open since 1961, delights tourists and locals alike. There's an air of authenticity to the Roman staples here, and the quality of the ingredients and the cooking mean booking ahead is a must. **Known for:** beautifully executed traditional Roman cooking; spaghetti alla gricia (with guanciale, pecorino cheese, and black pepper); good wine list. **$** *Average main: €16* ⊠ *Salita dei Crescenzi 31, Piazza Navona* ☎ *06/68803034* ⊕ *www.armandoalpantheon.it* ⊗ *Closed Sun. and Aug.*

★ Ba'Ghetto

$$ | **ITALIAN** | **FAMILY** | This well-established hot spot on the Jewish Ghetto's main promenade has pleasant indoor and outdoor seating. The kitchen is kosher (many places featuring Roman Jewish fare are not) and is known for its meat dishes. **Known for:** carciofi alla giudia (deep-fried artichokes) and other Roman-Jewish specialties; casual family atmosphere; tables on the pedestrianized street. [$] *Average main: €22* ✉ *Via del Portico d'Ottavia 57, Jewish Ghetto* ☎ *06/68892868* 🌐 *www.baghetto.com* 🕒 *Dinner Fri. and lunch Sat. are strictly for those who observe Shabbat with advance payment.*

BellaCarne

$$ | **ROMAN** | *Bellacarne* means "beautiful meat," and that's the focus of the menu here (though it's also what a Jewish Italian grandmother might say while pinching her grandchild's cheek). The kosher kitchen makes its own pastrami, but the setting is more fine dining than deli. **Known for:** pastrami; shabbat menu; outside seating. [$] *Average main: €17* ✉ *Via Portico d'Ottavia 51, Jewish Ghetto* ☎ *06/6833104* 🌐 *www.bellacarne.it* 🕒 *No dinner Fri. No lunch Sat. except limited Shabbat seating that must be pre-paid.*

★ Cul de Sac

$ | **WINE BAR** | This popular wine bar a stone's throw from Piazza Navona is among the city's oldest and has a book-length selection of wines from Italy, France, the Americas, and elsewhere. It offers great value and pleasant service and is a lovely spot for a light late lunch or an early dinner when most restaurants aren't open yet. **Known for:** great wine list (and wine bottle–lined interior); eclectic Italian and Mediterranean fare; relaxed atmosphere and outside tables. [$] *Average main: €12* ✉ *Piazza di Pasquino 73, Piazza Navona* ☎ *06/68801094* 🌐 *www.enotecaculdesacroma.it.*

Da Francesco

$$ | **ROMAN** | **FAMILY** | For good, hearty, Roman cuisine in an area filled with mediocre touristy restaurants, head to this trattoria that's been on the scene since the late 1950s. Stick with the classics, perhaps starting off with a mixed salumi plate featuring Parma ham and buffalo mozzarella before moving on to a *primi* (first course)—the amatriciana (with tomato sauce, guanciale, and pecorino cheese) is one of the standouts. **Known for:** authentic and informal atmosphere; outside tables in summer; traditional Roman cooking. [$] *Average main: €18* ✉ *Piazza del Fico 29, Piazza Navona* ☎ *06/6864009* 🌐 *www.dafrancesco.it.*

Dar Filettaro a Santa Barbara

$ | **ITALIAN** | The window reads "Filetti di Baccalà," but the official name of this small restaurant that specializes in one thing—deliciously battered and deep-fried fillets of salt cod—is Dar Filettaro a Santa Barbara. If it's in season, be sure to try the *puntarelle* (crisp chicory) tossed with garlic and anchovy dressing. **Known for:** filetti di baccalà; functional "hole-in-the-wall" interior; tables outside on the pretty square. [$] *Average main: €7* ✉ *Largo dei Librari 88, Campo de' Fiori* ☎ *06/6864018* 🌐 *www.facebook.com/FilettiDiBaccala* 🕒 *Closed Sun. and Aug. No lunch.*

Ditirambo

$$ | **ITALIAN** | Don't let the country-kitchen feel fool you. This little spot off the Campo de' Fiori goes a step beyond the ordinary with constantly changing offbeat takes on Italian classics. **Known for:** cozy and casual; hearty meat and pasta dishes; good vegetarian options. [$] *Average main: €16* ✉ *Piazza della Cancelleria 74, Campo de' Fiori* ☎ *06/6871626* 🌐 *www.ristoranteditirambo.it* 🕒 *Closed Aug.*

★ Emma

$$$ | **ROMAN** | **FAMILY** | Smack in the middle of the city, with the freshest produce right outside its door, this pizzeria features pies made with dough by Rome's

renowned family of bakers, the Rosciolis, as well as a good selection of pastas, mains, and local Lazio wines. **Known for:** light, airy, and casual; thin-crust Roman pizza; tasty fritti (classic fried Roman pizzeria appetizers). $ *Average main: €25* *Via Monte della Farina 28–29, Campo de' Fiori* 06/64760475 *www. emmapizzeria.com.*

Enoteca Corsi

$ | **ITALIAN** | Although this old-school, centro storico trattoria has been renovated, you wouldn't know it, and that's part of its charm. At lunchtime, it's often packed with a mix of civil servants from the nearby government offices, construction workers, and in-the-know tourists enjoying classic pastas, octopus salad, and *secondi* (second courses) such as roast veal with peas. **Known for:** casual atmosphere; Roman specialties; brusque but friendly service. $ *Average main: €12* *Via del Gesù 88, Piazza Navona* 06/6790821 *www.enotecacorsi.com* *Closed Sun. and 3 wks in Aug. No dinner Sat.*

★ Il Convivio Troiani

$$$$ | **MODERN ITALIAN** | The three Troiani brothers—Angelo in the kitchen and Giuseppe and Massimo presiding over the dining room and wine cellar—have been quietly redefining the experience of Italian *alta cucina* (haute cuisine) since 1990 at this well-regarded establishment in a tiny, nondescript alley north of Piazza Navona. The service is attentive without being overbearing, and the wine list is exceptional. **Known for:** fine dining in elegant surroundings; inventive modern Italian cooking with exotic touches; amazing wine cellar and a great sommelier. $ *Average main: €38* *Vicolo dei Soldati 31, Piazza Navona* 06/6869432 *www.ilconviviotroiani.it* *Closed Sun. and 1 wk in Aug. No lunch.*

Il Pagliaccio

$$$$ | **MODERN ITALIAN** | Some of the most innovative interpretations of fine Roman cookery can be found in this starkly chic restaurant on a backstreet between

upscale Via Giulia and the Campo de' Fiori. Chef Anthony Genovese was born in France to Calabrese parents and spent time cooking in Japan and Thailand, so his dishes make use of nontraditional spices, ingredients, and preparations— garnering him a loyal following and multiple accolades. **Known for:** elaborate tasting menus; fine dining in elegant surroundings; discreet location. $ *Average main: €110* *Via dei Banchi Vecchi 129a, Piazza Navona* 06/68809595 *www. ristoranteilpagliaccio.com* *Closed Sun., Mon., and Aug. No lunch Tues. and Wed.*

Il Sanlorenzo

$$$$ | **SEAFOOD** | A gorgeous space, with chandeliers and soaring original brickwork ceilings, is the setting for one of Rome's best seafood restaurants. Order à la carte, or if you're hungry, the eight-course tasting menu (given the quality of the fish, a relative bargain at €90), which might include cuttlefish-ink tagliatelle with mint, artichokes, and roe or shrimp from the island of Ponza with rosemary, bitter herbs, and porcini mushrooms. **Known for:** top-quality fish and seafood; spaghetti con ricci (sea urchins); elegant surroundings. $ *Average main: €40* *Via dei Chiavari 4/5, Campo de' Fiori* 06/6865097 *www.ilsanlorenzo. it* *Closed Sun. and 2 wks in Aug. No lunch Sat. and Mon.*

La Ciambella

$$ | **ITALIAN** | A large glass wall to the kitchen and massive skylight in the dining room hint at the contemporary leanings of this restaurant built atop the ruins of the Baths of Agrippa behind the Pantheon. The emphasis here is on high-quality ingredients and classic Italian culinary traditions interpreted for modern diners. **Known for:** elegant setting; sophisticated Italian cuisine; great location near the Pantheon. $ *Average main: €17* *Via dell'Arco della Ciambella 20, Piazza Navona* 06/6832930 *www.la-ciambella.it* *Closed Tues. and Wed.*

L'Angolo Divino

$ | **WINE BAR** | There's something about this cozy wine bar that makes it feel as if it's in a small university town instead of a bustling metropolis. The walls are lined with a tempting array of bottles from around the Italian peninsula, and the counter is stocked with cheese and salumi that can be sliced and piled on plates to order. **Known for:** excellent wine selection and advice; cozy atmosphere; late-night snacks. $ *Average main: €13* ✉ *Via dei Balestrari 12, Campo de' Fiori* ☎ *06/6864413* ⊕ *www.angolodivino.it* ⊘ *Closed 2 wks in Aug.*

Osteria dell'Ingegno

$$ | **MODERN ITALIAN** | This casual, trendy place—vibrant with colorful paintings by local artists—is a great spot to enjoy an ancient piazza while savoring a glass of wine or a gourmet meal. The simple but innovative menu includes dishes like Roman artichokes with baccalà, beef *tagliata* (sliced grilled steak) with a red-wine reduction, and a perfectly cooked duck breast with red fruit sauce. **Known for:** beautiful location on a pedestrian square; a great spot both for aperitifs and/or a meal; outdoor seating with views of ancient ruins. $ *Average main: €22* ✉ *Piazza di Pietra 45, Piazza Navona* ☎ *06/6780662* ⊕ *www.osteriadellingegno.com* ⊘ *Closed Mon.*

Pesci Fritti

$$ | **SOUTHERN ITALIAN** | This cute jewel box of a restaurant sits on the ruins of the ancient Theatre of Pompey just behind Campo de' Fiori (note the curve of the street). Step inside, and the whitewashed walls with touches of pale sea blue will make you feel like you've escaped to the Mediterranean coast for seafood favorites. **Known for:** fried fish and seafood choices; spaghetti with clams; cozy setting. $ *Average main: €18* ✉ *Via di Grottapinta 8, Campo de' Fiori* ☎ *06/68806170* ⊕ *pescifritti.business.site* ⊘ *Closed Mon. and Aug.*

★ Pianostrada

$$ | **MODERN ITALIAN** | This restaurant has an open kitchen, where you can watch the talented women owners cook up a storm of inventive delights—this is a "kitchen *lab*," after all, where top local ingredients are whipped into delicious plates. The spaghetti with tomato sauce, smoked ricotta, parmigiano, basil, and lemon peel is one of the signature dishes, and the amped-up traditional recipe is a delicious indication of how interesting the food can get. **Known for:** freshly baked focaccia with various toppings; creative burgers and salads; secret garden seating. $ *Average main: €20* ✉ *Via delle Zoccolette 22, Campo de' Fiori* ☎ *06/89572296* ⊘ *Closed Mon. No lunch Tues.–Fri.*

★ Pierluigi

$$$$ | **SEAFOOD** | This popular seafood restaurant is a fun spot on balmy summer evenings, where elegant diners sip crisp white wine at tables out on the pretty Piazza de' Ricci. As at most Italian restaurants, fresh fish is sold per hectogram (100 grams, or about 3.5 ounces), so you may want to double-check the cost after it's been weighed. **Known for:** top-quality fish and seafood; tables on the pretty pedestrianized piazza; elegant atmosphere with great service. $ *Average main: €38* ✉ *Piazza de' Ricci 144, Campo de' Fiori* ☎ *06/6868717* ⊕ *www.pierluigi.it.*

★ Roscioli Salumeria con Cucina

$$ | **WINE BAR** | The shop in front of this wine bar will beckon you in with top-quality comestibles like hand-sliced cured ham from Italy and Spain, more than 300 cheeses, and a dizzying array of wines—but venture farther inside to try an extensive selection of unusual dishes and interesting takes on the classics. There are tables in the cozy wine cellar downstairs, but try and bag a table at the back on the ground floor (reserve well ahead; Roscioli is very popular). **Known for:** extensive wine list; arguably Rome's

best spaghetti alla carbonara; best prosciutto in town. $ Average main: €22 ⊠ Via dei Giubbonari 21, Campo de' Fiori ☎ 06/6875287 ⊕ www.salumeriaroscioli. com ⊘ Closed 1 wk in Aug.

☕ Coffee and Quick Bites

Bar del Fico

$ | ITALIAN | FAMILY | Everyone in Rome knows Bar del Fico, located right behind Piazza Navona, so if you want to hang out with the locals, come here for a drink or something to eat at any time of day or night. In the mornings, chess players sit at tables outside under the shade of the fig tree that gives the bar its name; after sunset, the bar is packed with people sipping cocktails. **Known for:** outside tables in a pretty square; Italian-style brunch; buzzy atmosphere. $ Average main: €10 ⊠ Piazza del Fico 26, Piazza Navona ☎ 06/68891373 ⊕ www.bardelfico.com.

★ Gelateria Del Teatro

$ | ICE CREAM | FAMILY | In a window next to the entrance of this renowned gelateria, you can see the fresh fruit being used to create the day's flavors, which highlight the best of Italy—from Amalfi lemons to Alban hazelnuts. In addition to traditional options, look for interesting combinations like raspberry and sage or white chocolate with basil. **Known for:** sublime gelato; seasonal, all natural ingredients; charming location on a cobblestone street. $ Average main: €3 ⊠ Via dei Coronari 65/66, Piazza Navona ☎ 06/45474880 ⊕ www.gelateriadelteatro.it.

★ Giolitti

$ | ICE CREAM | FAMILY | Open since 1900, Giolitti near the Pantheon is Rome's old-school gelateria par excellence. Pay in advance at the register by the door; take your receipt to the counter; and choose from dozens of flavors, including chocolate, cinnamon, and pistachio. **Known for:** excellent gelato; old-school setting; wide selection of flavors. $ Average main: €3 ⊠ Via degli Uffici del Vicario 40, Piazza Navona ☎ 06/6991243 ⊕ www.giolitti.it.

Pasticceria Boccione

$ | BAKERY | FAMILY | This tiny, old-school bakery is famed for its Roman-Jewish sweet specialties. Service is brusque, choices are few, what's available depends on the season, and when it's sold out, it's sold out. **Known for:** ricotta and cherry tarts; pizza ebraica ("Jewish pizza," a dense baked sweet rich in nuts and raisins); no frills and no seats. $ Average main: €4 ⊠ Via del Portico d'Ottavia 1, Jewish Ghetto ☎ 06/6878637 ⊘ Closed Sat.

Sant'Eustachio il Caffè

$ | CAFÉ | FAMILY | Frequented by tourists and government officials from the nearby Senate alike, this café is considered by many to make Rome's best coffee. Take it at the counter Roman-style—servers are hidden behind a huge espresso machine, where they vigorously mix the sugar and coffee to protect their "secret method" for the perfectly prepared cup (if you want yours without sugar here, ask for it *senza zucchero*). **Known for:** gran caffè (large sugared espresso); old-school Roman coffee bar vibe; 1930s interior. $ Average main: €2 ⊠ Piazza Sant'Eustachio 82, Piazza Navona ☎ 06/68802048 ⊕ caffesanteustachio.com.

Hotels

Albergo Santa Chiara

$$$ | HOTEL | Guests choose this hotel, run by members of the same family for 200 years, not only for its prime location, but also its welcoming staff, top-notch service, and comfy beds. **Pros:** near the Pantheon and Santa Maria sopra Minerva; free Wi-Fi; lovely sitting area in front, overlooking the piazza. **Cons:** some rooms are on the small side and need updating; Wi-Fi can be slow; street-side rooms can be noisy. $ Rooms from: €210

✉ *Via Santa Chiara 21, Piazza Navona* ☎ *06/6872979* 🌐 *www.albergosantachiara.com* 🛏 *96 rooms* 🍴 *Free Breakfast.*

Casa di Santa Brigida

$ | **B&B/INN** | The friendly sisters of Santa Brigida oversee simple, straightforward, and centrally located accommodations in one of Rome's loveliest convents, with a rooftop terrace overlooking Palazzo Farnese. **Pros:** insider papal tickets; large library and sunroof; free Wi-Fi. **Cons:** weak air-conditioning; no TVs in the rooms (though there is a common TV room); payment at structure only. [$] *Rooms from: €50* ✉ *Piazza Farnese 96, entrance around the corner at Via Monserrato 54, Campo de' Fiori* ☎ *06/68892596* 🌐 *www.casabrigidaroma.it* 🛏 *20 rooms* 🍴 *Free Breakfast.*

D.O.M Hotel Roma

$$$$ | **HOTEL** | In an old convent on Via Giulia, one of Rome's romantic ivy-covered streets, the D.O.M (Deo Optimo Maximo) is an ultrachic luxury hotel that resembles an aristocratic *casa nobile.* **Pros:** complimentary Acqua di Parma toiletries; heated towel racks; hip decor. **Cons:** an armed guard at the anti-terrorism headquarters opposite the hotel may be off-putting for some; delicious but expensive cocktails; standard rooms are small for a five-star hotel. [$] *Rooms from: €480* ✉ *Via Giulia 131, Campo de' Fiori* ☎ *06/6832144* 🌐 *www.domhotelroma.com* 🛏 *18 rooms* 🍴 *Free Breakfast.*

Hotel Chapter Roma

$$$ | **HOTEL** | The edgy, of-the-moment design at this boutique hotel juxtaposes plush midcentury Italian furnishings with street art murals and industrial touches. **Pros:** trendy design; coworking space available; lively rooftop bar in summer. **Cons:** no gym; no spa; service can be spotty. [$] *Rooms from: €230* ✉ *Via di Santa Maria de' Calderari 47, Jewish Ghetto* ☎ *06/89935351* 🌐 *www.chapter-roma.com* 🛏 *47 rooms* 🍴 *Free Breakfast.*

Hotel de' Ricci

$$$$ | **HOTEL** | This intimate boutique hotel from the team behind the Pierluigi restaurant is a top spot for wine lovers. **Pros:** excellent wine cellar and wine tastings; great location on a quiet street; perks include complimentary aperitivo and priority reservations at Pierluigi. **Cons:** there's a charge of €50 per day to bring pets; there is a weekend crowd for the brunch; no spa or gym. [$] *Rooms from: €520* ✉ *Via della Barchetta 14, Campo de' Fiori* ☎ *06/6874775* 🌐 *www.hoteldericci.com* 🛏 *8 rooms* 🍴 *No Meals.*

Hotel Genio

$$ | **HOTEL** | Just off the beautiful Piazza Navona, this pleasant hotel has a lovely rooftop terrace that's the perfect place to enjoy a cappuccino or a glass of wine while taking in the view. **Pros:** breakfast buffet is abundant; moderate prices for the area; nice views from terrace. **Cons:** rooms facing the street can be noisy; spotty Wi-Fi; some furnishings need to be updated. [$] *Rooms from: €180* ✉ *Via Giuseppe Zanardelli 28, Piazza Navona* ☎ *06/6833781* 🌐 *www.hotelgenioroma.it* 🛏 *60 rooms* 🍴 *Free Breakfast.*

Hotel Ponte Sisto

$$$ | **HOTEL** | Situated in a remodeled Renaissance palazzo with one of the prettiest patio-courtyards in Rome, this hotel is a relaxing retreat close to Campo de' Fiori and Trastevere. **Pros:** rooms with views (and some with balconies and terraces); luxury bathrooms; beautiful courtyard garden. **Cons:** street-side rooms can be noisy; some upgraded rooms are small and not worth the price difference; carpets showing signs of wear. [$] *Rooms from: €260* ✉ *Via dei Pettinari 64, Campo de' Fiori* ☎ *06/6863100* 🌐 *www.hotelpontesisto.it* 🛏 *106 rooms* 🍴 *Free Breakfast.*

The Pantheon Iconic Rome Hotel, Autograph Collection

$$$$ | **HOTEL** | A member of Marriott's Autograph Collection, this boutique hotel is a sleek retreat in the center of the action. **Pros:** modern design and

amenities; restaurant by one of the city's best chefs; Marriott Bonvoy members can redeem points. **Cons:** some rooms lack external views; no spa or gym; design might be considered a bit cold and corporate. $ *Rooms from: €500* ⊠ *Via di Santa Chiara 4A, Piazza Navona* ☎ *06/87807070* ⊕ *www.thepantheonhotel.com* ⇴ *79 rooms* ❍| *No Meals.*

Nightlife

Enoteca al Parlamento Achilli
WINE BARS | The proximity of this traditional *enoteca* (wine bar) to Montecitorio, the Italian Parliament building, makes it a favorite with journalists and politicos, who often stop in for a glass of wine after work. But it's the tantalizing smell of truffles from the snack counter, where a sommelier waits to organize your tasting, that will probably lure you inside. There's also a celebrated restaurant where you can book a table and enjoy a parade of elegant Italian plates. Don't forget to check out the wine shop, too. ⊠ *Via dei Prefetti 15, Piazza Navona* ☎ *06/6873446* ⊕ *achilli.restaurant.*

Il Goccetto
WINE BARS | Specializing in the vintages produced by smaller vineyards from Sicily to Venice, this historical wine bar also has a menu of Italian delicacies (meats and cheeses) that likewise represents the entire Italian peninsula. The burrata with sun-dried tomatoes is a perennial favorite. The tiny bar is well designed but is always busy and never accepts reservations. If all the seats are taken, you might be able to sip wine on the step outside. ⊠ *Via dei Banchi Vecchi 14, Campo de' Fiori* ☎ *06/99448583* ⊕ *www.ilgoccetto.com.*

Jerry Thomas Speakeasy
COCKTAIL LOUNGES | One of just a handful of hidden bars in Rome, this intimate bar looks like a Prohibition-era haunt and serves the kind of classic cocktails you find in New York speakeasies. It's seating room only, so reservations must be made online in advance. Upon booking, you'll receive a password via email. Since it is a private club, the bar stays open late but patrons need to pay the €5 yearly membership fee once they arrive for the first time. Serious cocktail aficionados can also purchase specialty bitters and mixology tools at the Emporium across the alley from the drinks spot. ⊠ *Vicolo Cellini 30, Campo de' Fiori* ⊕ *www.thejerrythomasproject.it.*

The Sofa Bar Restaurant & Roof Terrace
BARS | The romantic rooftop terrace at Sofa has a 360-degree view of the Eternal City, so it's no surprise that it's a prime spot for a late-afternoon cocktail (weather permitting). Head downstairs in the cooler months for a wide selection of craft beers on tap inside the Hotel Indigo. ⊠ *Hotel Indigo Rome—St. George, Via Giulia 62, Campo de' Fiori* ☎ *06/68661846* ⊕ *www.hotelindigorome.com.*

Vinoteca Novecento
WINE BARS | Salami-and-cheese tasting menus and a seemingly unlimited selection of wines, Prosecco, vini santi, and grappe are highlights of this lovely (albeit tiny) enoteca with a very old-fashioned vibe. Inside, it's standing-room only; in good weather, you can sit outside at an oak barrique on a quiet cobblestone street leading to one of Rome's prettiest small squares. ⊠ *Piazza delle Coppelle 47, Piazza Navona* ☎ *06/6833078.*

🎭 Performing Arts

★ Teatro Argentina
THEATER | The 18th-century Teatro Argentina evokes glamour and sophistication with its velvet upholstery, large crystal chandeliers, and beautifully dressed theatergoers, who come to see international productions of stage and dance performances. ⊠ *Largo di Torre Argentina 52, Campo de' Fiori* ☎ *06/684000314* ⊕ *www.teatrodiroma.net.*

🛍 Shopping

BEAUTY

Antica Erboristeria Romana

OTHER HEALTH & BEAUTY | Complete with hand-labeled wooden drawers holding more than 200 varieties of herbs, flowers, and tinctures, Antica Erboristeria Romana has maintained its old-world apothecary feel (it's the oldest shop of its kind in Rome, dating back to 1752). The shop stocks an impressive array of teas and herbal infusions, more than 700 essential oils, bud derivatives, and powdered extracts. ⊠ *Via Torre Argentina 15, Piazza Navona* ☎ *06/6879493* ⊕ *www.anticaerboristeriaromana.it.*

CERAMICS AND DECORATIVE ARTS

⭐ INOR dal 1952

HOUSEWARES | For more than 50 years, INOR dal 1952 has served as a trusted friend for Romans in desperate need of an exclusive wedding gift, delicate stemware, or oh-so-perfect china place settings for a fancy Sunday lunch. Entrance is via a secluded 15th-century courtyard and up a flight of stairs. The store specializes in work handcrafted by the silversmiths of Pampaloni and Bastianelli in Florence. ⊠ *Via della Stelletta 23, Piazza Navona* ☎ *06/6878579* ⊕ *www.inor.it.*

CLOTHING

⭐ L'Archivio di Monserrato

WOMEN'S CLOTHING | Tailored jackets with exotic trims, dresses in eclectic prints and bold colors, and smart linen suits are some of the offerings at this airy, spacious boutique curated by Soledad Twombly (daughter-in-law of painter Cy Twombly). In addition to her original designs, look for a sophisticated mix of antique Turkish and Indian textiles, jewelry, shoes, and small housewares picked up on her travels. ⊠ *Via di Monserrato 150, Campo de' Fiori* ☎ *06/45654157* ⊕ *www.soledadtwombly.com.*

Le Tartarughe

WOMEN'S CLOTHING | A familiar face at the city's fashion shows, designer Susanna Liso, a Rome native, mixes raw silks or cashmere and fine merino wool to create captivating, enveloping garments that sometimes feature seductive or playful elements. Both her haute-couture and ready-to-wear lines are much loved by Rome's elite. ⊠ *Via Piè di Marmo 17, Piazza Navona* ☎ *06/6792240* ⊕ *www.letartarughe.eu.*

Morgana

WOMEN'S CLOTHING | When strolling down Via del Governo Vecchio, a street popular for funky and edgy clothing boutiques, you can't help but stop and stare at this shop's windows, where the family-run business displays some of its best hippie-chick and bridal-chic gowns. The highly original and highly coveted clothes are carefully crafted and hand-painted with one-of-a-kind designs. ⊠ *Via del Governo Vecchio 27, Piazza Navona* ☎ *334/7960281.*

Vestiti Usati Cinzia

MIXED CLOTHING | Vintage-clothes hunters, costume designers, and stylists alike love browsing through the racks at this fun, inviting shop, which is stocked wall-to-wall with funky 1960s and '70s apparel. There's definitely no shortage of goofy sunglasses, flower-power bell-bottoms, embroidered hippie tops, psychedelic boots, and other trippy merchandise from the days of peace and love. ⊠ *Via del Governo Vecchio 45, Piazza Navona* ☎ *06/6832945.*

FOOD AND WINE

Moriondo e Gariglio

CANDY | **FAMILY** | Dating from 1850 and adhering strictly to family recipes passed on from generation to generation, this shop makes some of Rome's finest chocolate delicacies and other sweet treats. The selection of more than 80 confections includes everything from dark-chocolate truffles to marrons glacés. The chocolates shaped like every letter of the alphabet are perennial favorites, though. ⊠ *Via Piè di Marmo 21, Piazza Navona* ☎ *06/6990856* ⊕ *moriondoegariglio.com.*

JEWELRY

Massimo Maria Melis

JEWELRY & WATCHES | Drawing heavily on ancient Roman and Etruscan designs, Massimo Maria Melis jewelry will carry you back in time. Working with 21-carat gold, he often incorporates antique coins in many of his exquisite bracelets and necklaces. Some of his pieces are done with an ancient technique, much loved by the Etruscans, in which tiny gold droplets are fused together to create intricately patterned designs. ⊠ *Via dell'Orso 57, Piazza Navona* ☎ *06/6869188* ⊕ *www. massimomariamelis.com.*

Quattrocolo

JEWELRY & WATCHES | Dating from 1938, this shop showcases exquisite, antique, micro-mosaic jewelry painstakingly crafted in the style perfected by the masters at the Vatican mosaic studio. You'll also find 18th- and 19th-century cameos and beautiful engraved stones as well as contemporary jewelry. The small works were beloved by cosmopolitan clientele of the Grand Tour age and offer modern-day shoppers a taste of yesteryear's grandeur. ⊠ *Via della Scrofa 48, Piazza Navona* ☎ *06/68801367* ⊕ *www.quattrocolo.com.*

SHOES AND ACCESSORIES

★ Chez Dede

OTHER SPECIALTY STORE | Husband-and-wife duo Andrea Ferolla and Daria Reina (he's a fashion illustrator, she's a photographer) curate a selection of clothes, bags, vintage jewelry, books, home decor, and anything else you might need in this cult favorite lifestyle-concept shop. Their signature bags are designed to go from the plane straight to the beach, and they regularly release collectible items featuring Ferolla's whimsical illustrations. ⊠ *Via di Monserrato 35, Campo de' Fiori* ☎ *06/83772934* ⊕ *www.chezdede.com.*

Ibiz

LEATHER GOODS | In business since 1972, this family team creates colorful, stylish leather handbags, belts, and sandals near Piazza Campo de' Fiori. Choose from the premade collection, or order something in the color of your choice; their workshop is visible in the boutique. ⊠ *Via dei Chiavari 39, Campo de' Fiori* ☎ *06/68307297* ⊕ *ibizroma.it.*

★ Maison Halaby

HANDBAGS | Lebanese designer and artist Gilbert Halaby was featured in fashion magazines like *Vogue* and created jewelry for Lady Gaga before giving up the rat race and opening his own shop, where the ethos is all about slow fashion. His boldly colored leather handbags incorporate suede, python, fringe, raffia, or jeweled handles, and his silk scarves are printed with his original watercolors, some of which are also on sale. The small, homey boutique—with a velvet sofa and lots of books, plants, and art—is mainly open by appointment, but if you pass by, ring the bell, and if Gilbert is there, he might just invite you in for coffee or Campari. ⊠ *Via di Monserrato 21, Campo de' Fiori* ☎ *06/96521585* ⊕ *www. maisonhalaby.com.*

STATIONERY

★ Cartoleria Pantheon dal 1910

STATIONERY | Instead of sending a postcard home, why not send a letter written on sumptuous, handmade, Amalfi paper purchased from this shop? It also sells hand-bound leather journals in an extraordinary array of colors and sizes. There are two locations in the neighborhood. ⊠ *Via della Maddalena 41, Piazza Navona* ☎ *06/6795633* ⊕ *www.cartoleria-pantheon.it.*

TOYS

Al Sogno

TOYS | FAMILY | This Navona jewel, around since 1945, is crammed top to bottom with artistic, well-crafted puppets, dolls, masks, stuffed animals, and other toys for children of all ages that encourage imaginative (and low-tech) play and learning. ⊠ *Piazza Navona 53, corner of Via Agonale, Piazza Navona* ☎ *06/6864198* ⊕ *www.alsogno.com.*

Piazza di Spagna

In spirit (and in fact) this section of the city is its most grandiose. The overblown Vittoriano monument, the labyrinthine treasure-chest palaces of Rome's surviving aristocracy, even the diamond-draped denizens of Via Condotti's shops—all embody the exuberant ego of a city at the center of its own universe. Here's where you'll see ladies in furs gobbling pastries at café tables and walk through a thousand snapshots as you climb the famous Spanish Steps, admired by generations from Byron to Versace. Cultural treasures abound around here: gilded 17th-century churches, glittering palazzi, and the greatest example of portraiture in Rome, Velázquez's incomparable *Innocent X* at the Galleria Doria Pamphilj. Have your camera ready—along with a coin or two—for that most beloved of Rome's landmarks, the Trevi Fountain.

GETTING HERE AND AROUND

Piazza di Spagna is a short walk from Piazza del Popolo, the Pantheon, and the Trevi Fountain. One of Rome's handiest subway stations, Spagna, is tucked just left of the steps. Buses No. 117 (from the Colosseum) and No. 119 (from Piazza del Popolo) hum through the area; the latter tootles up Via del Babuino, famed for its shopping.

Sights

★ Ara Pacis Augustae
(*Altar of Augustan Peace*)
MONUMENT | This pristine monument sits inside one of Rome's newer architectural landmarks: a gleaming, rectangular, glass-and-travertine structure designed by American architect Richard Meier. It overlooks the Tiber on one side and the

ruins of the marble-clad Mausoleo di Augusto (Mausoleum of Augustus) on the other and is a serene, luminous oasis right in the center of Rome.

This altar itself dates from 13 BC and was commissioned to celebrate the Pax Romana, the era of peace ushered in by Augustus's military victories. When viewing it, keep in mind that the spectacular reliefs would have been painted in vibrant colors, now long gone. The reliefs on the short sides portray myths associated with Rome's founding and glory; those on the long sides display a procession of the imperial family. Although half of his body is missing, Augustus is identifiable as the first full figure at the procession's head on the south-side frieze; academics still argue over exact identifications of most of the figures. Be sure to check out the small downstairs museum, which hosts rotating exhibits on Italian culture, with themes ranging from design to film. ⊠ *Lungotevere in Augusta, at the corner of Via Tomacelli, Piazza di Spagna* ☎ *06/0608* ⊕ *www.arapacis.it* ⛁ *€10.50, €13 when there's an exhibit* Ⓜ *Flaminio.*

★ Galleria d'Arte Moderna
ART MUSEUM | Access to this museum, which is housed in a former convent on the opposite side of Villa Borghese, is from an entrance above the Spanish Steps. A visit to it offers not only a look at modern Roman art but also at another side of the city—one where, in the near-empty halls, tranquility and contemplation reign. The permanent collection is too large to be displayed at once, so exhibits rotate. Nevertheless, the 18th-century building contains more than 3,000 19th- and 20th-century paintings, drawings, prints, and sculptures by artists including Giorgio de Chirico, Gino Severini, Scipione, Antonio Donghi, and Giacomo Manzù. ⊠ *Via Francesco Crispi 24, Piazza di Spagna* ☎ *06/0608* ⊕ *www. galleriaartemodernaroma.it* ⛁ *€7.50; €10 if there's a special exhibit* ☉ *Closed Mon.* Ⓜ *Spagna.*

Keats-Shelley Memorial House

HISTORIC HOME | Sent to Rome in a last-ditch attempt to treat his consumptive condition, English Romantic poet John Keats—celebrated for such poems as "Ode to a Nightingale" and "Endymion"—lived in this house at the foot of the Spanish Steps. At the time, this was the heart of Rome's colorful bohemian quarter, an area favored by English expats. He took his last breath here on February 23, 1821, and is now buried in the Non-Catholic Cemetery in Testaccio. On a visit to his final home, you can see his death mask, though local authorities had all his furnishings burned after his death as a sanitary measure. You'll also find a quaint collection of memorabilia of other English literary figures of the period—Lord Byron, Percy Bysshe Shelley, Joseph Severn, and Leigh Hun—and an exhaustive library of works on the Romantics. ⊠ *Piazza di Spagna 26, Piazza di Spagna* ☎ *06/6784235* ⊕ *ksh.roma.it* ✉ *€6* ⊙ *Closed Sun.* Ⓜ *Spagna.*

Mausoleo di Augusto

TOMB | The world's largest circular tomb certainly makes a statement about the glory of Augustus, Julius Caesar's successor. He was only 35 years old when he commissioned it following his victory over Marc Antony and Cleopatra. Though the ruins we see now are brick and stone, it was originally covered in marble and travertine, with evergreen trees planted on top, a colossal statue of the emperor at the summit, and a pair of bronze pillars inscribed with his achievements at the entrance. The mausoleum's innermost sepulchral chamber housed the ashes of several members of the Augustan dynasty, but it was subsequently raided and the urns were never found.

Between the 13th and 20th centuries, it lived several other lives as a garden, an amphitheater that hosted jousting tournaments, and a concert hall, which Mussolini tore down in 1936 in a bid to restore the monument to its imperial glory. His plans were interrupted by World War II, after which the mausoleum was all but abandoned until a recent restoration reopened it to the public.

It's best to book visits online as far in advance as possible because of the limited number of people allowed inside at any one time. Note, too, that this site has experienced closures owing to the construction of a new public piazza around it. ⊠ *Piazza Augusto Imperatore, Piazza di Spagna* ☎ *06/0608* ⊕ *www. mausoleodiaugusto.it* ✉ *€5* ⊙ *Closed Mon.* Ⓜ *Spagna.*

★ **Monumento a Vittorio Emanuele II, or Altare della Patria** (*Victor Emmanuel II Monument, or Altar of the Nation*)
MONUMENT | The huge white mass known as the "Vittoriano" is an inescapable landmark that has been likened to a giant wedding cake or an immense typewriter. Present-day Romans joke that you can only avoid looking at it if you are standing on it, but at the turn of the 20th century, it was the source of great civic pride. Built to honor the unification of Italy and the nation's first king, Victor Emmanuel II, it also shelters the eternal flame at the tomb of Italy's Unknown Soldier, killed during World War I. Alas, to create this elaborate marble behemoth and the vast surrounding piazza, its architects blithely destroyed many ancient and medieval buildings and altered the slope of the Campidoglio (Capitoline Hill), which abuts it.

The underwhelming exhibit inside the building tells the history of the country's unification, but the truly enticing feature of the Vittoriano is its rooftop terrace, which offers some of the best panoramic views of Rome. The only way up is by elevator (the entrance is located several flights of stairs up on the right as you face the monument). ⊠ *Entrances on Piazza Venezia, Piazza del Campidoglio, and Via di San Pietro in Carcere, Piazza di Spagna* ☎ *06/0608* ⊕ *vive.cultura.gov.it* ✉ *Main building free; €10 for the terrace* Ⓜ *Colosseo.*

★ Palazzo Colonna

CASTLE/PALACE | Rome's grandest private palace is a fusion of 17th- and 18th-century buildings that have been occupied by the Colonna family for more than 20 generations. The immense residence faces Piazza dei Santi Apostoli on one side and the Quirinale (Quirinal Hill) on the other—with a little bridge over Via della Pilotta linking to gardens on the hill—and contains an art gallery that's open to the public on Saturday morning or by guided tour on Friday morning.

The gallery is itself a setting of aristocratic grandeur; you might recognize the Sala Grande as the site where Audrey Hepburn meets the press in *Roman Holiday*. An ancient red marble *colonna* (column), which is the family's emblem, looms at one end, but the most spectacular feature is the ceiling fresco of the Battle of Lepanto painted by Giovanni Coli and Filippo Gherardi beginning in 1675. Adding to the opulence are works by Poussin, Tintoretto, and Veronese, as well as portraits of illustrious members of the family, such as Vittoria Colonna, Michelangelo's muse and longtime friend.

It's worth paying an extra fee to take the guided, English-language gallery tour, which will help you navigate through the array of madonnas, saints, goddesses, popes, and cardinals to see Annibale Carracci's lonely *Beaneater,* spoon at the ready and front teeth missing. The gallery also has a café with a pleasant terrace. ⊠ *Via della Pilotta 17, Piazza di Spagna* ☎ *06/6784350* ⊕ *www.galleriacolonna. it* ⊟ *€15 for gallery and gardens, €25 to also visit the Princess Isabelle Apartment, €30 for a guided tour of all public areas* ⊘ *Closed Sun.–Thurs.* Ⓜ *Barberini.*

★ Palazzo Doria Pamphilj

CASTLE/PALACE | Like the Palazzo Colonna and the Galleria Borghese, this dazzling 15th-century family palace provides a fantastic glimpse of aristocratic Rome. The understated beauty of the graceful facade barely hints at the interior's opulent halls and gilded galleries, which are filled with Old Master works. The 550 paintings here include three by Caravaggio: *St. John the Baptist, Mary Magdalene,* and the breathtaking *Rest on the Flight to Egypt.* Off the eye-popping Galleria degli Specchi (Gallery of Mirrors)—a smaller version of the one at Versailles—are the famous Velázquez *Pope Innocent X,* considered by some historians to be the greatest portrait ever painted, and the Bernini bust of the same Pamphilj pope. ⊠ *Via del Corso 305, Piazza di Spagna* ☎ *06/6797323* ⊕ *www.doriapamphilj.it* ⊟ *€14* ⊘ *Closed the 3rd Wed. of the month* ⚲ *Reservations required* Ⓜ *Barberini.*

★ Sant'Ignazio

CHURCH | Rome's second Jesuit church, this 17th-century landmark set on a Rococo piazza harbors some of the city's most magnificent trompe l'oeils. To get the full effect of the illusionistic ceiling by priest-artist Andrea Pozzo, stand on the small yellow disk set into the floor of the nave. The heavenly vision that seems to extend upward almost indefinitely represents the *Allegory of the Missionary Work of the Jesuits.* It's part of Pozzo's cycle of works in this church exalting the early history of the Jesuit order, whose founder was the reformer Ignatius of Loyola. The saint soars heavenward, supported by a cast of thousands, creating a jaw-dropping effect that was fully intended to rival that of the glorious ceiling by Baciccia in the nearby mother church of Il Gesù. Be sure to have coins handy for the machine that switches on the lights so you can marvel at the false dome, which is actually a flat canvas—a trompe l'oeil trick Pozzo used when the architectural budget drained dry.

Scattered around the nave are several awe-inspiring altars; their soaring columns, gold-on-gold decoration, and gilded statues are pure splendor. Splendid, too, are the occasional sacred music concerts performed by choirs from

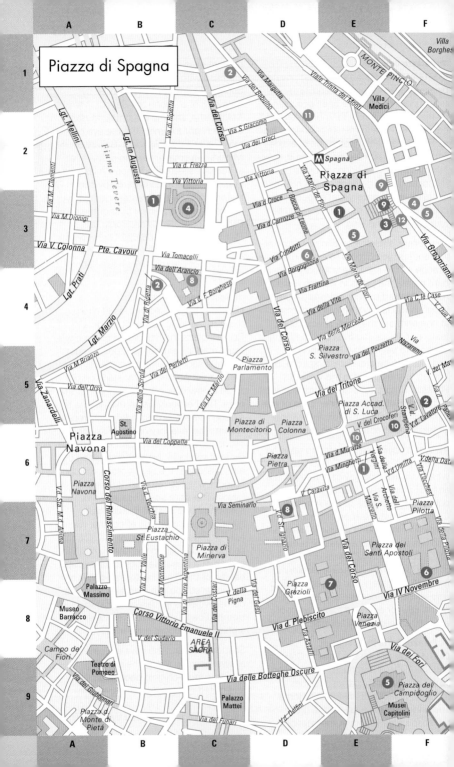

Piazza di Spagna

Sights ▼

1 Ara Pacis Augustae **B3**
2 Galleria d'Arte Moderna **G4**
3 Keats-Shelley Memorial House... **E3**
4 Mausoleo di Augusto **C3**
5 Monumento a Vittorio
  Emanuele II, or Altare
  della Patria **E9**
6 Palazzo Colonna **F7**
7 Palazzo Doria Pamphilj............ **E8**
8 Sant'Ignazio **D7**
9 The Spanish Steps................. **E3**
10 Trevi Fountain **F6**

Restaurants ▼

1 Baccano............................ **E6**
2 Il Marchese **B4**
3 Mirabelle **G2**
4 Moma **I3**
5 Ristorante Nino **E3**
6 Settimo............................. **G2**

Quick Bites ▼

1 Antico Caffè Greco................. **E3**
2 Il Gelato di San Crispino **F5**

Hotels ▼

1 Aleph Rome Hotel,
  Curio Collection by Hilton......... **H3**
2 Babuino 181 .... **C1**
3 Baglioni Hotel Regina **H2**
4 The Hassler....................... **F3**
5 Hotel de la Ville **F3**
6 Hotel d'Inghilterra **D3**
7 Hotel Eden........................ **G2**
8 Hotel Vilòn **C4**
9 Il Palazzetto **E2**
10 Maalot Roma **E6**
11 Margutta 19 .... **D2**
12 Scalinata di Spagna............... **F3**

KEY

1 Sights
1 Restaurants
1 Quick Bites
1 Hotels

all over the world. Look for posters by the main doors, or check the website for more information. ✉ *Via del Caravita 8A, Piazza Navona* ☎ *06/6794406* 🌐 *santignazio.gesuiti.it.*

★ The Spanish Steps

OTHER ATTRACTION | FAMILY | The iconic Spanish Steps (often called simply *la scalinata,* or "the staircase," by Italians) and the Piazza di Spagna from which they ascend both get their names from the Spanish Embassy to the Vatican on the piazza—even though the staircase was built with French funds in 1723. In honor of a diplomatic visit by the King of Spain, the hillside was transformed by architect Francesco de Sanctis to link the church of Trinità dei Monti at the top with the Via Condotti below. In an allusion to the church, the staircase is divided by three landings (beautifully lined with potted azaleas from mid-April to mid-May). Bookending the bottom of the steps are beloved holdovers from the 18th century, when the area was known as the "English Ghetto": the 18th-century Keats-Shelley House and Babington's Tea Rooms, both beautifully redolent of the Grand Tour era. ✉ *Piazza di Spagna* [M] *Spagna.*

★ Trevi Fountain

FOUNTAIN | FAMILY | Alive with rushing waters commanded by an imperious sculpture of Oceanus, the Fontana di Trevi has been all about theatrical effects from the start; it is an aquatic marvel in a city filled with them. The fountain's unique drama is largely due to its location: its vast basin is squeezed into the tight confluence of three little streets (the *tre vie,* which may give the fountain its name), with cascades emerging as if from the wall of Palazzo Poli.

Everyone knows the famous legend that if you throw a coin into the Trevi Fountain you will ensure a return trip to the Eternal City, but not everyone knows how to do it the right way. You must toss a coin with your right hand over your left shoulder, with your back to the fountain. One coin means you'll return to Rome; two, you'll return *and* fall in love; three, you'll return, find love, and marry. The fountain grosses some €600,000 a year, with every cent going to the Italian Red Cross. ✉ *Piazza di Trevi, Piazza di Spagna* [M] *Barberini.*

🍴 Restaurants

Baccano

$$$ | BRASSERIE | There are plenty of options for good food at reasonable prices around the Trevi Fountain, but this large brasserie—open for lunch, dinner, and everything in between—is a great bet. Although it emphasizes seafood, the extensive menu has something for everyone, from salads to pasta and entrées. **Known for:** oyster bar; excellent carbonara; classic international cocktails. [$] *Average main: €28* ✉ *Via delle Muratte 23, Piazza di Spagna* ☎ *06/69941166* 🌐 *www.baccanoroma.com* [M] *Barberini.*

★ Il Marchese

$$ | ITALIAN | This rustic-meets-glamorous bistro attracts locals for its flawless execution of Roman classics (many served photogenically in metal cooking pans) as well as original dishes. Its bar is known among amaro connoisseurs for having the largest selection in Rome, and the bitter liquors are the stars of the expertly crafted cocktail menu. **Known for:** beautiful design; well-executed classics; extensive selection of amaros and great cocktails. [$] *Average main: €18* ✉ *Via di Ripetta 162, Piazza di Spagna* ☎ *06/90218872* 🌐 *www.ilmarcheseroma.it* [M] *Spagna.*

Mirabelle

$$$$ | MODERN ITALIAN | Old-world elegance is the name of the game here—think white-jacketed waiters who attend to your every need, classic decor, and impeccable dishes, which are the most modern thing about this restaurant on the seventh floor of the Hotel Splendide Royal. Be sure to request a table on the terrace, which has panoramas of leafy Villa Borghese and the center of Rome. **Known for:** romantic atmosphere; panoramic terrace; top-notch food and service. $ *Average main: €54 ⊠ Hotel Splendide Royal, Via di Porta Pinciana 14, Piazza di Spagna ☎ 06/42168838 ⊕ www.mirabelle.it Ⓜ Spagna, Barberini.*

★ Moma

$$$ | MODERN ITALIAN | In front of the American embassy and a favorite of the design *trendoisie*, Michelin-starred Moma attracts well-heeled businessmen at lunch but turns into a more intimate affair for dinner. The kitchen turns out hits as it creates alta cucina (haute cuisine) made using Italian ingredients sourced from small producers. **Known for:** pasta with a twist; creative presentation; affordable fine dining. $ *Average main: €25 ⊠ Via San Basilio 42/43, Piazza di Spagna ☎ 06/42011798 ⊕ www.ristorantemoma.it ⊗ Closed Sun. No lunch Sat. Ⓜ Barberini.*

Ristorante Nino

$$$ | ITALIAN | A favorite among international journalists and the rich and famous since the 1930s, this eatery does not seem to have changed at all over the decades. The interior is Tuscan country rustic, and the menu, accordingly, sticks to the classics. **Known for:** warm crostini spread with pâté; upscale old-school Italian vibe; ribollita (Tuscan bean soup). $ *Average main: €26 ⊠ Via Borgognona 11, Piazza di Spagna ☎ 06/6786752 ⊕ ristorantenino.it ⊗ Closed Sun. and Aug. Ⓜ Spagna.*

Settimo

$$$ | ITALIAN | Crowning the Sofitel Rome Villa Borghese hotel, this chic restaurant serves fancy takes on Rome's *cucina povera* (peasant cooking) in a chic space with graphic punches of color. The terrace offers fantastic views that stretch from Villa Borghese to the dome of St. Peter's, but the interior dining room, with its floor-to-ceiling windows and terrazzo-inspired floors, is lovely, too. **Known for:** amped-up version of classic Roman

recipes; colorful, modern design; terrace with great views. $ *Average main: €26 ⊠ Sofitel Rome Villa Borghese, Via Lombardia 47, Piazza di Spagna ☎ 06/478021 ⊕ www.settimoristorante.it Ⓜ Barberini.*

☕ Coffee and Quick Bites

Antico Caffè Greco

$ | CAFÉ | The red-velvet chairs and marble tables of Rome's oldest café have seen the likes of Byron, Shelley, Keats, Goethe, and Casanova. Locals love basking in the more than 250 years of history held within its dark-wood walls lined with antique artwork; tourists appreciate its location amid the shopping madness of upscale Via Condotti. **Known for:** lavish historic design; perfect espresso; crystal goblets and high prices to match. $ *Average main: €12 ⊠ Via dei Condotti 86, Piazza di Spagna ☎ 06/6791700 ⊕ caffegreco.shop Ⓜ Spagna.*

Il Gelato di San Crispino

$ | ICE CREAM | FAMILY | Many people say this place—which is around the corner from the Trevi Fountain and had a cameo in the movie *Eat, Pray, Love*—serves the best gelato in Rome. Creative flavors like black fig, chocolate rum, Armagnac, and ginger-cinnamon all incorporate top-notch ingredients, and the shop is known for keeping its gelato hidden under metal covers to better preserve the quality. **Known for:** seasonal fruit flavors; offering only cups and no cones; wine-based gelato. $ *Average main: €4 ⊠ Via della Panetteria 42, Piazza di Spagna ☎ 06/69489518 ⊕ www.ilgelatodisancrispino.it Ⓜ Barberini.*

🛏 Hotels

Aleph Rome Hotel, Curio Collection by Hilton

$$$$ | HOTEL | Fashionable couples tend to favor the Aleph, a former bank–turned–luxury hotel, where the motto seems to be "more marble, everywhere." The abundant facilities include two pools (one in the spa and one on the roof), a cigar lounge, a cocktail bar, and two restaurants (one on the ground floor and one on the rooftop). **Pros:** free access to the spa for hotel guests; award-winning design; terrace with small pool. **Cons:** rooms are petite for the price; rooftop views don't showcase Rome's most flattering side; buffet breakfast not included. $ *Rooms from: €550* ✉ *Via San Basilio 15, Piazza di Spagna* ☎ *06/4229001* ⊕ *alephrome.com* ⤵ *88 rooms* ❚◯❚ *No Meals* Ⓜ *Barberini.*

Babuino 181

$$$ | HOTEL | On chic Via del Babuino, known for its high-end boutiques, jewelry stores, and antiques shops, this discreet and stylish hotel is an ideal pied-à-terre, with spacious rooms spread over two historic buildings. **Pros:** spacious suites; luxury Frette linens; iPhone docks and other handy in-room amenities. **Cons:** rooms can be a bit noisy; breakfast is nothing special; annex rooms feel removed from service staff. $ *Rooms from: €250* ✉ *Via del Babuino 181, Piazza di Spagna* ☎ *06/32295295* ⊕ *www. romeluxurysuites.com/it/babuino-181* ⤵ *24 rooms* ❚◯❚ *Free Breakfast* Ⓜ *Flaminio, Spagna.*

Baglioni Hotel Regina

$$$$ | HOTEL | The former home of Queen Margherita of Savoy, the Baglioni Hotel Regina, which enjoys a prime spot on the Via Veneto, is still a favorite among today's jet-setters. **Pros:** chic decor; luxury on-site spa; excellent on-site restaurant and bar. **Cons:** internal rooms overlook a/c ducts; extra charge for breakfast à la carte; location isn't as prestigious as it once was. $ *Rooms from: €420* ✉ *Via Veneto 72, Piazza di Spagna* ☎ *06/421111* ⊕ *www.baglionihotels.com/rome* ⤵ *114 rooms* ❚◯❚ *No Meals* Ⓜ *Barberini.*

★ The Hassler

$$$$ | HOTEL | When it comes to million-dollar views, the best place to stay in the whole city is the Hassler, so it's no surprise many of the rich and famous (Tom Cruise, Jennifer Lopez, and the Beckhams among them) are willing to pay top dollar for a room at this exclusive hotel atop the Spanish Steps. **Pros:** prime location and panoramic views; exceptional service; sauna access included with each reservation. **Cons:** VIP rates (10% VAT not included); gym and wellness area is tiny; rooms are updated on a rolling basis, leaving some feeling dated. $ *Rooms from: €1,010* ✉ *Piazza Trinità dei Monti 6, Piazza di Spagna* ☎ *06/699340, 800/223–6800 in U.S.* ⊕ *www.hotelhasslerroma.com* ⤵ *87 rooms* ❚◯❚ *Free Breakfast* Ⓜ *Spagna.*

★ Hotel de la Ville

$$$$ | HOTEL | Occupying a prime position atop the Spanish Steps, this glamorous sister property of the beloved Hotel de Russie near the Piazza del Popolo has as a Grand Tour–inspired design featuring antiques, custom wallpaper stamped with Piranesi prints, and plenty of silk. **Pros:** must-visit rooftop bar with panoramic views; prestigious location atop the Spanish Steps; pampering spa uses signature made-in-Italy organic products. **Cons:** some rooms are a bit small for the price; service can be a bit slow at the bar; no pets allowed. $ *Rooms from: €1,100* ✉ *Via Sistina 69, Piazza di Spagna* ☎ *06/977931* ⊕ *www.roccofortehotels.com* ⤵ *23 rooms* ❚◯❚ *No Meals* Ⓜ *Spagna.*

Hotel d'Inghilterra

$$$$ | HOTEL | Situated in a stately 16th-century building and founded in 1845, this storied hotel served as a guesthouse for aristocratic travelers visiting a noble family who once lived across the cobblestone street and has since been the home away from home for various monarchs, movie stars like Elizabeth Taylor, and several great writers— Lord Byron, John Keats, Mark Twain, and Ernest Hemingway among them. **Pros:** distinct character and opulence; turndown service (with chocolates); excellent in-house restaurant. **Cons:** elevator is small; the location, despite

soundproofing, is still noisy; some rooms badly in need of renovations and maintenance. [$] *Rooms from: €400* ✉ *Via Bocca di Leone 14, Piazza di Spagna* ☎ *06/699811* 🌐 *www.starhotelscollezione.com/en/our-hotels/hotel-d-inghilterra-rome* 🛏 *84 rooms* 🍴 *Free Breakfast* [M] *Spagna.*

★ Hotel Eden

$$$$ | **HOTEL** | At what was once a favorite haunt of Ingrid Bergman, Ginger Rogers, and Fellini, dashing elegance, exquisite decor, and stunning vistas of Rome combine with true Italian hospitality. **Pros:** gorgeous rooftop terrace restaurant; tranquil spa facilities; 24-hour room service. **Cons:** breakfast not included (and very expensive, at €45); gym is standard but small; some rooms overlook an unremarkable courtyard. [$] *Rooms from: €880* ✉ *Via Ludovisi 49, Piazza di Spagna* ☎ *06/478121* 🌐 *www.dorchestercollection.com/en/rome/hotel-eden* 🛏 *98 rooms* 🍴 *No Meals* [M] *Spagna.*

★ Hotel Vilòn

$$$$ | **HOTEL** | Set in a 16th-century mansion annexed to Palazzo Borghese and tucked behind a discreet entrance, this intimate hotel might be Rome's best-kept secret. **Pros:** gorgeous design; attentive staff; fantastic location. **Cons:** no spa or gym; some rooms are a bit small; not much communal space. [$] *Rooms from: €460* ✉ *Via dell'Arancio 69, Piazza di Spagna* ☎ *06/878187* 🌐 *www.hotelvilon.com* 🛏 *18 rooms* 🍴 *Free Breakfast* [M] *Spagna.*

Il Palazzetto

$$$ | **B&B/INN** | Formerly the retreat of a rich noble family, this 15th-century house is now one of Rome's most intimate and luxurious hotels, with gorgeous terraces and a rooftop bar affording views of the never-ending theater of the Spanish Steps. **Pros:** location and view; free Wi-Fi; guests have full access to the Hassler's services. **Cons:** often books up far in advance, particularly in high season; bedrooms do not access communal terraces; breakfast is served in the main building at the Hassler. [$] *Rooms from: €290* ✉ *Vicolo del Bottino 8, Piazza di Spagna* ☎ *06/69934560* 🌐 *www.hotelhasslerroma.com/en/il-palazzetto* 🛏 *4 rooms* 🍴 *Free Breakfast* [M] *Spagna.*

Maalot Roma

$$$$ | **HOTEL** | This boutique property inside the former residence of opera composer Gaetano Donizetto aims to be a restaurant with rooms above rather than a hotel with a restaurant below. **Pros:** chic design with original art; great food at Don Pasquale restaurant; central location just steps from the Trevi Fountain. **Cons:** no spa; service can be a bit slow; some rooms look directly onto the McDonald's across the street. [$] *Rooms from: €495* ✉ *Via delle Murate 78, Piazza di Spagna* ☎ *06/878087* 🌐 *www.hotelmaalot.com* 🛏 *30 rooms* 🍴 *Free Breakfast* [M] *Barberini.*

Margutta 19

$$$$ | **HOTEL** | At this all-suites property, tucked away on a leafy street known for its art galleries, the amenities are top drawer, the design is contemporary, the restaurant features a verdant terrace, and the accommodations have a hip New York–loft feel. **Pros:** studio-loft feel in the center of Rome; complete privacy; deluxe furnishings. **Cons:** no spa or gym; entry-level rooms lack views; no elevator in the annex to reach rooms on higher floors. [$] *Rooms from: €550* ✉ *Via Margutta 19, Piazza di Spagna* ☎ *06/97797979* 🌐 *www.romeluxurysuites.com/margutta-19* 🛏 *22 suites* 🍴 *Free Breakfast* [M] *Spagna.*

Scalinata di Spagna

$$ | **B&B/INN** | Perched atop the Spanish Steps, this charming boutique hotel is so popular that it's often booked far in advance. **Pros:** friendly and helpful concierge; fresh fruit in guest rooms; free Wi-Fi throughout. **Cons:** hike up the hill to the hotel; small rooms; no porter and no elevator. [$] *Rooms from: €250* ✉ *Piazza Trinità dei Monti 17, Piazza di Spagna*

☎ 06/45686150 ⊕ www.hotelscalinata. com ⇆ 30 rooms ◯| Free Breakfast Ⓜ Spagna.

 Nightlife

Antica Enoteca
WINE BARS | Piazza di Spagna's staple wine bar literally corners the market on prime people-watching. Cozy up to the counter to sip a drink under the charming frescoes, or snag a coveted outdoor table. In addition to a vast selection of wine, Antica Enoteca has delectable antipasti, perfect for a snack or a light lunch, as well as a full menu of pastas and pizzas. ⊠ Via della Croce 76/b, Piazza di Spagna ☎ 06/6790896 ⊕ www.anticae-noteca.com Ⓜ Spagna.

Wine Bar at the Palazzetto
WINE BARS | The prize for perfect aperitivo spot goes to the Palazzetto, with excellent drinks and appetizers, as well as a breathtaking view of the comings and goings on the Spanish Steps. Reach it by climbing the monumental staircase that it overlooks, or getting a lift from the elevator inside the Spagna Metro station. ⊠ Il Palazzetto, Vicolo del Bottino 8, Piazza di Spagna ⊹ The main entrance is a small gate at the top of the Spanish Steps ☎ 342/1507215 ⊕ www.hotelhasslerroma.com/en/il-palazzetto Ⓜ Spagna.

 Shopping

ACCESSORIES
Furla
HANDBAGS | Furla very well might be the best deal in Italian leather, selling high-quality purses and wallets at comparatively affordable prices. There are multiple locations throughout the Eternal City (including one at Fiumicino Airport), but its flagship store is in the heart of Piazza di Spagna. Be prepared to fight your way through crowds of passionate handbag lovers, all anxious to possess one of the delectable bags, wallets, or whimsical key chains in trendy sherbet hues or timeless bold color combos. ⊠ Piazza di Spagna 22, Piazza di Spagna ☎ 06/6797159 ⊕ www.furla.com Ⓜ Spagna.

CLOTHING
★ Brioni
MEN'S CLOTHING | Founded in 1945, Brioni is hailed for its impeccably crafted menswear. Italy's best tailors create bespoke suits to exacting standards, measured to the millimeter and completely personalized from a selection of more than 5,000 spectacular fabrics. A single made-to-measure wool suit will take a minimum of 32 hours to make. The brand's prêt-à-porter line is also praised for peerless cutting and stitching. Past and present clients include Clark Gable, Barack Obama, and, of course, James Bond. ⊠ Via Condotti 21A, Piazza di Spagna ☎ 06/6783428 ⊕ www.brioni. com Ⓜ Spagna.

Dolce & Gabbana
MIXED CLOTHING | Dolce and Gabbana met in 1980 when both were assistants at a Milan fashion atelier, and they opened their first store in 1982. With a modern aesthetic that screams sex appeal, the brand has always thrived on excess and is known for its bold, creative designs. The Rome store has a glass ceiling above a sparkling chandelier to allow natural light to spill in, illuminating the marble floors, antique brass accents, and (of course) the latest lines for men, women, and even children. It also has an expansive accessories area. ⊠ Via Condotti 49–51, Piazza di Spagna ☎ 06/69924999 ⊕ www.dolcegabbana.com Ⓜ Spagna.

Elena Mirò
WOMEN'S CLOTHING | Elena Mirò is a high-end brand that offers curvy women sophisticated, beautifully feminine clothes in sizes 46 (U.S. size 12, U.K. size 14) and up. There are several locations in Rome, including one on Via Nazionale. ⊠ Via Frattina 11, Piazza di Spagna ☎ 06/6784367 ⊕ www.elenamiro.com Ⓜ Spagna.

Fendi

MIXED CLOTHING | Fendi has been a fixture of the Roman fashion landscape since "Mamma" Fendi first opened shop with her husband in 1925. With an eye for crazy genius, she hired Karl Lagerfeld, who began working with the group at the start of his career. His furs and runway antics made him one of the most influential designers of the 20th century and brought international acclaim to Fendi. Although the atelier, now owned by the Louis Vuitton group, still symbolizes Italian glamour, it's also gotten new life in the Italian press for its "Fendi for Fountains" campaign, which included funding the restoration of Rome's Trevi Fountain, and for moving its global headquarters to a striking Mussolini-era building known as the "square Colosseum" in the city's EUR neighborhood. The flagship store in Rome is on the ground floor of Palazzo Fendi. Upper floors contain the brand's seven private suites (the first ever Fendi hotel), and the rooftop is home to Zuma, a modern Japanese restaurant with an oh-so-cool bar that has sweeping views across the city. ⊠ *Largo Carlo Goldoni 420, Piazza di Spagna* ☎ *06/33450896* ⊕ *www.fendi.com* Ⓜ *Spagna.*

Giorgio Armani

MIXED CLOTHING | One of the most influential designers of Italian haute couture, Giorgio Armani creates fluid silhouettes and dazzling evening gowns with sexy peek-a-boo cutouts; his signature cuts are made with the clever-handedness and flawless technique achievable only by working with tracing paper and Italy's finest fabrics over the course of a lifetime. His menswear collection uses traditional textiles like wide-ribbed corduroy and stretch jersey in nontraditional ways while staying true to a clean, masculine aesthetic. The iconic Italian brand has an Emporio Armani shop on Via del Babuino, but the flagship store is the best place to find pieces that range from exotic runway-worthy masterpieces to more wearable collections emphasizing casual Italian elegance with just the right touch of whimsy and sexiness. ⊠ *Via dei Condotti 77, Piazza di Spagna* ☎ *06/6991460* ⊕ *www.armani.com* Ⓜ *Spagna.*

Gucci

MIXED CLOTHING | Guccio Gucci opened his first leather shop selling luggage in Florence in 1921, and, more than 100 years later, the success of the double-G trademark is unquestionable. Tom Ford joined as creative director in 1994, helping the fashion house move into a new era that refreshed the label's aesthetic with reinterpretations of old-school favorites like horsebit loafers and Jackie Kennedy scarves. Now helmed by Sabato de Sarno, Gucci remains a fashion must for virtually every A-list celebrity, with clothing and accessory designs that are interesting, contemporary, and often gender-fluid takes on classic styles. ⊠ *Via Condotti 6–8, Piazza di Spagna* ☎ *06/6790405* ⊕ *www.gucci.com* Ⓜ *Spagna.*

★ Patrizia Pepe

WOMEN'S CLOTHING | Patrizia Pepe first emerged on the scene in Florence in 1993 with an aesthetic that's both minimalist and bold. Jackets with oversize lapels, playful pleats, mesmerizing mesh, and the occasional feathered poof set the designs apart. Spending time in the shop of this relative newcomer to the Italian fashion scene gives you the opportunity to pick up an item or two before the brand becomes the next fast-tracked craze. ⊠ *Via Frattina 44, Piazza di Spagna* ☎ *342/0005871* ⊕ *www.patriziapepe.com* Ⓜ *Spagna.*

Prada

MIXED CLOTHING | Besides the devil, plenty of serious shoppers wear Prada season after season, especially those willing to sell their souls for one of their ubiquitous handbags. If you are looking for that blend of old-world luxury with a touch of fashion-forward finesse, you'll hit it big here. Mario Prada founded the Italian luggage brand in 1913, but it has been his granddaughter, Miuccia, who updated the designs into the timeless investment pieces of today. You'll find the Rome store more service-oriented than the New York City branches—a roomy elevator delivers you to a series of thickly carpeted salons where a flock of discreet assistants will help you pick out dresses, shoes, lingerie, and fashion accessories. The men's store is located at Via Condotti 88/90, while the women's is down the street at 92/95. ⊠ *Via dei Condotti 88/90 and 92/95, Piazza di Spagna* ☎ *06/6790897* ⊕ *www.prada. com* Ⓜ *Spagna.*

Schostal
MIXED CLOTHING | A Piazza di Spagna fixture since 1870, this was once the go-to shop for corsets, petticoats, stockings, and bonnets. Today, it's the place to stop for essential basics that are increasingly difficult to find, like fine-quality shirts, underwear, and handkerchiefs made of wool and pure cashmere at affordable prices. ⊠ *Via della Fontanella di Borghese 29, Piazza di Spagna* ☎ *06/6791240* ⊕ *www.schostalroma1870.com* Ⓜ *Spagna.*

Valentino
MIXED CLOTHING | Since taking the reins, creative director Pierpaolo Piccioli has faced numerous challenges, the most basic of which is keeping Valentino true to Valentino after the designer's retirement in 2008. Piccioli served as accessories designer under Valentino for more than a decade and understands exactly how to make the next generation of Hollywood stars swoon. Valentino fills most of Piazza di Spagna, where the designer lived for decades in a lovely palazzo next to one of the multiple boutiques showcasing his eponymous designs with a romantic edginess—think studded heels or prêt-à-porter evening gowns worthy of the Oscars. Rock stars and other music lovers can also have their Valentino guitar straps personalized when they buy one at this enormous boutique. ⊠ *Piazza di Spagna 38, Piazza di Spagna* ☎ *06/94515710* ⊕ *www. valentino.com* Ⓜ *Spagna.*

Versace
MIXED CLOTHING | Versace's Rome flagship is a gem of architecture and design, with Byzantine-inspired mosaic floors, futuristic interiors with transparent walls, and merchandise that has a sexy rocker-Gothic-underground vibe. Here you'll find apparel, accessories, and home furnishings in designs every bit as flamboyant as Donatella and Allegra (Gianni's niece). ⊠ *Piazza di Spagna 12, Piazza di Spagna* ☎ *06/6784600* ⊕ *www.versace. com* Ⓜ *Spagna.*

DEPARTMENT STORES
★ La Rinascente
DEPARTMENT STORE | **FAMILY** | Set in a dazzling, seven-story space, Italy's best-known department store is packed topped to bottom with luxury goods, from cosmetics, handbags, and accessories to ready-to-wear designer sportswear to kitchen items and housewares. Even if you're not planning on buying anything, the basement excavations of a Roman aqueduct and the roof terrace bar with its splendid view are well worth a visit. There's also a location at Piazza Fiume. ⊠ *Via del Tritone 61, Piazza di Spagna* ☎ *02/91387388* ⊕ *www.rinascente.it* Ⓜ *Barberini.*

HEALTH & BEAUTY
Modàfferi Barber Shop
OTHER HEALTH & BEAUTY | Run by two friendly brothers, who took over the business from their father, this barbershop is preferred by actors performing at the nearby Teatro Sistina. It was founded in the 1970s and still has charmingly retro decor. They offer haircuts, beard care, manicures, pedicures, facials, and massages and have their own line of products. For extra privacy, you can request the private room. ⊠ *Via dei Cappuccini 11, Piazza di Spagna* ☎ *06/4817077* ⊕ *www.modafferibarbershop.it* Ⓜ *Barberini.*

JEWELRY

Bulgari

JEWELRY & WATCHES | Bulgari (also seen as Bvlgari) is to Rome what Tiffany is to New York and Cartier is to Paris. The jewelry giant has developed a reputation for meticulous craftsmanship melding noble metals with precious gems. In the middle of the 19th century, the great-grandfather of the current Bulgari brothers began working as a silver jeweler in his native Greece and is said to have moved to Rome with less than 1,000 lire in his pocket. This store's temple-inspired interior pays homage to the jeweler's ties to both places. Today, the mega-brand emphasizes colorful and playful jewelry, as evidenced by such popular collections as Bulgari-Bulgari and B.zero1. ⊠ *Via dei Condotti 10, Piazza di Spagna* ☎ *06/6792487* ⊕ *www.bulgari. com* Ⓜ *Spagna.*

SHOES

★ Braccialini

HANDBAGS | Founded in 1954 by Florentine stylist Carla Braccialini and her husband, Robert, this outfit makes bags that are authentic works of art in bright colors and delightful shapes, such as London black cabs or mountain chalets. The adorably quirky tote bags have picture-postcard scenes of luxury destinations made of brightly colored appliquéd leather. Be sure to check out the eccentric Temi (Theme) creature bags; the snail-shaped version made out of python skin makes a true fashion statement. There is another location on Via dei Condotti. ⊠ *Via Frattina, 117, Piazza di Spagna* ☎ *342/0338947* ⊕ *www.braccialini.it* Ⓜ *Spagna.*

Fausto Santini

SHOES | Shoe lovers with a passion for minimalist design flock to Fausto Santini to get their hands on his nerdy-chic footwear with its statement-making lines. Santini has been in business since 1970 and caters to a sophisticated, avant-garde clientele looking for elegant, classic shoes with a kick and a rainbow color palette. An outlet at Via Cavour 106, named for Fausto's father, Giacomo, sells last season's shoes at a big discount. ⊠ *Via Frattina 120, Piazza di Spagna* ☎ *06/6784114* ⊕ *www.faustosantini.com* Ⓜ *Spagna.*

Giuseppe Zanotti

SHOES | Giuseppe Zanotti creates sought-after men's and women's shoes ranging from colorful loafers to couture sneakers to pencil-thin stilettos (often with a bit of sparkle or other bling). The footwear here is placed on a literal pedestal so the craftsmanship can be admired from all angles. ⊠ *Piazza di Spagna, 33, Piazza di Spagna* ☎ *06/69924220* ⊕ *www.giuseppezanotti. com* Ⓜ *Spagna.*

★ Tod's

SHOES | Founded in the 1920s, Tod's has grown from a small family brand into a global powerhouse so wealthy that its owner Diego Della Valle donated €20 million to the Colosseum restoration project. The shoe baron is best known for his simple, classic, understated designs done in butter-soft leather, but his light, flexible Gommini line of driving shoes, with rubber-bottomed soles for extra driving-pedal grip, are popular as well. There is also a location on Via Condotti. ⊠ *Via della Fontanella di Borghese 56a–57, Piazza di Spagna* ☎ *06/68210066* ⊕ *www. tods.com* Ⓜ *Spagna.*

Repubblica and the Quirinale

This sector of Rome stretches down from the 19th-century district built up around the Piazza della Repubblica—originally laid out to serve as a monumental foyer between the Termini train station and the rest of the city—and over the rest of the Quirinale. The highest of ancient Rome's famed seven hills, the Quirinale is crowned by the massive

Palazzo Quirinale, home to the popes until 1870 and now Italy's presidential palace. Along the way, you can see ancient Roman sculptures, early Christian churches, and highlights from the 16th and 17th centuries, when Rome was conquered by the Baroque—and by Bernini.

Although Bernini's work feels omnipresent in much of the city center, the Renaissance-man range of his creations is particularly notable here. The artist as architect considered the church of Sant'Andrea al Quirinale one of his best; Bernini the urban designer and water worker is responsible for the muscle-bound sea god who blows his conch so provocatively in the fountain at the center of whirling Piazza Barberini. And Bernini the master gives religious passion a joltingly corporeal treatment in what is perhaps his greatest work, the *Ecstasy of St. Teresa,* in the church of Santa Maria della Vittoria.

GETTING HERE AND AROUND

Located between Termini station and the Spanish Steps, this area is about a 15-minute walk from either. Bus No. 40 will get you from Termini to the Quirinale in two stops; from the Vatican take Bus No. 64. The very central Repubblica Metro stop is on the piazza of the same name.

 Sights

Capuchin Museum

CEMETERY | Devoted to teaching visitors about the Capuchin order, this museum is mainly notable for its strangely touching and beautiful crypt under the church of Santa Maria della Concezione. The bones of some 4,000 monks are arranged in odd decorative designs around the shriveled and decayed remains of their kinsmen, a macabre reminder of the impermanence of earthly life. As one sign proclaims: "What you

are, we once were. What we are, you someday will be."

Upstairs in the church, the first chapel on the right contains Guido Reni's mid-17th-century *Archangel St. Michael Trampling the Devil.* The painting caused great scandal after an astute contemporary observer remarked that the face of the devil bore a surprising resemblance to Pope Innocent X, archenemy of Reni's Barberini patrons. Compare the devil with the bust of the pope that you saw in the Palazzo Doria Pamphilj and judge for yourself. ⊠ *Via Veneto 27, Quirinale* ☎ *06/88803695* ⊕ *museoecriptacappucci-ni.it* 🎫 *€8.50* Ⓜ *Barberini.*

Fontana delle Api (*Fountain of the Bees*)
FOUNTAIN | The upper shell and inscription of this fountain, which is decorated with the famous heraldic bees of the Barberini family, are from a fountain that Bernini designed for Pope Urban VIII; the rest was lost when the fountain was moved to make way for a new street. The inscription caused considerable uproar when the fountain was first built in 1644. It said that the fountain had been erected in the 22nd year of the pontiff's reign, although, in fact, the 21st anniversary of Urban's election to the papacy was still some weeks away. The last numeral was hurriedly erased, but to no avail—Urban died eight days before the beginning of his 22nd year as pope. The superstitious Romans, who had regarded the inscription as a foolhardy tempting of fate, were vindicated. ⊠ *Piazza Barberini, Quirinale* Ⓜ *Barberini.*

★ MACRO

ART MUSEUM | Formerly known as Rome's Modern and Contemporary Art Gallery, and before that as the Peroni beer factory, this redesigned industrial space has brought new life to the gallery and museum scene of a city hitherto hailed for its "then," not its "now." The collection here covers Italian contemporary artists from the 1960s through today. The goal is to bring current art to the public in innovative spaces and, not incidentally, to support and recognize Rome's contemporary art scene, which labors in the shadow of the city's artistic heritage. After a few days—or millennia—of dusty marble, it's a breath of fresh air.

■ TIP➔ **Check the website for occasional late-night openings and events.** ✉ *Via Nizza 138, Repubblica* ☎ *06/696271* ⊕ *www. museomacro.it* ✆ *Free* ☉ *Closed Mon.* Ⓜ *Castro Pretorio.*

★ Palazzo Barberini/Galleria Nazionale d'Arte Antica

ART MUSEUM | One of Rome's most splendid 17th-century buildings is a Baroque landmark. The grand facade was designed by Carlo Maderno (aided by his nephew, Francesco Borromini), but when Maderno died, Borromini was passed over in favor of his great rival, Gian Lorenzo Bernini. The palazzo is now home to the Galleria Nazionale d'Arte Antica, with a collection that includes Raphael's *La Fornarina,* a luminous portrait of the artist's lover (a resident of Trastevere, she was reputedly a baker's daughter). Also noteworthy are Guido Reni's portrait of the doomed *Beatrice Cenci* (beheaded in Rome for patricide in 1599)—Hawthorne called it "the saddest picture ever painted" in his Rome-based novel, *The Marble Faun*—and Caravaggio's dramatic *Judith Beheading Holofernes.*

The showstopper here is the palace's Gran Salone, a vast ballroom with a ceiling painted in 1630 by the third (and too-often-neglected) master of the Roman Baroque, Pietro da Cortona. It depicts the *Glorification of Urban VIII's Reign* and has the spectacular conceit of glorifying Urban VIII as the agent of Divine Providence, escorted by a "bomber squadron" (to quote art historian Sir Michael Levey) of huge Barberini bees, the heraldic symbol of the family. ✉ *Via delle Quattro Fontane 13, Quirinale* ☎ *06/4814591* ⊕ *www.barberinicorsini. org* ✆ *€12, includes Galleria Corsini* ☉ *Closed Mon.* Ⓜ *Barberini.*

★ Palazzo Massimo alle Terme

ART MUSEUM | The Museo Nazionale Romano, with items ranging from striking classical Roman paintings to marble bric-a-brac, has four locations: Palazzo Altemps, Crypta Balbi, the Museo delle Terme di Diocleziano, and this, the Palazzo Massimo alle Terme—a vast structure containing the great ancient treasures of the archaeological collection and also the coin collection. Highlights include the *Dying Niobid*, the famous bronze *Boxer at Rest*, and the *Discobolus Lancellotti.*

Among the museum's most intriguing attractions, however, are the ancient frescoes on view on the top floor. They're stunningly set up to "re-create" the look of the homes they once decorated, and their colors are remarkably preserved. You'll see stuccoes and wall paintings found in the area of the Villa Farnesina (in Trastevere), as well as those depicting a garden in bloom and an orchard alive with birds that once covered the walls of cool sunken rooms at Empress Livia's villa in Prima Porta, just outside the city. ✉ *Largo di Villa Peretti 2, Repubblica* ☎ *06/39967700* ⊕ *www.museonazionaleromano.beniculturali.it* ✆ *€10, or €14 for a combined ticket including access to Crypta Balbi, Museo delle Terme di Diocleziano, and Palazzo Altemps (valid for 1 wk)* ☉ *Closed Mon.* Ⓜ *Repubblica, Termini.*

Piazza del Quirinale

PLAZA/SQUARE | This strategic location atop the Quirinale has long been important. Indeed, it served as home of the Sabines in the 7th century BC—when they were deadly enemies of the Romans, who lived on the Campidoglio and Palatino (all of 1 km [½ mile] away). Today, it's the foreground for the presidential residence, Palazzo del Quirinale, and home to the Palazzo della Consulta, where Italy's Constitutional Court sits.

The open side of the piazza has a vista over the rooftops and domes of central Rome and St. Peter's. The Fontana di

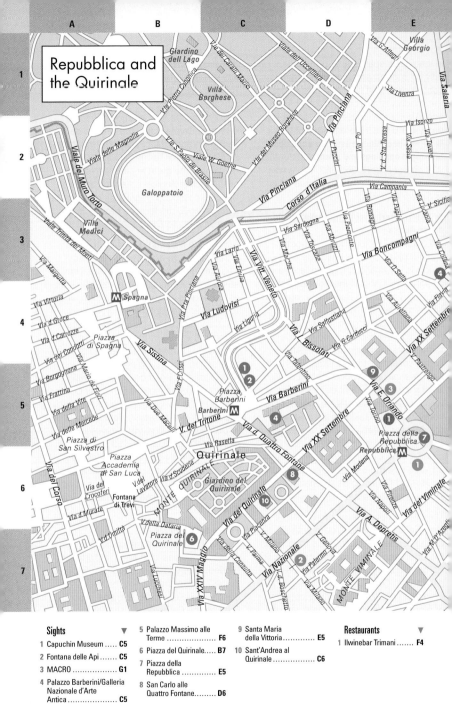

Repubblica and the Quirinale

| A | B | C | D | E |

1
Villa Georgio
Giardino del Lago
Villa Borghese

2
Galoppatoio
Corso d'Italia

3
Villa Medici
Via Boncompagni

4
Spagna M
Via Ludovisi
Piazza di Spagna
Via Vitt. Veneto
Via L. Bissolati

5
Piazza Barberini
Barberini M
Via Barberini
Via d. Quattro Fontane
Via XX Settembre
Piazza della Repubblica
Repubblica M

6
Piazza di San Silvestro
Piazza Accademia di San Luca
Fontana di Trevi
Quirinale
QUIRINALE
Giardino del Quirinale
MONTE VIMINALE

7
Piazza del Quirinale
Via Nazionale

Sights ▼

1 Capuchin Museum **C5**
2 Fontana delle Api **C5**
3 MACRO **G1**
4 Palazzo Barberini/Galleria Nazionale d'Arte Antica **C5**

5 Palazzo Massimo alle Terme **F6**
6 Piazza del Quirinale..... **B7**
7 Piazza della Repubblica **E5**
8 San Carlo alle Quattro Fontane......... **D6**

9 Santa Maria della Vittoria............. **E5**
10 Sant'Andrea al Quirinale **C6**

Restaurants ▼

1 Ilwinebar Trimani **F4**

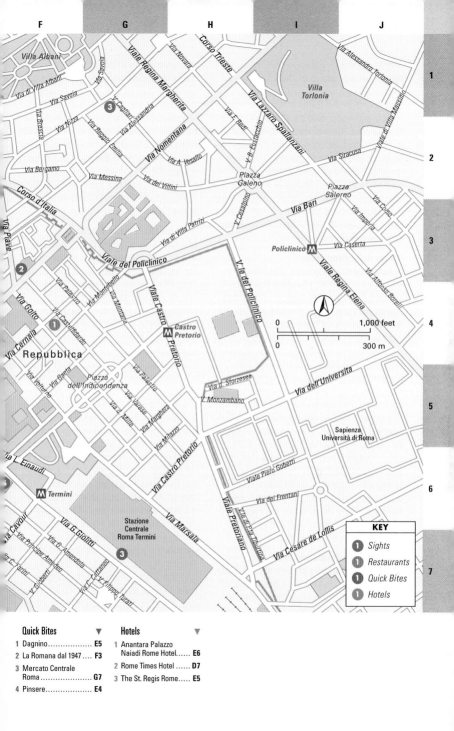

F	**G**	**H**	**I**	**J**

Villa Albani
Via di Villa Albani
Via Savoia
Via Brescia
Via Nizza
Viale Regina Margherita
Via Savoia
Via Novara
Corso Trieste
Via Alessandria
Via Catania
Via Regina Emilia
Via Lazzaro Spallanzani
Villa Torlonia
Via Alessandra Torlonia
Via di Villa Massimo
1

Via Bergamo
Via Messina
Via Nomentana
Via A. Vesallo
Via dei Villini
Via F. Redi
Via B. Eustacchio
Piazza Galeno
Via Siracusa
Piazza Salerno
Via Como
Via Imera
2

Corso d'Italia
Via Piave
Viale del Policlinico
Via di Villa Patrizi
Via Cesalpino
Via Bari
Policlinico Ⓜ
Via Caserta
Via Alfonso Borelli
Viale Regina Elena
3

Via Gotto
Via Palestro
Via Montebello
Via Mantara
Via Castelfidardo
Ⓜ Castro Pretorio
Castro Pretorio
Viale Castro Pretorio
V.le del Policlinico
0   1,000 feet
0   300 m
4

Via Cernaia
Repubblica
Via Gaeta
Piazza dell'Indipendenza
Via Varese
Via Palestro
Via d. Mille
Via Marghera
Via d. Storzesea
V. Monzambano
Via dell'Università
5

Via Volturno
Via L. Einaudi
Via Milazzo
Via Castro Pretorio
Sapienza Università di Roma
6

Ⓜ Termini
Via Cavour
Via Principe Amedeo
Via G. Giolitti
Via G. Amendola
Stazione Centrale Roma Termini
Via Marsala
Viale Pietro Gobetti
Via dei Frentani
Viale Pretoriano
Via di Pta Tiburtina
Via Cesare de Lollis
7

Via C. Tartini
Via C. Giobert
Via C. Cattaneo
Via Filippo Turati

KEY
① Sights
① Restaurants
① Quick Bites
① Hotels

Quick Bites ▼
1 Dagnino.................. **E5**
2 La Romana dal 1947 .... **F3**
3 Mercato Centrale Roma..................... **G7**
4 Pinsere.................. **E4**

Hotels ▼
1 Anantara Palazzo Naiadi Rome Hotel...... **E6**
2 Rome Times Hotel **D7**
3 The St. Regis Rome..... **E5**

Montecavallo, or Fontana dei Dioscuri, has a statuary group of Dioscuri trying to tame two massive marble steeds that was found in the Baths of Constantine, which once occupied part of the Quirinale's summit. Unlike many ancient statues in Rome, this group survived the Dark Ages intact, becoming one of the city's great sights during the Middle Ages. The obelisk next to the figures is from the Mausoleo di Augusto (Tomb of Augustus) and was put here by Pope Pius VI in the late 18th century. ✉ *Piazza del Quirinale, Quirinale* Ⓜ *Barberini.*

Piazza della Repubblica

PLAZA/SQUARE | Often the first view that spells "Rome" to weary travelers walking from Termini station, this round piazza was laid out in the late 1800s and follows the line of the caldarium of the vast ancient public baths, the Terme di Diocleziano. At its center, the exuberant Fontana delle Naiadi (Fountain of the Naiads) teems with voluptuous bronze ladies happily wrestling with marine monsters. The nudes weren't there when the pope unveiled the fountain in 1888—sparing him any embarrassment—but when the figures were added in 1901, they caused a scandal. It's said that the sculptor, Mario Rutelli, modeled them on the ample figures of two musical-comedy stars of the day. The colonnades now house the luxe hotel Anantara Palazzo Naiadi and various shops and cafés. ✉ *Repubblica* Ⓜ *Repubblica.*

San Carlo alle Quattro Fontane

CHURCH | Sometimes known as San Carlino because of its tiny size, this is one of Borromini's masterpieces. In a space no larger than the base of one of the piers of St. Peter's Basilica, he created a church that is an intricate exercise in geometric perfection, with a coffered dome that seems to float above the curves of the walls. Borromini's work is often bizarre, definitely intellectual, and intensely concerned with pure form. In San Carlo, he invented an original treatment of space

that creates an effect of rippling movement, especially evident in the double-S curves of the facade. Characteristically, the interior decoration is subdued, in white stucco with no more than a few touches of gilding, so as not to distract from the form. Don't miss the cloister: a tiny, understated Baroque jewel, with a graceful portico and loggia above, echoing the lines of the church. ✉ *Via del Quirinale 23, Quirinale* ☎ *06/48907729* Ⓜ *Barberini.*

★ Santa Maria della Vittoria

CHURCH | Designed by Carlo Maderno, this church is best known for Bernini's sumptuous Baroque decoration of the Cappella Cornaro (Cornaro Chapel, the last on the left as you face the altar), which houses his interpretation of divine love in the *Ecstasy of St. Teresa.* Bernini's masterly fusion of sculpture, light, architecture, painting, and relief is a multimedia extravaganza, with the chapel modeled as a theater, and one of the key examples of the Roman High Baroque. The members of the Cornaro family meditate on the communal vision of the great moment of divine love before them: the swooning saint's robes appear to be on fire, quivering with life, and the white marble group seems suspended in the heavens as golden rays illuminate the scene. An angel assists as Teresa abandons herself to the joys of heavenly love. To modern eyes, Bernini's representation of the saint's experience may seem more earthly than mystical. As the visiting French dignitary Charles de Brosses put it in the 18th century, "If this is divine love, I know all about it." ✉ *Via XX Settembre 17, Largo Santa Susanna, Repubblica* ☎ *06/42740571* Ⓜ *Repubblica.*

Sant'Andrea al Quirinale

CHURCH | Designed by Bernini, this small church is one of the triumphs of the Roman Baroque period. His son wrote that Bernini considered it his best work and that he used to come here occasionally, just to sit and contemplate.

Bernini's simple oval plan, a classic form in Baroque architecture, is given drama and movement by the decoration, which depicts St. Andrew's martyrdom and ascension into heaven and starts with the painting over the high altar, up past the figure of the saint above, to the angels at the base of the lantern and the dove of the Holy Spirit that awaits on high. ✉ *Via del Quirinale 30, Quirinale* ☎ *06/4819399* 🌐 *santandrea.gesuiti.it* 🕒 *Closed Mon.* [M] *Barberini.*

🍴 Restaurants

Ilwinebar Trimani

$$$ | **WINE BAR** | This wine bar is run by the Trimani family of wine merchants, whose shop next door has been in business for nearly two centuries. Hot food is served at lunch and dinner in the minimalist interior, and it is also perfect for an aperitif or an early supper (it opens for evening service at 6 pm). **Known for:** warmly lit second floor for sipping; torte salate (savory tarts); 5,000 wines from around the world. [$] *Average main: €30* ✉ *Via Cernaia 37/b, Repubblica* ☎ *06/4469630* 🌐 *www.trimani.com* 🕒 *Closed Sun. and 3 wks in Aug.* [M] *Castro Pretorio, Repubblica.*

☕ Coffee and Quick Bites

Dagnino

$ | **BAKERY** | **FAMILY** | Hidden inside a covered arcade, this Sicilian pasticceria, which opened in 1955, has pastry cases filled with cannoli, cassata, cakes, and marzipan. Go for breakfast, and try the cornetto filled with ricotta and chocolate chips—this might be the only place in Rome where you can find it. **Known for:** Sicilian desserts; midcentury modern design; cornetti filled with ricotta and chocolate chips. [$] *Average main: €3* ✉ *Via Vittorio Emanuele Orlando 75, Repubblica* ☎ *06/4818660* 🌐 *www.dagnino.com* [M] *Repubblica.*

La Romana dal 1947

$ | **ICE CREAM** | **FAMILY** | In summer, the line at this gelateria stretches out the door and around the corner. Though it's a franchise that originated in Rimini, it's loved by Romans for its rich, creamy gelato made with organic milk, fresh fruit, nuts, and chocolate. **Known for:** reasonably priced; big portions; modern decor. [$] *Average main: €3* ✉ *Via XX Settembre 60, Repubblica* ☎ *06/42020828* 🌐 *www.gelateriaromana.com* [M] *Repubblica.*

Mercato Centrale Roma

$ | **INTERNATIONAL** | **FAMILY** | This gourmet food hall is in the last place you'd expect—Termini Station—and it's great for a quick bite even if you're not catching a train. There are stalls from some of Rome's best food purveyors, including Stefano Callegari (of *trapizzino* fame), pizzaiolo Marco Quintili, and fritti by Arcangelo Dandini. **Known for:** gourmet food hall; trapizzino (stuffed triangle-shaped pizza dough) outpost; Sicilian specialties. [$] *Average main: €5* ✉ *Termini Station, Via Giovanni Giolitti 36, Repubblica* ☎ *06/46202900* 🌐 *www.mercatocentrale.it* [M] *Termini.*

Pinsere

$ | **PIZZA** | **FAMILY** | In Rome, you'll usually find either pizza tonda (round) or pizza al taglio (by the slice), but there's also pizza *pinsa*—an oval-shaped individual pie that's a little thicker than the classic Roman pizza. Pinsere is mostly a take-out shop, with people eating on the street for their lunch break, so it's the perfect quick meal. **Known for:** budget-friendly options; seasonal toppings; mortadella and pistachio pizzas. [$] *Average main: €6* ✉ *Via Flavia 98, Repubblica* ☎ *06/42020924* 🌐 *www.facebook.com/Pinsere* 🕒 *Closed weekends and 2 wks in Aug.* [M] *Castro Pretorio.*

Hotels

Anantara Palazzo Naiadi Rome Hotel

$$$$ | **HOTEL** | You'll experience exquisite service and pampering at this Neoclassical landmark on the Piazza della Repubblica built on the foundations of the Baths of Diocletian—it's now run by Anantara, a luxury hotel brand with roots in Thailand. **Pros:** top-notch concierge and staff; multiple romantic dining options; spa with both Asian and European-style treatments. **Cons:** food and beverages are expensive; beyond the immediate vicinity of many sights; rooms are a different style than public spaces. [$] *Rooms from: €400* ✉ *Piazza della Repubblica 47, Repubblica* ☎ *06/489381* 🌐 *www.anantara.com/en/palazzo-naiadi-rome* 🛏 *238 rooms* 🍴 *Free Breakfast* [M] *Repubblica, Termini.*

Rome Times Hotel

$$ | **HOTEL** | This modern hotel has large, soundproofed rooms with contemporary furnishings, hardwood floors, and huge fluffy beds. **Pros:** late checkout if booked through site; free use of Samsung smartphone for calls and Internet during your stay; large bright bathrooms. **Cons:** lower floors can be noisy; rooms in the annex don't come with all the benefits of the main hotel; lighting in rooms is not optimal. [$] *Rooms from: €180* ✉ *Via Milano 42, Quirinale* ☎ *06/99345101* 🌐 *www.rometimeshotel.com* 🛏 *81 rooms* 🍴 *No Meals* [M] *Repubblica.*

The St. Regis Rome

$$$$ | **HOTEL** | Originally opened by César Ritz in 1894, this grande dame has a Belle Epoque lobby filled with classic and contemporary art, a ballroom with painstakingly restored ceiling frescoes, and an intimate library where you can sip a cup of tea or something stronger. **Pros:** houses the Roman location of international art gallery Galleria Continua; every room comes with 24/7 butler service; the library lounge serves a lovely afternoon tea. **Cons:** food and drinks are pricey; breakfast is not included; restaurant feels more like a lounge than a proper restaurant. [$] *Rooms from: €650* ✉ *Via Vittorio E. Orlando 3, Repubblica* ☎ *06/47091* 🌐 *www.marriott.com* 🛏 *161 rooms* 🍴 *No Meals* [M] *Repubblica.*

Performing Arts

★ **Teatro dell'Opera**

OPERA | The company at this theater, a far younger sibling of La Scala in Milan and La Fenice in Venice, commands an audience during its mid-November–May season. In the hot summer months, it moves to the Terme di Caracalla for an outdoor opera series. As you might expect, the oft-preferred performance is *Aida*, for its spectacle, which once included real elephants. The company has lately taken a new direction, using projections atop the ancient ruins to create cutting-edge sets. ✉ *Piazza Beniamino Gigli 1, Repubblica* ☎ *06/481601, 06/4817003 tickets* 🌐 *www.operaroma.it* [M] *Repubblica.*

Villa Borghese and Environs

Touring Rome's artistic masterpieces while staying clear of its hustle and bustle can be, quite literally, a walk in the park. Some of the city's finest sights are tucked away in or next to green lawns and pedestrian piazzas, offering a breath of fresh air for weary sightseers, especially in the Villa Borghese park. One of Rome's largest, this park can alleviate gallery gout by offering an oasis in which to cool off under the ilex, oak, and umbrella pine trees. If you feel like a picnic, have an *alimentari* (food shop) make you some panini before you go; food carts within the park are overpriced.

GETTING HERE AND AROUND

The Metro stop for Piazza del Popolo is Flaminio on Line A. The Villa Giulia, the Galleria Nazionale d'Arte Moderna e Contemporanea, and the Bioparco in Villa Borghese are accessible from Via Flaminia, 1 km (½ mile) from Piazza del Popolo. Tram No. 19 and Bus No. 3 stop at each. Bus No. 160 and No. 628 connect Piazza del Popolo to Piazza Venezia. Bus No. 116 goes into Villa Borghese.

 # Sights

★ Galleria Borghese

ART MUSEUM | The luxury-loving Cardinal Scipione Borghese had this museum custom-built in 1612 as a showcase for his fabulous collection of both antiquities and more "modern" works. One of the collection's most famous works is Canova's Neoclassical sculpture, *Pauline Borghese as Venus Victorious.* Nearby are three key early Baroque sculptures by Bernini: *David, Apollo and Daphne,* and *The Rape of Persephone.* You'll also find masterpieces by Caravaggio, Raphael (including his moving *Deposition*), Pinturicchio, Perugino, Bellini, and Rubens. Probably the gallery's most famous painting is Titian's allegorical *Sacred and Profane Love.*
■**TIP→ Admission to the Galleria Borghese is by reservation only. Visitors are admitted in two-hour shifts 9–5. Prime-time slots sell out days in advance, so reserve and directly (and early) through the museum's website.** ⊠ *Piazzale Scipione Borghese 5, off Via Pinciana, Villa Borghese* ☎ *06/32810 reservations, 06/8413979 info* ⊕ *galleria-borghese.beniculturali.it* ⊠ *€15, including €2 reservation fee; increased fee during temporary exhibitions* ⊗ *Closed Mon.* ⚇ *Reservations essential.*

★ MAXXI—Museo Nazionale delle Arti del XXI Secolo (*National Museum of 21st-Century Arts*)

ART MUSEUM | Designed by the late Iraqi-British architect Zaha Hadid, this modern building plays with lots of natural light and has curving and angular lines,

big open spaces, glass ceilings, and steel staircases that twist through the air—all meant to question the division between "within" and "without." The MAXXI hosts temporary exhibitions of art, architecture, film, and more. The permanent collection, displayed on a rotating basis, has more than 350 works from modern and contemporary artists, including Andy Warhol, Francesco Clemente, and Gerhard Richter. ⊠ *Via Guido Reni 4/A, Flaminio* ☎ *06/3201954* ⊕ *www.maxxi.art* ⊠ *€12* ⊗ *Closed Mon.* Ⓜ *Flaminio, then Tram No. 2 to Apollodoro.*

★ Piazza del Popolo

PLAZA/SQUARE | **FAMILY** | With its obelisk and twin churches, this immense square marks what was, for centuries, Rome's northern entrance, where all roads from the north converged and where visitors, many of them pilgrims, got their first impression of the Eternal City. The desire to make this entrance to Rome something special was a pet project of popes and their architects for more than three centuries. Although it was once crowded with fashionable carriages, the piazza today is a pedestrian zone. At election time, it's the scene of huge political rallies, and on New Year's Eve, Rome stages a mammoth alfresco party here. ⊠ *Piazza del Popolo* Ⓜ *Flaminio.*

★ Santa Maria del Popolo

CHURCH | Standing inconspicuously in a corner of the vast Piazza del Popolo, this church often goes unnoticed, but the treasures inside make it a must for art lovers. Bramante enlarged the apse, which was rebuilt in the 15th century on the site of a much older place of worship. Inside, in the first chapel on the right, you'll see some frescoes by Pinturicchio from the mid-15th century; the adjacent Cybo Chapel is a 17th-century exercise in decorative marble.

Raphael designed the famous Chigi Chapel, the second on the left, with vault mosaics—showing God the Father in Benediction—as well as statues of

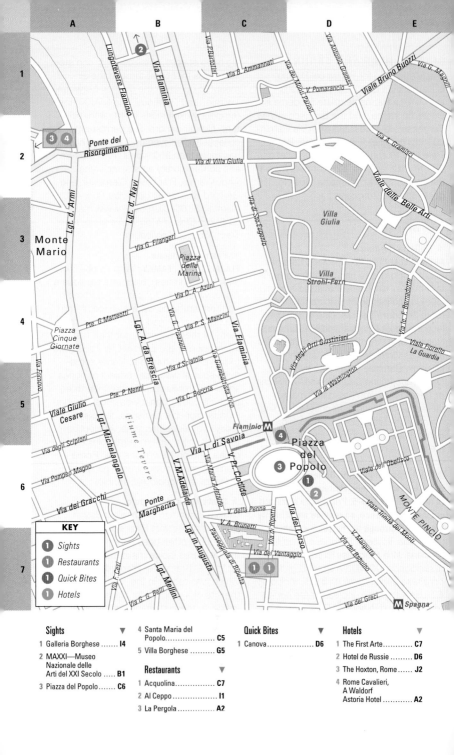

	A	B	C	D	E

Sights ▼

1 Galleria Borghese **I4**
2 MAXXI—Museo
Nazionale delle
Arti del XXI Secolo **B1**
3 Piazza del Popolo **C6**
4 Santa Maria del
Popolo **C5**
5 Villa Borghese **G5**

Restaurants ▼

1 Acquolina **C7**
2 Al Ceppo **I1**
3 La Pergola **A2**

Quick Bites ▼

1 Canova **D6**

Hotels ▼

1 The First Arte............ **C7**
2 Hotel de Russie **D6**
3 The Hoxton, Rome **J2**
4 Rome Cavalieri,
A Waldorf
Astoria Hotel **A2**

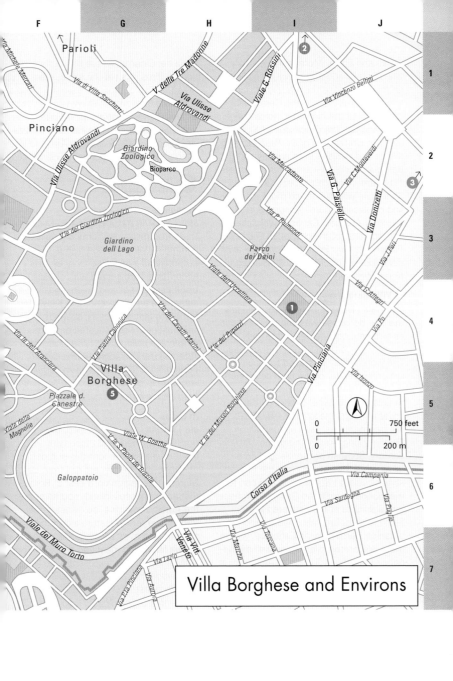

Villa Borghese and Environs

F G H I J

1 2 3 4 5 6 7

Parioli

Via di Villa Sacchetti

V. delle Tre Madonne

Via Ulisse Aldrovandi

Viale G. Rossini

Via Vincenzo Bellini

Pinciano

Via Ulisse Aldrovandi

Giardino Zoologico

Bioparco

Via Mercadante

Via C. Monteverdi

Via G. Paisiello

Via Donizetti

V.le del Giardino Zoologico

Via P. Raimondi

Giardino del Lago

Parco dei Daini

Via G. Allegri

Via I. Pizzi

Viale dell'Uccelliera

Via G. Allegri

V.le dei Cavalli Marini

V.le Fiorello La Guardia

V.le dei Pupazzi

Via Po

V.le Pietro Canonica

Via Pinciana

Via Isonzo

Villa Borghese

Piazzale d. Canestre

Viale delle Magnolie

Viale W. Goethe

V.le del Museo Borghese

Viale dell'Aranciera

V.le di S. Paolo del Brasile

Galoppatoio

Corso d'Italia

Via Campania

Via Sardegna

Via Puglie

Via Toscana

Viale del Muro Torto

Via Vitt. Veneto

Via Marche

Via Lazio

Via Pta Pinciana

Via Aurora

0   750 feet
0   200 m

Jonah and Elijah. More than a century later, Bernini added the oval medallions on the tombs and the statues of Daniel and Habakkuk. Finally, the Cerasi Chapel, to the left of the high altar, holds two Caravaggios: *The Crucifixion of St. Peter* and *The Conversion of St. Paul.* Exuding drama and realism, both are key early Baroque works that show how "modern" 17th-century art can appear. Compare their style with the much more restrained and classically "pure" *Assumption of the Virgin* by Annibale Carracci, which hangs over the altar of the chapel. ⊠ *Piazza del Popolo 12, near Porta del Popolo, Piazza del Popolo* ☎ *06/3610836* ⊕ *www.agostiniani.it* Ⓜ *Flaminio.*

★ **Villa Borghese**

CITY PARK | FAMILY | Rome's Central Park, the Villa Borghese was originally laid out as a recreational garden in the early 17th century by Cardinal Scipione Borghese. The word "villa" was used to mean suburban estate, of the type developed by the ancient Romans and adopted by Renaissance nobles. Today's gardens cover a much smaller area—by 1630, the perimeter wall was almost 5 km (3 miles) long. At the end of the 18th century, Scottish painter Jacob More remodeled the gardens into the English style popular at the time. In addition to the gloriously restored Galleria Borghese, the highlights of the park are Piazza di Siena, a graceful amphitheater, and the botanical garden on Via Canonica, where there is a pretty little lake as well as the neoclassical faux–Temple of Aesculapius, the Biopark zoo, Rome's own replica of London's Globe Theatre, and the Villa Giulia museum.

The Carlo Bilotti Museum (⊕ *www.museocarlobilotti.it*) is particularly attractive for Giorgio de Chirico fans, and there is more modern art in the nearby Galleria Nazionale d'Arte Moderna e Contemporanea. The 63-seat children's movie theater, Cinema dei Piccoli, shows films for adults in the evening. There's also Casa del Cinema, where film buffs can screen films or sit at the sleek, cherry-red, indoor-outdoor café (you can find a schedule of events at ⊕ *www.casadelcinema.it*). ⊠ *Main entrances at Porta Pinciana, the Pincio, Piazzale Flaminio (Piazza del Popolo), Viale delle Belle Arti, and Via Mercadante, Villa Borghese* Ⓜ *Flaminio.*

 Restaurants

Acquolina

$$$$ | MODERN ITALIAN | This two-Michelin-starred restaurant turns out delicious and high-quality seafood dishes that surprise and evoke a sensory experience. Tortelli are served with cheese, black pepper, eel, and onion, and all the dishes are artfully presented. **Known for:** elaborate tasting menus; spaghetti with langoustines; sophisticated desserts. Ⓢ *Average main: €50* ⊠ *The First Roma Arte, Via del Vantaggio 14, Piazza del Popolo* ☎ *06/3201590* ⊕ *www.acquolinaristorante.it* ⏱ *Closed Sun. and Mon. No lunch* Ⓜ *Flaminio.*

Al Ceppo

$$$ | ITALIAN | The well-heeled, the business-minded, and those with refined palates frequent this outpost of tranquility. The owners hail from Le Marche, the region northeast of Rome that encompasses inland mountains and the Adriatic coastline, so dishes from their native region feature alongside seafood and meats ready to be grilled. **Known for:** grilled meat and fish; authentic Le Marche cuisine; excellent wine list. Ⓢ *Average main: €30* ⊠ *Via Panama 2, Villa Borghese* ☎ *06/8419696* ⊕ *www.ristorantealceppo.it* ⏱ *No lunch Mon. Closed 3 wks in Aug.*

★ **La Pergola**

$$$$ | MODERN ITALIAN | Dinner here is a truly spectacular and romantic event, with incomparable views across the city matched by a stellar dining experience that includes top-notch service as well as sublimely inventive fare. The difficulty comes in choosing from among Michelin-starred chef Heinz Beck's *alta cucina* (high cuisine) specialties. **Known for:** fagotelli La Pergola stuffed with pecorino, eggs, and cream with guanciale and zucchini; award-winning wine list; weekend reservations that book up three months in advance. $ *Average main: €75* ✉ *Rome Cavalieri, A Waldorf Astoria Resort, Via Alberto Cadlolo 101, Monte Mario* ☎ *06/35092152* ⊕ *www.hilton.com* ⊘ *Closed Sun. and Mon., 3 wks in Aug., and Jan. No lunch* ⏚ *Jacket required.*

Coffee and Quick Bites

Canova
$$ | ITALIAN | FAMILY | Esteemed director Federico Fellini, who lived around the corner on Via Margutta, used to come here all the time and even had an office in the back. His drawings and black-and-white stills from his films remain on display in the hallway that leads to the interior dining room, but the best place to sit for people-watching with a coffee, light lunch, or aperitivo is on the terrace out front. **Known for:** great people-watching; sandwiches and other light fare; Fellini's old hangout. $ *Average main: €15* ✉ *Piazza del Popolo 16, Piazza del Popolo* ☎ *06/3612231* ⊕ *www.canovapiazzadel-popolo.it* Ⓜ *Flaminio.*

Hotels

The First Arte
$$$$ | HOTEL | Set in a 19th-century Neo-classical palace, this cozy boutique hotel was remodeled to feature high-tech, elegant guest rooms while keeping the core structure, including unique windows and tall ceilings, intact. **Pros:** fitness room with Technogym equipment; staff that is eager to please; more than 200 works of art on display from Galleria Mucciaccia. **Cons:** some rooms can be dark; rooftop bar can get quite crowded; not a lot of in-room storage for luggage. $ *Rooms from: €500* ✉ *Via del Vantaggio 14, Piazza*

del Popolo ☎ *06/45617070* ⊕ *www.pavil-ionshotels.com/rome/thefirstarte* ⥹ *29 rooms* ⍟ *Free Breakfast* Ⓜ *Flaminio.*

★ Hotel de Russie
$$$$ | HOTEL | Occupying a 19th-century hotel that once hosted royalty, Picasso, and Cocteau, the Hotel de Russie is now the first choice in Rome for government bigwigs and Hollywood high rollers seeking ultimate luxury in a secluded retreat. **Pros:** big potential for celebrity sightings; well-equipped gym and world-class spa; excellent Stravinskij cocktail bar has courtyard tables. **Cons:** faster Internet comes at a fee; breakfast not included; very expensive. $ *Rooms from: €1,100* ✉ *Via del Babuino 9, Piazza del Popolo* ☎ *06/328881* ⊕ *www.roccofortehotels. com/hotels-and-resorts/hotel-de-russie* ⥹ *120 rooms* ⍟ *No Meals* Ⓜ *Flaminio.*

The Hoxton, Rome
$$ | HOTEL | British brand The Hoxton's first foray into Italy is a design lover's dream filled with 1970s-inspired bespoke furniture, art tomes, and plants that transform the large lobby into intimate seating nooks perfect for socializing and coworking. **Pros:** stylish design; friendly staff; great food and drinks. **Cons:** far from main sights, with the closest Metro stop a mile away; rooms have little storage space for clothes; no gym or spa. $ *Rooms from: €189* ✉ *Largo Benedetto Marcello 220, Parioli* ☎ *06/94502700* ⊕ *thehoxton.com/rome* ⥹ *192 rooms* ⍟ *No Meals.*

Rome Cavalieri, A Waldorf Astoria Hotel
$$$$ | RESORT | FAMILY | Set in a quiet residential neighborhood amid 15 acres of lush Mediterranean parkland, the Rome Cavalieri is a true hilltop oasis with magnificent views as well as three outdoor pools, one indoor pool, and a palatial spa. **Pros:** famed art collection, including a Tiepolo triptych from 1725; complimentary shuttle to city center; impressive on-site restaurant. **Cons:** you definitely pay for the luxury of staying here—everything is expensive; outside the city center; not all

rooms have great views. $ *Rooms from: €330* ✉ *Via Alberto Cadlolo 101, Monte Mario* ☎ *06/35091* ⊕ *www.hilton.com* ⤸ *370 rooms* ❘◯❘ *No Meals.*

Nightlife

★ **Stravinskij Bar at the Hotel de Russie**

COCKTAIL LOUNGES | The Stravinskij Bar, in the Hotel de Russie, is the best place to sample la dolce vita. Celebrities, blue bloods, and VIPs hang out in the gorgeous courtyard garden where mixed drinks and cocktails are well above par. There are also healthy smoothies and bites if you need to refuel. ✉ *Hotel de Russie, Via del Babuino 9, Piazza del Popolo* ☎ *06/3288874* ⊕ *www.roccoforte-hotels.com* Ⓜ *Flaminio.*

Performing Arts

★ **Auditorium Parco della Musica**

CONCERTS | Architect Renzo Piano conceived and constructed the Auditorium Parco della Musica, a futuristic complex made up of three enormous, pod-shaped concert halls, which have hosted some of the world's greatest music acts. The Sala Santa Cecilia is a massive hall for grand orchestra and choral concerts; the Sala Sinopoli is more intimately scaled for smaller troupes; and the Sala Petrassi was designed for alternative events. All three are arrayed around the Cavea (amphitheater), a vast outdoor Greco-Roman-style theater. The Auditorium also hosts seasonal festivals, including the Rome Film Fest. ✉ *Viale Pietro de Coubertin 30, Flaminio* ☎ *06/80241281* ⊕ *www.auditorium.com* Ⓜ *Flaminio, then Tram No. 2 to Apollodoro.*

Teatro Olimpico

THEATER | Part of Rome's theater circuit, the 1930s-era Teatro Olimpico is one of the main venues for cabaret, contemporary dance companies, visiting international ballet companies, and touring Broadway shows. ✉ *Piazza Gentile da Fabriano 17, Flaminio* ☎ *06/32659916*

⊕ *www.teatroolimpico.it* Ⓜ *Flaminio, then Tram 2 to Mancini.*

Shopping

★ **Il Marmoraro**

OTHER SPECIALTY STORE | This tiny shop is a holdout of Via Margutta's days as a street full of artists and artisans. Sandro Fiorentino's father opened the shop in 1969 (he carved plaques like the one that marks Federico Fellini's house up the street), and Sandro still engraves the marble by hand. The shop is packed full of plaques, many with clever phrases, which make a great souvenir. Sandro will also engrave a message of your choice upon request. ✉ *Via Margutta 53B, Piazza del Popolo* ☎ *06/3207660* Ⓜ *Spagna.*

Trastevere

Across the Tiber from the Jewish Ghetto is Trastevere (literally "across the Tiber"), long cherished as Rome's Greenwich Village and now subject to rampant gentrification. In spite of this, Trastevere remains about the most tightly knit community in the city, the Trasteverini proudly proclaiming their descent from the ancient Romans. Ancient bridges—the Ponte Fabricio and the Ponte Cestio—link Trastevere and the Ghetto to Isola Tiberina (Tiber Island), a diminutive sandbar and one of Rome's most picturesque sights.

GETTING HERE AND AROUND

From the Vatican or Spanish Steps, expect a 30- to 40-minute walk to reach Trastevere. From Termini station, take Bus No. 40 Express or No. 64 to Largo di Torre Argentina, where you can switch to Tram No. 8 to get to Trastevere. If you don't feel like climbing the steep Gianicolo, take Bus No. 115 from Largo dei Fiorentini, then enjoy the walk down to the northern reaches of Trastevere or explore the leafy residential area of Monteverde Vecchio on the other side of the hill.

Sights

Isola Tiberina (*Tiber Island*)

ISLAND | FAMILY | It's easy to overlook this tiny island in the Tiber, but you shouldn't. In terms of history and sheer loveliness, charming Isola Tiberina—shaped like a boat about to set sail—gets high marks. Cross onto the island via Ponte Fabricio, Rome's oldest remaining bridge, constructed in 62 BC. On the north side of the island crumbles the romantic ruin of the Ponte Rotto (Broken Bridge), which dates from 179 BC. Descend the steps to the lovely river embankment to see a Roman relief of the intertwined-snakes symbol of Aesculapius, the great god of healing.

In imperial times, Romans sheathed the entire island with marble to make it look like Aesculapius's ship, replete with a towering obelisk as a mast. Amazingly, a fragment of the ancient sculpted ship's prow still exists. You can marvel at it on the downstream end of the embankment. Today, medicine still reigns here. The island is home to the hospital of Fatebenefratelli (literally, "Do good, brothers"). Nearby is San Bartolomeo, built at the end of the 10th century by the Holy Roman Emperor Otto III and restored in the 18th century. ⊠ *Trastevere* ✦ *Isola Tiberina can be accessed by Ponte Fabricio or Ponte Cestio.*

Palazzo Corsini

ART MUSEUM | A brooding example of Baroque style, the palace (once home to Queen Christina of Sweden) is across the road from the Villa Farnesina and houses part of the 16th- and 17th-century sections of the collection of the Galleria Nazionale d'Arte Antica. Among the star paintings in this manageably sized collection are Rubens's *St. Sebastian Healed by Angels* and Caravaggio's *St. John the Baptist.* Stop in if only to climb the 17th-century stone staircase, itself a drama of architectural shadows and sculptural voids. Behind, but separate

from, the palazzo is the University of Rome's Orto Botanico, home to 3,500 species of plants, with various greenhouses around a stairway/fountain with 11 jets. ⊠ *Via della Lungara 10, Trastevere* ☎ *06/68802323 Galleria Corsini, 06/32810 Galleria Corsini tickets, 06/49917107 Orto Botanico* ⊕ *www.barberinicorsini.org* 🎟 *€12 Galleria Corsini, including entrance to Palazzo Barberini within 20 days; €4 Orto Botanico* ⊗ *Closed Mon.*

★ Santa Cecilia in Trastevere

CHURCH | This basilica commemorates the aristocratic St. Cecilia, patron saint of musicians. One of ancient Rome's most celebrated early Christian martyrs, she was most likely put to death by the Emperor Diocletian just before the year AD 300. After an abortive attempt to suffocate her in the baths of her own house (a favorite means of quietly disposing of aristocrats in Roman days), she was brought before the executioner. But not even three blows of the executioner's sword could dispatch the young girl. She lingered for several days, converting others to the Christian cause, before finally dying. In 1595, her body was exhumed—it was said to look as fresh as if she still breathed—and the heart-wrenching sculpture by eyewitness Stefano Maderno that lies below the main altar was, he insisted, exactly how she looked.

Time your visit in the morning to enter the cloistered convent to see what remains of Pietro Cavallini's *Last Judgment,* dating from 1293. It's the only major fresco in existence known to have been painted by Cavallini, a contemporary of Giotto. To visit the frescoes, ring the bell of the convent to the left of the church entrance between 10 am and 12 pm. ⊠ *Piazza di Santa Cecilia 22, Trastevere* ☎ *06/5899289* ⊕ *www.benedettinesantacecilia.it* 🎟 *Frescoes €2.50, underground €2.50* ⊗ *Access to frescoes closed in the afternoon.*

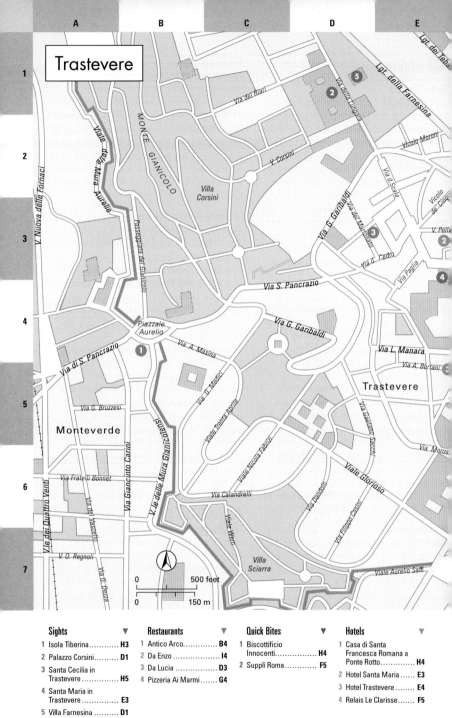

Trastevere

| A | B | C | D | E |

Sights ▼

1 Isola Tiberina............ **H3**
2 Palazzo Corsini.......... **D1**
3 Santa Cecilia in Trastevere **H5**
4 Santa Maria in Trastevere **E3**
5 Villa Farnesina **D1**

Restaurants ▼

1 Antico Arco.............. **B4**
2 Da Enzo **I4**
3 Da Lucia **D3**
4 Pizzeria Ai Marmi....... **G4**

Quick Bites ▼

1 Biscottificio Innocenti................. **H4**
2 Supplì Roma **F5**

Hotels ▼

1 Casa di Santa Francesca Romana a Ponte Rotto............. **H4**
2 Hotel Santa Maria **E3**
3 Hotel Trastevere **E4**
4 Relais Le Clarisse....... **F5**

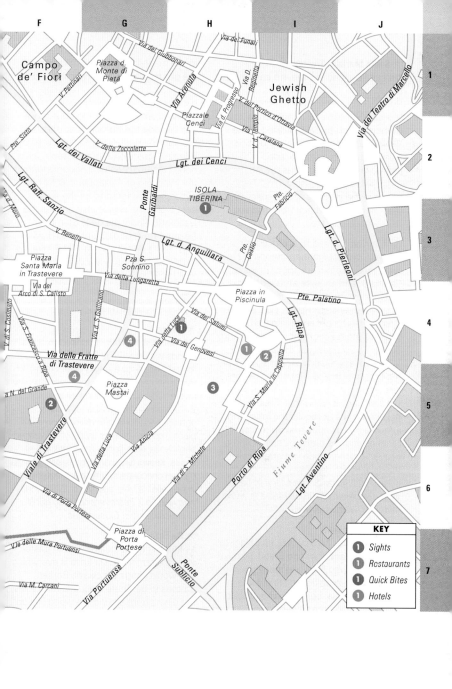

★ Santa Maria in Trastevere

CHURCH | Built during the 4th century and rebuilt in the 12th century, this is one of Rome's oldest and grandest churches. It is also the earliest foundation of any Roman church to be dedicated to the Virgin Mary. The 18th-century portico draws attention to the facade's 800-year-old mosaics, which represent the parable of the Wise and Foolish Virgins. They enhance the whole piazza, especially at night, when the church front and bell tower are illuminated.

With a nave framed by a processional of two rows of gigantic columns (22 in total) taken from the ancient Baths of Caracalla, and an apse studded with gilded mosaics, the interior conjures the splendor of ancient Rome. Overhead is Domenichino's gilded ceiling (1617). The church's most important mosaics, Pietro Cavallini's six panels of the *Life of the Virgin,* cover the semicircular apse. Note the building labeled "Taberna Meritoria" just under the figure of the Virgin in the Nativity scene, with a stream of oil flowing from it; it recalls the legend that a fountain of oil appeared on this spot, prophesying the birth of Christ. Off the piazza's northern side is a street called Via delle Fonte dell'Olio in honor of this miracle. ⊠ *Piazza Santa Maria in Trastevere, Trastevere* ☎ *06/5814802* ⊕ *www. santamariaintrastevere.it.*

★ Villa Farnesina

CASTLE/PALACE | Money was no object to the extravagant Agostino Chigi, a banker from Siena who financed many papal projects. His munificence is evident in this elegant villa, built for him in about 1511. Agostino entertained the popes and princes of 16th-century Rome, impressing his guests at riverside suppers by having his servants clear the table by casting the precious silver and gold dinnerware into the Tiber (indeed, nets were unfurled a foot or two beneath the water's surface to retrieve the valuable ware).

In the magnificent Loggia of Psyche on the ground floor, Giulio Romano and others created the frescoes from Raphael's designs. Raphael's lovely *Galatea* is in the adjacent room. On the floor above you can see the trompe-l'oeil effects in the aptly named Hall of Perspectives by Peruzzi. Agostino Chigi's bedroom, next door, was frescoed by Il Sodoma with the *Wedding of Alexander and Roxanne,* which is considered to be the artist's best work. The palace also houses the Gabinetto Nazionale delle Stampe, a treasure trove of old prints and drawings. ⊠ *Via della Lungara 230, Trastevere* ☎ *06/68027268* ⊕ *www.villafarnesina.it* ⊠ *€10* ⊗ *Closed Sun.*

🍴 Restaurants

★ Antico Arco

$$$ | **MODERN ITALIAN** | Founded by three friends with a passion for wine and fine food, Antico Arco attracts diners from Rome and beyond with its refined culinary inventiveness. The location on top of the Janiculum Hill makes for a charming setting, and inside, the dining rooms are plush, modern spaces, with whitewashed brick walls, dark floors, and black velvet chairs. **Known for:** changing seasonal menu; molten chocolate soufflé cake; extensive wine cellar. Ⓢ *Average main: €29* ⊠ *Piazzale Aurelio 7, Trastevere* ☎ *06/5815274* ⊕ *anticoarco.it* ⊗ *Closed Tues.*

★ Da Enzo

$ | **ROMAN** | In the quieter part of Trastevere, the family-run Da Enzo is everything you would imagine a classic Roman trattoria to be. There are just a few tables, but diners from around the world line up to eat here—a testament to the quality of the food. **Known for:** cacio e pepe (pasta with pecorino-cheese sauce and black pepper), carbonara, and other Roman classics; boisterous, authentic atmosphere; small space with long waits. Ⓢ *Average main: €14* ⊠ *Via dei Vascellari 29, Trastevere* ☎ *06/5812260* ⊕ *www.daenzoal29. com* ⊗ *Closed Sun. and 2 wks in Aug.*

Da Lucia

$ | **ROMAN** | **FAMILY** | There's no shortage of old-school trattorias in Trastevere, but this one has a strong following. Both locals and expats enjoy the brusque but "authentic" service and the hearty Roman fare; snag a table outside in warm weather for the true Roman experience of cobblestone-terrace dining. **Known for:** bombolotti (a tubular pasta) all'amatriciana; spaghetti cacio e pepe; involtini (beef rolls). $ *Average main: €14* ⊠ *Vicolo del Mattonato 2, Trastevere* ☎ *06/5803601* ⊗ *Closed Mon., Tues., and Aug. No lunch Wed.–Sat.*

Pizzeria Ai Marmi

$ | **PIZZA** | **FAMILY** | This place is packed pretty much every night with diners munching on crisp pizzas that come out of the wood-burning ovens at top speed. It's best not to go during peak dining hours, so go early or late if you don't want to wait. **Known for:** excellent wood-oven pizzas; fried starters such as supplì (breaded fried rice balls); open until midnight for a late-night bite. $ *Average main: €12* ⊠ *Viale Trastevere 53, Trastevere* ☎ *06/5800919* ⊗ *Closed Wed. and 3 wks in Aug.*

☕ Coffee and Quick Bites

Biscottificio Innocenti

$ | **ITALIAN** | **FAMILY** | The scent of cookies wafts out into the street as you approach this family-run bakery, where a small team makes sweet treats the old-school way in a massive oven bought in the 1960s. There are dozens of varieties of baked goods, mostly sweet but some savory. **Known for:** old-school family-run bakery; dozens of varieties of baked goods; brutti ma buoni ("ugly but good") cookies. $ *Average main: €3* ⊠ *Via della Luce 21, Trastevere* ☎ *06/5803926* ⊕ *www.facebook.com/BiscottificioInnocenti* ⊗ *Closed 2 wks in Aug.*

Suppli Roma

$ | **ROMAN** | **FAMILY** | Trastevere's best supplì (Roman-style rice croquettes) have been served at this hole-in-the-wall take-out spot since 1979. At lunchtime, the line spills out onto the street with locals who've come for the namesake treats, as well as fried baccalà fillets and stuffed zucchini flowers. **Known for:** old-fashioned baked pizza with spicy marinara sauce; gnocchi on Thursday (the traditional day for it in Rome); classic fried risotto ball with ragù or cacio e pepe. $ *Average main: €5* ⊠ *Via di San Francesco a Ripa 137, Trastevere* ☎ *06/5897110* ⊕ *www.suppliroma.it* ⊗ *Closed Sun. and 2 wks in Aug.*

Hotels

Casa di Santa Francesca Romana a Ponte Rotto

$ | **HOTEL** | In the heart of Trastevere but tucked away from the hustle and bustle of the medieval quarter, this comfortable, affordable hotel in a former monastery is centered on a lovely green courtyard. **Pros:** rates can't be beat; triple rooms for small groups; away from rowdy tourist side of Trastevere. **Cons:** a bit far from Metro, but there are tram and bus stops nearby; few amenities besides TV room and reading room; spotty Wi-Fi. $ *Rooms from: €98* ⊠ *Via dei Vascellari 61, Trastevere* ☎ *06/5812125* ⊕ *www.sfromana.it* ⇥ *37 rooms* ❑ *Free Breakfast.*

Hotel Santa Maria

$$ | **HOTEL** | A Trastevere treasure with a pedigree going back four centuries, this ivy-covered, mansard-roofed, rosy-brick-red, erstwhile Renaissance-era convent—just steps away from the glorious Santa Maria in Trastevere church and a few blocks from the Tiber—has sweet and simple guest rooms: a mix of brick walls, "cotto" tile floors, oak furniture, and matching bedspreads and curtains. **Pros:** a quaint and pretty oasis in a central location; free bicycles to use during your stay; lovely rooftop terrace with views across the city. **Cons:** tricky to find; not the best value for money; some rooms can be noisy. $ *Rooms from: €170* ✉ *Vicolo del Piede 2, Trastevere* ☎ *06/5894626* ⊕ *www.hotelsantamariatrastevere.it* ⬡ *20 rooms* ❖ *Free Breakfast.*

Hotel Trastevere
$$ | **HOTEL** | This hotel captures the villagelike charm of the Trastevere district and offers basic, clean, comfortable rooms. **Pros:** good rates for location; convenient to tram and bus; friendly staff. **Cons:** rooms are a little worn around the edges; few amenities; standard rooms are quite small. $ *Rooms from: €130* ✉ *Via Luciano Manara 24/a, Trastevere* ☎ *06/5814713* ⊕ *www.hoteltrastevere. net* ⬡ *14 rooms* ❖ *Free Breakfast.*

Relais Le Clarisse
$$ | **B&B/INN** | Set within the former cloister grounds of the Santa Chiara order, with beautiful gardens, Le Clarisse makes you feel like a personal guest at a friend's villa, thanks to the comfortable size of the guest rooms and personalized service. **Pros:** spacious rooms with comfy beds; high-tech showers/tubs with good water pressure; complimentary high-speed Wi-Fi. **Cons:** this part of Trastevere can be noisy at night; check when booking as you may be put in neighboring building; no restaurant or bar. $ *Rooms from: €140* ✉ *Via Cardinale Merry del Val 20, Trastevere* ☎ *06/58334437* ⊕ *www. leclarissetrastevere.com* ⬡ *17 rooms* ❖ *Free Breakfast.*

 Nightlife

★ Freni e Frizioni
COCKTAIL LOUNGES | This hipster hangout is great for a sunset aperitivo or for late-night socializing. Though the vibe is artsy and laid-back, the bartenders take their cocktails seriously—and have the awards to prove it. In warmer weather, the crowd overflows into the large terrazzo overlooking the Tiber and the side streets of Trastevere. ✉ *Via del Politeama*

4, Trastevere ☎ *06/45497499* ⊕ *www. frenifrizioni.com.*

 Shopping
BOOKSTORES
Almost Corner Bookshop
BOOKS | Bursting at the seams with not an inch of space left on its shelves, this tiny little bookshop is a favorite meeting point for English speakers in Trastevere. Irish owner Dermot O'Connell goes out of his way to find what you're looking for, and if he doesn't have it in stock he'll make a special order for you. The shop carries everything from popular best sellers to translated Italian classics, as well as lots of good books about Rome. ✉ *Via del Moro 45, Trastevere* ☎ *06/5836942* ⊕ *www.facebook.com/ AlmostCornerBookshop.*

MARKETS
Porta Portese
MARKET | FAMILY | One of the biggest flea markets in Italy welcomes shoppers in droves every Sunday from 7 am to 2 pm. Treasure seekers and bargain hunters love scrounging around tents for new and vintage clothing and accessories, antique furniture, used books, and other odds 'n' ends. Bring your haggling skills, and cash (preferably small bills—it'll work in your favor when driving a bargain); many stallholders don't accept credit cards, and the nearest ATM is a hike. ✉ *Via Portuense and adjacent streets between Porta Portese and Via Ettore Rolli, Trastevere.*

Aventino and Testaccio

The **Aventino** district is somewhat rarefied, where some houses still have their own bell towers and private gardens are called "parks," without exaggeration. Like the emperors of old on the Palatine, the fortunate residents here look out over the Circus Maximus and the river, winding its way far below. **Testaccio** is perhaps the world's only district built on broken pots:

the hill of the same name was born from discarded pottery used to store oil, wine, and other goods loaded from nearby Ripa, when Rome had a port and the Tiber was once a mighty river to an empire. It's quiet during the day, but on Saturday buzzes with the loud music from rows of discos and clubs.

Sights

★ Centrale Montemartini

ART MUSEUM | A decommissioned early-20th-century power plant is now this intriguing exhibition space for the overflow of ancient art from the Musei Capitolini collection. Getting here is half the fun. A 15-minute walk from the heart of Testaccio iwill lead you past walls covered in street art to the urban district of Ostiense. Head southwest and saunter under the train tracks passing buildings adorned with four-story-high murals until you reach the often-uncrowded Centrale Montemartini, where Roman sculptures and mosaics are set amid industrial machinery and pipes.

Unusually, the collection is organized by the area in which the ancient pieces were found. Highlights include the former boiler room filled with ancient marble statues that once decorated Rome's private villas, such as the beautiful *Esquiline Venus*, as well as a large mosaic of a hunting scene. ⊠ *Via Ostiense 106, Testaccio* ☎ *06/0608* ⊕ *www.centralemontemartini.org* ☒ *€10* ⊘ *Closed Mon.* Ⓜ *Garbatella.*

★ Gran Priorato di Roma dell'Ordine di Malta

RELIGIOUS BUILDING | **FAMILY** | Although the line to peek through the keyhole of a nondescript green door in the Gran Priorato, the walled compound of the Knights of Malta, sometimes snakes around Piazza dei Cavalieri di Malta, the enchanting view is worth the wait. Far across the city, you'll see the dome of St. Peter's Basilica flawlessly framed by the keyhole

and tidily trimmed hedges that lie just beyond the locked door. The priory and the square are the work of Giovanni Battista Piranesi, an 18th-century engraver who is more famous for etching Roman views than for orchestrating architecture, but he fancied himself a bit of an architect and did not disappoint.

Founded in the Holy Land during the Crusades, the Knights of Malta is the world's oldest and most exclusive order of chivalry. The knights amassed huge tracts of land in the Middle East and were based on the Mediterranean island of Malta from 1530 until 1798, when Napoléon expelled them. In 1834, they established themselves in Rome, where ministering to the sick became their raison d'être. ■ **TIP→ Private, guided tours of the Gran Priorato are usually offered on Friday morning, but you must prebook by email.** ⊠ *Via Santa Sabina and Via Porta Lavernale, Aventino* ✍ *visitorscentre@ orderofmalta.int* ⊕ *www.ordinedimaltaitalia.org/gran-priorato-di-roma* ☒ *From €5 per person (min. of 10 people), plus the cost of the required guide, €80 in Italian, €100 in any other language. If a group has already formed, then anyone may join for the regular entry fee* ⚄ *Reservations required* Ⓜ *Circo Massimo; Tram No. 3.*

★ Santa Maria in Cosmedin

CHURCH | **FAMILY** | One of Rome's oldest churches—built in the 6th century and restored in the late 19th century—is on the Piazza della Bocca della Verità, originally the location of the Forum Boarium, ancient Rome's cattle market and later the site of public executions. Although the church has a haunting interior and contains the flower-crowned skull of St. Valentine, who is celebrated every February 14th, it plays second fiddle to the renowned artifact installed out in its portico.

The Bocca della Verità (Mouth of Truth) is in reality nothing more than an ancient drain cover, unearthed during the Middle

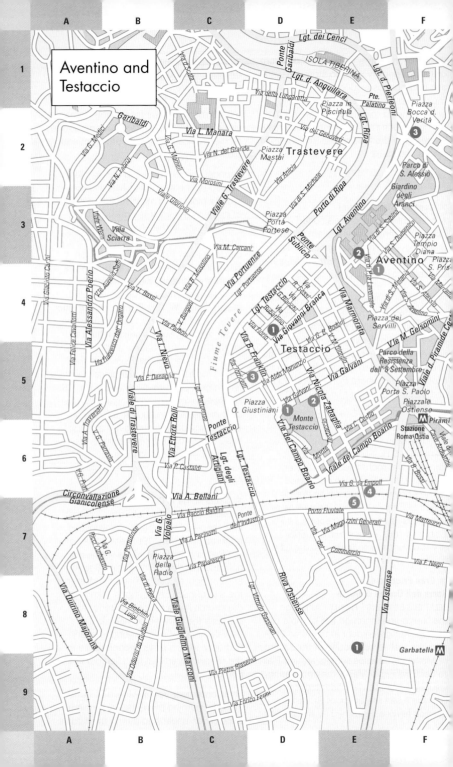

Aventino and Testaccio

A
B
C
D
E
F

1
2
3
4
5
6
7
8
9

Lgt. dei Cenci
ISOLA TIBERINA
Ponte Garibaldi
Lgt. d. Anguillara
Lgt. d. Pierleoni
Pte. Palatino
Via della Lungaretta
Via Arenula
Piazza in Piscinula
Piazza Bocca d. Verità ❸

Via G. Medici
Garibaldi
Via L. Manara
Via N. del Grande
Piazza Mastai
Trastevere
Parco di S. Alessio

Via M. Fanini
Via C. Manzini
Via Morosini
Viale G. Trastevere
Via Amicia
Via S. Michele
Porto di Ripa
Lgt. Aventino
Giardino degli Aranci

Viale Glorioso
Villa Sciarra
Viale G. Trastevere
Piazza Porta Portese
Ponte Sublicio
Via di S. Sabina
Via S. Domenico
Piazza Tempio Diana
Aventino ❷ ❶
Piazza S. Pris

Viale delle Mura Aurelie
Via Giacinto Carini
Via Alessandro Poerio
Via M. Carcani
Lgt. Portuense
Via Portuense
Lgt. Testaccio
Via Marmorata
Piazza dei Servilii

Via Felice Cavallotti
Via Francesco dell'Ongaro
Via T. Bassi
Via L. Bargoni
Via B. Franklin
Via Alardo
Via Giovanni Branca ❶
Testaccio
Via G. B. Bodoni
Via Galvani
V/le M. Gelsomini
Parco della Resistenza dell' 8 Settembre

Via A. Traversari
Viale di Trastevere
Via I. Nievo
Via F. Denaglia
Via Aldo Manunzio
Via Nicola Zabaglia
Piazza Porta S. Paolo
Piazzale Ostiense
Via d. Piramide Cestia

Via G. Sassi
Viale di Trastevere
Lgt. Portuense
Piazza O. Giustiniani
Via Galvani ❶
Monte Testaccio ❷
Via C. Cestio
M Piram

Circonvallazione Gianicolense
Via Ettore Rolli
Ponte Testaccio
Lgt. degli Argiani
Via del Campo Boario
Stazione Roma-Ostia

Via P. Castaldi
Via A. Bellani
Lgt. Testaccio
Viale del Campo Boario
Via G. da Empoli ❹

Via G. Volpato
Via Baccio Baldini
Ponte dell'Industria
Porto Fluviale ❺
Via Magazzini Generali
Via Matteucci

Via G. Chiabrera
Via Portuense
Via A. Pacinotti
Commercio
Via F. Negri

Via Quirino Majorana
Piazza della Radio
Via Papareschi
Riva Ostiense

Via Brichini Luigi
Viale Guglielmo Marconi
Lgt. Vittorio Gassman

Via Pietro Blaserna
Garbatella M ❶

Via Enrico Fermi

Fiume Tevere

Map Labels

Parco Traiano

M Colosseo

Colosseo

Viale Domus Aurea

MONTE PALATINO

Via Labicana

Via C. Vibenna

Via Ostia

Via C.d'Africa

ROMAN FORUM (FORO ROMANO)

Via di S. Gregorio

Parco del Celio

Via Annia

Circo Massimo

Via dei Cerchi

Basilica Santi Giovanni e Paolo

Via della Navicella

Piazza go la alfa

Via del Circo Massimo

Basilica di Santo Stefano Retondo

Via delle Terme di Diocleziano

Villa Celimontana

Via di Sant'Erasmo

Via Fonte di Fauno

M Circo Massimo

Via delle Terme di Caracalla

Piazzale Metronio

Viale Aventino

Parco di Porta Capena

Via Antoniana

Via Druso

Via S. Saba

Via B. Peruzzi

Viale Guido Baccelli

Via Via E. Rosa

Piazza L. Bernini

Viale Giotto

Via di Villa Pepoli

V.le Guido Baccelli

Via di Porta San Sebastiano

Viale di Porta Ardeatina

Via Guerrieri

Via Fabio L.Cilone

Via C. Baltrani

Viale di Porta Ardeatina

Via delle Terme di Caracalla

iazza dei artigiani

Viale Marco Polo

Via Gerolamo Dandini

Viale Odd. Beccari

Villa Osio

Piazzale 12 Ottobre 1492

Via Palos

Via Cristoforo Colombo

Via Antonio Pigafetta

Via Capitan Bavastro

Via della Moletta

Via P. Felter

Via Campania

Circonvallazione Ostiense

Via Caffaro

Via Ignazio Persico

Sights ▼

1 Centrale Montemartini.............**E8**
2 Gran Priorato di Roma dell'Ordine di Malta.................**E3**
3 Santa Maria in Cosmedin..........**F2**
4 Terme di Caracalla.................**H4**

Restaurants ▼

1 Checchino dal 1887.................**D5**
2 Flavio al Velavevodetto **D5**
3 La Torricella **C5**
4 Marigold **E6**
5 Porto Fluviale.......................**E7**

Quick Bites ▼

1 Trapizzino **D4**

Hotels ▼

1 Hotel San Anselmo **E4**

3

Rome AVENTINO AND TESTACCIO

KEY

1 Sights
1 Restaurants
1 Quick Bites
1 Hotels

0 —— 1,000 feet
0 —— 300 m

Ages. Legend has it, however, that the teeth will clamp down on a liar's hand if they dare to tell a fib while holding their fingers up to the fearsome mouth. Hordes of tourists line up to take the test every day (kids especially get a kick out of it). ✉ *Piazza della Bocca della Verità 18, Aventino* ☎ *06/6787759* 🌐 *www.cosmedin.org* [M] *Circo Massimo.*

Terme di Caracalla (*Baths of Caracalla*)
RUINS | FAMILY | The Terme di Caracalla are some of Rome's most massive—yet least visited—ruins. Begun in AD 206 by the emperor Septimius Severus and completed by his son, Caracalla, the 28-acre complex could accommodate 1,600 bathers at a time. Along with an Olympic-size swimming pool and baths, the complex also had two gyms, a library, and gardens. The impressive baths depended on slave labor, particularly the unseen stokers who toiled in subterranean rooms to keep the fires roaring in order to heat the water.

Rather than a simple dip in a tub, Romans turned "bathing" into one of the most lavish leisure activities imaginable. A bath began in the sudatoria, a series of small rooms resembling saunas, which then led to the caldarium, a circular room that was humid rather than simply hot. Here a strigil, or scraper, was used to get the dirt off the skin. Next stop: the warm(-ish) tepidarium, which helped start the cool-down process. Finally, it ended with a splash around the frigidarium, a chilly swimming pool.

Although some black-and-white mosaic fragments remain, most of the opulent mosaics, frescoes, and sculptures have found their way into Rome's museums. Nevertheless, the towering walls and sheer size of the ruins give one of the best glimpses into ancient Rome's ambitions. If you're here in summer, don't miss the chance to catch an open-air opera or ballet in the baths, put on by the Teatro dell'Opera di Roma. ✉ *Viale delle Terme di Caracalla 52, Aventino* ☎ *06/39967702* 🌐 *www.coopculture.it* 🎟 *€8 (includes Villa dei Quintili and Tomba di Cecilia Metella)* 🕒 *Closed Mon.* [M] *Circo Massimo.*

🍴 Restaurants

Checchino dal 1887
$$ | ROMAN | Literally carved into the side of a hill made up of ancient shards of amphorae, this upscale, family-run establishment has an exceptional wine cellar and stellar contemporary cocktails that incorporate traditional local ingredients. One of the first restaurants to open near Testaccio's (now long-closed) slaughterhouse, it still serves classic offal dishes—though the white-jacketed waiters are happy to suggest other options. **Known for:** old-school Roman cooking; old-school Roman waiters; coda alla vaccinara (Roman-style oxtail). [$] *Average main: €23* ✉ *Via di Monte Testaccio 30, Testaccio* ☎ *06/5743816* 🌐 *www.checchino-dal-1887.com* 🕒 *Closed Mon. and Tues., Aug., and 1 wk at Christmas* [M] *Piramide.*

★ **Flavio al Velavevodetto**
$$ | ROMAN | It's everything you're looking for in a true Roman eating experience: authentic, in a historic setting, and filled with Italians eating good food at good prices. In this very *romani di Roma* (Rome of the Romans) neighborhood, surrounded by discos and bars, you can enjoy classic local dishes, from vegetable antipasto to cacio e pepe (said to be the best version in the city) and lamb chops. **Known for:** authentic Roman atmosphere and food; outdoor covered terrace in summer; polpette di bollito (fried breaded meatballs). [$] *Average main: €16* ✉ *Via di Monte Testaccio 97, Testaccio* ☎ *06/5744194* 🌐 *www.ristorantevelavevodetto.it* [M] *Piramide.*

La Torricella
$$ | SEAFOOD | FAMILY | This family-run institution has been serving seafood in the working-class Testaccio neighborhood

for more than 40 years, and if you visit the local market early enough you might spot the owner selecting the freshest fish, which mainly arrives from Gaeta, south of Rome. The menu changes every day, but look for house specialties like *paccheri* (a very large, tubular pasta) with *totani* (baby calamari), pasta with *telline* (small clams), or the wondrously simple spaghetti with lobster. **Known for:** fresh, local seafood; relaxed but refined setting with outdoor seating; polpette di pesce al sugo (fish balls in tomato sauce). $ *Average main: €18* ✉ *Via Evangelista Torricelli 2/12, Testaccio* ☎ *06/5746311* ⊕ *www.la-torricella.com* ⊗ *Closed Mon.* Ⓜ *Piramide.*

★ Marigold

$ | **SCANDINAVIAN** | Run by a husband-and-wife team (she's Danish, he's Italian), this hip restaurant has a Scandinavian-meets-Italian design and menu. It draws a young, international crowd who come for the sourdough, cinnamon buns, and veggie-forward dishes. **Known for:** breads and other baked goods; weekend brunch; minimalist design. $ *Average main: €13* ✉ *Via Giovanni da Empoli 37, Testaccio* ☎ *06/87725679* ⊕ *marigoldroma.com* ⊗ *Closed Mon. and Tues., 3 wks in Aug., and 2 wks in Dec. No dinner* Ⓜ *Ostiense.*

Porto Fluviale

$ | **ITALIAN** | Set in a structure so massive that it takes up the better part of a block on a street that's gone from gritty clubland to popular nightspot, Porto Fluviale is a bar, café, pizzeria, lunch buffet, and lively evening restaurant. The menu is all-encompassing, too, with dishes that highlight cuisine from all over Italy. **Known for:** good cocktails; pizza from wood-burning oven; cicheti (Venetian-style tapas). $ *Average main: €13* ✉ *Via del Porto Fluviale 22, Testaccio* ☎ *06/5743199* ⊕ *www.portofluviale.com* Ⓜ *Piramide.*

 Coffee and Quick Bites

Trapizzino

$ | **ROMAN** | **FAMILY** | Stefano Callegari is one of Rome's most famous pizza makers, but at Trapizzino he's doing something a bit different. The name of the restaurant is derived from the Italian words for sandwich (*tramezzino*) and pizza, and the result is something like an upscale pizza pocket, stuffed on the spot with local specialties like chicken alla cacciatore, or *trippa* (tripe), or roast pumpkin, pecorino, and almonds. **Known for:** casual setting, with seating available next door; eggplant parmigiana and meatball sandwiches; Italian craft beer. $ *Average main: €5* ✉ *Via Giovanni Branca 88, Testaccio* ☎ *06/43419624* ⊕ *www.trapizzino.it* ⊗ *Closed 1 wk in Aug.* Ⓜ *Piramide.*

Hotels

Hotel San Anselmo

$ | **HOTEL** | Set in a *molto* charming garden atop the Aventine Hill, this refurbished 19th-century villa is a romantic retreat. **Pros:** free Wi-Fi; historic building with artful interior; garden where you can enjoy breakfast. **Cons:** some rooms are quite small; limited public transportation; no full restaurant. $ *Rooms from: €120* ✉ *Piazza San Anselmo 2, Aventino* ☎ *06/570057* ⊕ *www.aventinohotels.com/sananselmo* ⇥ *34 rooms* ⦿ *Free Breakfast* Ⓜ *Circo Massimo.*

Nightlife

★ Tram Depot

CAFÉS | A coffee stand by day and cocktail bar by night, this outdoor establishment began life as a city tram car back in 1903. Now the historic carriage has been converted to a kiosk permanently stationed on a park corner with retro tables and garden seating. A trendy crowd descends at sunset, and seats are at a premium until the wee hours of the morning. But since it is entirely outside,

Tram Depot is mainly open in the warmer months of the year (April through November). ⊠ *Via Marmorata 13, Testaccio* Ⓜ *Piramide.*

Shopping

★ Volpetti

FOOD | A Roman institution for 50 years, Volpetti sells excellent cured meats and salami from its buzzing deli counter. The rich aromas and flavors are captivating from the moment you enter the store. The food selection also includes genuine buffalo-milk mozzarella, fresh pasta, Roman pecorino, olive oils, balsamic vinegars, and fresh bread. It's also a great place for assembling gift baskets, and it offers worldwide shipping. ⊠ *Via Marmorata 47, Testaccio* ☎ *375/5130898* ⊕ *www.volpetti.com* Ⓜ *Piramide.*

Esquilino and Via Appia Antica

Esquilino, covering Rome's most sprawling hill—the Esquiline—lies at the edge of the tourist maps, near the Termini station. Today, culturally diverse inhabitants of different nationalities live and work in the area. It's not the cobblestone-street atmosphere that most think of when they think of Rome. Far south lies catacomb country—the haunts of the fabled underground graves of Rome's earliest Christians, arrayed to either side of the Queen of Roads, the Via Appia Antica (Appian Way). Strewn with classical ruins and dotted with grazing sheep, the road stirs images of chariots and legionnaires returning from imperial conquests. It was completed in 312 BC by Appius Claudius, who laid it out to connect Rome with settlements in the south, in the direction of Naples. Though time and vandals have taken their toll on the ancient relics along the road, the catacombs remain to cast their spirit-warm spell. Today, the dark,

gloomy catacombs contrast strongly with the Appia Antica's fresh air, verdant meadows, and evocative classical ruins.

GETTING HERE AND AROUND
The Esquilino Hill can be reached via the Vittorio Emanuele subway station, one stop from Termini station. Bus No. 150F runs from Piazza del Popolo to Esquilino.

The initial stretch of the Via Appia Antica is not pedestrian-friendly—there is fast, heavy traffic and no sidewalk all the way from Porta San Sebastiano to the Catacombe di San Callisto. To reach the catacombs, take Bus No. 218 from San Giovanni in Laterano. Alternatively, take Metro Line A to Colli Albani and then Bus No. 660 to the Tomba di Cecilia Metella.

Sights

Catacombe di San Callisto
(*Catacombs of St. Calixtus*)
CEMETERY | Burial place of several very early popes, this is Rome's oldest and best-preserved underground cemetery. One of the (English-speaking) friars who acts as custodian of the catacomb will guide you through its crypts and galleries, some adorned with early Christian frescoes. Watch out for wrong turns: this catacomb is five stories deep! ▪ TIP→ **This site has a large parking area and is favored by big groups; it can get busy.** ⊠ *Via Appia Antica 110, Via Appia Antica* ☎ *06/5130151* ⊕ *www.catacombe-sancallisto.it* 🎫 *€10* 🕐 *Closed Wed. and mid-Jan.–Feb.*

★ Catacombe di San Sebastiano
(*Catacombs of St. Sebastian*)
CEMETERY | The 4th-century church at this site was named after the saint who was buried in its catacomb, which burrows underground on four different levels. This was the only early Christian cemetery to remain accessible during the Middle Ages, and it was from here that the term "catacomb" is derived—it's in a spot where the road dips into a hollow, known to the Romans as a *catacumba* (Greek for

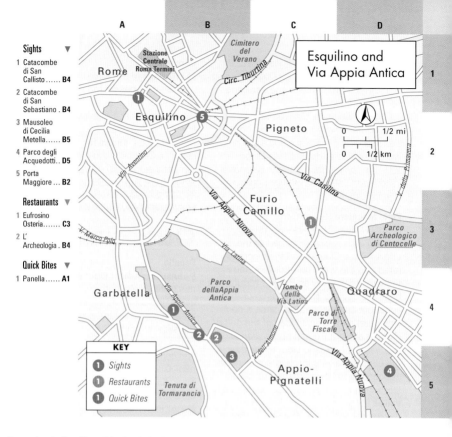

Sights ▼

1 Catacombe di San Callisto **B4**

2 Catacombe di San Sebastiano . **B4**

3 Mausoleo di Cecilia Metella **B5**

4 Parco degli Acquedotti .. **D5**

5 Porta Maggiore ... **B2**

Restaurants ▼

1 Eufrosino Osteria **C3**

2 L' Archeologia . **B4**

Quick Bites ▼

1 Panella **A1**

Esquilino and Via Appia Antica

KEY
- ① Sights
- ① Restaurants
- ① Quick Bites

"near the hollow"). ✉ *Via Appia Antica 136, Via Appia Antica* ☎ *06/7850350* ⊕ *www. catacombe.org* 🎟 *€10* ⊘ *Closed Dec.*

Mausoleo di Cecilia Metella

CEMETERY | For centuries, sightseers have flocked to this famous landmark, one of the most complete surviving tombs of ancient Rome. One of the many round mausoleums that once lined the Appian Way, this tomb is a smaller version of the Mausoleum of Augustus, but impressive nonetheless. It was the burial place of a Roman noblewoman: the wife of the son of Crassus, who was one of Julius Caesar's rivals and known as the richest man in the Roman Empire (infamously entering the English language as "crass").

The original decoration includes a frieze of bulls' skulls near the top. The travertine stone walls were made higher, and the medieval-style crenellations were added

when the tomb was transformed into a fortress by the Caetani family in the 14th century. An adjacent chamber houses a small museum with exhibits on the area's geological phases. Entrance to this site also includes access to the splendid Villa dei Quintili. ✉ *Via Appia Antica 161, Via Appia Antica* ☎ *06/7886254* ⊕ *www. parcoarcheologicoappiaantica.it* 🎟 *€8, includes all the sites in the Parco dell'Appia Antica (Villa dei Quintili, Antiquarium di Lucrezia Romana, Complesso di Capo di Bove, Tombe della Via Latina, and the Villa dei Setti Bassi)* ⊘ *Closed Mon.*

★ Parco degli Acquedotti

CITY PARK | FAMILY | This massive park, technically part of the Parco dell'Appia Antica, was named for the six remaining aqueducts that formed part of the famously elaborate system that carried water to ancient Rome. The park has some serious film cred: it was featured in the opening scene of *La Dolce Vita* and in a rather memorable scene depicting some avant-garde performance art in *La Grande Bellezza*. On weekends, it's a popular place for locals to picnic, exercise, and generally enjoy a day out with their kids or dogs. ⊠ *Via Lemonia 221, Via Appia Antica* ⊕ *www.parcodegliacquedotti.it* ⊇ *Free* Ⓜ *Giulio Agricola, Subaugusta.*

Porta Maggiore (*Great Gate*)
RUINS | FAMILY | The massive, 1st-century-AD arch was built as part of the original Aqua Claudia and then incorporated into the walls hurriedly erected in the late 3rd century as Rome's fortunes began to decline. The great arch of the aqueduct subsequently became a *porta* (city gate) and gives an idea of the grand scale of ancient Roman public works. On the Piazzale Labicano side, to the east, is the curious Baker's Tomb, erected in the 1st century BC by a prosperous baker (predating both the aqueduct and the city walls); it's shaped like an oven to signal the deceased's trade. The site is now in the middle of a public transport node and is close to Rome's first tram depot (going back to 1889). ⊠ *Piazza di Porta Maggiore, Esquilino* Ⓜ *Tram No. 5, 14, or 19.*

🍴 Restaurants

Eufrosino Osteria
$$ | ITALIAN | FAMILY | At this welcoming osteria run by three young owners, wood-paneled walls, terrazzo floors, and green pendant lamps evoke 1970s nostalgia. Romans come here to sample such regional dishes as Tuscan fried chicken or Sicilian-style fusilli with broccoli, pine nuts, raisins, and anchovies. **Known for:** regional Italian dishes; slow-food principles; neighboring pizzeria. Ⓢ *Average main: €16* ⊠ *Via di Tor Pignattara 188, Via Appia Antica* ☎ *348/5883932* ⊕ *www.facebook.com/EufrosinoRoma* ⊙ *Closed Tues.* Ⓜ *Malatesta, Porta Furba.*

L'Archeologia
$$ | ITALIAN | In this circa-1804 farmhouse you can dine beside the fireplace in cool weather or in the garden under age-old vines in summer. Specialties include fillet of beef in a hazelnut sauce and fresh seafood. **Known for:** ancient wine cellar La Cantina; hand-painted frescoes; romantic setting. Ⓢ *Average main: €24* ⊠ *Via Appia Antica 139, Via Appia Antica* ☎ *06/7880494* ⊕ *www.larcheologia.it* ⊙ *Closed Tues. No lunch weekdays.*

☕ Coffee and Quick Bites

Panella
$ | BAKERY | FAMILY | Opened in 1929, this bakery sells both sweet and savory items, including more than 70 types of bread. Line up for the pizza al taglio (by the slice) at lunchtime, or sit down at one of the outdoor tables for a cappuccino and cornetto or an aperitivo replete with mini sandwiches made on homemade buns. **Known for:** one of Rome's best bakeries; crostata, tartlets, and other sweet treats; espresso with zabaione. Ⓢ *Average main: €10* ⊠ *Via Merulana 54, Esquilino* ☎ *06/4872435* ⊕ *panellaroma.com* Ⓜ *Vittorio Emanuele.*

Chapter 4

VENICE

Updated by
Liz Humphreys

◉ Sights	🍴 Restaurants	🛏 Hotels	⊕ Shopping	🍸 Nightlife
★★★★★	★★★★☆	★★★★★	★★★☆☆	★★☆☆☆

WELCOME TO VENICE

TOP REASONS TO GO

★ **Cruising the Grand Canal:** The beauty of its palaces, enhanced by the play of light on the water, make a trip down Venice's "Main Street" unforgettable.

★ **Basilica di San Marco:** Don't miss the gorgeous mosaics inside—they're worth standing in line for.

★ **Santa Maria Gloriosa dei Frari:** Its austere, cavernous interior houses Titian's *Assumption*—one of the world's most beautiful altarpieces—plus several other spectacular art treasures.

★ **Gallerie dell'Accademia:** Legendary masterpieces of Venetian painting will overwhelm you in this fabled museum.

★ **Sipping wine and snacking at a bacaro:** For a sample of tasty local snacks and excellent Veneto wines in a uniquely Venetian setting, head for one of the city's many wine bars.

1 **San Marco.** The neighborhood at the center of Venice is filled with fashion boutiques, art galleries, and grand hotels.

2 **Dorsoduro.** This graceful residential area is home to renowned art galleries; the Campo Santa Margherita is a lively student hangout.

3 **San Polo and Santa Croce.** These bustling *sestieri* (districts) have all sorts of shops, several major churches, and the Rialto fish and produce markets.

4 **Cannaregio.** This sestiere has some of the sunniest open-air canal-side walks in town; the Jewish Ghetto has a fascinating history.

5 **Castello.** With its gardens, park, and narrow, winding walkways, it's the sestiere least influenced by Venice's tourist culture.

6 **San Giorgio Maggiore and Giudecca.** San Giorgio is graced with its magnificent namesake church, and Giudecca has wonderful views of Venice.

7 **Islands of the Lagoon.** Each island in Venice's northern lagoon has its own allure.

EATING AND DRINKING WELL IN VENICE

Pescheria (fish market)

The catchword in Venetian restaurants is "fish." How do you learn about the catch of the day? A visit to the Rialto's *pescheria* (fish market) is more instructive than any book, and when you're dining at a well-regarded restaurant, ask for a recommendation.

Traditionally, fish is served with a bit of salt, maybe some chopped parsley, and a drizzle of olive oil—no lemon; lemon masks the flavor. Ask for an entire wild-caught fish; it's much more expensive than its farmed cousin but certainly worth it. Antipasto may be prosciutto *di San Daniele* (from the Veneto region) or *sarde in saor* (fresh panfried sardines marinated with onions, raisins, and pine nuts). Risotto, cooked with shellfish or veggies, is a great first course. Pasta? Enjoy it with seafood: this is *not* the place to order spaghetti with tomato sauce. Other pillars of regional cooking include *pasta e fagioli* (thick bean soup with pasta); polenta, often with *fegato alla veneziana* (liver with onion); and that dessert invented in the Veneto, tiramisu.

GOING BACARO

You can sample regional wines and scrumptious *cicheti* (small snacks) in *bacari* (wine bars), a great Venetian tradition. Crostini and *polpette* (meat, fish, or vegetable croquettes) are popular cicheti, as are small sandwiches, seafood salads, *baccalà mantecato* (creamy, whipped salt cod), and toothpick-speared items like roasted peppers, marinated artichokes, and mozzarella balls.

SEAFOOD

Granseola (crab), *moeche* (tiny, locally caught soft-shell crabs), sweet *canoce* (mantis shrimp), *capelunghe* (razor clams), calamari, and *seppie* or *seppioline* (cuttlefish) are all prominently featured, as well as *rombo* (turbot), *branzino* (sea bass), *San Pietro* (John Dory), *sogliola* (sole), *orate* (gilthead bream), and *triglia* (mullet). Trademark dishes include sarde in saor, *frittura mista* (tempura-like fried fish and vegetables), and baccalà mantecato.

RISOTTO, PASTA, POLENTA

As a first course, Venetians favor the creamy rice dish risotto *all'onda* ("undulating," as opposed to firm), prepared with vegetables or shellfish. When pasta is served, it's generally accompanied by seafood sauces, too: *pasticcio di pesce* is lasagna-type pasta baked with fish, and *bigoli* is a strictly local whole-wheat pasta shaped like thick spaghetti, usually served *in salsa* (an anchovy-onion sauce with a dash of cinnamon), or with *nero di seppia* (cuttlefish-ink sauce). *Pasta e fagioli* is another classic first course, and polenta is a staple—served creamy or fried in wedges, generally as an accompaniment to stews or *seppie in nero* (cuttlefish in black ink).

Linguine with clam sauce

VEGETABLES

The larger islands of the lagoon are known for their legendary vegetables, such as the Sant'Erasmo *castraure*, sinfully expensive but heavenly tiny white artichokes that appear for a few days in spring. Spring treats include the fat white asparagus from neighboring Bassano or Verona, and artichoke bottoms (*fondi*), usually sautéed with olive oil, parsley, and garlic. From December to March the prized local radicchio *di Treviso* is grilled and frequently served with a bit of melted Taleggio cheese from Lombardy. Fall brings small wild mushrooms called *chiodini* and *zucca di Mantova,* a yellow squash with a gray-green rind used in soups, puddings, and ravioli stuffing.

SWEETS

Tiramisu lovers will have ample opportunity to sample this creamy delight made from ladyfingers soaked in espresso and rum or brandy and covered with mascarpone cream and cinnamon. Gelato, *sgroppino* (prosecco, vodka, and lemon sorbet), and *semifreddo* (soft homemade ice cream) are other sweets frequently seen on Venetian menus, as are almond cakes and dry cookies served with dessert wine. Try *focaccia veneziana,* a sweet raised cake made in the late fall and winter.

Tiramisu

Venice is often called La Serenissima, or "the most serene," a reference to the majesty, wisdom, and power of this city that was for centuries a leader in trade between Europe and Asia and a major center of European culture. Built on water by people who saw the sea as defender and ally, and who constantly invested in its splendor with magnificent architectural projects, Venice is a city unlike any other.

No matter how often you've seen it in photos and films, the real thing is more dreamlike than you could ever imagine. Its most notable landmarks, the Basilica di San Marco and the Palazzo Ducale, are exotic mixes of Byzantine, Romanesque, Gothic, and Renaissance styles, reflecting Venice's ties with the rest of Italy and with Constantinople to the east. Shimmering sunlight and silvery mist soften every perspective here; it's easy to understand how the city became renowned in the Renaissance for its artists' use of color. It's full of secrets, inexpressibly romantic, and frequently given over to pure, sensuous enjoyment.

You'll see Venetians going about their daily affairs in vaporetti, in the *campi* (squares), and along the *calli* (narrow streets). Despite their many challenges (including more frequent flooding and overcrowding), they are proud of their city and its history and are still quite helpful to those who show proper respect for Venice and its way of life.

Planning

Getting Oriented

Venice proper is quite compact, and you should be able to walk across it in a couple of hours, even counting a few minutes for getting lost. Vaporetti will save wear and tear on tired feet but won't always save you much time.

Venice is divided into six sestieri: Cannaregio, Castello, Dorsoduro, San Marco, San Polo, and Santa Croce. More sedate outer islands float around them—San Giorgio Maggiore and Giudecca just to the south; beyond them the Lido, the barrier island; and to the north, Murano, Burano, and Torcello.

Getting Here and Around

AIR
CONTACT Aeroporto Marco Polo.
☎ *041/2609260* ⊕ *www.veniceairport.it.*

LAND TRANSFERS
CONTACT ATVO. ☎ *0421/5944* ⊕ *www.atvo.it.*

WATER TRANSFERS
From Marco Polo terminal, it's a mostly covered seven-minute walk to the dock where boats depart for Venice's historic center. The ride is in a closed boat so you won't get much of a view; plus, it's more expensive and generally slower than the bus to Piazzale Roma (unless your hotel is near a boat station).

CONTACT Alilaguna. ☎ *041/2401701* ⊕ *www.alilaguna.it.*

CAR
Venice is at the end of the SR11, just off the east–west A4 autostrada. There are no cars in Venice; if possible, return your rental when you arrive.

A warning: don't be waylaid by illegal touts, often wearing fake uniforms, who try to flag you down and offer to arrange parking and hotels; use one of the established garages, mainly clustered at Piazzale Roma. Consider reserving a space in advance. The **Autorimessa Comunale** (☎ *041/2722394* ⊕ *avm.avmspa.it*) costs €30 for 24 hours with online reservations. **Garage San Marco** (☎ *041/5232213* ⊕ *parclick.it*) costs €18 from 5 pm to 5 am, and €45 for 24 hours with online reservations. For brief stays, opt for **Parcheggio Sant'Andrea** (☎ *041/2722384* ⊕ *avm.avmspa.it*), where up to two hours costs €7. On its own island, **Isola del Tronchetto** (☎ *041/5207555* ⊕ *www.tronchettoparking.it*) charges €25 for 24 hours. Watch for signs coming over the bridge—you turn right just before Piazzale Roma.

Many hotels and the casino have guest discounts with the San Marco or Tronchetto garages. A perfectly convenient alternative is to park in Mestre, on the mainland, and take a train (10 minutes, €1.40) or bus into Venice. The garage across from the station and the Bus 2 stop costs €22 for up to 24 hours.

PUBLIC TRANSPORTATION
WATER BUSES
CONTACT ACTV. ☎ *041/041041* ⊕ *www.actv.it.*

WATER TAXIS
A *motoscafo* isn't cheap: you'll spend about €70 for a short trip in town, €90 to the Lido, and €100 or more per hour to visit the outer islands. It is strongly suggested to book through the **Consorzio Motoscafi Venezia** (☎ *041/2406712 Mon.–Fri. 9 am–6 pm, Sat. 9 am–4 pm; 041/5222303 Mon.–Fri. 6 pm–9 am, Sat. 4 pm–6 pm, Sun. and holidays 9 am–4 pm* ⊕ *www.motoscafivenezia.com*) to avoid an argument with your driver over prices. A water taxi can carry up to 10 passengers, with an additional charge of €10 per person for more than four people, so if you're traveling in a group, it may not be that much more expensive than a vaporetto.

TRAIN
Venice has rail connections with many major cities in Italy and Europe. Note that Venice's train station is **Venezia Santa Lucia,** not to be confused with Venezia Mestre, which is the mainland stop prior to arriving in the historic center. Some trains don't continue beyond the Mestre station; in such cases you can catch the next Venice-bound train. Get a ticket on the Trenitalia app or a paper ticket from the kiosk on the platform and validate it (in the yellow time-stamp machine) to avoid a fine.

Making the Most of Your Time

The hordes of tourists here are legendary, especially in spring and fall but during other seasons, too—there's really no "off-season" in Venice. Unfortunately, tales of impassable tourist-packed streets and endless queues to get into the Basilica di San Marco are not exaggerated. A little bit of planning, however, will help you avoid the worst of the crowds.

Most tourists do little more than take the vaporetto down the Grand Canal to Piazza San Marco, see the piazza and the basilica, and walk up to the Rialto and back to the station. You'll want to visit these areas, too, but do so in the early morning, before most tourists have finished their breakfast cappuccinos. Because many tourists are other Italians who come for a weekend outing, you can further decrease your competition for Venice's pleasures by choosing to visit the city on weekdays.

Away from San Marco and the Rialto, the streets and quays of Venice's beautiful medieval and Renaissance residential districts receive only a moderate amount of traffic. Besides the Grand Canal and the Piazza San Marco, and perhaps Torcello, the other historically and artistically important sites are seldom overcrowded. Even on weekends you probably won't have to queue up for the Gallerie dell'Accademia.

Restaurants

Dining options in Venice range from ultra-high-end establishments, where jackets are required, to very casual eateries. Once staunchly traditional, many restaurants have revamped their dining rooms and their menus, creating dishes that blend classic elements with ingredients and methods less common to the region. Mid- and upper-range restaurants often offer innovative options as well as mainstays like sarde in saor and fegato alla veneziana.

Unfortunately, Venice also has its share of overpriced, mediocre eateries. Restaurants catering to tourists have little motivation to maintain quality since most diners are one-time patrons. You are better off at a restaurant frequented by locals, who are interested in the food, not the views. Avoid places with cajoling waiters outside, as well as those that don't display their prices or have showy tourist menus translated into a dozen languages. For the same €15–€20 you'd spend at such places, you could do better at a bacaro making a meal of cicheti.

Hotels

Venetian magic lingers when you retire for the night, whether you're staying in a grand hotel or budget *locanda* (inn). Hotels usually occupy very old buildings, often without elevators or lounge areas. It's not at all unusual for each room to be different, even on the same floor: windows overlooking charming canals and bleak alleyways are both common. Venice is one of the most popular destinations on Earth—so book your lodging as far in advance as possible.

In terms of location, the area in and around San Marco is the most crowded and expensive. Still convenient but more tranquil areas include Dorsoduro, Santa Croce, and Cannaregio (though the area around the train station can be hectic), or even Castello in the area beyond the Pietà church. Also take into consideration the proximity of a vaporetto stop, especially if you have heavy baggage. Regardless of where you stay, it's essential that you have detailed directions to your hotel: note not only its street address but also its sestiere as well as a nearby landmark or two. Even if you arrive by water taxi, you may still have a bit of a walk.

⇨ *Hotel and restaurant reviews have been shortened. For full information, visit Fodors.com. Prices in the lodging reviews are the lowest cost of a standard double room in high season. Prices in the dining reviews are the average cost of a main course at dinner, or, if dinner is not served, at lunch.*

What It Costs in Euros			
$	$$	$$$	$$$$
HOTELS			
under €125	€125–€200	€201–€300	over €300
RESTAURANTS			
under €15	€15–€24	€25–€35	over €35

Nightlife

Nightlife offerings in Venice are, even by rather sedate standards, fairly tame. Most bars must close by midnight, especially those that offer outdoor seating. Piazza San Marco is a popular meeting place in nice weather, when the cafés stay open relatively late and all seem to compete to offer the best live music. The younger crowd, Venetians and visitors alike, tend to gravitate toward the area around the Ponte di Rialto, with Campi San Bartolomeo and San Luca on one side and Campo Rialto Nuovo on the other. Especially popular with university students and young people from the mainland are the bars around Campo Santa Margherita.

Passes and Discounts

Avoid lines and hassle with the online **Venezia Unica City Pass** (⊕ *www.veneziaunica.it*). This all-in-one pass can be used for public transportation and entry to museums, churches, and other attractions; you only pay for the services you wish to add. You'll receive an email with the pass, which you can show for entry at sights, though you'll still need to physically collect your transportation pass at an ACTV automatic ticket machine or ticket point located around the city.

Fifteen of Venice's most significant churches covered by the Venezia Unica City Pass are part of the **Chorus Foundation** umbrella group (☎ *041/2750462* ⊕ *www.chorusvenezia.org*), which coordinates their administration, hours, and admission fees. Churches in this group are open to visitors all day except Sunday morning. Single church entry costs €3; you have a year to visit all 15 with the €12 Chorus Pass, which you can get at any participating church or online.

The Museum Pass (€40) from **Musei Civici** (☎ *041/2405211* ⊕ *www.visitmuve.it/en/tickets*) includes single entry to 11 Venice city museums for six months.

Performing Arts

Visit ⊕ *www.agendavenezia.org* for a preview of musical, artistic, and sporting events. *Venezia News* (*VENews*), available at newsstands, has similar information but also includes in-depth articles about noteworthy events. The tourist office publishes a handy, free quarterly *Calendar* in Italian and English, listing daily events and current museum and venue hours. *Venezia da Vivere* (⊕ *www.veneziadavivere.com/en*) is a seasonal guide listing cool cultural happenings and places. And don't ignore the posters you see plastered on the walls as you walk—often they contain the most up-to-date information you can find.

⇨ *For more information on festivals in Venice, see On the Calendar in Travel Smart.*

CARNEVALE

Although Carnevale has traditionally been associated with the time leading up to the Roman Catholic period of Lent, it originally started out as a principally secular annual period of partying and feasting to celebrate Venice's victory over Ulrich II, Patriarch of Aquileia, in 1162. To commemorate the annual tribute Ulrich was forced to pay, a bull and 12 pigs were slaughtered in Piazza San Marco each year on the day before Lent. Since then, the city has marked the days preceding *Quaresima* (Lent) with abundant feasting and wild celebrations. The word *carnevale* is derived from the words *carne* (meat) and *levare* (to remove), as eating meat was restricted during Lent. The use of masks for Carnevale was first mentioned in 1268, and its direct association with Lent was not made until the end of the 13th century.

Venice earned its international reputation as the "city of Carnevale" in the 18th century, when partying would begin several months before Lent and the city seemed to be one continuous masquerade. During this time, income from tourists became a major source of funds in La Serenissima's coffers. With the Republic's fall in 1797, Carnevale was prohibited by the French and the Austrians. From Italian reunification in 1866 until the fall of Fascism in the 1940s, the event was alternately allowed or banned, depending on the government's stance.

It was revived for good in the 1970s, when residents began taking to the calli and campi in their own impromptu celebrations. It didn't take long for the tourist industry to embrace Carnevale as a means to stimulate business in low season. And their faith is well placed: each year over the 10- to 12-day Carnevale period (ending on the Tuesday before Ash Wednesday), more than a half-million people attend concerts, theater and street performances, masquerade balls, historical processions, fashion shows, and contests. Since 2008 Carnevale has been organized by **Venezia Marketing & Eventi** (⊕ *www.carnevale.venezia.it*). Stop by any tourist office (☎ *041/2424* ⊕ *www. veneziaunica.it*) for information, but be aware it can be mobbed. If you're not planning on joining in the revelry, you'd be wise to choose another time to visit Venice. Crowds throng the streets (which become one-way, with police directing foot traffic), bridges are designated "no-stopping" zones to avoid gridlock, and prices skyrocket.

Shopping

Alluring shops abound in Venice. You'll find countless vendors of such trademark wares as glass, lace, and high-end textiles. The authenticity of some goods can be suspect, but they're often pleasing to the eye, regardless of origin. You will also find interesting craft and art studios with high-quality, one-of-a-kind articles. Antiques, especially antique Venetian glass, are almost invariably cheaper outside of Venice, because Venetians are ready to pay high prices for their own heritage.

The San Marco area is full of shops and couture boutiques, such as Armani, Missoni, Valentino, Fendi, and Versace. Leading from Piazza San Marco, you'll find some of Venice's busiest shopping streets—Le Mercerie, the Frezzeria, Calle dei Fabbri, and Calle Larga XXII Marzo. Other good shopping areas surround Calle del Teatro and Campi San Salvador, Manin, San Fantin, and San Bartolomeo. You can find somewhat less expensive, more varied, and more imaginative shops between the Ponte di Rialto and San Polo and in Santa Croce, and art galleries in Dorsoduro from the Salute to the Accademia. Regular store hours are usually 9 to 12:30 and 3:30 or 4 to 7:30; some stores close Saturday afternoon or Monday morning.

Tours

Venice has a variety of tours with expert guides; just be sure to choose a guide that's authorized if you book a private tour. Some excursions also include a boat tour as a portion of a longer walking tour. And, of course, a gondola ride is always an excellent way to take in the sights of the city.

GONDOLA RIDES
The best location to hire a gondola depends on your preference. For a waterside view of Grand Canal palaces, board a boat at one of the main gondola stations, such as Santa Maria del Giglio or San Toma. For a quieter experience, start your tour from a peaceful *fondamenta* (quay) in Cannaregio or Castello, like the Fondamenta S. Severo. The price of a 40-minute ride is €80 for up to six passengers, increasing to €100 between 7 pm and 8 am. Every 20 minutes extra is an additional €40. ■TIP→ **Agree with your gondolier on price and duration of the ride beforehand to avoid confusion and unexpected costs.**

PRIVATE TOURS
A Guide in Venice
GUIDED TOURS | This popular company offers a wide variety of innovative, entertaining, and informative themed tours—including master artisan, art, and architecture tours—for private groups of up to eight people. Guided tours generally last two to three hours, with a fee of €85 per hour, which does not include admissions or transportation fees. ☎ *0348/5927974* ⊕ *www.aguideinvenice.com.*

See Venice
GUIDED TOURS | Luisella Romeo is a delightful guide capable of bringing to life even the most convoluted aspects of Venice's art and history. She can customize tours depending on guests' areas of interest, including Murano and glass art, music in Venice, and photography tours. ☎ *0349/0848303* ⊕ *www.seevenice.it.*

Walks Inside Venice
GUIDED TOURS | For a host of particularly creative group and private tours—from history to art to gastronomy—check out Walks Inside Venice. The maximum group size is six, and tour guides include people with advanced university degrees and published authors. ☎ *0347/2530560, 0335/5229714* ⊕ *www.walksinside-venice.com.*

Visitor Information

The multilingual staff of the Venice tourism office (☎ *041/2424* ⊕ *www.veneziaunica.it*) can provide directions and up-to-the-minute information. Branches can be found at Marco Polo Airport; the Venezia Santa Lucia train station; Garage Comunale, on Piazzale Roma; and at Piazza San Marco near Museo Correr at the southwest corner. The train station branch is open daily 8 am–6:30 pm; other branches have similar hours.

San Marco

Extending from Piazza San Marco (St. Mark's Square) to the Ponte di Rialto, this sestiere is the historical and commercial heart of Venice. Restaurants in its eponymous square—the only one in Venice given full stature as a "piazza" and, hence, often referred to simply as "the Piazza"—heave with tourists, but enjoying an *aperitivo* (pre-dinner drink) here is an unforgettable experience.

This sestiere is also graced with some of Venice's loveliest churches, best-endowed museums, and finest hotels (often with Grand Canal views). In addition, it's the city's main shopping district. Some of the famous Venetian glass producers from Murano have boutiques in San Marco, as do many Italian designers. Its mazes of streets are also lined with shops that sell elegantly wrought jewelry among other items.

TIMING

You can easily spend several days seeing the historical and artistic monuments in and around Piazza San Marco alone, but at a bare minimum, plan on at least an hour for the basilica and its wonderful mosaics. Add on another half hour if you want to see its Pala d'Oro, Galleria, and Museo di San Marco. You'll want at least an hour to appreciate the Palazzo Ducale. Leave another hour for the Museo Correr, through which you also enter the archaeological museum and the Libreria Sansoviniana. If you choose to simply take in the piazza itself from a café table at an establishment with an orchestra, keep in mind there will be an additional charge for the music.

Sights

★ Basilica di San Marco

(*St. Mark's Basilica*)

CHURCH | The Basilica di San Marco is not only the religious center of a great city, but also an expression of the political, intellectual, and economic aspiration and accomplishments of a place that, for centuries, was at the forefront of European culture. It is a monument not just to the glory of God, but also to the glory of Venice. The basilica was the doges' personal chapel, linking its religious function to the political life of the city, and was endowed with all the riches the Republic's admirals and merchants could carry off from the Orient (as the Byzantine Empire was then known), earning it the nickname "Chiesa d'Oro" (Golden Church). When the present church was begun in the 11th century, rare colored marbles and gold-leaf mosaics were used in its decoration. The 12th and 13th centuries were a period of intense military expansion, and by the early 13th century, the facades began to bear testimony to Venice's conquests, including gilt-bronze ancient Roman horses taken from Constantinople in 1204.

The glory of the basilica is, of course, its medieval mosaic work; about 30% of the mosaics survive in something close to their original form. The earliest date from the late 12th century, but the great majority date from the 13th century. The taking of Constantinople in 1204 was a deciding moment for the mosaic decoration of the basilica. Large amounts of mosaic material were brought in, and a Venetian school of mosaic decoration began to develop. Moreover, a 4th- or 5th-century treasure—the Cotton Genesis, the earliest illustrated Bible—was brought from Constantinople and supplied the designs for the exquisite mosaics of the Creation and the stories of Abraham, Joseph, and Moses that adorn the narthex (entrance hall). They are among the most beautiful and best preserved in all the basilica.

Remember that this is a sacred place: guards may deny admission to people in shorts, sleeveless dresses, and tank tops. ⊠ *Piazza San Marco, San Marco 328, San Marco* ☎ *041/2708311* ⊕ *www. basilicasanmarco.it* ✉ *Standard tickets: Basilica €3, Pala d'Oro €5, museum and Loggia dei Cavalli €7, bell tower €10. Skip-the-line tickets: Basilica €6, Pala d'Oro €12, museum and Loggia dei Cavalli €15, full ticket (Basilica, museum, Loggia dei Cavalli) €20, bell tower €12* Ⓜ *Vaporetto: Zaccaria, Vallaresso.*

Campanile di San Marco

(*St. Mark's Bell Tower*)

VIEWPOINT | Construction of Venice's famous brick bell tower (325 feet tall, plus the angel) began in the 9th century; it took on its present form in 1514. During the 15th century, the tower was used as a place of punishment: immoral clerics were suspended in wooden cages from the tower, some forced to subsist on bread and water for as long as a year; others were left to starve. In 1902, the tower unexpectedly collapsed, taking with it Jacopo Sansovino's marble loggia (1537–49) at its base. The largest original

Continued on page 160

CRUISING THE GRAND CANAL

THE BEST INTRODUCTION TO VENICE IS A TRIP DOWN MAIN STREET

Venice's Grand Canal is one of the world's great thoroughfares. It winds its way from Piazzale Roma to Piazza San Marco, passing 200 palazzi built from the 13th to the 18th centuries by Venice's richest and most powerful families. There's a theatrical quality to a boat ride on the canal: it's as if each pink- or gold-tinted facade is trying to steal your attention from its rival across the way.

In medieval and Renaissance cities, wars and sieges required defense to be an element of design; but in rich, impregnable Venice, you could safely show off what you had. But more than being simply an item of conspicuous consumption, a Venetian's palazzo was an embodiment of his person—not only his wealth, but also his erudition and taste.

The easiest and cheapest way to see the Grand Canal is to take the Line 1 *vaporetto* (water bus) from Piazalle Roma to San Marco. The ride takes about 35 minutes. Invest in a day ticket and you can spend the better part of a day hopping on and off at the vaporetto's many stops, visiting the sights along the banks. Keep your eyes open for the highlights listed here; some have fuller descriptions later in this chapter.

FROM PIAZZALE ROMA TO RIALTO

Palazzo Labia
Tiepolo's masterpiece, the cycle of Antony and Cleopatra, graces the grand ballroom in this palazzo. The Labia family, infamous for their ostentation, commissioned the frescos to celebrate a marriage and had Tiepolo use the face of the family matriarch, Maria Labia, for that of Cleopatra. Luckily, Maria Labia was known not only for her money, but also for her intelligence and her beauty.

Santa Maria di Nazareth

Ponte di Scalzi

R. DI BIASIO

Stazione Ferrovia Santa Lucia

FERROVIA

SANTA CROCE

Ponte di Calatrava

After you pass the Ferrovia, the baroque church immediately to your left is the baroque **Santa Maria di Nazareth**, called the Chiesa degli Scalzi (Church of the Barefoot).

After passing beneath the Ponte di Scalzi, ahead to the left, where the Canale di Cannaregio meets the Grand Canal, you'll spy **Palazzo Labia**, an elaborate 18th-century palace built for the social-climbing Labia family.

Known for their ostentation even in this city where modesty was seldom a virtue, the Labias chose a location that required three facades instead of the usual one.

A bit farther down, across the canal, is the 13th-century **Fondaco dei Turchi**, an elegant residence that served as a combination commercial center and ghetto for the Turkish community. Try not to see the side towers and the crenellations; they were

added during a 19th-century restoration.

Beyond it is the obelisk-topped **Ca' Belloni-Battagia**, designed for the Belloni family by star architect Longhena. Look for the family crest he added prominently on the facade.

On the opposite bank is architect Mauro Codussi's magnificent **Palazzo Vendramin-Calergi**, designed just before 1500. Codussi ingeniously married the fortress-like Renaissance style of the Florentine Alberti's Palazzo Rucellai to the lacy delicacy of the Venetian Gothic, creating the prototype of the Venetian Renaissance palazzo. The palazzo is now Venice's casino.

Palazzo Vendramin-Calergi
Venice's first Renaissance palazzo. Immediately recognized as a masterpiece, it was so highly regarded that later, when its subsequent owners, the Calergi, were convicted of murder and their palace was to be torn down as punishment, the main building was spared.

Ca' d'Oro
Inspired by stories of Nero's Domus Aurea (Golden House) in Rome, the first owner had parts of the facade gilded with 20,000 sheets of gold leaf. The gold has long worn away, but the Ca' D'Oro is still Venice's most beautiful Gothic palazzo.

Ca' da Mosto
Venice's oldest surviving palazzo gives you an idea of Marco Polo's Venice. More than any other Byzantine palazzo in town, it maintains its original 13th-century appearance.

GHETTO

S. MARCUOLA

Ca' Belloni-Battagia

S. STAE

Ca' Pesaro

Fondaco dei Turchi

Depositi del Megio

San Stae Church

SAN POLO

Ca' Corner della Regina

CA' D'ORO

Pescheria
Stop by in the morning to see the incredible variety of fish for sale. Produce stalls fill the adjacent fondamenta. Butchers and cheesemongers occupy the surrounding shops.

Rialto Mercato

Fondaco dei Tedeschi

Ca' dei Camerlenghi

RIALTO

SAN MARCO

The whimsically Baroque church of **San Stae** on the right bank is distinguished by a host of marble saints on its facade.

Farther along the bank is one of Longhena's Baroque masterpieces, **Ca' Pesaro**. It is now the Museum of Modern Art.

Next up on the left is **Ca' d'Oro** (1421-1438), the canal's most spendid example of Venetian Gothic domestic design. Across from this palazzo is the loggia of the neo-Gothic *pescheria*, Venice's fish market.

Slightly farther down, on the bank opposite from the vegetable market, is the early 13th-century **Ca' da Mosto**, the oldest building on the Grand Canal. The upper two floors are later additions, but the ground floor and piano nobile give you a good idea of a rich merchant's house during the time of Marco Polo.

As you approach the Rialto Bridge, to the left, just before the bridge, is the

Fondaco dei Tedeschi. German merchants kept warehouses, offices, and residences here; its facade was originally frescoed by Titian and Giorgione.

FROM RIALTO TO THE PONTE DELL' ACCADEMIA

SAN POLO

Ponte di Rialto

△ RIALTO

Ca' Foscari
The canal's most imposing Gothic masterpiece, Ca' Foscari was built to blot out the memory of a traitor to the Republic.

Palazzo Barzizza

Ca' Loredan

S. SILVESTRO △

Ca' Farsetti

Palazzo Pisani Moretta

Ca' Grimani

S. ANGELO

TOMA △

Ca' Garzoni

Ca' Balbi

Palazzo Grassi

Ca' Rezzonico

SAN MARCO

REZZONICO △

ACCADEMIA △

Gallerie dell'Accademia

DORSODURO

The shop-lined **Ponte di Rialto** was built in stone after former wooden bridges had burned or collapsed. As you pass under the bridge, on your left stands star architect Sansovino's Palazzo Dolfin Manin. The white stone–clad Renaissance palace was built at huge expense and over the objections of its conservative neighbors.

A bit farther down stand **Ca' Loredan** and **Ca' Farsetti**, 13th-century Byzantine palaces that today make up Venice's city hall.

Along the same side is the **Ca' Grimani**, by the Veronese architect Sanmichele. Legend has it that the palazzo's oversized windows were demanded by the young Grimani's fiancée, who insisted that he build her a palazzo on the Canale Grande with windows larger than the portal of her own house.

At the Sant'Angelo landing, the vaporetto passes close to Codussi's **Ca' Corner-Spinelli**. Back on the right bank, in a lovely salmon color, is the graceful **Palazzo Pisani Moretta**, built in the mid-15th century and typical of the Venetian Gothic palazzo of the generation after the Ca' D'Oro.

A bit farther down the right bank, crowned by obelisks, is **Ca' Balbi**. Niccolò Balbi built this elegant palazzo in order to upstage his former landlord, who had insulted him in public.

Farther down the right bank, where the Canale makes a sharp turn, is the imposing **Ca' Foscari**. Doge Francesco Foscari tore down an earlier palazzo on this spot and built this splendid palazzo to erase memory of the traitorous former owner. It is now the seat of the University of Venice.

Continuing down the right bank you'll find Longhena's **Ca' Rezzonico**, a magnificent baroque palace. Opposite stands the Grand Canal's youngest palace, Giorgio Massari's **Palazzo Grassi**, commissioned in 1749. It houses part of the François Pinot contemporary art collection.

Near the canal's fourth bridge, is the former church and monastery complex that houses the world-renowned **Gallerie dell'Accademia**, the world's largest and most distinguished collection of Venetian art.

ARCHITECTURAL STYLES ALONG THE GRAND CANAL

BYZANTINE: 13th century
Distinguishing characteristics: high, rounded arches, relief panels, multicolored marble.
Examples: Fondaco dei Turchi, Ca' Loredan, Ca' Farsetti, Ca' da Mosto

GOTHIC: 14th and 15th centuries
Distinguishing characteristics: pointed arches, high ceilings, and many windows.
Examples: Ca' d'Oro, Ca' Foscari, Palazzo Pisani Moretta, Ca' Barbaro (and, off the canal, Palazzo Ducale)

RENAISSANCE: 16th century
Distinguishing characteristics: classically influenced emphasis on harmony and motifs taken from classical antiquity.

Examples: Palazzo Vendramin-Calergi, Ca' Grimani, Ca' Corner-Spinelli, Ca' dei Camerlenghi, Ca' Balbi, Palazzo Corner della Ca' Granda, Palazzo Dolfin Manin, and, off the canal, Libreria, Sansoviniana on Piazza San Marco

BAROQUE: 17th century
Distinguishing characteristics: Renaissance order wedded with a more dynamic style, achieved through curving lines and complex decoration.

Examples: churches of Santa Maria di Nazareth, San Stae, and Santa Maris della Salute; Ca' Belloni Battaglia, Ca' Pesaro, Ca' Rezzonico

FROM THE PONTE DELL'ACCADEMIA TO SAN ZACCARIA

Ca' Barbaro
John Singer Sargent, Henry James, and Cole Porter are among the guests who have stayed at Ca' Barbaro. It was a center for elegant British and American society during the turn of the 20th century.

Santa Maria Della Salute
Baldessare Longhena was only 26 when he designed this church, which was to become one of Venice's major landmarks. Its rotunda form and dynamic Baroque decoration predate iconic Baroque churches in other Italian cities.

SAN MARCO

Ponte dell' Accademia

Ca' Pisani-Gritti

Palazzo Corner della Ca' Granda

ACCADEMIA

Casetta Rossa

S. M. DEL GIGLIO

DORSODURO

Ca' Barbarigo

SALUTE

Palazzo Salviati

Palazzo Venier dei Leoni
Eccentric art dealer Peggy Guggenheim's personal collection of modern art is here. At the Grand Canal entrance to the palazzo stands Marino Marini's sexually explicit equestrian sculpture, the Angel of the Citadel. Numerous entertaining stories have been spun around the statue and Ms. Guggenheim's overtly libertine ways.

S. Maria della Salute

Ca' Dario
Graceful and elegant Ca' Dario is reputed to carry a curse. Almost all its owners since the 15th century have met violent deaths or committed suicide. It was, nevertheless, a center for elegant French society at the turn of the 20th century.

Down from the Accademia Bridge, on the left bank next door to the fake Gothic Ca' Franchetti, is the beautiful **Ca' Barbaro**, designed by Giovanni Bon, who was also at work about that time on the Ca' D'Oro.

Farther along on the left bank Sansovino's first work in Venice, the **Palazzo Corner della Ca' Granda**, begun in 1533, still shows the influence of his Roman Renaissance contemporaries, Bramante and Giulio Romano. It faces the uncompleted **Palazzo Venier dei Leoni**, which holds the Peggy Guggenheim Collection, a good

cross-section of the visual arts from 1940 to 1960.

Ca' Dario a bit farther down, was originally a Gothic palazzo, but in 1487 it was given an early Renaissance multicolored marble facade.

At this point on the canal the cupola of **Santa Maria della Salute** dominates the scene. The commission for the design of the church to celebrate the Virgin's

rescuing Venice from the disastrous plague of 1630, was given to the 26-year-old Longhena. The young architect stressed the new and inventive aspects of his design, likening the rotunda shape to a crown for the Virgin.

Basilica di S. Marco

PIAZZA SAN MARCO

Palazzo Ducale

S. ZACCARIA

VALLARESSO

Palazzo Dandolo a San Moise

Punta della Dogana

The Grand Canal is 2½ miles long, has an average depth of 9 feet, and is 76 yards wide at its broadest point and 40 yards at its narrowest.

SAN GIORGI MAGGIORE

Across from the Salute, enjoying the magnificent view across the canal, are a string of luxury hotels whose historic facades have either been radically modified or are modern neo-Gothic fantasies. The main interest here is the rather unimposing Hotel Monaco e Gran Canal, the former Palazzo Dandolo a San Moise, which contains Europe's first casino, the famous ridotto, founded in 1638. It was a stomping ground of Casanova, and was closed by the Republic in 1774 because too much money was being lost to foreigners.

At the **Punta della Dogana** on the tip of Dorsoduro, Japanese architect Tadao Ando, using Zen-inspired concepts of space, has transformed a 17th–century customs house into a museum for contemporary art. It is a fitting coda to the theme of Venice as living center for international artistic creativity, as set by Calatrava's bridge at the beginning of the Grand Canal.

At the Vallaresso vaporetto stop you've left the Grand Canal, but stay on board for a view of the **Palazzo Ducale**, with **Basilica di San Marco** behind it, then disembark at San Zaccaria.

Let's Get Lost

Getting around Venice presents some unusual problems: the city's layout has few straight lines; house numbering seems nonsensical; and the six sestieri of San Marco, Cannaregio, Castello, Dorsoduro, Santa Croce, and San Polo all duplicate each other's street names. What's more, addresses in Venice are given by sestiere rather than street, making them of limited help in getting around. Venetians commonly give directions by pinpointing a major landmark, such as a church, and telling you where to go from there.

The numerous vaporetto lines can be bewildering, too, and often the only option for getting where you want to go is to walk. Yellow signs, posted on many busy corners, point toward the major landmarks—San Marco, Rialto, Accademia, and so forth—but don't count on finding such markers once you're deep into residential neighborhoods. Even buying a good map at a newsstand—the kind showing all street names and vaporetto routes—won't necessarily keep you from getting lost. To make matters worse, map apps on smart phones, for some reason, give frequently erroneous results for Venice.

Fortunately, as long as you maintain your patience, getting lost in Venice can be a pleasure. For one thing, being lost is a sign that you've escaped the tourist throngs. And although you might not find the Titian masterpiece you'd set out to see, you could wind up coming across an ageless bacaro (a traditional wine bar) or a quirky shop that turns out to be the highlight of your afternoon. Opportunities for such serendipity abound. Keep in mind that the city is self-contained: sooner or later, perhaps with the help of a patient native, you can rest assured you'll regain your bearings.

bell, called the Marangona, survived. The crushed loggia was promptly reconstructed, and the new tower, rebuilt to the old plan, reopened in 1912. On a clear day the stunning view includes the Lido, the lagoon, and the mainland as far as the Alps, but strangely enough, none of the myriad canals that snake through the city. ⊠ *Piazza San Marco, San Marco* ☎ *041/2708311* ⊕ *www.basilicasanmarco.it* 🎟 *€10, skip-the-line tickets €12* Ⓜ *Vaporetto: San Zaccaria, Vallaresso.*

★ **Museo Correr**

HISTORY MUSEUM | This museum of Venetian art and history contains an impressive sculpture collection by Antonio Canova and important paintings by Giovanni Bellini, Vittore Carpaccio (Carpaccio's famous painting of the Venetian courtesans is here), and other major local painters. There are nine sumptuously decorated Imperial Rooms, where the Empress of Austria once stayed, and several rooms convey the city's proud naval history through highly descriptive paintings and numerous maritime objects, including ships' cannons and some surprisingly large iron mast-top navigation lights. ⊠ *Piazza San Marco 52, Ala Napoleonica, opposite Basilica, San Marco* ☎ *041/2405211* ⊕ *correr.visitmuve.it* 🎟 *Museums of San Marco Pass €30, includes Museo Correr, Museo Archeologico, Biblioteca Nazionale Marciana, and Palazzo Ducale. Museum Pass €40, includes all four museums plus seven civic museums* Ⓜ *Vaporetto: San Zaccaria, Vallaresso.*

★ **Palazzo Ducale** (*Doge's Palace*)
CASTLE/PALACE | Rising majestically above Piazzetta San Marco, this Gothic fantasia of pink-and-white marble—the doges' residence from the 10th century and the central administrative center of the Venetian Republic—is a majestic expression of Venetian prosperity and power. Upon entering, you'll find yourself in an immense courtyard with some of the first evidence of Venice's Renaissance architecture, including Antonio Rizzo's 15th-century Scala dei Giganti (Stairway of the Giants). The palace's sumptuous chambers have walls and ceilings covered with works by Venice's greatest artists. In the Anticollegio you'll find *The Rape of Europa* by Veronese and Tintoretto's *Bacchus and Ariadne Crowned by Venus*. The ceiling of the Sala del Senato (Senate Chamber), featuring *The Triumph of Venice* by Tintoretto, is magnificent, but it's dwarfed by his masterpiece *Paradise* in the Sala del Maggiore Consiglio (Great Council Hall), the world's largest oil painting. The popular Secret Itineraries tour lets you visit the doge's private apartments and hidden passageways. ✉ *Piazza San Marco 1, San Marco* 🕾 *041/42730892 tickets* ⊕ *palazzoducale. visitmuve.it* 🎫 *Museums of San Marco Pass €30, includes Palazzo Ducale, Museo Correr, Museo Archeologico, and Biblioteca Nazionale Marciana. Museum Pass €40, includes all four museums plus seven civic museums. Secret Itineraries tour €32* Ⓜ *Vaporetto: San Zaccaria, Vallaresso.*

★ **Palazzo Grassi**
ART MUSEUM | Built between 1748 and 1772 by Giorgio Massari for a Bolognese family, this palace is one of the last of the great noble residences on the Grand Canal. Once owned by auto magnate Gianni Agnelli, it was bought by French businessman François Pinault in 2005 to showcase his highly esteemed collection of modern and contemporary art (which

has now grown so large that Pinault rented the Punta della Dogana, at the entryway to the Grand Canal, for his newest acquisitions). Pinault brought in Japanese architect Tadao Ando to remodel the Grassi's interior. Check online for a schedule of temporary art exhibitions. ✉ *Campo San Samuele 3231, San Marco* 🕾 *041/2401308* ⊕ *www.palazzograssi. it* 🎫 *€15, includes Punta della Dogana* 🕙 *Closed Tues.* Ⓜ *Vaporetto: San Samuele, Sant'Angelo.*

★ **Piazza San Marco** (*St. Mark's Square*)
PLAZA/SQUARE | **FAMILY** | One of the world's most beautiful squares, Piazza San Marco (St. Mark's Square) is the spiritual and artistic heart of Venice, a vast open space bordered by an orderly procession of arcades marching toward the fairy-tale cupolas and marble lacework of the Basilica di San Marco. From midmorning on, it is generally packed with tourists. (If Venetians have business in the piazza, they try to conduct it in the early morning, before the crowds swell.) At night the piazza can be magical, especially in winter, when mists swirl around the lampposts and the campanile.

Facing the basilica, on your left, the long, arcaded building is the Procuratie Vecchie, renovated to its present form in 1514 as offices and residences for the powerful procurators, or magistrates.

On your right is the Procuratie Nuove, built half a century later in a more imposing, classical style. It was originally planned by Venice's great Renaissance architect Jacopo Sansovino (1486–1570), to carry on the look of his Libreria Sansoviniana (Sansovinian Library), but he died before construction on the Nuove had begun. Vincenzo Scamozzi (circa 1552–1616), a pupil of Andrea Palladio (1508–80), completed the design and construction. Still later, the Procuratie Nuove was modified by architect

San Marco

A B C D E

1
C. Larga Pezzana
C. llo Zen
Campo di S. Polo
C. Cavalli
San Polo
Campo S. Aponal
R. d. Ravano
C. Paradiso
Campo dei Frari
Rio Terrà
San Polo
Campo di S. Silvestro
C. d. Silvestro

2
Santa Maria Gloriosa dei Frari
R. Doanetta
Saliz. S. Polo
C. del Magazen
C. d. Shiavchiari
Palazzo Barzizza
Rio Terrà dei Nomboli
C. dei Saoneri
C. d. Traghetto d. Madonnetta
S. Silvestro
C. d. Cristo
C. dei Nomboli
Campo S. Tomà

3
Grand Canal
S. Angelo
C. Pesaro
Saliz. del Teatro
C. d. S. Andrea
Rio Malpaga
Cam Man
S. Tomà

4
C. Lezze
C. d. Traghetto Garzoni
C. del Pestrin
C. del Magazen
C. d. Mandola
R. Terrà degli Assassini
C. Morolin
C. Mocenigo Casa Nova
C. Cornar
Prco. S. Samuele
C. llo Nuovo
Campo S. Angelo
C. del Caffettier
R. d. Madonna

5
R. Grassi
Saliz. S. Samuele
Campo San Barnaba
Santo Stefano
C. d. Cristo
Calle della Verona
Ramo della Verona
C. d. Fenice
C. Farsetti
C. delle Carozze
C. dei Zotti
Campo S. Samuele
S. Samuele
Campo S. Stefano
C. Caotoria
R. d. Veste
Ca' Rezzonico
C. del Teatro

6
Palazzo Falier
C. Vetturi
C. Giustinian
Rio di S. Vidal
Calle delle Munaghe
Campo S. Vidal
Campo Pidani
Calle dello Spezier
C. Zaguri
Fond. Corner Zaguri
Fond. Malvasia
Campo S. Maurizio
Campo S. Maria Zobenigo
Rio del Santissimo Gritti
C. Vicenza
C. del Pestrin

7
Accademia
Campo d. Carità
Calle Doge da Ponte
Fond. Barbaro
C. Gritti o del Campanile
Giglio

Sights ▼		Restaurants ▼	Quick Bites ▼
1 Basilica di San Marco.......... **I4**	4 Palazzo Ducale........... **I5**	1 Enoteca al Volto........ **E3**	1 Bar all'Angolo............ **C5**
2 Campanile di San Marco.......... **H5**	5 Palazzo Grassi **A5**	2 Harry's Bar **G6**	2 Caffè Florian............. **H5**
3 Museo Correr **G5**	6 Piazza San Marco **H5**	3 Ristorante Quadri....... **H4**	3 Gelatoteca Suso **H1**
	7 Ponte di Rialto........... **G1**		4 Gran Caffè Quadri **H4**

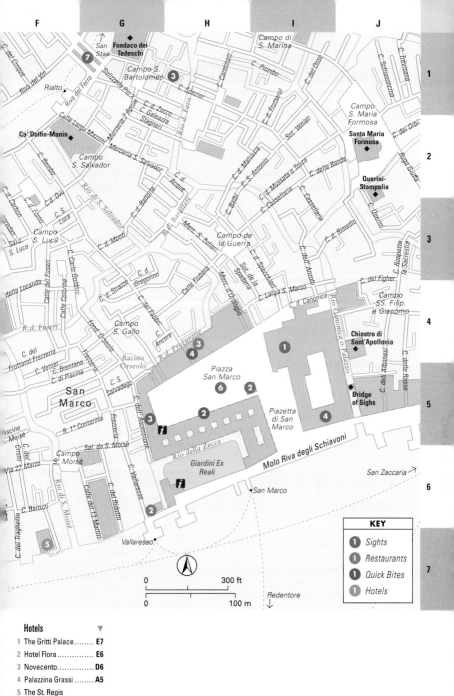

F G H I J

San Stae
Fondaco dei Tedeschi
Campo di S. Marina
C. Trevisana
C. d. Ospiti
C. Schiavoncini
1

Riva del Vin
Rialto
Riva del Ferro
Salizada Pio X
Campo S. Bartolomeo
C. Spezier
C. dt Zocco
C. Galeazza
Stagneri
Rio di S. Lio
C. Fruttariol
C. Piombo
C. Venier
Sot. Venier
Campo S. Maria Formosa
C. del Orbi
Ruga Giuffa

Ca' Dolfin-Manin
Calle Larga Mazzini
Merceria 2 Aprile
Mercerie
Mercerie S. Salvador
C. d. Acque
C. d. Matvasia
C. S. Antonio
C. Balbi
C. S. Mussata o Tosca
C. Cassellana
C. della Bande
Casselleria
Santa Maria Formosa
Querini-Stampalia
C. Querini
2

Campo S. Salvador
Rio di S. Salvador
C. d. Monti
C. t. Battotta
C. Bembo
C. d. Ovo
C. S. Luca
R. d. Barbieri
Merc. S. Zulian
C. dell Anzolo
C. d. Rimedin
3

C. Cartoni
Salit. S. Luca
Campo S. Luca
C. d. Fuseri
C. d. Strazze
C. d. Gregolino
Calle Fiubera
Merc. d'Orologio
Campo de la Guerra
Sot. della Spadaria
C. Spechieri
C. Larga S. Marco
C. dell Anzolo
Rio Canonica o Palazzo
Campo SS. Filip. e Giacomo
C. Riapetta
la Sacristia
4

Stella Locanda
C. del Fruttarol Frezzeria
C. Venier
C. di Piscina
Fond. Orseolo
Bacino Orseolo
Campo S. Gallo
C. Ancora
R. d. Procuratie
Piazza San Marco
Chiostro di Sant'Apollonia
C. del Figher
C. d. Canonica
C. dell Athanasi
C. delle Rasse
4

San Marco
C. S. Salvadego
Frezzeria
C. dell Ascensione
R. d. Fuseri
Piazzetta di San Marco
Bridge of Sighs
5

R. 1° Contarina
Cascine
C. Moisè
Campo S. Moisè
Sal. da S. Moisè
Rio della Zecca
Giardini Ex Reali
Molo Riva degli Schiavoni
San Zaccaria →
6

Via 22 Marzo
C. del Cristo
Rio di S. Moisè
C. del Ridotto
C. Barozzi
Calle del 13 Martiri
San Marco
Vallaresso
7

Redentore ↓

KEY

❶ Sights
❶ Restaurants
❶ Quick Bites
❶ Hotels

0 ——— 300 ft
0 ——— 100 m

Hotels ▼

1 The Gritti Palace **E7**
2 Hotel Flora **E6**
3 Novecento **D6**
4 Palazzina Grassi **A5**
5 The St. Regis
   Venice **F7**

Taking a Gondola Ride

Riding a gondola along the canals is an iconic Venetian experience—and one that's still very much worth doing, despite the expense. It's not hard to find a gondolier, donned in traditional striped garb, beckoning from the helm of a docked boat to take you on a relaxing ride along the city's waterways. Venture away from the busy area around the Grand Canal and look for a boat on one of the smaller, quieter waterways so you can nestle into the plushly upholstered seats and float by Venice's legendary facades without being distracted by the crowds. Go in the morning to watch the city come to life, in the late afternoon when the colors of the buildings are especially vibrant, or at sunset for maximum romance. Boats sit six people, and signs posted on the red-and-white striped poles throughout the city list the standard rates for a 30-minute gondola ride (€80 during the day, €100 after 7 pm; 20-minute increments can be added for an additional fee).

Baldassare Longhena (1598–1682), one of Venice's Baroque masters.

When Napoléon (1769–1821) entered Venice with his troops in 1797, he expressed his admiration for the piazza and promptly gave orders to alter it. His architects demolished a church with a Sansovino facade in order to build the Ala Napoleonica (Napoleonic Wing), or Fabbrica Nuova (New Building), which linked the two 16th-century procuratie and effectively enclosed the piazza.

Piazzetta San Marco is the "little square" leading from Piazza San Marco to the waters of Bacino San Marco (St. Mark's Basin); its *molo* (landing) once served as the grand entrance to the Republic. Two imposing columns tower above the waterfront. One is topped by the winged lion, a traditional emblem of St. Mark that became the symbol of Venice itself; the other supports St. Theodore, the city's first patron, along with his dragon. (A third column fell off its barge and ended up in the bacino before it could be placed alongside the others.) Although the columns are a glorious vision today, the Republic traditionally executed convicts here—and some superstitious Venetians still avoid walking between them. ⊠ *Piazza San Marco, San Marco* Ⓜ *Vaporetto: San Zaccaria, Vallaresso.*

★ **Ponte di Rialto** (*Rialto Bridge*)
BRIDGE | FAMILY | The competition to design a stone bridge across the Grand Canal attracted the best architects of the late 16th century, including Michelangelo, Palladio, and Sansovino, but the job went to the less famous (if appropriately named) Antonio da Ponte (1512–95). His pragmatic design, completed in 1591, featured shop space and was high enough for galleys to pass beneath. Putting practicality and economy over aesthetic considerations—unlike the classical plans proposed by his more famous contemporaries—da Ponte's bridge essentially followed the design of its wooden predecessor. But it kept decoration and cost to a minimum at a time when the Republic's coffers were low, due to continual wars against the Turks and competition brought about by the Spanish and Portuguese opening of oceanic trade routes. Along the railing you'll enjoy one of the city's most famous views: the Grand Canal vibrant with boat traffic. ⊠ *San Marco* Ⓜ *Vaporetto: Rialto.*

🍴 Restaurants

Enoteca al Volto

$$ | VENETIAN | A short walk from the Ponte di Rialto, this bar has been around since 1936, and the satisfying cicheti and primi have a lot to do with its staying power. Grab a table out front, or take refuge in one of the two small, dark rooms with a ceiling plastered with wine labels that provide a classic backdrop for simple fare, including a delicious risotto that is served daily from noon, plus a solid wine list of both Italian and foreign vintages. **Known for:** great local and international wine selection; tasty and inexpensive cicheti; fantastic main courses, including risotto and pasta with seafood. $ Average main: €17 ✉ Calle Cavalli, San Marco 4081, San Marco ☎ 041/5228945 ⊕ enotecaalvolto.com Ⓜ Vaporetto: Rialto.

★ Harry's Bar

$$$$ | VENETIAN | For those who can afford it, lunch or dinner at Harry's Bar is as much a part of a visit to Venice as a walk across Piazza San Marco or a vaporetto ride down the Grand Canal. Inside, the suave, subdued beige-on-white decor is unchanged from the 1930s, and the classic Venetian fare is carefully and excellently prepared. **Known for:** being the birthplace of the Bellini cocktail; see-and-be-seen atmosphere; signature crepes flambées and famous Cipriani chocolate cake. $ Average main: €58 ✉ Calle Vallaresso, San Marco 1323, San Marco ☎ 041/5285777 ⊕ www.cipriani.com Ⓜ Vaporetto: Vallaresso.

★ Ristorante Quadri

$$$$ | VENETIAN | Although the lavish interior has been updated by designer Philippe Starck, this restaurant above the famed café of the same name is still steeped in Venetian ambience and history (it was where Turkish coffee was introduced to the city in the 1700s). When the Alajmo family (of the celebrated Le Calandre near Padua) took over, they put their accomplished sous-chef from Padua in charge of the kitchen, resulting in the addition of dishes—best sampled with a tasting menu—that are complex and sophisticated, with a wonderful wine list to match. **Known for:** sophisticated and modern Italian cuisine; seasonal tasting menus; revitalized designer decor. $ Average main: €60 ✉ Piazza San Marco 121, San Marco ☎ 041/5222105 ⊕ alajmo.it ⊘ Closed Mon., Tues., and late Jan. No lunch Wed.–Fri. Ⓜ Vaporetto: Giardinetti, Vallaresso.

☕ Coffee and Quick Bites

Bar all'Angolo

$ | CAFÉ | This corner of Campo Santo Stefano is a pleasant place to sit and watch the Venetian world go by. The café staff are in constant motion, so you'll receive your coffee, spritz, panino (a sandwich warmed on a griddle), or tramezzino (sandwich on untoasted white bread, usually with a mayonnaise-based filling) in short order; consume it at your leisure at one of the outdoor tables, at the bar, or at the tables in the back. **Known for:** simple yet satisfying fare, like tramezzini and panini; tasty homemade desserts, including tiramisu and cakes; good people-watching. $ Average main: €10 ✉ Campo Santo Stefano, San Marco 3464, just in front of Santo Stefano church, San Marco ☎ 041/5220710 ⊘ Closed Sun. and Jan. Ⓜ Vaporetto: Sant'Angelo.

★ Caffè Florian

$$ | CAFÉ | Florian is not only Italy's first café (1720), but also one of its most beautiful, with glittering, neo-Baroque decor and 19th-century wall panels depicting Venetian heroes. The coffee, drinks, and snacks are good, but most people come for the atmosphere and history: this was the only café to serve women during the 18th century; it was frequented by artistic notables like Wagner, Goethe, Goldoni, Lord Byron, Marcel Proust, and Charles Dickens; and it was the birthplace of the international

art exhibition that became the Venice Biennale. **Known for:** prime location on St. Mark's Square; beautiful, historic interior; hot chocolate, coffee, and quick nibbles. [$] *Average main: €16* ✉ *Piazza San Marco 57, San Marco* ☎ *041/5205641* 🌐 *www.caffeflorian.com* 🕓 *Closed early Jan.* [M] *Vaporetto: Giardinetti, Vallaresso.*

Gelatoteca Suso

$ | **ICE CREAM** | **FAMILY** | Try this fun shop for gelato that's out of the ordinary: think walnut cream with caramelized fig, or vanilla with rum raisins and Malaga wine; sorbets and milkshakes are also on offer. There's a second location on Salizada S Giovanni Grisostomo, in Cannaregio. **Known for:** unusual flavors; vegan ice cream options; convenient location on way to Rialto Bridge. [$] *Average main: €5* ✉ *Sotoportego de la Bissa, San Marco 5453, San Marco* ☎ *041/3084136* 🌐 *suso.gelatoteca.it* [M] *Vaporetto: Rialto.*

★ **Gran Caffè Quadri**

$$ | **CAFÉ** | Come for breakfast, a pre-dinner aperitivo, or anything in between at this always lively historic coffeehouse—opened in 1775 and taken over by the famous culinary Alajmo family in 2011—in the center of the action on Piazza San Marco. Choose from a wide selection of pastries at breakfast (though the cappuccino and brioche combo is always a classic), pizzas at lunch, and tramezzini all day long, including one with lobster. **Known for:** extensive (though pricey) aperitivo; celebrity owners; prime people-watching. [$] *Average main: €17* ✉ *Piazza San Marco 121, San Marco* ☎ *049/630303* 🌐 *alajmo.it* [M] *Vaporetto: Giardinetti, Vallaresso.*

Hotels

★ **The Gritti Palace**

$$$$ | **HOTEL** | With handblown chandeliers, sumptuous textiles, and sweeping canal views, this grande dame (whose history dates from 1525, when it was built as the residence of the prominent Gritti family) represents aristocratic Venetian living at its best. **Pros:** truly historical property; Grand Canal location; classic Venetian experience. **Cons:** major splurge; food served at the hotel gets mixed reviews; few spa amenities. [$] *Rooms from: €1450* ✉ *Campo Santa Maria del Giglio 2467, San Marco* ☎ *041/794611* 🌐 *www.thegrittipalace.com* 🛏 *82 rooms* 🍴 *No Meals* [M] *Vaporetto: Giglio.*

Hotel Flora

$$$ | **HOTEL** | The elegant and refined facade announces a charming, and reasonably priced, place to stay; the hospitable staff, the tastefully decorated rooms, and the lovely garden, where guests can breakfast or drink, do not disappoint. **Pros:** central location; peaceful hidden garden; excellent breakfast. **Cons:** some rooms can be on the small side; no water views; old-fashioned lobby doesn't invite hanging out. [$] *Rooms from: €235* ✉ *Calle Bergamaschi, San Marco 2283/A, just off Calle Larga XXII Marzo, San Marco* ☎ *041/5205844* 🌐 *www.hotelflora.it* 🛏 *40 rooms* 🍴 *Free Breakfast* [M] *Vaporetto: Vallaresso.*

★ **Novecento**

$$$ | **HOTEL** | A stylish yet intimate retreat tucked away on a quiet *calle* (street) midway between Piazza San Marco and the Accademia Bridge offers exquisite rooms tastefully decorated with original furnishings and tapestries from the Mediterranean and Far East. **Pros:** intimate, romantic atmosphere; unique design sensibility; complimentary afternoon tea. **Cons:** most rooms only have showers, not tubs; no elevator; some rooms can be noisy. [$] *Rooms from: €259* ✉ *Calle del Dose, San Marco 2683/84, off Campo San Maurizio, San Marco* ☎ *041/2413765* 🌐 *www.novecento.biz* 🛏 *9 rooms* 🍴 *Free Breakfast* [M] *Vaporetto: Santa Maria del Giglio.*

Palazzina Grassi

$$$$ | **HOTEL** | The only hotel in Italy outfitted by famed French designer Philippe Starck boasts a clubby atmosphere, over-the-top contemporary rooms lined with Murano glass, and so-close-you-can-touch-them Grand Canal views. **Pros:** fun, modern take on Venetian design; next door to Palazzo Grassi art space and walking distance to St. Mark's; friendly, helpful service. **Cons:** food in restaurant not up to par; bathrooms smaller than they should be; can be loud when parties are in full swing. [$] *Rooms from: €436* ✉ *Ramo Grassi, San Marco* ☎ *041/5284644* 🌐 *www.palazzinagrassi.com* 🛏 *26 rooms* 🍴 *Free Breakfast* [M] *Vaporetto: San Samuele.*

★ **The St. Regis Venice**

$$$$ | **HOTEL** | Whimsical design details evoking the Venetian landscape abound in this elegant, contemporary hotel constructed from five historic palazzi with phenomenal views onto the Grand Canal. **Pros:** wonderful central location; terraces with unbeatable views; St. Regis butler service for all guests. **Cons:** sleek modern style not for fans of Venetian opulence; standard rooms on the small side; few spa amenities (no pool or saunas). [$] *Rooms from: €1151* ✉ *San Marco 2159, San Marco* ☎ *041/2400001* 🌐 *www.marriott.com* 🛏 *169 rooms* 🍴 *No Meals* [M] *Vaporetto: Vallaresso.*

Nightlife

Bacarando in Corte dell'Orso

WINE BARS | It is easy to see why this place is popular with the locals, offering fairly priced cocktails, a reasonable assortment of cicheti, and a good selection of Italian wine, but the warm ambience, friendly staff, and occasional live jazz are the main draws. The kitchen stays open until late. ✉ *Corte Dell'Orso, San Marco 5495, San Marco* ✥ *Tucked away in alley across from Church of San Giovanni Grisostomo* ☎ *041/5238280* 🌐 *www.bacarando.com* [M] *Vaporetto: Rialto.*

Bacaro Jazz

BARS | This Venetian-style dive bar has strong cocktails, a jazz soundtrack, and hundreds of bras hanging from the ceiling. The lively daily happy hour is a great time to visit. ✉ *San Marco 5546, San Marco* ☎ *041/5285249* 🌐 *bacarojazz.it* [M] *Vaporetto: Rialto.*

★ **Bar Longhi**

BARS | The Gritti Palace is home to one of the most exclusive watering holes in town (though thankfully open to the public), lined with 18th-century paintings and Murano chandeliers. You can also enjoy your cocktail on the patio with prime views onto the Grand Canal. ✉ *The Gritti Palace, Campo Santa Maria del Giglio, San Marco 2467, San Marco* ☎ *041/794611* 🌐 *www.thegrittipalace.com* [M] *Vaporetto: Giglio.*

Shopping

★ **Al Duca d'Aosta**

MIXED CLOTHING | The most stylish of Venetians and visitors alike come here for women's and men's designer labels for every taste. Brands include Burberry, Givenchy, Jil Sander, Lanvin, Moncler, and many others; be prepared to be wowed. ✉ *San Marco 284, San Marco* ☎ *041/5220733* 🌐 *www.alducadaosta.com* [M] *Vaporetto: San Marco, Zaccaria.*

★ **Atelier Segalin di Daniela Ghezzo**

SHOES | This artist turned master shoemaker produces one-of-a-kind creations from exotic leathers. Though the shoes start at €650 and usually take at least six weeks to finish, you'll truly feel like you're wearing a masterpiece. ✉ *Calle dei Fuseri, San Marco 4365, San Marco* ☎ *041/5222115* 🌐 *www.danielaghezzo.it* [M] *Vaporetto: Rialto.*

★ **Dittura Massimo**

SHOES | Run by a second-generation shoemaker, this shop is one of the only places left in the city still producing Venice's iconic *friulane* slippers, invented in the 19th century and hand-stitched from velvet and rubber. The shoes are still worn by gondoliers today. ⊠ *Calle Fiubera, San Marco 943, San Marco* ☎ *041/5231163* Ⓜ *Vaporetto: San Marco.*

★ Giuliana Longo
HATS & GLOVES | A hat shop that's been around since 1901 offers an assortment of Venetian and gondolier straw hats, Panama hats from Ecuador, caps and berets, and some select scarves of silk and fine wool; there's even a special corner dedicated to accessories for antique cars. ⊠ *Calle del Lovo, San Marco 4813, San Marco* ☎ *041/5226454* ⊕ *www.giulianalongo.com* Ⓜ *Vaporetto: San Marco.*

★ Jesurum Venezia 1870
FABRICS | A great deal of so-called Burano Venetian lace is now machine-made in China—and there really is a difference. Unless you have some experience, you're best off going to a trusted place. Jesurum has been the major producer of handmade Venetian lace since 1870. Its lace is, of course, all modern production, but if you want an antique piece, the people at Jesurum can point you in the right direction. ⊠ *Calle Veste, San Marco 2024, San Marco* ☎ *041/5238969* ⊕ *www.jesurum.it* Ⓜ *Vaporetto: Vallaresso.*

★ MuranoVitrum
GLASSWARE | You'll find Murano-made glassworks, including glasses, vases, chandeliers, mirrors, and sculptures, in this friendly family-owned shop. ⊠ *San Marco 1229, San Marco* ☎ *041/5206358* ⊕ *www.muranovitrum.com* Ⓜ *Vaporetto: Vallaresso.*

T Fondaco dei Tedeschi
DEPARTMENT STORE | This 15th-century Renaissance commercial center served as Venice's main post office for many years, but was remodeled and returned to its historical roots as a luxury department store. Here you can find a large assortment of high-end jewelry, clothing, and other luxury items. Plus, fabulous views can be had from the rooftop terrace—book a free 15-minute visit online.

⊠ *Calle Fondaco dei Tedeschi, near San Marco end of Ponte di Rialto, San Marco* ☎ *041/3142000* ⊕ *www.dfs.com* Ⓜ *Vaporetto: Rialto.*

Dorsoduro

The sestiere Dorsoduro (named for its "hard back" solid clay foundation) is across the Grand Canal to the south of San Marco. It is a place of meandering canals, the city's finest art museums, monumental churches, and *scuole* (Renaissance civic institutions) filled with works by Titian, Veronese, and Tiepolo, and a promenade called the Zattere, where on sunny days you'll swear half the city is out for *passeggiata* (a stroll). The eastern tip of the peninsula, the Punta della Dogana, is capped by the dome of Santa Maria della Salute and was once the city's customs point; the old customs house is now a museum of contemporary art.

TIMING
You can easily spend a full day in the neighborhood. Devote at least a half hour to admiring the Titians in the imposing and monumental Santa Maria della Salute, and another half hour to the wonderful Veroneses in the peaceful, serene church of San Sebastiano. The Gallerie dell'Accademia demands a few hours, but if time is short an audio guide can help you cover the highlights in about an hour. Ca' Rezzonico deserves at least an hour, as does the Peggy Guggenheim Collection.

Sights

★ Ca' Rezzonico
HISTORY MUSEUM | Designed by Baldassare Longhena in the 17th century, this gigantic palace was completed nearly 100 years later by Giorgio Massari and became the last home of English poet Robert Browning (1812–89). Stand on the bridge by the Grand Canal entrance to

Venetian Art Glass

The glass of Murano is Venice's number one product, and you'll be confronted by mind-boggling displays of traditional and contemporary glassware—much of it kitsch and not made in Venice. Traditional Venetian glass is hot blown glass, not lead crystal; it comes in myriad forms that range from the classic ornate goblets and chandeliers, to beads, vases, sculpture, and more. Beware of paying "Venetian" prices for glass made elsewhere. A piece claiming to be made in Murano may guarantee its origin, but not its value or quality; the prestigious Venetian glassmakers—like Venini, Seguso, Salviati, and others—sign their pieces, but never use a "made in Murano" label. To make a smart purchase, take your time and be selective. You can learn a great deal without sales pressure at the Museo del Vetro (⊕ *museovetro.visitmuve. it*) on Murano; unfortunately, you'll likely find the least attractive glass where public demonstrations are offered. Although prices in Venice and on Murano are comparable, shops in Venice with wares from various glassworks may charge slightly less.

■ TIP→ **A "free" taxi to Murano always comes with sales pressure. Take the vaporetto included in your transit pass, and, if you prefer, a private guide who specializes in the subject but has no affinity to any specific furnace.**

4

Venice DORSODURO

spot the plaque with Browning's poetic excerpt, "Open my heart and you will see graved inside of it, Italy…," on the left side of the palace. The spectacular centerpiece is the eye-popping Grand Ballroom, which has hosted some of the grandest parties in the city's history, from its 18th-century heyday to the 1969 Bal Fantastica (a Save Venice charity event that attracted every notable of the day, from Elizabeth Taylor to Aristotle Onassis).

Today the upper floors of the Ca' Rezzonico are home to the especially delightful Museo del Settecento (Museum of Venice in the 1700s). Its main floor successfully retains the appearance of a magnificent Venetian palazzo, decorated with period furniture and tapestries in gilded salons, as well as Gianbattista Tiepolo ceiling frescoes and oil paintings. Upper floors contain a fine collection of paintings by 18th-century Venetian artists, including the famous Pulcinella frescoes by Tiepolo's son, Giandomenico, moved here from the Villa di Zianigo.

There's even a restored apothecary, complete with powders and potions. ⊠ *Fondamenta Rezzonico, Dorsoduro 3136, Dorsoduro* 🕾 *041/2410100* ⊕ *carezzonico. visitmuve.it* ✉ *€10 (free with Museum Pass)* 🕑 *Closed Mon.–Wed.* Ⓜ *Vaporetto: Ca' Rezzonico.*

Campo Santa Margherita

PLAZA/SQUARE | Lined with cafés and restaurants generally filled with students from the two nearby universities, Campo Santa Margherita also has produce vendors and benches where you can sit and take in the bustling local life of the campo. Also close to Ca' Rezzonico and the Scuola Grande dei Carmini, and only a 10-minute walk from the Gallerie dell'Accademia, the square is the center of Dorsoduro social life. It takes its name from the church to one side, closed since the early 19th century and now used as an auditorium. On weekend evenings, especially in the summer, it attracts hordes of students, even from the mainland. ⊠ *Campo Santa Margherita, Dorsoduro* Ⓜ *Vaporetto: Zattere, Ca' Rezzonico.*

★ Gallerie dell'Accademia

ART MUSEUM | The greatest collection of Venetian paintings in the world hangs in these galleries founded by Napoléon in 1807 on the site of a religious complex he had suppressed. The galleries were carefully and subtly restructured between 1945 and 1959 by the renowned Venetian architect Carlo Scarpa. Highlights include works by Jacopo Bellini, the father of the Venetian Renaissance, as well as the richly colored paintings of his more accomplished son Giovanni; *The Tempest* by Giorgione, a revolutionary work that has intrigued viewers and critics for centuries; *Feast in the House of Levi,* which got Veronese summoned to the Inquisition; and several of Tintoretto's finest works. Don't miss the views of 15th- and 16th-century Venice by Carpaccio and Gentile Bellini, Giovanni's brother—you'll recognize many places you've seen on your walks. Booking tickets in advance isn't essential but only costs an additional €1.50. ⊠ *Campo de la Carità, Dorsoduro 1050, Campo della Carità just off Accademia Bridge, Dorsoduro* ☎ *041/5222247, 041/5243354 reservations when calling from outside Italy* ⊕ *www.gallerieacca-demia.it/en* ☞ *€12; subject to increases for special exhibitions* Ⓜ *Vaporetto: Accademia, Zattere.*

Gesuati

(*Church of Santa Maria del Rosario*) CHURCH | After the Dominicans took over the church of Santa Maria della Visitazione from the suppressed order of Gesuati laymen in 1668, Giorgio Massari, the last of the great Venetian Baroque architects, was commissioned to build this structure between 1726 and 1735. It has an important Gianbattista Tiepolo (1696–1770) illusionistic ceiling and several other of his works, plus those of his contemporaries Giambattista Piazzetta (1683–1754) and Sebastiano Ricci (1659–1734). Outside on the right-hand wall above a small staircase is a bronze door decorated with a series of panels showing scenes from the life of Jesus by noted Venetian sculptor Francesco Scarpabolla. ⊠ *Fondamenta Zattere ai Gesuati, Dorsoduro* ☎ *041/5205921 church office, 041/2750462* ⊕ *www.chorusven-ezia.org* ☞ *€3 (free with Chorus Pass)* ⊘ *Closed Sun.* Ⓜ *Vaporetto: Zattere.*

Peggy Guggenheim Collection

ART MUSEUM | FAMILY | Housed in the incomplete but nevertheless charming Palazzo Venier dei Leoni, this choice selection of 20th-century painting and sculpture represents the taste and extraordinary style of the late heiress Peggy Guggenheim. Through wealth, social connections, and a sharp eye for artistic trends, Guggenheim (1898–1979) became an important art dealer and collector from the 1930s through the 1950s, and her personal collection here includes works by Picasso, Kandinsky, Pollock, Motherwell, and Ernst (her onetime husband). The museum serves beverages, snacks, and light meals in its refreshingly shady and artistically sophisticated garden. ⊠ *Fondamenta Venier dei Leoni, Dorsoduro 701-704, Dorsoduro* ☎ *041/2405411* ⊕ *www.gug-genheim-venice.it* ☞ *€16* ⊘ *Closed Tues.* Ⓜ *Vaporetto: Accademia, Salute.*

★ Punta della Dogana

ART MUSEUM | Funded by the billionaire who owns a major share in Christie's Auction House, the François Pinault Foundation commissioned Japanese architect Tadao Ando to redesign this fabled customs house—sitting at the *punta,* or point of land, at the San Marco end of the Grand Canal—now home to a changing roster of works from Pinault's renowned collection of contemporary art. The streaming light, polished surfaces, and clean lines of Ando's design contrast beautifully with the massive columns, sturdy beams, and brick of the original Dogana. Even if you aren't into contemporary art, a visit is worthwhile just to see Ando's amazing architectural transformation. Be sure to walk down to the punta for a magnificent view of the Venetian basin. Check online for a schedule of temporary exhibitions. ✉ *Punta della Dogana, Dorsoduro* ☎ *041/2401308* 🌐 *www.palazzograssi.it* 🎫 *€15 with Palazzo Grassi* 🕒 *Closed Tues.* [M] *Vaporetto: Salute.*

★ San Sebastiano

CHURCH | Paolo Veronese (1528–88), though still in his twenties, was already the official painter of the Republic when he began the ceiling oil panels and wall frescoes at San Sebastiano in 1555. For decades he continued to embellish the church with very beautiful illusionistic scenes. The cycles of scenes in San Sebastiano are considered to be his supreme accomplishment. His three oil paintings in the center of the ceiling depict scenes from the life of Esther, a rare theme in Venice. Veronese is buried beneath his bust near the organ. ✉ *Campazzo San Sebastiano, Dorsoduro* ☎ *041/2750462* 🌐 *www.chorusvenezia.org* 🎫 *€3 (free with Chorus Pass)* 🕒 *Closed Sun.* [M] *Vaporetto: San Basilio.*

★ Santa Maria della Salute

CHURCH | The most iconic landmark of the Grand Canal, La Salute (as this church is commonly called) is best viewed from the Riva degli Schiavoni at sunset or from the Accademia Bridge by moonlight. Baldassare Longhena (later Venice's most important Baroque architect) won a competition in 1631 to design a shrine honoring the Virgin Mary for saving Venice from a plague that over two years (1629–30) killed 47,000 residents, or one-third of the city's population. Outside, this ornate white Istrian stone octagon is topped by a colossal cupola with snail-like ornamental buttresses. Check the website for information on guided tours. ✉ *Punta della Dogana, Dorsoduro* ☎ *041/2743928* 🌐 *basilicasalutevenezia.it* 🎫 *Church free, sacristy €6, sacristy and art gallery €12, balustrade of the prophets €5, dome €8* [M] *Vaporetto: Salute.*

Scuola Grande dei Carmini

HISTORIC SIGHT | When the order of Santa Maria del Carmelo commissioned Baldassare Longhena to finish the work on the Scuola Grande dei Carmini in the 1670s, their confraternity was one of the largest and wealthiest in Venice. Little expense was spared in the stuccoed ceilings and carved wooden paneling, and the artwork is remarkable. The paintings by Gianbattista Tiepolo that adorn the Baroque ceiling of the **Sala Capitolare** (Chapter House) are particularly alluring. In what many consider his best work, the artist's nine canvases vividly transform some rather conventional religious themes into dynamic displays of color and movement. ✉ *Campo dei Carmini, Dorsoduro 2617, Dorsoduro* ☎ *041/5289420* 🌐 *www.scuolagrandecarmini.it* 🎫 *€7* [M] *Vaporetto: Ca' Rezzonico.*

🍴 Restaurants

★ Estro Vino e Cucina

$$$ | **MODERN ITALIAN** | Wine lovers shouldn't miss this cozy and compact eatery run by the Spezzamonte brothers, which offers a fantastic selection of organic wines along with modern takes on classic Venetian dishes, such as *scampi in saor* (marinated langoustines) and grilled local amberjack. If you can't choose, let the helpful servers suggest the perfect vino from their list of more than 700 bottles to pair with your à la carte dishes or tasting menu. **Known for:** extensive natural wine list; ambitious local cuisine; vibrant atmosphere. [$] *Average main: €28* ✉ *Crosera San Pantalon, Dorsoduro 3778, Dorsoduro* ☎ *041/4764914* 🌐 *www.estrovenezia.com* 🕒 *Closed Tues.* [M] *Vaporetto: San Tomà.*

Impronta

$$$ | **VENETIAN** | This sleek café is a favorite lunchtime haunt for professors from the nearby university and local businesspeople, when you can easily have a beautifully prepared *primo* (first course)

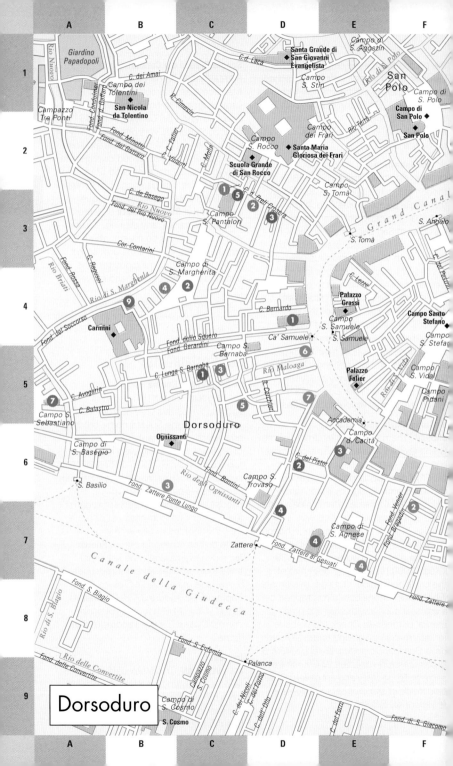

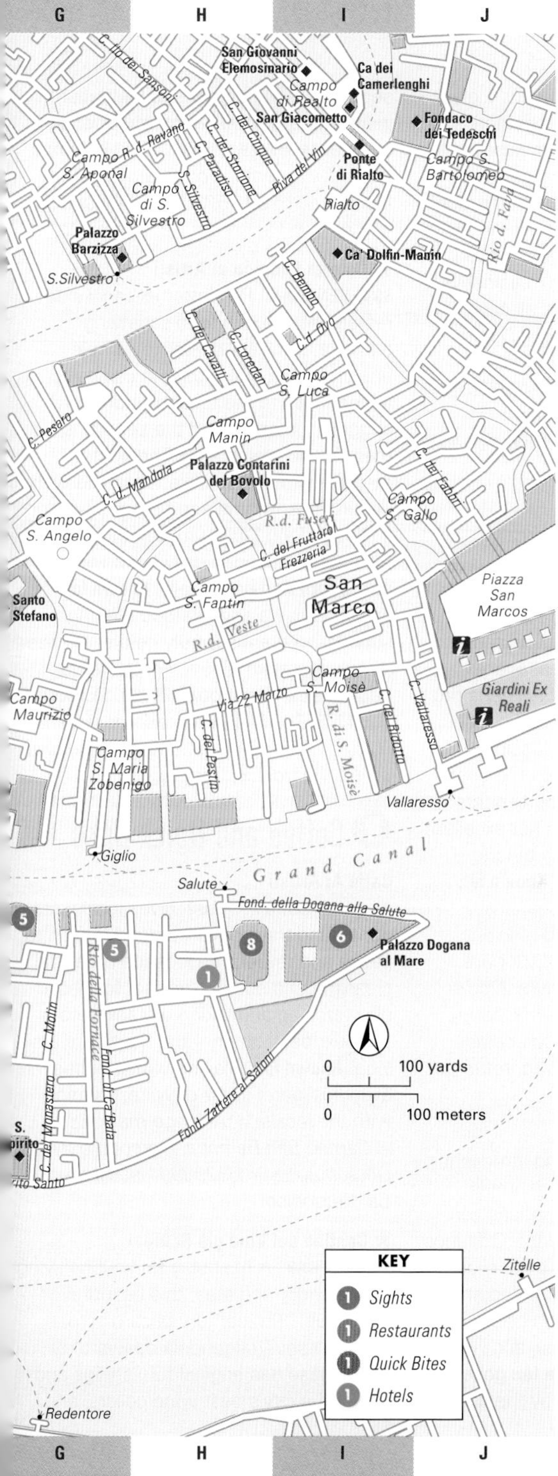

Sights ▼

1 Ca' Rezzonico **D4**
2 Campo Santa Margherita **C4**
3 Gallerie dell'Accademia **E6**
4 Gesuati............................. **D7**
5 Peggy Guggenheim Collection... **G6**
6 Punta della Dogana **I6**
7 San Sebastiano **A5**
8 Santa Maria della Salute **H6**
9 Scuola Grande dei Carmini....... **B4**

Restaurants ▼

1 Estro Vino e Cucina................ **C2**
2 Impronta **D3**
3 La Bitta............................ **C5**
4 Osteria alla Bifora **B4**
5 Osteria Enoteca ai Artisti **C5**

Quick Bites ▼

1 Caffè Ai Artisti **C5**
2 Cantine del Vino già Schiavi...... **D6**
3 Imagina Cafè **D3**
4 Osteria al Squero **D7**
5 Pasticceria Tonolo................. **C3**

Hotels ▼

1 Ca Maria Adele **H7**
2 Hotel American Dinesen........... **F7**
3 Il Palazzo Experimental **B6**
4 La Calcina **E7**
5 Locanda Ca' Zose................. **G6**
6 Palazzo Stern..................... **D5**
7 Pensione Accademia
Villa Maravege................... **D5**

4

Venice DORSODURO

KEY
1 Sights
1 Restaurants
1 Quick Bites
1 Hotels

or *secondo* (second course), plus a glass of wine, for a reasonable price; there's also a good selection of sandwiches and salads. Unlike most local eateries, this spot is open from breakfast through late dinner, and you can dine well in the evening on imaginative pasta, seafood, and meat dishes. **Known for:** imaginative dishes; contemporary decor; all-day dining. [$] *Average main: €25* ✉ *Dorsoduro 3815, Calle Crosera and Calle San Pantalon, Dorsoduro* ☎ *041/2750386* 🌐 *www.improntacafevenice.com* 🕓 *Closed Sun. and 2 wks in Aug.* [M] *Vaporetto: San Tomà.*

★ La Bitta

$$ | NORTHERN ITALIAN | For a break from all the fish and seafood options in Venice, this is your place; the meat- and veggie-focused menu (inspired by the cuisine of the Venetian mainland) presents a new temptation at every course, and market availability keeps the dishes changing almost every day. The homemade desserts are all luscious (it's been said that La Bitta serves the best panna cotta in town), and you can trust the owner's selections from her excellent wine and grappa lists, which tend to favor small local producers. **Known for:** meat dishes (no seafood); seasonally inspired menus; friendly and efficient service. [$] *Average main: €23* ✉ *Calle Lunga San Barnaba, Dorsoduro 2753/A, Dorsoduro* ☎ *041/5230531* 🌐 *facebook.com/labittavenezia* 💳 *No credit cards* 🕓 *Closed Sun. No lunch* [M] *Vaporetto: Ca' Rezzonico, Zattere.*

★ Osteria alla Bifora

$$ | VENETIAN | A beautiful and atmospheric bacaro, Alla Bifora has such ample, satisfying fare that most Venetians consider it a full-fledged restaurant. Offerings include overflowing trays of cold, sliced meats and cheeses; various preparations of *baccalà* (cod); and Venetian classics, such as *polpette* (croquettes), and marinated anchovies. **Known for:** good selection of regional wines by the glass; seppie in nero con polenta (cuttlefish in ink with polenta); warm and friendly owners. [$] *Average main: €18* ✉ *Campo Santa Margherita, Dorsoduro 2930, Dorsoduro* ☎ *041/5236119* 🕓 *Closed Jan. and Aug.* [M] *Vaporetto: Ca' Rezzonico.*

★ Osteria Enoteca ai Artisti

$$$ | VENETIAN | Pop into this canal-side restaurant at lunch for a satisfying primo or come for dinner to sample fine and fresh offerings; the candlelit tables that line the fondamenta (quay) suggest romance, and the service is friendly and welcoming. The posted menu—with choices like tagliatelle with porcini mushrooms and tiger prawns, or a filleted John Dory with tomatoes and pine nuts—changes daily (spot the date at the top) and seasonally. **Known for:** delicious pasta and seafood offerings; superlative tiramisu; truly helpful service. [$] *Average main: €25* ✉ *Fondamenta della Toletta, Dorsoduro 1169a, Dorsoduro* ☎ *041/5238944* 🌐 *www.enotecaartisti.com* 🕓 *Closed Sun. and Mon.* [M] *Vaporetto: Ca' Rezzonico, Zattere.*

☕ Coffee and Quick Bites

Caffè Ai Artisti

$ | CAFÉ | Caffè Ai Artisti gives locals, students, and travelers alike good reason to pause and refuel. The location is central, pleasant, and sunny—perfect for people-watching and taking a break before the next destination—and the hours are long. **Known for:** relaxing with a coffee; evening Aperol spritz or wine; chilling with the locals. [$] *Average main: €8* ✉ *Campo San Barnaba, Dorsoduro 2771, Dorsoduro* ☎ *041/5238994* [M] *Vaporetto: Ca' Rezzonico.*

★ Cantine del Vino già Schiavi

$ | WINE BAR | A mainstay for anyone living or working in the area, this beautiful, family-run, 19th-century bacaro across from the *squero* (gondola boatyard) of San Trovaso has original furnishings and one of the city's best wine cellars, and

the walls are covered floor to ceiling with bottles for purchase. The *cicheti* (small plates) here are some of the most inventive—and freshest—in Venice (feel free to compliment the signora, who makes them up to twice a day); everything's eaten standing up, as there's no seating. **Known for:** excellent quality cicheti; plenty of wine choices; boisterous local atmosphere. $ *Average main: €8* ✉ *Fondamenta Nani, Dorsoduro 992, Dorsoduro* ☎ *041/5230034* ⊕ *www.cantinaschiavi.com* ⊘ *Closed Sun. and 3 wks in Aug.* Ⓜ *Vaporetto: Accademia, Zattere.*

Imagina Cafè

$ | **ITALIAN** | This friendly café and art gallery, located between Campo Santa Margherita and Campo San Barnaba, is a great place to stop for a spritz, or even for a light lunch or dinner. The highlights are the freshly made salads, but their panini and tramezzini are also among the best in the area. **Known for:** tasty sandwiches and salads; good wines and cocktails; pleasant outdoor seating. $ *Average main: €10* ✉ *Rio Terà Canal, Dorsoduro 3126, Dorsoduro* ☎ *041/2410625* ⊕ *www.imaginacafe.it* Ⓜ *Vaporetto: Ca' Rezzonico.*

Osteria al Squero

$$ | **ITALIAN** | It wasn't long after this lovely little wine bar (not, as its name implies, a restaurant) appeared across from Squero San Trovaso that it became a neighborhood—and citywide—favorite. The Venetian owner has created a personal vision of what a good bar should offer: a variety of sumptuous cicheti, panini, and cheeses to be accompanied by just the right regional wines (ask for his recommendation). **Known for:** tasty cicheti; good veggie options; pretty canal views. $ *Average main: €20* ✉ *Fondamenta Nani, Dorsoduro 943/944, Dorsoduro* ☎ *335/6007513 mobile* ⊕ *osteriaalsquero.wordpress.com* ⊘ *Closed Sun.* Ⓜ *Vaporetto: Zattere, Accademia.*

Pasticceria Tonolo

$ | **BAKERY** | One of Venice's premier confectioneries has been in operation since 1886. During Carnevale it's still one of the best places in town for *frittelle,* or fried doughnuts (traditional raisin or cream-filled), and at Christmas and Easter, this is where Venetians order their focaccia veneziana, the traditional raised cake—well in advance. **Known for:** arguably the best pastries in Venice; excellent coffee; can't-miss doughnuts. $ *Average main: €5* ✉ *Calle San Pantalon, Dorsoduro 3764, Dorsoduro* ☎ *041/5237209* ⊕ *pasticceria-tonolo-venezia.business.site* ⊘ *Closed Mon.* Ⓜ *Vaporetto: San Tomà.*

Hotels

★ Ca Maria Adele

$$$$ | **HOTEL** | One of the city's most intimate and elegant getaways blends terrazzo floors, dramatic Murano chandeliers, and antique-style furnishings with contemporary touches, particularly in the African-wood reception area and breakfast room. **Pros:** quiet and romantic; imaginative decor; tranquil yet convenient spot near Santa Maria della Salute. **Cons:** no elevator and lots of stairs; bathrooms on the small side; no restaurant (just breakfast room). $ *Rooms from: €419* ✉ *Campo Santa Maria della Salute, Dorsoduro 111, Dorsoduro* ☎ *041/5203078* ⊕ *www.camariaadele.it* ⊘ *Closed 3 wks in Jan.* ⇨ *12 rooms* ⦿❘ *Free Breakfast* Ⓜ *Vaporetto: Salute.*

Hotel American Dinesen

$$$ | **HOTEL** | If you're in Venice to see art, you can't beat the location of this hotel, where all the spacious rooms have brocade fabrics and Venetian-style lacquered furniture. **Pros:** near Gallerie dell'Accademia and Peggy Guggenheim Collection; on a bright, quiet, exceptionally picturesque canal; some rooms have canal-view terraces. **Cons:** canal-view rooms are more expensive; style could be too understated for those expecting Venetian opulence; bathrooms can feel

cramped. $ *Rooms from: €221* ✉ *Fondamenta Bragadin, Dorsoduro 628, Dorsoduro* ☎ *041/5204733* ⊕ *www.hotelamerican.it* ↻ *34 rooms* ⦿ *No Meals* Ⓜ *Vaporetto: Accademia, Salute, Zattere.*

Il Palazzo Experimental

$$$ | **HOTEL** | Of-the-moment Parisian designer Dorothée Meilichzon composed the striped pastel color palette at this hip boutique hotel—the first Experimental Group property in Italy—hidden inside a Renaissance palazzo facing the Giudecca Canal. **Pros:** fun, whimsical decor; quiet location away from the Venice crowds; trendy cocktail bar on-site. **Cons:** not all rooms have water views; little storage space in bathrooms; no gym. $ *Rooms from: €279* ✉ *Fondamenta Zattere Al Ponte Lungo, Dorsoduro 1411, Dorsoduro* ☎ *041/0980200* ⊕ *www.palazzoexperimental.com* ↻ *32 rooms* ⦿ *No Meals* Ⓜ *Vaporetto: Zattere, San Basilio.*

La Calcina

$$ | **HOTEL** | Many notables (including Victorian-era art critic John Ruskin) have stayed at this hotel, though they might not recognize it after its series of upscale renovations; it has an enviable location along the sunny Zattere, as well as comfy rooms and apartments with parquet floors, original 19th-century furniture, and firm beds. **Pros:** panoramic views from some rooms; quiet, peaceful atmosphere; well-regarded restaurant with terrace over the Giudecca Canal. **Cons:** not for travelers who prefer ultramodern surroundings; no elevator; most rooms on the small side. $ *Rooms from: €149* ✉ *Zattere, Dorsoduro 780, Dorsoduro* ☎ *041/5206466* ⊕ *www.lacalcina.com* ↻ *25 rooms* ⦿ *Free Breakfast* Ⓜ *Vaporetto: Zattere.*

Locanda Ca' Zose

$$ | **HOTEL** | The idea that the Campanati sisters named the 15 rooms in their renovated 17th-century locanda after the stars and constellations of the highest magnitude in the Northern Hemisphere

says something about how personally this place is run. **Pros:** canal views; quiet but convenient location; efficient, personal service. **Cons:** no outdoor garden or terrace; no Wi-Fi in rooms (but free in lounge, as is computer use); unimpressive breakfast. $ *Rooms from: €127* ✉ *Calle del Bastion, Dorsoduro 193/B, Dorsoduro* ☎ *041/5226635* ⊕ *www.hotelcazose.com* ↻ *15 rooms* ⦿ *No Meals* Ⓜ *Vaporetto: Salute.*

★ Palazzo Stern

$$$ | **HOTEL** | This opulently refurbished neo-Gothic palazzo features marble-column arches, terrazzo floors, frescoed ceilings, mosaics, and a charming carved staircase, and some rooms have tufted walls and parquet flooring. **Pros:** excellent hotel service; lovely views from many rooms; modern renovation retains historic ambience. **Cons:** standard rooms don't have views; Grand Canal–facing rooms can be a bit noisy; no restaurant, gym, or spa. $ *Rooms from: €280* ✉ *Calle del Traghetto, Dorsoduro 2792, Dorsoduro* ☎ *041/2770869* ⊕ *www.palazzostern.com* ↻ *24 rooms* ⦿ *No Meals* Ⓜ *Vaporetto: Ca' Rezzonico.*

Pensione Accademia Villa Maravege

$$ | **HOTEL** | Behind iron gates in one of the most densely packed parts of the city is this renowned Gothic-style villa with gardens and charmingly decorated accommodations with Venetian-style antique reproductions and fine tapestry. **Pros:** a unique villa in the heart of Venice; two gardens where guests can breakfast, drink, and relax; complimentary drinks and snacks at the bar. **Cons:** no guest rooms have Grand Canal views; bathrooms can be on the small side; no restaurant. $ *Rooms from: €185* ✉ *Fondamenta Bollani, Dorsoduro 1058, Dorsoduro* ☎ *041/5210188* ⊕ *www.pensioneaccademia.it* ↻ *27 rooms* ⦿ *Free Breakfast* Ⓜ *Vaporetto: Accademia.*

Nightlife

Al Chioschetto

BARS | Although this popular place consists only of a kiosk set up to serve some outdoor tables, it is located on the Zattere and thus provides a wonderful view of the Giudecca Canal. It's a handy meet-up spot for locals, especially students from the nearby university, and a useful stop-off for tourists in nice weather for a spritz or a panino. Keep in mind, though, that "the kiosk" exists for quick refreshments and not for lingering. The view and the sunshine (and especially the sunset) are the main draw; the food and drink, while acceptable, are not exceptional. ⊠ *Fondamenta delle Zattere, Dorsoduro 1406/A, Dorsoduro* ☎ *348/3968466* Ⓜ *Vaporetto: San Basilio, Zattere.*

★ Il Caffè Rosso (*Bar Rosso*)

BARS | The sign above the door simply says "CAFFÈ," but it has long since been called "Bar Rosso" for its bright-red exterior. The ideal people-watching spot on one of the busiest campos, it has far more tables outside than inside. A favorite with students and faculty from the nearby university, it's a good place to start the day with coffee and croissant, or to enjoy a drink. ⊠ *Campo Santa Margherita, Dorsoduro 2963, Dorsoduro* ☎ *041/5287998* ⊕ *facebook.com/cafferosso.venezia* Ⓜ *Vaporetto: Ca' Rezzonico.*

Orange

BARS | Modern, hip, and complemented by an internal garden, this welcoming bar anchors the south end of Campo Santa Margherita, the liveliest campo in Venice. You can have *piadine* (thin flatbread) sandwiches, salads, and drinks while watching soccer games on a massive screen inside, or sit at the tables facing the campo. Despite being close to the university, Orange is frequented primarily by young working people from the mainland and tourists. ⊠ *Campo Santa Margherita, Dorsoduro 3054/A, Dorsoduro* ☎ *041/5234740* ⊕ *facebook.com/orangevenezia* Ⓜ *Vaporetto: Ca' Rezzonico.*

Venice Jazz Club

LIVE MUSIC | Owner Federico is on the piano while his band plays live jazz in styles including classic, modern, Latin jazz, and bossa nova at this intimate venue. Concerts usually start at 9 pm every night except Sunday and Monday, and dinner is available beforehand for an extra charge. ⊠ *Fondamenta del Squero, Dorsoduro* ☎ *041/5232056* ⊕ *www.venicejazzclub.com* ☞ *€25 entrance fee includes 1 drink* Ⓜ *Vaporetto: Ca' Rezzonico.*

Shopping

Il Grifone

HANDBAGS | Of Venice's few remaining artisan leather shops, Il Grifone is the standout with respect to quality, tradition, and the guarantee of an exquisite product. For more than 30 years, Antonio Peressin has been making bags, purses, belts, and smaller leather items that have a wide following because of his precision and attention to detail. His goods remain reasonably and accessibly priced. ⊠ *Fondamenta del Gafaro, Dorsoduro 3516, Dorsoduro* ☎ *041/5229452* ⊕ *www.ilgrifonevenezia.it* Ⓜ *Vaporetto: Piazzale Roma.*

Marina e Susanna Sent

JEWELRY & WATCHES | The beautiful and elegant glass jewelry of Marina and Susanna Sent has been featured in *Vogue.* Look also for vases and other exceptional design pieces. Other locations are on the Fondamenta Serenella on Murano and in San Polo under the Sotoportego dei Oresi at Rialto. ⊠ *Campo San Vio, Dorsoduro 669, Dorsoduro* ☎ *041/5208136* ⊕ *www.marinaesusannasent.com* Ⓜ *Vaporetto: Salute, Accademia, Zattere.*

San Polo and Santa Croce

The two smallest of Venice's six sestieri, San Polo and Santa Croce, were named after their main churches, although the Chiesa di Santa Croce was demolished in 1810. The city's most famous bridge, the Ponte di Rialto, unites San Marco (east) with San Polo (west). The Rialto takes its name from Rivoaltus, the high ground on which it was built. You'll find some of Venice's most lauded restaurants here, and shops abound in the area surrounding the Ponte di Rialto. On the San Marco side you'll find fashion, on the San Polo side, food.

TIMING

To do the area justice requires at least half a day. If you want to take part in the food shopping, come early to beat the crowds. Campo San Giacomo dell'Orio, west of the main thoroughfare that takes you from the Ponte di Rialto to Santa Maria Gloriosa dei Frari, is a peaceful place for a drink and a rest. The museums of Ca' Pesaro are a time commitment—you'll want at least two hours to see them both.

 Sights

Ca' Pesaro

ART MUSEUM | Baldassare Longhena's grand Baroque palace, begun in 1676, is the beautifully restored home of two impressive collections. The Galleria Internazionale d'Arte Moderna has works by 19th- and 20th-century artists, such as Klimt, Kandinsky, Matisse, and Miró. It also has a collection of representative works from the Venice Biennale that amounts to a panorama of 20th-century art. The pride of the Museo Orientale is its collection of Japanese art—and especially armor and weapons—of the Edo period (1603–1868). It also has a small but striking collection of Chinese and Indonesian porcelains and musical instruments. ⊠ *Fondamenta Pesaro, Santa Croce 2076, Santa Croce* ☎ *041/721127 Galleria, 041/5241173 Museo Orientale* ⊕ *capesaro.visitmuve. it* ⊠ *€10, includes both museums (free with Museum Pass)* ⊗ *Closed Mon.–Wed.* Ⓜ *Vaporetto: San Stae.*

Campo San Polo

PLAZA/SQUARE | Only Piazza San Marco is larger than this square, and the echo of children's voices bouncing off the surrounding palaces makes the space seem even bigger. Campo San Polo once hosted bullfights, fairs, military parades, and packed markets, and now comes especially alive on summer nights, when it's home to the city's outdoor cinema.

The Chiesa di San Polo has been restored so many times that little remains of the original 9th-century church, and the 19th-century alterations were so costly that, sadly, the friars sold off many great paintings to pay bills. Although Gianbattista Tiepolo is represented here, his work is outdone by 16 paintings by his son Giandomenico (1727–1804), including the *Stations of the Cross* in the oratory to the left of the entrance. The younger Tiepolo also created a series of expressive and theatrical renderings of the saints. Look for altarpieces by Tintoretto and Veronese that managed to escape auction.

San Polo's bell tower (begun 1362), across the street from the entrance to the church, remained unchanged over the centuries—don't miss the two lions, playing with a disembodied human head and a serpent, on the wall just above the tower's doorway. Tradition has it that the head refers to that of Marino Faliero, the doge executed for treason in 1355. ⊠ *Campo San Polo, San Polo* ☎ *041/2750462* ⊕ *www.chorusvenezia. org* ⊠ *Chiesa di San Polo €3 (free with Chorus Pass)* ⊗ *Closed Sun.* Ⓜ *Vaporetto: San Silvestro, San Tomà.*

San Giacomo dall'Orio

PLAZA/SQUARE | This lovely square was named after a laurel tree (*orio*), and today trees lend it shade and character. Add benches and a fountain (with a drinking bowl for dogs), and the pleasant, oddly shaped campo becomes a welcoming place for friendly conversation and neighborhood kids at play. The church of San Giacomo dall'Orio was founded in the 9th century on an island still populated (the legend goes) by wolves. The current church dates from 1225. ⊠ *Campo San Giacomo dall'Orio, Santa Croce* ☎ *041/2750462* ⊕ *www.chorusvenezia. org* 🎫 *Church €3 (free with Chorus Pass)* 🕙 *Church closed Sun.* Ⓜ *Vaporetto: San Stae, Riva de Biasio.*

San Giovanni Elemosinario

CHURCH | Storefronts make up the facade, and market guilds—poulterers, messengers, and fodder merchants—built the altars at this church intimately bound to the Rialto markets. The original church was completely destroyed by a fire in 1514 and rebuilt in 1531 by Scarpagnino, who had also worked on the Scuola di San Rocco. During a more recent restoration, workers stumbled upon a frescoed cupola by Pordenone (1484–1539) that had been painted over centuries earlier. Don't miss Titian's *St. John the Almsgiver* and Pordenone's *Sts. Catherine, Sebastian, and Roch.* ⊠ *Rialto Ruga Vecchia San Giovanni, San Polo 480, San Polo* ☎ *041/2750462* ⊕ *www.chorusvenezia.org* 🎫 *€3 (free with Chorus Pass)* 🕙 *Closed Fri.–Tues.* Ⓜ *Vaporetto: San Silvestro, Rialto Mercato.*

San Stae

CHURCH | The church of San Stae—the Venetian name for Sant'Eustachio (St. Eustace)—was reconstructed in 1687 by Giovanni Grassi and given a new facade in 1707 by Domenico Rossi. Renowned Venetian painters and sculptors of the early 18th century decorated this church around 1717 with the legacy left by Doge Alvise II Mocenigo, who's buried in the center aisle. San Stae affords a good opportunity to see the early works of Gianbattista Tiepolo, Sebastiano Ricci, and Piazzetta, as well as those of the previous generation of Venetian painters, with whom they had studied. ⊠ *Campo San Stae, Santa Croce* ☎ *041/2750462* ⊕ *www.chorusvenezia.org* 🎫 *€3 (free with Chorus Pass)* 🕙 *Closed Fri.–Tues.* Ⓜ *Vaporetto: San Stae.*

★ Santa Maria Gloriosa dei Frari

CHURCH | Completed in 1442, this immense Gothic church of russet-color brick, known locally as "I Frari," is famous for its array of spectacular Venetian paintings and historic tombs. In the sacristy, see Giovanni Bellini's 1488 triptych *Madonna and Child with Saints.* The Corner Chapel is graced by Bartolomeo Vivarini's altarpiece *St. Mark Enthroned* and *Saints John the Baptist, Jerome, Peter, and Nicholas.* In the first south chapel of the chorus, there is a fine sculpture of St. John the Baptist by Donatello, dated 1438, with a psychological intensity rare for early Renaissance sculpture. Titian's *Assumption*, unveiled in 1518, is at the far end of the nave. ⊠ *Campo dei Frari, San Polo* ☎ *041/2728611* ⊕ *www.basilicadeifrari.it* 🎫 *€3 (free with Chorus Pass)* Ⓜ *Vaporetto: San Tomà.*

★ Scuola Grande di San Rocco

ART MUSEUM | This elegant example of Venetian Renaissance architecture was built between 1516 and 1549 for the essentially secular charitable confraternity bearing the saint's name. The Venetian *scuole* were organizations that sometimes had loose religious affiliations, through which the artisan class could exercise some influence upon civic life. San Rocco was a protector against the plague, and his scuola was one of the city's most magnificent. While the building is bold and dramatic outside, its contents are even more stunning—a series of more than 60 paintings by Tintoretto. *Moses Striking Water from the*

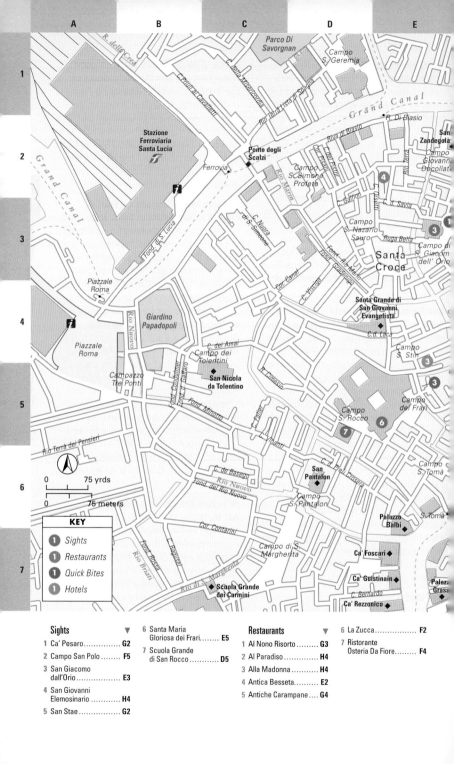

Sights ▼

1 Ca' Pesaro.............. **G2**
2 Campo San Polo **F5**
3 San Giacomo
dall'Orio................. **E3**
4 San Giovanni
Elemosinario **H4**
5 San Stae................ **G2**

6 Santa Maria
Gloriosa dei Frari........ **E5**
7 Scuola Grande
di San Rocco **D5**

Restaurants ▼

1 Al Nono Risorto **G3**
2 Al Paradiso.............. **H4**
3 Alla Madonna **H4**
4 Antica Besseta.......... **E2**
5 Antiche Carampane **G4**

6 La Zucca................ **F2**
7 Ristorante
Osteria Da Fiore......... **F4**

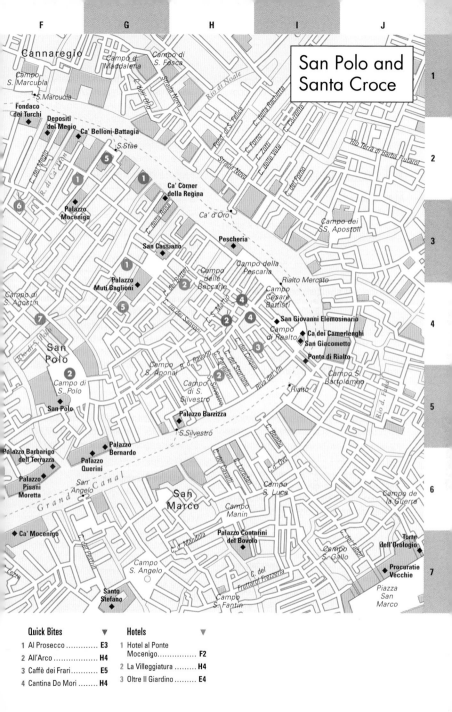

San Polo and Santa Croce

Cannaregio

Campo d. Maddalena
Campo di S. Fosca

Campo S. Marcuola
S. Marcuola

Fondaco dei Turchi
Depositi del Megio
Ca' Belloni-Battagia
S.Stae
Ca' Corner della Regina
Ca' d'Oro
Campo dei SS. Apostoli

Palazzo Mocenigo
San Cassiano
Pescheria
Campo della Pescaria
Campo delle Beccarie
Rialto Mercato
Campo Cesare Battisti

Palazzo Muti Baglioni
San Giovanni Elemosinario
Campo di S. Agostin
San Polo
Campo S. Aponal
Campo di Realto
Ca dei Camerlenghi
San Giacometto
Ponte di Rialto
Rialto
Campo S Bartolomeo

Campo di S. Polo
San Polo
Campo di S. Silvestro
Palazzo Barzizza
S.Silvestro

Palazzo Barbarigo dell Terrazza
Palazzo Bernardo
Palazzo Querini
Palazzo Pisani Moretta
San Angelo
Grand Canal
San Marco
Campo Manin
Campo S. Luca
Campo de la Guerra

Ca' Mocenigo
Palazzo Contarini del Bovolo
Torre dell'Orologio
Procuratie Vecchie

Campo S. Angelo
Campo S. Gallo
Piazza San Marco

Santo Stefano
Campo S Fantin

Quick Bites ▼

1 Al Prosecco **E3**
2 All'Arco **H4**
3 Caffè dei Frari **E5**
4 Cantina Do Morì **H4**

Hotels ▼

1 Hotel al Ponte Mocenigo **F2**
2 La Villeggiatura **H4**
3 Oltre Il Giardino **E4**

Rock, The Brazen Serpent, and *The Fall of Manna* represent three afflictions—thirst, disease, and hunger—that San Rocco sought to relieve. ✉ *Campo San Rocco, San Polo 3052, San Polo* ☎ *041/5234864* 🌐 *www.scuolagrandesanrocco.it* 🎟 *€10* [M] *Vaporetto: San Tomà.*

🍴 Restaurants

Al Nono Risorto
$$ | **VENETIAN** | **FAMILY** | This friendly trattoria popular with the locals is only a short walk from the Rialto markets. The pizza—not a Venetian specialty, generally speaking—is pretty good here, but the star attractions are the generous appetizers and excellent shellfish pastas. **Known for:** traditional starters and pastas; quite tasty pizzas; pretty outdoor garden seating. [$] *Average main: €16* ✉ *Sotoportego de Siora Bettina, Santa Croce 2338, Santa Croce* ☎ *041/5241169* 🌐 *alnonorisorto-venezia.com* 🕒 *Closed Jan.* [M] *Vaporetto: Rialto Mercato.*

★ Al Paradiso
$$$ | **MODERN ITALIAN** | In a small dining room made warm and cozy by its pleasing and unpretentious decor, proprietor Giordano makes all diners feel like honored guests. Unlike many elegant restaurants, Al Paradiso serves generous portions, and many of the delicious antipasti and primi are quite satisfying; you may want to follow the traditional Italian way of ordering and wait until you've finished your antipasto or your primo before you order your secondo. **Known for:** large appetizer and pasta portions; tasty meat and fish mains; central location near the Ponte di Rialto. [$] *Average main: €26* ✉ *Calle del Paradiso, San Polo 767, San Polo* ☎ *041/5234910* 🌐 *www.ristoranteal-paradiso.com* 🕒 *Closed 3 wks Jan.–Feb.* [M] *Vaporetto: San Silvestro.*

Alla Madonna
$$ | **VENETIAN** | "The Madonna" used to be world-famous as *the* classic Venetian trattoria, but in recent decades has settled into middle age. Owned and operated by the Rado family since 1954, this Venetian institution looks like one, with wood beams, stained-glass windows, and a panoply of paintings on white walls. **Known for:** freshly prepared seafood; traditional Venetian cuisine; old-time atmosphere. [$] *Average main: €18* ✉ *Calle della Madonna, San Polo 594, San Polo* ☎ *041/5223824* 🌐 *www.ristoranteallamadonna.com* 🕒 *Closed Wed. and Jan.* [M] *Vaporetto: San Silvestro, Rialto Mercato.*

Antica Besseta
$$$ | **VENETIAN** | Tucked away in a quiet corner of Santa Croce, with a few tables under an ivy shelter, the Antica Besseta dates from the 19th century, and it retains some of its old feel. The menu focuses on vegetables and fish, according to what's at the market, with some pasta and meat dishes, too. **Known for:** classic Italian pastas, like spaghetti con vongole (with clams); simple menu of fish and meat choices; charming old-fashioned feel. [$] *Average main: €30* ✉ *Salizzada de Ca' Zusto, Santa Croce 1395, Santa Croce* ☎ *041/721687* 🌐 *www.anticabesseta.it* 🕒 *Closed Tues.* [M] *Vaporetto: Riva de Biasio.*

★ Antiche Carampane
$$$ | **SEAFOOD** | Judging by its rather modest and unremarkable appearance, you wouldn't guess that Piera Bortoluzzi Librai's trattoria is among the finest fish restaurants in the city both because of the quality of the ingredients and because of the chef's creative magic. You can choose from a selection of classic dishes with a modern and creative touch. **Known for:** superlative fish and seafood; modernized Venetian dishes; popular with visitors and locals (so book ahead). [$] *Average main: €30* ✉ *Rio Terà delle Carampane, San Polo 1911, San Polo* ☎ *041/5240165* 🌐 *www.antichecarampane.com* 🕒 *Closed Sun. and Mon., 10 days in Jan., and 3 wks July–Aug.* [M] *Vaporetto: Rialto Mercato, San Silvestro.*

La Zucca

$$$ | **NORTHERN ITALIAN** | Simple place settings, wood lattice walls, and a mélange of languages make La Zucca (The Pumpkin) feel much like a typical, somewhat sophisticated vegetarian restaurant that you could find in any European city. What makes La Zucca special is simply great cooking and the use of fresh, local ingredients—many of which, like the particularly sweet zucca itself, aren't normally found outside northern Italy. **Known for:** seasonal vegetarian-focused dishes; home-style Italian cooking; flan di zucca (pumpkin pudding). $ *Average main: €25* ⊠ *Calle del Tentor, at Ponte del Megio, Santa Croce 1762, Santa Croce* ☎ *041/5241570* ⊕ *www.lazucca.it* ⊘ *Closed Sun.* Ⓜ *Vaporetto: San Stae.*

★ Ristorante Osteria Da Fiore

$$$$ | **VENETIAN** | The understated atmosphere, simple decor, and quiet elegance featured alongside Da Fiore's modern take on traditional Venetian cuisine certainly merit its international reputation. With such beautifully prepared cuisine, you would expect the kitchen to be run by a chef with a household name; however, the kitchen is headed by owner Maurizio Martin's wife, Mara, who learned to cook from her grandmother. **Known for:** sophisticated traditional Venetian dishes; delicious tasting menus; reservations required. $ *Average main: €54* ⊠ *Calle del Scaleter, San Polo 2202, San Polo* ☎ *041/721308* ⊕ *www.ristorantedafiore.com* ⊘ *Closed 3 wks in Jan. and Sun.* Ⓜ *Vaporetto: San Tomà, San Silvestro.*

☕ Coffee and Quick Bites

Al Prosecco

$$ | **WINE BAR** | Locals drop into this friendly bacaro to explore wines from this region and elsewhere in Italy, which accompany a carefully chosen selection of meats, cheeses, and other food from small, artisanal producers, used in tasty panini like the *porchetta romane verdure* (roasted pork with greens) and

in elegant cold platters. A young, friendly staff reel off the day's specials with ease. **Known for:** great selection of biodynamic wines, including prosecco; lovely meat and cheese platters; outdoor seating on the lively campo. $ *Average main: €20* ⊠ *Campo San Giacomo dall'Orio, Santa Croce 1503, Santa Croce* ☎ *041/5240222* ⊕ *www.alprosecco.com* ⊘ *Closed Sun.* Ⓜ *Vaporetto: San Stae.*

All'Arco

$ | **WINE BAR** | Just because it's noon and you only have enough time between sights for a sandwich doesn't mean that it can't be a satisfying, even awe-inspiring, one. There's no menu at All'Arco, but a scan of what's behind the glass counter is all you need; order what entices you, or have Roberto or Matteo (father and son) suggest a cicheto or panino. **Known for:** top-notch cicheti; platters of meats and cheeses; friendly and helpful service. $ *Average main: €8* ⊠ *Calle Arco, San Polo 436, San Polo* ☎ *041/5205666* ⊘ *Closed Wed.* Ⓜ *Vaporetto: Rialto Mercato, San Silvestro.*

Caffè dei Frari

$ | **CAFÉ** | Just over the bridge in front of the Frari church is this old-fashioned place where you'll find an assortment of sandwiches and snacks, but it is the atmosphere, and not the food, that is the main attraction. Established in 1870, it's one of the last Venetian tearooms with its original decor, and while prices are a bit higher than in cafés in nearby Campo Santa Margherita, the vibe and the friendly "retro" atmosphere make the added cost worthwhile. **Known for:** lovely historic setting; well-made cocktails; quality cicheti. $ *Average main: €8* ⊠ *Fondamenta dei Frari, San Polo 2564, San Polo* ☎ *347/8293158* ⊘ *Closed Sun. and Mon. No dinner* Ⓜ *Vaporetto: San Tomà.*

Cantina Do Mori

$ | **WINE BAR** | This is the original bacaro, in business continually since 1462; cramped but warm and cozy under hanging antique copper pots, it has served generations of workers from the Rialto markets. In addition to young local whites and reds, the well-stocked cellar offers reserve labels, many available by the glass; between sips you can choose to munch the wide range of cicheti on offer, or a few tiny well-stuffed tramezzini, appropriately called *francobolli* (postage stamps). **Known for:** good choice of wines by the glass; fine selection of cicheti and sandwiches; delicious baccalà mantecato, with or without garlic and parsley. [$] *Average main: €8* ✉ *Calle dei Do Mori, San Polo 429, San Polo* ☎ *041/5225401* 🕒 *Closed Sun.* [M] *Vaporetto: Rialto Mercato.*

Hotels

★ Hotel al Ponte Mocenigo

$$ | HOTEL | At this hotel—once home to the Santa Croce branch of the Mocenigo family, which counts a few doges in its lineage—a columned courtyard welcomes you, and guest room decor nods to the building's history, with canopied beds, striped damask fabrics, lustrous terrazzo flooring, and gilt-accented furnishings. **Pros:** fantastic value; friendly and helpful staff; enchanting courtyard (the perfect spot for an aperitivo). **Cons:** beds are on the hard side; standard rooms are small; rooms in the annex can be noisy. [$] *Rooms from: €140* ✉ *Salizzada San Stae, Santa Croce 1985, Santa Croce* ☎ *041/5244797* 🌐 *www.alpontemocenigo.com* 🛏 *11 rooms* 🍴 *Free Breakfast* [M] *Vaporetto: San Stae.*

La Villeggiatura

$$ | HOTEL | If eclectic Venetian charm is what you seek, this luminous residence near the Rialto has it: each of the individually decorated guest rooms has its own theater-theme wall painting by a local artist. **Pros:** relaxed atmosphere and friendly, personalized service; meticulously maintained; well located near markets, artistic monuments, and restaurants. **Cons:** no elevator and lots of stairs; no view to speak of, despite the climb; no restaurant (though breakfast is served). [$] *Rooms from: €140* ✉ *Calle dei Botteri, San Polo 1569, San Polo* ☎ *041/5244673* 🌐 *www.lavilleggiatura.it* 🛏 *6 rooms* 🍴 *Free Breakfast* [M] *Vaporetto: Rialto Mercato.*

★ Oltre il Giardino

$$$$ | HOTEL | Behind a brick wall, just over the bridge from the Frari church, this palazzo is hard to find but well worth the effort: a sheltered location, large garden, and individually decorated guest rooms make it feel like a country house. **Pros:** peaceful, gracious, and convenient setting; glorious walled garden; friendly owners happy to share their Venice tips. **Cons:** a beautiful, but not particularly Venetian, ambience; rooms book up quickly; no in-house restaurant (though breakfast served). [$] *Rooms from: €330* ✉ *Fondamenta Contarini, San Polo 2542, San Polo* ☎ *041/2750015* 🌐 *www.oltreilgiardino-venezia.com* 🕒 *Closed Jan.* 🛏 *6 rooms* 🍴 *Free Breakfast* [M] *Vaporetto: San Tomà.*

Nightlife

★ Il Mercante

COCKTAIL LOUNGES | When the clock strikes 6 pm, historic Caffè dei Frari transforms into this lively craft cocktail bar that will dazzle your inner adventurer. Relax on a velvet sofa while savoring remarkably inventive drinks paired with flavorful small bites. Each pairing has a distinctive name; "Amatriciana" is composed of vodka, dry vermouth, and black tea, served with Parmesan foam, pineapple gel, and balsamic vinegar (billed as "strong, smoky, tasty"). ✉ *Fondamenta dei Frari, San Polo 2564, San Polo* ☎ *347/8293158 mobile* 🌐 *www.ilmercantevenezia.com* [M] *Vaporetto: San Tomà.*

Naranzaria

BARS | At the friendliest of the several bar-restaurants that line the Erbaria, near the Rialto markets, enjoy a cocktail outside, along the Canal Grande, or at a cozy table inside the renovated

16th-century warehouse. Although the food is acceptable, the ambience is really the main attraction. After the kitchen closes at 10:30, light snacks are served until midnight, and there is live music (usually jazz, Latin, or rock) occasionally on Sunday evening. On summer evenings, especially the weekend, the market area draws crowds of young people from Venice, the lagoon islands, and the mainland. ✉ *L'Erbaria, San Polo 130, San Polo* ☎ *041/7241035* ⊕ *www.naranzaria.it* Ⓜ *Vaporetto: Rialto Mercato.*

🛍 Shopping

Gilberto Penzo

CRAFTS | The gondola and lagoon boat expert in Venice creates scale models of a wide variety of Venetian boats in his nearby *laboratorio* (workshop). (If the retail shop is closed, a sign posted on the door will explain how to find Signor Penzo.) When he's not busy sawing and sanding, Mr. Penzo writes historical and technical books about traditional Venetian boats, including the gondola. Here you'll also find gondola model kits, as well as some *forcole* (Venetian rowing oarlocks). ✉ *Calle Seconda dei Saoneri, San Polo 2681, San Polo* ☎ *041/5246139* ⊕ *www.veniceboats.com* Ⓜ *Vaporetto: San Tomà.*

★ Il Tabarro San Marco di Monica Daniele

OTHER SPECIALTY STORE | This petite shop is the best place in town to find traditional Venetian wool capes, known as *tabarro*, and classic hats, such as the Ezra Pound (curved hat with a brim), the *tricorno* (three-cornered hat), and the *cilindro* (top hat). ✉ *Calle del Scaleter, San Polo 2235, San Polo* ☎ *041/5246242* ⊕ *www.monicadaniele.com* Ⓜ *Vaporetto: San Stae, San Silvestro.*

Laberintho

JEWELRY & WATCHES | A tiny bottega near Campo San Polo is run by a team of young goldsmiths and jewelry designers specializing in inlaid stones. The work on display in their shop is exceptional, and they also create customized pieces. ✉ *Calle del Scaleter, San Polo 2236, San Polo* ☎ *041/710017* ⊕ *www.laberintho.com* Ⓜ *Vaporetto: San Stae, San Silvestro.*

★ Tessitura Luigi Bevilacqua

FABRICS | This renowned studio has kept the weaving tradition alive in Venice since 1875, using 18th-century hand looms for its most precious creations. Its repertoire of 3,500 different patterns and designs yields a ready-to-sell selection of hundreds of brocades, Gobelins, damasks, velvets, taffetas, and satins. You'll also find tapestry, cushions, and braiding. ✉ *Santa Croce 1320, Santa Croce* ☎ *041/721566* ⊕ *luigi-bevilacqua.com* Ⓜ *Vaporetto: Riva de Biasio.*

Cannaregio

Seen from above, this part of town seems like a wide field plowed by several long, straight canals linked by perpendicular streets—not typical of Venice, where the shape of the islands usually defines the shape of the canals. Cannaregio's main thoroughfare, the Strada Nova (New Street, converted from a canal in 1871), is the longest street in Venice; it runs parallel to the Grand Canal.

TIMING

Although it's more residential and less sight-rich than other Venice neighborhoods, you'll still need several hours here to explore the Ca' d'Oro palace and Madonna dell'Orto and Santa Maria dei Miracoli churches, and to wander the Jewish Ghetto. Cannaregio is a great place to spend a morning before taking the vaporetto to Murano and Burano, which departs from the Fondamente Nove stop.

Sights

★ Ca' d'Oro

HISTORY MUSEUM | One of the classic postcard sights of Venice, this exquisite Venetian Gothic palace was once literally a "Golden House," when its marble tracery and ornaments were embellished with gold. It was created by Giovanni and Bartolomeo Bon between 1428 and 1430 for the patrician Marino Contarini, who had read about the Roman emperor Nero's golden house in Rome, the Domus Aurea, and wished to imitate it as a present to his wife. Her family owned the land and the Byzantine *fondaco* (palace-trading house) previously standing on it; you can still see the round Byzantine arches incorporated into the Gothic building's entry porch. ✉ *Calle Ca' d'Oro, Cannaregio 3933, Cannaregio* ☎ *041/5200345* ⊕ *www.cadoro.org* 🖃 *€6* Ⓜ *Vaporetto: Ca' d'Oro.*

★ Gesuiti

(*Chiesa di Santa Maria Assunta*) **CHURCH** | The interior walls of this early-18th-century church (1715–30) resemble brocade drapery, and only touching them will convince skeptics that rather than embroidered cloth, the green-and-white walls are inlaid marble. This trompe-l'oeil decor is typical of the late Baroque's fascination with optical illusion. Toward the end of his life, Titian tended to paint scenes of suffering and sorrow in a nocturnal ambience. A dramatic example of this is on display above the first altar to the left: Titian's daring *Martyrdom of St. Lawrence* (1578), taken from an earlier church that stood on this site. Tintoretto's *Assumption* (1555), originally commissioned for the destroyed Crociferi church, demands reverence. The Crociferi's surviving oratory, or prayer hall (Oratorio dei Crociferi), located across from the church, features some of Palma Giovane's best work, painted between 1583 and 1591. The oratory can be visited only by advance reservation by phone. ✉ *Campo dei Gesuiti, Cannaregio* ☎ *041/5231610 Gesuiti, 041/3096605 oratory* ⊕ *www.gioiellinascostidivenezia. it* 🖃 *Gesuiti €1; Oratorio dei Crociferi €3* ♿ *Reservations needed to visit oratory* Ⓜ *Vaporetto: Fondamente Nove.*

★ Jewish Ghetto

HISTORIC DISTRICT | The very first Jewish ghetto in Europe also contains the continent's highest density of Renaissance-era synagogues, and visiting them on a guided tour is interesting not only culturally but also aesthetically. In 1516, the Venetian Senate voted to confine Jews to an island in Cannaregio, whose gates were locked at night and whose canals were patrolled. In the 16th century, the community grew with refugees from the Inquisition. Although the gates were pulled down after Napoléon's 1797 arrival, the ghetto was reinstated during the Austrian occupation. Full freedom wasn't realized until 1866 with the founding of the Italian state. Many Jews fled Italy after Mussolini's 1938 racial laws, but of the remainder, all but eight were killed by the Nazis. You can visit some of the historic buildings of the ghetto on guided tours, which run in English every hour from 10 am to 5 pm (starting 9 am on Fridays) every day except Saturday. ✉ *Campo del Ghetto Nuovo, Cannaregio* ☎ *055/2989815* ⊕ *www.ghettovenezia. com* 🖃 *€12 for guided tour* ☉ *No guided tours on Sat. or Jewish holidays.*

★ Madonna dell'Orto

CHURCH | Though built toward the middle of the 14th century, this church takes its character from its beautiful late-Gothic facade, added between 1460 and 1464; it's one of the most beautiful Gothic churches in Venice. Tintoretto lived nearby, and this, his parish church, contains some of his most powerful work. Lining the chancel are two huge (45 feet by 20 feet) canvases, *Adoration of the Golden Calf* and *Last Judgment.* In glowing contrast to this awesome spectacle is Tintoretto's *Presentation of the Virgin at the Temple* and the simple chapel where he and his children, Marietta and Domenico, are buried. Paintings by Domenico, Cima da Conegliano, Palma Giovane, Palma Vecchio, and Titian also hang in the church. A chapel displays a photographic reproduction of a precious *Madonna and Child* by Giovanni Bellini. The original was stolen one night in 1993. Don't miss the beautifully austere, late-Gothic cloister (1460), which you enter through the small door to the right of the church; it is frequently used for exhibitions but may be open at other times as well. ✉ *Campo della Madonna dell'Orto, Cannaregio* ☎ *041/719933* 🎟 *€3* 🕓 *Closed Sun.* [M] *Vaporetto: Orto.*

Palazzo Vendramin-Calergi

CASINO | Hallowed as the site of Richard Wagner's death and today Venice's most glamorous casino, this magnificent edifice found its fame centuries earlier: Venetian star architect Mauro Codussi (1440–1504) essentially invented Venetian Renaissance architecture with this design. Built for the Loredan family around 1500, Codussi's palace married the fortresslike design of the Florentine Alberti's Palazzo Rucellai with the lightness and delicacy of Venetian Gothic. Note how Codussi beautifully exploits the flickering light of Venetian waterways to play across the building's facade and to pour in through the generous windows. Consult the website to book a guided tour of the small Museo Wagner upstairs, where an archive, events, and concerts may interest Wagnerians.

Venice has always prized the beauty of this palace. In 1652 its owners were convicted of a rather gruesome murder, and the punishment would have involved, as was customary, the demolition of their palace. The murderers were banned from the Republic, but the palace, in view of its beauty and historical importance, was spared. Only a newly added wing was torn down. ✉ *Cannaregio 2040, Cannaregio* ☎ *041/5297111* 🌐 *www.casinovenezia.it* 🎟 *Casino €5–€10; free for visitors staying at a Venice hotel (with prior written confirmation from the hotel, by 6 pm that day)* [M] *Vaporetto: San Marcuola.*

★ **Santa Maria dei Miracoli**

CHURCH | Tiny yet harmoniously proportioned, this Renaissance gem, built between 1481 and 1489, is sheathed in marble and decorated inside with exquisite marble reliefs. Architect Pietro Lombardo (circa 1435–1515) miraculously compressed the building to fit its lot, then created the illusion of greater size by varying the color of the exterior, adding extra pilasters on the building's canal side and offsetting the arcade windows to make the arches appear deeper. The church was built to house *I Miracoli*, an image of the Virgin Mary by Niccolò di Pietro (1394–1440) that is said to have performed miracles—look for it on the high altar. ✉ *Campo Santa Maria Nova, Cannaregio* ☎ *041/2750462* 🌐 *www.chorusvenezia.org* 🎟 *€3 (free with Chorus Pass)* 🕓 *Closed Sun.* [M] *Vaporetto: Rialto.*

🍴 Restaurants

★ **Algiubagiò**

$$$ | **ITALIAN** | Established in 1950, this restaurant along the quiet, northern outlier of Fondamente Nove has grandstand views of the San Michele island and various menus showcasing seasonal fish, meat, and pasta dishes. The friendly staff also serve ice cream, drinks, and sandwiches, making its modern bar, chic dining rooms, and lagoon-side platform restful environs to pause any time of day. **Known for:** airy respite for lunch or a snack; romantic spot for dinner; lovely waterfront seating with views of the Dolomites. [$] *Average main: €33* ✉ *Fondamente Nove, Cannaregio 5039, Cannaregio* ☎ *041/5236084* 🌐 *www.algiubagio.net* 🕓 *Closed Tues.* [M] *Vaporetto: Fondamente Nove.*

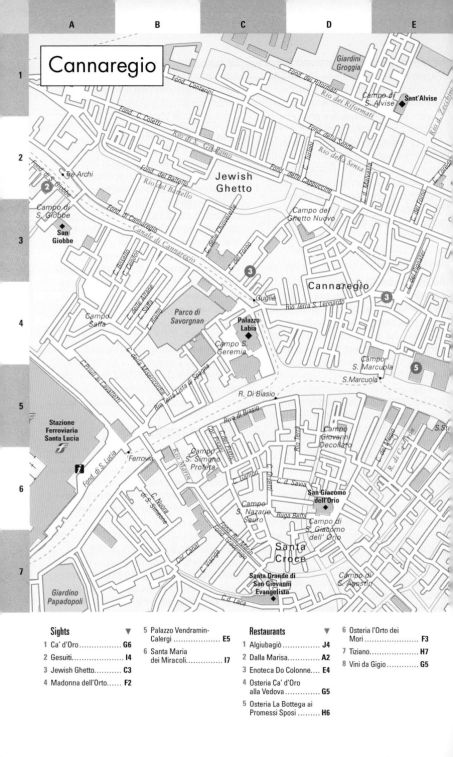

Cannaregio

Sights ▼

1 Ca' d'Oro G6
2 Gesuiti I4
3 Jewish Ghetto C3
4 Madonna dell'Orto F2

5 Palazzo Vendramin-
  Calergi E5
6 Santa Maria
  dei Miracoli I7

Restaurants ▼

1 Algiubagiò J4
2 Dalla Marisa A2
3 Enoteca Do Colonne E4
4 Osteria Ca' d'Oro
  alla Vedova G5
5 Osteria La Bottega ai
  Promessi Sposi H6

6 Osteria l'Orto dei
  Mori F3
7 Tiziano H7
8 Vini da Gigio G5

F   G   H   I   J

Madonna
dell'Orto

KEY

1 Sights
1 Restaurants
1 Quick Bites
1 Hotels

0   100 yards
0   100 meters

Canale delle Navi

1

2

3

4

Campo della
Madonna
dell'Orto

Sacca della
Misericordia

Fond. Nuove

Campo S.
Marziale

Campo di
S. Fosca
Maddalene

Rio della Sensa

Canale della Misericordia

Fond. S. Caterina

Fond.
Nuove

Fond. Nuove

Strada Nova

Rio di Noale

Grand Canal

Campo dei
SS. Apostoli

S. Canciano

Campo
S. Maria
Nova

Rio Terra di Barba Frutarol

C. d. Volti
C. Venier

Ca. D'oro

San
Cassiano

Pescheria

Campo della
Pescaria

Rialto Mercato

Palazzo Muti
Baglioni

Campo
delle
Beccarie

Campo
Cesare
Bettisti

San Giovanni
Elemosinario

Campo
di Rialto

Ca' da Mosto

Ca dei Camerlenghi

Campo Santi
Giovanni e Paolo

5 Locanda Ca' Amadi..... **H7**

6 Palazzo Abadessa **G5**

7 3749 Ponte Chiodo...... **G5**

Quick Bites	Hotels
1 Vino Vero **G4**	1 Al Palazzetto **G5**
	2 Al Ponte Antico **H7**
	3 Ca' Sagredo Hotel **G6**
	4 Hotel Antico Doge **H6**

★ Dalla Marisa

$$ | ITALIAN | This is the most famous restaurant in Venice for the city's working class; if you can get a table for lunch, you'll eat, without any choice, what Marisa prepares for her local clientele—generally, enormous portions of excellent pasta followed by a hearty roast meat course (frequently game, more infrequently fish), for an inexpensive fixed price. Dinner is a bit more expensive, and you may have some choice, but not much; for the authentic "Marisa experience," go for lunch. **Known for:** Venetian classics like baccalà mantecato; limited menu choices and cramped inside; genuine local atmosphere and gruff service. $ *Average main: €15* ✉ *Fondamenta di San Giobbe 652B, Cannaregio* ☎ *041/720211* ⊕ *trattoria-daa-marisa.business.site* ⊗ *No dinner Sun., Mon., and Wed.*

Enoteca Do Colonne

$ | WINE BAR | Venetians from the neighborhood frequent this friendly bacaro, not just for a glass of very drinkable wine, but also because of its excellent selection of traditional Venetian cicheti for lunch. There's a large assortment of sandwiches and panini, as well as luscious tidbits like grilled vegetables, breaded and fried sardines and shrimp, and a superb version of baccalà mantecato, along with Venetian working-class specialties, such as *musetto* (a sausage made from pigs' snouts served warm with polenta) and *nervetti* (veal tendons with lemon and parsley). **Known for:** a cozy place for locals to hang out; classic cicheti and sandwiches; the best musetto in town. $ *Average main: €10* ✉ *Rio Terà Cristo, Cannaregio 1814, Cannaregio* ☎ *041/5240453* ⊕ *www.docolonne.it* Ⓜ *Vaporetto: San Marcuola.*

Osteria Ca' d'Oro alla Vedova

$ | VENETIAN | "The best polpette in town," you'll hear fans of the venerable Vedova say, and that explains why it's an obligatory stop on any *giro d'ombra* (bacaro tour); the polpette are always hot and crunchy—and also gluten-free, as they're made with polenta. Ca' d'Oro is a full-fledged trattoria as well, but make sure to reserve ahead: it's no secret to those seeking traditional Venetian fare at reasonable prices, locals and travelers alike. **Known for:** famous polpette; classic Venetian cuisine; house wine served in tiny traditional glasses. $ *Average main: €14* ✉ *Calle del Pistor, Cannaregio 3912, off Strada Nova, Cannaregio* ☎ *041/5285324* ⊕ *www.facebook.com/allavedova* ⊗ *Closed Thurs. and Sun. morning* Ⓜ *Vaporetto: Ca' d'Oro.*

Osteria La Bottega ai Promessi Sposi

$$ | VENETIAN | Join locals at the *banco* (counter) premeal for an *ombra* (small glass of wine) and cicheti like polpette or violet eggplant rounds, or reserve a table for a full meal in the dining room or the intimate courtyard. A varied, seasonal menu includes local standards like calf's liver, along with creative variations on classic Venetian fare, such as homemade ravioli stuffed with radicchio di Treviso or orecchiette with a scrumptious minced-duck sauce. **Known for:** creative cicheti and wine; regularly changing menu with both traditional and modern choices; friendly, helpful service. $ *Average main: €20* ✉ *Calle de l'Oca, just off Campo Santi Apostoli, Cannaregio 4367, Cannaregio* ☎ *041/2412747* ⊗ *No lunch Mon.* Ⓜ *Vaporetto: Ca' d'Oro.*

Osteria l'Orto dei Mori

$$$ | ITALIAN | This small, popular neighborhood osteria—located canal-side, just under the nose of the campo's famous corner statue—specializes in creative versions of classic Italian (but not necessarily Venetian) dishes; don't skip dessert, as the tiramisu wins raves. Dine in the artsy and atmospheric interior or outside in the intimate, echoing square for a truly memorable experience. **Known for:** traditional Italian dishes with modern accents; choice local wine selection; buzzing atmosphere with locals and tourists alike.

$ Average main: €26 ⊠ Campo dei Mori, Fondamenta dei Mori, Cannaregio 3386, Cannaregio ☎ 041/5243677 ⊕ www. osteriaortodeimori.com ☉ Closed Tues. and Wed. Ⓜ Vaporetto: Orto, Ca' d'Oro, San Marcuola.

Tiziano

$ | ITALIAN | A fine variety of excellent tramezzini (sandwiches made of untoasted white bread triangles) lines the display cases at this *tavola calda* (roughly the Italian equivalent of a cafeteria) on the main thoroughfare from the Rialto to Santi Apostoli; inexpensive salad plates and daily pasta specials are also served. This is a great place for a light meal or snack before a performance at the nearby Teatro Malibran. **Known for:** quick meals or snacks, especially tramezzini; modest prices; efficient (if occasionally grumpy) service. *$ Average main: €8 ⊠ Salizada San Giovanni Crisostomo, Cannaregio 5747, Cannaregio ☎ 041/5235544 ⊕ bartiziano.business.site Ⓜ Vaporetto: Rialto.*

★ Vini da Gigio

$$ | VENETIAN | A brother-sister team run this refined trattoria, where you're made to feel as if you've been personally invited to lunch or dinner. Indulge, perhaps, in rigatoni with duck sauce or arugula-stuffed ravioli, seafood risotto made to order, or sesame-encrusted tuna. Just note, though, that it's the meat dishes that steal the show: the steak with red-pepper sauce and the *tagliata di agnello* (sautéed lamb fillet with a light, crusty coating) are both superb, and you'll never enjoy a better *fegato alla veneziana* (liver with onion). **Known for:** superb meat dishes like fegato alla veneziana; one of the city's best wine cellars; helpful and professional service. *$ Average main: €23 ⊠ Fondamenta San Felice, Cannaregio 3628/A, Cannaregio ☎ 041/5285140 ⊕ www.vinidagigio.com ☉ Closed Mon., Tues., and 2 wks in Aug. Ⓜ Vaporetto: Ca' d'Oro.*

Coffee and Quick Bites

★ Vino Vero

$ | WINE BAR | Swing by this pint-sized wine bar for cicheti and crostini that are just a bit different and fresher than what you'll find elsewhere, along with a fine selection of natural wines. Though there's not much space inside, try to snag one of the coveted seats by the canal. **Known for:** large selection of both Italian and international natural wines; delectable small bites; pretty canal-side seating. *$ Average main: €12 ⊠ Fondamenta de la Misericordia, Cannaregio 2497, Cannaregio ☎ 041/2750044 ⊕ vinovero.wine ☉ No lunch Mon. Ⓜ Vaporetto: Madonna dell'Orto, Ca' d'Oro.*

🛏 Hotels

Al Palazzetto

$$ | B&B/INN | FAMILY | Understated Venetian decor, original exposed-beam ceilings and terrazzo flooring, and large rooms suitable for families or small groups are hallmarks of this intimate, family-owned guesthouse. **Pros:** authentic 18th-century palace; clean and quiet; good value. **Cons:** old-fashioned decor; not many amenities; a bit rough around the edges. *$ Rooms from: €149 ⊠ Calle delle Vele, Cannaregio 4057, Cannaregio ☎ 041/2750897 ⊕ www.guesthouse.it ⤴ 5 rooms ⦿❙ Free Breakfast Ⓜ Vaporetto: Ca' d'Oro.*

★ Al Ponte Antico

$$$$ | HOTEL | This hospitable 16th-century palace inn has lined its Gothic windows with tiny white lights, creating an inviting glow that's emblematic of the luxurious, distinctively Venetian warmth inside. **Pros:** upper-level terrace overlooks Grand Canal; family-run warmth; excellent service. **Cons:** in one of the busiest areas of the city (although not particularly noisy); beds a little hard for some; books up quickly. *$ Rooms from: €350 ⊠ Calle dell'Aseo, Cannaregio 5768, Cannaregio ☎ 041/2411944 ⊕ www.alponteantico. com ⤴ 9 rooms ⦿❙ Free Breakfast Ⓜ Vaporetto: Rialto.*

Ca' Sagredo Hotel

$$$$ | **HOTEL** | This expansive palace has been the Sagredo family residence since the mid-1600s and has the decor to prove it: a massive staircase has Longhi wall panels soaring above it; large common areas are adorned with original art by Tiepolo, Longhi, and Ricci; and a traditional Venetian style dominates guest rooms, many of which have canal views and some of which have original art and architectural elements. **Pros:** excellent location; some of the city's best preserved interiors; rooftop terrace and indoor bar. **Cons:** more opulent than intimate, heat in rooms controlled by front desk; no coffee- or tea-making facilities in rooms. $ *Rooms from: €374* ✉ *Campo Santa Sofia, Cannaregio 4198/99, Cannaregio* ☎ *041/2413111* ⊕ *www.casagredohotel.com* 🛏 *42 rooms* ❍❘ *No Meals* Ⓜ *Vaporetto: Ca' d'Oro.*

Hotel Antico Doge

$$$$ | **HOTEL** | Once the home of Marino Faliero, a 14th-century doge who was executed for treason, this palazzo has been attentively "modernized" in elegant 18th-century Venetian style: all rooms are adorned with brocades, damask-tufted walls, gilt mirrors, and parquet floors—even the breakfast room has a stuccoed ceiling and Murano chandelier. **Pros:** romantic, atmospheric decor; convenient to the Rialto and beyond; some rooms have whirlpool tubs. **Cons:** no outdoor garden or terrace; no elevator; area outside hotel can get very busy. $ *Rooms from: €360* ✉ *Campo Santi Apostoli, Cannaregio 5643, Cannaregio* ☎ *041/7799990* ⊕ *www.anticodoge.com* 🛏 *20 rooms* ❍❘ *No Meals* Ⓜ *Vaporetto: Ca' d'Oro, Rialto.*

Locanda Ca' Amadi

$$ | **HOTEL** | A historic 13th-century palazzo near the Rialto markets is a welcome retreat on a tranquil *corte* (court), and individually decorated rooms have tufted walls and views of a lively canal or a quiet courtyard. **Pros:** classic Venetian style; some canal-view rooms; handy for sightseeing. **Cons:** rooms vary a lot in size and quality; no restaurant (simple continental breakfast served, though); reception staff not always helpful or available. $ *Rooms from: €171* ✉ *Corte Amadi, Cannaregio 5815, Cannaregio* ☎ *041/5285210* ⊕ *www.caamadi.it* 🛏 *6 rooms* ❍❘ *Free Breakfast* Ⓜ *Vaporetto: Rialto.*

★ Palazzo Abadessa

$$ | **HOTEL** | At this late-16th-century palazzo, you can experience warm hospitality, a luxurious atmosphere, a lush private garden, and unusually spacious guest rooms well appointed with antique-style furniture, frescoed or stuccoed ceilings, and silk fabrics. **Pros:** enormous walled garden, a rare and delightful treat in crowded Venice; unique and richly decorated guest rooms; superb guest service. **Cons:** some bathrooms are small and plain; no restaurant (buffet breakfast served); Wi-Fi can be iffy. $ *Rooms from: €172* ✉ *Calle Priuli, Cannaregio 4011, off Strada Nova, Cannaregio* ☎ *041/2413784* ⊕ *www.abadessa.com* ⊙ *Closed last 2 wks in Jan.* 🛏 *15 rooms* ❍❘ *Free Breakfast* Ⓜ *Vaporetto: Ca' d'Oro.*

3749 Ponte Chiodo

$$ | **B&B/INN** | Spending time at this charming guesthouse near the Ca' d'Oro vaporetto stop is like staying with a friend: service is warm and helpful, with lots of suggestions for dining and sightseeing. **Pros:** highly attentive service; relaxed atmosphere; pretty private garden. **Cons:** some bathrooms are smallish; no restaurant, though breakfast is served in the garden; not for those looking for large-hotel amenities (no spa or gym). $ *Rooms from: €135* ✉ *Calle Racheta, Cannaregio 3749, Cannaregio* ☎ *041/2413935, 348/2473520 mobile* ⊕ *www.pontechiodo.it* 🛏 *6 rooms* ❍❘ *Free Breakfast* Ⓜ *Vaporetto: Ca' d'Oro.*

Nightlife

El Sbarlefo

WINE BARS | The odd name is Venetian for "smirk," although you'll be hard-pressed to find one at this cheery, familiar bacaro with a wine selection as ample as the cicheti on offer. The spread of delectables ranges from classic polpette of meat and tuna to tomino cheese rounds to speck and robiola rolls, and the selection of wines is equally intriguing. There's often live jazz and blues on Friday and Saturday nights. El Sbarlefo has a second location in Dorsoduro, in the calle just behind the church of San Pantalon. ⊠ *Salizada del Pistor, off Campo Santi Apostoli, Cannaregio 4556/C, Cannaregio* ☎ *041/5246650* ⊕ *www.elsbarlefo.it* Ⓜ *Vaporetto: Ca' d'Oro.*

TiME Social Bar

COCKTAIL LOUNGES | The seasonal cocktails at this charming mixology bar, many of which use fruit and homemade bitters, win rave reviews from visitors and locals alike. There are also small nibbles on offer if hunger strikes. ⊠ *Rio Terà Farsetti, Cannaregio 1414, Cannaregio* ☎ *338/3636951 mobile* ⊕ *www.facebook.com/venicecocktail* Ⓜ *Vaporetto: San Marcuola Casino.*

Un Mondo di Vino

WINE BARS | Recharge with some wine or a cicheto or two—meat, fish, and vegetarian choices are on offer—at this cozy, friendly spot near the Miracoli church. Numerous wines are available by the glass, and the helpful servers are often happy to crack open a bottle for sampling if there's something you fancy. ⊠ *Salizzada San Cancian, Cannaregio* ☎ *041/5211093* ⊕ *www.bacarounmondodivino.it* Ⓜ *Vaporetto: Rialto, Ca' d'Oro.*

Shopping

★ Gianni Basso Stampatore

STATIONERY | Beloved of artists and celebrities, this traditional printer creates handmade business cards, stationery, and invitations using vintage letterpress machinery. You can choose from the selection on offer or have your own custom-designed and shipped to you at home. ⊠ *Calle del Fumo, Cannaregio 5306, Cannaregio* ☎ *041/5234681* Ⓜ *Vaporetto: Fondamente Nove.*

Vittorio Constantini

ANTIQUES & COLLECTIBLES | **FAMILY** | This glass artist's workshop features unusual, intricate pieces inspired by nature—birds, butterflies, beetles, and other insects—appreciated by adults and children alike. ⊠ *Calle del Fumo, Cannaregio 5311, Cannaregio* ☎ *041/5222265* ⊕ *www.vittoriocostantini.com* Ⓜ *Vaporetto: Fondamente Nove.*

Castello

Castello, Venice's largest sestiere, includes all of the land from east of Piazza San Marco to the city's easternmost tip. Its name probably comes from a fortress that once stood on one of the eastern islands. Not every well-off Venetian family could find a spot or afford to build a palazzo on the Grand Canal. Many who couldn't instead settled in western Castello, taking advantage of its proximity to the Rialto and San Marco, and built the noble palazzi that today distinguish this area from the fisher's enclave in the more easterly streets of the sestiere. During the days of the Republic, eastern Castello was the primary neighborhood for workers in the shipbuilding Arsenale located in its midst and now home to the Venice Biennale. Foodies flock here for some of the city's most creative modern Italian cuisine.

TIMING

Unless you're here during the Biennale—in which case, you'll be spending at least a full day or two at the Arsenale—you can check out the neighborhood's three gorgeous churches (San Francesco della Vigna, Santi Giovanni e Paolo, and San Zaccaria), as well as the lovely rooms in the Scuola di San Giorgio degli Schiavoni (if it's open, which it isn't always), in half a day.

Sights

Arsenale

MILITARY SIGHT | Visible from the street, the Porta Magna (1460), an impressive Renaissance gateway designed by Antonio Gambello, was the first classical structure to be built in Venice. It is guarded by four lions—war booty of Francesco Morosini, who took the Peloponnese from the Turks in 1687. The Arsenale is said to have been founded in 1104 on twin islands. The immense facility that evolved—it was the largest industrial complex in Europe built prior to the Industrial Revolution—was given the old Venetian dialect name *arzanà*, borrowed from the Arabic *darsina'a,* meaning "workshop." At the height of its activity, in the early 16th century, it employed as many as 16,000 *arsenalotti,* workers who were among the most respected shipbuilders in the world. The Arsenale developed a type of pre–Industrial Revolution assembly line, which allowed it to build ships with astounding speed and efficiency. The Arsenale's efficiency was confirmed time and again—whether building 100 ships in 60 days to battle the Turks in Cyprus (1597) or completing one perfectly armed warship, start to finish, while King Henry III of France attended a banquet. ⊠ *Campo de la Tana 2169, Castello* Ⓜ *Vaporetto: Arsenale.*

★ San Francesco della Vigna

CHURCH | Although this church contains some interesting and beautiful paintings and sculptures, it's the architecture that makes it worth the hike through a lively, middle-class residential neighborhood. The Franciscan church was enlarged and rebuilt by Jacopo Sansovino in 1534, giving it the first Renaissance interior in Venice; its proportions are said to reflect the mystic significance of the numbers three and seven dictated by Renaissance neo-Platonic numerology. The soaring but harmonious facade was added in 1562 by Palladio. The church represents a unique combination of the work of the two great stars of 16th-century Veneto architecture. ⊠ *Campo di San Francesco della Vigna, Castello* ☎ *041/5206102* ⊕ *www.facebook.com/sanfrancescodellavignavenezia* Ⓜ *Vaporetto: Celestia.*

★ San Zaccaria

CHURCH | More a museum than a church, San Zaccaria has a striking Renaissance facade, with central and upper portions representing some of Mauro Codussi's best work. The lower portion of the facade and the interior were designed by Antonio Gambello. The original structure of the church was 14th-century Gothic, with its facade completed in 1515, some years after Codussi's death in 1504, and it retains the proportions of the rest of the essentially Gothic structure. Inside is one of the great treasures of Venice, Giovanni Bellini's celebrated altarpiece, *La Sacra Conversazione,* easily recognizable in the left nave. Completed in 1505, when the artist was 75, it shows Bellini's ability to incorporate the aesthetics of the High Renaissance into his work. ⊠ *Campo San Zaccaria, 4693 Castello, Castello* ☎ *041/5221257* 🖃 *Church free, chapels and crypt €3 (free with Chorus Pass)* ⊙ *Closed Sun. morning* Ⓜ *Vaporetto: San Zaccaria.*

★ Santi Giovanni e Paolo

CHURCH | This gorgeous Italian Gothic church of the Dominican order, consecrated in 1430, looms over one of the most picturesque squares in Venice: the Campo Giovanni e Paolo, centered around the magnificent 15th-century equestrian statue of Bartolomeo Colleoni by the Florentine Andrea Verrocchio. Bartolomeo Bon's portal, combining Gothic and classical elements, was added between 1458 and 1462, using columns salvaged from Torcello. The 15th-century Murano stained-glass window near the side entrance is breathtaking for its beautiful colors and figures. ✉ *Campo dei Santi Giovanni e Paolo, Castello* ☎ *041/5235913* 🌐 *www.santigiovanniepaolo.it* 🎫 *€3.50* 🕒 *Closed weekends* [M] *Vaporetto: Fondamente Nove, Rialto.*

★ **Scuola di San Giorgio degli Schiavoni**
HISTORIC SIGHT | Founded in 1451 by the Dalmatian community, this small scuola, or confraternity, was, and still is, a social and cultural center for migrants from what is now Croatia. It contains one of Italy's most beautiful rooms, harmoniously decorated between 1502 and 1507 by Vittore Carpaccio. Although Carpaccio generally painted legendary and religious figures against backgrounds of contemporary Venetian architecture, here is perhaps one of the first instances of "Orientalism" in Western painting. **TIP→ Opening hours are quite flexible. Since this is a must-see site, book in advance so you won't be disappointed.** ✉ *Calle dei Furlani, Castello 3259/A, Castello* ☎ *041/5228828* 🌐 *www.scuoladalmatavenezia.com* 🎫 *€5* [M] *Vaporetto: Arsenale, San Zaccaria.*

🍴 Restaurants

Al Covo
$$$ | **VENETIAN** | For years, Diane and Cesare Binelli's Al Covo has set the standard of excellence for traditional, refined Venetian cuisine; the Binellis are dedicated to providing their guests with the freshest, highest-quality fish from the Adriatic, and vegetables, when at all possible, from the islands of the Venetian Lagoon and the fields of the adjacent Veneto region. Although their cuisine could be correctly termed "classic Venetian," it always offers surprises, like the juicy crispness of their legendary fritto misto (fried mixed seafood and vegetables)—reliant upon an unconventional secret ingredient in the batter—or the heady aroma of their fresh anchovies marinated in wild fennel, an herb somewhat foreign to Veneto. **Known for:** sophisticated Venetian flavors; top-notch local ingredients; Diane's chocolate cake for dessert. [$] *Average main: €30* ✉ *Campiello Pescaria, Castello 3968, Castello* ☎ *041/5223812* 🌐 *www.ristorantealcovo.com* 🕒 *Closed Tues. and Wed., 3 wks. in Jan., and 10 days in Aug.* [M] *Vaporetto: Arsenale.*

★ **Alle Testiere**
$$$ | **VENETIAN** | The name is a reference to the old headboards that adorn the walls of this tiny, informal restaurant, but the food (not the decor) is undoubtedly the focus. Local foodies consider this one of the most refined eateries in the city thanks to chef Bruno Gavagnin's gently creative take on classic Venetian fish dishes; the chef's artistry seldom draws attention to itself but simply reveals new dimensions of familiar fare, creating dishes that stand out for their lightness and balance. **Known for:** daily changing fish offerings, based on what's fresh at the market; excellent pasta with seafood; wonderful wine selection. [$] *Average main: €28* ✉ *Calle del Mondo Novo, Castello 5801, Castello* ☎ *041/5227220* 🌐 *www.osterialletestiere.it* 🕒 *Closed Sun. and Mon., 3 wks in Jan. and Feb., and 4 wks in July and Aug.*

★ **Corte Sconta**
$$$ | **SEAFOOD** | The heaping seafood antipasti alone is reason enough to visit this classic seafood-focused eatery close to the Biennale—think tuna and swordfish carpaccio, spider crab, clams, crab pâté, and a variety of fish. But you'll also want to stay for the excellent mains, particularly soft-shell crab, mixed grilled fish, and spaghetti vongole, plus the lovely courtyard setting. **Known for:** some of the best seafood in town; charming

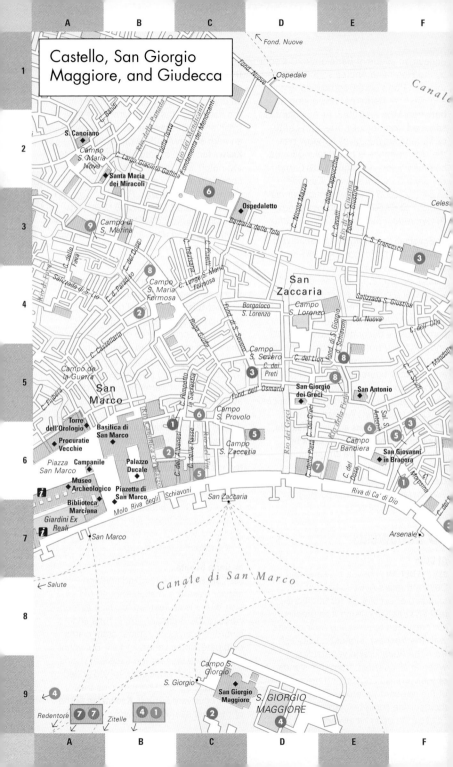

Castello, San Giorgio Maggiore, and Giudecca

S. Canciano
Campo S. Maria Nova
Santa Maria dei Miracoli
Ospedaletto
Campo di S. Marina
Campo S. Maria Formosa
San Zaccaria
Borgoloco S. Lorenzo
Campo S. Lorenzo
Campo S. Severo
C. dei Preti
San Giorgio dei Greci
San Antonio
San Giovanni in Bragora
Campo Bandiera
San Marco
Torre dell'Orologio
Procuratie Vecchie
Basilica di San Marco
Campo S. Provolo
Campo S. Zaccaria
Campanile
Piazza San Marco
Palazzo Ducale
Museo Archeologico
Biblioteca Marciana
Piazzetta di San Marco
Giardini Ex Reali
San Marco
Molo Riva degli Schiavoni
San Zaccaria
Riva di Ca' di Dio
Arsenale

Fond. Nuove
Ospedale
Canale
Celes
Barbaria delle Tole
Salizzada di S. Lio
C. Cassetteria
Campo de la Guerra
Fond. dell' Osmarin
Canale di San Marco

Campo S. Giorgio
S. Giorgio
San Giorgio Maggiore
S. GIORGIO MAGGIORE
Redentore
Zitelle
Salute

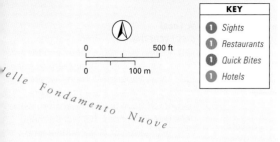

KEY

1 Sights
1 Restaurants
1 Quick Bites
1 Hotels

| 0 | 500 ft |
| 0 | 100 m |

Venice CASTELLO

4

Sights ▼

1 Arsenale **I7**
2 Fondazione Giorgio Cini **C9**
3 San Francesco della Vigna **F3**
4 San Giorgio Maggiore **D9**
5 San Zaccaria **D6**
6 Santi Giovanni e Paolo **C3**
7 Santissimo Redentore **A9**
8 Scuola di San Giorgio
   degli Schiavoni **E5**

Restaurants ▼

1 Al Covo **F6**
2 Alle Testiere **B4**
3 Corte Sconta **F6**
4 Cip's Club & Oro **B9**
5 CoVino **F6**
6 Il Ridotto **C5**
7 La Palanca **A9**
8 Local **E5**
9 Osteria di Santa Marina **A3**

Quick Bites ▼

1 Aciugheta **C5**
2 El Rèfolo **H8**
3 Wine Bar 5000 ....**D5**

Hotels ▼

1 Belmond Hotel Cipriani **B9**
2 Ca' dei Dogi **B6**
3 Ca' di Dio **F7**
4 Hilton Molino Stucky Venice **A9**
5 Hotel Danieli **C6**
6 Hotel La Residenza **E6**
7 Metropole **E6**
8 Ruzzini Palace Hotel **B4**

Bacini →

delle Fondamento Nuove

nd Case Nuove

dell'Oratorio
ampo
della
lestia

Canale delle Galeazze

o della Gome

Darsena
Arsenale Vecchio

Arsenale

Darsena
Grande

ampo
dell
senale

Castello

Tana

o dell'Arsenale

C. S. Biagio

Rio della Tana

Campo della Tana

Fond. della Tana

Rio di S. Daniele

Fond. S. Gioacchino
Fond. di S. Anna

Via Giuseppe Garibaldi

C. Nuova
C. dei Preti
C. del Pistor

C. Cabotto

C. Erizzo
C. Col. Colonna
C. Schiavoca

C. Vechia

Via S. Domenico

Via Giuseppe Garibaldi

C. della Stua
C. delle Strazze
C. Nicoli

C. di S. Giorgio

Secco Marina

Riva S. Biagio

Riva dei Sette Martiri

Giardini
Garibaldi

Fond. di S.
Giuseppe

Campo di
S. Giuseppe

Giardini
Pubblici

Viale Trento

Giardini •

S. Elena →

G   H   I   J

atmosphere with outdoor seating; service with a sense of humor. [$] *Average main: €28* ✉ *Calle del Pestrin, Castello 3886, Castello* ☎ *041/5227024* 🌐 *www.cortescontavenezia.com* 🕒 *Closed Sun. and Mon.* [M] *Vaporetto: Arsenale.*

CoVino

$$$ | ITALIAN | A charming new concept in Venetian eateries, diminutive CoVino offers a fixed-price, three-course menu, from which you'll choose among several traditionally inspired antipasti, secondi, and desserts with innovative—and satisfying—twists. At this Slow Food presidio, you can watch the cook construct your sliced tuna dressed with Bronte pistachios and eggplant; Bra sausage "imported" from the Piedmont alla Valpolicella with tiny green beans; or perhaps even fresh gazpacho. **Known for:** locally sourced ingredients; wine selection; light lunch option for €30. [$] *Average main: €33* ✉ *Calle del Pestrin, Castello 3829a-3829, Castello* ☎ *041/2412705* 🌐 *www.covinovenezia.com* 💳 *No credit cards* 🕒 *Closed Tues. and Wed. No lunch Thurs.* [M] *Vaporetto: Arsenale.*

★ Il Ridotto

$$$$ | MODERN ITALIAN | Longtime restaurateur Gianni Bonaccorsi (proprietor of the popular Aciugheta nearby) has established an eatery where he can pamper a limited number of lucky patrons with his imaginative cuisine and impeccable taste in wine. *Ridotto* means "small, private place," which this very much is, evoking an atmosphere of secrecy and intimacy; the innovative menus tend toward lighter but wonderfully tasty versions of classic dishes. **Known for:** some of the most creative cuisine in Venice; excellent five- or seven-course tasting menus; extensive wine recommendations. [$] *Average main: €40* ✉ *Campo SS. Filippo e Giacomo, Castello 4509, Castello* ☎ *041/5208280* 🌐 *www.ilridotto.com* 🕒 *Closed Wed. No lunch Tues. and Thurs.* [M] *Vaporetto: San Zaccaria.*

★ Local

$$$$ | VENETIAN | In a simple yet charming setting with beamed ceilings and terrazzo floors, a sister and brother team oversee their "New Venetian Cuisine," where local ingredients are used to prepare reinvented traditional dishes, often with Japanese influences. It's tasting-menu only, with seven or nine courses (or a less expensive three-course option at weekday lunch), and wine pairings from their extensive list are a recommended treat. **Known for:** tiramigiù dessert: coffee, marsala, and mascarpone; ingredients from Italian producers and daily catch; highly attentive staff. [$] *Average main: €130* ✉ *Salizzada dei Greci, Castello 3303, Castello* ☎ *041/2411128* 🌐 *www.ristorantelocal.com* 🕒 *Closed Tues. and Wed. No lunch Sun. and Thurs.* [M] *Vaporetto: San Zaccaria.*

★ Osteria di Santa Marina

$$$$ | VENETIAN | The candlelit tables on this romantic campo are inviting enough, but it's the intimate restaurant's imaginative kitchen that's likely to win you over; you can order consistently excellent pasta, fish, or meat dishes à la carte or opt for one of the rewarding tasting menus. The wine list is ample and well thought out, and the service is gracious, warm, and professional. **Known for:** innovative and artfully presented modern Venetian food; charming setting; wonderful wine pairings. [$] *Average main: €36* ✉ *Campo Santa Marina, Castello 5911, Castello* ☎ *041/5285239* 🌐 *www.osteriadisantamarina.com* 🕒 *Closed Sun. and 2 wks in Aug. No lunch Mon.* [M] *Vaporetto: Rialto.*

☕ Coffee and Quick Bites

Aciugheta

$$ | WINE BAR | Almost an institution, the "Tiny Anchovy" (as the name translates) doubles as a pizzeria-trattoria, but the real reason for coming is the bar's tasty cicheti, like the eponymous anchovy minipizzas, the *arancioni* (stuffed fried rice balls), and the polpette. Wines by the glass change daily, but there is always a good selection of local wines on hand, as well as some Tuscan and Piedmontese choices thrown in for good measure. **Known for:** pizzetta con l'acciuga (minipizza with anchovy); mix of traditional and more modern cicheti; good selection of Italian wines by the glass. [$] *Average main: €17* ✉ *Campo SS. Filippo e Giacomo, Castello 4357, Castello* ☎ *041/5224292* 🌐 *www.aciugheta.com* [M] *Vaporetto: San Zaccaria.*

El Rèfolo

$$ | **WINE BAR** | At this contemporary cantina and hip hangout in a very Venetian neighborhood, the owner pairs enthusiastically chosen wines and artisanal beers with select meat, savory cheese, and seasonal vegetable combos. With outside-only seating (not particularly comfortable), it's more appropriate for an aperitivo and a light meal. **Known for:** good selection of wine and beer; filling meat and cheese plates; boisterous atmosphere outside in nice weather. [$] *Average main: €16* ✉ *Via Garibaldi, Castello 1580, Castello* ☎ *344/1636759 mobile* ⏲ *Closed Mon.* [M] *Vaporetto: Arsenale.*

Wine Bar 5000

$ | **WINE BAR** | Nibble on a selection of cicheti or a cheese or meat plate at this cozy wine bar on Campo San Severo, near the Basilica dei Frari. You can either dine inside the brick-walled, Murano glass–chandeliered space, or watch the gondolas sail by at a table outdoors next to the quiet adjacent Severno canal. **Known for:** large wine list, including biodynamic options; lovely outdoor seating area; small but well-prepared choice of cicheti. [$] *Average main: €12* ✉ *Campo San Severo, Castello 5000, Castello* ☎ *041/3097891* 🌐 *winebar5000.it* ⏲ *Closed Wed.* [M] *Vaporetto: San Zaccaria.*

Hotels

★ Ca' dei Dogi

$$ | **HOTEL** | A quiet courtyard secluded from the San Marco melee offers an island of calm in six guest rooms and two apartments (some with private terraces overlooking the Doge's Palace, one with a Jacuzzi), which are individually decorated with contemporary furnishings and accessories. **Pros:** amazing location close to Doge's Palace and Piazza San Marco; balconies with wonderful views; traditional Italian restaurant on-site. **Cons:** rooms are on the small side; no elevator and lots of stairs; bathrooms can feel cramped. [$] *Rooms from: €164* ✉ *Corte Santa Scolastica, Castello 4242, Castello* ☎ *041/2413751* 🌐 *www.cadeidogi.it* ⏲ *Closed 3 wks. in Dec.* 🛏 *6 rooms* 🍴 *Free Breakfast* [M] *Vaporetto: San Zaccaria.*

Ca' di Dio

$$$$ | **HOTEL** | Housed in a palace dating from 1272, with interiors updated by of-the-moment architect Patricia Urquiola, this deluxe hotel offers rooms with views of San Giorgio Maggiore island, two restaurants, and two internal courtyards, all within striking distance of the Venice Biennale grounds. **Pros:** on-site gym and spa; convenient to the Biennale; most guest rooms are suites. **Cons:** a walk from traditional Venetian sights; not for fans of traditional design; quite expensive. [$] *Rooms from: €456* ✉ *Riva Ca' di Dio, Castello 5866, Castello* ☎ *041/0980238* 🌐 *vretreats.com/en/ca-di-dio* 🛏 *66 rooms* 🍴 *Free Breakfast* [M] *Vaporetto: Arsenale.*

★ Hotel Danieli

$$$$ | **HOTEL** | One of the city's most famous lodgings—built in the 14th century and run as a hotel since 1822—lives up to its reputation: the chance to explore the wonderful, highly detailed lobby is itself a reason to book an overnight stay, plus the views along the lagoon are fantastic, the rooms gorgeous, and the

food fabulous. **Pros:** historical and inviting lobby; amazing rooftop views; tasty cocktails at Bar Dandolo. **Cons:** lots of American tourists; some rooms feel dated; service can be indifferent. [$] *Rooms from: €1200* ✉ *Riva degli Schiavoni, Castello 4196, Castello* ☎ *041/5226480* 🌐 *hoteldanieli.com* 🛏 *210 rooms* 🍴 *No Meals* [M] *Vaporetto: San Zaccaria.*

Hotel La Residenza

$$ | **HOTEL** | Set in a quiet campo, this renovated 15th-century Gothic-Byzantine palazzo has simple but spacious rooms and lovely public spaces filled with chandeliers, 18th-century paintings, and period reproduction furnishings. **Pros:** lavish salon and breakfast room; quiet residential area, steps from Riva degli Schiavoni and 10 minutes from Piazza San Marco; affordable rates. **Cons:** no elevator; basic guest rooms; sparse breakfast. [$] *Rooms from: €190* ✉ *Campo Bandiera e Moro, Castello 3608, Castello* ☎ *041/5285315* 🌐 *www.venicelaresidenza.com* 🛏 *15 rooms* 🍴 *No Meals* [M] *Vaporetto: Arsenale.*

★ **Metropole**

$$$$ | **HOTEL** | Atmosphere prevails in this labyrinth of opulent, intimate spaces featuring classic Venetian decor combined with Eastern influences: common areas and sumptuously appointed guest rooms are filled with an assortment of antiques and curiosities. **Pros:** hotel harkens back to the gracious Venice of a bygone era; suites have private roof terraces with water views; great food and cocktails in the gorgeous Oriental Bar & Bistrot. **Cons:** one of the most densely touristed locations in the city; rooms with views are considerably more expensive; quirky, eccentric collections on display not for everyone. [$] *Rooms from: €355* ✉ *Riva degli Schiavoni, Castello 4149, Castello* ☎ *041/5205044* 🌐 *www.hotelmetropole.com* 🛏 *67 rooms* 🍴 *Free Breakfast* [M] *Vaporetto: San Zaccaria.*

Ruzzini Palace Hotel

$$$ | **HOTEL** | Renaissance- and Baroque-style common areas are soaring spaces with Venetian terrazzo flooring, frescoed and exposed beam ceilings, and Murano chandeliers; guest rooms tastefully mix historical style with contemporary furnishings and appointments. **Pros:** a luminous, aristocratic ambience; located on a lively Venetian campo not frequented by tourists; great buffet breakfast (not included in all rates). **Cons:** plain bathrooms; relatively far from a vaporetto stop; no restaurant on-site. [$] *Rooms from: €207* ✉ *Campo Santa Maria Formosa, Castello 5866, Castello* ☎ *041/2410447* 🌐 *www.ruzzinipalace.com* 🛏 *28 rooms* 🍴 *No Meals* [M] *Vaporetto: San Zaccaria, Rialto.*

🍸 Nightlife

Bar Dandolo

COCKTAIL LOUNGES | Even if you're not staying at Hotel Danieli, it's worth a stop to marvel at its bar's over-the-top decor inside a 14th-century palace. Though pricey, it's a highly atmospheric place to sample their signature Vesper martini or another cocktail of your choice, usually accompanied by live piano music. ✉ *Hotel Danieli, Riva degli Schiavoni, Castello 4196, Castello* ☎ *041/5226480* 🌐 *www.hoteldanieli.com* [M] *Vaporetto: San Zaccaria.*

Zanzibar

CAFÉS | This kiosk bar is very popular on warm summer evenings with Venetians and tourists. Although there's food, it's mostly limited to conventional Venetian sandwiches and commercial ice cream. The most interesting thing about the place is its location with a view of the church of Santa Maria Formosa, which makes it a pleasant place for a drink and a good place for people-watching. ✉ *Campo Santa Maria Formosa, Castello 5840, Castello* ☎ *345/2885654* 🌐 *www.facebook.com/zanzibar5840* [M] *Vaporetto: San Zaccaria.*

🛍 Shopping

⭐ Banco Lotto No. 10

WOMEN'S CLOTHING | All the one-of-a-kind clothes and bags on sale at this vintage-inspired boutique were designed and created by residents of the women's prison on Giudecca island. ✉ *Salizada Sant'Antonin, Castello 3478/A, Castello* ☎ *041/5221439* ⊕ *www.facebook.com/bancolotto10* Ⓜ *Vaporetto: San Zaccaria.*

⭐ Papier Mache—Laboratorio di Artigianato Artistico

OTHER SPECIALTY STORE | **FAMILY** | If you're looking for an authentic Venetian mask, this is the place to go. Owner Stefano and his talented team of artists create exquisite handmade masks that can be custom-ordered if you don't see what you want, as well as shipped worldwide. ✉ *Calle Lunga Santa Maria Formosa, Castello 5174/B, Castello* ☎ *041/5229995* ⊕ *www.papiermache.it* Ⓜ *Vaporetto: Ospedale.*

San Giorgio Maggiore and Giudecca

Beckoning travelers across St. Mark's Basin is the island of San Giorgio Maggiore, separated by a small channel from Giudecca. A tall brick campanile on that distant bank nicely complements the Campanile of San Marco. Beneath it looms the stately dome of one of Venice's greatest churches, San Giorgio Maggiore, the creation of Andrea Palladio. To the west, on Giudecca, is Palladio's other masterpiece, the church of the Santissimo Redentore.

You can reach San Giorgio Maggiore via Vaporetto Line 2 from San Zaccaria. The next three stops on the line take you to Giudecca. The island's past may be shrouded in mystery, but despite recent gentrification by artists and well-to-do bohemians, it's still down-to-earth and one of the city's few remaining primarily working-class neighborhoods. Interestingly, you find that most Venetians don't even consider the Giudecchini Venetians at all.

TIMING

A half day should be plenty of time to visit the area. Allow about a half hour to see each of the churches and an hour or two to look around Giudecca.

👁 Sights

⭐ Fondazione Giorgio Cini
(*Cini Foundation*)

OTHER MUSEUM | Adjacent to San Giorgio Maggiore is a complex that now houses the Cini Foundation, established in 1951 as a cultural center dedicated to humanist research. It contains a beautiful cloister designed by Palladio in 1560, his refectory, a library designed by Longhena, and various archives. In a woodland area you can wander amid 10 "Vatican Chapels" created for the 2018 Architecture Biennale by renowned architects, including Norman Foster. Another stunning feature is the Borges Labyrinth, a 1-km (½-mile) path through a boxwood hedge that allows visitors to take a 45-minute contemplative walk. It was designed by Randoll Coate and inspired by the Jorge Luis Borges short story "The Garden of Forking Paths." An evocative audio guide, composed by Antonio Fresa and performed by Teatro La Fenice's orchestra, may accompany your pensive stroll. Guided tours are given daily (except Wednesday, November through mid-March), and reservations are required. ✉ *Isola di San Giorgio Maggiore* ☎ *366/4202181 WhatsApp for info and tour reservations* ⊕ *www.cini.it* 🎟 *€15 for Tour 1 (Foundation buildings), Tour 2 (Borges Labyrinth), or Tour 3 (The Vatican Chapels with Teatro Verde); €22 for two tours combined; €28 for three tours combined* ⊘ *Closed Wed. Nov.–mid-Mar.* ⚐ *Reservations required* Ⓜ *Vaporetto: San Giorgio.*

Did You Know?

The nobility in Venice used to be extremely competitive about their gondolas, decorating them in flamboyant colors and over-the-top ornaments. A law in the 16th century put an end to that. Today, all gondolas in Venice must be painted boring black, though they are allowed three flourishes: a curly tail, a pair of seahorses, and a multi-pronged prow.

★ San Giorgio Maggiore
CHURCH | There's been a church on this island since the 8th century. Today's refreshingly airy and simply decorated church of brick and white marble was begun in 1566 by Palladio and displays his architectural hallmarks of mathematical harmony and classical influence. *The Last Supper* and the *Gathering of Manna,* two of Tintoretto's later works, line the chancel. To the right of the entrance hangs *The Adoration of the Shepherds* by Jacopo Bassano. Ask to see Carpaccio's *St. George and the Dragon,* which hangs in a private room. The campanile (bell tower) dates from 1791. **TIP→ Climb to the top of the campanile for unparalleled 360-degree views of the lagoon, islands, and Venice itself.** ✉ *Isola di San Giorgio Maggiore* ☎ *041/5227827* 🌐 *www.abbaziasangiorgio.it* 🎫 *Church free, campanile €6* [M] *Vaporetto: San Giorgio.*

Santissimo Redentore
CHURCH | After a plague in 1576 claimed some 50,000 people—nearly one-third of the city's population (including Titian)—Andrea Palladio was asked to design a commemorative church. Giudecca's Capuchin friars offered land and their services, provided the building's design was in keeping with the simplicity of their hermitage. Consecrated in 1592, after Palladio's death, the Redentore (considered Palladio's supreme achievement in ecclesiastical design) is dominated by a dome and a pair of slim, almost minaretlike bell towers. Its deceptively simple, stately facade leads to a bright, airy interior. There aren't any paintings or sculptures of note, but the harmony and elegance of the interior makes a visit worthwhile. ✉ *Fondamenta San Giacomo* ☎ *041/5231415* 🌐 *www.chorusvenezia.org* 🎫 *€3 (free with Chorus Pass)* 🕓 *Closed Sun.* [M] *Vaporetto: Redentore.*

🍴 Restaurants

Cip's Club & Oro
$$$$ | **VENETIAN** | Located on the water's edge, looking out at the Venice skyline, the Belmond Cipriani's exclusive outdoor-indoor Cip's Club and Oro restaurant is best known for its breathtaking views, but the exquisite tasting menu of Venetian classics and extensive wine list certainly don't play second fiddle. Taking the complimentary 10-minute boat ride to and from San Marco also adds to the thoroughly James Bond sense of drama and romance. **Known for:** sublime Venice vistas with a Bellini; sophisticated service; relaxing lunch destination. [$] *Average main: €100* ✉ *Belmond Hotel Cipriani, Giudecca 10* ☎ *041/240801* 🌐 *www.belmond.com* [M] *Vaporetto: Zitelle.*

★ La Palanca
$$ | **ITALIAN** | It's all about the views at this classic, informal wine bar–restaurant, where tables perched on the water's edge are often filled with chatty patrons, particularly at lunchtime. The homemade pasta and fish dishes are highly recommended, and although they don't really serve dinner, a filling selection of cicheti is offered in the evening. **Known for:** sea bass ravioli, grilled seafood, and baccalà; good, affordable wine list; superlative views. [$] *Average main: €16* ✉ *Isola della Giudecca 448* ☎ *041/5287719* 🌐 *www.facebook.com/lapalancagiudecca* 🕓 *Closed Sun.* [M] *Vaporetto: Palanca.*

🛏 Hotels

★ Belmond Hotel Cipriani
$$$$ | **HOTEL** | With amazing service, wonderful rooms, fab restaurants, and a large pool and spa—all just a five-minute boat ride from Piazza San Marco (the hotel water shuttle leaves every 15 minutes, 24 hours a day)—the Cipriani is Venetian luxe at its best. **Pros:** old-world charm meets modern luxury; Olympic-size heated saltwater pool; Michelin-starred restaurant. **Cons:** very expensive; may

be too quiet for some; gym not open 24 hours. $ *Rooms from: €1400* ⌧ *Giudecca 10* ☎ *041/240801* ⊕ *www.belmond. com* ☾ *Closed mid-Nov.–late Mar.* ⤳ *96 rooms* ⦿ *Free Breakfast* Ⓜ *Vaporetto: Zitelle.*

Hilton Molino Stucky Venice

$$$ | **HOTEL** | **FAMILY** | Wooden beams and iron columns are some of the original details still visible in this redbrick former flour mill–turned-hotel, which also features sublime views across the lagoon to Venice, particularly from the lively rooftop bar. **Pros:** extremely helpful staff; shuttle boat to San Marco; ample breakfast buffet. **Cons:** can hear noise from other rooms; hotel itself a bit confusing to navigate; food offerings on the pricey side. $ *Rooms from: €292* ⌧ *Giudecca 810* ☎ *041/2723311* ⊕ *www.hilton.com/en/ hotels/vcehihi-hilton-molino-stucky-venice* ⤳ *379 rooms* ⦿ *No Meals* Ⓜ *Vaporetto: Palanca.*

 ## Nightlife

★ Skyline Rooftop Bar

COCKTAIL LOUNGES | For arguably the best views of Venice anywhere, visit this buzzy eighth-floor hotel cocktail bar. There are regular DJ and live music events during the summer months. ⌧ *Hilton Molino Stucky Venice, Giudecca 810* ☎ *041/2723316* ⊕ *www.skylinebar-venice.it* Ⓜ *Vaporetto: Palanca.*

 ## Shopping

Fortuny Tessuti Artistici

FABRICS | The original Fortuny textile factory, built on former convent grounds, has been converted into a showroom. Prices are over-the-top, but it's worth a trip to see the extraordinary colors and textures of their hand-printed silks and velvets. Call in advance to arrange a tour of the buildings and gorgeous gardens. ⌧ *Fondamenta San Biagio, Giudecca 805* ☎ *041/5287697* ⊕ *fortuny.com* Ⓜ *Vaporetto: Palanca.*

Islands of the Lagoon

The perfect vacation from your Venetian vacation is an escape to Murano, Burano, and sleepy Torcello, the islands of the northern lagoon, or to the Lido, Venice's barrier island that forms the southern border of the Venetian Lagoon. Torcello is legendary for its beauty and breathing room, and makes a wonderful destination for a picnic (be sure to pack a lunch). Burano, which has a long history of lace production, is an island of fishing traditions and houses painted in a riot of colors—blue, yellow, pink, ocher, and dark red. Murano is renowned for its glass, and you can tour a glass factory here, but be warned that you will be pressured to buy. San Michele, a vaporetto stop on the way to Murano, is the cemetery island of Venice, the resting place of many international artists who have chosen to spend eternity in this beautiful city. Finally, the Lido, which protects Venice from the waters of the Adriatic, forms the beach of Venice, and is home to a series of elegant bathing establishments.

TIMING

Hitting all the sights on all the islands takes a busy, full day. If you limit yourself to Murano and San Michele, you can easily explore for an ample half day; the same goes for Burano and Torcello. In summer the express Vaporetto Line 7 will take you to Murano from San Zaccaria (the Jolanda landing) in 25 minutes; Line 3 will take you from Piazzale Roma to Murano via the Canale di Cannaregio in 21 minutes; otherwise, local Line 4.1 makes a 45-minute trip from San Zaccaria every 20 minutes, circling the east end of Venice, stopping at Fondamente Nove and San Michele on the way. To see glassblowing, get off at Colonna; the Museo stop will put you near the Museo del Vetro.

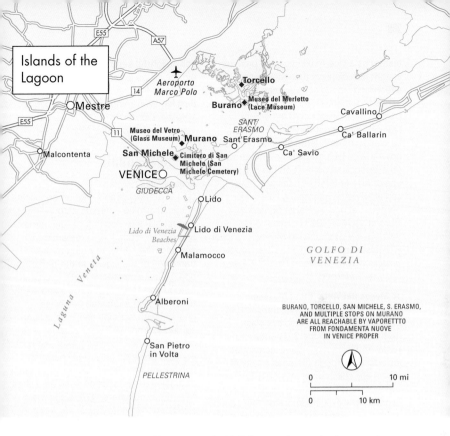

Islands of the Lagoon

E55
A57
14 Aeroporto Marco Polo
Mestre
E55
11 Museo del Vetro (Glass Museum) Murano
Malcontenta
San Michele
VENICE
GIUDECCA
Lido di Venezia Beaches
Lido di Venezia
Malamocco
Alberoni
San Pietro in Volta
PELLESTRINA
Laguna Veneta

Torcello
Museo del Merletto (Lace Museum)
Burano
SANT' ERASMO
Sant'Erasmo
Cimitero di San Michele (San Michele Cemetery)
Cavallino
Ca' Ballarin
Ca' Savio
Lido

GOLFO DI VENEZIA

BURANO, TORCELLO, SAN MICHELE, S. ERASMO, AND MULTIPLE STOPS ON MURANO ARE ALL REACHABLE BY VAPORETTTO FROM FONDAMENTA NUOVE IN VENICE PROPER

0   10 mi
0   10 km

Line 12 goes from Fondamente Nove direct to Murano and Burano every 30 minutes (from there, Torcello is a five-minute ferry ride on Line 9); the full trip takes 45 minutes each way. To get to Burano and Torcello from Murano, pick up Line 12 at the Faro stop (Murano's lighthouse). Line 1 runs from San Marco to the Lido in about 20 minutes.

 Sights

★ Cimitero di San Michele (San Michele Cemetery)

CEMETERY | It's no surprise that serenity prevails on San Michele in Venice's northern lagoon. The city's island cemetery is surrounded by ocher brick walls and laced with cypress-lined pathways amid plots filled with thousands of graves; there's also a modern extension completed by British architect David Chipperfield

in 2017. Among those who have made this distinctive island their final resting place are such international arts and science luminaries as Igor Stravinsky, Sergei Diaghilev, Ezra Pound, and the Austrian mathematician Christian Doppler (of the Doppler effect). You're welcome to explore the grounds if you dress respectfully and adhere to a solemn code of conduct. Photography and picnicking are not permitted. ⊠ *Isola di San Michele, San Michele* ☎ *041/7292841* 🎫 *Free* Ⓜ *Vaporetto: San Michele.*

Museo del Merletto (Lace Museum)

HISTORY MUSEUM | FAMILY | Home to the Burano Lace School from 1872 to 1970, the palace of Podestà of Torcello now houses a museum dedicated to the craft for which this island is known. Detailed explanations of the manufacturing process and Burano's distinctive history as a lace-making capital provide insight into displays that showcase everything from black Venetian Carnival capes to fingerless, elbow-length "mitten gloves" fashionable in 17th-century France. Portraits of Venice's aristocracy as well as embroidered silk and brocade gowns with lace embellishments provide greater societal context on the historical use of lace in European fashion. You can also watch interesting lace-making demonstrations. ✉ *Piazza Galuppi 187, Burano* ☎ *041/730034* 🌐 *museomerletto.visitmuve.it* 🎟 *€5, Island Museums Ticket €12 (also includes Murano Glass Museum), free with Museum Pass* 🕒 *Closed Mon.* [M] *Vaporetto: Burano.*

★ Museo del Vetro (Glass Museum)
ART MUSEUM | FAMILY | This compact yet informative museum displays glass items dating from the 3rd century to today. You'll learn all about techniques introduced through the ages (many of which are still in use), including 15th-century gold-leaf decoration, 16th-century filigree work that incorporated thin bands of white or colored glass into the crystal, and the 18th-century origins of Murano's iconic chandeliers. A visit here will help you to understand the provenance of the glass you'll see for sale—and may be tempted to buy—in shops around the island. ✉ *Fondamenta Marco Giustinian 8, Murano* ☎ *041/2434914 tickets, 041/739586 office* 🌐 *museovetro.visitmuve.it* 🎟 *€10; Island Museums Ticket €12 (also includes Burano Lace Museum); free with Museum Pass* [M] *Vaporetto: Murano Museo.*

Beaches

Lido di Venezia Beaches
BEACH | FAMILY | Most hotels on the Lido have access to charming beach clubs with cabanas, striped umbrellas, and chaise longues—all of which are often available for nonguests to use for a fee. On either end of the long barrier island, the public beaches offer a more rustic but still delightful setting for nature lovers to dig their toes in the sand. **Amenities:** food and drink; lifeguards; showers; toilets. **Best for:** swimming; walking. ✉ *Lido di Venezia, Lido* ☎ *041/8627117* 🌐 *www.visitlido.it* [M] *Vaporetto: Lido.*

🍴 Restaurants

Acquastanca
$$$ | VENETIAN | Grab a seat among locals at this charming, intimate eatery—the perfect place to pop in for a lunchtime primo or to embark on a romantic evening. The name, referring to the tranquility of the lagoon at the turn of the tide, reflects this restaurant's approach to food and service, and you'll find such tempting seafood-based dishes as gnocchi with scallops and zucchini and curried scampi with black rice; tasteful decor sets the mood with exposed brick, iron and glass accents, and charming fish sculptures. **Known for:** light and fresh traditional food; focus on seafood dishes; relaxing atmosphere. [$] *Average main: €28* ✉ *Fondamenta Manin 48, Murano* ☎ *041/3195125* 🌐 *www.acquastanca.it* 🕒 *Closed Sun. No dinner Tues.–Thurs. and Sat.* [M] *Vaporetto: Murano Colonna, Murano Faro.*

Busa alla Torre da Lele
$$ | VENETIAN | If you're shopping for glass on Murano and want to sample some first-rate home cooking for lunch, you can't do better than stopping in this unpretentious trattoria in the island's central square. Friendly waiters will bring you ample portions of pasta, with freshly made seafood-based sauces, and a substantial variety of carefully grilled or baked fish. **Known for:** tasty local fish and seafood; reliable lunch stop in Murano; outdoor dining on a square. [$] *Average main: €20* ✉ *Campo Santo Stefano 3, Murano* ☎ *041/739662* 🕒 *No dinner* [M] *Vaporetto: Murano Colonna.*

Locanda Cipriani Restaurant

$$$$ | **VENETIAN** | A nearly legendary restaurant—Hemingway came here often to eat, drink, and brood under the veranda's greenery—established by a nephew of Giuseppe Cipriani (the founder of Harry's Bar), this inn profits from its idyllic location on the island of Torcello. The food is not exceptional, especially considering the high prices, but dining here is more about getting lost in Venetian magic; the menu features pastas and lots of seafood. **Known for:** wonderful historic atmosphere; traditional Venetian cuisine, with a focus on seafood; a peaceful lunch choice when you want to get away from Venice. $ *Average main: €40* ⊠ *Piazza Santa Fosca 29, Torcello* ☎ *041/730150* ⊕ *www.locandacipriani.com* ⊗ *Closed Tues. and early Jan.–mid-Feb. No dinner Sun.–Thurs.* Ⓜ *Vaporetto: Torcello.*

Trattoria Al Gatto Nero

$$$ | **SEAFOOD** | Since 1965, Al Gatto Nero has offered the best fish on Burano. No matter what you order, though, you'll savor the pride the owner and his family have in their lagoon, their island, and the quality of their *cucina* (maybe even more so when enjoying it on the picturesque fondamenta). **Known for:** the freshest fish and seafood around; risotto Burano style, using local ghiozzi fish; tagliolini (thin spaghetti) with spider crab. $ *Average main: €33* ⊠ *Fondamenta della Giudecca 88, Burano* ☎ *041/730120* ⊕ *www.gattonero. com* ⊗ *Closed Mon., 1 wk in July, and 3 wks in Nov. No dinner Sun., Wed., and Thurs.* Ⓜ *Vaporetto: Burano.*

★ Venissa

$$$$ | **MODERN ITALIAN** | Stroll across the bridge from Burano to the islet of Mazzorbo to see some of the Venetian islands' only working vineyards, amid which sits this charming restaurant where seasonal dishes incorporate vegetables, herbs, and flowers fresh from the garden and fish fresh from the lagoon, served in seven- to 10-course tasting menus (there's also a more casual osteria). To accompany your meal, pick out a local wine like the Dorona di Venezia, made with the island's native grape. **Known for:** creative, sometimes avant-garde dishes; relaxed setting with tables overlooking the vines; perfect wine pairings. $ *Average main: €150* ⊠ *Fondamenta Santa Caterina 3, Mazzorbo* ☎ *041/5272281* ⊕ *www.venissa.it* ⊗ *Closed Wed. in Sept.; Tues. and Wed. the rest of the year; 10 days in late July and late Nov., and early Jan.–mid-Mar.* Ⓜ *Vaporetto: Mazzorbo.*

Hotels

Hotel Excelsior Venice Lido Resort

$$$$ | **HOTEL** | **FAMILY** | Built in 1908, this grand hotel with Moorish decor has old-fashioned charm and loads of amenities—from a private beach with white cabanas and a seasonal bar and restaurant to a swimming pool, gym, and tennis courts (though, oddly, no spa). **Pros:** lovely beachfront location; convenient water shuttle every 30 minutes to and from Venice proper; friendly, welcoming staff. **Cons:** could do with a refresh; restaurants on the expensive side; can get very busy in summer and around the Venice Film Festival. $ *Rooms from: €585* ⊠ *Lungomare Marconi 41, Lido* ☎ *041/5260201* ⊕ *www.hotelexcelsiorvenezia.com* ⤴ *196 rooms* ⦿ *Free Breakfast* Ⓜ *Vaporetto: Lido.*

★ Hyatt Centric Murano Venice

$$$ | **HOTEL** | Befitting its location on Murano, this well-situated hotel is in a former glassmaking factory and has vitreous works of art throughout; it also has spacious, contemporary guest rooms with dark-wood floors and brown-and-cream color schemes. **Pros:** excellent breakfast buffet; vaporetto stop right outside the hotel, free airport transfers; easy walk to restaurants and shops. **Cons:** most rooms have no views; gym is basic; extra charge for using wellness center. $ *Rooms from: €210* ⊠ *Riva Longa 49, Murano* ☎ *041/2731234* ⊕ *www.hyatt.*

com/hyatt-centric/vcect-hyatt-centric-mu-rano-venice ⊒ *119 rooms* ¶◯| *No Meals*
Ⓜ *Vaporetto: Murano Museo.*

★ JW Marriott Venice Resort & Spa
$$$$ | **RESORT** | Once you get a taste of the resort's lush gardens, fabulous spa, and fantastic pools—all set on an exclusive island called Isole Delle Rose, a 20-minute boat ride from Venice—you may find yourself quickly settling into *la dolce vita.* **Pros:** relaxed vibe; spacious rooms; loads of amenities. **Cons:** getting to and from Venice can feel like a hassle; not much Venetian style in rooms; extra charge for spa. $ *Rooms from: €509* ⊠ *Isola delle Rose, Laguna di San Marco, Venezia Succursale 12, Venice* ☎ *041/8521300* ⊕ *www.jwvenice.com* ⊘ *Closed mid-Nov.–Feb.* ⊒ *266 rooms* ¶◯| *Free Breakfast.*

Shopping

★ Davide Penso
JEWELRY & WATCHES | This Venice-born, Murano-based artist makes gorgeous glass necklaces, earrings, and bracelets using the lampwork technique, where he shapes colored glass rods over a flame. ⊠ *Fondamenta Riva Longa 48, Murano* ☎ *041/739819* ⊕ *www.davidepenso.info* Ⓜ *Vaporetto: Museo Murano.*

★ Emilia Burano
FABRICS | This is not your grandmother's lace—these fourth-generation lace makers have updated their designs to produce exquisite bed linens, lampshades, and other items. ⊠ *Piazza Galuppi 205, Burano* ☎ *041/9345738* ⊕ *emiliaburano.it* Ⓜ *Vaporetto: Burano.*

★ MaMa Salvadore Murano
GLASSWARE | To see more of glassmaking's artistic side, visit this gallery/shop that highlights works from international contemporary glass artists. ⊠ *Fondamenta da Mula 148, Murano* ☎ *331/6224359 mobile* ⊕ *www.mamamurano.com* Ⓜ *Vaporetto: Murano.*

★ Salviati
GLASSWARE | One of the oldest and most prestigious Italian glassmakers (founded in 1859), Salviati partners with renowned international designers, including Tom Dixon, to create beautiful contemporary pieces. ⊠ *Fondamenta Radi 16, Murano* ☎ *041/5274085* ⊕ *www.salviati.com* Ⓜ *Vaporetto: Murano Museo, Murano Navagero.*

★ Simone Cenedese
GLASSWARE | This talented second-generation glass master produces intricately designed and often whimsical glass chandeliers and sculptures. ⊠ *Calle Bertolini 6, Murano* ☎ *041/5274455* ⊕ *simonecenedese.it* Ⓜ *Vaporetto: Murano Faro, Murano Colonna.*

NORTHERN ITALY

Updated by
Robert Andrews,
Nick Bruno, and Liz Shemaria

⊙ Sights	🎔 Restaurants	🛏 Hotels	🛍 Shopping	🍸 Nightlife
★★★★★	★★★★★	★★★★★	★★★★☆	★★★☆☆

WELCOME TO NORTHERN ITALY

TOP REASONS TO GO

★ **Giotto's frescoes in the Cappella degli Scrovegni:** In this Padua chapel, Giotto's expressive and innovative frescoes foreshadowed the Renaissance.

★ **Leonoardo's Last Supper:** Behold one of the world's most famous works of art for yourself housed within Santa Maria delle Grazie in Milan.

★ **Hiking in the Cinque Terre:** Hike the famous Cinque Terre trails past gravity-defying vineyards, colorful, rock-perched villages, and the deep blue Mediterranean Sea.

★ **The signature food of Emilia-Romagna:** This region's food—prosciutto crudo, Parmigiano-Reggiano, balsamic vinegar, and above all, pasta—makes the trip to Italy worthwhile.

★ **Breathtaking mosaics:** The intricate tiles in Ravenna's Mausoleo di Galla Placidia, in brilliantly well-preserved colors, depict vivid portraits and pastoral scenes.

Northern Italy holds some of the country's most memorable towns, cities, and regions. The Veneto region, just west of Venice, holds the beautiful, artistically rich cities of Padua, Vicenza, and Verona. Farther west, Milan is a major transportation hub and may be your point of entry into the country. South of Milan, you'll find the gorgeous beaches of the Italian Riviera, with the colorful villages of the Cinque Terre being a highlight. Between Florence and Venice, the region of Emilia-Romagna holds prosperous, highly cultured cities, where the locals have mastered the art of living—and especially eating—well.

1 **Padua.** A city of both high-rises and history, Padua is most noted for Giotto's frescoes in the Cappella degli Scrovegni.

2 **Verona.** One of the best preserved and most beautiful cities in Italy.

3 **Vicenza.** This elegant art city bears the signature of the great 16th-century architect Andrea Palladio.

4 **Milan.** The country's center of finance and commerce is constantly looking to the future. Home of the Italian stock exchange, it's also one of the world's fashion capitals and has cultural and artistic treasures that rival those of Florence and Rome.

5 **Riomaggiore.** The first of the Cinque Terre villages has a small harbor and coastal views.

6 Manarola. Terraced vineyards, olive trees, and pastel houses fill the town.

7 Corniglia. Climb (365 steps) to the most remote Cinque Terre town.

8 Vernazza. Enjoy lively piazzas and a postcard-worthy port view.

9 Monterosso al Mare. Come here for festivals, beaches, clear water, and plentiful hotels.

10 Bologna. Emilia's principal cultural and intellectual center is famed for its arcaded sidewalks, medieval towers, and sublime restaurants.

11 Ferrara. This prosperous, tidy town north of Bologna has a rich medieval past and distinctive cuisine.

12 Ravenna. The main attractions of this well-preserved Romagna city are its mosaics—glittering treasures left from Byzantine rule.

EATING AND DRINKING WELL IN THE VENETO AND FRIULI–VENEZIA GIULIA

Baked sea bream

With the decisive seasonal changes of the Venetian Arc, it's little wonder that many restaurants shun printed menus. Elements from field and forest define much of the region's cuisine, including white asparagus, herbs, chestnuts, radicchio, and wild mushrooms.

Restaurants of the Venetian Arc tend to cling to tradition, not only in the food they serve, but also when they serve it. From 2:30 in the afternoon until about 7:30 in the evening most places are closed (though you can pick up a snack at a bar during these hours), and on Sunday afternoon restaurants are packed with Italian families and friends indulging in the weekly ritual of lunching out.

Meals are still sacred for most Italians, so don't be surprised if you get disapproving looks as you gobble down a sandwich or a slice of pizza while seated on the church steps or a park bench. (In many places it's actually illegal to do so.)

THE BEST IN BEANS

Pasta e fagioli (a thick bean soup with pasta, served slightly warm or at room temperature) is made all over Italy. Folks in the Veneto, though, take special pride in their version, made from particularly fine beans grown around the village of Lamon, near Belluno. *Il fagiolo di Lamon* derives from the *Borlotto di Vigevano* bean and was first introduced by a monk in the 1500s via the Spanish court's colonial links to Mexico and Guatemela.

FISH

The catch of the day is always a good bet, whether it's sweet and succulent Adriatic shellfish, sea bream, bass, or John Dory, or freshwater fish from Lake Garda, near Verona. A staple in the Veneto is *baccalà*: this is dried salt cod, which, alongside *stoccafisso*, air-dried cod, was introduced to Italy during the Renaissance by northern European traders. Dried cod is soaked in water or milk and then prepared in a different way in each city. In Vicenza, baccalà *alla vicentina* confusingly uses stoccafisso, which is cooked with onions, milk, and cheese, and is generally served with polenta.

Creamed salted cod

MEAT

In the Veneto, traditional dishes feature offal as much as the prime cuts. Beef (including veal), pork, rabbit, horse, and donkey meat are standard, while goose, duck, and guinea fowl are common poultry options. In Friuli–Venezia Giulia, menus show the influence of Austria-Hungary: you may find deer and hare on the menu, as well as Eastern European–style goulash. One unusual treat served throughout the Veneto is *nervetti*—cubes of gelatin from a calf's knee prepared with onions, parsley, olive oil, and lemon.

PASTA, RISOTTO, POLENTA

For *primi* (first courses), the Veneto dines on *bigoli* (thick whole-wheat pasta), generally served with an anchovy-onion sauce delicately flavored with cinnamon, or creamy risotto flavored with vegetables or shellfish. Polenta is everywhere, whether it's a stiff porridge topped with Gorgonzola, or a stew, or a patty grilled and served alongside meat or fish.

RADICCHIO DI TREVISO

In fall and winter be sure to try the radicchio di Treviso, a red endive grown near that town but popular all over the region. Cultivation is very labor-intensive, so it can be expensive. It's best in a veal or chicken stew, in a risotto, or just grilled or baked with a drizzle of olive oil and perhaps a little Taleggio cheese from neighboring Lombardy.

WINE

The Veneto produces more D.O.C. (Denominazione di Origine Controllata) wines than any other region in Italy. Amarone, the region's crowning achievement, is a robust, full-bodied red. The best of the whites are Soave, prosecco, and *pinot bianco* (pinot blanc). In Friuli–Venezia Giulia, local wines include *friulano*, a dry, lively white made from the sauvignon vert grape, and *picolit*, a dessert wine.

Radicchio

EATING AND DRINKING WELL IN EMILIA-ROMAGNA

Homemade tortellini

Italians rarely agree about anything, but many concede that some of the country's finest foods originated in Emilia-Romagna. Tortellini, fettuccine, Parmesan cheese, prosciutto crudo, and balsamic vinegar are just a few of the Italian delicacies born here.

One of the beauties of Emilia-Romagna is that its exceptional food can be had without breaking the bank. Many trattorias serve up classic dishes, mastered over the centuries, at reasonable prices. Cutting-edge restaurants and wine bars are often more expensive; their inventive menus are full of *fantasia*—reinterpretations of the classics. For the budget-conscious, Bologna, a university town, has great places for cheap eats.

Between meals, you can sustain yourself with the region's famous sandwich, the *piadina*. It's made with pitalike thin bread, usually filled with prosciutto or mortadella, cheese, and vegetables, then put under the grill and served hot, with the cheese oozing at the sides. These addictive sandwiches can be savored at sit-down places or ordered to go.

THE REAL RAGÙ

Emilia-Romagna's signature dish is *tagliatelle al ragù* (flat noodles with meat sauce), which inspired the "spaghetti Bolognese" eaten outside Italy. This *primo* (first course) is on every menu, and no two versions are the same. The sauce starts in a sauté pan with finely diced carrots, onions, and celery. Purists add nothing but minced beef, but some use *guanciale* (pork cheek), sausage, veal, or chicken. Broth is added, and sometimes wine, milk, or cream.

PORK PRODUCTS

It's not just mortadella and cured pork products like prosciutto crudo and *culatello* that Emilia-Romagnans go crazy for—they're wild about the whole hog. You'll frequently find *cotechino* and *zampone*, both *secondi* (second courses), on menus. Cotechino is a savory, thick, fresh sausage served with lentils on New Year's Eve (the combination is said to augur well for the new year) and with mashed potatoes year-round. Zampone, a stuffed pig's foot, is redolent of garlic and deliciously fatty.

Pumpkin-stuffed tortelli

BOLLITO MISTO

The name means "mixed boil," and they do it exceptionally well in this part of Italy. According to Emilia-Romagnans, *bollito misto* was invented here, although other Italians—especially those from Milan, Verona, and Piedmont—might dispute this claim. Chicken, beef, tongue, and zampone are tossed into a stockpot and boiled; they're then removed from the broth and served with a fragrant *salsa verde* (green sauce), made with parsley and spiced with anchovies, garlic, and capers. This simple yet rich dish is usually served with mashed potatoes on the side, and savvy diners will mix some of the piquant salsa verde into the potatoes as well.

Cotechino sausage

STUFFED PASTA

Among the many Emilian variations on stuffed pasta, tortellini are the smallest. *Tortelli* and *cappellacci* are larger pasta "pillows," about the size of a brussels sprout, but with the same basic form as tortellini. They're often filled with pumpkin or spinach and cheese. *Tortelloni* are, in theory, even bigger, although their size varies. Stuffed pastas are generally served simply, with melted butter, sage, and Parmigiano-Reggiano cheese or, in the case of tortellini, *in brodo* (in beef, chicken, or capon broth or some combination thereof), which brings out the subtle richness of the filling.

WINES

Emilia-Romagna's wines accompany the region's fine food rather than vying with it for accolades. The best-known is *Lambrusco*, a sparkling red produced on the Po Plain that has some admirers and many detractors. It's praised for its tartness and condemned for the same; it does, however, pair brilliantly with the local fare. The region's best wines include Sangiovese di Romagna (somewhat similar to Chianti), from the Romagnan hills, and Barbera from the Colli Piacentini and Apennine foothills. Castelluccio, Bonzara, Zerbina, Leone Conti, and Tre Monti are among the region's top producers.

The prosperous north has Italy's most diverse landscape, highly cultured cities, along with exceptional cuisine—from French-influenced fare to the Italian classics prepared with unrivaled skill in Emilia-Romagna.

Venice is a rare jewel of a city, complete with canals, churches, and charming bridges, while the nearby Veneto region is where you'll find the artistically rich cities of Padua, Verona, and Vicenza. Milan is a center of commerce and style and the towns that make up the Cinque Terre, including Riomaggiore, Manarola, and Corniglia, are located along a rugged portion of the Italian Riviera, known for its spectacular vistas and world-class hiking.

MAJOR REGIONS

The Veneto. For centuries influenced by the city of Venice on the marshy Adriatic coast, the Veneto is a prosperous region dotted by fortified cities with captivating history and undulating vineyards. Padua's alluring architecture, art, and canal network may reflect the Venetian influence as the closest terra firma dominion, but its ancient, pioneering university—famed for its humanist alumni—creates a beguiling buzz of cycling students, food markets, and commerce. With the cooling Dolomite Alpine waters of the Adige River snaking through its medieval, Roman, and Venetian heart, Verona combines splendor with intimacy. Perfectly formed and wealthy Vicenza is where the peerless Palladio put his harmonious architectural plans into bricks, mortar, and gleaming marble.

Milan. To the west of the Veneto lies Milan, the country's economic engine,

home to the Italian stock exchange as well as world-famous fashion houses and cultural treasures.

The Cinque Terra. South, on the Gulf of Genoa, are five isolated seaside villages known collectively as the Cinque Terre. Stunningly beautiful, this region attracts hikers and nature lovers.

Emilia-Romagna. Gourmets the world over claim that Emilia-Romagna's greatest contribution to humankind has been gastronomic, but Bologna's palaces, Ferrara's medieval alley, and the Byzantine beauty of mosaic-rich Ravenna are all breathtaking.

Planning

When to Go

The ideal times to visit are late spring and early summer (May and June) and in early fall (September and October). Summers tend to be hot and humid—though if you're an opera buff, it's worth tolerating the heat in order to see a performance at the Arena di Verona (where the season runs from July through September).

Winter is a good time to avoid travel to these regions; although the dense fog can be beautiful, it makes for bad driving conditions, and wet, bone-chilling cold isn't unusual November through March. That being said, you'll get some of the best rates and some of the smallest crowds if you do decide to visit during this time.

Planning Your Time

Lined up in a row west of Venice are Padua, Vicenza, and Verona—three prosperous small cities that are each worth at least a day on a northern Italy itinerary. Verona has the most charm and the widest selection of hotels and restaurants, so it's probably the best choice for a base in the area, even though it also draws the most tourists. The hills north of Venice make for good drives, with appealing villages set amid a visitor-friendly wine country.

Italy's commercial hub isn't usually at the top of the list for visiting tourists, but Milan is the nation's most modern city, with its own sophisticated appeal: its fashionable shops rival those of New York and Paris, its soccer teams are Italy's answer to the Yankees and the Mets, its opera performances set the standard for the world, and its art treasures are well worth the visit.

The Italian Riviera and Cinque Terre region is extremely seasonal. From April to October, the area's bustling with shops, cafés, clubs, and restaurants that stay open late. In high season (Easter and June–August), it can be very crowded and lively. Yet, the rest of the year, the majority of resorts close down, and you'll be hard-pressed to find accommodations or restaurants open.

Plan on spending at least two days in Bologna, the region's cultural and historical capital. Also plan on visiting Ferrara, a misty, mysterious medieval city. If you have time, go to Ravenna for its memorable Byzantine mosaics and Modena for its harmonious architecture and famous balsamic vinegar.

Getting Here and Around

Aeroporto Malpensa, 50 km (31 miles) northwest of Milan, is the major northern Italian hub for intercontinental flights and also sees substantial European and domestic traffic. Venice's Aeroporto Marco Polo also serves international destinations. There are regional airports in Turin, Genoa, Bologna, Verona, Trieste, Treviso, Bolzano, and Parma, and Milan has a secondary airport, Linate. You can reach all of these on connecting flights from within Italy and from other European cities. You can also get around northern Italy by train using the Italian national rail system, FS-Trenitalia (⊕ *www.trenitalia. com*). Shuttle buses run three times an hour (less often after 10 pm) between Malpensa and Milan's main train station, Stazione Centrale; the trip takes about 75 minutes, depending on traffic. The Malpensa Express Train, which leaves twice an hour, takes 40 minutes and delivers you to Cadorna metro station in central Milan.

The cities in these regions are connected by well-maintained highways and an efficient railway system. A car provides added freedom, but city driving and parking can be a challenge.

Restaurants

You'll find lots of traditional northern Italian restaurants in this region, and can pretty much count on menus divided into pasta, fish, and meat options. As in the rest of Italy, it's common for dishes to feature seasonal and local ingredients. Although the Veneto is not considered one of Italy's major cuisine areas, the region offers many opportunities for exciting gastronomic adventures. The fish offerings are among the most varied and freshest in Italy, and possibly Europe, and the vegetables from the islands in the Venetian lagoon are considered a national treasure. Take a break from pasta and try the area's wonderful, creamy risottos and hearty polenta. Meal prices in Milan tend to be higher than in the rest of the region (and quite high for European cities in general), though this is also where you'll see examples of the latest food trends and more adventurous choices on the menus. While fine dining can be found in Cinque Terre, you are more likely to enjoy a casual atmosphere, often with an amazing sea view. Expect both the decor and dishes to be simple but flavorful.

In Emilia-Romagna, dining options range from mom-and-pop-style informal trattorias to three-star Michelin restaurants. Food here is not for the faint of heart (or those on diets): it is rich, creamy, and cheesy. Local wines pair remarkably well with this sumptuous fare. You may want to rethink Lambrusco, as it marries well with just about everything on the menu.

Hotels

Rates tend to be higher in Padua and Verona; in Verona especially, seasonal rates vary widely and soar during trade fairs and the opera season. There are fewer good lodging choices in Vicenza, perhaps because more overnighters are drawn to the better restaurant scenes in Verona and Padua. *Agriturismo* (farm stay) information is available at tourist offices and sometimes on their websites. High-season in Milan depends on what fairs and exhibitions are being staged. Prices in almost all hotels can go up dramatically during the Furniture Fair in early April. Fashion, travel, and tech fairs also draw big crowds throughout the year, raising prices. In contrast to other cities in Italy, however, you can often find discounts on weekends. In Cinque Terre, lodging tends to be pricey in high season, particularly June to August; reservations for this region should also be made far in advance as places book up very quickly. Emilia-Romagna has a reputation for demonstrating a level of efficiency

uncommon in most of Italy. Even the smallest hotels are usually well-run, with high standards of quality and service. Bologna is very much a businessperson's city, and many hotels here cater to the business traveler, but there are smaller, more intimate hotels as well. It's smart to book in advance—the region hosts many fairs and conventions that can fill up hotels even during low season.

⇨ *Prices in the dining reviews are the average cost of a main course at dinner, or, if dinner is not served, at lunch. Prices in the reviews are the lowest cost of a standard double room in high season. Restaurant and hotel reviews have been shortened. For full information, visit Fodors.com.*

What It Costs in Euros

	$	$$	$$$	$$$$
RESTAURANTS				
	under €15	€15–€24	€25–€35	over €35
HOTELS				
	under €125	€125–€200	€201–€300	over €300

Padua

42 km (25 miles) west of Venice.

A romantic warren of arcaded streets, Padua has long been one of the major cultural centers of northern Italy. It has first-rate artistic monuments and, along with Bologna, is one of the few cities in the country where you can catch a glimpse of student life.

Its university, founded in 1222 and Italy's second oldest, attracted such cultural icons as Dante (1265–1321), Petrarch (1304–74), and Galileo Galilei (1564–1642), thus earning the city the sobriquet *La Dotta* (The Learned). Padua's Basilica di Sant'Antonio, begun around 1238, attracts droves of pilgrims, especially on his feast day, June 13. Three great artists—Giotto (1266–1337), Donatello (circa 1386–1466), and Mantegna (1431–1506)—left significant works in Padua, with Giotto's Scrovegni Chapel being one of the best-known, and most meticulously preserved, works of art in the country. Today, a cycle-happy student body—some 60,000 strong—flavors every aspect of local culture. Don't be surprised if you spot a *laurea* (graduation) ceremony marked by laurel leaves, mocking lullabies, and X-rated caricatures.

GETTING HERE AND AROUND

The train trip between Venice and Padua is short, and regular bus service originates from Venice's Piazzale Roma. By car from Venice, Padua is on the Autostrada Torino–Trieste A4/E70. Take the San Carlo exit and follow Via Guido Reni to Via Tiziano Aspetti into town. Regular bus service connects Venice's Marco Polo airport with downtown Padua.

Padua is a walker's city. If you arrive by car, leave your vehicle in one of the parking lots on the outskirts or at your hotel. Unlimited bus service is included with the PadovaCard (€18 or €24, valid for 48 or 72 hours), which allows entry to all the city's principal sights (€1 extra for a Scrovegni Chapel reservation). It's available at tourist information offices and at some museums and hotels.

VISITOR INFORMATION

CONTACT Padua Tourism Office. ✉ *Padova Railway Station, Piazzale Stazione, Padua* ☎ *049/5207415* ⊕ *www.turismopadova.it.*

Sights

Abano Terme

HOT SPRING | A very popular hot-springs spa town about 12 km (7 miles) southwest of Padua, Abano Terme lies at the foot of the Euganean Hills among hand-tilled vineyards. If a bit of pampering sounds better than traipsing through yet another church or castle, indulge yourself with a soak, a massage, or mud

treatments, which are especially recommended for joint aches. A good-value day pass (€35) is available at Hotel Antiche Terme Ariston Molino Buja (⊕ *aristonmolino.it*). ✉ *Abano Terme* ✛ *Take Padua West exit off A4, or Terme Euganee exit off A13* ☎ *049/8669061* ⊕ *www.abano.it; aristonmolino.it.*

★ **Basilica di Sant'Antonio** (*Basilica del Santo*)

CHURCH | Thousands of faithful make the pilgrimage here each year to pray at the tomb of St. Anthony, while others come to admire works by the 15th-century Florentine master Donatello. His equestrian statue (1453) of the condottiere Erasmo da Narni, known as Gattamelata, in front of the church is one of the great masterpieces of Italian Renaissance sculpture. The huge church, which combines elements of Byzantine, Romanesque, and Gothic styles, was probably begun around 1238, seven years after the death of the Portuguese-born saint. The Cappella del Santo (housing the tomb of the saint) dates from the 16th century. ✉ *Piazza del Santo, Padua* ☎ *049/8225652* ⊕ *www.basilicadelsanto. it* 🎫 *Basilica free, museum complex €7* ☾ *Museum complex closed Mon.*

Burchiello Excursion, Brenta Canal

BODY OF WATER | During the 16th century the Brenta was transformed into a mainland version of Venice's Grand Canal with the building of nearly 50 waterside villas. Back then, boating parties viewed them from *burchielli*—beautiful river barges. Today the Burchiello excursion boat makes full- and half-day tours along the Brenta in season, departing from Padua and Venice; tickets can also be bought at travel agencies. You visit three houses, including the Villas Pisani and Foscari, with a lunchtime break in Oriago (€23 or €30 extra). Note that most houses are on the left side coming from Venice, or the right from Padua. ✉ *Via Porciglia 34, Padua* ☎ *049/8760233* ⊕ *www.ilburchiello.it*

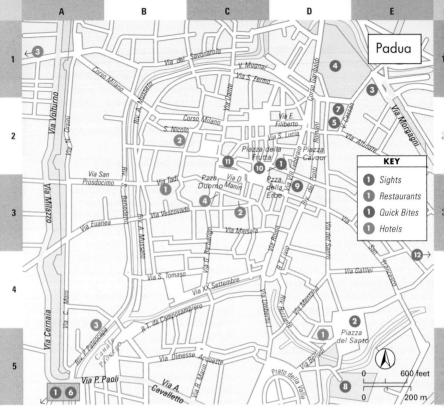

Padua

KEY

1 Sights
1 Restaurants
1 Quick Bites
1 Hotels

0 ——— 600 feet
0 ——— 200 m

Sights ▼

1 Abano Terme........... **A5**
2 Basilica di Sant'Antonio **E4**
3 Burchiello Excursion, Brenta Canal **E1**
4 Cappella degli Scrovegni............... **D1**
5 Chiesa degli Eremitani................ **D2**
6 Montegrotto Terme..... **A5**
7 Musei Civici degli Eremitani................ **D2**
8 Orto Botanico **D5**
9 Palazzo del Bo **D3**
10 Palazzo della Ragione **C2**
11 Piazza dei Signori........ **C2**
12 Villa Pisani............... **E4**

Restaurants ▼

1 Enoteca dei Tadi........ **B3**
2 L'Anfora **C3**
3 Le Calandre.............. **A1**
4 Osteria dal Capo **C3**

Quick Bites ▼

1 Bar Romeo................ **C2**

Hotels ▼

1 Al Fagiano **D5**
2 Albergo Verdi **B2**
3 Methis Hotel & Spa..... **A4**

The Venetian Arc, Past and Present

Long before Venetians made their presence felt on the mainland in the 15th century, Ezzelino III da Romano (1194–1259) laid claim to Verona, Padua, and the surrounding lands and towns. He was the first of a series of brutal and aggressive rulers who dominated the cities of the region until the rise of Venetian rule.

After Ezzelino was ousted, powerful families, such as Padua's Carrara and Verona's Della Scala (Scaligeri), vied throughout the 14th century to dominate these territories. With the rise of Venetian rule came a time of relative peace, when noble families from the lagoon and the mainland commissioned Palladio and other accomplished architects to design their palazzi and villas. This rich classical legacy, superimposed upon medieval castles and fortifications, is central to the identities of present-day Padua, Vicenza, and Verona.

The region remained under Venetian control until the Napoleonic invasion and the fall of the Venetian Republic in 1797. The Council of Vienna ceded it, along with Lombardy, to Austria in 1815. The region revolted against Austrian rule and joined the Italian Republic in 1866.

Friuli–Venezia Giulia's complicated history is reflected in its architecture, language, and cuisine. It's been marched through, fought over, hymned by patriots, and romanticized by writers who include James Joyce, Rainer Maria Rilke, Ernest Hemingway, Pier Paolo Pasolini, Italo Svevo, and Jan Morris. The region has seen Fascists and Communists, Romans, Hapsburgs, and Huns. It survived by forging sheltering alliances—Udine beneath the wings of San Marco (1420), Trieste choosing Duke Leopold of Austria (1382) over Venetian domination.

Some of World War I's fiercest fighting took place in Friuli–Venezia Giulia, where memorials and cemeteries commemorate the hundreds of thousands who died before the arrival of Italian troops in 1918 finally liberated Trieste from Austrian rule. Trieste, along with the whole of Venezia Giulia, was annexed to Italy in 1920. During World War II, Germany occupied the area and placed Trieste in an administrative zone along with parts of Slovenia. The only Nazi extermination camp on Italian soil, the Risiera di San Sabba, was in a suburb of Trieste. After the war, during a period of Cold War dispute, Trieste was governed by an Allied military administration; it was officially re-annexed to Italy in 1954, when Italy ceded the Istrian peninsula to the south to Yugoslavia. These arrangements were not finally ratified by Italy and Yugoslavia until 1975.

✉ €75 half day, €119 full day; lunch extra
🕙 Closed Mon. and Nov.–Feb.

★ **Cappella degli Scrovegni**
(The Arena Chapel)
CHURCH | The emotional intensity and naturalism of the frescoes illustrating the lives of Mary and Jesus in

this world-famous chapel broke new ground in Western art. Enrico Scrovegni commissioned these frescoes to atone for the sins of his deceased father, Reginaldo, the usurer condemned to the Seventh Circle of the Inferno in Dante's *Divine Comedy*. Giotto and his assistants worked on the frescoes from 1303 to 1305, arranging them in tiers to be read from left to right. To preserve the artwork, doors are opened only every 15 minutes. ⊠ *Piazza Eremitani 8, Padua* ☏ *049/2010020 reservations* ⊕ *www. cappelladegliscrovegni.it* ⛁ *€14, includes Musei Civici and Palazzo Zuckermann.*

Chiesa degli Eremitani

CHURCH | This 13th-century church houses substantial fragments of Andrea Mantegna's frescoes (1448–50), which were damaged by Allied bombing in World War II. Despite their fragmentary condition, Mantegna's still beautiful and historically important depictions of the martyrdom of St. James and St. Christopher show the young artist's mastery of extremely complex problems of perspective. ⊠ *Piazza Eremitani, Padua* ☏ *049/8756410.*

Montegrotto Terme

HOT SPRING | At this spa town about 13 km (8 miles) southwest of Padua, you can luxuriate in thermal mineral pools. Montegrotto Terme has several hotels whose treatments vary from simple massage and thermal and mud baths to hydrokinetic therapy. Scuba enthusiasts head here for the world's deepest indoor pool, Y-40 Deep Joy. The nearest railway stop, on the Bologna–Padua line, is Terme Euganee–Montegrotto. Taxis are available outside the station. ⊠ *Montegrotto Terme* ⊹ *Terme Euganee exit off A13* ☏ *049/8928311* ⊕ *www.visitabanomontegrotto.com.*

★ Musei Civici degli Eremitani (*Civic Museum*)

OTHER MUSEUM | Usually visited along with the neighboring Cappella degli Scrovegni, this former monastery houses a rich array of exhibits and has wonderful cloister gardens with a mix of ancient architectural fragments and modern sculpture. The Pinacoteca displays works of medieval and modern masters, including some by Tintoretto, Veronese, and Tiepolo. Standouts are the *Giotto Crucifix,* which once hung in the Cappella degli Scrovegni, and the *Portrait*

of a Young Senator, by Giovanni Bellini (1430–1516). ⊠ *Piazza Eremitani 8, Padua* ☏ *049/8204551* ⊕ *www.padovanet.it* ⛁ *€10, €14 with Scrovegni Chapel and Palazzo Zuckermann; free with PadovaCard* ⊙ *Closed Mon.*

Orto Botanico (*Botanical Garden*)

GARDEN | The Venetian Republic ordered the creation of Padua's botanical garden in 1545 to supply the university with medicinal plants, and it retains its original layout. You can stroll the arboretum—still part of the university—and wander through hothouses and beds of plants that were introduced to Italy in this late-Renaissance garden. A St. Peter's palm, planted in 1585, inspired Goethe to write his 1790 essay, "The Metamorphosis of Plants." ⊠ *Via Orto Botanico 15, Padua* ☏ *049/8273939* ⊕ *www.ortobotanicopd.it* ⛁ *€10 (€5 with PadovaCard)* ⊙ *Closed Mon.*

★ Palazzo del Bo

CASTLE/PALACE | The University of Padua, founded in 1222, centers on this predominantly 16th-century palazzo with an 18th-century facade. It's named after the Osteria del Bo (*bo* means "ox"), an inn that once stood on the site. It's worth a visit to see the perfectly proportioned anatomy theater (1594), the beautiful Old Courtyard, and a hall with a lectern used by Galileo. You can enter only as part of a guided tour; weekend/public holiday tours allow access to other parts of the university; most guides speak English, but it is worth checking ahead by phone. ⊠ *Via 8 Febbraio, Padua* ☏ *049/8275111 university switchboard, 049/8273939* ⊕ *www.unipd.it* ⛁ *€7; €12 extended tour weekends and public holidays.*

Palazzo della Ragione

CASTLE/PALACE | Also known as Il Salone, the spectacular arcaded reception hall in Padua's original law courts is as notable for its grandeur—it's 85 feet high—as for its colorful setting, surrounded by shops, cafés, and open-air fruit and vegetable markets. Nicolò Miretto and Stefano da Ferrara, working from 1425 to 1440, painted the frescoes after Giotto's plan, which was destroyed by a fire in 1420. The stunning space hosts art shows, and an enormous wooden horse, crafted for a public tournament in 1466, commands pride of place. It is patterned after the famous equestrian statue by Donatello in front of the Basilica di Sant'Antonio, and may, in fact, have been designed by Donatello himself in the last year of his life. ✉ *Piazza della Ragione, Padua* ☎ *049/8205006* 🌐 *padovacultura.padovanet.it* 🎫 *€7 (free with PadovaCard)* 🕒 *Closed Mon.*

Piazza dei Signori

PLAZA/SQUARE | Some fine examples of 15th- and 16th-century buildings line this square. On the west side, the **Palazzo del Capitanio** (facade constructed 1598–1605) has an impressive **Torre dell'Orologio,** with an astronomical clock dating from 1344 and a portal made by Falconetto in 1532 in the form of a Roman triumphal arch. The 12th-century **Battistero del Duomo** (Cathedral Baptistry), with frescoes by Giusto de' Menabuoi (1374–78), is a few steps away. ✉ *Piazza dei Signori, Padua* ☎ *049/656914* 🌐 *www.battisteropadova.it* 🎫 *Battistero €8 (free with PadovaCard).*

Villa Pisani

CASTLE/PALACE | **FAMILY** | Extensive grounds with rare trees, ornamental fountains, and garden follies surround this extraordinary palace in Stra, 13 km (8 miles) southeast of Padua. Built in 1721 for the Venetian doge Alvise Pisani, it recalls Versailles more than a Veneto villa. This was one of the last and grandest of many stately residences constructed along the Brenta River from the 16th to 18th centuries by wealthy Venetians. Gianbattista Tiepolo's (1696–1770) spectacular fresco on the ballroom ceiling, *The Apotheosis of the Pisani Family* (1761), alone is worth the visit. For a relaxing afternoon, explore the gorgeous park and maze. ✉ *Via Doge Pisani 7, Stra* ☎ *049/502074* 🌐 *villapisani.beniculturali.it* 🎫 *€8, €5 park only* 🕒 *Closed Mon.*

Cocktail Hour on Padua's Piazzas 🍴

A great Padua tradition is the outdoor consumption of *aperitivi*—a *spritz* (a mix of Aperol or Campari, soda water, and wine), prosecco, or wine—in the Piazza delle Erbe and Piazza delle Frutta. Several bars there provide drinks in plastic cups so you can take them outside and mingle among the crowds. The ritual begins at 6 or so, and may be accompanied with tasty cocktail stick–pierced appetizers known to the Padovani as *spunciotti*. Bars generally close shortly after midnight.

🍴 Restaurants

★ Enoteca dei Tadi

$$ | **ITALIAN** | In this cozy and atmospheric cross between a wine bar and a restaurant, you can put together a fabulous, inexpensive dinner from various classic dishes from all over Italy. Portions are small, but prices are reasonable—just follow the local custom and order a selection, perhaps starting with fresh *burrata* (mozzarella's creamier cousin) with tomatoes, or a selection of prosciutti or salami. **Known for:** several kinds of lasagna; intimate and rustic setting; bountiful wine and grappa list. [$] *Average main: €22* ✉ *Via dei Tadi 16, Padua* ☎ *338/4083434 mobile* 🌐 *www.enotecadeitadi.it* 🕒 *Closed Mon. No dinner Sun.*

L'Anfora

$$ | **WINE BAR** | This mix between a traditional *bacaro* (wine bar) and an osteria is a local institution, opened in 1922. Stand at the bar with a cross section of Padovano society, from construction workers to professors, and peruse the reasonably priced menu of simple *casalinga* (home-cooked dishes), plus salads and a selection of cheeses. **Known for:** atmospheric art-filled osteria with wood interior; no-nonsense traditional Veneto food; very busy at lunchtime. $ *Average main: €19* ✉ *Via Soncin 13, Padua* ☎ *049/656629* ⊕ *osteria-lanfora.eatbu.com* ⊗ *Closed Sun. (except in Dec.).*

Le Calandre

$$$$ | **MODERN ITALIAN** | Traditional Veneto recipes are given a highly sophisticated and creative treatment here, and the whole theatrical tasting-menu experience and gorgeous table settings can seem by turns revelatory or overblown at this high-profile place. Owner-chef Massimiliano Alajmo's creative, minis-cule-portion dishes, passion for design (bespoke lighting, carved wooden tables, and quirky plates), and first-class wine list make this an option for a pricey celebratory meal. **Known for:** theatrical, sensory dining experience; playful (or to some, pretentious) touches; reservations essential. $ *Average main: €200* ✉ *Via Liguria 1, Sarmeola* ⊹ *7 km (4 miles) west of Padua* ☎ *049/630303* ⊕ *www.calandre.com* ⊗ *Closed Sun. and Mon. No lunch Tues.*

Osteria dal Capo

$$ | **VENETIAN** | Located in the heart of what used to be Padua's Jewish ghetto, this friendly trattoria serves almost exclusively traditional Veneto dishes, and it does so with refinement and care. Everything from the well-crafted dishes to the unfussy ship's dining cabin–like decor and elegant plates reflect decades of Padovano hospitality. **Known for:** intimate and understated dining at decent prices; meaty-sauced pasta dishes; limited tables mean reservations essential. $ *Average main: €23* ✉ *Via degli Obizzi 2, Padua* ☎ *049/663105* ⊕ *www.osteriadal-capo.it* ⊗ *Closed Sun. No lunch Mon.*

 Coffee and Quick Bites

Bar Romeo

$ | **NORTHERN ITALIAN** | Deep in the atmospheric Sotto Salone market, this busy bar does a fab selection of filled *tramezzini* (triangular sandwiches), panini, and other snacks. Ask behind the bar or one of the locals about the various wines and snacks chalked on the board. It's a great place to hear the local dialect and mingle with the market workers and shoppers any time of day; grab a breakfast coffee and brioche, a glass of Falanghina, or a bit later—after 11 am perhaps—an aperitivo with snacks. **Known for:** good-value sandwiches; friendly staff and Padovano vibe; superb selection of wine by the glass. $ *Average main: €5* ✉ *26 Sotto Salone, Padua* ☎ *340/5560611 mobile.*

Hotels

Al Fagiano

$ | **HOTEL** | The refreshingly funky surroundings in this self-styled art hotel include sponge-painted walls, brush-painted chandeliers, and views of the spires and cupolas of the Basilica di Sant'Antonio. **Pros:** great for art lovers or those after a unique ambience; relaxed, quirky, homey atmosphere; convenient location. **Cons:** not all rooms have views; some find the way-out-there (some risqué) art a bit much; lots of stairs. $ *Rooms from: €112* ✉ *Via Locatelli 45, Padua* ☎ *049/8750073* ⊕ *www.alfagiano.com* ⊷ *40 rooms* ⊙ *No Meals.*

Albergo Verdi

$ | **HOTEL** | One of the best-situated hotels in the city provides understated modern rooms and public areas that tend toward the minimalist without being severe, while the intimate breakfast room with stylish Eames Eiffel chairs and adjoining terrace is a tranquil place to start the day. **Pros:** excellent location close to Piazza dei Signori; bountiful breakfast selection; 24-hour bar service. **Cons:** student noise in piazza-facing rooms; few views; steep stairs and small elevator. $ *Rooms from: €110* ⊠ *Via Dondi dell'Orologio 7, Padua* ☎ *049/8364163* ⊕ *www.albergoverdipa-dova.it* ⤵ *14 rooms* ⦿ *Free Breakfast.*

Methis Hotel & Spa

$ | **HOTEL** | Four floors of modern design reflect nature's elements at this modern spa hotel: there are gentle earth tones and fiery red in the classic rooms; watery, cool blues in superior rooms; and airy white in the top-floor suites. **Pros:** superb canal walks nearby; better views of canal across road from front rooms; gym, sauna, Turkish bath, and spa treatments. **Cons:** 15-minute walk from major sights and restaurants; public spaces lack some character; tired decor and unkempt corners. $ *Rooms from: €120* ⊠ *Riviera Paleocapa 70, Padua* ☎ *049/8725555* ⊕ *www.methishotel.it* ⤵ *59 rooms* ⦿ *Free Breakfast.*

 Nightlife

★ Caffè Pedrocchi

CAFÉS | No visit to Padua is complete without taking time to sit in this historic café and iconic Padovano venue, patronized by luminaries like the French novelist Stendhal in 1831. Nearly 200 years later, it remains central to the city's social life. The café was built in the Egyptian Revival style, and it's now famed for its innovative aperitivi and signature mint coffee. The accomplished, innovative restaurant serves breakfast, lunch, and dinner. The grand salons and terrace provide a backdrop for the occasional jazz, swing, and cover bands. ⊠ *Piazzetta Pedrocchi, Padua* ☎ *049/8781231* ⊕ *www.caffeped-rocchi.it.*

 Shopping

★ Mercato Sotto il Salone

FOOD | Under the Salone there's an impressive food market where shops sell choice salami and cured meats, local cheeses, wines, coffee, and tea. With the adjacent Piazza delle Erbe fruit and vegetable market, you can pick up all the makings of a fine picnic. On weekends and public holidays, the piazza is often filled with fabulous street food, as well as wine and beer stalls. ⊠ *Piazza della Ragione, Padua* ⊕ *mercatosottoilsalone. it.*

Zotti Antiquariato

ANTIQUES & COLLECTIBLES | Owned by antiques dealer Pietro Maria Zotti—who has worked for more than 40 years in the trade—this always-changing shop has fascinating finds from Venetian artworks to stylish mid-century furniture, plus lots of smaller, more affordable items, including books, prints, jewelry, militaria, and coins. ⊠ *Selciato San Nicolò 5, Padua* ☎ *338/2930830 mobile* ⊕ *www.zottianti-quariato.it.*

Verona

114 km (71 miles) west of Venice, 60 km (37 miles) west of Vicenza.

On the banks of the fast-flowing River Adige, enchanting Verona has timeless monuments, a picturesque town center, and a romantic reputation as the setting of Shakespeare's *Romeo and Juliet*. With its lively Venetian air and proximity to Lake Garda, it attracts hordes of tourists, especially Germans and Austrians. Tourism peaks during summer's renowned season of open-air opera in the arena and during spring's Vinitaly, one of the world's most important wine expos. For five days you can sample the wines of more than 3,000 wineries from dozens of countries.

Verona grew to power and prosperity within the Roman Empire as a result of its key commercial and military position in northern Italy. With its Roman arena, theater, and city gates, it has the most significant monuments of Roman antiquity north of Rome. After the fall of the empire, the city continued to flourish under the guidance of barbarian kings, such as Theodoric, Alboin, Pepin, and

Berenger I, reaching its cultural and artistic peak in the 13th and 14th centuries under the della Scala (Scaligero) dynasty. (Look for the *scala,* or ladder, emblem all over town.) In 1404 Verona traded its independence for security and placed itself under the control of Venice. (The other recurring architectural motif is the lion of St. Mark, a symbol of Venetian rule.)

If you're going to visit more than one or two sights, it's worth purchasing a VeronaCard, available at museums, churches, and tobacconists for €20 (for 24 hours) or €25 (48 hours). It buys a single admission to most of the city's significant museums and churches, plus you can ride free on city buses. If you're mostly interested in churches, a €8 cumulative ticket is sold at Verona's major houses of worship and gains you entry to the Duomo, San Fermo Maggiore, San Zeno Maggiore, and Sant'Anastasia. Note that Verona's churches strictly enforce their dress code: no sleeveless shirts, shorts, or short skirts.

GETTING HERE AND AROUND

Verona is midway between Venice and Milan. Several trains per hour depart from any point on the Milan–Venice line. By car, from Venice, take the Autostrada Trieste–Torino A4/E70 to the SS12 and follow it north into town.

VISITOR INFORMATION

CONTACT Verona Tourism Office (IAT Verona). ⊠ *Via degli Alpini 9, Piazza Bra, Verona* ☎ *045/8068680* ⊕ *www.veronatouristoffice.it/en.*

 Sights

Arche Scaligere

TOMB | On a little square off Piazza dei Signori are the fantastically sculpted Gothic tombs of the della Scala family, who ruled Verona during the late Middle Ages. The 19th-century English traveler and critic John Ruskin described the tombs as graceful places where people

who have fallen asleep live. The tomb of Cangrande I (1291–1329) hangs over the portal of the adjacent church and is the work of the Maestro di Sant'Anastasia. The tomb of Mastino II, begun in 1345, has an elaborate baldachin, originally painted and gilded, and is surrounded by an iron grillwork fence and topped by an equestrian statue. The latest and most elaborate tomb is that of Cansignorio (1375), the work principally of Bonino da Campione. The major tombs are all visible from the street. ⊠ *Via Arche Scaligere, Verona.*

★ Arco dei Gavi

RUINS | This stunning structure is simpler and less imposing, but also more graceful, than the triumphal arches in Rome. Built in the 1st century by the architect Lucius Vitruvius Cerdo to celebrate the accomplishments of the patrician Gavia family, it was highly esteemed by several Renaissance architects, including Palladio. ⊠ *Corso Cavour, Verona.*

Arena di Verona

RUINS | **FAMILY** | Only Rome's Colosseum and Capua's arena would dwarf this amphitheater, built for gymnastic competitions, choreographed sacrificial rites, and games involving hunts, fights, battles, and wild animals. Although four arches are all that remain of the arena's outer arcade, the main structure is complete and dates from AD 30. In summer, you can join up to 16,000 for spectacular opera productions and pop or rock concerts (extra costs for these events). ■TIP→ **The opera's the main thing here: when there is no opera performance, you can still enter the interior, but the arena is less impressive inside than the Colosseum or other Roman amphitheaters.** ⊠ *Piazza Bra 5, Verona* ☎ *045/8005151 performance tickets, 045/8003204 visit* ⊕ *www.arena.it* ☎ *€10 (free with VeronaCard); €11 includes entrance to nearby Museo Lapidario Maffeiano.*

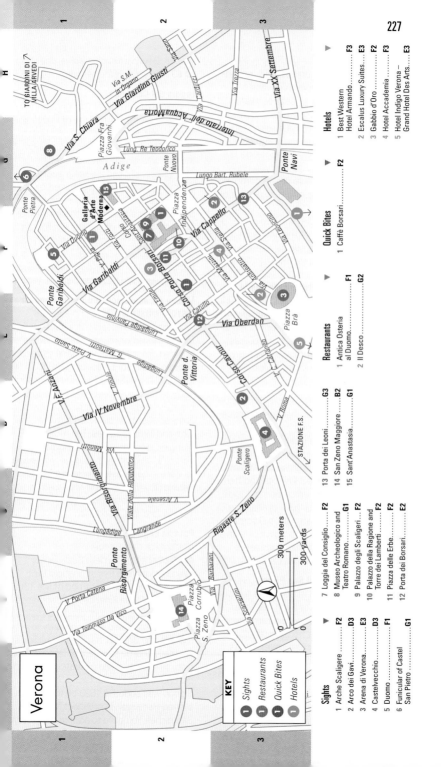

Verona

227

KEY

- 1️⃣ Sights
- 1️⃣ Restaurants
- 1️⃣ Quick Bites
- 1️⃣ Hotels

▸ **Sights**

1 Arche Scaligere F2
2 Arco dei Gavi D3
3 Arena di Verona E3
4 Castelvecchio D3
5 Duomo F1
6 Funicular of Castel San Pietro G1
7 Loggia del Consiglio F2
8 Museo Archeologico and Teatro Romano G1
9 Palazzo degli Scaligeri F2
10 Palazzo della Ragione and Torre dei Lamberti F2
11 Piazza delle Erbe F2
12 Porta dei Borsari E2
13 Porta dei Leoni G3
14 San Zeno Maggiore B2
15 Sant'Anastasia G1

▸ **Restaurants**

1 Antica Osteria al Duomo F1
2 Il Desco G2

▸ **Quick Bites**

1 Caffè Borsari F2

▸ **Hotels**

1 Best Western Hotel Armando F3
2 Escalus Luxury Suites E3
3 Gabbio d'Oro F2
4 Hotel Accademia F3
5 Hotel Indigo Verona – Grand Hotel Des Arts E3

300 meters
300 yards

★ Castelvecchio

CASTLE/PALACE | This crenellated, russet brick building with massive walls, towers, turrets, and a vast courtyard was built for Cangrande II della Scala in 1354 and presides over a street lined with attractive old buildings and palaces of the nobility. Only by going inside the Museo di Castelvecchio can you really appreciate this massive castle complex with its vaulted halls. You also get a look at a significant collection of Venetian and Veneto art, medieval weapons, and jewelry. The interior of the castle was restored and redesigned as a museum between 1958 and 1975 by Carlo Scarpa, one of Italy's most accomplished architects. ∎ TIP→ **Behind the castle is the fortified Ponte Scaligero (1355), which spans the River Adige and is a fab spot for taking photos.** ⊠ *Corso Castelvecchio 2, Verona* ☎ *045/7110129* ⊕ *museodicastelvecchio.comune.verona.it* 🔖 *€6 (free with VeronaCard)* ⊗ *Closed Mon.*

Duomo

CHURCH | The present church was begun in the 12th century in the Romanesque style; its later additions are mostly Gothic. On pilasters guarding the main entrance are 12th-century carvings thought to represent Oliver and Roland, two of Charlemagne's knights and heroes of several medieval epic poems. Inside, Titian's *Assumption* (1530) graces the first chapel on the left. ⊠ *Via Duomo, Verona* ☎ *045/592813* ⊕ *www.chieseverona.it* 🔖 *€4, (€8 Church Cumulative Ticket or free with VeronaCard).*

★ Funicular of Castel San Pietro

VIEWPOINT | Opened in 2017, this funicular ride ascends 500 feet from near the Teatro Romano up to a panoramic terrace in just 90 seconds, affording fabulous Veronese views. For the adventurous, there's scope for long walks around the parkland paths and quiet lanes crisscrossing the elevated city walls. ⊠ *Via Fontanelle S. Stefano, Verona* ☎ *342/8966695*

mobile ⊕ *www.funicolarediverona.it* 🔖 *€3 round-trip, €2 one-way.*

Loggia del Consiglio

GOVERNMENT BUILDING | This graceful structure on the north flank of Piazza dei Signori was finished in 1492 and built to house city council meetings. Although the city was already under Venetian rule, Verona still had a certain degree of autonomy, which was expressed by the splendor of the loggia. Very strangely for a Renaissance building of this quality, its architect remains unknown, but it's the finest surviving example of late-15th-century architecture in Verona. The building is not open to the public, but the exterior is worth a visit. ⊠ *Piazza dei Signori, Verona.*

Museo Archeologico and Teatro Romano

HISTORY MUSEUM | The archaeological holdings of this museum in a 15th-century former monastery consist largely of the donated collections of Veronese citizens proud of their city's classical past. You'll find few blockbusters here, but there are some noteworthy pieces (especially among the bronzes), and it is interesting to see what cultured Veronese collected between the 17th and 19th centuries. The museum complex includes the Teatro Romano, Verona's 1st-century theater, which is open to visitors. ⊠ *Rigaste del Redentore 2, Verona* ☎ *045/7110129* ⊕ *museoarcheologico.comune.verona.it* 🔖 *€4.50 (free with VeronaCard)* ⊗ *Closed Mon.*

Palazzo degli Scaligeri

(*Palazzo di Cangrande*)

CASTLE/PALACE | The della Scala family ruled Verona from this stronghold built (over Roman ruins) at the end of the 13th century and then inhabited by Cangrande I. At that time Verona controlled the mainland Veneto from Treviso and Lombardy to Mantua and Brescia, hence the building's alternative name as a seat of Domini di Terraferma (Venetian administration): Palazzo del Podestà. The portal facing Piazza dei Signori was added in 1533 by the accomplished Renaissance architect Michele Sanmicheli. You have to admire the palazzo from the outside, as it's not open to the public. ⊠ *Piazza dei Signori, Verona.*

★ Palazzo della Ragione and Torre dei Lamberti

VIEWPOINT | An elegant 15th-century pink-marble staircase leads up from the *mercato vecchio* (old market) courtyard to the magistrates' chambers in this 12th-century palace, built at the intersection of the main streets of the ancient Roman city. The interior now houses exhibitions of art from the **Galleria d'Arte Moderna Achille Forti.** You can get the highest view in town from atop the attached 270-foot-high Romanesque Torre dei Lamberti. About 50 years after a lightning strike in 1403 knocked its top off, it was rebuilt and extended to its current height. ⊠ *Piazza dei Signori, Verona* ☎ *045/9273027* ⊕ *torredeilamberti.it* 🎟 *Gallery and tower €8 (free with VeronaCard); €4 gallery only; €6 tower only* ☾ *Gallery closed Mon.* ⚐ *Book the tower visit in advance by phone.*

Piazza delle Erbe

PLAZA/SQUARE | Frescoed buildings surround this medieval square, where a busy Roman forum once stood; during the week it's still bustling, as vendors sell produce and trinkets, much as they have been doing for generations. Eyes are drawn to the often sun-sparkling Madonna Verona fountain (1368) and its Roman statue (the body is from AD 380, with medieval additions). ⊠ *Piazza delle Erbe, Verona.*

★ Porta dei Borsari

RUINS | As its elegant decoration suggests, this is the main entrance to ancient Verona—dating, in its present state, from the 1st century. It's at the beginning of the narrow, pedestrianized Corso Porta Borsari, now a smart shopping street leading to Piazza delle Erbe. ⊠ *Corso Porta Borsari, Verona.*

Porta dei Leoni

RUINS | The oldest of Verona's elegant and graceful Roman portals, the Porta dei Leoni (on Via Leoni, just a short walk from Piazza delle Erbe) dates from the 1st century BC, but its original earth-and-brick structure was sheathed in local marble during the early imperial era. It has become the focus of a campaign against violence—there are often flowers and messages by the monument—in memory of the murder of a young Veronese here in 2009. ⊠ *Via Leoni, Verona.*

★ San Zeno Maggiore

CHURCH | One of Italy's finest Romanesque churches is filled with treasures, including a rose window by the 13th-century sculptor Brioloto that represents a wheel of fortune, with six of the spokes formed by statues depicting the rising and falling fortunes of mankind. The 12th-century porch is the work of Maestro Niccolò; it's flanked by marble reliefs by Niccolò and Maestro Guglielmo depicting scenes from the Old and New Testaments and from the legend of Theodoric. The bronze doors date from the 11th and 12th centuries; some were probably imported from Saxony, and some are from Veronese workshops. They combine allegorical representations with scenes from the lives of saints.

Inside, look for the 12th-century statue of San Zeno to the left of the main altar. In modern times it has been dubbed the "Laughing San Zeno" because of a misinterpretation of its conventional Romanesque grin. A famous *Madonna and Saints* triptych by Andrea Mantegna (1431–1506) hangs over the main altar, and a peaceful cloister (1120–38) lies to the left of the nave. The detached bell tower was finished in 1173. ⊠ *Piazza San Zeno, Verona* ☎ *045/592813* ⊕ *www.chieseverona.it* 🎟 *€4 (€8 Church Cumulative Ticket or free with VeronaCard).*

Sant'Anastasia

CHURCH | Verona's largest church, begun in 1290 but only consecrated in 1471, is a fine example of Gothic brickwork and has a grand doorway with elaborately carved biblical scenes. The main reason for visiting this church, however, is *St. George and the Princess* (dated 1434, but perhaps earlier) by Pisanello (1377–1455). It's above the Pellegrini Chapel off the main altar. As you come in, look also for the *gobbi* (hunchbacks) supporting the holy-water basins. ⊠ *Piazza Sant'Anastasia, Verona* ☎ *045/592813* ⊕ *www.chieseverona.it* 🎫 *€4 (€8 Church Cumulative Ticket or free with VeronaCard).*

🍴 Restaurants

★ Antica Osteria al Duomo

$$ | **NORTHERN ITALIAN** | This side-street eatery, lined with old wood paneling and decked out with musical instruments, serves traditional Veronese classics, like *bigoli* (thick whole wheat spaghetti) with donkey ragù and *pastissada con polenta* (horse-meat stew with polenta). Don't be deterred by the unconventional meats—they're tender and delicious, and this is probably the best place in town to sample them. **Known for:** blackboard menu, bar, and wooden interiors; occasional live music; rustic courtyard. 💲 *Average main: €20* ⊠ *Via Duomo 7/A, Verona* ☎ *045/8004505* ⊕ *alduomoosteria.altervista.org* 🕙 *Closed Sun. except in Dec. and during wine fair.*

★ Il Desco

$$$$ | **MODERN ITALIAN** | Opened in 1981 by Elia Rizzo, the nationally renowned fine-dining Desco cuisine is now crafted by talented son Matteo. True to Italian and Rizzo culinary traditions, he preserves natural flavors through careful ingredient selection, adding daring combinations inspired by stints in kitchens around the world. **Known for:** inventive, colorful plates of food; elegant, arty surroundings fit for a modern opera; pricey tasting menus. 💲 *Average main: €110* ⊠ *Via Dietro San Sebastiano 7, Verona* ☎ *045/595358* ⊕ *www.ristoranteildesco.it* 🕙 *Closed Sun. and Mon. (open for dinner Mon. in July, Aug., and Dec.).*

☕ Coffee and Quick Bites

★ Caffè Borsari

$ | **NORTHERN ITALIAN** | This bustling café-bar is famed for its excellent creamy coffee and freshly made brioche—it's cheek-by-jowl *al banco* (at the counter/bar), with Veronese patrons spilling outside. The narrow space on the charming Corso Borsari cobbles is packed with coffee- and tea-making pots and cups, as are its walls with colorful gifts and oddities according to the time of year. **Known for:** indulgent hot chocolate; selection of coffee, tea, candies, and chocolates to take away; fab staff may decorate your schiuma (froth). 💲 *Average main: €4* ⊠ *Corso Portoni Borsari 15, Verona* ☎ *045/8031313* ⊕ *facebook.com/caffeborsari.*

🛏 Hotels

Best Western Hotel Armando

$$ | **HOTEL** | In a residential area a few minutes' walk from the Arena, this contemporary Best Western hotel offers respite from the busy city as well as easier parking. **Pros:** large rooms for Italy; good breakfast; free Wi-Fi. **Cons:** no parking valet; simple room decor; noise from neighboring restaurant. 💲 *Rooms from: €175* ⊠ *Via Dietro Pallone 1, Verona* ☎ *045/8000206* ⊕ *www.hotelarmando.it* 🕙 *Closed 2 wks late Dec.–early Jan.* ↵ *28 rooms* ⏵❙ *Free Breakfast.*

Escalus Luxury Suites

$$$ | **HOTEL** | **FAMILY** | Near the Arena and Verona's marble-paved main shopping street, Via Mazzini, these suites and mini-apartments offer contemporary minimalist style in muted colors; the larger ones have handy kitchenettes, and all have swank bathrooms. **Pros:** chic location near sights and shopping; family-friendly Glamour Deluxe Suite with balcony; large showers. **Cons:** checkout is before 11 am; constant passeggiata hum from Via Mazzini; minimalist decor not to everyone's taste. 💲 *Rooms from:*

€275 ✉ *Vicolo Tre Marchetti 12, Verona* ☎ *045/8036754* 🌐 *www.escalusverona.com* 🛏 *6 suites* 🍴 *Free Breakfast.*

Gabbia d'Oro

$$$$ | HOTEL | Occupying a historic building off Piazza delle Erbe in the ancient heart of Verona, this hotel is a romantic fantasia of ornamentation, rich fabrics, and period-style furniture. **Pros:** central location; great breakfast; romantic atmosphere. **Cons:** some very small rooms, especially considering the price; small bathrooms; some guests may find the decor overly ornate, even stuffy. [$] *Rooms from: €364* ✉ *Corso Porta Borsari 4/a, Verona* ☎ *045/8003060* 🌐 *www.hotelgabbiadoro.it* 🛏 *27 rooms* 🍴 *Free Breakfast.*

Hotel Accademia

$$$ | HOTEL | The Palladian facade of columns and arches here hint at the well-proportioned interior layout: expect an elegant contemporary take on Art Deco in public spaces and immaculate if impersonal traditional-style decor in guest rooms. **Pros:** central location; good fitness room; rooftop solarium. **Cons:** expensive parking; some may find the decor lacking; service can be patchy. [$] *Rooms from: €294* ✉ *Via Scala 12, Verona* ☎ *045/596222* 🌐 *www.hotelaccademiaverona.it* 🛏 *96 rooms* 🍴 *Free Breakfast.*

Hotel Indigo Verona – Grand Hotel Des Arts

$$$ | HOTEL | Handily placed near both the Arena and train station, the art-inspired Indigo is a handsome 1920s Stile Liberty palazzo with stylish design touches and a sophisticated loungy feel throughout. **Pros:** warm customer service; cool bar and courtyard; good parking and transport links. **Cons:** on busy Corso Porta Nuova; limited breakfast choice; some rooms a bit small. [$] *Rooms from: €261* ✉ *Corso Porta Nuova 105, Verona* ☎ *0800/9880220* 🌐 *www.ihg.com/hotelindigo* 🛏 *62 rooms* 🍴 *Free Breakfast.*

Vicenza

74 km (46 miles) west of Venice, 43 km (27 miles) west of Padua.

A visit to Vicenza is a must for any student or fan of architecture. This elegant, prosperous city bears the distinctive signature of the 16th-century architect Andrea Palladio, whose name has been given to the "Palladian" style of architecture. He emphasized the principles of order and harmony using the classical style of architecture established by Renaissance architects, such as Brunelleschi, Alberti, and Sansovino. He used these principles and classical motifs not only for public buildings but also for private dwellings. His elegant villas and palaces were influential in propagating classical architecture in Europe, especially Britain, and later in America—most notably at Thomas Jefferson's Monticello.

In the mid-16th century Palladio was commissioned to rebuild much of Vicenza, which had been greatly damaged during wars waged against Venice by the League of Cambrai (1505), an alliance of the papacy, France, the Holy Roman Empire, and several neighboring city-states. He made his name with the renovation of the basilica, begun in 1549 in the heart of Vicenza, and then embarked on a series of lordly buildings, all of which adhere to the same classicism and principles of harmony.

GETTING HERE AND AROUND

Vicenza is midway between Padua and Verona; several trains leave from Venice every hour. By car, take the Autostrada Brescia–Padova/Torino–Trieste A4/E70 to SP247 North directly into Vicenza.

VISITOR INFORMATION

CONTACT Vicenza Tourism Office. ✉ *Piazza Giacomo Matteotti 12, Vicenza* ☎ *0444/994770* 🌐 *www.vicenzae.org.*

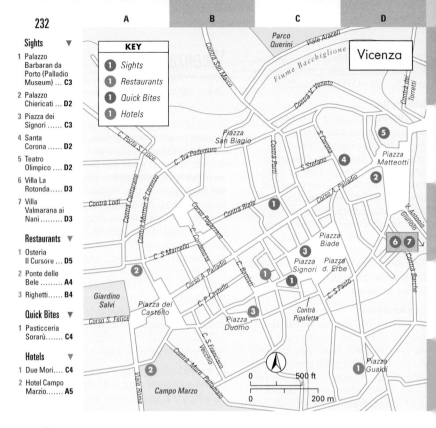

Sights ▼

1 Palazzo Barbaran da Porto (Palladio Museum) ... **C3**

2 Palazzo Chiericati ... **D2**

3 Piazza dei Signori **C3**

4 Santa Corona **D2**

5 Teatro Olimpico **D2**

6 Villa La Rotonda..... **D3**

7 Villa Valmarana ai Nani **D3**

Restaurants ▼

1 Osteria Il Cursore ... **D5**

2 Ponte delle Bele **A4**

3 Righetti...... **B4**

Quick Bites ▼

1 Pasticceria Sorarù....... **C4**

Hotels ▼

1 Due Mori.... **C4**

2 Hotel Campo Marzio....... **A5**

KEY

1 Sights

1 Restaurants

1 Quick Bites

1 Hotels

◉ Sights

Palazzo Barbaran da Porto (Palladio Museum)

CASTLE/PALACE | Palladio executed this beautiful city palace for the Vicentine noble Montano Barbarano between 1570 and 1575. The noble patron, however, did not make things easy for Palladio; the architect had to incorporate at least two preexisting medieval houses, with irregularly shaped rooms, into his classical, harmonious plan. It also had to support the great hall of the *piano nobile* (moving floor) above the fragile walls of the original medieval structure. The wonder of it is that this palazzo is one of Palladio's most harmonious constructions; the viewer has little indication that this is actually a transformation of a medieval structure. The palazzo also contains a museum dedicated to Palladio

and is the seat of a center for Palladian studies. ⊠ *Contrà Porti 11, Vicenza* ☎ *0444/323014* ⊕ *www.palladiomuseum. org* ⊡ *€8; €20 Vicenza Card, includes Palazzo Chiericati and Teatro Olimpico, plus others* ⊙ *Closed Mon. and Tues.*

Palazzo Chiericati

CASTLE/PALACE | This imposing Palladian palazzo (1550) would be worthy of a visit even if it didn't house Vicenza's **Museo Civico.** Because of the ample space surrounding the building, Palladio combined elements of an urban palazzo with those he used in his country villas. The museum's important Venetian holdings include significant paintings by Cima, Tiepolo, Piazzetta, and Tintoretto, but its main attraction is an extensive collection of rarely found works by painters from the Vicenza area, among them Jacopo Bassano (1515–92) and the eccentric and innovative Francesco Maffei (1605–60), whose work foreshadowed important currents of Venetian painting of subsequent generations. ⊠ *Piazza Matteotti, Vicenza* ☎ *0444/222811* ⊕ *www.museicivicivicenza.it* 🖃 *€7; €20 Vicenza Card, includes Palazzo Barbaran da Porto and Teatro Olimpico, plus others* ⊘ *Closed Mon.*

Piazza dei Signori

PLAZA/SQUARE | At the heart of Vicenza, this square contains the Palazzo della Ragione (1549), the project with which Palladio made his name by successfully modernizing a medieval building, grafting a graceful two-story exterior loggia onto the existing Gothic structure. Commonly known as Palladio's basilica, the palazzo served as a courthouse and public meeting hall (the original Roman meaning of the term "basilica") and is now open only when it houses exhibits. The main point of interest, though, the loggia, is visible from the piazza. Take a look also at the Loggia del Capitaniato, opposite, which Palladio designed but never completed. ⊠ *Piazza dei Signori, Vicenza.*

Santa Corona

CHURCH | An exceptionally fine *Baptism of Christ* (1502), a work of Giovanni Bellini's maturity, hangs over the altar on the left, just in front of the transept of this church. Santa Corona also houses the elegantly simple Valmarana chapel, designed by Palladio. ⊠ *Contrà S. Corona, Vicenza* ☎ *0444/320854* ⊕ *www.museicivicivicenza.it* 🖃 *€3 (free with Vicenza Card)* ⊘ *Closed Mon.*

★ Teatro Olimpico

PERFORMANCE VENUE | Palladio's last, perhaps most spectacular work was begun in 1580 and completed in 1585, after his death, by Vincenzo Scamozzi (1552–1616). Based closely on the model of ancient Roman theaters, it represents an important development in theater and stage design and is noteworthy for its acoustics and the cunning use of perspective in Scamozzi's permanent backdrop. The anterooms are frescoed with images of important figures in Venetian history. One of the few Renaissance theaters still standing, it can be visited (with guided tours) during the day and is used for concerts, operas, and other performances. ⊠ *Ticket office, Piazza Matteotti 12, Vicenza* ☎ *0444/964380* ⊕ *www.teatrolimpicovicenza.it* 🖃 *€11; €20 Vicenza Card, includes Palazzo Barbaran da Porto and Palazzo Chiericati, plus others* ⊘ *Closed Mon.*

★ Villa La Rotonda (*Villa Almerico Capra*)

HISTORIC HOME | Commissioned in 1556 as a suburban residence for Paolo Almerico, this beautiful Palladian villa is the purest expression of Palladio's architectural theory and aesthetic. More a villa-temple than a residence, it contradicts the rational utilitarianism of Renaissance architecture and demonstrates the priority Palladio gave to the architectural symbolism of celestial harmony over practical considerations. A visit to view the interior can be difficult to schedule—the villa remains privately owned, and visiting hours are limited and constantly change—but this is a worthwhile stop, if only to see how Palladio's harmonious arrangement of smallish interconnected rooms around a central domed space paid little attention to the practicalities of living. The interior decoration, mainly later Baroque stuccowork, contains some allegorical frescoes in the cupola by Palladio's contemporary, Alessandro Maganza.

Even without a peek inside, experiencing the exterior and the grounds is a must for any visit to Vicenza. The villa is a 20-minute walk from town or a cab (€12) or bus ride (No. 8) from Vicenza's Piazza Roma. Private tours are by appointment; see their website for the latest visiting details. ⊠ *Via della Rotonda, Vicenza* ☎ *0444/321793* ⊕ *www.villalarotonda.it* 🖃 *€15 with guided tour* ⊘ *Interior closed Mon.–Thurs. late Mar.–late Nov.*

★ **Villa Valmarana ai Nani**

HISTORIC HOME | Inside this 17th- to 18th-century country house, named for the statues of dwarfs adorning the garden, is a series of frescoes executed in 1757 by Gianbattista Tiepolo depicting scenes from classical mythology, the *Iliad*, Tasso's *Jerusalem Delivered*, and Ariosto's *Orlando furioso* (The Frenzy of Orlando). They include his *Sacrifice of Iphigenia*, a major masterpiece of 18th-century painting. The neighboring *foresteria* (guesthouse) is also part of the museum; it contains frescoes showing 18th-century life at its most charming and scenes of chinoiserie popular in the 18th century, by Tiepolo's son Giandomenico (1727–1804). The garden dwarfs are probably taken from designs by Giandomenico. You can reach the villa on foot by following the same path that leads to Palladio's Villa La Rotonda. ✉ *Via dei Nani 2/8, Vicenza* ☎ *0444/321803* 🌐 *www.villavalmarana.com* 🎫 *€12.*

🍴 Restaurants

★ **Osteria Il Cursore**

$$ | **NORTHERN ITALIAN** | This cozy 19th-century *locale storico* (historic hostelry) is steeped in Vicentina atmosphere, from the bar serving local wines and *sopressa* (premium salami) to the intimate dark-wood restaurant serving hearty classics. Grab a table out back for a sit-down meal of robust dishes like *bigoli* (thick, egg-enriched spaghetti) with duck, spaghetti with baccalà (cod), and, in spring, *risi e bisi* (rice with peas). **Known for:** great-value pasta; buzzy atmosphere, especially on Vicenza soccer-match days; quality wine and cold cuts. [$] *Average main: €16* ✉ *Stradella Pozzetto 10, Vicenza* ☎ *0444/323504* 🌐 *www.osteriacursore.it* 🕒 *Closed Tues.*

Ponte delle Bele

$$ | **NORTHERN ITALIAN** | Many of Vicenza's wealthier residents spend at least part of the summer in the Alps to escape the heat, and the dishes of this popular and friendly trattoria reflect the hearty Alpine influences on local cuisine. The house specialty, *stinco di maiale al forno* (roast pork shank), is wonderfully fragrant, with herbs and aromatic vegetables. **Known for:** hearty Vicentina classics, including baccalà served with polenta; unfussy, relaxed atmosphere and kitschy Alpine decor; mountain cheeses and cold cuts. [$] *Average main: €15* ✉ *Contrà Ponte delle Bele 5, Vicenza* ☎ *0444/320647* 🌐 *www.pontedellebele.it* 🕒 *Closed Sun. and 2 wks in Aug.*

Righetti

$ | **ITALIAN** | Vicentini of all generations gravitate to this popular self-service cafeteria for classic dishes that don't put a dent in your wallet. Expect hearty helpings of fare such as *orzo e fagioli* (barley and bean soup) and baccalà alla vicentina (stockfish Vicenza style). **Known for:** classic dishes; very popular, especially for lunch; entertaining local atmosphere. [$] *Average main: €12* ✉ *Piazza Duomo 3, Vicenza* ☎ *0444/543135* 🌐 *www.selfrighetti.it* 🕒 *Closed weekends and 1 wk in Jan. and Aug.*

☕ Coffee and Quick Bites

Pasticceria Soraru̇

$ | **NORTHERN ITALIAN** | Nestled under the porticoes of Piazzetta Palladio, the historic Pasticceria Sorarù occupies the former Cafeteria Palladio (1870) and is an ever-reliable spot for the freshest breakfast brioche with cappuccino, and a cornucopia of pastry delights. Inside, you can lean on the handsome old wooden counter and sample a pastry or three while admiring the glass jars filled with colorful candies. **Known for:** traditional Vicentino pastries and gelato; zaèti (polenta and raisin) biscuits and famous plum cake; seating under the porticoes. [$] *Average main: €5* ✉ *Piazzetta Andrea Palladio 17, Vicenza* ☎ *0444/320915* 🌐 *www.facebook.com/pasticceriasoraru.*

Hotels

Due Mori
$ | **HOTEL** | The public areas and guest rooms at one of the oldest (1883) hotels in the city, just off Piazza dei Signori, are filled with turn-of-the-20th-century antiques, and regulars favor the place because the high ceilings in the main building make it feel light and airy. **Pros:** tastefully furnished rooms in central location; rate same year-round; free Wi-Fi. **Cons:** no a/c, although ceiling fans minimize the need for it; no help with luggage; no TVs in rooms. [$] *Rooms from: €100* ✉ *Contrà Do Rode 24, Vicenza* ☎ *0444/321886* 🌐 *www.albergoduemori.it* 🕒 *Closed 2 wks in early Aug. and 2 wks in late Dec.* 🛏 *30 rooms* 🍴 *No Meals.*

★ **Hotel Campo Marzio**
$$ | **HOTEL** | Rooms at this comfortable full-service hotel—a five-minute walk from the train station and right in front of the city walls—are ample in size, with a mix of contemporary and traditional accents. **Pros:** great location; free bike hire; set back from the street, so it's quiet and bright. **Cons:** breakfast room a tad uninspiring; businesslike exterior; no in-room tea- or coffeemaking facilities. [$] *Rooms from: €140* ✉ *Viale Roma 21, Vicenza* ☎ *0444/5457000* 🌐 *www.hotelcampomarzio.com* 🛏 *36 rooms* 🍴 *Free Breakfast.*

Milan

Rome may be bigger and wield political power, but Milan and the affluent north are what really make the country go. Leonardo da Vinci's *The Last Supper* and other great works of art are here, as well as a spectacular Gothic Duomo, the finest of its kind.

And yet, Milan hasn't won the battle for hearts and minds when it comes to tourism. Most visitors prefer Tuscany's hills and Venice's canals to Milan's hectic efficiency and wealthy indifference. But its secrets reveal themselves slowly to those who look. A side street conceals a garden complete with flamingos (Giardini Invernizzi, on Via dei Cappuccini, just off Corso Venezia; closed to the public, but you can still catch a glimpse), and a renowned 20th-century-art collection hides modestly behind an unspectacular facade a block from Corso Buenos Aires (the Casa-Museo Boschi di Stefano).

Virtually every invader in European history—Gaul, Roman, Goth, Lombard, and Frank—as well as a long series of rulers from France, Spain, and Austria, took a turn at ruling the city. After being completely sacked by the Goths in AD 539 and by the Holy Roman Empire under Frederick Barbarossa in 1157, Milan became one of the first independent city-states of the Renaissance. Its heyday of self-rule proved comparatively brief. From 1277 until 1500 it was ruled first by the Visconti and then the Sforza dynasties. These families were known, justly or not, for a peculiarly aristocratic mixture of refinement, classical learning, and cruelty; much of the surviving grandeur of Gothic and Renaissance art and architecture is their doing. Be on the lookout in your wanderings for the Visconti family emblem—a viper, its jaws straining wide, devouring a child.

GETTING HERE AND AROUND

The city center is compact and walkable; trolleys and trams make it even more accessible, and the efficient Metropolitana (subway) and buses provide access to locations farther afield. Driving in Milan is difficult and parking a real pain, so a car is a liability. In addition, drivers within the second ring of streets (the *bastioni*) must pay a daily congestion charge on weekdays between 7:30 am and 7:30 pm (until 6 pm on Thursday). You can pay the charge at news vendors, tobacconists, Banca Intesa Sanpaolo ATMs, or with the EasyPark app (🌐 *www.easyparkitalia.it*);

Palladio's Architecture

Wealthy 16th-century patrons commissioned Andrea Palladio to design villas that would reflect their sense of cultivation and status. Using a classical vocabulary of columns, arches, and domes, he gave them a series of masterpieces in the towns and hills of the Veneto that exemplify the neo-Platonic ideals of harmony and proportion. Palladio's creations are the perfect expression of how a learned 16th-century man saw himself and his world, and as you stroll through them today, their serene beauty is as powerful as ever. Listen closely and you might even hear that celestial harmony, the music of the spheres, that so moved Palladio and his patrons.

Town and Country

Although the *villa*, or country residence, was still a relatively new phenomenon in the 16th century, it quickly became all the rage once the great lords of Venice turned their eyes from the sea toward the fertile plains of the Veneto. They were forced to do this once their trade routes had faltered when Ottoman Turks conquered Constantinople in 1456 and Columbus opened a path for Spain to the riches of America in 1492. In no time, canals were built, farms were laid out, and the fashion for villeggiatura became a favored lifestyle. As a means of escaping an overheated Rome, villas had been the original brainchild of the ancient emperors, and it was no accident that the Venetian lords wished to emulate this palatial style of country residence. Palladio's method of evaluating the standards, and standbys, of ancient Roman life through the eye of the Italian Renaissance, combined with

his innate sense of proportion and symmetry, became the lasting foundation of his art. In turn, Palladio threw out the mélange of styles prevalent in Venetian architecture—Byzantine, Gothic, and Renaissance—for the pure, noble lines found in the buildings of the Caesars.

Andrea Palladio (1508–80)

"Face dark, eyes fiery. Dress rich. His appearance that of a genius." So was Palladio described by his wealthy mentor, Count Trissino. Trissino encouraged the young student to trade in his birth name, Andrea di Pietro della Gondola, for the elegant Palladio. He did, and it proved a wise move indeed. Born in Padua in 1508, Andrea moved to nearby Vicenza in 1524 and was quickly taken up by the city's power elite. He experienced a profound revelation on his first trip, in 1541, to Rome, where he sensed the harmony of the ancient ruins and saw the elements of classicism that were working their way into contemporary architecture. This experience led to his spectacular conversion of Vicenza's Palazzo della Ragione into a Roman basilica, recalling the great meeting halls of antiquity. In years to come, after relocating to Venice, he created some memorable churches, such as San Giorgio Maggiore (1564). Despite these varied projects, Palladio's unassailable position as one of the world's greatest architects is tied to the countryside villas, which he spread across the Veneto plains like a firmament of stars. Nothing else in the Veneto illuminates more clearly the idyllic beauty of the region than these elegant residences, their stonework now nicely mellowed and suntanned after five centuries.

Vicenza

To see Palladio's pageant of palaces, head for Vicenza. His Palazzo della Ragione marks the city's heart, the Piazza dei Signori. This building rocketed young Palladio from an unknown to an architectural star. Across the way is his redbrick Loggia del Capitaniato. One block past the loggia is Vicenza's main street, appropriately named Corso Andrea Palladio. Just off this street is the Contrà Porti, where you'll find the Palazzo Barbaran da Porto (1570) at No. 11, with its fabulously rich facade erupting with Ionic and Corinthian pillars. Today, this is the Centro Internazionale di Studi di Architettura Andrea Palladio (www.palladiomuseum.org), a study center that mounts impressive temporary exhibitions. A few steps away, on the Contrà San Gaetano Thiene, is the Palazzo Thiene (1542–58), designed by Giulio Romano and completed by Palladio. Doubling back to Contrà Porti 21, you find the Palazzo Iseppo da Porto (1544), the first palazzo where you can see the neoclassical effects of young Palladio's trip to Rome. Following the Contrà Riale, you come to Corso Fogazzaro 16 and the Palazzo Valmarana Braga (1565). Its gigantic pilasters were a first for domestic architecture. Returning to the Corso Palladio, head left to the opposite end of the Corso, about five blocks, to the Piazza Matteotti and Palazzo Chiericati (1550). This was practically a suburban area in the 16th century, and for the palazzo Palladio combined elements of urban and rural design. The pedestal raising the building and the steps leading to the entrance— unknown in urban palaces—were to protect from floods and to keep cows from wandering in the front door. Across the Corso Palladio is Palladio's last and one of his most spectacular works, the Teatro Olimpico (1580). By careful study of ancient ruins and architectural texts, he reconstructed a Roman theater with archaeological precision. Palladio died before it was completed, but he left clear plans for the project. Although it's on the outskirts of town, the Villa Almerico Capra, better known as La Rotonda or Villa della Rotonda (1566), is an indispensable part of any visit to Vicenza. It's the iconic Palladian building, the purest expression of his aesthetic.

Palladio Country

At the Villa Barbaro (1554) near the town of Maser in the province of Treviso, 48 km (30 miles) northeast of Vicenza, you can see the results of a onetime collaboration between two of the greatest artists of their age. Palladio was the architect, and Paolo Veronese decorated the interior with an amazing cycle of trompe-l'oeil frescoes—walls dissolve into landscapes, and illusions of courtiers and servants enter rooms and smile down from balustrades. Legend has it a feud developed between Palladio and Veronese, with Palladio feeling the illusionistic frescoes detracted from his architecture; but there is practically nothing to support the idea of such a rift. It's also noteworthy that Palladio for the first time connected the two lateral granaries to the main villa. This was a working farm, and Palladio thus created an architectural unity by connecting the working parts of the estate to the living quarters with graceful arcades, bringing together the Renaissance dichotomy of the active and the contemplative.

238

parking meters and parking garages in the area also include it in the cost. There is also a public bike sharing system called BikeMi (⊕ *www.bikemi.com*).

BICYCLE
CONTACT BikeMi. ☎ *02/48607607* ⊕ *www.bikemi.com.*

PUBLIC TRANSPORTATION
A standard public transit ticket within the central zones of Milan costs €2 and is valid for a 90-minute trip on a subway, bus, or tram. An all-inclusive subway, bus, and tram pass costs €11.50 for 24 hours or €17.50 for 48 hours. Another option is a Carnet (€18), good for 10 tram, bus, or subway rides. Individual tickets and passes can be purchased from news vendors, tobacconists, at ticket machines at all subway stops, at ticket offices at the Duomo and other subway stops, and on your phone via the ATM Milano app. You can also pay for a subway ride using a contactless credit card at the turnstile to avoid ticket purchasing lines.

Once you have your ticket, either stamp it or insert it into the slots in station turnstiles or on poles inside trolleys and buses. (Electronic tickets won't function if they become bent or demagnetized. If you have a problem, contact a station manager, who can usually issue a new ticket.) Trains run from 6 am to 12:30 am.

CONTACTS ATM. (*Azienda Trasporti Milanesi*) ☎ *02/48607607* ⊕ *www.atm. it/en.* **Radiobus.** ☎ *02/48034803* ⊕ *www. atm.it/en.*

TAXI
Taxi fares in Milan are higher than in American cities; a short ride can run about €15 during rush hour or fashion week. You can get a taxi at a stand with an orange "Taxi" sign, or by calling one of the taxi companies. Most also have apps you can download to order taxis from your phone; some let you text or use WhatsApp to hail a cab. Dispatchers may speak some English; they'll ask for the phone number you're calling from, and

they'll tell you the number of your taxi and how long it'll take to arrive. If you're in a restaurant or bar, ask the staff to call a cab for you.

CONTACTS 026969. ☎ *02/6969* ⊕ *www.026969.it.* **Taxi028585.** ☎ *02/8585* ⊕ *www.milanoradiotaxi.it.* **Taxiblu.** ☎ *02/4040* ⊕ *www.taxiblu.it.*

TOURS
CONTACT City Sightseeing Milano. ☎ *02/867131* ⊕ *www.city-sightseeing.it/ en/milan.*

VISITOR INFORMATION
CONTACT Milan Tourism Office. ✉ *Piazza del Duomo 14, next to Palazzo Reale, Duomo* ☎ *02/88455555* ⊕ *www.yesmilano.it.*

Duomo

Milan's main streets radiate out from the massive Duomo, a late-Gothic cathedral begun in 1386. Heading north is the handsome Galleria Vittorio Emanuele II, an enclosed shopping arcade that opens at one end to the world-famous opera house known as La Scala. Via Manzoni leads northeast from La Scala to the Quadrilatero della Moda, or fashion district. Heading northeast from the Duomo is the pedestrian-only street Corso Vittorio Emanuele II. Northwest of the Duomo is Via Dante, at the top of which is the imposing outline of the Castello Sforzesco.

Sights

Battistero Paleocristiano/Baptistry of San Giovanni alle Fonti
CHURCH | More specifically known as the Baptistry of San Giovanni alle Fonti, this 4th-century baptistry is one of two that lie beneath the Duomo. Although opinion remains divided, it is widely believed to be where Ambrose, Milan's first bishop and patron saint, baptized Augustine. Tickets also include a visit to

the Duomo and its museum. ⊠ *Piazza del Duomo, enter through Duomo, Duomo* ☎ *02/72023375* ⊕ *www.duomomilano. it* 🎟 *€10, including admission to Duomo and museum; €20, including Duomo, museum, and roof with elevator, valid for 72 hrs* Ⓜ *Duomo.*

★ Duomo

CHURCH | There is no denying that for sheer size and complexity, the Duomo is unrivaled in Italy. It is the second-largest church in the country—the largest being St. Peter's in Rome. This intricate Gothic structure has been fascinating and exasperating visitors and conquerors alike since it was begun by Gian Galeazzo Visconti III (1351–1402), first duke of Milan, in 1386. Consecrated in the 15th or 16th century, it was not completed until just before the coronation of Napoléon as king of Italy in 1809.

The building is adorned with 135 marble spires and 2,245 marble statues. The Duomo's most famous sculpture is the gruesome but anatomically instructive figure of *San Bartolomeo* (St. Bartholomew), who was flayed alive. As you enter the apse to admire those splendid windows, glance at the sacristy doors to the right and left of the altar. The lunette on the right dates from 1393 and was decorated by Hans von Fernach. ⊠ *Piazza del Duomo, Duomo* ☎ *02/72023375* ⊕ *www.duomomilano.it* 🎟 *Cathedral €7; museum €7; cathedral, museum, and archaeological area €10; stairs to roof €15; elevator €20* Ⓜ *Duomo.*

★ Galleria Vittorio Emanuele II

STORE/MALL | This spectacular late-19th-century Belle Époque tunnel is essentially one of the planet's earliest and most select shopping malls, with upscale tenants that include Gucci and Prada. This is the city's heart, midway between the Duomo and La Scala. It teems with life, which makes for great people-watching from the tables that spill out from bars and restaurants, where you can enjoy an overpriced coffee. Books,

clothing, food, hats, and jewelry are all for sale. Known as Milan's "parlor," the Galleria is often viewed as a barometer of the city's well-being. ⊠ *Piazza del Duomo, Duomo* Ⓜ *Duomo.*

Milano Osservatorio—Fondazione Prada

OTHER MUSEUM | This contemporary photography and visual languages exhibition space, developed in partnership with Fondazione Prada, is spread over two floors in the Galleria Vittorio Emanuele II. Exhibitions, which rotate several times a year, explore the cultural and social implications of expression. The space itself, bombed after World War II and then fully restored, is worth visiting just for the unique view of the Galleria dome through the large windows. You can reach the gallery via the elevator next to the Prada store. ⊠ *Galleria Vittorio Emanuele II, Piazza del Duomo, Duomo* ☎ *02/56662611* ⊕ *www.fondazioneprada. org/visit/milano-osservatorio* 🎟 *€10; €15, including Fondazione Prada* ⊗ *Closed Tues.* Ⓜ *Duomo.*

Museo del Novecento

ART MUSEUM | Ascend a Guggenheim-esque spiral walkway to reach the modern works at this petite yet dense collection of Italian contemporary art, adjacent to the Duomo. The museum highlights 20th-century Italian artists, including a strong showing of Futurists, like Boccioni and Severini, and sculptures from Marini, along with a smattering of works by other European artists, including Picasso, Braque, and Matisse. ⊠ *Via Marconi 1, Duomo* ☎ *02/88444061* ⊕ *www.museodelnovecento.org* 🎟 *€5 (free every 1st and 3rd Tues. of month after 2)* ⊗ *Closed Mon.* Ⓜ *Duomo.*

★ Palazzo Reale

ART MUSEUM | Elaborately decorated with painted ceilings and grand staircases, this former royal palace close to the Duomo is almost worth a visit in itself; however, it also functions as one of Milan's major art galleries, with a focus on modern artists. Exhibitions have highlighted works

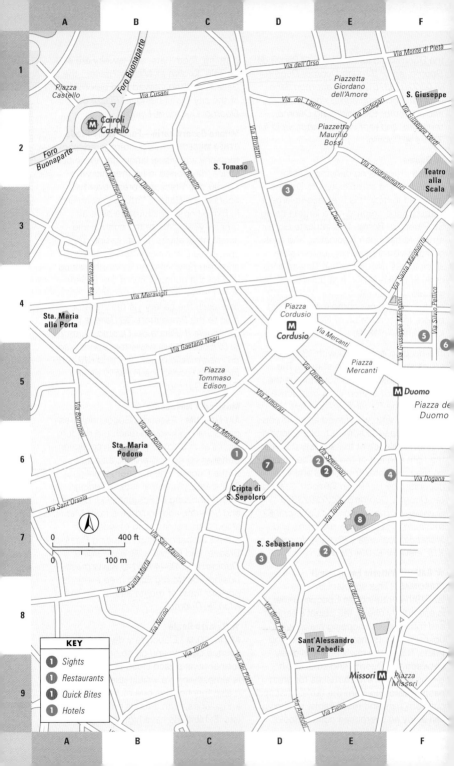

Sights ▼

1. Battistero Paleocristiano/
Baptistry of San Giovanni
alle Fonti **H5**
2. Duomo **H5**
3. Galleria Vittorio
Emanuele II......................... **G4**
4. Milano Osservatorio—
Fondazione Prada **G4**
5. Museo del Novecento **G6**
6. Palazzo Reale **H7**
7. Pinacoteca Ambrosiana **D6**
8. Santa Maria Presso
San Satiro **E7**

Restaurants ▼

1. Giacomo Arengario............... **G6**
2. La Vecchia Latteria **E7**
3. Piz **D7**

Quick Bites ▼

1. Camparino in Galleria **G5**
2. Piccolo Peck **E6**
3. Rinascente Food Hall............. **H5**

Hotels ▼

1. Hotel Gran Duca di York............ **C6**
2. Hotel Spadari al Duomo............ **E6**
3. Hotel Star **D3**
4. Maison Milano |
UNA Esperienze **F6**
5. Park Hyatt Milan.................... **F4**
6. Room Mate Giulia.................. **F5**

by Picasso, Chagall, Warhol, Pollock, and Kandinsky. Check the website before you visit to see what's on; purchase tickets online in advance to save time in the queues, which are often long and chaotic. ✉ *Piazza del Duomo 12, Duomo* ☎ *02/88445181* 🌐 *www.palazzorealemilano.it* 🎟 *Varies by exhibition* ⏲ *Closed Mon.* [M] *Duomo.*

Pinacoteca Ambrosiana

ART MUSEUM | Cardinal Federico Borromeo, one of Milan's native saints, founded this picture gallery in 1618 with the addition of his personal art collection to a bequest of books to Italy's first public library. The core works of the collection include such treasures as Caravaggio's *Basket of Fruit,* Raphael's monumental preparatory drawing (known as a "cartoon") for *The School of Athens,* which hangs in the Vatican, and Leonardo da Vinci's *Portrait of a Musician.* The highlight for many is Leonardo's *Codex Atlanticus,* which features thousands of his sketches and drawings. ✉ *Piazza Pio XI 2, Duomo* ☎ *02/806921* 🌐 *www.ambrosiana.it/en* 🎟 *€16.50* ⏲ *Closed Mon.* [M] *Duomo.*

Santa Maria Presso San Satiro

CHURCH | Just a few steps from the Duomo, this architectural gem was first built in 876 and later perfected by Bramante (1444–1514), demonstrating his command of proportion and perspective—hallmarks of Renaissance architecture. Bramante tricks the eye with a famous optical illusion that makes a small interior seem extraordinarily spacious and airy, while accommodating a beloved 13th-century fresco. ✉ *Via Torino 17–19, Duomo* ☎ *02/874683* [M] *Duomo; Tram No. 2, 3, 4, 12, 14, 19, 20, 24, or 27.*

🍴 Restaurants

Giacomo Arengario

$$$ | **ITALIAN** | Join businesspeople, ladies who lunch, and in-the-know travelers at this elegant restaurant atop the Museo del Novecento and with a glorious Duomo view (be sure to request a window table, though, or risk being relegated to a viewless back room). To complement the vistas, choose from a selection of well-prepared seafood, pasta, and meat courses for lunch and dinner; the servers are happy to recommend pairings from the extensive wine list. **Known for:** amazing Duomo views from tables by the windows; contemporary Milanese dishes; wine pairings. [$] *Average main: €30* ✉ *Via Marconi 1, Duomo* ☎ *02/72093814* 🌐 *www.giacomomilano.com/location/arengario* [M] *Duomo.*

La Vecchia Latteria

$$ | **VEGETARIAN** | In its two small dining rooms, this family-owned lunch spot serves an impressive amount of vegetarian cuisine. Nestled on a small street just steps away from the Duomo, it offers an array of freshly prepared seasonal selections from a daily-changing menu; try the *misto forno* (mixed plate), which offers a taste of several different small dishes. **Known for:** Italian-focused vegetarian cuisine; varied menu; retro '50s atmosphere. [$] *Average main: €15* ✉ *6 Via dell'Unione, Duomo* ☎ *02/874401* 🌐 *www.facebook.com/la.vecchia.latteria* ⏲ *Closed Sun. No dinner* [M] *Duomo or Missori.*

★ Piz

$ | **PIZZA** | Fun, lively, and full of locals, this casual and inexpensive pizzeria on a side street near the Duomo has just three kinds of thin-crust pizza on the menu—luckily, all are excellent. Choose from margherita, bianca (white, with no tomato), and marinara (with no mozzarella); although you'll inevitably need to wait, you'll likely get a free glass of prosecco and a slice of pizza while you do. **Known for:** seasonal changing bianca pizza; free before- and after-dinner drinks; bustling vibe. [$] *Average main: €9* ✉ *Via Torino 34, Duomo* ☎ *02/86453482* 🌐 *www.facebook.com/pizmilano* [M] *Duomo; Tram No. 2, 3, or 14.*

☕ Coffee and Quick Bites

Camparino in Galleria

$$$ | CAFÉ | One thing has remained constant in the Galleria: the Camparino, whose inlaid counter, mosaics, and wrought-iron fixtures have been welcoming tired shoppers since 1867. Small plates to be enjoyed with a Campari aperitif are served in pretty Bar di Passo downstairs, while a more extensive range of Campari cocktails paired with food for aperitivo or dinner is available in elegant Sala Spiritello upstairs. **Known for:** contemporary versions of Campari cocktails; high-end aperitivo; prime people-watching. $ *Average main: €30* ✉ *Galleria Vittorio Emanuele, Piazza del Duomo 21, Duomo* ☎ *02/86464435* ⊕ *www.camparino.com* Ⓜ *Duomo.*

Piccolo Peck

$$ | SANDWICHES | The café at this foodie paradise near the Duomo features Italian specialty foods such as excellent cheeses, charcuterie, vegetables in olive oil, seafood, and sandwiches. It also reinterprets classic dishes like Russian salad and pâté, which can be washed down with a fine selection of wines by the glass or a bottle from its cellar of global labels. **Known for:** wide bakery selection, including classic brioche; delicious Italian treats from the famed Peck deli; casual atmosphere. $ *Average main: €20* ✉ *Via Spadari 9, Duomo* ☎ *02/8023161* ⊕ *www.peck.it/en/restaurants/piccolo-peck* Ⓜ *Tram No. 2, 12, 14, 16, or 19.*

Rinascente Food Hall

$$ | ECLECTIC | The seventh floor of this famous Italian department store is a gourmet food market surrounded by several small restaurants that can be a good option for lunch, an aperitivo overlooking the Duomo, or dinner after a long day of shopping. There are several places to eat, including the popular mozzarella bar Obicà, God Save the Food for juices and healthy bowls, and the sophisticated Maio restaurant. **Known for:** culinary gifts to take home; inexpensive meals and snacks; terrace overlooking the Duomo. $ *Average main: €15* ✉ *Piazza Duomo, Duomo* ☎ *02/91387388* ⊕ *www.rinascente.it* Ⓜ *Duomo.*

🛏 Hotels

Hotel Gran Duca di York

$$$ | HOTEL | The spare but classically elegant and efficient rooms at this hotel are arranged around a courtyard—four have private terraces—and offer good value for pricey Milan. **Pros:** central location; friendly staff; good breakfast. **Cons:** limited amenities (no restaurant or gym); many rooms on the small side; showers can be tiny. $ *Rooms from: €240* ✉ *Via Moneta 1, Duomo* ☎ *02/874863* ⊕ *www.ducadiyork.com* ⇨ *33 rooms* ⦿ *Free Breakfast* Ⓜ *Cordusio or Duomo; Tram No. 2, 12, 14, 16, or 27.*

Hotel Spadari al Duomo

$$$ | HOTEL | That this chic city-center inn is owned by an architect's family comes through in details like the custom-designed furniture and paintings by young Milanese artists in the stylish guest rooms. **Pros:** good breakfast; central location; attentive staff. **Cons:** some rooms on the small side; street noise can be a problem; no restaurant. $ *Rooms from: €299* ✉ *Via Spadari 11, Duomo* ☎ *02/72002371* ⊕ *www.spadarihotel.com* ⇨ *40 rooms* ⦿ *Free Breakfast* Ⓜ *Duomo; Tram No. 2, 3, 12, 14, 16, 24, or 27.*

Hotel Star

$$$ | HOTEL | The staff are helpful and the rooms are well equipped and comfortable, some with touches like whirlpool tubs and balconies. **Pros:** centrally located near key attractions; friendly staff; breakfast is included. **Cons:** quirky animal prints in some rooms not for everyone; street noise can be an issue; some bathrooms are extremely small. $ *Rooms from: €220* ✉ *Via dei Bossi 5, Duomo* ☎ *02/801501* ⊕ *www.hotelstar.it* ⇨ *30*

rooms 🍴 *Free Breakfast* [M] *Cordusio or Duomo.*

Maison Milano | UNA Esperienze

$$$ | **HOTEL** | Inside this faithfully restored palazzo dating from the early 1900s, spaciousness is accentuated with soft white interiors, muted fabrics and marble, and contemporary lines. **Pros:** the warmth of a residence and the luxury of a design hotel; lovely bathrooms; friendly staff. **Cons:** breakfast not included; not much of a lobby; no restaurant or bar. [$] *Rooms from: €247* ✉ *Via Mazzini 4, Duomo* ☎ *02/69826949* 🌐 *www.gruppouna.it/esperienze/maison-milano* 🛏 *27 rooms* 🍴 *No Meals* [M] *Duomo; Tram No. 2, 3, 12, 14, 16, 24, or 27.*

★ **Park Hyatt Milan**

$$$$ | **HOTEL** | Extensive use of warm travertine stone and modern art creates a sophisticated yet inviting backdrop at the Park Hyatt, where spacious, opulent guest rooms have walk-in closets and bathrooms with double sinks, glass-enclosed rain showers, and separate soaking tubs. **Pros:** central location; contemporary decor and amenities; excellent restaurant. **Cons:** not particularly intimate; very expensive; some rooms showing a little wear. [$] *Rooms from: €1024* ✉ *Via Tommaso Grossi 1, Duomo* ☎ *02/88211234* 🌐 *www.hyatt.com/en-US/hotel/italy/park-hyatt-milan/milph* 🛏 *106 rooms* 🍴 *No Meals* [M] *Duomo; Tram No. 1.*

★ **Room Mate Giulia**

$$$$ | **HOTEL** | For hip, design-focused lodging with a friendly feel and prime location right next to the Galleria and around the corner from the Duomo, you can't do much better than the city's first outpost from Spanish hotel chain Room Mate. **Pros:** amazing location; fresh, appealing design; spa. **Cons:** breakfast room a bit cramped; gym on the small side; busy location means some noise in rooms. [$] *Rooms from: €302* ✉ *Via Silvio Pellico 4, Duomo* ☎ *02/80888900* 🌐 *www.room-matehotels.com/en/giulia* 🛏 *85 rooms* 🍴 *No Meals* [M] *Duomo; Tram No. 1.*

Nightlife

Bar STRAF

BARS | This architecturally stimulating but dimly lit place has such artistic features as recycled fiberglass panels and vintage 1970s furnishings. The music is an eclectic mix of chill-out tunes during the daytime, with more upbeat and vibrant tracks pepping it up at night. Located on a quiet side street near the Duomo, STRAF, inside the hotel of the same name, draws a young and lively, if tourist-heavy, crowd. ✉ *Via San Raffaele 3, Duomo* ☎ *02/805081* 🌐 *www.straf.it/bar* [M] *Duomo.*

Performing Arts

Conservatorio

MUSIC | The two halls belonging to the Conservatorio host some of the leading names in classical music. Series are organized by several organizations, including the venerable chamber music society the **Società del Quartetto**. ✉ *Via del Conservatorio 12, Duomo* ☎ *02/762110,* 🌐 *www.consmilano.it* [M] *San Babila; Tram No. 9, 12, 23, or 27; Bus No. 60 or 73.*

★ **Teatro alla Scala**

OPERA | You need know nothing of opera to sense that La Scala is closer to a cathedral than a concert hall. Hearing opera sung in this magical setting is an unparalleled experience: it is, after all, where Verdi established his reputation and where Maria Callas sang her way into opera lore. It stands as a symbol—both for the performer who dreams of singing here and for the opera buff—and its notoriously demanding audiences are apt to jeer performers who do not measure up. At the Museo Teatrale alla Scala you can admire an extensive collection of librettos, paintings of the famous names of Italian opera, posters, costumes, antique instruments, and

design sketches for the theater. ✉ *Piazza della Scala, Largo Ghiringhelli 1, Duomo* ☎ *02/72003744 theater, 02/88797473 museum* ⊕ *www.teatroallascala.org* ✉ *Museum €12* Ⓜ *Duomo or Cordusio; Tram No. 1.*

Shopping

Borsalino

HATS & GLOVES | The kingpin of milliners, Borsalino has managed to stay trendy since it opened in 1857. ✉ *Galleria Vittorio Emanuele II 92, Duomo* ☎ *02/89015436* ⊕ *www.borsalino.com* Ⓜ *Duomo; Tram No. 1.*

Gucci

MIXED CLOTHING | This Florence-born brand attracts lots of fashion-forward tourists in hot pursuit of its monogrammed bags, shoes, and accessories. ✉ *Galleria Vittorio Emanuele II, Duomo* ☎ *02/8597991* ⊕ *www.gucci.com* Ⓜ *Duomo; Tram No. 1.*

La Rinascente

DEPARTMENT STORE | The flagship location of this always bustling and very central department store—adjacent to both the Duomo and the Galleria Vittorio Emanuele II—carries a wide range of Italian and international brands (both high-end and casual) for men, women, and children. There's also a fine selection of beauty and home products. ✉ *Piazza Duomo, Duomo* ☎ *02/91387388* ⊕ *www.rinascente.it* Ⓜ *Duomo; Tram No. 1, 2, 12, 14, 16, or 27.*

Trussardi

MIXED CLOTHING | This Milan-based label offers sleek, fashion-forward accessories, leather goods, and clothes. ✉ *Galleria San Carlo angolo, Corso Europa, 6, Duomo* ☎ *02/783909* ⊕ *www.trussardi.com* Ⓜ *Duomo; Tram No. 1.*

Castello

This 15th-century castle is home to crypts, battlements, tunnels, and an interesting array of museums.

Sights

Castello Sforzesco

HISTORIC SIGHT | Wandering the grounds of this tranquil castle and park near the center of Milan is a great respite from the often-hectic city, and the interesting museums inside are an added bonus. Highlights include the Sala delle Asse, a frescoed room attributed to Leonardo da Vinci (1452–1519), and Michelangelo's unfinished *Rondanini Pietà*, believed to be his last work. The *pinacoteca* (picture gallery) features 230 paintings from medieval times to the 18th century, and the Museo dei Mobili e delle Sculture Lignee (Furniture Museum) includes a delightful collection of Renaissance treasure chests. ✉ *Piazza Castello, Castello* ☎ *02/88463700* ⊕ *www.milanocastello. it* ✉ *Castle free, museums €5 (free every 1st and 3rd Tues. of month after 2, and 1st Sun. of month)* 🕐 *Museums closed Mon.* Ⓜ *Cadorna, Lanza, or Cairoli; Tram No. 1, 2, 4, 12, 14, or 19; Bus No. 18, 37, 50, 58, 61, or 94.*

🎭 Performing Arts

Teatro Dal Verme

CONCERTS | Frequent classical, rock, and jazz concerts by international artists are staged here from October to May. ✉ *Via San Giovanni sul Muro 2, Castello* ☎ *02/87905* ⊕ *www.ipomeriggi.it* Ⓜ *Cairoli; Tram No. 1 or 4.*

Sempione

Just beyond the Sforzesco Castle grounds is a large park that holds an aquarium, the Triennale museum, and the Torre Branca.

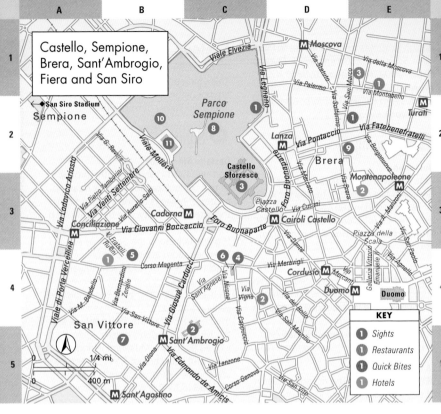

Castello, Sempione,
Brera, Sant'Ambrogio,
Fiera and San Siro

Sights ▼

1 Acquario Civico
di Milano.................C2

2 Basilica di
Sant'Ambrogio...........C5

3 Castello Sforzesco.......C3

4 Chiesa di
San Maurizio al
Monastero Maggiore ...C4

5 The Last Supper/
Il Cenacolo/Santa Maria
delle Grazie..............B4

6 Museo Civico
Archeologico C4

7 Museo Nazionale della
Scienza e Tecnologia
Leonardo da Vinci B5

8 Parco Sempione.........C2

9 Pinacoteca di Brera....D2

10 Torre Branca B2

11 Triennale
Design Museum B2

Restaurants ▼

1 Cittamani.................E1

2 DaDa in Taverna C4

3 Fioraio Bianchi Caffè....E1

Quick Bites ▼

1 N'Ombra de Vin E2

Hotels ▼

1 Antica Locanda
Leonardo B4

2 Bulgari Hotel Milano E3

Sights

Acquario Civico di Milano

(*Civic Aquarium of Milan*)

AQUARIUM | FAMILY | The third-oldest aquarium in Europe, opened in 1906, is known as much for its Art Nouveau architecture as for its small but interesting collection of marine life. You'll find 36 pools that house more than 100 species of fish, including an emphasis on Italian freshwater fish and their habitat, and one tank of species from the Red Sea. ⊠ *Viale Gerolamo Gadio 2, Sempione* ☎ *02/88465750* ⊕ *www.acquariodimilano.it* ⊠ *€5; free every 1st and 3rd Tues. of month after 2* ⊗ *Closed Mon.* Ⓜ *Lanza; Tram No. 2, 4, 12, or 14; Bus No. 57.*

Parco Sempione

CITY PARK | FAMILY | Originally the gardens and parade grounds of the Castello Sforzesco, this open space was reorganized during the Napoleonic era, when the arena on its northeast side was constructed, and then turned into a park during the building boom at the end of the 19th century. It is still the lungs of the city's fashionable western neighborhoods, and the **Aquarium** still attracts Milan's schoolchildren. The park became a bit of a design showcase in 1933 with the construction of the Triennale. ⊠ *Piazza Sempione, Sempione* ☎ *02/88467383* ⊕ *www.yesmilano.it/en/see-and-do/itineraries/explore-parco-sempione* ⊠ *Free* Ⓜ *Cairoli, Lanza or Cadorna; Tram No. 1, 2, 4, 12, 14, 19, or 27; Bus No. 43, 57, 61, 70, or 94.*

Torre Branca

VIEWPOINT | It is worth visiting Parco Sempione just to see the Torre Branca. Designed by architect Gio Ponti (1891–1979), who was behind so many of the projects that made Milan the design capital that it is, this steel tower rises 330 feet over the Triennale. Take the elevator to get a nice view of the city, then have a drink at the glitzy Just Cavalli Restaurant and Club at its base. ⊠ *Parco Sempione, Sempione* ☎ *02/3314120* ⊕ *www.museobranca.it/torre-branca* ⊠ *€6* ⊗ *Closed Mon., Tues., and Thurs.; and mid-May–mid-Nov.* Ⓜ *Cadorna; Tram No. 1; Bus No. 61.*

Triennale Design Museum

ART MUSEUM | In addition to honoring Italy's design talent, the Triennale also offers a regular series of exhibitions on design from around the world. A spectacular bridge entrance leads to a permanent collection, an exhibition space, and a stylish café and rooftop restaurant with expansive views. The Triennale also manages the fascinating museum-studio of designer Achille Castiglioni, in nearby Piazza Castello (hour-long guided tours Tuesday through Friday at 10, 11, and noon, and one Saturday a month; €15. Call or email in advance to book: ☎ *02/8053606* ✉ *info@achillecastiglioni.it*). ⊠ *Via Alemagna 6, Sempione* ☎ *02/72434244* ⊕ *www.triennale.org* ⊠ *Prices start at €5* ⊗ *Closed Mon.* Ⓜ *Cadorna; Bus No. 61.*

Brera

To the north of the Duomo lie the winding streets of this elegant neighborhood, once the city's bohemian quarter.

Sights

★ **Pinacoteca di Brera** (*Brera Art Gallery*)
ART MUSEUM | The collection here is star-studded even by Italian standards. Highlights include the somber *Cristo Morto* (Dead Christ) by Mantegna, which dominates Room VI with its sparse palette of umber and its foreshortened perspective, Raphael's (1483–1520) *Sposalizio della Vergine* (Marriage of the Virgin) and *La Vergine con il Bambino e Santi* (Madonna with Child and Saints), by Piero della Francesca (1420–92), an altarpiece commissioned by Federico da Montefeltro (shown kneeling, in full armor, before the Virgin). ⊠ *Via Brera 28, Brera* ☎ *02/72105141* ⊕ *www.*

The Pinacoteca di Brera in Milan features masterpieces from the 13th to 20th centuries.

pinacotecabrera.org 🖅 €15 🕙 *Closed Mon.* Ⓜ *Montenapoleone or Lanza; Tram No. 1, 4, 12, 14, or 27; Bus No. 61.*

🍴 Restaurants

★ Cittamani
$$ | MODERN INDIAN | Celebrity chef Ritu Dalmia runs well-regarded Italian restaurants in India, so it's no surprise that her first restaurant in Italy offers a mash-up of modern Indian food with Italian and international ingredients; even the decor, with shelves of pottery and terrazzo floors, is a cultural combo. Look for unexpected flavors and a mix of small plates, more substantial mains, and utterly delicious fusion desserts. **Known for:** Indian food quite different from the norm; nontraditional naans; sleek contemporary setting. $ *Average main: €21* ✉ *Piazza Mirabello 5, Brera* ☎ *02/38240935* ⊕ *www.cittamani.com* 🕙 *Closed Sun.* Ⓜ *Moscova or Turati; Bus No. 43 or 94.*

Fioraio Bianchi Caffè
$$$ | MODERN ITALIAN | A French-style bistro in the heart of Milan, Fioraio Bianchi Caffè was opened more than 40 years ago by Raimondo Bianchi, a great lover of flowers; in fact, eating at this restaurant is a bit like dining in a Parisian boutique with floral decor. Despite the French atmosphere, the dishes have Italian flair and ensure a classy, inventive meal. **Known for:** charming, flower-filled, shabby-chic setting; creative Italian-style bistro food; great spot for morning coffee and pastries. $ *Average main: €28* ✉ *Via Montebello 7, Brera* ☎ *02/29014390* ⊕ *www.fioraiobianchicaffe.it* 🕙 *Closed Sun. and 3 wks in Aug.* Ⓜ *Turati.*

☕ Coffee and Quick Bites

N'Ombra de Vin
$ | WINE BAR | This enoteca serves wine by the glass and, in addition to the plates of *salumi* (Italian cold cuts) and cheese nibbles, has light food and not-so-light desserts. It's a great place for people-watching on Via San Marco, while

indoors offers a more dimly lit, romantic setting; check out the impressive vaulted basement, where bottled wines and spirits are sold. **Known for:** atmospheric setting in an Augustinian refectory; Italian and French wines; solid tapas dishes. [$] *Average main: €14* ✉ *Via S. Marco 2, Brera* ☎ *02/6599650* 🌐 *www.nombradevin.it* [M] *Lanza, Turati, or Montenapoleone; Tram No. 1, 2, 4, 12, or 14.*

🛏 Hotels

Bulgari Hotel Milano

$$$$ | **HOTEL** | Housed in an 18th-century palazzo on a quiet street a short stroll from Brera and Montenapoleone shopping, the Bulgari offers up chic yet restrained rooms, an enormous garden, and a celebrity-chef-helmed restaurant. **Pros:** excellent spa, with heated pool, sauna, and Jacuzzi; trendy and fashionable guests; convenient location for sightseeing. **Cons:** rooms are a bit bland; service not quite up to par; extremely expensive. [$] *Rooms from: €1700* ✉ *Via Privata Fratelli Gabba 7b, Brera* ☎ *02/8058051* 🌐 *www.bulgarihotels.com/en_US/milan* 🛏 *61 rooms* 🍴 *No Meals* [M] *Montenapoleone.*

🍸 Nightlife

Il Bar at Bulgari Hotel Milano

BARS | Having drinks or a light lunch at the Bulgari Hotel bar lets you step off the asphalt and into one of the city's most impressive private urban gardens—even indoors you seem to be outside, separated from the elements by a spectacular wall of glass. The Bar is a great place to run into international hotel guests and jet-setting Milanese, and the staff mix up a wide range of traditional and novel drinks—including the Bulgari Cocktail with gin, Aperol, and orange, pineapple, and lime juices. ✉ *Via Privata Fratelli Gabba 7/b, Brera* ☎ *02/8058051* 🌐 *www.bulgarihotels.com/en_US/milan/bar-and-restaurant/il-bar* [M] *Montenapoleone; Tram No. 1.*

🛍 Shopping

Mercato di Via S. Marco

MARKET | The Monday- and Thursday-morning markets here cater to the wealthy residents of the central Brera neighborhood. In addition to food stands where you can get cheese, roast chicken, and dried beans and fruits, there are several clothing and shoe stalls that are important stops for some of Milan's most elegant women. ✉ *Via San Marco, near Via Castelfidardo, Brera* [M] *Lanza; Tram No. 2, 4, 12, or 14.*

Sant'Ambrogio

If the part of the city to the north of the Duomo is dominated by shopping, Sant'Ambrogio and other parts to the south are known for art. The most famous piece is *Il Cenacolo*—known in English as *The Last Supper.* If you have time for nothing else, make sure you see this masterpiece, which is housed in the refectory of Santa Maria delle Grazie. Reservations are required to see it, and you should make yours at least three weeks before you depart for Italy, so you can plan the rest of your time in Milan.

👁 Sights

Basilica di Sant'Ambrogio
(*Basilica of St. Ambrose*)

CHURCH | Milan's bishop, St. Ambrose (one of the original Doctors of the Catholic Church), consecrated this church in AD 387. St. Ambroeus, as he is known in Milanese dialect, is the city's patron saint, and his remains—dressed in elegant religious robes, a miter, and gloves—can be viewed inside a glass case in the crypt below the altar. Until the construction of the more imposing Duomo, this was Milan's most important church. Much restored and reworked over the centuries (the gold-and-gem-encrusted altar dates from the 9th century), Sant'Ambrogio still preserves its Romanesque characteristics, including 5th-century mosaics. The church is often closed for weddings on Saturdays. ⊠ *Piazza Sant'Ambrogio 15, Sant'Ambrogio* ☎ *02/86450895* ⊕ *www.basilicasantambrogio.it* Ⓜ *Sant'Ambrogio; Bus No. 50, 58, or 94.*

Chiesa di San Maurizio al Monastero Maggiore

CHURCH | Next to the Museo Civico Archeologico, you'll find this little gem of a church, constructed starting in 1503 and decorated almost completely with magnificent 16th-century frescoes. The modest exterior belies the treasures inside, including a concealed back room once used by nuns that includes a fascinating fresco of Noah loading the ark with animals, including two unicorns. ⊠ *Corso Magenta 15, Sant'Ambrogio* ☎ *02/88445208* ⊕ *www.museoarcheologicomilano.it/oltre-il-museo/la-chiesa-s.-maurizio-al-monastero-maggiore* Ⓜ *Cadorna or Cairoli; Tram No. 16 or 27; Bus No. 50, 58, or 94.*

★ The Last Supper/Il Cenacolo/Santa Maria delle Grazie

CHURCH | Leonardo da Vinci's *The Last Supper,* housed in this church and former Dominican monastery, has had an almost unbelievable history of bad luck and neglect. Its near destruction in an American bombing raid in August 1943 was only the latest chapter in a series of misadventures, including—if one 19th-century source is to be believed—being whitewashed over by monks. After years of restorers patiently shifting from one square centimeter to another, Leonardo's masterpiece is free of centuries of retouching, grime, and dust. Astonishing clarity and luminosity have been regained, helped by lighting, and a timed entry system where small groups are ushered into climate-controlled rooms with automatic glass doors, to prevent humidity.

Despite Leonardo's carefully preserved preparatory sketches, in which the apostles are clearly labeled by name, there still remains some small debate about a few identities in the final arrangement. There can be no mistaking Judas, however—small and dark, isolated from the terrible confusion that has taken the hearts of the others. Reservations are required to view the work. Viewings are in 15-minute timed-entry slots, and visitors must arrive 30 minutes before. Reservations can be made online. Reserve at least three weeks ahead if you want a Saturday slot, two weeks for a weekday slot. Some city bus tours include a visit in their regular circuit, which may be a good option. ⊠ *Piazza Santa Maria delle Grazie 2, off Corso Magenta, Sant'Ambrogio* ☎ *02/92800360 reservations, 02/4676111 church* ⊕ *www.cenacolovinciano.net* 🎫 *Last Supper €15* ⏱ *Closed Mon.* Ⓜ *Cadorna or Conciliazione; Tram No. 18.*

Museo Civico Archeologico (*Municipal Archaeological Museum*)

HISTORY MUSEUM | Appropriately situated in the heart of Roman Milan, this museum housed in a former monastery displays everyday utensils, jewelry, silver plate, and several fine examples of mosaic pavement from Mediolanum, the ancient Roman name for Milan. The museum opens into a garden that is flanked by the square tower of the Roman circus and the polygonal Ansperto tower, adorned with frescoes dating to the end of the 13th and 14th centuries that portray St. Francis and other saints receiving the stigmata. ⊠ *Corso Magenta 15, Sant'Ambrogio* ☎ *02/88445208* ⊕ *www.museoarcheologicomilano.it* 🎫 *€5 (free every 1st and 3rd Tues. of month after 2, and 1st Sun. of month)* ⏱ *Closed Mon.* Ⓜ *Cadorna or Cairoli; Tram No. 16 or 27; Bus No. 50, 58, or 94.*

Museo Nazionale della Scienza e Tecnologia Leonardo da Vinci (*National Museum of Science and Technology*)
SCIENCE MUSEUM | FAMILY | This converted cloister is best known for the collection of models based on Leonardo da Vinci's sketches. One of the most visited rooms features interactive, moving models of the famous *vita aerea* (aerial screw) and *ala battente* (beating wing), thought to be forerunners of the modern helicopter and airplane, respectively. The museum also houses a varied collection of industrial artifacts, including trains, and several reconstructed workshops, including a watchmaker's, a lute maker's, and an antique pharmacy. ⊠ *Via San Vittore 21, Sant'Ambrogio* ☎ *02/02485551* ⊕ *www.museoscienza.org* 🎫 *€10, €18 including tour of submarine (€20 when reserved in advance)* 🕑 *Closed Mon.* Ⓜ *Sant'Ambrogio; Bus No. 50, 58, or 94.*

 **Restaurants**

DaDa in Taverna
$$ | MODERN ITALIAN | This wood-paneled taverna near the stock exchange, within a house from the 14th century, was transformed into a contemporary restaurant and cocktail bar; it's the perfect spot to enjoy a mix of both traditional and more innovative fare. Pastas such as carbonara and robust secondi like roasted leg of lamb are available at dinner. **Known for:** inventive dishes; fantastic wine and cocktail selection; historical setting with a bright and modern edge. $ *Average main: €21* ⊠ *Via Morigi 8, Sant'Ambrogio* ☎ *02/36755232* ⊕ *www.dadaintaverna.com* 🕑 *Closed Sun.* Ⓜ *Cairoli or Cordusio; Tram 1, 2, 4, 12, 14, 16, or 27.*

 Hotels

Antica Locanda Leonardo
$$ | HOTEL | A feeling of relaxation prevails in this 19th-century building, and the neighborhood—the church that houses *The Last Supper* is a block away—is one

of Milan's most desired and historic. **Pros:** very quiet and homey; breakfast is ample; friendly, helpful staff. **Cons:** more like a bed-and-breakfast than a hotel; old-fashioned decor; breakfast is an extra fee. $ *Rooms from: €168* ⊠ *Corso Magenta 78, Sant'Ambrogio* ☎ *02/48014197* ⊕ *www.anticalocandaleonardo.com* 🕑 *Closed 1st wk in Jan. and 3 wks in Aug.* ⏎ *24 rooms* 🍴 *No Meals* Ⓜ *Conciliazione, Sant'Ambrogio, or Cadorna; Tram No. 1, 16, 19, or 27.*

Fiera and San Siro

Fiera is a quiet suburb northwest of the city center. Neighboring San Siro is home to Stadio Meazza (commonly known as San Siro Stadium), where AC and Inter Milan play their home matches.

 Activities

San Siro Stadium (Stadio Meazza)
SOCCER | FAMILY | AC Milan and Inter Milan, two of the oldest and most successful teams in Europe, vie for the heart of soccer-mad Lombardy. They share the use of San Siro Stadium (Stadio Meazza) during their August–May season. With more than 60,000 of the 80,000 seats appropriated by season-ticket holders and another couple of thousand allocated to visiting fans, tickets to Sunday games can be difficult to come by. Buy advance AC Milan tickets at ⊕ *www.acmilan.com*, at the Casa Milan ticket office at Via Aldo Rossi 8, or at VivaTicket sales points. They're also sold at the stadium booth on match days. Inter tickets are available at ⊕ *www.inter.it.* Tours are also available (⊕ *www.sansirostadium.com/en/museum-tour*). ⊠ *Piazzale Angelo Moratti, San Siro* ☎ *02/48798201* ⊕ *www.sansirostadium.com* Ⓜ *San Siro Stadio; Tram No. 16; Bus No. 49.*

Quadrilatero

Via Manzoni, which lies northeast of La Scala, leads to Milan's Quadrilatero della Moda, or fashion district.

Sights

Museo Bagatti Valsecchi

HISTORIC HOME | Glimpse the lives of 19th-century Milanese aristocrats in a visit to this lovely historic house museum, once the home of two brothers, Barons Fausto and Giuseppe Bagatti. Family members inhabited the house until 1974; it opened to the public as a museum in 1984. The house is decorated with the brothers' fascinating collection of 15th- and 16th-century Renaissance art, furnishings, and objects, including armor, musical instruments, and textiles. The detailed audio guide included with admission provides a thorough insight into the history of the artworks and intriguing stories of the family itself. ⊠ *Via Gesu 5, Quadrilatero* ☎ *02/76006132* ⊕ *www. museobagattivalsecchi.org* 🎟 *€12* ⊙ *Closed Mon. and Tues.* Ⓜ *Montenapoleone; Tram No. 1.*

Museo Poldi-Pezzoli

ART MUSEUM | This exceptional museum, opened in 1881, was once a private residence and collection, and contains not only pedigreed paintings but also porcelain, textiles, and a cabinet with scenes from Dante's life. The gem is undoubtedly *Portrait of a Lady,* by Piero del Pollaiolo (1431–98), one of the city's most prized treasures and the source of the museum's logo. The collection also includes masterpieces by Botticelli (1445–1510), Andrea Mantegna (1431–1506), Giovanni Bellini (1430–1516), and Fra Filippo Lippi (1406–69). ⊠ *Via Manzoni 12, Quadrilatero* ☎ *02/794889* ⊕ *www.museopoldipezzoli.it* 🎟 *€14* ⊙ *Closed Tues.* Ⓜ *Montenapoleone or Duomo; Tram No. 1.*

 Restaurants

Don Carlos

$$$$ | **ITALIAN** | One of the few restaurants open after La Scala lets out, Don Carlos, in the Grand Hotel et de Milan, is nothing like its indecisive operatic namesake (whose betrothed was stolen by his father). Flavors are bold, presentation is precise and full of flair, service is attentive, and the walls are blanketed with sketches of the theater. **Known for:** veal Milanese; homemade pasta; late-night hours. Ⓢ *Average main: €39* ⊠ *Grand Hotel et de Milan, Via Manzoni 29, Quadrilatero* ☎ *02/72314640* ⊕ *www. ristorantedoncarlos.it/en* ⊙ *No lunch* Ⓜ *Montenapoleone; Tram No. 1 or 2.*

★ Seta

$$$$ | **MODERN ITALIAN** | Modern Italian cuisine made using interesting ingredients is the draw at this restaurant with sophisticated brown-and-turquoise decor in Milan's Mandarin Oriental Hotel. The best way to experience the intricate dishes is through the seven-course tasting menu; for a less expensive option, opt for the three-course "carte blanche" lunch menu. **Known for:** ultracreative dishes; wonderful Italo-centric wine list; top-notch service. Ⓢ *Average main: €150* ⊠ *Via Andegari 9, Quadrilatero* ☎ *02/87318897* ⊕ *www.mandarinoriental.com/milan/la-scala/fine-dining/restaurants/italian-cuisine/seta* ⊙ *Closed Sun. and Mon.,1st wk of Jan., and 3 wks in Aug.* Ⓜ *Montenapoleone; Tram No. 1.*

☕ Coffee and Quick Bites

Chic & Go Milano

$ | **MODERN ITALIAN** | Step into these stylish and trendy surroundings (next door to a Balenciaga office and down the street from Giorgio Armani) for a quick sandwich as exquisite as the fashions and fashionistas in the nearby shops. Though the lobster panini will run you a pretty penny, other top-notch items—like crab, salmon, prosciutto, Angus tartare, and

mozzarella *di bufala*—are not a bad deal.
Known for: gourmet sandwiches; regional
meats; convenient location near shopping. Ⓢ *Average main: €8* ⊠ *Via Montenapoleone 25, Quadrilatero* ☎ *02/782648*
⊕ *www.facebook.com/chicandgomilano*
Ⓜ *Montenapoleone; Tram No. 1.*

 # Hotels

★ Armani Hotel Milano

$$$$ | **HOTEL** | This minimalist boutique
hotel looks like it has been plucked from
the pages of a sleek magazine, and it
should: it was designed by fashion icon
Giorgio Armani to evoke the same sculptural, streamlined aesthetic—and tailored
comfort—as his signature clothing.
Pros: complimentary (except for alcohol)
minibar; lovely spa area and 24-hour
gym; great location near major shopping
streets. **Cons:** breakfast (only included in
some rates) not up to par; some noise
issues from neighboring rooms; a few
signs of wear and tear. Ⓢ *Rooms from:
€1050* ⊠ *Via Manzoni 31, Quadrilatero*
☎ *02/88838888* ⊕ *www.armanihotelm-
ilano.com* ⤴ *95 rooms* ⦿ *No Meals*
Ⓜ *Montenapoleone.*

Four Seasons Hotel Milano

$$$$ | **HOTEL** | Built in the 15th century as a
convent, with a colonnaded cloister, this
sophisticated retreat certainly exudes a
feeling that is anything but urban. **Pros:**
quiet, elegant setting that feels removed
from noisy central Milan; friendly and
helpful staff; large rooms. **Cons:** decor is a
bit old-fashioned; breakfast isn't included
in the rate; expensive. Ⓢ *Rooms from:
€1231* ⊠ *Via Gesù 6–8, Quadrilatero*
☎ *02/77088* ⊕ *www.fourseasons.com/
milan* ⤴ *118 rooms* ⦿ *No Meals* Ⓜ *Montenapoleone; Tram No. 1.*

Grand Hotel et de Milan

$$$$ | **HOTEL** | Only blocks from La Scala,
you'll find everything you would expect
from a traditionally elegant European
hotel, where tapestries and persim-
mon velvet enliven a 19th-century look

without sacrificing dignity and luxury.
Pros: traditional and elegant; great location off Milan's main shopping streets;
staff go above and beyond to meet guest
needs. **Cons:** gilt decor may not suit
those who like more modern design; no
spa; some small rooms. Ⓢ *Rooms from:
€682* ⊠ *Via Manzoni 29, Quadrilatero*
☎ *02/723141* ⊕ *www.grandhoteletdemi-
lan.it* ⤴ *72 rooms, 23 suites* ⦿ *No Meals*
Ⓜ *Montenapoleone.*

Hotel Senato

$$$$ | **HOTEL** | The central courtyard of
this boutique hotel near Milan's fashion
district is covered in a layer of water, a
cheeky nod to the Naviglio Grande canal
that once ran in front of the 19th-century
palace, which now has a sleek, minimalist design and artsy touches like brass
ginkgo biloba-leaf lamps, serpentine
mosaic floor patterns, and flowers and
music selected by curators. **Pros:** cool
designer touches; lovely breakfast buffet
with local products; convenient location.
Cons: some rooms on the small side;
noise can be an issue; basic gym facilities. Ⓢ *Rooms from: €309* ⊠ *Via Senato
22, Quadrilatero* ☎ *02/781236* ⊕ *www.
senatohotelmilano.it* ⤴ *43 rooms* ⦿ *Free
Breakfast* Ⓜ *Turati or Palestro; Tram No.
1; Bus No. 61 or 94.*

★ Mandarin Oriental, Milan

$$$$ | **HOTEL** | **FAMILY** | A sense of refined
luxury pervades the guest rooms and
public spaces of this sophisticated hotel,
located just off the main Via Montenapoleone shopping street; from the elegant
bedrooms with supercomfortable beds
and oversize bathrooms with underfloor
heating to the highly rated restaurant
and one of the largest spas in Milan
(9,700 square feet), you'll be taken care
of here. **Pros:** wonderful and attentive service; tranquil spa and 24-hour
fitness center; top restaurant on-site.
Cons: very expensive; only some rooms
have views; can be difficult to find.
Ⓢ *Rooms from: €1249* ⊠ *Via Andegari
9, Quadrilatero* ☎ *02/87318888* ⊕ *www.*

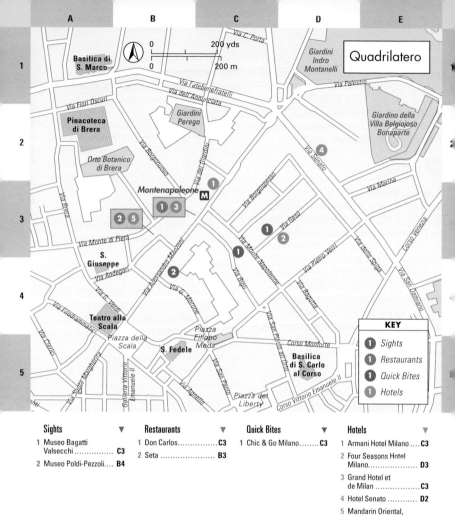

Sights ▼

1 Museo Bagatti
  Valsecchi **C3**
2 Museo Poldi-Pezzoli.... **B4**

Restaurants ▼

1 Don Carlos **C3**
2 Seta **B3**

Quick Bites ▼

1 Chic & Go Milano **C3**

Hotels ▼

1 Armani Hotel Milano **C3**
2 Four Seasons Hotel
  Milano **D3**
3 Grand Hotel et
  de Milan **C3**
4 Hotel Senato **D2**
5 Mandarin Oriental,
  Milan **B3**

mandarinoriental.com *70 rooms, 34 suites* ⦿*No Meals* Ⓜ *Montenapoleone; Tram No. 1.*

Ⓨ Nightlife

Armani/Bamboo Bar

BARS | With high ceilings, louvered windows, and expansive views of the city's rooftops, this modern architectural marvel is a great spot to enjoy a relaxing cup of tea or a predinner aperitivo. ✉ *Via Manzoni 31, Quadrilatero* ☎ *02/88838703* ⊕ *www.armanihotelmilano.com/dine/ armani-bamboo-bar* Ⓜ *Montenapoleone; Tram No. 1.*

Shopping

Armani Megastore

OTHER SPECIALTY STORE | Armani Junior, Emporio Armani, Armani Fiori (flowers), Armani Dolci (chocolate), and Armani Libri (books) are all under this monumental store's roof. ✉ *Via Manzoni 31, Quadrilatero* ☎ *02/62312600* ⊕ *www.armani. com* Ⓜ *Montenapoleone; Tram No. 1.*

★ DMAG Outlet

MIXED CLOTHING | This store has some of the best prices in the area for luxury items, such as Prada, Gucci, Lanvin, and Cavalli. DMAG has two other locations, at Via Forcella 13 and Via Bigli 4. ✉ *Via Manzoni 44, Quadrilatero* ☎ *02/36514365* ⊕ *www.dmag.eu* Ⓜ *Montenapoleone; Tram No. 1.*

★ Dolce & Gabbana

MIXED CLOTHING | This fabulous duo has created an empire based on sultry designs for men and women. The gorgeous three-story flagship store features clothing for both, plus accessories. ✉ *Via della Spiga 2, Quadrilatero* ☎ *02/795747* ⊕ *www.dolcegabbana.it* Ⓜ *San Babila; Tram No. 61 or 94.*

Dondup

MIXED CLOTHING | Started in 1999, Dondup is a Milanese brand that has captured the essence of casual chic. But it's no longer just a brand for denim lovers: its flagship store houses menswear, women's wear, accessories, and shoe collections. ✉ *Via della Spiga 50, Quadrilatero* ☎ *02/20242232* ⊕ *www.dondup.com* Ⓜ *Montenapoleone; Tram No. 1.*

Giorgio Armani

MIXED CLOTHING | Find Armani's apparel and accessories for both men and women in the brand's boutique. ✉ *Via Sant'Andrea 9, Quadrilatero* ☎ *02/76003234* ⊕ *www.armani.com* Ⓜ *San Babilo.*

Missoni

MIXED CLOTHING | Famous for their kaleidoscope-pattern knits, this family-run brand sells whimsical designs for men and women. ✉ *Via Sant'Andrea, angolo Via Bagutta, Quadrilatero* ☎ *02/76003555* ⊕ *www.missoni.com* Ⓜ *Montenapoleone or San Babila; Tram No. 1.*

Miu Miu

MIXED CLOTHING | Prada's more upbeat, youthful brand has a wide offering of boldly printed women's fashions and accessories. ✉ *Via Sant'Andrea 21, Quadrilatero* ☎ *02/76001799* ⊕ *www.miumiu. com* Ⓜ *Montenapoleone, San Babila, or Palestro; Tram No. 1.*

Moschino

MIXED CLOTHING | Known for its bold prints, colors, and appliqués, Moschino is a brand for daring fashionistas. ✉ *Via della Spiga 26, Quadrilatero* ☎ *02/76022639* ⊕ *www.moschino.com* Ⓜ *Montenapoleone, San Babila, or Palestro; Tram No. 1.*

Prada

MIXED CLOTHING | Founded in Milan in 1913 selling steamer trunks and handbags, Prada has several locations throughout the city. Its stores on Via Montenapoleone showcase its women's (✉ *Via Montenapoleone 8*) and men's fashions (✉ *Via Montenapoleone 6*). ✉ *Via Montenapoleone 8, Quadrilatero* ☎ *02/7771771* ⊕ *www.prada. com* Ⓜ *Montenapoleone, San Babila, or Palestro; Tram No. 1.*

Roberto Cavalli

MIXED CLOTHING | Famous for his wild-animal prints, Roberto Cavalli creates sexy designs for men and women. ✉ *Via Montenapoleone 6, Quadrilatero* ☎ *02/7630771* ⊕ *www.robertocavalli.com* Ⓜ *San Babila.*

Salvatore Ferragamo Donna

LEATHER GOODS | This Florence-based brand is a leader in leather goods and accessories, and carries designs for women in this store. ✉ *Via Montenapoleone 3, Quadrilatero* ☎ *02/76000054* ⊕ *www.ferragamo.com* Ⓜ *San Babila.*

Salvatore Ferragamo Uomo

LEATHER GOODS | Ferragamo's men's accessories, leather goods, and ties are a staple for Milan's male fashion set. ✉ *Via Montenapoleone 20/4, Quadrilatero* ☎ *02/76006660* ⊕ *www.ferragamo.com* Ⓜ *Montenapoleone; Tram No. 1.*

Tod's

LEATHER GOODS | This leather-goods leader sells luxury handbags as well as a variety of shoes for men and women. It also offers men's and women's clothing. ✉ *Via Montenapoleone 13, Quadrilatero* ☎ *02/76002423* ⊕ *www.tods.com* Ⓜ *Montenapoleone, San Babila, or Palestro; Tram No. 1.*

Valentino

MIXED CLOTHING | Even after the departure of its founding father, Valentino Garavani, this fashion brand still flourishes. ✉ *Via Montenapoleone 20, Quadrilatero* ☎ *02/76006182* ⊕ *www.valentino.com* Ⓜ *Montenapoleone; Tram No. 1.*

Versace

MIXED CLOTHING | Run by flamboyant Donatella Versace and known for its rock-and-roll styling, the first store of this fashion house opened on Via della Spiga in 1978, not far from its current location in the Quadrilatero della Moda shopping district. ✉ *Via Monte Napoleone, 11, Quadrilatero* ☎ *02/76008528* ⊕ *www.versace.com* Ⓜ *San Babila or Montenapoleone.*

Porta Garibaldi

This stylish, upscale, and buzzing district is home to the emblematic 10 Corso Como concept store and the colorful and lively Piazza Gae Aulenti, which is a study in Milan's modern architecture, including the 757-foot UniCredit Tower. New construction, stylish restaurants, and urban parks provide a modern break from historical sightseeing.

Sights

ADI Design Museum Compasso d'Oro

OTHER MUSEUM | More than 350 of the most renowned Italian industrial design objects are showcased in this former Enel electricity plant, which opened as a museum in 2021. The items in the permanent collection were selected during biennial judging for Compasso d'Oro (Golden Compass) awards from 1954 until today. Some of the exhibits are grouped by category, like cars (1960 Abarth-Fiat Monza Zagato, 1959 Fiat 500, and 2014 Ferrari F12berlinetta) and coffeemakers (Alessi's 9090 from 1979 and Napoletana from 1981). ✉ *Piazza Compasso d'Oro, 1, Garibaldi* ☎ *02/36693790* ⊕ *www.adidesignmuseum.org* 🎫 *€12* 🕐 *Closed Mon.* ☞ *Tickets may be purchased online, or at the museum with a credit card or mobile wallet (no cash accepted)* Ⓜ *Garibaldi.*

Piazza Gae Aulenti

PLAZA/SQUARE | Welcome to the modern era. The piazza named for the famed Italian female architect is a stroll into the future of architectural design. Here you'll find Italy's tallest skyscraper (the 757-foot mirrored and spired UniCredit Tower), IBM Studios (a curved and wood-slatted innovation lab), a Tesla dealership, and an LED tree surrounded by reflective pools. Linger through a botanical garden, Biblioteca degli Alberi (library of trees), and join locals picnicking when the weather cooperates. ✉ *Piazza Gae Aulenti, Garibaldi* Ⓜ *Garibaldi.*

Restaurants

★ Ceresio 7 Pools & Restaurant

$$$$ | **CONTEMPORARY** | Book well in advance for one of Milan's most fashionable eateries, where the tables are lacquered red and modern artwork crowds the walls—exactly what you'd expect from the twin brothers, Dean and Dan Caten, behind the fashion label Dsquared2. The food cred matches the scene—with fresh, creative, sophisticated pastas and other dishes. **Known for:** luxe ingredients like lobster, king crab, and truffles; place for seeing and being seen; swimming pools and terrace views. $ *Average main: €37* ✉ *Via Ceresio 7, Garibaldi* ☎ *02/31039221* ⊕ *www. ceresio7.com* Ⓜ *Garibaldi; Tram No. 2, 4, 12, or 14; Bus No. 37 or 190.*

Ratanà

$$ | **NORTHERN ITALIAN** | Chef Cesare Battisti infuses the Milanese dishes of his childhood with a contemporary twist at this lively restaurant. Its two patios face a park with skyline views, and its dining room is decorated with vintage items (like an Olivetti typewriter and Scandalli accordion). **Known for:** meat- and fish-focused menu with contemporary and traditional dishes; setting in a former historical house; more than 500 wines. $ *Average main: €24* ✉ *Via Gaetano de Castillia, 28, Garibaldi* ☎ *02/87128855* ⊕ *www.ratana.it* ⊗ *Closed 2 wks in Aug. and 2 wks in Dec.* Ⓜ *Gioia.*

☕ Coffee and Quick Bites

Zàini

$ | **BAKERY** | The Zàini family opened its chocolate factory here in 1913, on a side street off Corso Como. Today, its black-and-white marble-tile-floored and chandelier-lit café is found just past flagship stores for Dsquared2 and Moschino. **Known for:** decadent hot chocolate; artfully wrapped chocolate gifts; elegant breakfast spot. $ *Average main: €10* ✉ *Via Carlo de Cristoforis, 5, Garibaldi* ☎ *02/694914449* ⊕ *www.zainimilano. com* Ⓜ *Garibaldi.*

 Hotels

Hotel VIU Milan

$$$$ | **HOTEL** | A short walk from trendy Corso Como and the historic Cimitero Monumentale, this sleek business-focused hotel features vertical gardens outside and contemporary Italian-designed furnishings within—but its true pièce de résistance is an inviting rooftop pool with panoramic views. **Pros:** stylish modern decor; spacious bathrooms; high-quality food. **Cons:** out-of-the-way location for central Milan; hotel has a signature scent, which may bother perfume-averse guests; rooftop terrace sometimes not useable due to events. $ *Rooms from: €306* ✉ *Via Aristotile Fioravanti 6, Garibaldi* ☎ *02/80010910* ⊕ *www.hotelviumilan. com* ⇨ *124 rooms* ⦿ *No Meals* Ⓜ *Monumentale; Tram No. 10, 12, or 14.*

▼ Nightlife

★ Blue Note

LIVE MUSIC | The first European branch of the famous New York nightclub features regular performances by some of the most famous names in jazz, as well as blues and rock concerts. Dinner is also available. ✉ *Via Borsieri 37, Garibaldi* ☎ *02/69016888* ⊕ *www.bluenotemilano. com* Ⓜ *Isola; Tram No. 7, 31, or 33.*

Dry Milano

BARS | A hot spot for both classic and creative cocktails, this trendy industrial space packed with hip locals has a pizza joint in the back if you get hungry. ✉ *Via Solferino 33, Garibaldi* ☎ *02/63793414* ⊕ *www.drymilano.it* Ⓜ *Moscova, Turati, or Repubblica; Tram No. 1, 9, or 33; Bus No. 37.*

258

Shopping

⭐ **10 Corso Como**
OTHER SPECIALTY STORE | A shrine to Milan's creative fashion sense, the concept store 10 Corso Como was founded by the former fashion editor and publisher Carla Sozzani. The clothing and design establishment also includes a restaurant-café, gallery, bookstore, and small hotel. ⊠ *Corso Como 10, Corso Como* ☎ *02/29002674* ⊕ *www.10corsocomo.com* Ⓜ *Porta Garibaldi.*

Repubblica

Some of the city's best hotels can be found around the Piazza della Repubblica.

Restaurants

Mercato Centrale
$ | **ITALIAN** | Without traveling across the city, you can try the creations of some of the most well-known food purveyors in Milan. Follow neon signs with sketches of the type of food on offer to pick from standbys such as risotto from Sergio Barzetti and fish from Pescheria Pedol at the newest opening of the concept food hall that's also in Florence, Rome, and Turin. **Known for:** late-night dining; wide variety of Italian street food; high-quality for affordable prices. Ⓢ *Average main: €10* ⊠ *Via Giovanni Battista Sammartini 2, Repubblica* ☎ *02/37928400* ⊕ *www.mercatocentrale.it/milano* Ⓜ *Central Station; Tram No. 5, 9, or 10.*

Coffee and Quick Bites

⭐ **Pavè**
$ | **BAKERY** | Your main problem at Pavè will be deciding what to order among rows of cakes, tarts, classic Italian brioches (with sweet fillings like cream and jam), and other pastries. When everything is this drool-worthy, your best strategy is to come with friends and share your favorites. **Known for:** chocolate and fruit-filled tarts; vegan pastries; sandwiches and crostini on homemade bread. Ⓢ *Average main: €10* ⊠ *Via Felice Casati 27, Repubblica* ☎ *02/37905491* ⊕ *www.pavemilano.com* Ⓜ *Repubblica.*

Hotels

Hotel Principe di Savoia Milano
$$$$ | **HOTEL** | Milan's grande dame has all the exquisite trappings of a traditional luxury hotel: lavish mirrors, drapes, and carpets; limousine services; and some of the city's largest guest rooms, outfitted with eclectic fin de siècle furnishings. **Pros:** substantial health club–spa; close to Central Station; shuttle to Duomo and shopping district. **Cons:** located in a not-very-attractive neighborhood; not near major sites; breakfast and other meals overly expensive; showing a bit of wear and tear. Ⓢ *Rooms from: €605* ⊠ *Piazza della Repubblica 17, Repubblica* ☎ *02/91387010* ⊕ *www.dorchestercollection.com/en/milan/hotel-principe-di-savoia* 🛏 *301 rooms* ⑂ *No Meals* Ⓜ *Repubblica; Tram No. 1, 9, or 33.*

ME Milan Il Duca
$$$$ | **HOTEL** | This outpost of the Spanish hotel brand ME by Meliá has a lively party atmosphere, with rousing music playing in the lobby, a design-conscious vibe, and a happening rooftop bar with panoramic city views. **Pros:** great rooftop bar; spacious rooms; young, vibrant atmosphere. **Cons:** no spa; may feel overdesigned to some; can be noisy. Ⓢ *Rooms from: €450* ⊠ *Piazza della Repubblica 13, Repubblica* ☎ *02/84220108* ⊕ *www.melia.com/en/hotels/italy/milan/me-milan-il-duca/index.htm* 🛏 *132 rooms* ⑂ *No Meals* Ⓜ *Repubblica; Tram No. 1, 5, 9, 10, or 33.*

Westin Palace
$$$ | **HOTEL** | Don't be fooled by the functional 1950s-era exterior of one of Milan's premier business addresses: inside, rooms have a contemporary look with soothing gray walls and marble

bathrooms. **Pros:** full-service hotel with extensive amenities; renovated rooms in both modern and more traditional styles; good-size gym open 24/7. **Cons:** lacking in local character; not in the most central or attractive location; Wi-Fi can be spotty in some rooms. [$] *Rooms from: €248* ✉ *Piazza della Repubblica 20, Repubblica* ☎ *02/63361* 🌐 *www.marriott.com/hotels/travel/milwi-the-westin-palace-milan* 🛏 *231 rooms* 🍴 *No Meals* [M] *Repubblica; Tram No. 1, 5, 9, or 33.*

Nightlife

Radio Rooftop Bar

COCKTAIL LOUNGES | Some of Milan's most beautiful people congregate for an Aperol spritz and a selection of international tapas on this terrace with panoramic views of the city. Located at the top of the ME Milan Il Duca, the bar has heat lamps to keep visitors here even in cooler weather. ✉ *Piazza della Repubblica 13, Repubblica* ☎ *02/35403218* 🌐 *www.melia.com/en/hotels/italy/milan/me-milan-il-duca/restaurants.htm* [M] *Repubblica; Tram No. 1, 5, 9, 10, or 33.*

Cinque Giornate

Located just east of the city center, Cinque Giornate marks the location of the Five Days revolt against Austrian rule in Milan.

Restaurants

Da Giacomo

$$$ | **ITALIAN** | The fashion and publishing crowds, as well as international bankers and businesspeople, favor this Milanese-Ligurian restaurant. The emphasis is on fish, and with its tile floor and bank of fresh seafood, the place has a refined neighborhood-bistro style. **Known for:** sophisticated dining; specialty gnocchetti alla Giacomo (with seafood and tomato); extensive wines, cocktails, and after-dinner drinks. [$] *Average main: €32* ✉ *Via P. Sottocorno 6, entrance in Via Cellini, Cinque Giornate* ☎ *02/76023313* 🌐 *www.giacomomilano.com* [M] *Tram No. 9, 12, 23, or 27; Bus No. 60 or 73.*

Palestro

Nestled just below the Giardini Pubblici Indro Montanelli park, Palestro is filled with galleries, museums, and historical landmarks.

Sights

GAM: Galleria d'Arte Moderna/Villa Reale

HISTORIC HOME | One of the city's most beautiful buildings is an outstanding example of neoclassical architecture, built between 1790 and 1796. After it was donated to Napoléon, who lived here briefly with Empress Josephine, it became known as the Villa Reale. The collection consists of works donated by prominent Milanese art collectors. It emphasizes 18th- and 19th-century Italian works, but also has a smattering of 20th-century Italian pieces. ✉ *Via Palestro 16, Palestro* ☎ *02/88445947* 🌐 *www.gam-milano.com* 🎟 *€5 (free every 1st and 3rd Tues. of month after 2)* 🕒 *Closed Mon.* [M] *Palestro or Turati; Tram No. 1 or 2; Bus No. 94 or 61.*

Villa Necchi Campiglio

NOTABLE BUILDING | In 1932, architect Piero Portaluppi designed this sprawling estate in an Art Deco style, with inspiration coming from the decadent cruise ships of the 1920s. Once owned by the Necchi Campiglio industrial family, the tasteful and elegant three-level home and garden—which sits on Via Mozart, one of Milan's most exclusive streets—is a reminder of the refined, modern culture of the nouveaux riches who accrued financial power in Milan during that era. There is also a café on the grounds that is open 10 am–6 pm. ■ **TIP→ An audio tour is included with the entrance fee, and can be listened to on a mobile device. Tours**

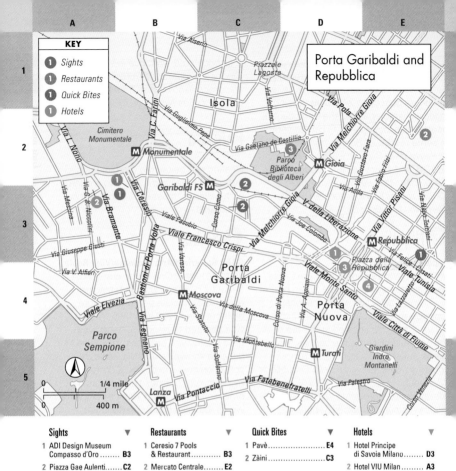

Porta Garibaldi and Repubblica

KEY
- ① Sights
- ① Restaurants
- ① Quick Bites
- ① Hotels

Sights ▼	Restaurants ▼	Quick Bites ▼	Hotels ▼
1 ADI Design Museum Compasso d'Oro **B3**	1 Ceresio 7 Pools & Restaurant **B3**	1 Pavè **E4**	1 Hotel Principe di Savoia Milano **D3**
2 Piazza Gae Aulenti **C2**	2 Mercato Centrale **E2**	2 Zàini **C3**	2 Hotel VIU Milan **A3**
	3 Ratanà **D2**		3 ME Milan Il Duca **D4**
			4 Westin Palace **E4**

in English are available on Saturday at 11:30 am and 2:30 pm with advanced booking. ✉ *Via Mozart 14, Palestro* ☎ *02/76340121* 🌐 *www.fondoambiente.it/villa-necchi-campiglio-eng* 🎫 *From €15 for guided visits; garden-only €4.* 🕒 *Closed Mon. and Tues.* [M] *Palestro, San Babila, or Montenapoleone; Bus No. 54, 61, or 94.*

Porta Venezia

This district is home to parks and gardens, museums, galleries, and one end of the famed Corso Buenos Aires shopping street.

👁 Sights

Fondazione Luigi Rovati

ART MUSEUM | This isn't your typical Etruscan history museum. A seven-year project led by the Luigi Rovati foundation transformed two levels of a palazzo commissioned by the Prince of Piombino in 1871 into a stone-carved contemporary museum where ancient artifacts stand alongside those from the 20th century and beyond. Digital installations translate Etruscan into English and Italian on some of the objects, while an immersive moving floor map shows the civilization's major cities before its Roman conquest. A rotating display of contemporary exhibits along with permanent works on the main floor continues the play of ancient and modern, such as with Andy Warhol's interpretation of an Etruscan scene in the same room as archaeological finds. Giardino Padiglione, and its adjoining Andrea Aprea Bistrot, is an ideal spot for an afternoon aperitif or coffee. ✉ *Corso Venezia 52, Porta Venezia* ☎ *02/38273001* 🌐 *www.fondazioneluigirovati.org* 🎫 *€16* 🕒 *Closed Mon. and Tues.* [M] *Porta Venezia; Tram No. 9.*

Giardini Pubblici Indro Montanelli (*Public Gardens Indro Montanelli*)

GARDEN | **FAMILY** | Giuseppe Piermarini, architect of La Scala, laid out these gardens across Via Palestro from the Villa Reale in 1770. Designed as public pleasure gardens, today they are still popular with families who live in the city center. Generations of Milanese have taken pony rides and gone on the miniature train and merry-go-round. The park also contains a small planetarium and the **Museo Civico di Storia Naturale** (Municipal Natural History Museum). ✉ *Corso Venezia 55, Porta Venezia* ☎ *02/88463337* 🌐 *www.comune.milano.it/aree-tematiche/verde/verde-pubblico/parchi-cittadini/giardini-indro-montanelli* 🎫 *Gardens free, museum €5 (free every 1st and 3rd Tues. of month after 2 and 1st Sun. of month)* 🕒 *Museum closed Mon.* [M] *Palestro; Tram No. 9, 29, or 30.*

🍴 Restaurants

Joia

$$$$ | **VEGETARIAN** | At this hushed, haute-cuisine vegetarian haven near Piazza della Repubblica, delicious dishes—all without eggs and many without flour—are served in a minimalist beige room that puts the focus solely on the artistry of the food. Vegetarians, who often get short shrift in Italy, will marvel at the variety of culinary offerings made from many organic and biodynamic ingredients. **Known for:** imaginative presentations; ever-changing menu; well-thought-out wine selection. [$] *Average main: €60* ✉ *Via Panfilo Castaldi 18, Porta Venezia* ☎ *02/29522124* 🌐 *joia.it/en* 🕒 *Closed Sun. and Mon., 2 wks in Aug., and Dec. 24–Jan. 6* [M] *Repubblica or Porta Venezia; Tram No. 1, 5, 9, or 33.*

LùBar

$$ | **SICILIAN** | Dining at LùBar, which was started by three children of Milan fashion designer Luisa Beccaria and which is tucked into the side of the Galleria d'Arte Moderna, feels like eating inside a greenhouse—only with fashionable people among the trees and plants. The cozy, chic environs lend themselves perfectly to nibbling on small plates of modern

Sicilian food—for lunch, an afternoon snack, or a light dinner—many served on Caltagirone ceramics straight from Sicily. **Known for:** Sicilian street food like arancini and polpette (meatballs); LùBar Spritz made with Amara, a Sicilian blood orange amaro; charming, relaxed atmosphere. [$] *Average main: €16* ✉ *Via Palestro 16, Porta Venezia* ☎ *02/83527769* 🌐 *www.lubar.it* [M] *Palestro or Turati; Tram No. 1 or 2; Bus No. 94 or 61.*

Buenos Aires

This street in northeastern Milan is one of the busiest in the city and has more than 350 stores and outlets to choose from.

👁 Sights

Casa-Museo Boschi di Stefano (*Boschi di Stefano House and Museum*)
HISTORIC HOME | To most people, Italian art means Renaissance art, but the 20th century in Italy was also a time of artistic achievement. An apartment on the second floor of a stunning Art Deco building designed by Milan architect Portaluppi houses this collection, which was donated to the city of Milan in 2003 and is a tribute to the enlightened private collectors who replaced popes and nobles as Italian patrons. The walls are lined with the works of postwar greats, such as Fontana, de Chirico, and Morandi. Along with the art, the museum holds distinctive postwar furniture, sculptures, and stunning Murano glass chandeliers. ✉ *Via Jan 15, Buenos Aires* ☎ *02/88463614* 🌐 *www.casamuseoboschidistefano.it* 🎫 *Free* 🕒 *Closed Mon.* [M] *Lima; Tram No. 33; Bus No. 60.*

Formula 1 Racing

Italian Grand Prix. Italy's Formula 1 fans are passionate and huge numbers converge in early September for the Italian Grand Prix, held 15 km (9 miles) northeast of Milan in Monza. The racetrack was built in 1922 within the **Parco di Monza**. Check the website for dates, as well as for special category races, like classic cars and motorcycles. Visitors are allowed to zoom around the track on certain days—guided by a professional driver, of course. ✉ *Monza Eni Circuit, Via Vedano 5, Parco di Monza, Monza* ☎ *24821 in Italy* 🌐 *www.monzanet.it.*

☕ Coffee and Quick Bites

★ **Marghe**
$ | **NEOPOLITAN** | At Marghe, crafting Neapolitan-style pizza is art—as the line of people outside the restaurant each night suggests. Book in advance to grab a table in the rustic and lively dining room with exposed concrete walls, floral-tiled floors, and pendant lights, where pizzas are delivered quickly and piping hot. **Known for:** ingredients from Naples and the Amalfi Coast; local atmosphere; delicious pizza. [$] *Average main: €10* ✉ *Via Plinio 6, Buenos Aires* ☎ *02/2047117* 🌐 *www.marghepizza.com* [M] *Lima.*

Loreto

Located in the northeastern part of the city, Piazzale Loreto has a rather grim recent history: In August 1944, the Gestapo in Milan publicly executed 15 Italian resistance fighters here. Less than a year later, Benito Mussolini and a number of other high-ranking fascists, were captured and shot, with their bodies displayed here. There are no placards or signs to mark this history.

🍴 Restaurants

Da Abele

$ | **ITALIAN** | The superb risotto dishes at this neighborhood trattoria change with the season; you'll find at least three on the menu—meat, fish, and vegetarian—and it's tempting to try them all. The setting is relaxed and the service is informal. **Known for:** meat-focused main courses like tripe; cozy neighborhood favorite; reasonable prices. [$] *Average main: €13* ✉ *Via Temperanza 5, Loreto* ☎ *02/2613855* 🕒 *Closed Mon. No lunch* [M] *Pasteur.*

Bicocca

This university and business district plays host to musicals and concerts as well as art installations.

👁 Sights

Pirelli HangarBicocca

ARTS CENTER | Anselm Kiefer's *The Seven Heavenly Palaces*—seven cement towers extending 43–52 feet high, along with five of Kiefer's large-scale paintings—is the must-see permanent installation at this impressive gallery in a former train factory. There are also temporary exhibitions of contemporary art throughout the year; check the website for the latest showings. ✉ *Via Chiese 2, Bicocca* ☎ *02/66111573* 🌐 *www.pirellihangarbicocca.org* 🎫 *Free* 🕒 *Closed Mon.–Wed.* [M] *Via Chiese; Bus No. 87 or 51.*

Porta Romana

Porta Romana is a hip and vibrant neighborhood.

👁 Sights

★ **Fondazione Prada**

ART MUSEUM | New structures of metal and glass and revamped buildings once part of a distillery from the 1910s now contain this museum's roughly 205,000 square feet. The modern art showcased here is not for the faint of heart. Permanent pieces, such as *Haunted House,* featuring works by Louise Bourgeois and Robert Gober, are avant-garde and challenging, and temporary exhibitions highlight cutting-edge Italian and international artists. Don't hesitate to ask one of the helpful, knowledgeable staffers for guidance navigating the expansive grounds, which can be confusing. And don't miss the Wes Anderson–designed café, Bar Luce, for a drink or snack, or the restaurant Torre for an aperitivo or a full meal with panoramic views from on high. The Fondazione is a hike from the city center; expect a 10-minute walk from the metro station to the galleries. ✉ *Largo Isarco 2, Porta Romana* ☎ *02/56662611* 🌐 *www.fondazioneprada.org* 🎫 *€12 for full visit admission, which includes a ticket to Milano Osservatorio* 🕒 *Closed Tues.* [M] *Lodi TIBB; Tram No. 24; Bus No. 65.*

🍴 Restaurants

U Barba

$ | **NORTHERN ITALIAN** | Simple, fresh, authentic Ligurian specialties will take you back to lazy summer days on the Italian Riviera—even during Milan's gray winters. Such coastal classics as *trofie al pesto* (an egg-free pasta served with pesto) and *bagnun di acciughe* (anchovy soup), coupled with a basket of warm

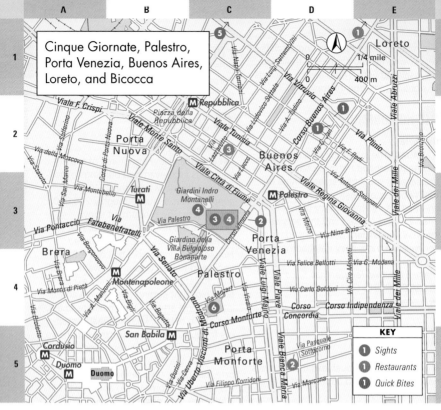

Cinque Giornate, Palestro,
Porta Venezia, Buenos Aires,
Loreto, and Bicocca

Sights ▼

1 Casa-Museo
   Boschi di Stefano **D2**
2 Fondazione
   Luigi Rovati **C3**
3 GAM: Galleria d'Arte
   Moderna/Villa Reale **C3**
4 Giardini Pubblici
   Indro Montanelli **C3**
5 Pirelli
   HangarBicocca **C1**
6 Villa Necchi
   Campiglio **C4**

Restaurants ▼

1 Da Abele **E1**
2 Da Giacomo **D5**
3 Joia **C2**
4 LùBar **C3**

Quick Bites ▼

1 Marghe **D2**

KEY

1 *Sights*
1 *Restaurants*
1 *Quick Bites*

focaccia or a side of *farinata* (a chickpea pancake) reign supreme in this Milan favorite. **Known for:** fresh pasta, also available to take home; charming setting with vintage furniture; seasonal changing menu. $ *Average main: €14 ⊠ Via Pier Candido Decembrio 33, Porta Romana ☎ 02/45487032 ⊕ www.ubarba.it ⊗ No lunch weekdays Ⓜ Lodi TIBB; Tram No. 16; Bus No. 90.*

Ticinese

This boho district is also home to the Basilica di San Lorenzo Maggiore and the Basilica di Sant'Eustorgio.

Sights

MUDEC (Museo delle Culture)
ART MUSEUM | Home to a permanent collection of ethnographic displays as well as temporary exhibitions of big-name artists such as Basquiat and Miró, MUDEC is in the vibrant Zona Tortona area of the city. British architect David Chipperfield designed the soaring space in a former factory. The permanent collection includes art, objects, and documents from Africa, Asia, and the Americas. Book in advance for the most popular temporary exhibits. There's also a highly rated restaurant, Enrico Bartolini Mudec, as well as a more casual bistro. ⊠ *Via Tortona 56, Ticinese ☎ 02/54917 ⊕ www. mudec.it 🔁 Permanent collection free, special exhibitions from €12 ⊗ Closed Mon. until 2:30 pm Ⓜ Sant'Agostino or Porta Genova; Tram No. 2 or 14; Bus No. 68 or 90/91.*

San Lorenzo Maggiore alle Colonne
CHURCH | Sixteen ancient Roman columns line the front of this sanctuary; remnants of 4th-century Paleo-Christian mosaics survive in the Cappella di Sant'Aquilino (Chapel of St. Aquilinus). ⊠ *Corso di Porta Ticinese 35, Ticinese ☎ 02/89404129 ⊕ www.sanlorenzomaggiore.com 🔁 Mosaics €2 Ⓜ Missori.*

"Let's Go to the Columns"

Andiamo al Le Colonne, in Milanese youthspeak, is the cue to meet up at the sober Roman columns in front of the Basilica San Lorenzo Maggiore. Attracted to the Corso di Porta Ticinese by its bars and shops, hipsters spill out on the street to chat and drink. Neighbors may complain about the noise and confusion, but students and nighthawks find it indispensable for socializing at all hours. It's a street—no closing time.

Restaurants

★ [bu:r] di Eugenio Boer
$$$$ | **MODERN ITALIAN** | Named after the phonetic spelling of the Dutch-Italian chef's last name, this innovative, high-concept restaurant, whose quiet dining rooms are done up in gray and gold, offers a choice of interesting tasting menus and à la carte options. Boer's contemporary Italian food is beautifully presented and full of complex flavors, and the well-matched wines lean toward the natural. **Known for:** personalized cuisine; traditional dishes with an ultramodern spin; helpful and well-informed service. $ *Average main: €65 ⊠ Via Mercalli 22, Ticinese ☎ 02/62065383 ⊕ www.restaurantboer.com ⊗ Closed Sun. No lunch Ⓜ Crocetta; Tram No. 15; Bus No. 94.*

🛏 Hotels

★ Aethos Milan
$$$ | **HOTEL** | The decor in this eclectic, extremely hip hotel at the foot of the lively Corso di Porta Ticinese and by the Navigli canals features sports memorabilia from golf, horseback riding, boxing, and others. **Pros:** contemporary flair;

interesting location near many restaurants and bars; very friendly staff. **Cons:** lacking some of the amenities of large hotels; about a half-hour hike from the Duomo and central attractions; bar noise can be heard in some rooms. $ *Rooms from: €255* ✉ *Piazza XXIV Maggio 8, Porta Ticinese* 🕿 *02/89415901* ⊕ *www.aethoshotels.com/milan* 🛏 *32 rooms* ⍥ *No Meals* Ⓜ *Tram No. 3 or 9.*

Navigli

One of the oldest neighborhoods in the city, Navigli is a quiet, artistic hub during the weekdays and a lively hot spot on nights and weekends.

👁 Sights

★ Navigli District
HISTORIC DISTRICT | In medieval times, a network of *navigli,* or canals, crisscrossed the city. Almost all have been covered over, but two—Naviglio Grande and Naviglio Pavese—are still navigable. The area's chock-full of boutiques, art galleries, cafés, bars, and restaurants, and at night the Navigli serves up a scene about as close as you will get to southern Italian–style street life in Milan. On weekend nights, it is difficult to walk among the youthful crowds thronging the narrow streets along the canals. Check out the antiques fair on the last Sunday of the month from 9 to 6. ◼ **TIP➜ During the summer months, be sure to put on some mosquito repellent.** ✉ *South of Corso Porta Ticinese, Navigli* Ⓜ *Porta Genova; Tram No. 2, 3, 9, 14, 15, 29, or 30.*

🍴 Restaurants

142
$$ | **ITALIAN** | From day to night, step into the chic living room of 142 for whatever you are craving. Drink coffee and eat a homemade brioche at a bar decorated in crown caps or eat lunch or dinner at tables with a hand-painted Pollock flourish, while browsing a selection of art books. **Known for:** playful plating and setting; all day and late-night dining; seafood dishes with flair. $ *Average main: €20* ✉ *Corso Cristoforo Colombo 6, Navigli* 🕿 *02/47758490* ⊕ *www.142.restaurant* ⍥ *Closed Mon. No dinner Sun.* Ⓜ *Porto Genova: Tram No. 2, 9, 10, or 14.*

🍸 Nightlife

Rita
BARS | Though it's a bit difficult to find, on a side street in the popular aperitivo haunt of Navigli, the expertly mixed cocktails, well-prepared snacks, and excellent playlist make this classic worth the hunt. It also serves burgers, sandwiches, and more substantial plates for dinner. ✉ *Via Angelo Fumagalli 1, Navigli* 🕿 *02/8372865* ⊕ *www.ritacocktails.com* Ⓜ *Porta Genova; Tram No. 2.*

★ Ugo Bar
BARS | Flanked by a long bar and tables lit by candles, and featuring floral wallpaper and eclectic framed paintings of animals, this bar has a moody living-room vibe. It's a charming place for a drink, if you can squeeze past the crowds. There is also a handful of outdoor tables for prime people-watching. ✉ *Via Corsico 12, Navigli* 🕿 *02/39811337* ⊕ *www.ugobar.it* Ⓜ *Porta Genova; Tram No. 9 or 10.*

🎭 Performing Arts

Auditorium di Milano Fondazione Cariplo
CONCERTS | This modern hall, known for its excellent acoustics, is home to the **Orchestra Sinfonica di Milano Giuseppe Verdi** (Symphonic Orchestra) and **Coro Sinfonico di Milano Giuseppe Verdi** (Symphonic Choir). The season, which runs from September to June, includes many top international performers and rotating guest conductors. ✉ *Largo Gustav Mahler, at Corso San Gottardo, Navigli* 🕿 *02/83389401* ⊕ *www.laverdi.org* Ⓜ *Tram No. 3 or 15; Bus No. 59 or 91.*

Shopping

Antonioli
MIXED CLOTHING | Antonioli raises the bar for Milan's top trendsetters. Uniting the most cutting-edge looks of each season, it is among the fashion-forward concept stores in the city. Aside from Italian brands like Valentino, it also stocks a competitive international array of designers, like Ann Demeulemeester, Rick Owens, Givenchy, Maison Margiela, and Vetements. ✉ *Via Pasquale Paoli 1, Navigli* ☎ *02/36561860* 🌐 *www.antonioli.eu* [M] *Porta Genova; Tram No. 2.*

Tortona

Tortona's former factories, warehouses, and workshops are now a creative hub packed with shops, studios, and the MUDEC, a museum with modern and contemporary art and special exhibitions.

Sights

Armani/Silos
OTHER MUSEUM | About 600 pieces, from about 1980 to the present, by famed Milanese fashion designer Giorgio Armani are displayed on four floors of this airy 48,000-square-foot museum, housed in a 1950s building that was formerly a Nestlé cereal storage facility. The collection is divided by theme: Ethnicities; Androgynous, including many of Armani's famous suits; and Stars, with clothes worn to the Oscars and other celebrity-studded events. A digital archive lets you explore Armani's full body of work, and a café lets you stop for a restorative espresso. Temporary exhibitions explore photography, architecture, and other themes related to design. ✉ *Via Bergognone 40, Ticinese* ☎ *02/91630010* 🌐 *www.armanisilos.com* 🎟 *€12* 🕒 *Closed Mon. and Tues.* [M] *Sant'Agostino or Porta Genova; Tram No. 2 or 14; Bus No. 68 or 90/91.*

Hotels

Hotel Magna Pars Suites Milano
$$$$ | **HOTEL** | This ultrastylish all-suites boutique hotel in a former perfume factory has Italian-designed furnishings; paintings by local Brera Academy artists; and sleek, white accommodations—each with its own signature scent (such as fruity, woodsy, or floral) and all overlooking one of two tranquil courtyards. **Pros:** modern, design-y feel; attentive service; wonderful food at the attached restaurant. **Cons:** spa on the small side; a bit of a trek to central attractions; perfumed rooms not for everyone. [$] *Rooms from: €397* ✉ *Via Forcella 6, Tortona* ☎ *02/8338371* 🌐 *www.magnapars.it* 🛏 *60 suites* 🍴 *Free Breakfast* [M] *Porta Genova; Tram No. 2, 9, or 19.*

Riomaggiore

17 km (11 miles) southwest of La Spezia, 101 km (60 miles) southeast of Genoa.

At the eastern end of the Cinque Terre, Riomaggiore is built into a river gorge (hence the name, which means "major river") and is easily accessible from La Spezia by train or car. The landscape is terraced and steep—be prepared for many stairs!—and leads to a small harbor, protected by large slabs of alabaster and marble that serve as tanning beds for sunbathers. The harbor is also the site of several outdoor cafés with fine views. According to legend, the settlement of Riomaggiore dates as far back as the 8th century, when Greek religious refugees came here to escape persecution by the Byzantine emperor.

The village is divided into two parts. If you arrive by train, you will have to pass through a tunnel that flanks the train tracks to reach the historic side of town. To avoid the crowds and get a great view of the Cinque Terre coast, walk straight uphill as soon as you exit the station.

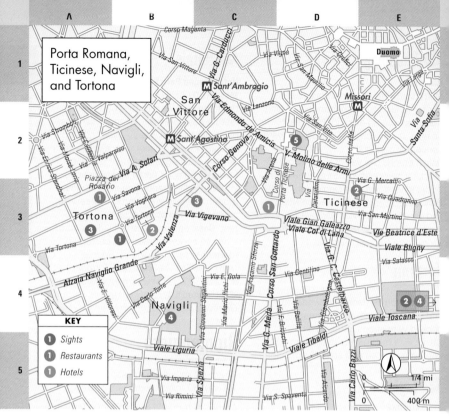

Porta Romana,
Ticinese, Navigli,
and Tortona

Sights ▼

1 Armani/Silos............. **B3**
2 Fondazione Prada **E4**
3 MUDEC (Museo delle
  Culture) **A3**
4 Navigli District **B4**
5 San Lorenzo Maggiore
  alle Colonne **D2**

Restaurants ▼

1 Al Fresco................. **A3**
2 [bu:r] di Eugenio Boer ... **E3**
3 142....................... **B3**
4 U Barba **E4**

Hotels ▼

1 Aethos Milan............. **C3**
2 Hotel Magna Pars
  Suites Milano **B3**

This winding road takes you over the hill to the 14th-century **church of St. John the Baptist,** toward the medieval town center and the Genovese-style tower houses that dot the village. Follow Via Roma (the Old Town's main street) downhill, pass under the train tracks, and you'll arrive in the charming fishermen's port. Lined with traditional fishing boats and small trattorias, this is a lovely spot for a romantic lunch or dinner. Unfortunately, Riomaggiore doesn't have as much old-world charm as its sister villages; its easy accessibility has brought traffic and more construction here than elsewhere in the Cinque Terre.

GETTING HERE AND AROUND
The enormous parking problems presented by these cliff-dwelling villages have been mitigated somewhat by a large, covered parking structure at La Spezia Centrale station, which costs around €2.50 per hour in summer. It's clean and secure (you cannot enter without a ticket code to open the door), and it's open 24/7. This is a good backup solution for those with cars, although others may choose to take a day trip from Pisa or Lucca and rely on bus and train services. Arrive early, as it can fill up by mid-morning, especially in high season.

VISITOR INFORMATION
CONTACT Riomaggiore Welcome Center. ⊠ *Riomaggiore train station, Piazza Rio Finale 26, Riomaggiore* ☎ *0187/760515* ⊕ *www.parconazionale5terre.it.*

 ## Sights

Riomaggiore
TOWN | This village at the eastern end of the Cinque Terre is built into a river gorge (hence the name, which means "river major"). It has a tiny harbor protected by large slabs of alabaster and marble, which serve as tanning beds for sunbathers as well as being the site of several outdoor cafés with fine views. According to legend, the settlement of

Riomaggiore dates as far back as the 8th century, when Greek religious refugees came here to escape persecution by the Byzantine emperor. ⊠ *Riomaggiore* ☎ *0187/920633* ⊕ *www.lamialiguria.it/en.*

Manarola

16 km (10 miles) southwest of La Spezia, 117 km (73 miles) southeast of Genoa.

The enchanting pastel houses of Manarola spill down a steep hill overlooking a spectacular turquoise swimming cove and a bustling harbor. The whole town is built on black rock. Above the town, ancient terraces still protect abundant vineyards and olive trees. This village is the center of wine and olive oil production in the region, and its streets are lined with shops selling local products.

Surrounded by steep terraced vineyards, Manarola's one road tumbles from the Chiesa di San Lorenzo (14th century) high above the village, down to the rocky port. Since the Cinque Terre wine cooperative is located in Groppo, a hamlet overlooking the village (reachable by foot or by the green park bus; ask at park offices for schedules), the vineyards are accessible. If you'd like to snap a shot of the most famous view of the town, you can walk from the port area to the cemetery above. Along the way you'll pass the town's playground, uncrowded bathrooms, and a tap with clean drinking water.

GETTING HERE AND AROUND
Though it's possible to drive and park (in a lot above town, which means walking down), it's much easier to arrive by often overly crowded train. Trains run from La Spezia or Levanto; both are very short journeys and cost around €5.

Continued on page 274

Hiking the Cinque Terre

Though often described as relaxing and easy, the Cinque Terre also have several hiking options if you wish to exert yourself a little. Many people do not realize just how demanding parts of these trails can be—it's best to come prepared. We recommend bringing a Cinque Terre Card and cash (smaller shops, eateries, and the park entrances do not accept credit cards).

When all trails are completely open, a hike through the entire region takes about four to five hours; add time for exploring each village and taking a lunch break—it's an all-day, if not two-day, trek. We recommend an early start, especially in summer when midday temperatures can rise to 90°F. Note that only Sentiero Azzurro (Trail No. 2) requires the Cinque Terre Card. The other 20-plus trails in the area are free. All trails are well marked with a red-and-white sign. Trails from village to village get progressively steeper from south (Riomaggiore) to north (Monterosso). If you're a day-tripper with a car, use the underground lot at La Spezia Centrale train station (€2.50 per hour in summer) and take the train to Riomaggiore (6–8 minutes).

Our Favorites

Other trails to consider include **Monterosso to Santuario Madonna di Soviore**, a fairly strenuous but rewarding 1½ hours up to a lovely 8th-century sanctuary. There is also a restaurant and a priceless view. **Riomaggiore to Montenero and Portovenere** is one hour up to the sanctuary and another three hours to Portovenere, passing through some gorgeous, less-traveled terrain. **Manarola to Volastra to Corniglia** runs high above the main trail and through vineyards and lesser-known villages. **Monterosso to Levanto** is a good 2½-hour hike, passing over Punta Mesco with glorious views of the Cinque Terre to the south, Corsica to the west, and the Alps to the north.

Each town has something that passes for a beach (usually with lots of pebbles or slabs of terraced rock), but there is only one option for both sand and decent swimming—in Monterosso, just across from the train station. It's equipped with chairs, umbrellas, and snack bars.

Precautions

If you're hitting the trails, carry water with you, wear sturdy shoes (hiking boots are best), and have a hat and sunscreen handy. Note that the lesser-used trails aren't as well maintained as Trail No. 2. If you're undertaking the full Trail No. 1 hike, bring something to snack on as well as your water bottle. Note that currently the Via dell'Amore and the portion of Trail No. 2 between Manarola and Corniglia are closed indefinitely due to landslides.

■ TIP→ **Check weather reports, especially in late fall and winter; thunderstorms can make shelterless trails slippery and dangerous. Rain in October and November can cause landslides and close trails altogether.**

HIKING THE CINQUE TERRE

FIVE REMOTE VILLAGES MAKE ONE MUST-SEE DESTINATION

"Charming" and "breathtaking" are adjectives that get a workout when you're traveling in Italy, but it's rare that both apply to a single location. The Cinque Terre is such a place, and this combination of characteristics goes a long way toward explaining its tremendous appeal.

The area is made up of five tiny villages (Cinque Terre literally means "Five Lands") clinging to the cliffs along a gorgeous stretch of the Ligurian coast. The terrain is so steep that for centuries footpaths were the only way to get from place to place. It just so happens that these paths provide beautiful views of the rocky coast tumbling into the sea, as well as access to secluded beaches and grottoes.

Backpackers "discovered" the Cinque Terre in the 1970s, and its popularity has been growing ever since. Despite summer crowds, much of the original appeal is intact. Each town has maintained its own distinct charm, and views from the trails in between are as breathtaking as ever.

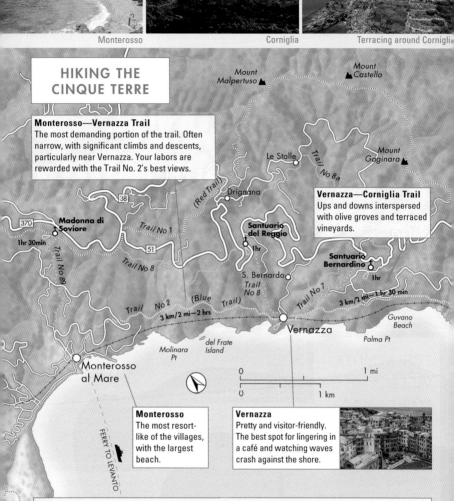

Monterosso

Corniglia

Terracing around Corniglia

HIKING THE CINQUE TERRE

Mount Malpertuso

Mount Castello

Monterosso—Vernazza Trail
The most demanding portion of the trail. Often narrow, with significant climbs and descents, particularly near Vernazza. Your labors are rewarded with the Trail No. 2's best views.

Le Stalle

Trail No 8a

Mount Goginara

(Red Trail)

Drignana

Vernazza—Corniglia Trail
Ups and downs interspersed with olive groves and terraced vineyards.

38

Santuario del Reggio

370

Madonna di Soviore

Trail No 1

1hr

Santuario Bernardino

1hr 30min

51

S. Bernardo

1hr

Trail No 8

Trail No 89

Trail No 8

Trail No 7

3 km/2 mi—1 hr 30 min

Trail No 2 (Blue Trail)

3 km/2 mi—2 hrs

Vernazza

Guvano Beach

del Frate Island

Molinara Pt

Palma Pt

Monterosso al Mare

0   1 mi

0   1 km

FERRY TO LEVANTO

Monterosso
The most resort-like of the villages, with the largest beach.

Vernazza
Pretty and visitor-friendly. The best spot for lingering in a café and watching waves crash against the shore.

THE CLASSIC HIKE

Hiking is the most popular way to experience the Cinque Terre, and Trail No. 2, the Sentiero Azzurro (Blue Trail), is the most traveled path. To cover the entire trail is a full day: it's approximately 13 km (8 miles) in length, takes you to all five villages, and requires about five hours, not including stops, to complete. The best approach is to start at the eastern-most town of Riomaggiore and warm up your legs on the easiest segment of the trail. As you work your way west, the hike gets progressively more demanding. Between Corniglia and Manarola take the ferry (which provides its own beautiful views) or the inland train running between the towns instead.

Manarola   Along Lovers' Lane   Via dell'Amore

Corniglia—Manarola Trail
This section of the trail is currently closed.

Manarola—Riomaggiore Trail
Known as the Via dell'Amore (Lovers' Lane). A wide, paved, flat path with fine views.

KEY

····················	*Major footpaths*
- - - - - - -	*Sanctuary footpaths*
· · · · · · ·	*Connecting footpaths*
⟶ 45min ⟶	*Hiking times*
⚲	*Sanctuaries*

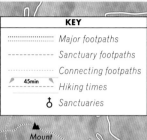

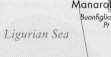

Corniglia
Perched on a cliff 300 feet above the sea, reached by a switchback path (or by shuttle bus).

Manarola
The most photogenic of the villages, best seen from the cemetery a few minutes up the path toward Corniglia.

Riomaggiore
Cliff-clinging buildings are almost as striking as those in Manarola. Stairs to the left of the train station entrance cross over the tracks and lead to the trailhead.

BEYOND TRAIL NO.2

Trail No. 2 is just one of a network of trails crisscrossing the hills. If you're a dedicated hiker, spend a few nights and try some of the other routes. Trail No. 1, the Sentiero Rosso (Red Trail), climbs from Portovenere (east of Riomaggiore) and returns to the sea at Levanto (west of Monterosso al Mare). To hike its length takes from 9 to 12 hours; the ridge-top trail provides spectacular views from high above the villages, each of which can be reached via a steep path. Other shorter trails go from the villages up into the hills, some leading to religious sanctuaries. Trail No. 9, for example, starts from the old section of Monterosso and ends at the Madonna di Soviore Sanctuary.

Accessing Cinque Terre Trails

When to Go

The ideal times to visit the Cinque Terre are September and May, when the weather is mild and the summer tourist season isn't in full swing (June through August can be unbearably hot and crowded).

Getting Here and Around

Between mid-March and mid-October there is a local train between La Spezia and Levanto that stops at each of the Cinque Terre villages, and runs approximately every 30 minutes throughout the day. Tickets for each leg of the journey (around €5) are available at all five train stations. In Corniglia, the only one of the Cinque Terre that isn't at sea level, a shuttle service (€2) is provided for those who don't wish to climb (or descend) the 300-plus steps that link the train station with the cliff-top town.

The Explora 5 Terre shuttle-bus operates a daily service between La Spezia and the villages; a day ticket costs €18.50.

Along the Cinque Terre coast two ferry lines operate. From June to September, Golfo Paradiso runs from Genoa and Camogli to Monterosso al Mare and Vernazza (a round-trip ticket costs €45). Other tours are also available. From late March to October, the smaller but more frequent Golfo

dei Poeti stops at each village from Lerici (east of Riomaggiore) to Monterosso, with the exception of Corniglia, two to five times a day (a round-trip ticket costs €28–€39); you can also purchase one-way tickets.

Admission

Entrance tickets for using the trails are available at ticket booths located at the start of each section of Trail No. 2, and at information offices in the Levanto, Monterosso, Vernazza, Corniglia, Manarola, Riomaggiore, and La Spezia train stations. A one-day Cinque Terre Card costs €7.50, which includes a trail map and an information leaflet; a two-day pass is €14.50.

The Cinque Terre Carta Treno, which allows access to the park plus unlimited daily use of the regional train between La Spezia, the five villages, and Levanto just north of Monterosso, costs €18.20 for a one-day pass, €33 for a two-day pass, and €47 for a three-day pass.

For More Information

⊕ www.cinqueterre.com; www. lecinqueterre.org; www.parconazionale5terre.it; www.rebuildmonterosso. com; www.savevernazza.com; www. littleparadiso.com (blog); www. explora5terre.it; www.golfoparadiso.it; www.navigazionegolfodeipoeti.it.

VISITOR INFORMATION
CONTACT Manarola Welcome Center.
✉ Manarola train station, Via dell'Amore, Manarola ☎ 0187/760511 ⊕ www.parconazionale5terre.it.

Sights

Manarola

TOWN | Enchanting pastel houses spill down a steep hill overlooking a spectacular turquoise swimming cove and a bustling harbor. The whole town is built on black rock. Above the town, ancient terraces still protect abundant vineyards and olive trees. This village is the center of the wine and olive oil production of the region, and its streets are lined with shops selling local products. ⊠ *Manarola* ☎ *0187/760511* ⊕ *www.lamialiguria.it/en, www.parconazionale5terre.it.*

Hotels

★ La Torretta

$$$$ | **HOTEL** | One of the Cinque Terre's few "boutique" hotels is in a 17th-century tower that sits high on the hill above the rainbow-hue village of Manarola, with truly lovely views of the terraced vineyards, colorful village homes, and the Mediterranean sea; inside, decor is chic, sleek, and antiques-bedecked. **Pros:** no-smoking policy; free luggage transfer; stellar staff. **Cons:** steep walk up to the hotel; some rooms are small; books up quickly. $ *Rooms from: €330* ⊠ *Vico Volto 20, Cinque Terre, Manarola* ☎ *0187/920327* ⊕ *www.torrettas.com* ◷ *Closed Nov.–Mar.* ⌁ *15 rooms* ⍾ *Free Breakfast.*

Corniglia

27 km (17 miles) northwest of La Spezia, 100 km (60 miles) southeast of Genoa.

The buildings, narrow lanes, and stairways of Corniglia are strung together amid vineyards high on the cliffs. On a clear day, views of the entire coastal strip are excellent, from Elba in the south to the Italian Alps in the north. The high perch and lack of harbor make this farming community the most remote and therefore least crowded of the Cinque Terre. In fact, the 365 steps that lead up from the train station to the town center dissuade many tourists from making the hike to the village. You can also take the green park bus, but they run infrequently and are usually packed with tired hikers.

Corniglia is built along one road edged with small shops, bars, gelaterias, and restaurants. Midway along Via Fieschi is the **Largo Taragio,** the main square and heart of the village. Shaded by leafy trees and umbrellas, this is a lovely spot for a mid-hike gelato break. Here you'll find the 14th-century Chiesa di San Pietro. The church's rose window of marble imported from Carrara is impressive, particularly considering the work required to get it here!

GETTING HERE AND AROUND

This town has very limited parking and it's much simpler to take the train from either La Spezia or Levanto.

VISITOR INFORMATION
CONTACT Corniglia Welcome Center. ⊠ *Corniglia train station, Via alla Stazione, Corniglia* ☎ *0187/812523* ⊕ *www. parconazionale5terre.it.*

Sights

Corniglia

TOWN | Stone buildings, narrow lanes, and stairways are strung together amid vineyards high on the cliffs; on a clear day views of the entire coastal strip are excellent. The high perch and lack of harbor make this farming community the most remote of the Cinque Terre. ⊠ *Corniglia* ☎ *0187/812523* ⊕ *www.lamialiguria.it/en, www.parconazionale5terre.it.*

San Pietro

CHURCH | On a pretty pastel square sits the 14th-century church of San Pietro. The rose window of marble imported from Carrara is impressive, particularly considering the work required to get it here. ⊠ *Via Fieschi 19, Corniglia* ⛺ *Free.*

Vernazza

27 km (17 miles) west of La Spezia, 96 km (59 miles) southeast of Genoa.

With its narrow streets and small squares, Vernazza is arguably the most charming of the Cinque Terre towns, and usually the most crowded. Historically, it was the most important of them and—since Vernazza was the only one fortunate enough to have a natural port—the wealthiest, as evidenced by the elaborate arcades, loggias, and marble work lining Via Roma and Piazza Marconi.

The village's pink slate-roof houses and colorful squares contrast with the remains of the medieval fort and castle, including two towers, in the old town. The Romans first inhabited this rocky spit of land in the 1st century. Today, Vernazza has a fairly lively social scene. Piazza Marconi looks out across Vernazza's small sandy beach to the sea, toward Monterosso. The numerous restaurants and bars crowd their tables and umbrellas on the outskirts of the piazza, creating a patchwork of sights and sounds that form one of the most unique and beautiful places in the world.

GETTING HERE AND AROUND
Driving to Vernazza is complicated, and it's much easier to take a short train ride from either La Spezia or Levanto. Trains run frequently.

VISITOR INFORMATION
CONTACT Vernazza Welcome Center. ✉ *Vernazza train station, Via Roma 51, Vernazza* ☎ *0187/028316* ⊕ *www.parconazionale-5terre.it.*

 ## Sights

Vernazza
TOWN | With narrow streets and small squares, the village that many consider to be the most charming of the five towns has the best access to the sea—a geographic reality that made the village wealthier than its neighbors, as evidenced by the elaborate arcades, loggias, and marble work. The village's pink, slate-roof houses and colorful squares contrast with the remains of the medieval fort and castle, including two towers, in the old town. The Romans first inhabited this rocky spit of land in the 1st century.

Today, Vernazza has a fairly lively social scene. It's a great place to refuel with a hearty seafood lunch or linger in a café between links of the seaside hike. ✉ *Vernazza* ☎ *0187/028316* ⊕ *www.lamialiguria.it/en, www.parconazionale5terre.it.*

 ## Restaurants

Gambero Rosso
$$$ | **LIGURIAN** | Relax on Vernazza's main square at this fine trattoria looking out onto the church of Santa Maria d'Antiochi. Enjoy such delectable dishes as shrimp salad, vegetable torte, and *risotto alla ciccio* (with squid, prawns, and mussels). **Known for:** piazza view; fresh seafood; pesto dishes. $ *Average main: €33* ✉ *Piazza Marconi 7, Vernazza* ☎ *0187/812265* ⊕ *www.ristorantegamberorosso.net* ⊘ *Closed Thurs. and Nov.–late Mar.*

★ Ristorante Belforte
$$ | **LIGURIAN** | High above the sea in one of Vernazza's remaining medieval stone towers is this unique spot serving delicious Cinque Terre cuisine such as branzino *sotto sale* (cooked under salt), *tagliolini al nero di seppia con gamberi* (fresh pasta with squid ink sauce and prawns), and *polpo di scoglio alla griglia* (grilled octopus). The setting is magnificent, so try for an outdoor table. **Known for:** incredible views; grilled octopus; lively atmosphere. $ *Average main: €20* ✉ *Via Guidoni 42, Vernazza* ☎ *0187/812222* ⊕ *www.ristorantebelforte.it* ⊘ *Closed Tues. and Nov.–late Mar.*

 ## Hotels

La Malà
$$ | **B&B/INN** | A cut above other lodging options in the Cinque Terre, these small guest rooms are equipped with flat-screen TVs, air-conditioning, marble showers, and comfortable bedding and have views of the sea or the port, which can also be enjoyed at their most bewitching from a shared terrace literally

suspended over the Mediterranean. **Pros:** clean, fresh-feeling rooms; views; helpful, attentive staff. **Cons:** some stairs are involved; books up quickly; child-friendly (either a pro or a con). $ *Rooms from: €170* ✉ *Via San Giovanni Battista 29, Vernazza* ☎ *334/2875718 mobile* ⊕ *www. lamala.it* ⊙ *Closed early Jan.–late Feb.* ⤳ *4 rooms* ⑩ *Free Breakfast.*

Monterosso al Mare

32 km (20 miles) northwest of La Spezia, 89 km (55 miles) southeast of Genoa.

It's the combined draw of beautiful beaches, rugged cliffs, crystal clear turquoise waters, and plentiful small hotels and restaurants that has made Monterosso al Mare the largest of the Cinque Terre villages (population 1,800) and also the busiest in midsummer.

And Monterosso has festivals enough to match its size. They start with the Lemon Feast on the Saturday before Ascension Sunday. Then, on the second Sunday after Pentecost, comes the Flower Festival of Corpus Christi: during the afternoon, the streets and alleyways of the historic center are decorated with thousands of colorful flower petals, set in beautiful designs, over which an evening procession passes. Finally, the Salted Anchovy and Olive Oil Festival takes place each year during the second weekend of September.

GETTING HERE AND AROUND
The largest of the "Five Lands," it's possible to drive and park nearby, but it's best to take the train either from La Spezia or Levanto.

VISITOR INFORMATION
CONTACT Monterosso al Mare Welcome Center. ✉ *Monterosso al Mare train station, Via Fegina 40, Monterosso al Mare* ☎ *0187/817059* ⊕ *www.parconazionale-5terre.it.*

Restaurants

★ Enoteca Internazionale
$ | **WINE BAR** | Located on the main street, this bar offers a large selection of wines, both local and from farther afield, plus delicious light fare; its umbrella-covered patio is a welcoming spot to recuperate after a day of hiking. Susanna, the owner, is a certified sommelier who's always forthcoming with helpful suggestions on pairing local wines with their tasty bruschettas. **Known for:** extensive wine list; patio dining; helpful staff. $ *Average main: €13* ✉ *Via Roma 62, Monterosso al Mare* ☎ *0187/817278* ⊕ *www.enotecainternazionale.com* ⊙ *Closed Jan. and Feb.*

★ Miky
$$$ | **SEAFOOD** | This is arguably the best restaurant in Monterosso, specializing in tasty, fresh seafood dishes like grilled calamari and monkfish ravioli. If their *catalana* (poached lobster and shrimp with sliced raw fennel and carrot) happens to be on the menu, know that it's a winner. **Known for:** sunny seaside setting; fresh seafood; fine dining. $ *Average main: €28* ✉ *Via Fegina 104, Monterosso al Mare* ☎ *0187/817608* ⊕ *www.ristorantemiky.it* ⊙ *Closed Tues. and Nov.–Mar.*

Hotels

Bellambra
$$$ | **B&B/INN** | Modern rooms with charm and comfort in the heart of the old town make this place a terrific base for exploring the Cinque Terre. **Pros:** an apartment for up to six people; spacious rooms and bathrooms; central location. **Cons:** can be a bit noisy; no elevator with steep, narrow stairs; books up quickly. $ *Rooms from: €250* ✉ *Via Roma 64, Monterosso al Mare* ☎ *392/0121912 mobile* ⊕ *www. bellambra5terre.com* ⤳ *4 rooms* ⑩ *Free Breakfast.*

★ Il Giardino Incantato

$$ | **B&B/INN** | With wood-beam ceilings and stone walls, the stylishly restored and updated rooms in this 16th-century house in the historic center of Monterosso ooze comfort and old-world charm. **Pros:** spacious rooms; gorgeous garden; excellent hosts. **Cons:** no views; no under-14s or pets; there are only four rooms so books up quickly. [$] *Rooms from: €200* ✉ *Via Mazzini 18, Monterosso al Mare* ☎ *0187/818315* 🌐 *www.ilgiardinoincantato.net* 🕒 *Closed Nov.–Mar.* 🛏 *4 rooms* 🍴 *Free Breakfast.*

Porto Roca

$$$ | **HOTEL** | Far from the madding crowds, one of Cinque Terre's only high-end hotels is perched on the famous terraced cliffs right over the main beach, with large balconies to savor panoramic views of the magnificent sea. **Pros:** unobstructed sea views; tranquil location; shuttle bus into town (though walking there is eminently possible). **Cons:** two- or three-night minimum stay in high season; back-facing rooms can be a bit dark; somewhat removed from town. [$] *Rooms from: €210* ✉ *Via Corone 1, Monterosso al Mare* ☎ *0187/817502* 🌐 *www.portoroca.it* 🕒 *Closed early Nov.–early Apr.* 🛏 *43 rooms* 🍴 *Free Breakfast.*

Bologna

117 km (72 miles) north of Florence in Tuscany, 57 km (35 miles) southeast of Modena.

Bologna, a city rich with cultural jewels, has long been one of the best-kept secrets in northern Italy. Tourists in the know bask in the shadow of its leaning medieval towers and devour the city's wonderful food.

The charm of the centro storico, with its red-arcaded passageways and sidewalks, can be attributed to wise city counselors who, at the beginning of the 13th century, decreed that roads couldn't be built without *portici* (porticoes). Were these counselors to return to town eight centuries later, they'd marvel at how little has changed.

Bologna, with a population of about 388,000, has a university-town vibe—and it feels young and lively in a way that many other Italian cities don't.

GETTING HERE AND AROUND

Frequent train service from Florence to Bologna makes getting here easy. The Italo and Frecciarossa and Frecciargento (high-speed trains) run several times an hour and take just under 40 minutes. Otherwise, you're left with the *regionale* (regional) trains, which putter along and get you to Bologna in around 1¾ hours. The historic center is an interesting and relatively effortless walk from the station—though it takes about 20 minutes.

If you're driving from Florence, take the A1, exiting onto the A14, and then get on the RA1 to Exit 7–Bologna Centrale. The trip takes about an hour. From Milan, take the A1, exiting to the A14 as you near the city; from there, take the A13 and exit at Bologna; then follow the RA1 to Exit 7–Bologna Centrale. The trip takes just under three hours.

VISITOR INFORMATION

Bologna Welcome card (from €25) offers free and discounted entry to many sights, including the Musei Civici for up to 15 days (🌐 *www.bolognawelcome.com/en/information/bologna-welcome-card-eng*).

CONTACT Bologna Tourism Offices. ✉ *Piazza Maggiore 1/e, Bologna* ☎ *051/6583111* 🌐 *www.bolognawelcome.com.*

Sights

Basilica di San Petronio

CHURCH | Construction on this vast cathedral began in 1390; and the work still isn't finished more than 600 years later. Above the center of the door is a Madonna and Child flanked by Saints Ambrose and Petronius, the city's patrons. Michelangelo, Giulio Romano, and Andrea Palladio (among others), submitted designs for the facade, which were all eventually rejected. The Bolognesi had planned an even bigger church but had to tone down construction when the university seat was established next door in 1561. The most important art in the church is in the fourth chapel on the left: these frescoes by Giovanni di Modena date to 1410–15. ⊠ *Piazza Galvani 5, Piazza Maggiore* ☎ *051/231415* ⊕ *www. basilicadisanpetronio.org* ⊡ *Free* ⊙ *Museo di San Petronio closed Mon.*

Fontana del Nettuno

FOUNTAIN | Sculptor Giambologna's elaborate 1563–66 Baroque fountain and monument to Neptune occupying Piazza Nettuno has been aptly nicknamed "Il Gigante" (The Giant). Its exuberantly sensual mermaids and undraped god of the sea drew fire when it was constructed—but not enough, apparently, to dissuade the populace from using the fountain as a public washing stall for centuries. ⊠ *Piazza del Nettuno, next to Palazzo Re Enzo, Piazza Maggiore.*

Le Due Torri

NOTABLE BUILDING | FAMILY | Two landmark medieval towers, mentioned by Dante in *The Inferno*, stand side by side in the compact Piazza di Porta Ravegnana. Once, every family of importance had a tower as a symbol of prestige and power (and as a potential fortress). Now only 24 remain out of nearly 100 that once presided over the city. Torre Garisenda (late 11th century), which tilts 10 feet off perpendicular, was shortened to 157 feet in the 1300s and is now closed to visitors. Torre degli Asinelli (1119) is 318 feet tall and leans 7½ feet. If you're up to a serious physical challenge—and not claustrophobic—you may want to climb its 498 narrow, wooden steps to get the view over Bologna. ⊠ *Piazza di Porta Ravegnana, East of Piazza Maggiore* ☎ *051/6583111* ⊕ *www.duetorribologna. com* ⊡ *€5* ⚠ *Reservations essential.*

★ MAMbo and Museo Morandi

ART MUSEUM | The museum—the name stands for Museo d'Arte Moderna di Bologna, or Bologna's Museum of Modern Art—houses a permanent collection of modern art. All of this is set within the sleek minimalist structure built in 1915 as the Forno del Pane, a large bakery. Seek out the powerful Arte e Ideologia section for Guttuso's *Funerali di Togliatti* (1972), a charged symbol of pride and pain for many Bolognesi and Italiani. The work of Bologna's celebrated abstract painter Giorgio Morandi (1890–64), known for his muted still life paintings of domestic objects and landscapes, can be viewed at the Museo Morandi here. The fab bookshop and MAMbo Cafè complete the complex. ⊠ *Via Don Minzoni 14, Bologna* ☎ *051/6496611* ⊕ *www.mambo-bologna. org* ⊡ *€6 permanent collection; €6 temporary shows* ⊙ *Closed Mon.*

Museo Internazionale e Biblioteca della Musica di Bologna

OTHER MUSEUM | The music museum in the spectacular Palazzo Aldini-Sanguinetti, with its 17th- and 18th-century frescoes, offers among its exhibits a 1606 harpsichord and a collection of beautiful music manuscripts dating from the 1500s. ⊠ *Strada Maggiore 34, University area* ☎ *051/2757711* ⊕ *www.museibologna.it/musica* ⊡ *€5* ⊙ *Closed Mon.*

Palazzo Comunale

GOVERNMENT BUILDING | When Bologna was an independent city-state, this huge palace dating from the 13th to 15th century was the seat of government—a function it still serves today in a building that is a mélange of styles. Over the door is a statue of Bologna-born Pope Gregory XIII (reigned 1572–85), most famous for reorganizing the calendar. The Collezioni Comunali d'Arte museum exhibits medieval paintings as well as some Renaissance works by Luca Signorelli (circa 1445–1523) and Tintoretto (1518–94). ⊠ *Piazza Maggiore 6, Piazza Maggiore* ☎ *051/2193998 Collezioni Comunali*

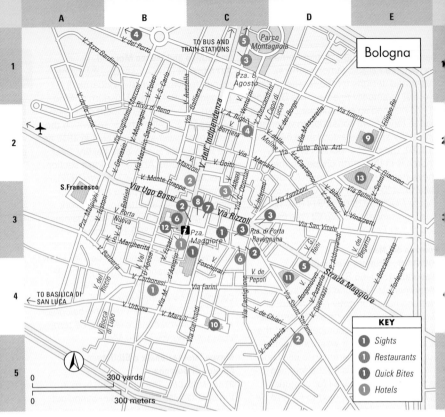

Bologna

Sights ▼

1 Basilica di
San Petronio **C3**

2 Fontana del Nettuno..... **C3**

3 Le Due Torri.............. **C3**

4 MAMbo and
Museo Morandi......... **B1**

5 Museo Internazionale
e Biblioteca della
Musica di Bologna **D4**

6 Palazzo Comunale **B3**

7 Palazzo del Podestà..... **C3**

8 Palazzo Re Enzo.......... **C3**

9 Pinacoteca Nazionale... **E2**

10 San Domenico **C4**

11 Santo Stefano........... **D4**

12 Torre dell'Orologio
(Clock Tower)............ **B3**

13 Università di Bologna ... **E2**

Restaurants ▼

1 Da Cesari **B4**

2 Drogheria della Rosa... **D4**

3 Ristorante I Portici....... **C1**

4 Trattoria
Caffè del Rosso **C2**

5 Trattoria di Via Serra **C1**

6 Trattoria Gianni
a la Vecia Bulagna....... **C3**

Quick Bites ▼

1 Mercato di Mezzo **C3**

2 Sfoglia Rina.............. **C3**

3 Tamburini **C3**

Hotels ▼

1 Art Hotel Orologio **B3**

2 Grand Hotel
Majestic già Baglioni.... **C3**

3 Hotel Corona D'Oro...... **C3**

d'Arte, 051/2194400 Sala Borsa ⊕ www. museibologna.it ✉ Collezioni Comunali d'Arte €6; Sala Borsa free ☉ Collezioni Comunali d'Arte closed Mon.; Sala Borsa closed Sun.

Palazzo del Podestà
NOTABLE BUILDING | This classic Renaissance palace facing the Basilica di San Petronio was erected from 1484–94, and attached to it is the soaring Torre dell'Arengo. The bells in the tower have rung whenever the city has celebrated, mourned, or called its citizens to arms. It may not be open to the public, but head under the palazzo's atmospheric vaulted arches to experience the resonant magic of the Voltone del Podestà: whisper into the right-angled brick walls below a saintly statue to communicate with a pal opposite. ✉ *Piazza Maggiore 1, Piazza Maggiore.*

Palazzo Re Enzo
CASTLE/PALACE | Built in 1244, this palace became home to King Enzo of Sardinia, who was imprisoned here in 1249 after he was captured during the fierce battle of Fossalta. He died here 23 years later. The palace has other macabre associations as well: common criminals received last rites in the tiny courtyard chapel before being executed in Piazza Maggiore. The colonnaded courtyard is worth a peek, and its two grand *saloni* (salons) are used for events including concerts. ✉ *Piazza del Nettuno 1/c, Piazza Maggiore* ☎ *051/6583192* ⊕ *www. palazzoreenzo.com.*

Pinacoteca Nazionale
ART GALLERY | Bologna's principal art gallery contains many works by the immortals of Italian painting; its prize possession is the *Ecstasy of St. Cecilia* by Raphael (1483–1520). There's also a beautiful polyptych by Giotto (1267–1337), as well as *Madonna with Child and Saints Margaret, Jerome, and Petronius* (altarpiece of St. Margaret) by Parmigianino (1503–40); note the rapt eye contact between St. Margaret and

the Christ child. ✉ *Via delle Belle Arti 56, University area* ☎ *051/4209411* ⊕ *www. pinacotecabologna.beniculturali.it* ✉ *€8* ☉ *Closed Mon.*

San Domenico
CHURCH | The tomb of St. Dominic, who died here in 1221, is called the Arca di San Domenico and is found in this church in the sixth chapel on the right. Many artists participated in its decoration, notably Niccolò di Bari, who was so proud of his 15th-century contribution that he changed his name to Niccolò dell'Arca to recall this famous work. The young Michelangelo (1475–1564) carved the angel on the right and the image of San Petronio. In the right transept of the church is a tablet marking the last resting place of hapless King Enzo, the Sardinian ruler imprisoned in the Palazzo Re Enzo. The attached museum contains religious relics. ✉ *Piazza San Domenico 13, off Via Garibaldi, South of Piazza Maggiore* ☎ *051/6400411* ⊕ *www.sandomenicobologna.it.*

★ Santo Stefano
CHURCH | This splendid and unusual basilica contains between four and seven connected churches (authorities differ). A 4th-century temple dedicated to Isis originally occupied this site, but much of what you see was erected between the 10th and 12th centuries. Just outside the church, which probably dates from the 5th century (with later alterations), is the Cortile di Pilato (Pilate's Courtyard), named for the basin in the center. Despite the fact that the basin was probably crafted around the 8th century, legend has it that Pontius Pilate washed his hands in it after condemning Christ. ✉ *Piazza Santo Stefano, Via Santo Stefano 24, University area* ☎ *051/4983423* ⊕ *www.santostefanobologna.it* ☉ *Closed during services.*

Torre dell'Orologio (Clock Tower)
CLOCK | For a spectacular view of Piazza Maggiore and the Bolognesi hills from two terraces as well as a look at how

Bologna's oldest clock keeps the city punctual, climb the Torre dell'Orologio, or d'Arccursio tower. Opened to the public in 2021, it was built in 1249 as University of Bologna law professor Accursio da Bagnolo's monumental timepiece for his home in the piazza. The clock mechanism you'll see dates from 1773, as found on the horologist's inscription "Rinaldo Gandofli Accademic Clementi Fece 1773," among the clock's movement, gears, and swinging pendulum. ✉ *Piazza Maggiore 6, Bologna* ☎ *051/6583111* 🌐 *www.bolognawelcome.com* 🎟 *€8* 🕒 *Closed Mon.* ✍ *Reservations required.*

★ Università di Bologna

COLLEGE | Take a stroll through the streets of the university area: a jumble of buildings, some dating as far back as the 15th century and most to the 17th and 18th. The neighborhood, as befits a college town, is full of bookshops, coffee bars, and inexpensive restaurants. Political slogans and sentiments are scrawled on walls all around the university and tend to be ferociously leftist, sometimes juvenile, and often entertaining. Among the 15 university museums, the most interesting is the Museo di Palazzo Poggi, which displays scientific instruments plus paleontological and botanical artifacts. ✉ *Via Zamboni 33, University area* ☎ *051/2099610 museum* 🌐 *sma.unibo.it/it/il-sistema-museale/museo-di-palazzo-poggi* 🎟 *€7 museum* 🕒 *Closed Mon.*

🍴 Restaurants

★ Da Cesari

$$ | **EMILIAN** | Host Paolino Cesari has been presiding over his eatery since 1962, and he and his staff go out of their way to make you feel at home. The food's terrific, and if you love pork products, try anything on the menu with *mora romagnola*: Paolino has direct contact with the people who raise this breed that nearly became extinct (he calls it "my pig"). **Known for:** pork dishes like flavorful salame; wine list with lots of local bottles; traditional setting. [$] *Average main: €19* ✉ *Via de' Carbonesi 8, South of Piazza Maggiore* ☎ *051/237710* 🌐 *www.da-cesari.it* 🕒 *Closed Sun., Aug., and 1 wk in Jan.*

Drogheria della Rosa

$$ | **EMILIAN** | Chef Emanuele Addone, who presides over his intimate little restaurant set in an ex-pharmacy, hits the food markets every day and buys what looks good, ensuring seasonality. He sauces his tortelli stuffed with *squacquerone* and *stracchino* (two creamy, fresh cow's-milk cheeses) with artichokes, zucchini flowers, or mushrooms, depending on the time of year. **Known for:** idiosyncratic surroundings; seasonal filled tortelli; no written menu. [$] *Average main: €19* ✉ *Via Cartoleria 10, University area* ☎ *051/222529* 🌐 *www.drogheriadellarosa.it* 🕒 *No dinner Sun. Closed Mon.*

Ristorante I Portici

$$$$ | **EMILIAN** | The frescoed ceiling, parquet flooring, and live classical music are clues that this sophisticated restaurant (part of the hotel of the same name) occupies a former theater and *café-chantant,* or musical venue, from the late 19th century. It's the perfect setting for an evening of fine dining featuring mainly Emilian-inspired dishes with modern touches and the vision of young chef Nicola Annunziata. **Known for:** sumptuous surroundings in a former theater; sophisticated culinary offerings; refined and attentive service. [$] *Average main: €50* ✉ *Via dell'Indipendenza 69, North of Piazza Maggiore* ☎ *051/42185* 🌐 *www.iporticihotel.com* 🕒 *Closed Sun. and Mon. No lunch.*

Trattoria Caffè del Rosso

$ | **EMILIAN** | Here, in the mirrored interior, a mostly young crowd chows down on classic regional fare at affordable prices. Nimble staff bearing multiple plates sashay neatly between the closely spaced tables delivering such standards as tortellini in brodo and *cotoletta alla Bolognese* (veal with Parmigiano-Reggiano and prosciutto). **Known for:** student haunt with great-value regional food; affordable wine list; fun atmosphere. $ Average main: €14 ⊠ Via Augusto Righi 30/A, University area ☎ 051/236730 ⊕ trattoria-caffe-del-rosso-bologna.business.site ⊗ No dinner Sun.

Trattoria di Via Serra

$$ | **EMILIAN** | At this simple trattoria off the main tourist circuit, much care has been taken with the decor: the rooms, overseen by host Flavio, are small and intimate, and the wooden walls painted a creamy whitish gray. Chef Tommaso gives equal care to the menu and deftly turns out Bolognese classics, as well as dishes with a modern twist—among the antipasti, his *tosone fresco avvolto nella pancetta* incorporates Parmigiano-Reggiano, unsmoked bacon, and greens. **Known for:** all locally sourced ingredients; modern riffs on classic dishes; convivial atmosphere. $ Average main: €18 ⊠ Via Serra 9B, Beyond the City Center ☎ 051/6312330 ⊕ www.trattoriadiviaserra.it ⊗ Closed Sun., Mon., and Aug.

★ Trattoria Gianni a la Vecia Bulagna

$$ | **EMILIAN** | At the bottom of an alley off Piazza Maggiore, this unassuming place—known to locals as simply "Da Gianni"—is all about food. The usual starters are on hand—including a tasty tortellini in brodo—in addition to daily specials; bollito misto (mixed boiled meat) is a fine option here, and the *cotechino con puré di patate* (pork sausage with mashed potatoes) is elevated to sublimity by the accompanying salsa verde. **Known for:** tortellini in brodo; efficient and friendly service; busy local spot. $ Average main: €20 ⊠ Via Clavature 18, Piazza Maggiore ☎ 051/229434 ⊕ www.trattoria-gianni.it ⊗ Closed Mon. and 1 wk in early Jan. No dinner Sun.

☕ Coffee and Quick Bites

Mercato di Mezzo

$ | **ITALIAN** | **FAMILY** | This former fruit and vegetable market, established in medieval times and transformed into a covered market after unification, has now morphed into a fancy gourmet food hall. Various outlets offer quality Bologna classics plus some innovations, including tortellini and tortelloni at DeGusto Coop; pizza at Rossopomodoro; panini, pasta, and cold cuts at L'Antica Bottega; and fried fish and quirky fish hamburgers at Pescheria del Pavaglione. **Known for:** great wines by the glass; buzzy Bolognesi atmosphere; its pork and cheese products. $ Average main: €14 ⊠ Via Clavature 12, Piazza Maggiore ☎ 379/1855172 mobile ⊕ www.facebook.com/mercatodimezzobologna ⊗ Closed Mon.

Sfoglia Rina

$ | **ITALIAN** | **FAMILY** | The *pastaio* (pasta-maker) tradition in this bright honeycomb tiled pasta shop and restaurant—which often has a line around the block—started nearly 60 years ago in a town about 9½ km (6 miles) southwest of Bologna. There, Rina De Franceschi rolled *sfoglia* (dough) following family recipes. **Known for:** fresh pasta in many varieties; weekly vegetarian-friendly specials; affordable and wide-ranging menu. $ Average main: €11 ⊠ Via Castiglione 5/b, Bologna ☎ 051/9911710 ⊕ www.sfogliarina.it.

★ Tamburini

$ | **WINE BAR** | Two small rooms inside plus kegs and bar stools outside make up this lively, packed little spot. The overwhelming plate of *affettati misti* is crammed with top-quality local cured meats and succulent cheeses, and the adjacent salumeria offers many wonderful items to take away. **Known for:** cheese and cured meat plates; abundant portions; lively atmosphere with a vast wine selection. $ Average main: €12 ⊠ Via Caprarie

1, Piazza Maggiore ☎ *051/234726* 🌐 *www.tamburini.com.*

Hotels

★ Art Hotel Orologio

$$ | **HOTEL** | **FAMILY** | The location of this stylish and welcoming family-run hotel can't be beat: it's right around the corner from Piazza Maggiore on a quiet piazza. **Pros:** central location; family-friendly rooms; welcomes all animals. **Cons:** some street noise; pet-friendly environment may not appeal to allergy sufferers; limited facilities. [$] *Rooms from: €199* ✉ *Via IV Novembre 10, Piazza Maggiore* ☎ *051/7457411* 🌐 *www.art-hotel-orologio.com* 🛏 *34 rooms* 🍴 *Free Breakfast.*

Grand Hotel Majestic già Baglioni

$$$$ | **HOTEL** | From the marble lobby to the luxury rooftop-terrace suites, Bologna's oldest and grandest hotel, set in an 18th-century palazzo impresses with its classical aristocratic French decor and top-notch food. **Pros:** central location; spa and gym; sophisticated Carracci restaurant dining. **Cons:** poor soundproofing and street noise in some rooms; breakfast could be better; service may feel aloof to some. [$] *Rooms from: €400* ✉ *Via dell'Indipendenza 8, Piazza Maggiore* ☎ *051/225445* 🌐 *grandhotelmajestic.duetorrihotels.com* 🛏 *106 rooms* 🍴 *Free Breakfast.*

Hotel Corona D'Oro

$$$$ | **HOTEL** | Elegance and historic charm are the keynotes of this converted medieval palazzo once belonging to the powerful Azzoguidi family, just a short stroll from Piazza Maggiore and all the main attractions. **Pros:** helpful, friendly staff; spacious and silent rooms; historic character. **Cons:** steps on some floors are not ideal for anyone with mobility issues; no restaurant; some rooms are small. [$] *Rooms from: €399* ✉ *Via Oberdan 12, Bologna* ☎ *051/7457611* 🌐 *www.hco.it* 🛏 *40 rooms* 🍴 *Free Breakfast.*

Nightlife

BARS

Le Stanze

BARS | At Le Stanze you can sip an aperitivo or a late-night drink amid a young and noisy clientele. The incredibly grand decor includes 17th-century frescoes in what was once the private chapel of the Palazzo Bentivoglio. The adjoining restaurant offers a small selection of Bologna favorites. ✉ *Via del Borgo di San Pietro 1, University area* ☎ *051/228767* 🌐 *www.lestanzecafe.it.*

Nu Lounge Bar

BARS | This high-energy tiki bar draws a cocktail-loving crowd that enjoys fun drinks such as "Hellvis," made with lime, agave syrup, rum, grenadine, ginger, and Angostura. ✉ *Via de' Musei 6, off Buca San Petronio, Piazza Maggiore* ☎ *051/222532* 🌐 *www.nuloungebar.com.*

★ Osteria del Sole

WINE BARS | Although "osteria" in an establishment's name suggests that food will be served, such is not the case here. This place is all about drinking wine; the entrance door has warnings such as "He who doesn't drink will please stay outside." It's been around since 1465, and locals pack in, bearing food from outside to accompany the wine. ✉ *Vicolo Ranocchi 1/d, Piazza Maggiore* ☎ *347/9680171 mobile* 🌐 *www.osteriadelsole.it.*

CAFÉS

★ Zanarini

CAFÉS | Chic Bolognesi congregate at this bar and sit outside on gorgeous Piazza Galvani sipping coffee in the morning and swanky aperitivi with *stuzzichini* snacks come evening. Tasty sandwiches, cold cuts, and cute pastries are also available. ✉ *Piazza Galvani 1, Piazza Maggiore* ☎ *051/2750041* 🌐 *antoniazzi.biz.*

MUSIC VENUES

Bravo Caffè

LIVE MUSIC | Rub shoulders with artsy celebs, locals, and visitors who dine while listening to intimate jazz, funk, rock, and pop artists from Italy and beyond. It can be a special, intimate place to see legends like Luca Carboni, Tullio de Piscopo, Nicola Conte, Suzanne Vega, Lisa Stansfield, Billy Cobham, and Roy Ayers. ✉ *Via Mascarella 1 Bologna, North of Piazza Maggiore* ☎ *051/266112* ⊕ *www. bravocaffe.it.*

Cantina Bentivoglio
LIVE MUSIC | With live music including jazz staged nearly every evening since 1987, Cantina Bentivoglio is one of Bologna's most renowned nightspots. You can enjoy light and more substantial meals here as well. ✉ *Via Mascarella 4/B, University area* ☎ *051/265416* ⊕ *www. cantinabentivoglio.it.*

Osteria Buca delle Campane
LIVE MUSIC | In a 13th-century building, this underground tavern has good, inexpensive food, and the after-dinner scene is popular with locals, including students, who come to listen to the live music on weekends and some other nights. The kitchen stays open until long past midnight. Reservations are strongly advised. ✉ *Via Benedetto XIV 4, University area* ☎ *051/220918* ⊕ *www.bucadellecampane.it.*

Performing Arts
MUSIC AND OPERA
Teatro Comunale
MUSIC | This 18th-century theater presents concerts by Italian and international orchestras throughout the year, but the highly acclaimed opera performances from January to July and October to December are the main attraction. Reserve seats for those performances well in advance. ✉ *Largo Respighi 1, University area* ☎ *051/529019* ⊕ *www. tcbo.it.*

🛍 Shopping
CLOTHING
Castel Guelfo The Style Outlets
OUTLET | If you don't feel like paying Galleria Cavour prices, this mall is about 20 minutes outside Bologna. It includes more than 50 stores, among them such top brands as Swarovski. ✉ *Via del Commercio 4/2, Loc. Poggio Piccolo* ⊕ *Take the A14 toward Imola, Castel San Pietro Terme exit; 980 feet after tollbooth, turn right onto Via San Carlo* ☎ *0542/670765* ⊕ *www.thestyleoutlets.it.*

Galleria Cavour
MALL | Opened in 1959, the upscale Galleria houses many of the fashion giants, including Armani, Gucci, Saint Laurent, and Tod's. ✉ *Via Luigi Carlo Farini, South of Piazza Maggiore* ☎ *051/226889* ⊕ *www.galleriacavour.it.*

WINE AND FOOD
Enoteca Italiana
WINE/SPIRITS | Consistently recognized as one of the best wine stores in the country, Enoteca Italiana (est.1972) lives up to its reputation—as it says, "every good bottle has a good story"—with shelves lined with excellent selections from all over Italy at reasonable prices. In addition, the delicious plates of cured meats served with wines by the glass, make a great light lunch. ✉ *Via Marsala 2/b, North of Piazza Maggiore* ☎ *051/235989* ⊕ *www.enotecaitaliana.it.*

La Baita Vecchia Malga
FOOD | Fresh tagliolini, tortellini, and other Bolognese pasta delicacies are sold here, along with sublime food to eat at small tables here or take away. The cheese counter is laden with superlative local specimens. ✉ *Via Pescherie Vecchie 3/a, Piazza Maggiore* ☎ *051/223940* ⊕ *www. vecchiamalganegozi.com.*

Majani
CANDY | Classy Majani has been producing chocolate since 1796. Its staying power may be attributed to high-quality

confections that are as pretty to look at as they are to eat. ✉ *Via de' Carbonesi 5, Piazza Maggiore* ☎ *051/234302* ⊕ *www.majani.it.*

Mercato delle Erbe

FOOD | This food market and food hall that opened in 1910 bustles year-round. ✉ *Via Ugo Bassi 23, Piazza Maggiore* ☎ *335/4112427* ⊕ *www.mercatodelleerbe.it.*

Paolo Atti & Figli

FOOD | This place has been producing some of Bologna's finest pastas, cakes, and other delicacies since 1868. There's a second branch at Via Drapperie 6. ✉ *Via Caprarie 7, Piazza Maggiore* ☎ *051/220425* ⊕ *www.paoloatti.com.*

★ Roccati

CANDY | Sculptural works of chocolate, as well as basic bonbons and simpler sweets, have been crafted here since 1909. ✉ *Via Clavature 17/a, Piazza Maggiore* ☎ *051/261964* ⊕ *www.roccaticioccolato.com.*

Ferrara

47 km (29 miles) northeast of Bologna, 74 km (46 miles) northwest of Ravenna.

When the legendary Ferrarese filmmaker Michelangelo Antonioni called his beloved hometown "a city that you can see only partly, while the rest disappears to be imagined," perhaps he was referring to the low-lying mist that rolls in off the Adriatic each winter and shrouds Ferrara's winding knot of medieval alleyways, turreted palaces, and ancient wine bars—once frequented by the likes of Copernicus—in a ghostly fog. But perhaps Antonioni was also suggesting that Ferrara's striking beauty often conceals a dark and tortured past.

Today you're likely to be charmed by Ferrara's prosperous air and meticulous cleanliness, its excellent restaurants and chic bars (for coffee and any other liquid

refreshment), and its lively wine-bar scene. You'll find aficionados gathering outside any of the wine bars near the Duomo even on the foggiest of weeknights. Although Ferrara is a UNESCO World Heritage site, the city draws amazingly few tourists—which only adds to its appeal.

GETTING HERE AND AROUND

Train service is frequent from Bologna (usually three trains per hour) and takes either a half hour or 50 minutes, depending on which train type you take. It's around 35 minutes from Florence to Bologna, and then about a half hour from Bologna to Ferrara. The walk from the station is easy (about 20 minutes) and not particularly interesting. You can also take Bus No. 1, No. 6 or No. 9 from the station to the center; buy your ticket at the newsagent inside and remember to stamp your ticket upon boarding the bus.

If you're driving from Bologna, take the RA1 out of town, then the A13 in the direction of Padua, exiting at Ferrara Nord. Follow the SP19 directly into the center of town. The trip should take about 45 minutes.

VISITOR INFORMATION

CONTACT Ferrara Tourism Office. ✉ *Castello Estense, Piazza Castello, Ferrara* ☎ *0532/209370* ⊕ *www.ferrarainfo.com.*

 Sights

Casa Romei

CASTLE/PALACE | Built by the wealthy banker Giovanni Romei (1402–83), this vast structure with a graceful courtyard ranks among Ferrara's loveliest Renaissance palaces. Mid-15th-century frescoes adorn rooms on the ground floor; the piano nobile contains detached frescoes from local churches as well as lesser-known Renaissance sculptures. The Sala delle Sibille has a very large 15th-century fireplace and beautiful coffered wood ceilings. ✉ *Via Savonarola 30, Ferrara*

The Castello Estense, a fortress dating from the 14th century, dominates the center of Ferrara.

☎ 0532/234130 ⊕ www.ferraraterraeac-qua.it ✉ €5.

★ Castello Estense
CASTLE/PALACE | The former seat of Este power, this massive castle dominates the center of town, a suitable symbol for the ruling family: cold and menacing on the outside, lavishly decorated within. The public rooms are grand, but deep in the bowels of the castle are dungeons where enemies of the state were held in wretched conditions. The prisons of Don Giulio, Ugo, and Parisina have some fascinating features, like 15th-century graffiti. Lovers Ugo and Parisina (stepmother and stepson) were beheaded in 1425 because Ugo's father, Niccolò III, didn't like the fact that his son was cavorting with his stepmother.

The castle was established as a fortress in 1385, but work on its luxurious ducal quarters continued into the 16th century. Representative of Este grandeur are the Sala dei Giochi, painted with athletic scenes, and the Sala dell'Aurora, decorated to show the times of the day. The terraces of the castle and the hanging garden have fine views of the town and countryside. You can traverse the castle's drawbridge and wander through many of its arcaded passages whenever the castle gates are open. ✉ Piazza Castello, Ferrara ☎ 0532/419180 ⊕ www.castel-loestense.it ✉ €12 🕓 Closed Tues.

Duomo
CHURCH | The magnificent Gothic cathedral, a few steps from the Castello Estense, has a three-tier facade of slender arches and beautiful sculptures over the central door. Work began in 1135 and took more than 100 years to complete. The interior was completely remodeled in the 17th century. At the time of writing, the Duomo is undergoing major restoration after the 2012 earthquake: the interior is only partially open with a multimedia display outlining the works. ✉ Piazza della Cattedrale, Ferrara ☎ 0532/207449 ⊕ www.cattedralediferrara.it.

Museo della Cattedrale
ART MUSEUM | Some of the original decorations of the town's main church,

the former church, and the cloister of San Romano reside in the Museo della Cattedrale, across the piazza from the Duomo. Inside you'll find 22 codices commissioned between 1477 and 1535; early-13th-century sculptures by the Maestro dei Mesi; a mammoth oil on canvas by Cosmè Tura from 1469; and an exquisite Jacopo della Quercia, the *Madonna della Melagrana*. Although this last work dates from 1403 to 1408, the playful expression on the Christ child seems very 21st century. ⊠ *Via San Romano 1, Ferrara* ☎ *0532/761299* ⊕ *www.ferrarainfo.com* ☜ *€6* ⊗ *Closed Mon.*

Museo Nazionale dell'Ebraismo Italiano e della Shoah (*Museum of Italian Judaism and the Shoah*)

OTHER MUSEUM | The collection of ornate religious objects and multimedia installations at this museum (commonly known as MEIS) bears witness to the long history of the city's Jewish community. This history had its high points—1492, for example, when Ercole I invited the Jews to come over from Spain—and its lows, notably 1627, when Jews were enclosed within the ghetto, where they were forced to live until the advent of a united Italy in 1860. The triangular warren of narrow cobbled streets that made up the ghetto originally extended as far as Corso Giovecca (originally Corso Giudecca, or Ghetto Street). When it was enclosed, the neighborhood was restricted to the area between Via Scienze, Via Contrari, and Via di San Romano. The museum is located about a 15-minute walk from the former Jewish ghetto. Guided tours may be booked in advance by emailing or calling the museum. ⊠ *Via Piangipane 81, Ferrara* ☎ *0532/769137* ⊕ *www. meisweb.it* ☜ *€10* ⊗ *Closed Mon.*

Palazzo dei Diamanti
(*Palace of Diamonds*)

ART MUSEUM | Named for the 8,500 small pink-and-white marble pyramids (or "diamonds") that stud its facade, this

building was designed to be viewed in perspective—both faces at once—from diagonally across the street. Work began in the 1490s and finished around 1504. Inside the palazzo is the Pinacoteca Nazionale which houses 13th- to 17th-century Ferrarese painting, plus temporary shows. ⊠ *Corso Ercole I d'Este 21, Ferrara* ☎ *0532/244949* ⊕ *www.palazzo-diamanti.it* ☜ *€15* ⊗ *Closed Mon.*

★ Palazzo Schifanoia

HISTORIC SIGHT | The oldest, most characteristic area of Ferrara is south of the Duomo, stretching between the Corso Giovecca and the city's ramparts. Here various members of the Este family built pleasure palaces, the best known of which is the Palazzo Schifanoia (*schifanoia* means "carefree" or, literally, "fleeing boredom"). Begun in the late 14th century, the palace was remodeled between 1464 and 1469. Inside is Museo Schifanoia, with its lavish interior—particularly the Salone dei Mesi, which contains an extravagant series of frescoes showing the months of the year and their mythological attributes. ⊠ *Via Scandiana 23, Ferrara* ☎ *0532/244949* ⊕ *www.ferrarainfo.com* ☜ *€12* ⊗ *Closed Mon.*

Via delle Volte

STREET | One of the best-preserved medieval streets in Europe, the Via delle Volte clearly evokes Ferrara's past. The series of ancient *volte* (arches) along the narrow cobblestone alley once joined the merchants' houses on the south side of the street to their warehouses on the north side. The street ran parallel to the banks of the Po River, which was home to Ferrara's busy port. ⊠ *Via delle Volte, Ferrara.*

 Restaurants

★ Enoteca al Brindisi

$ | WINE BAR | Ferrara is a city of wine bars, beginning with this one (allegedly Europe's oldest), which opened in 1435—Copernicus drank here while a student in the late 1400s, and the place still has an undergraduate aura. The twentysomething staff pours well-chosen wines by the glass, and they serve *cappellacci di zucca* (pasta stuffed with squash) with two different sauces (ragù or butter and sage). **Known for:** set menus at great prices; characterful interior; full of locals, students, and visitors. $ *Average main: €12* ✉ *Via Adelardi 11, Ferrara* ☎ *0532/473744* ⊕ *www.albrindisi.net* ⊗ *Closed Mon. and 1 wk in late Jan.*

Il Mandolino

$$ | EMILIAN | At this idiosyncratic trattoria on the historic Via delle Volte try tearing your attention away from the countless paintings, photographs, and musical instruments that cover the walls, and instead focusing on the excellent fare on offer. Typical dishes include the classic cappellacci di zucca, and the lasagna may be one of the best you'll ever have. **Known for:** fascinating decor; local home cooking like excellent lasagna; friendly staff. $ *Average main: €16* ✉ *Via delle Volte 52, Ferrara* ☎ *0532/760080* ⊕ *www. ristoranteilmandolino.it* ⊗ *Closed Tues. No dinner.*

Il Sorpasso

$$ | EMILIAN | Named after a 1962 cult movie, *Il Sorpasso* (*The Easy Life*) serves terrific, honestly priced food in an unassuming space: white walls lined with movie posters, and white floors. No matter—the fine cooking and the sourcing of local ingredients whenever possible help this trattoria surpass many others. **Known for:** excellent pasta and desserts; using local ingredients whenever possible; vegan and vegetarian options. $ *Average main: €18* ✉ *Via Saraceno 118, Ferrara* ☎ *0532/790289* ⊕ *www. trattoriailsorpasso.it* ⊗ *Closed Mon. and Tues.*

★ L'Oca Giuliva

$$ | EMILIAN | Food, service, and ambience harmonize blissfully at this casual but elegant restaurant inside a 12th-century building. The chef shows a deft hand with area specialties and shines with the fish dishes. **Known for:** creative antipasti and seafood dishes; cappellacci di zucca (pumpkin-stuffed pasta); Ferrarese and seafood tasting menus. $ *Average main: €20* ✉ *Via Boccacanale di Santo Stefano 38/40, Ferrara* ☎ *0532/207628* ⊕ *www. ristorantelocagiuliva.it* ⊗ *Closed Tues. No lunch Thurs.*

Molto Più Che Centrale

$$ | EMILIAN | A winning combination of traditional and innovative dishes is the big draw at this colorful, contemporary restaurant with splashy modern art spread over two floors. Young chef Giacomo Garutti delivers Ferrarese classics like *salamina da sugo con purè* (salami atop creamy mashed potatoes) alongside fried and grilled seafood, and innovations like cappellacci pasta filled with pumpkin, orange, and ginger. There's a good wine list, too. **Known for:** local dishes with modern flourishes; upbeat, contemporary setting; attentive waitstaff. $ *Average main: €18* ✉ *Via Boccaleone 8, Ferrara* ☎ *0532/1880070* ⊕ *www.moltopiu-checentrale.it* ⊗ *Closed Thurs.*

★ Quel Fantastico Giovedì

$$ | EMILIAN | Locals and other cognoscenti frequent this sleek eatery just minutes away from Piazza del Duomo, where chef Gabriele Romagnoli uses prime local ingredients to create gustatory sensations on a menu that changes daily. Fish and seafood figure prominently among his dishes, such as with a *gratinato* (similar to a French au gratin) with seafood. **Known for:** seasonal menu; notable fish and seafood dishes; excellent service. $ *Average main: €18* ✉ *Via Castelnuovo 9, Ferrara* ☎ *0532/760570* ⊗ *Closed Wed. No lunch Thurs.*

 Hotels

Hotel Annunziata

$$ | HOTEL | Brightly colored fittings enliven the white-walled, hardwood-floor guest rooms—think minimalism with a splash—at this hotel on a quiet little

piazza near the forbiddingly majestic Castello Estense. **Pros:** perfect location (you can't get much more central); stellar staff; terrific buffet breakfast. **Cons:** few facilities and limited public spaces; some rooms have uninspiring views; annex 500 feet from main building. $ *Rooms from: €130* ⊠ *Piazza Repubblica 5, Ferrara* ☎ *0532/201111* ⊕ *www.annunziata.it* ⤶ *27 rooms* ⎮○⎮ *Free Breakfast.*

★ **Locanda Borgonuovo**

$ | **B&B/INN** | In the early 18th century this lodging began life as a convent (later suppressed by Napoléon), but now it's a delightful city-center bed-and-breakfast, popular with performers at the city's Teatro Comunale. **Pros:** phenomenal breakfast featuring local foods and terrific cakes made in-house; bicycles can be borrowed for free; knowledgeable local advice. **Cons:** steep stairs to reception area and rooms; must reserve far in advance as this place books quickly; decor may be a bit over-fussy for some. $ *Rooms from: €100* ⊠ *Via Cairoli 29, Ferrara* ☎ *0532/211100* ⊕ *www.borgonuovo.com* ⤶ *5 rooms* ⎮○⎮ *Free Breakfast.*

Maxxim Hotel

$ | **HOTEL** | **FAMILY** | Though given a stylish modern makeover, the courtyards, vaulted brick lobby, and breakfast room of this 15th-century palazzo retain much of their lordly Renaissance flair. **Pros:** beyond-helpful staff; good choice for families; tasteful modern makeover. **Cons:** split-level loft rooms impractical for some; occasional noise from neighboring rooms; some bathrooms are on the small side. $ *Rooms from: €80* ⊠ *Via Ripagrande 21, Ferrara* ☎ *0532/1770700* ⊕ *www.maxxim.it* ⤶ *40 rooms* ⎮○⎮ *Free Breakfast.*

Ravenna

80 km (50 miles) northwest of San Marino, 93 km (58 miles) southeast of Ferrara.

A small, quiet, and well-heeled city, Ravenna has brick palaces, cobblestone streets, magnificent monuments, and spectacular Byzantine mosaics. The high point in its civic history occurred in the 5th century, when Pope Honorious moved his court here from Rome. Gothic kings Odoacer and Theodoric ruled the city until it was conquered by the Byzantines in AD 540. Ravenna later fell under the sway of Venice, and then, inevitably, the Papal States.

Because Ravenna spent much of its past looking east, its greatest art treasures show that Byzantine influence. Churches and tombs with the most unassuming exteriors contain within them walls covered with sumptuous mosaics. These beautifully preserved Byzantine mosaics put great emphasis on nature, which you can see in the delicate rendering of sky, earth, and animals. Outside Ravenna, the town of Classe hides even more mosaic gems.

GETTING HERE AND AROUND

By car from Bologna, take the SP253 to the RA1, and then follow signs for the A14/E45 in the direction of Ancona. From here, follow signs for Ravenna, taking the A14dir Ancona–Milano–Ravenna exit. Follow signs for the SS16/E55 to the center of Ravenna. From Ferrara the drive is more convoluted, but also more interesting. Take the SS16 to the RA8 in the direction of Porto Garibaldi, taking the Roma/Ravenna exit. Follow the SS309/E55 to the SS309dir/E55, taking the SS253 Bologna/Ancona exit. Follow the SS16/E55 into the center of Ravenna.

By train, there are one or two direct services hourly from Bologna, taking 70 minutes.

VISITOR INFORMATION

CONTACT Ravenna Tourism Office. ⊠ *Piazza San Francesco 7, Ravenna* ☎ *0544/35755* ⊕ *www.turismo.ra.it.*

Sights

★ Basilica di San Vitale

CHURCH | The octagonal church of San Vitale was built in AD 547, after the Byzantines conquered the city, and its interior shows a strong Byzantine influence. The area behind the altar contains the most famous works, depicting Emperor Justinian and his retinue on one wall, and his wife, Empress Theodora, with her retinue, on the opposite one. Notice how the mosaics seamlessly wrap around the columns and curved arches on the upper sides of the altar area. **■TIP→ School groups can sometimes swamp the site from March through mid-June.** ⊠ *Via San Vitale, off Via Salara, Ravenna* ☎ *0544/541688* ⊕ *www.ravennamosaici.it* ⧆ *€11 combination ticket, includes 4–5 diocesan monuments.*

Battistero Neoniano

CHURCH | Next door to Ravenna's 18th-century cathedral, this baptistery has one of the town's most important mosaics. It dates from the beginning of the 5th century AD, with work continuing through the century. In keeping with the building's role, the great mosaic in the dome shows the baptism of Christ, and beneath are the Apostles. The lowest register of mosaics contains Christian symbols, the Throne of God, and the Cross. Note the naked figure kneeling next to Christ—he is the personification of the River Jordan. ⊠ *Piazza Duomo, Ravenna* ☎ *0544/541688* ⊕ *www. ravennamosaici.it* ⧆ *€11 combination ticket, includes 4–5 diocesan monuments* ⧉ *Reservations essential.*

Classis Ravenna – Museo della Città e del Territorio

OTHER MUSEUM | FAMILY | In Classe, a short distance outside Ravenna, this museum dazzlingly illustrates the history of Ravenna and its environs from the pre-Roman era to the Lombard conquest in AD 751. The museum occupies a refurbished sugar refinery, and with the help of multimedia presentations and panels in Italian and English, it chronicles the Roman, Ostrogoth, and Byzantine periods. Displays include bronze statuettes, stone sculptures, glassware, and mosaic fragments. A separate room summarizes the building's more recent history. It's an easy walk from Sant'Apollinare in Classe. **■TIP→ To get here from Ravenna, take Bus No. 4 from the station or the local train to Classe, or use the cycle path from the city center.** ⊠ *VIa Classense 29, off SS71, Classe* ☎ *0544/473717* ⊕ *www.classisravenna.it* ⧆ *€7.*

Domus dei Tappeti di Pietra
(*House of the Stone Carpets*)

RUINS | This archaeological site with lovely mosaics was uncovered in 1993 during digging for an underground parking garage near the 18th-century church of Santa Eufemia. Ten feet below ground level lie the remains of a Byzantine palace dating from the 5th and 6th centuries AD. Its beautiful and well-preserved network of floor mosaics displays elaborately designed patterns, creating the effect of luxurious carpets. ⊠ *Via Barbiani 16, enter through Sant'Eufemia church, Ravenna* ☎ *0544/473678* ⊕ *www. domusdeitappetidipietra.it* ⧆ *€4.*

★ Mausoleo di Galla Placidia

CHURCH | The little tomb and the great church stand side by side, but the tomb predates the Basilica di San Vitale by at least 100 years: these two adjacent sights are decorated with the best-known, most elaborate mosaics in Ravenna. Galla Placidia was the sister of the Roman emperor Honorius, who moved the imperial capital to Ravenna in AD 402. This mid-5th-century mausoleum is her memorial.

The simple redbrick exterior only serves to enhance by contrast the richness of

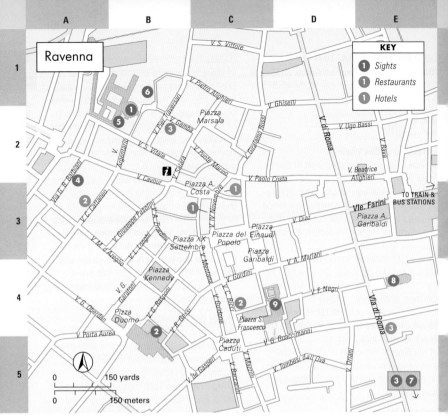

Ravenna

KEY
- 1 Sights
- 1 Restaurants
- 1 Hotels

TO TRAIN &
BUS STATIONS

0 ———— 150 yards
0 ———— 150 meters

Sights ▼

1 Basilica di San Vitale... **B2**
2 Battistero Neoniano.... **B4**
3 Classis Ravenna –
  Museo della Città e del
  Territorio **E5**
4 Domus dei Tappeti
  di Pietra **A2**
5 MAR-Museo Nazionale
  di Ravenna.............. **B2**
6 Mausoleo di Galla
  Placidia **B1**
7 Sant'Apollinare in
  Classe.................... **E5**
8 Sant'Apollinare
  Nuovo **E4**
9 Tomba di Dante **D4**

Restaurants ▼

1 Bella Venezia............. **C3**
2 Ca' de Vèn **C4**
3 Osteria del
  Tempo Perso **B2**

Hotels ▼

1 Albergo Cappello **C3**
2 Hotel Sant'Andrea...... **A3**
3 Palazzo Bezzi............. **E4**

the interior mosaics, in deep midnight blue and glittering gold. The tiny central dome is decorated with symbols of Christ, the evangelists, and striking gold stars. Eight of the Apostles are represented in groups of two on the four inner walls of the dome; the other four appear singly on the walls of the two transepts. There are three sarcophagi in the tomb, none of which are believed to actually contain the remains of Galla Placidia. ■ TIP→ **Visit early or late in the day to avoid the school groups that can sometimes swamp the Mausoleo from March through mid-June.** ⊠ *Via San Vitale, 17, off Via Salara, Ravenna* ☎ *0544/541688* ⊕ *www. ravennamosaici.it* ▱ *€11 combination ticket, includes 4–5 diocesan monuments (€2 supplement for mausoleum).*

MAR-Museo Nazionale di Ravenna (National Museum of Ravenna)

OTHER MUSEUM | Next to the Church of San Vitale and housed in a former Benedictine monastery, the museum contains artifacts from ancient Rome, Byzantine fabrics and carvings, and pieces of early Christian art. The collection is well displayed and artfully lighted. In the first cloister are marvelous Roman tomb slabs from excavations nearby; upstairs, you can see a reconstructed 18th-century pharmacy. ⊠ *Via San Vitale 17, Ravenna* ☎ *0544/213902* ⊕ *ravennantica.it/ en/national-museum-of-ravenna* ▱ *€5* ☉ *Closed Mon.*

Sant'Apollinare in Classe

CHURCH | This church about 5 km (3 miles) southeast of Ravenna is landlocked now, but when it was built, it stood in the center of the busy shipping port known to the ancient Romans as Classis. The arch above and the area around the high altar are rich with mosaics. Those on the arch, older than the ones behind it, are considered superior. They show Christ in Judgment and the 12 lambs of Christianity leaving the cities of Jerusalem and Bethlehem. In the apse is the figure of Sant'Apollinare himself, a bishop of

Ravenna, and above him is a magnificent Transfiguration against blazing green grass, animals in odd perspective, and flowers. ⊠ *Via Romea Sud 224, off SS71, Classe* ☎ *0544/527308* ⊕ *info.raven-nantica.it* ▱ *€5 or €8 including Classis Ravenna museum* ☉ *Closed Mon.*

Sant'Apollinare Nuovo

CHURCH | The mosaics displayed in this church date from the early 6th century, making them slightly older than those in San Vitale. Since the left side of the church was reserved for women, it's only fitting that the mosaics on that wall depict 22 virgins offering crowns to the Virgin Mary. On the right wall, 26 men carry the crowns of martyrdom; they approach Christ, surrounded by angels. ⊠ *Via Roma 53, at Via Guaccimanni, Ravenna* ☎ *0544/541688* ⊕ *www.raven-namosaici.it* ▱ *€11 combination ticket, includes 4–5 diocesan monuments.*

Tomba di Dante

TOMB | Exiled from his native Florence, the author of *The Divine Comedy* died here in 1321, and Dante's tomb is in a small neoclassical building next door to the large church of St. Francis. The Florentines have been trying to reclaim their famous son for hundreds of years, but the Ravennans refuse to give him up, arguing that since Florence did not welcome Dante in life, it does not deserve him in death. Perhaps as penance, every September the Florentine government sends olive oil that's used to fuel the light hanging in the chapel's center. ⊠ *Via Dante Alighieri 9, Ravenna* ☎ *0544/215676* ⊕ *vivadante.it* ▱ *Free.*

Restaurants

Bella Venezia

$$ | ITALIAN | Pastel walls, crisp white tablecloths, and warm light provide the backdrop for some seriously good Romagnolo dishes. The menu offers local specialties, but also gives a major nod to Venice—Ravenna's conqueror of long ago. **Known for:** truffle dishes, depending on the season; outdoor dining; family owned and operated since 1969. [$] *Average main: €17* ✉ *Via IV Novembre 16, Ravenna* ☎ *0544/212746* 🌐 *www.ristorantebellavenezia.it* 🕒 *Closed Sun.*

Ca' de Vèn

$$ | **ITALIAN** | These buildings, joined by a glass-ceilinged courtyard, date from the 15th century, so the setting itself is reason enough to come; that the food is so good makes a visit here all the more satisfying. At lunchtime Ca' de Vèn teems with locals tucking in to *piadine* (a typical Romagnolo flatbread) stuffed or topped with various ingredients, and the grilled dishes—including *tagliata di pollo* (sliced chicken breast tossed with arugula and set atop exquisitely roasted potatoes)—are among the highlights. **Known for:** grilled meats; weekly menu of Romagnolo specialties; majestic, high-ceilinged lively setting. [$] *Average main: €18* ✉ *Via Corrado Ricci 24, Ravenna* ☎ *0544/30163* 🌐 *www.cadeven.it* 🕒 *Closed Mon.*

★ Osteria del Tempo Perso

$$ | **ITALIAN** | A couple of jazz-, rock-, and food-loving friends joined forces to open this smart little restaurant in the center. The interior's warm terra-cotta-sponged walls give off an orange glow, and wine bottles line the walls, interspersed with photographs of musical greats—but the food is what counts. **Known for:** terrific seafood dishes; fine wine list; homemade pastas. [$] *Average main: €22* ✉ *Via Gamba 12, Ravenna* ☎ *0544/215393* 🌐 *www.osteriadeltempoperso.it* 🕒 *No lunch weekdays.*

Hotels

Albergo Cappello

$$ | **HOTEL** | Originally opened in the late 19th century and restored a century later, this small, charming place exhibits a Venetian influence, with Murano chandeliers hanging from the high coffered wood ceilings in common rooms. **Pros:** good location in historic area and near sights; accommodating staff; wine bar and good restaurant. **Cons:** patchy air-conditioning; parking sometimes hard to find; occasional street noise in some rooms. [$] *Rooms from: €149* ✉ *Via IV Novembre 41, Ravenna* ☎ *0544/219813* 🌐 *www.albergocappello.it* 🛏 *7 rooms* 🍴 *Free Breakfast.*

Hotel Sant'Andrea

$ | **B&B/INN** | **FAMILY** | For a quiet and welcoming lodging on a residential street a stone's throw from the Basilica di San Vitale, look no further—it even has a delightful garden. **Pros:** quiet neighborhood; good-size guest rooms and family suites, some with terraces; cheery and helpful staff. **Cons:** can get a little noisy; reception closes at 9 pm; few facilities. [$] *Rooms from: €110* ✉ *Via Carlo Cattaneo 33, Ravenna* ☎ *0544/215564* 🌐 *www.santandreahotel.com* 🛏 *12 rooms* 🍴 *Free Breakfast.*

Palazzo Bezzi

$$ | **HOTEL** | Set in a historic, central palazzo, Bezzi is the best bet in town for reliable, friendly customer service, and a comfortable stay amid modern surroundings, a quiet garden, and panoramic rooftop solarium. **Pros:** reliable service, cleanliness, and maintenance; small spa and gym; central yet quiet location. **Cons:** some may find the decor soulless; no bar or restaurant; pricey garage parking. [$] *Rooms from: €180* ✉ *Via di Roma 45, Ravenna* ☎ *0544/36926* 🌐 *palazzobezzi.it* 🛏 *32 rooms* 🍴 *Free Breakfast.*

Performing Arts

Teatro di Tradizione Dante Alighieri

ARTS CENTERS | Operas and dance productions are staged here from November to April, as well as classical, jazz, and blues concerts year-round. If your Italian is up to it, you could also attend any of the theatrical productions. ✉ *Via Mariani 2, Ravenna* ☎ *0544/249244* 🌐 *www.teatroalighieri.org.*

Chapter 6

FLORENCE

6

Updated by
Elizabeth Shemaria

Sights	Restaurants	Hotels	Shopping	Nightlife
★★★★★	★★★★★	★★★★★	★★★★★	★★★★☆

WELCOME TO FLORENCE

TOP REASONS TO GO

★ **Galleria degli Uffizi:** Italian Renaissance art doesn't get much better than this vast collection bequeathed in 1737 by the last Medici, Anna Maria Luisa.

★ **Brunelleschi's Dome:** His work of engineering genius is the city's undisputed centerpiece.

★ **Michelangelo's** *David*: One look, up close, and you'll know why this is one of the world's most famous sculptures.

★ **The view from Piazzale Michelangelo:** From this perch the city is laid out before you. The colors at sunset heighten the experience.

★ **Piazza Santa Croce:** After you've had your fill of Renaissance masterpieces, idle here and watch the world go by.

1 **Around the Duomo.** You're in the heart of Florence here. Among the numerous highlights are the city's greatest museum (the Uffizi) and arguably its most impressive square (Piazza della Signoria).

2 **San Lorenzo.** The complex of the basilica of San Lorenzo, the Palazzo Medici-Riccardi, and the Galleria dell'Accademia bears the imprints of the Medici and of Michelangelo, culminating in the latter's masterful statue *David*. Just to the north, the former convent of San Marco is an oasis of artistic treasures decorated with ethereal frescoes.

3 **Santa Maria Novella.** This part of town includes the train station, 16th-century palaces, and the city's swankest shopping street, Via Tornabuoni.

4 **Santa Croce.** The district centers on its namesake basilica, which is filled with the tombs of Renaissance (and other) luminaries. The area is also known for its leather shops.

5 **The Oltrarno.** Across the Arno you encounter the massive Palazzo Pitti and the narrow streets of the Santo Spirito neighborhood.

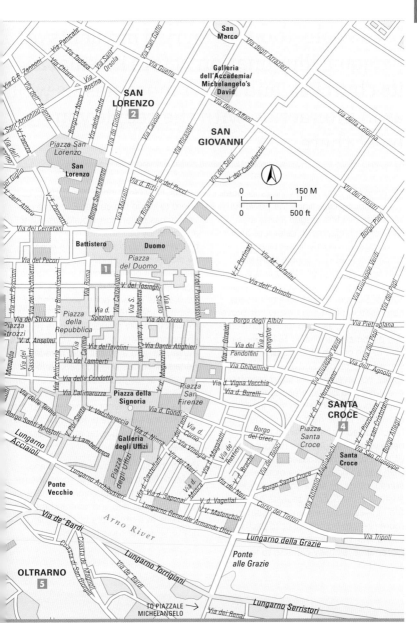

Its magical combination of beauty and history has drawn people to Florence for centuries, and then it draws them back again. It offers myriad moments of personal illumination before its palazzi, its churches, and its art museums, as well as in interaction with the people you meet there.

Florence has captivated visitors for ages now, probably ever since the powerful Medici family first staged jousts and later lavish pageants to celebrate their weddings. Its mostly sober beauty continued to attract people from all over Europe intent on taking in the achievements of the past on their Grand Tour of Europe. Sometimes this heady combination of art and beauty has proven overwhelming, as it did for French author and diplomat Stendhal in 1817, whose visit to the church of Santa Croce occasioned palpitations and a fainting spell. Today, however, visitors are more often overwhelmed by the press of their own numbers intent on taking it all in before moving on to the next stop on their tightly scheduled tours. Florence has always been visitor-friendly—the historical center of the city can be crossed on foot in less than half an hour, and the picturesque surrounding hills are a short bus ride away. But the flood of tourists has made the natives more reticent. A visitor is more likely to bump into or to exchange views with other visitors than with native Florentines, all busy catering to tourists'

needs. Few Florentines, these days, can afford to live in the center. Even the university has pulled some buildings out to a suburb. By day, the city is overrun with busloads of day-trippers; come evening by droves of U.S. study-abroad students intent on immersion in the native *aperitivo* (pre-dinner drink) culture. Where have all the Italians gone, you wonder? Fear not, they still come out on Sundays to walk in family groups along the major shopping streets, school groups still pack museums, and they still hold parades in Renaissance costume to mark various historical or religious occasions. Caffè culture still thrives. All this will be revealed to the attentive visitor who sees past the crowds and takes the time to look around the corner onto a quieter street, piazza, or neighborhood.

When the sun sets over the Arno and, as Mark Twain described it, "overwhelms Florence with tides of color that make all the sharp lines dim and faint and turn the solid city to a city of dreams," it's hard not to fall under the city's spell.

Planning

Getting Here and Around

AIR

To get into the city center from the airport by car, take the autostrada A11. The T2 tram will take you directly to and from the airport and the center of town. Buy tickets at machines outside the tram stops.

CONTACTS Aeroporto A. Vespucci. ✉ *10 km (6 miles) northwest of Florence, Florence* ☎ *055/30615* ⊕ *www.aeroporto. firenze.it.* **Aeroporto Galileo Galilei.** ✉ *12 km (7 miles) south of Pisa and 80 km (50 miles) west of Florence, Florence* ☎ *050/849300* ⊕ *www.pisa-airport.com.*

BIKE AND MOPED

Brave souls (cycling in Florence is difficult at best) may rent bicycles at easy-to-spot locations at Fortezza da Basso, the Stazione Centrale di Santa Maria Novella, and Piazza Pitti. Otherwise, try **Alinari** (✉ *Via San Zanobi 38/r, San Marco* ☎ *055/280500* ⊕ *www. alinarirental.com*). You'll be up against hordes of tourists and those pesky *motorini* (mopeds). (For a safer ride, try Le Cascine, a former Medici hunting ground turned into a large public park with paved pathways.) The historic center can be circumnavigated via bike paths lining the *viali,* the ring road surrounding the area. If you want to go native and rent a noisy Vespa (Italian for "wasp") or other make of motorcycle or *motorino,* you can do so at **Massimo** (✉ *Via Campo d'Arrigo 16/r* ☎ *055/573689* ⊕ *www.massimoautonoleggio.com*).

BUS

Florence's flat, compact city center is made for walking, but when your feet get weary you can use the efficient bus system, which includes small electric buses making the rounds in the center. Buses also climb to Piazzale Michelangelo and San Miniato south of the Arno.

Maps and timetables are available for a small fee at the ATAF (Azienda Trasporti Area Fiorentina) booth next to the train station or for free at visitor information offices. Tickets must be bought in advance from tobacco shops, newsstands, automatic ticket machines near main stops, or ATAF booths. The ticket must be validated in the machine immediately upon boarding.

You have several ticket options, all valid for one or more rides on all lines. A €1.20 ticket is good for one hour from the time it is first canceled. A multiple ticket—four tickets, each valid for 70 minutes—costs €5.40. See ⊕ *www.at-bus.it* for more info.

Long-distance buses provide inexpensive service between Florence and other cities in Italy and Europe. **ATAF** and **Flixbus** (☎ *02/94759208* ⊕ *www.flixbus.com/bus/ florence*) are the major lines.

CAR

Florence is connected to the north and south of Italy by the Autostrada del Sole (A1). It takes about 1½ hours of driving on scenic roads to get to Bologna (although heavy truck traffic over the Apennines often makes for slower going), about 3 hours to Rome, and 3–3½ hours to Milan. The Tyrrhenian Coast is an hour west on the A11.

An automobile in Florence is a major liability. If your itinerary includes parts of Italy where you'll want a car (such as Tuscany), pick the vehicle up on your way out of town.

TAXI

Taxis usually wait at stands throughout the city (in front of the train station and in Piazza della Repubblica, for example). You can also call radio dispatch (☎ *055/4390, 055/4242*) for one to pick you up wherever you are.

The meter starts at €3.30 if you get a taxi at a stand or €5.40 if you call for one. Extra charges apply at night, on Sunday, and for luggage. Women out on the town after midnight are entitled to a 10% discount on the fare; you must, however, request it or call radio dispatch (☎ 055/4378557).

TRAIN
Florence is on the principal Italian train route between most European capitals and Rome, and within Italy it is served frequently from Milan, Venice, and Rome by Intercity (IC) and nonstop Eurostar trains. Avoid trains that stop only at the Campo di Marte or Rifredi station, which are not convenient to the city center.

CONTACT Stazione Centrale di Santa Maria Novella. ✉ *Piazza della Stazione, Santa Maria Novella* ☎ *055/8922021 Trenitalia in Italy (fee for call)* ⊕ *www.trenitalia. com.*

Making the Most of Your Time

With some planning, you can see Florence's most famous sights in a couple of days. Start off at the city's most awe-inspiring architectural wonder, the **Duomo,** climbing to the top of the dome if you have the stamina (and are not claustrophobic: it gets a little tight going up and coming back down). On the same piazza, check out Ghiberti's bronze doors at the **Battistero.** (They're actually high-quality copies; the Museo dell'Opera del Duomo has the originals.) Set aside the afternoon for the **Galleria degli Uffizi,** making sure to reserve tickets in advance.

On Day 2, visit Michelangelo's *David* in the **Galleria dell'Accademia**—reserve tickets here, too. Linger in **Piazza della Signoria,** Florence's central square, where a copy of *David* stands in the spot the original occupied for centuries, then head east a couple of blocks to **Santa Croce,**

the city's most artistically rich church. Double back and walk across Florence's landmark bridge, the **Ponte Vecchio.**

Do all that, and you'll have seen some great art, but you've just scratched the surface. If you have more time, put the **Bargello,** the **Museo di San Marco,** and the **Cappelle Medicee** at the top of your list. When you're ready for an art break, stroll through the **Boboli Gardens** or explore Florence's lively shopping scene, from the food stalls of the **Mercato Centrale** to the chic boutiques of the **Via Tornabuoni.**

HOURS
Florence's sights keep tricky hours. Some are closed Wednesday, some Monday, some every other Monday. Quite a few shut their doors each day (or on most days) by 2 in the afternoon. Things get even more confusing on weekends. Make it a general rule to check the hours closely for any place you're planning to visit; if it's someplace you have your heart set on seeing, it's worthwhile to call to confirm.

Here's a selection of major sights that might not be open when you'd expect (⇨ *consult the Sights listings within this chapter for full details*). And be aware that, as always, hours can and do change. Also note that on the first Sunday of the month, all state museums are free. That means that the Accademia and the Uffizi, among others, do not accept reservations. Unless you are a glutton for punishment (i.e., large crowds), these museums are best avoided on that day.

The **Accademia** and the **Uffizi** are both closed Monday. Note, too, that on the first Sunday of the month, all state museums, including these two, are free and do not accept reservations.

The **Bargello** is closed on Tuesday and the second and fourth Sunday of the month. Otherwise, it's open from 8:15 am until 1:50 pm (until 6:50 pm on Saturday).

The **Battistero** is open daily 8:30 am to 7:45 pm.

The **Cappelle Medicee** are closed Tuesday.

The **Duomo** is open from 10:15 am to 6:45 pm.

Museo di San Marco closes at 1:50—except for alternating Sundays and Mondays, when it's closed entirely.

Palazzo Medici-Riccardi is closed Wednesday.

RESERVATIONS

At most times of day a line of people snakes around the Uffizi. They're waiting to buy tickets, and you don't want to be one of them. Instead, call ahead for a reservation (☎ 055/294883).

You'll be given a reservation number and an admission time—the sooner you call, the more time slots you'll have to choose from. Go to the museum's reservation door 10 minutes before the appointed hour (at least 30 minutes before in high season), give the clerk your number, pick up your ticket, and go inside. You'll pay €4 for this privilege, but it's money well spent.

You can also book through the ticketing website (⊕ www.b-ticket.com/b-ticket/uffizi). The process takes some patience, but it works, and money-saving combo tickets are available as well. Use the same reservation service to book tickets for the Galleria dell'Accademia, where lines rival those of the Uffizi.

Reservations can also be made for the Palazzo Pitti, the Bargello, and several other sights, but they usually aren't needed—although, lately, in summer, lines can be long at Palazzo Pitti. An alternative strategy is to check with your hotel—many will handle reservations.

Restaurants

Florence's popularity with tourists means that, unfortunately, there's a higher percentage of mediocre restaurants here than you'll find in most Italian towns (Venice, perhaps, might win that prize). Some restaurant owners cut corners and let standards slip, knowing that a customer today is unlikely to return tomorrow, regardless of the quality of the meal. So, if you're looking to eat well, it pays to do some research, starting with the recommendations here. Dining hours start at around 1 for lunch and 8 for dinner. Many of Florence's restaurants are small, so reservations are a must. You can sample such specialties as creamy fegatini (a chicken-liver spread) and ribollita (minestrone thickened with bread and beans and swirled with extra-virgin olive oil) in a bustling, convivial trattoria, where you share long wooden tables set with paper place mats, or in an upscale *ristorante* with linen tablecloths and napkins.

Hotels

Florence is equipped with hotels for all budgets; for instance, you can find both budget and luxury hotels in the *centro storico* (historic center) and along the Arno. Florence has so many famous landmarks that it's not hard to find lodging with a panoramic view. The equivalent of the genteel *pensioni* of yesteryear can still be found, though they are now officially classified as "hotels." Generally small and intimate, they often have a quaint appeal that usually doesn't preclude modern plumbing. Florence's importance not only as a tourist city but also as a convention center and the site of the Pitti fashion collections guarantees a variety of accommodations.

The high demand also means that, except in winter, reservations are a must.

⇨ *Hotel and restaurant reviews have been shortened. For full information, visit Fodors.com. Prices in the hotel reviews are the lowest cost of a standard double room in high season. Prices in the dining reviews are the average cost of a main course at dinner, or, if dinner is not served, at lunch.*

What It Costs in Euros

	$	$$	$$$	$$$$
HOTELS				
	under €125	€125–€200	€201–€300	over €300
RESTAURANTS				
	under €15	€15–€24	€25–€35	over €35

Shopping

Window-shopping in Florence is like visiting an enormous contemporary-art gallery. Many of today's greatest Italian artists are fashion designers, and most keep shops in Florence. Discerning shoppers may find bargains in the street markets.

■ TIP→ **Do not buy any knockoff goods from any of the hawkers plying their fake Prada (or any other high-end designer) on the streets. It's illegal, and fines are astronomical if the police happen to catch you. (You pay the fine, not the vendor.)**

Shops are generally open 9–1 and 3:30–7:30, and are closed Sunday and Monday mornings most of the year. Summer (June to September) hours are usually 9–1 and 4–8, and some shops close Saturday afternoon instead of Monday morning. When looking for addresses, you'll see two color-coded numbering systems on each street. The red numbers are commercial addresses and are indicated, for example, as "31/r." The blue or black numbers are residential addresses. Most shops take major credit cards and ship purchases, but because

of possible delays it's wise to take your purchases with you.

Visitor Information

The Florence tourist office (☎ *039/055000* ⊕ *www.feelflorence.it*), has branches at the airport, just outside Piazza Santa Croce, across the street from Stazione di Santa Maria Novella (the main train station), and at the Bigallo in Piazza del Duomo. The offices are generally open from 9 am until 7 pm. The multilingual staff will answer questions, give you directions, and provide information on the latest performing-arts happenings and other events. The website also provides information in English.

Around the Duomo

The heart of Florence, stretching from the Piazza del Duomo south to the Arno, is as dense with artistic treasures as any place in the world. Its churches, medieval towers, Renaissance palaces, and world-class museums and galleries contain some of the most outstanding achievements of Western art.

Much of the centro storico is closed to automobile traffic, but you still must dodge mopeds, cyclists, and masses of fellow tourists as you walk the narrow streets, especially in the area bounded by the Duomo, Piazza della Signoria, Galleria degli Uffizi, and the Ponte Vecchio. Via dei Calzaiuoli, between Piazza del Duomo and Piazza della Signoria, is the city's favorite passeggiata.

 Sights

Bargello

ART MUSEUM | This building started out in the Middle Ages as the headquarters for the *capitano del popolo* (captain of the people) during the Middle Ages and was later a prison. Today, it houses the Museo

Nazionale, home to what is probably the finest collection of Renaissance sculpture in Italy. The remarkable masterpieces by Michelangelo (1475–1564), Donatello (circa 1386–1466), and Benvenuto Cellini (1500–71) are distributed amid an eclectic collection of arms, ceramics, and miniature bronzes, among other things. ⊠ *Via del Proconsolo 4, Bargello* ☎ *055/0649440* ⊕ *www.museodelbargello.it* ✉ *€9* ⊘ *Closed Tues. and 2nd and 4th Sun. of the month.*

Battistero (*Baptistery*)

RELIGIOUS BUILDING | The octagonal Baptistery is one of the supreme monuments of the Italian Romanesque style and one of Florence's oldest structures. The round Romanesque arches on the exterior date from the 11th century, and the interior dome mosaics from the beginning of the mid-13th century are justly renowned, but they could never outshine the building's famed bronze Renaissance doors decorated with panels crafted by Lorenzo Ghiberti. Michelangelo declared them so beautiful that they could serve as the Gates of Paradise. ⊠ *Piazza del Duomo, Duomo* ☎ *055/2645789* ⊕ *duomo.firenze.it* ✉ *Admission is via one of 3 combo tickets, each valid for 3 days: €30 Brunelleschi Pass (with Campanile, Cupola of the Duomo, Museo dell'Opera del Duomo, and Santa Reparata Basilica Cripta); €20 Giotto Pass (with Campanile, Museo dell'Opera, and Cripta); €15 Ghiberti Pass (with Museo dell'Opera and Cripta).*

Campanile

NOTABLE BUILDING | **FAMILY** | The Gothic bell tower designed by Giotto (circa 1266–1337) is a soaring structure of multicolor marble originally decorated with sculptures by Donatello and reliefs by Giotto, Andrea Pisano, and others (which are now in the Museo dell'Opera del Duomo). A climb of 414 steps rewards you with a close-up of Brunelleschi's cupola on the Duomo next door and a sweeping view of the city. ⊠ *Piazza del Duomo, Duomo* ☎ *055/2645789* ⊕ *duomo.firenze.it* ✉ *Admission is via one of 2 combo tickets, each valid for 3 days: €30 Brunelleschi Pass (with Battistero, Cupola of the Duomo, Museo dell'Opera del Duomo, and Santa Reparata Basilica Cripta); €20 for Giotto Pass (with Battistero, Museo dell'Opera, and Cripta).*

★ Duomo

(*Cattedrale di Santa Maria del Fiore*)
CHURCH | In 1296, Arnolfo di Cambio was commissioned to build "the loftiest, most sumptuous edifice human invention could devise" in the Romanesque style. The immense Duomo was not completed until 1436, the year it was consecrated. The imposing facade dates only from the 19th century; its neo-Gothic style somewhat complements Giotto's genuine Gothic 14th-century campanile. The real glory of the Duomo, however, is Filippo Brunelleschi's dome, presiding over the cathedral with a dignity and grace that few domes to this day can match.

Brunelleschi's cupola was one of the great engineering breakthroughs of all time: most of Europe's later domes, including that of St. Peter's in Rome, were built employing Brunelleschi's methods, and today the Duomo has come to symbolize Florence in the same way that the Eiffel Tower symbolizes Paris. The interior is a fine example of Florentine Gothic, though much of the cathedral's best-known art has been moved to the nearby Museo dell'Opera del Duomo. ⊠ *Piazza del Duomo, Duomo* ☎ *055/2645789* ⊕ *duomo.firenze. it* ✉ *Church is free. Admission to the cupola is via the €30 Brunelleschi Pass, a 3-day combo ticket that also includes the Battistero, Campanile, Museo dell'Opera del Duomo, and Santa Reparata Basilica Cripta* ⊘ *Closed Sun.* ⚐ *Timed-entry reservations required for the cupola.*

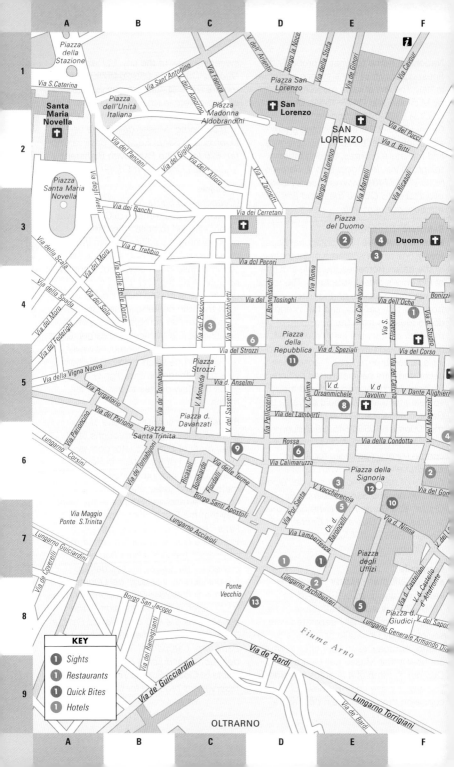

KEY

- 1 Sights
- 1 Restaurants
- 1 Quick Bites
- 1 Hotels

Around the Duomo

Santa Maria degli Angeli

Piazza Santa Maria Nuova

SAN GIOVANNI

Piazza San Firenze

Piazza Santa Croce

Santa Croce

Cappella de'Pazzi

Biblioteca Nazionale

Piazza Cavalleggeri

Piazza Mentana

Ponte alle Grazie

Sights ▼

1 Bargello............................ G6
2 Battistero E3
3 Campanile E3
4 Duomo E3
5 Galleria degli Uffizi E8
6 Mercato Nuovo D6
7 Museo dell'Opera del Duomo G3
8 Orsanmichele E5
9 Palazzo Davanzati C6
10 Palazzo Vecchio F7
11 Piazza della Repubblica........... D5
12 Piazza della Signoria E6
13 Ponte Vecchio D8

Restaurants ▼

1 Coquinarius........................ F4
2 Gucci Osteria...................... F6
3 Rivoire............................. E6

Quick Bites ▼

1 'ino................................ E7

Hotels ▼

1 Hermitage E7
2 Hotel degli Orafi.................. E8
3 Hotel Helvetia and Bristol........ C4
4 Hotel Renaissance F6
5 In Piazza della Signoria E7
6 Palazzo Vecchietti D4

★ **Galleria degli Uffizi**

ART MUSEUM | The Medici installed their art collections at Europe's first modern museum, open to the public (at first only by request) since 1591. Among the highlights are Paolo Uccello's *Battle of San Romano*; the *Madonna and Child with Two Angels* by Fra Filippo Lippi; *Birth of Venus* and *Primavera* by Sandro Botticelli; the portraits of the Renaissance duke Federico da Montefeltro and his wife Battista Sforza by Piero della Francesca; the *Madonna of the Goldfinch* by Raphael; Michelangelo's *Doni Tondo*; the *Venus of Urbino* by Titian; and the splendid *Bacchus* by Caravaggio. Late in the afternoon is usually the least crowded time to visit. For a €4 fee, advance tickets (recommended) can be reserved by phone, online, or, once in Florence, at the Uffizi's reservation booths (⊠ *Uffizi presale booth, Piazza Pitti* ☎ *055/294883*), at least one day in advance of your visit. ⊠ *Piazzale degli Uffizi 6, Piazza della Signoria* ☎ *055/294883* ⊕ *www.uffizi.it* ◱ *From €12* ⊘ *Closed Mon.*

Mercato Nuovo (*New Market*)

MARKET | FAMILY | The open-air loggia, built in 1551, teems with souvenir stands, but the real attraction is a copy of Pietro Tacca's bronze *Porcellino* (which translates as "little pig" despite the fact the animal is, in fact, a wild boar). The sculpture is Florence's equivalent of the Trevi Fountain: put a coin in his mouth, and if it falls through the grate below (according to one interpretation), it means you'll return to Florence someday. What you're seeing is a copy of a copy: Tacca's original version, in the Museo Bardini, is actually a copy of an ancient Greek work. ⊠ *Via Por Santa Maria at Via Porta Rossa, Piazza della Repubblica* ☎ *339/3271143 mobile* ⊕ *www.mercatodelporcellino.it.*

★ **Museo dell'Opera del Duomo**
(*Cathedral Museum*)

ART MUSEUM | A seven-year restoration, completed in 2015, gave Florence one of its most modern, up-to-date museums. The exhibition space was doubled, and the old facade of the cathedral, torn down in the 1580s, was re-created with a 1:1 relationship to the real thing. Both sets of Ghiberti's doors adorn the same room. Michelangelo's *Pietà* finally has the space it deserves, as does Donatello's *Mary Magdalene*. ⊠ *Piazza del Duomo 9, Duomo* ☎ *055/2302885* ⊕ *duomo.firenze.it* ◱ *Admission is via one of 3 combo tickets, each valid for 3 days: €30 Brunelleschi Pass (with Battistero, Campanile, Cupola of the Duomo, and Santa Reparata Basilica Cripta); €20 Giotto Pass (with Battistero, Campanile, and Cripta); €15 Ghiberti Pass (with Battistero and Cripta)* ⊘ *Closed 1st Tues. of month.*

Orsanmichele

CHURCH | This structure has served multiple purposes. Built in the 8th century as an oratory, in 1290, it was turned into an open-air loggia for selling grain. Destroyed by fire in 1304, it was rebuilt as a loggia-market. Between 1367 and 1380 its arcades were closed and two stories were added above. Finally, at century's end, it was turned into a church.

Although the interior contains a beautifully detailed 14th-century Gothic tabernacle by Andrea Orcagna (1308–68), it's the exterior that is most interesting. Niches contain sculptures (all copies) dating from the early 1400s to the early 1600s by Donatello and Verrocchio (1435–88), among others, which were paid for by the guilds. ⊠ *Via dei Calzaiuoli, Piazza della Repubblica* ☎ *055/0649450* ⊕ *www.bargellomusei.beniculturali.it* ◱ *€4* ⊘ *Closed Sun., Mon., and Wed.–Fri.* ⚠ *Reservations recommended.*

Continued on page 313

Florence through the Ages

Guelph vs. Ghibelline. Although Florence can lay claim to a modest importance in the ancient world, it didn't come into its own until the Middle Ages. In the early 1200s the city, like most of the rest of Italy, was rent by civic unrest. Two factions, the Guelphs and the Ghibellines, competed for power. The Guelphs supported the papacy, and the Ghibellines supported the Holy Roman Empire. Bloody battles—most notably one at Montaperti in 1260—tore Florence and other Italian cities apart. By the end of the 13th century the Guelphs ruled securely and the Ghibellines had been vanquished. This didn't end civic strife, however: the Guelphs split into the Whites and the Blacks for reasons still debated by historians. Dante, author of *the Divine Comedy*, was banished from Florence in 1301 because he was a White.

The Guilded Age. Local merchants had organized themselves into guilds by some time beginning in the 12th century. In 1250, they proclaimed themselves the *primo popolo* (literally, "first people"), making a landmark attempt at elective, republican rule. Though the episode lasted only 10 years, it constituted a breakthrough in Western history. Such a daring stance by the merchant class was a by-product of Florence's emergence as an economic powerhouse. Florentines were papal bankers; they instituted the system of international letters of credit, and the gold florin became the international standard of currency. With this economic strength came a building boom. Sculptors such as Ghiberti and Donatello decorated the new churches; painters such as Giotto and Masaccio frescoed their walls.

Mighty Medici. Though ostensibly a republic, Florence was blessed (or cursed) with one very powerful family, the Medici, who came to prominence in 1434 and were initially the de facto rulers and then the absolute rulers of Florence for several hundred years. It was under patriarch Cosimo il Vecchio (1389–1464) that the Medici's position in Florence was securely established. Florence's golden age occurred during the reign of his grandson Lorenzo de' Medici (1449–92). Lorenzo was not only an astute politician but also a highly educated man and a great patron of the arts. Called "Il Magnifico" (the Magnificent), he gathered around him poets, artists, philosophers, architects, and musicians.

Lorenzo's son Piero (1471–1503) proved inept at handling the city's affairs. He was run out of town in 1494, and Florence briefly enjoyed its status as a republic while dominated by the Dominican friar Girolamo Savonarola (1452–98). After a decade of internal unrest, the republic fell and the Medici returned to power, but Florence never regained its former prestige. By the 1530s most of the major artistic talent had left the city—Michelangelo, for one, had settled in Rome. The now-ineffectual Medici, eventually attaining the title of grand dukes, remained nominally in power until the line died out in 1737, after which time Florence passed from the Austrians to the French and back again until the unification of Italy (1865–70), when it briefly became the capital under King Vittorio Emanuele II.

THE DUOMO

FLORENCE'S BIGGEST MASTERPIECE

For all its monumental art and architecture, Florence has one undisputed centerpiece: the Cathedral of Santa Maria del Fiore, better known as the Duomo. Its cupola dominates the skyline, presiding over the city's rooftops like a red hen over her brood. Little wonder that when Florentines feel homesick, they say they have "*nostalgia del cupolone.*"

The Duomo's construction began in 1296, following the design of Arnolfo di Cambio, Florence's greatest architect of the time. By modern standards, construction was slow and haphazard—it continued through the 14th and into the 15th century, with some dozen architects having a hand in the project.

In 1366, Neri di Fioravante created a model for the hugely ambitious cupola: it was to be the largest dome in the world, surpassing Rome's Pantheon. But when the time finally came to build the dome in 1418, no one was sure how—or even if—it could be done. Florence was faced with a 143 foot hole in the roof of its cathedral, and one of the greatest challenges in the history of architecture.

Fortunately, local genius Filippo Brunelleschi was just the man for the job. Brunelleschi won the 1418 competition to design the dome, and for the next 18 years he oversaw its construction. The enormity of his achievement can hardly be overstated. Working on such a large scale (the dome weighs 37,000 tons and uses 4 million bricks) required him to invent hoists and cranes that were engineering marvels. A "dome within a dome" design and a novel herringbone bricklaying pattern were just two of the innovations used to establish structural integrity. Perhaps most remarkably, he executed the construction without a supporting wooden framework, which had previously been thought indispensable.

Brunelleschi designed the lantern atop the dome, but he died soon after its first stone was laid in 1446; it wouldn't be completed until 1461. Another 400 years passed before the Duomo received its facade, a 19th-century neo-Gothic creation.

DUOMO TIMELINE

1296 Work begins, following design by Arnolfo di Cambio.

1302 Arnolfo dies; work continues, with sporadic interruptions.

1331 Management of construction taken over by the Wool Merchants guild.

1334 Giotto appointed project overseer, designs campanile.

1337 Giotto dies; Andrea Pisano takes leadership role.

1348 The Black Plague; all work ceases.

1366 Vaulting on nave completed; Neri di Fioravante makes model for dome.

1417 Drum for dome completed.

1418 Competition is held to design the dome.

1420 Brunelleschi begins work on the dome.

1436 Dome completed.

1446 Construction of lantern begins; Brunelleschi dies.

1461 Antonio Manetti, a student of Brunelleschi, completes lantern.

1469 Gilt copper ball and cross added by Verrocchio.

1587 Original facade is torn down by Medici court.

1871 Emilio de Fabris wins competition to design new facade.

1887 Facade completed.

WHAT TO LOOK FOR INSIDE THE DUOMO

The interior of the Duomo is a fine example of Florentine Gothic with a beautiful marble floor, but the space feels strangely barren—a result of its great size and the fact that some of the best art has been moved to the nearby **Museo dell'Opera del Duomo**.

Notable among the works that remain are two towering equestrian frescoes of famous mercenaries: Niccolò da Tolentino (1456) by Andrea del Castagno, and Sir John Hawkwood (1436) by Paolo Uccello. There's also fine terra-cotta work by Luca della Robbia. Ghiberti, Brunelleschi's great rival, is responsible for much of the stained glass, as well as a reliquary urn with gorgeous reliefs. A vast fresco of the Last Judgment, painted by Vasari and Zuccari, covers the dome's interior. Brunelleschi had wanted mosaics to go there; it's a pity he didn't get his wish.

In the crypt beneath the cathedral, you can explore excavations of a Roman wall and mosaic fragments from the late 6th century; entry is near the first pier on the right. On the way down you pass Brunelleschi's modest tomb.

1. Entrance; stained glass by Ghiberti
2. Fresco of Niccolò da Tolentino by Andrea del Castagno
3. Fresco of John Hawkwood by Paolo Uccello
4. Dante and the Divine Comedy by Domenico di Michelino
5. Lunette: Ascension by Luca della Robbia
6. Above altar: two angels by Luca della Robbia. Below the altar: reliquary of St. Zenobius by Ghiberti
7. Lunette: Resurrection by Luca della Robbia
8. Entrance to dome
9. Bust of Brunelleschi by Buggiano
10. Stairs to crypt
11. Campanile

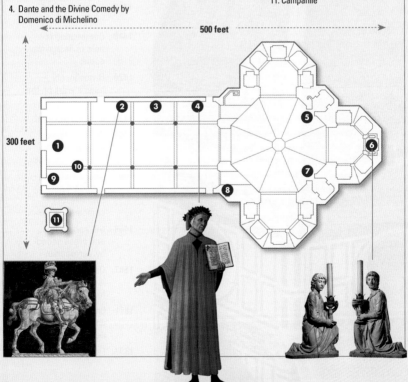

500 feet

300 feet

MAKING THE CLIMB

Climbing the 463 steps to the top of the dome is not for the faint of heart—or for the claustrophobic—but those who do it will be rewarded a smashing view of Florence (left). Keep in mind that the way up is also the way down, which means that while you're huffing and puffing in the ascent, people very close to you in a narrow staircase (below) are making their way down.

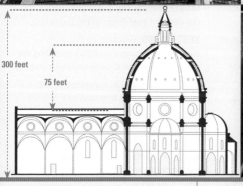

300 feet

75 feet

DUOMO BASICS

- Admission to the church is free, but there's a fee to visit the cupola, and timed-entry reservations are required.

- For an alternative to the dome, consider climbing the less trafficked campanile, which gives you a view from on high of the dome itself.

- Dress code essentials: covered shoulders, no short shorts, and hats off upon entering.

THE CRYPT

The crypt is worth a visit: computer modeling allows visitors to see its ancient Roman fabric and subsequent rebuilding. A transparent plastic model shows exactly what the earlier church looked like.

BRUNELLESCHI vs. GHIBERTI
The Rivalry of Two Renaissance Geniuses

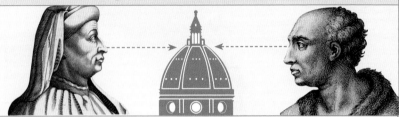

In Renaissance Florence, painters, sculptors, and architects competed for major commissions, with the winner earning the right to undertake a project that might occupy him (and keep him paid) for a decade or more. Stakes were high, and the resulting rivalries fierce—none more so than that between Filippo Brunelleschi and Lorenzo Ghiberti.

The two first clashed in 1401, for the commission to create the bronze doors of the Baptistery. When Ghiberti won, Brunelleschi took it hard, fleeing to Rome, where he would remain for 15 years. Their rematch came in 1418, over the design of the Duomo's cupola, with Brunelleschi triumphant. For the remainder of their lives, the two would miss no opportunity to belittle each other's work.

FILIPPO BRUNELLESCHI (1377–1446)

MASTERPIECE: The dome of Santa Maria del Fiore.

BEST FRIENDS: Donatello, whom he stayed with in Rome after losing the Baptistery doors competition; the Medici family, who rescued him from bankruptcy.

SIGNATURE TRAITS: Paranoid, secretive, bad tempered, practical joker, inept businessman.

SAVVIEST POLITICAL MOVE: Feigned sickness and left for Rome after his dome plans were publicly criticized by Ghiberti, who was second-in-command. The project proved too much for Ghiberti to manage on his own, and Brunelleschi returned triumphant.

MOST EMBARRASSING MOMENT: In 1434, he was imprisoned for two weeks for failure to pay a small guild fee. The humiliation might have been orchestrated by Ghiberti.

OTHER CAREER: Shipbuilder. He built a huge vessel, *Il Badalone*, to transport marble for the dome up the Arno. It sank on its first voyage.

INSPIRED: The dome of St. Peter's in Rome.

LORENZO GHIBERTI (1378–1455)

MASTERPIECE: The Gates of Paradise, the ten-paneled east doors of the Baptistery.

BEST FRIEND: Giovanni da Prato, an underling who wrote diatribes attacking the dome's design and Brunelleschi's character.

SIGNATURE TRAITS: Instigator, egoist, know-it-all, shrewd businessman.

SAVVIEST POLITICAL MOVE: During the Baptistery doors competition, he had an open studio and welcomed opinions on his work, while Brunelleschi labored behind closed doors.

OTHER CAREER: Collector of classical artifacts, historian.

INSPIRED: The Gates of Hell by Auguste Rodin.

The Gates of Paradise detail

Palazzo Davanzati

CASTLE/PALACE | The prestigious Davizzi family owned this 14th-century palace in one of Florence's swankiest medieval neighborhoods (it was sold to the Davanzati in the 15th century). The place is a delight, as you can wander through the surprisingly light-filled courtyard and climb the steep stairs to the piano nobile (there's also an elevator), where the family did most of its living. The beautiful Sala dei Pappagalli (Parrot Room) is adorned with trompe-l'oeil tapestries and gaily painted birds. ⊠ *Piazza Davanzati 13, Piazza della Repubblica* ☎ *055/0649460* ⊕ *www.bargellomusei.beniculturali.it* ⛵ *€9* ⊘ *Closed Mon. and 1st, 3rd, and 5th Sun. of month.*

Palazzo Vecchio (*Old Palace*)

CASTLE/PALACE | **FAMILY** | Florence's forbidding, fortresslike city hall was begun in 1299, presumably designed by Arnolfo di Cambio, and its massive bulk and towering campanile dominate Piazza della Signoria. It was built as a meeting place for the guildsmen governing the city at the time; today, it is still City Hall. The main attraction is on the second floor, the opulently vast Sala dei Cinquecento (Room of the Five Hundred), named for the 500-member Great Council that met here. ⊠ *Piazza della Signoria, Piazza della Signoria* ☎ *055/2768325* ⊕ *museicivici-fiorentini.comune.fi.it* ⛵ *From €12.50.*

Piazza della Repubblica

PLAZA/SQUARE | The square marks the site of an ancient forum, which was the core of the original Roman settlement and which was replaced in the Middle Ages by the Mercato Vecchio (Old Market). The current piazza, constructed between 1885 and 1895 as a neoclassical showpiece, is lined with outdoor cafés, affording an excellent opportunity for people-watching. ⊠ *Piazza della Repubblica, Florence.*

Piazza della Signoria

PLAZA/SQUARE | This is by far the most striking square in Florence. It was here, in 1497 and 1498, that the famous "bonfire of the vanities" took place, when the fanatical Dominican friar Savonarola induced his followers to hurl their worldly goods into the flames. The statues in the square and in the 14th-century Loggia dei Lanzi on the south side vary in quality. Cellini's famous bronze *Perseus* holding the severed head of Medusa is certainly the most important. ⊠ *Piazza della Signoria, Florence.*

Ponte Vecchio (*Old Bridge*)

BRIDGE | This charmingly simple bridge was built in 1345 to replace an earlier bridge swept away by flood. Its shops first housed butchers, then grocers, blacksmiths, and other merchants. But in 1593, the Medici grand duke Ferdinand I, whose private corridor linking the Medici palace (Palazzo Pitti) with the Medici offices (the Uffizi) crossed the bridge atop the shops, decided that all this plebeian commerce under his feet was unseemly. So he threw out the butchers and blacksmiths and installed 41 goldsmiths and eight jewelers. The bridge has been devoted solely to these two trades ever since. The Corridoio Vasariano (⊠ *Piazzale degli Uffizi 6, Piazza della Signoria* ☎ *055/294883*), the private Medici elevated passageway, was built by Vasari in 1565. It was most likely designed so that the Medici family wouldn't have to walk amid the commoners. As of this writing the corridor is closed to visitors. ⊠ *Florence.*

🍴 Restaurants

Coquinarius

$$ | **ITALIAN** | This rustically elegant space, which has served many purposes over the past 600 years, offers some of the tastiest food in town at great prices. It's the perfect place to come if you aren't sure what you're hungry for, as they offer a little bit of everything: salad lovers will have a hard time choosing from among the lengthy list (the Scozzese, with poached chicken, avocado, and bacon, is a winner); those with a yen for pasta will face agonizing choices (the ravioli with pecorino and pears is particularly good). **Known for:** marvelous salads; reasonably priced wine list; inconsistent service. [$] *Average main: €18* ✉ *Via delle Oche 11/r, Duomo* ☎ *055/2302153* 🌐 *www. coquinarius.it* 🕓 *Closed Sun.*

★ Gucci Osteria

$$$ | FUSION | Chef, artist, and visionary Massimo Bottura has joined forces with the creative folk at Gucci to develop a marvelous menu that is both classic and innovative. Though he trained with Ducasse and Adrià, his major influence was his grandmother's cooking. **Known for:** tortellini in crema di Parmigiano Reggiano; an ever-changing menu; outdoor seating in one of Florence's most beautiful squares. [$] *Average main: €35* ✉ *Piazza della Signoria 10, Piazza della Signoria* ☎ *055/75927038* 🌐 *www. gucciosteria.com.*

★ Rivoire

$$ | ITALIAN | One of the best spots in Florence for people-watching offers stellar service, light snacks, and terrific aperitivi. It's been around since the 1860s, and has been famous for its hot and cold chocolate (with or without cream) for more than a century. **Known for:** hot chocolate; friendly bartenders; the view on the piazza. [$] *Average main: €15* ✉ *Piazza della Signoria 5/r, Piazza della Signoria* ☎ *055/214412* 🌐 *rivoire.it/en.*

Coffee and Quick Bites

★ 'ino

$ | ITALIAN | This is the perfect place to grab a bite and/or a glass of wine after a visit to the nearby Uffizi. Only the very best ingredients go into owner Alessandro Frassica's delectable panini. **Known for:** delicious bread; interesting panini combinations; top-notch ingredients. [$] *Average main: €8* ✉ *Via dei Georgofili 3/r–7/r, Piazza della Signoria* ☎ *055/214154* 🌐 *www.inofirenze.com* 🕓 *Closed Mon. and Tues.*

Hotels

Hermitage

$$$ | HOTEL | Some rooms here have views of the Palazzo Vecchio, and others of the Arno; the rooftop terrace, where you can have breakfast or an aperitivo, is decked with flowers. **Pros:** views; friendly staff; enviable position a stone's throw from the Ponte Vecchio. **Cons:** short flight of stairs to reach elevator; might be time for a refurbishing; street noise sometimes a problem. [$] *Rooms from: €245* ✉ *Vicolo Marzio 1, Piazza della Signoria* ☎ *055/287216* 🌐 *www.hermitagehotel. com* 🛏 *28 rooms* 🍴 *Free Breakfast.*

Hotel degli Orafi

$$$$ | HOTEL | A key scene in *A Room with a View* was shot in this pensione, which is today a luxury hotel adorned with chintz and marble. **Pros:** stellar Arno views; rooftop bar; quiet location during the evenings. **Cons:** some street noise in river-facing rooms; on the path of many tour groups during the day; somewhat pricey. [$] *Rooms from: €327* ✉ *Lungarno Archibusieri 4, Piazza della Signoria* ☎ *055/26622* 🌐 *www.hoteldegliorafi.it* 🛏 *50 rooms* 🍴 *Free Breakfast.*

Hotel Helvetia and Bristol

$$$$ | HOTEL | From the cozy yet sophisticated lobby with its stone columns to the guest rooms decorated with prints, you might feel as if you're a guest in a sophisticated manor house. **Pros:** central location; excellent restaurant; old-world charm. **Cons:** rooms facing the street get some noise; breakfast is not always included in the price of a room; books up quickly. [$] *Rooms from: €675* ✉ *Via dei Pescioni 2, Piazza della Repubblica* ☎ *055/26651* 🌐 *collezione.starhotels.com* 🛏 *89 rooms* 🍴 *No Meals.*

Hotel Renaissance

$$ | HOTEL | Nestled in an old building just a stone's throw from the main civic square (Piazza Signoria), this charming little boutique hotel offers peace in quiet elegance. **Pros:** the staff; the sumptuous breakfast; the location. **Cons:** steps up to the elevator; some street noise in some rooms; books up quickly. $ *Rooms from: €180* ✉ *Via della Condotta 4, Piazza della Signoria* ☎ *055/213996* ⊕ *www.hotelrenaissancefirenze.com* ⤳ *9 rooms* ⦿ *No Meals.*

★ In Piazza della Signoria

$$$$ | B&B/INN | In this home that is part of a 15th-century palazzo, a cozy feeling permeates the charming rooms, all of which are uniquely decorated and lovingly furnished; some have damask curtains, others fanciful frescoes in the bathroom. **Pros:** marvelous staff; tasty breakfast with a view of Piazza della Signoria; some rooms easily accommodate three. **Cons:** short flight of stairs to reach elevator; some of the rooms have steps up into showers and bathtubs; books up quickly during high season. $ *Rooms from: €320* ✉ *Via dei Magazzini 2, Piazza della Signoria* ☎ *055/2399546* ⊕ *www.boutiquehotelinpiazza.com* ⤳ *13 rooms* ⦿ *Free Breakfast.*

Palazzo Vecchietti

$$$$ | HOTEL | If you're looking for a swank setting, and the possibility of staying in for a meal (each room has a tiny kitchenette), look no further than this hotel which, while thoroughly modern, dates to the 15th century. **Pros:** great service; central location; public room has a Renaissance fireplace and high ceilings. **Cons:** no restaurant; some street noise a possibility; it's expensive. $ *Rooms from: €1194* ✉ *Via degli Strozzi 4, Duomo* ☎ *055/2302802* ⊕ *www.palazzovecchietti.com* ⤳ *14 rooms* ⦿ *Free Breakfast.*

Nightlife

Hard Rock Cafe

LIVE MUSIC | Hard Rock packs in young Florentines and travelers eager to sample the music hall chain's take on classic American grub. ✉ *Via De' Brunelleschi 1, Piazza della Repubblica* ☎ *055/277841* ⊕ *www.hardrock.com.*

Yab

DANCE CLUBS | Yab never seems to go out of style, though it increasingly becomes the haunt of Florentine high school and university students intent on dancing and doing vodka shots. ✉ *Via Sassetti 5/r, Piazza della Repubblica* ☎ *055/215160* ⊕ *www.yab.it.*

 Performing Arts

Orchestra da Camera Fiorentina

MUSIC | This orchestra performs various concerts of classical music throughout the year at Orsanmichele, the grain-market–turned–church. ✉ *Via Monferrato 2, Piazza della Signoria* ☎ *055/783374* ⊕ *orchestradacamerafiorentina.it.*

Shopping

★ Bernardo

MEN'S CLOTHING | Come here for men's trousers, cashmere sweaters, and shirts with details like mother-of-pearl buttons. ✉ *Via Porta Rossa 87/r, Piazza della Repubblica* ☎ *055/283333* ⊕ *www.bernardofirenze.it.*

Carlo Piccini

JEWELRY & WATCHES | Still in operation after four generations, this Florentine institution sells antique jewelry and makes pieces to order; you can also get old jewelry reset here. ✉ *Ponte Vecchio 31/r, Piazza della Signoria* ☎ *055/292030* ⊕ *www.carlopiccini.com.*

Diesel

MIXED CLOTHING | Trendy Diesel started in Vicenza; its gear is on the "must have" list of many Italian teens. ⊠ *Via degli Speziali 16/r, Piazza della Signoria* ☎ *055/2399963* ⊕ *www.diesel.com.*

Gherardi

JEWELRY & WATCHES | Florence's king of coral, Gherardi has the city's largest selection of finely crafted pieces, as well as cultured pearls, jade, and turquoise. ⊠ *Ponte Vecchio 36/r, Piazza della Signoria* ☎ *055/211809* ⊕ *www.gherardigioielli.it.*

Mandragora Art Store

MUSEUM SHOP | This is one of the first attempts in Florence to cash in on the museum-store craze. Look for reproductions of valued works of art and jewelry. ⊠ *Piazza del Duomo 50/r, Duomo* ☎ *055/292559* ⊕ *www.mandragora.it.*

Mercato dei Fiori (*Flower Markete*)

MARKET | Every Thursday morning from September through June the covered loggia in Piazza della Repubblica hosts this lively market—a riot of plants, flowers, and difficult-to-find herbs. ⊠ *Piazza della Repubblica, Florence.*

Mercato del Porcellino

MARKET | FAMILY | If you're looking for cheery, inexpensive trinkets to take home, roam through the stalls under the loggia of the Mercato del Porcellino. ⊠ *Via Por Santa Maria at Via Porta Rossa, Piazza della Repubblica* ☎ *339/3271143 mobile* ⊕ *www.mercatodelporcellino.it.*

Missoni Boutique

MIXED CLOTHING | Shop for knitwear at the Florence outpost of the Italian brand known for its bold pieces. ⊠ *Via Porta Rossa 77–79/r, Piazza della Repubblica* ☎ *055/215774* ⊕ *www.missoni.com.*

Oro Due

JEWELRY & WATCHES | Gold jewelry and other beauteous objects are priced according to the level of craftsmanship and the value of gold bullion that day.

⊠ *Via Lambertesca 12/r, Piazza della Signoria* ☎ *055/292143.*

Patrizia Pepe

WOMEN'S CLOTHING | The Florentine designer has clothes for those with a tiny streak of rebelliousness. Sizes run extremely small. ⊠ *Piazza San Giovanni 12/r, Duomo* ☎ *055/2645056* ⊕ *www.patriziapepe.com.*

★ Pegna

FOOD | This shop has been selling both Italian and non-Italian food since 1860. If you're tired of mozzarella and feel the need for some cheddar, this is the place to find it. ⊠ *Via dello Studio 8, Duomo* ☎ *055/282701* ⊕ *www.pegna.sangiustosrl.com.*

★ Penko

JEWELRY & WATCHES | Renaissance goldsmiths provide the inspiration for this dazzling jewelry with a contemporary feel. ⊠ *Via Ferdinando Zannetti 14–16/r, Duomo* ☎ *055/211661* ⊕ *www.paolopenko.com.*

Quercioli & Lucherini

LINGERIE | This shop has been vending high-quality clothing—the kind that goes next to bare skin—since 1895. Remember that luxury comes at a price. ⊠ *Via Porta Rossa 45/r, Piazza della Repubblica* ☎ *055/292035.*

San Lorenzo

A sculptor, painter, architect, and poet, Florentine native son Michelangelo was a consummate genius, and some of his finest creations remain in his hometown. The Biblioteca Medicea Laurenziana is perhaps his most fanciful work of architecture. A key to understanding Michelangelo's genius can be found in the magnificent Cappelle Medicee, where both his sculptural and architectural prowess can be clearly seen. Planned frescoes were never completed, sadly, for they would have shown in one space the artistic triple threat that he certainly was. The towering yet graceful *David,* perhaps his most famous work, resides in the Galleria dell'Accademia.

Sights

Basilica di San Lorenzo
CHURCH | Filippo Brunelleschi designed this basilica, as well as that of Santo Spirito in the Oltrarno, in the 15th century. He never lived to see either finished. The two interiors are similar in design and effect. San Lorenzo, however, has a grid of dark, inlaid marble lines on the floor, which considerably heightens the dramatic effect. Brunelleschi's Sagrestia Vecchia (Old Sacristy) has stucco decorations by Donatello; it's at the end of the left transept. ⊠ *Piazza San Lorenzo, San Lorenzo* ☎ *055/214042* ⊕ *sanlorenzofirenze.it* 🎟 *€9* 🕑 *Closed Sun.*

Biblioteca Medicea Laurenziana
(*Laurentian Library*)
LIBRARY | Michelangelo the architect was every bit as original as Michelangelo the sculptor. He was interested in experimentation, invention, and the expression of a personal vision that was at times highly idiosyncratic. It was never more idiosyncratic than in the Laurentian Library, begun in 1524 and finished in 1568 by Bartolomeo Ammannati. Its famous *vestibolo,* a strangely shaped anteroom, has had scholars scratching their heads for centuries. In a space more than two stories high, why did Michelangelo limit his use of columns and pilasters to the upper two-thirds of the wall? Why didn't he rest them on strong pedestals instead of on huge, decorative curlicue scrolls, which rob them of all visual support? Why did he recess them into the wall, which makes them look weaker still? The architectural elements give the room a soft, rubbery look that is one of the strangest effects ever achieved by 16th-century architecture. ⊠ *Piazza San Lorenzo 9, entrance to left of San Lorenzo, San Lorenzo*

☎ *055/2937911* ⊕ *www.bmlonline.it* 🎟 *Special exhibitions €3* 🕑 *Check ahead on opening days and times as this site has seen temporary closures.*

Cappelle Medicee (*Medici Chapels*)
CHURCH | This magnificent complex includes the Cappella dei Principi, the Medici chapel and mausoleum begun in 1605 that kept marble workers busy for several hundred years, and the Sagrestia Nuova (New Sacristy), designed by Michelangelo and so called to distinguish it from Brunelleschi's Sagrestia Vecchia (Old Sacristy). Michelangelo received the commission for the New Sacristy in 1520 from Cardinal Giulio de' Medici, who later became Pope Clement VII. ⊠ *Piazza di Madonna degli Aldobrandini 6, San Lorenzo* ☎ *055/294883 reservations* ⊕ *www.bargellomusei.beniculturali.it* 🎟 *€9* 🕑 *Closed Tues.*

Galleria dell'Accademia
(*Accademia Gallery*)
ART MUSEUM | **FAMILY** | The collection of Florentine paintings, dating from the 13th to the 18th century, is largely unremarkable, but the sculptures by Michelangelo are worth the price of admission. The unfinished *Slaves,* fighting their way out of their marble prisons, were meant for the tomb of Michelangelo's overly demanding patron Pope Julius II. But the focal point is the original *David,* commissioned in 1501 by the Opera del Duomo (Cathedral Works Committee), which gave the 26-year-old sculptor a leftover block of marble that had been ruined 40 years earlier by two other sculptors. ⊠ *Via Ricasoli 58/60, San Marco* ☎ *055/294883 reservations, 055/0987100 gallery* ⊕ *www.galleriaaccademiafirenze.it* 🎟 *€12* 🕑 *Closed Mon.*

★ Mercato Centrale
MARKET | **FAMILY** | Some of the food at this huge, two-story market hall is remarkably exotic. The ground floor contains meat and cheese stalls, as well as some very good bars that have panini. The upstairs food hall is eerily reminiscent of food

Florence's Trial by Fire

One of the most striking figures of Renaissance Florence was Girolamo Savonarola, a Dominican friar who, for a moment, captured the spiritual conscience of the city. In 1491 he became prior of the convent of San Marco, where he adopted a life of austerity and delivered sermons condemning Florence's excesses and the immorality of his fellow clergy. Following the death of Lorenzo de' Medici in 1492, Savonarola was instrumental in the re-formation of the republic of Florence, ruled by a representative council with Christ enthroned as monarch. In one of his most memorable acts he urged Florentines to toss worldly possessions—from sumptuous dresses to Botticelli paintings—onto a "bonfire of the vanities" in Piazza della Signoria. Savonarola's antagonism toward church hierarchy led to his undoing: he was excommunicated in 1497, and the following year was hanged and burned on charges of heresy. Today, at the Museo di San Marco, you can visit Savonarola's cell.

halls everywhere, but the quality of the food served more than makes up for this. The downstairs market is closed on Sunday; the upstairs food hall is always open. ☒ *Piazza del Mercato Centrale, San Lorenzo* ☎ *055/2399798* ⊕ *www.mercatocentrale.it/firenze.*

Museo di Casa Martelli

HISTORIC HOME | The wealthy Martelli family, long associated with the all-powerful Medici, lived, from the 16th century, in this palace on a quiet street near the Basilica of San Lorenzo. The last Martelli died in 1986, and, in October 2009, the *casa-museo* (house-museum) opened to the public. It's the only nonreconstructed example of such a house in all of Florence, and for that reason alone it's worth a visit. The family collected art, and while most of the stuff is B-list, a few gems by Beccafumi, Salvatore Rosa, and Piero di Cosimo adorn the walls. ☒ *Via Zanetti 8, San Lorenzo* ☎ *055/0649420* ⊕ *www.bargellomusei.beniculturali.it* ☑ *Free* ⊘ *Closed Sun., Mon., Tues. morning, Wed.–Fri., and Sat. afternoon* ⚓ *Reservations suggested.*

Museo di San Marco

ART MUSEUM | A former Dominican convent adjacent to the church of San Marco houses this museum, which contains many stunning works by Fra Angelico (circa 1400–55), the Dominican friar famous for his piety as well as for his painting. When the friars' cells were restructured between 1439 and 1444, he decorated many of them with frescoes meant to spur religious contemplation. His unostentatious and direct paintings exalt the simple beauties of the contemplative life. Don't miss the famous *Annunciation,* on the upper floor, and the works in the gallery off the cloister as you enter. Here you can see his beautiful *Last Judgment*; as usual, the tortures of the damned are far more inventive and interesting than the pleasures of the redeemed. ☒ *Piazza San Marco 3, San Lorenzo* ☎ *055/0882000* ⊕ *www.polomusealetoscana.beniculturali.it* ☑ *€8* ⊘ *Closed 1st, 3rd, and 5th Sun. and 2nd and 4th Mon. of month.*

Palazzo Medici-Riccardi

CASTLE/PALACE | The main attraction of this palace, begun in 1444 by Michelozzo for Cosimo de' Medici, is the interior chapel, the Cappella dei Magi, on the piano nobile (main floor). Painted on its walls is

Benozzo Gozzoli's famous *Procession of the Magi,* finished in 1460 and celebrating both the birth of Christ and the greatness of the Medici family. The building also hosts rotating exhibits. ✉ *Via Cavour 1, San Lorenzo* ☎ *055/2760552* 🌐 *www.palazzomediciriccardi.it* 🎟 *Museum only €7, plus exhibits €10* 🕒 *Closed Wed.*

Santissima Annunziata

CHURCH | Dating from the mid-13th century, this church was restructured in 1447 by Michelozzo, who gave it an uncommon (and lovely) entrance cloister with frescoes by Andrea del Sarto (1486–1530), Pontormo (1494–1556), and Rosso Fiorentino (1494–1540). Another fresco is note is the very fine *Holy Trinity with St. Jerome* in the second chapel on the left. Done by Andrea del Castagno (circa 1421–57), it shows a wiry and emaciated St. Jerome with Paula and Eustochium, two of his closest followers. ✉ *Piazza di Santissima Annunziata, San Lorenzo* ☎ *055/266181* 🎟 *Free.*

Spedale degli Innocenti

ART MUSEUM | **FAMILY** | The building built by Brunelleschi in 1419 to serve as an orphanage takes the historical prize as the very first Renaissance building. Brunelleschi designed its portico with his usual rigor, constructing it from the two shapes he considered mathematically (and therefore philosophically and aesthetically) perfect: the square and the circle. Below the level of the arches, the portico encloses a row of perfect cubes; above the level of the arches, the portico encloses a row of intersecting hemispheres. The entire geometric scheme is articulated with Corinthian columns, capitals, and arches borrowed directly from antiquity.

At the time he designed the portico, Brunelleschi was also designing the interior of San Lorenzo, using the same basic ideas. But because the portico was finished before San Lorenzo, the Spedale degli Innocenti can claim the honor of ushering in Renaissance architecture. The 10 ceramic medallions depicting swaddled infants that decorate the portico are by Andrea della Robbia (1435–1525/28), done in about 1487.

Within the building is the small Museo degli Innocenti. Although most of the objects are minor works by major artists, they're still worth a look. Of note is Domenico Ghirlandaio's (1449–94) *Adorazione dei Magi* (*Adoration of the Magi*), executed in 1488. ✉ *Piazza di Santissima Annunziata 13, San Lorenzo* ☎ *055/2037122* 🌐 *www.museodeglinnocenti.it* 🎟 *€16.*

🍴 Restaurants

La Mescita

$ | **TUSCAN** | Come early (or late) to grab a seat at this tiny spot frequented by Florentine university students and businesspeople, who come to enjoy the day's primi (the lasagna is terrific), perhaps followed by the *polpettone* (meat loaf) and tomato sauce. Though seats are cramped, and the wine is no great shakes, the service is friendly and the food hits the spot. **Known for:** its longevity (it's been around since the 1920s); delicious pastas at rock-bottom prices; jovial staff. [$] *Average main: €10* ✉ *Via degli Alfani 70/r, Florence* ☎ *347/7951604 mobile* 🌐 *vini-la-mescita.business.site* 🕒 *Closed Wed. No dinner.*

★ Mario

$ | **TUSCAN** | Florentines flock to this narrow, family-run trattoria near San Lorenzo to feast on Tuscan favorites served at simple tables under a wooden ceiling dating from 1536. A distinct cafeteria feel and genuine Florentine hospitality prevail: you'll be seated wherever there's room, which often means with strangers. **Known for:** grilled meats; roasted potatoes; festive atmosphere. [$] *Average main: €13* ✉ *Via Rosina 2/r, corner of Piazza del Mercato Centrale, San Lorenzo* ☎ *055/218550* 🌐 *www.trattoriamario.com* 🕒 *Closed Sun. and Aug. No dinner Mon.–Wed. and Sat.*

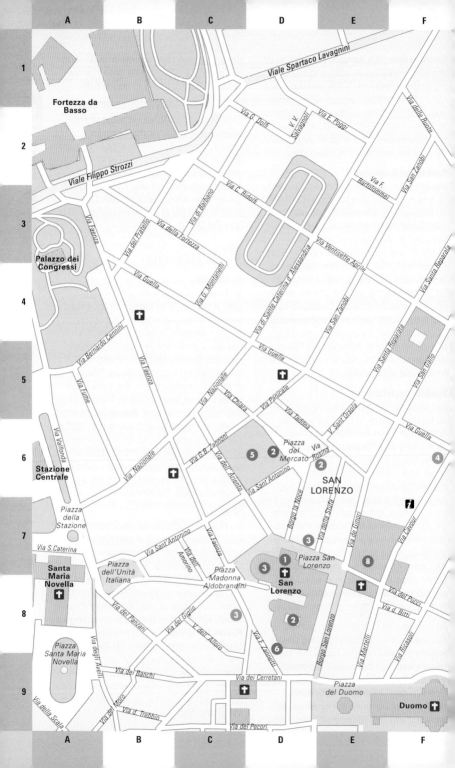

Florence SAN LORENZO

6

San Lorenzo

Sights ▼
1 Basilica di San Lorenzo **D7**
2 Biblioteca Medicea
   Laurenziana **D8**
3 Cappelle Medicee **D7**
4 Galleria dell'Accademia **H5**
5 Mercato Centrale **D6**
6 Museo di Casa Martelli **D8**
7 Museo di San Marco **H4**
8 Palazzo Medici-Riccardi **E7**
9 Santissima Annunziata **I6**
10 Spedale degli Innocenti **I6**

Restaurants ▼
1 La Mescita **H7**
2 Mario **D6**
3 Trattoria Sergio Gozzi **D7**

Quick Bites ▼
1 Alfio e Beppe **G5**
2 da Nerbone **D6**
3 Shake **G5**

Hotels ▼
1 Antica Dimora Firenze **H2**
2 Antica Dimora Johlea **H2**
3 Firenze Number Nine **C8**
4 Il Guelfo Bianco **F6**

KEY
1 Sights
1 Restaurants
1 Quick Bites
1 Hotels

0   300 ft
0   100 m

★ Trattoria Sergio Gozzi

$ | **TUSCAN** | This restaurant just across the way from the Basilica of San Lorenzo and run by the Gozzi family since 1915 serves food that's as delicious as it is affordable. The short menu changes daily, though the *lombatina alla griglia* (grilled veal T-bone steak) is almost always available, and meat eaters should not miss it. **Known for:** local favorite; ever-changing menu; terrific pastas. [$] *Average main: €12* ✉ *Piazza San Lorenzo 8/r, San Lorenzo* ☎ *055/281941* 🌐 *www.facebook.com/TrattoriaGozzi* 🕒 *Closed Sun. No dinner.*

Coffee and Quick Bites

Alfio e Beppe

$ | **ITALIAN** | Watch chickens roast over high flames while you decide which of the delightful side dishes you'd like to enjoy as well. Although this place is strictly takeout (there are no tables), it's open on Sunday when many places are not. **Known for:** good ribs; delicious roasted potatoes; roasted chicken to go. [$] *Average main: €9* ✉ *Via Cavour 118/r, San Marco* ☎ *055/214108* 🕒 *Closed Sat.*

★ da Nerbone

$ | **TUSCAN** | This *tavola calda* (cafeteria) in the middle of the covered Mercato Centrale has been serving Florentines since 1872. Tasty primi and secondi are always available, as are *bollitos* (boiled beef sandwiches), but the cognoscenti come for the *panino con il lampredotto* (tripe sandwich)—best when it's prepared *bagnato* (with the bread quickly dipped in the tripe cooking liquid) and served slathered with green and/or spicier red sauce. **Known for:** tripe sandwich; frequented by locals (and everyone else); favorite dishes sell out fast. [$] *Average main: €10* ✉ *Piazza Mercato Centrale, Florence* ☎ *055/6480251* 🕒 *Closed Sun. No dinner.*

Shake

$ | **ITALIAN** | Handily located between Piazza San Marco and Piazza San Lorenzo, Shake serves up creative juices, tasty baked goods, wonderful salads, and great bowls. It's committed to sustainability and to keeping its carbon footprint small. **Known for:** remarkable way with juices (the De-Tox is especially good); nice, cheerful staff; courtyard seating. [$] *Average main: €7* ✉ *Via Camillo Cavour 67/69r, San Lorenzo* ☎ *055/0515418* 🌐 *www.shakecafe.bio.*

Hotels

Antica Dimora Firenze

$$ | **B&B/INN** | Each simply furnished room in this *residenza* (guesthouse) is painted a different pastel color—peach, rose, powder-blue—and double-glazed windows ensure a peaceful night's sleep. **Pros:** ample DVD library; honor bar with Antinori wines; complimentary coffee, tea, and fresh fruit available all day in the sitting room. **Cons:** books up quickly; some might consider it too small; might be too removed for some. [$] *Rooms from: €178* ✉ *Via San Gallo 72, San Marco* ☎ *055/4627296* 🌐 *www.antichedimorefiorentine.it* 🛏 *6 rooms* 🍴 *Free Breakfast.*

★ Antica Dimora Johlea

$$$ | **B&B/INN** | In addition to guest rooms with four-poster beds and sweeping drapes, this 19th-century palazzo has a charming, flower-filled terrace where you can sip a glass of wine while taking in a view of Brunelleschi's cupola. **Pros:** great staff; cheerful rooms; honor bar. **Cons:** staff goes home at 7:30; staircase to roof terrace is narrow; steps to breakfast room. [$] *Rooms from: €263* ✉ *Via San Gallo 80, San Marco* ☎ *055/4633292* 🌐 *www.antichedimorefiorentine.it* 🛏 *6 rooms* 🍴 *Free Breakfast.*

Firenze Number Nine

$$$ | HOTEL | At this elegant hotel, swank reception rooms have comfortable couches and contemporary artwork, and guest rooms feature parquet floors, high ceilings, and furnishings that combine Scandinavian sleekness with the Italian love for fine fabric (think: damask draperies). **Pros:** historic center location; walk-in gym and spa; sumptuous breakfast. **Cons:** some street noise; might be too trendy for some; books up quickly. $ *Rooms from: €342* ⊠ *Via del Conti 9, San Lorenzo* ☎ *055/293777* ⊕ *www.firenzenumbernine.com* ⟿ *45 rooms* ⦿ *Free Breakfast.*

Il Guelfo Bianco

$$ | HOTEL | The 15th-century building has all modern conveniences, but Renaissance charm still shines in the high-ceiling rooms. **Pros:** great staff; beautiful floors made of either parquet or marble; sumptuous breakfast. **Cons:** rooms facing the street can be noisy; might be too removed for some; not all rooms are well lit. $ *Rooms from: €189* ⊠ *Via Cavour 29, San Marco* ☎ *055/288330* ⊕ *www.ilguelfobianco.it* ⟿ *40 rooms* ⦿ *Free Breakfast.*

Shopping

★ Baroni Alimentari

FOOD | The cheese selection at Baroni may be the most comprehensive in Florence. It also sells high-quality truffle products, vinegars, and other delicacies, many of which are, or can be, packed for shipping. ⊠ *Mercato Central, enter at Via Signa, San Lorenzo* ☎ *055/289576* ⊕ *www.facebook.com/baronialimentari.*

Mercato Centrale

MARKET | FAMILY | This huge indoor food market offers a staggering selection of all things edible. Downstairs is full of vendors hawking their wares—meat, fish, fruit, vegetables—upstairs (daily 8 am–midnight) is full of food stalls serving up the best of what Italy has to offer.

⊠ *Piazza del Mercato Centrale, San Lorenzo* ☎ *055/2399798* ⊕ *www.mercatocentrale.it/firenze.*

Mercato di San Lorenzo

MARKET | FAMILY | The clothing and leather-goods stalls at Mercato di San Lorenzo in the streets next to the San Lorenzo church have bargains for shoppers on a budget. ⊠ *Via dell'Ariento, Florence.*

Santa Maria Novella

Piazza Santa Maria Novella is a gorgeous, pedestrian-only square, with grass (laced with roses) and plenty of places to sit and rest your feet. The streets in and around the piazza have their share of architectural treasures, including some of Florence's most tasteful palaces. Between Santa Maria Novella and the Arno is Via Tornabuoni, Florence's swankiest shopping street.

Sights

Museo Novecento

ART MUSEUM | It began life as a 13th-century Franciscan hostel offering shelter to tired pilgrims. It later became a convalescent home, and in the late 18th century it was a school for poor girls. Now the former Ospedale di San Paolo houses a museum devoted to Italian art of the 20th century. Admittedly, most of these artists are not exactly household names, but the museum is so beautifully well done that it's worth a visit. The second floor contains works by artists from the second half of the century; start on the third floor and go directly to the collection of Alberto della Ragione, a naval engineer who was determined to be on the cutting edge of art collecting. ⊠ *Piazza Santa Maria Novella 10, Santa Maria Novella* ☎ *055/2768224* ⊕ *www.museonovecento.it* ⛝ *€9.50* ⊗ *Closed Thurs.*

Meet the Medici

The Medici were the dominant family of Renaissance Florence, wielding political power and financing some of the world's greatest art. You'll see their names at every turn around the city. These are some of the more notable family members.

Cosimo il Vecchio (1389–1464): incredibly wealthy banker to the popes and the first in the family line to act as de facto ruler of Florence. He was a great patron of the arts and architecture; he was the moving force behind the family palace and the Dominican complex of San Marco.

Lorenzo il Magnifico (1449–92): grandson of Cosimo il Vecchio who presided over a Florence largely at peace with its neighbors. A collector of cameos, a writer of sonnets, and a lover of ancient texts, he was the preeminent Renaissance man and, like his grandfather, the de facto ruler of Florence.

Leo X (1475–1521): also known as Giovanni de' Medici, he became the first Medici pope, helping extend the family power base to include Rome and the Papal States. His reign was characterized by a host of problems, the biggest one being a former friar named Martin Luther.

Catherine de' Medici (1519–89): was married by her great uncle Pope Clement VII to Henry of Valois, who later became Henry II of France. Wife of one king and mother of three, she was the first Medici to marry into European royalty. Lorenzo il Magnifico, her great-grandfather, would have been thrilled.

Cosimo I (1537–74): the first grand duke of Tuscany, not to be confused with his ancestor, Cosimo il Vecchio.

Museo Salvatore Ferragamo

ART MUSEUM | A shrine to footwear, the shoes in this dramatically displayed collection were designed by Salvatore Ferragamo (1898–1960) beginning in the early 20th century. Born in southern Italy, Ferragamo jump-started his career in Hollywood by creating shoes for the likes of Mary Pickford and Rudolph Valentino. He then returned to Florence and set up shop in the 13th-century Palazzo Spini Ferroni. The collection includes about 16,000 shoes, and those on display are frequently rotated. Special exhibitions are also mounted here and are well worth visiting—past shows have been devoted to Audrey Hepburn, Greta Garbo, and Marilyn Monroe. ⊠ *Piazza Santa Trinita 5/r, Santa Maria Novella* ☎ *055/3562846* ⊕ *museo.ferragamo.com* 🎫 *€8.*

Museo Stibbert

ART MUSEUM | Frederick Stibbert (1838–1906), born in Florence to an Italian mother and an English father, liked to collect things. Over a lifetime of doing so, he amassed some 50,000 objects. This museum, which was also his home, displays many of them. He had a fascination with medieval armor, as well as costumes, particularly Uzbek costumes, which are exhibited in a room called the Moresque Hall. These are mingled with an extensive collection of swords and guns. ⊠ *Via Federico Stibbert 26, Florence* ☎ *055/475520* ⊕ *www.museostibbert.it* 🎫 *€10* ⊗ *Closed Thurs.*

Palazzo Strozzi

CASTLE/PALACE | The Strozzi family built this imposing palazzo in an attempt to outshine the nearby Palazzo Medici. The exterior is simple, severe, and massive: it's a testament to the wealth of a patrician, 15th-century Florentine family. The interior courtyard is another matter altogether. It is here that the classical vocabulary—columns, capitals, pilasters, arches, and cornices—is given uninhibited and powerful expression. Inside, find rotating exhibits with a focus on contemporary art. ✉ *Via Tornabuoni, Piazza della Repubblica* ☎ *055/2645155* 🌐 *www.palazzostrozzi.org* 🎟 *Courtyard free; exhibits €15.*

Santa Maria Novella

CHURCH | The facade of this church looks distinctly clumsy by later Renaissance standards, and with good reason: it is an architectural hybrid. The lower half was completed mostly in the 14th century and about 100 years later (around 1456), architect Leon Battista Alberti was called in to complete the job, adding architectural motifs in an entirely different style. Highlights include the 14th-century, stained-glass-rose window depicting the *Coronation of the Virgin*; the Cappella Filippo Strozzi, containing late-15th-century frescoes and stained glass by Filippino Lippi; and the *cappella maggiore,* displaying frescoes by Ghirlandaio. ✉ *Piazza Santa Maria Novella 18, Santa Maria Novella* ☎ *055/2768224* 🌐 *www.smn.it/en* 🎟 *€7.50* 🕒 *Closed Sun. morning.*

Santa Trinita

CHURCH | Started in the 11th century by Vallombrosian monks and originally Romanesque in style, this church underwent a Gothic remodeling during the 14th century. (Remains of the Romanesque construction are visible on the interior front wall.) The major works are the fresco cycle and altarpiece in the Cappella Sassetti, the second to the high altar's right, painted by Ghirlandaio between 1480 and 1485. His work here possesses graceful decorative appeal and proudly depicts his native city, as most of the cityscapes show 15th-century Florence in all its glory. The wall frescoes illustrate scenes from the life of St. Francis, and the altarpiece, depicting the *Adoration of the Shepherds,* veritably glows. ✉ *Piazza Santa Trinita, Santa Maria Novella* ☎ *055/216912* 🕒 *Closed noon–4 pm.*

🍴 Restaurants

Buca Lapi

$$$$ | **ITALIAN** | The Antinori family started selling wine from their palace's basement in the 15th century, and, 600 years later, this *buca* (hole) is a lively, subterranean spot filled with Florentine aristocrats chowing down on what might be the best—and the most expensive—bistecca fiorentina (flavorful, lightly seasoned beef) in town. The classic Tuscan menu has the usual suspects: *crostino di cavolo nero* (black cabbage on toasted garlic bread), along with ribollita (vegetable, bean, and bread soup) and pappa al pomodoro (tomato and bread soup). **Known for:** gargantuan bistecca fiorentina; adherence to Tuscan classics; pet-friendly. [$] *Average main: €40* ✉ *Via del Trebbio 1r* ☎ *055/213768* 🌐 *www.bucalapi.com/en* 🕒 *Closed Sun. No lunch.*

Cantinetta Antinori

$$$ | **TUSCAN** | After a morning of shopping on Via Tornabuoni, stop for lunch in this 15th-century palazzo, a place to see and be seen as well as to dine. The panache of the clientele is matched by that of the food, with dishes such as *tramezzino con pane di campagna al tartufo* (bread served with country pâté and truffles) and *insalata di gamberoni e gamberetti con carciofi freschi* (crayfish and prawn salad with shaved raw artichokes). **Known for:** chic clientele; most ingredients come from the family farm; outdoor seating in a 15th-century courtyard. [$] *Average main: €31* ✉ *Piazza Antinori 3, Santa Maria Novella* ☎ *055/292234* 🌐 *www.cantinetta-antinori.com/en* 🕒 *Closed Sun.*

★ La Sostanza

$$ | **TUSCAN** | Since opening its doors in 1869, this trattoria has been serving top-notch, unpretentious food to Florentines

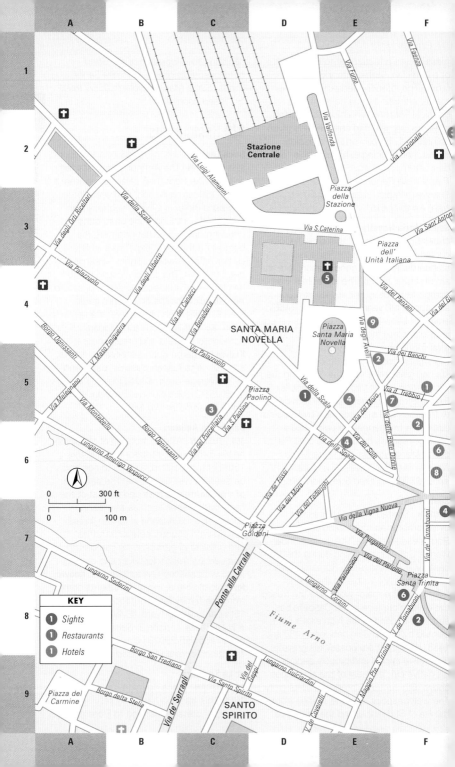

Santa Maria Novella

Sights ▼

1	Museo Novecento................	**D5**
2	Museo Salvatore Ferragamo......	**F8**
3	Museo Stibbert	**G1**
4	Palazzo Strozzi	**F7**
5	Santa Maria Novella	**E4**
6	Santa Trinita.......................	**F8**

Restaurants ▼

1	Buca Lapi...........................	**F5**
2	Cantinetta Antinori	**F6**
3	La Sostanza	**C5**
4	La Spada...........................	**E6**
5	Mangiafoco	**G8**
6	Obicà...............................	**F6**
7	Osteria Belle Donne................	**E5**
8	Procacci...........................	**F6**
9	Vincanto	**E4**

Hotels ▼

1	Gallery Hotel Art	**G9**
2	Hotel L'Orologio	**E5**
3	Nuova Italia	**F2**
4	The Place Firenze..................	**E5**

6

Florence SANTA MARIA NOVELLA

Map labels:

Via Nazionale · Via Guelfa · Via Panicale · Via Chiara · Via Taddea · Via Sant'Orsola · Via San Gallo · Via Guelfa · T. G. B. Zannoni · Piazza del Mercato · Via Rosina · Via Cavour

SAN GIOVANNI

Via dell'Ariento · Borgo la Noce · Via della Stufa · Via de' Ginori · Via Ricasoli

Via Faenza · Piazza San Lorenzo · Via dei Servi

Piazza Madonna Aldobrandini · San Lorenzo · Via del Pucci

Via F. Zannetti · Borgo San Lorenzo · Via Martelli · Via Ricasoli · Via d. Bitti

dell' Alloro

Via dei Cerretani · Piazza del Duomo · Duomo

Via del Pecori

Via dei Vecchietti · Via del Tosinghi · Via Roma · Via dell'Oche · Via dello Studio

V. Brunelleschi · Via S. Elisabetta · Via del Corso

Via del Strozzi · Piazza della Repubblica · Via d. Speziali

azza rozzi · Via d. Anselmi · Via Calima · V. d. Orsanmichele · V. d. Tavolini · Via del Corso · Via Dante Alighieri

Via Pellicceria · Via del Lamberti · Via dei Magazzini

P'za d. Davanzati · Rossa · Via della Condotta

Via Calimaruzza · Piazza della Signoria · Piazza San Firenze

Via delle Terme · V. Vacchereccia · Via del Gondi

Fiordaliso · V. Por S.ta · Ch. d. Baroncelli · Via d. Ninna · Via dei Leoni

rgo Santi Apostoli · Via Lambertesca · Galleria degli Uffizi · Via Vinegia

ingarno Acciaioli · Piazza degli Uffizi · Via dei Neri

who like their bistecca very large and, of course, very rare, as that's the only way to eat it. The *tartino di carciofi* (artichoke tart) and the *pollo al burro* (chicken with butter) are signature dishes. **Known for:** Tuscan classics; delicious desserts (especially the semifreddo); no-frills, 19th-century decor. $ *Average main: €17* ✉ *Via del Porcellana 25/r, Lungarno North* ☎ *055/212691* ⊕ *www.facebook.com/trattoriasostanzailtroia* ⊟ *No credit cards* ⊘ *Closed Sun.*

La Spada

$ | **ITALIAN** | **FAMILY** | Near Santa Maria Novella is La Spada. Walk in and inhale the fragrant aromas of meats cooking in the wood-burning oven. **Known for:** grilled meats and aromatic pastas; adherence to Tuscan cuisine; eat in or order takeout. $ *Average main: €11* ✉ *Via della Spada 62/r, Santa Maria Novella* ☎ *055/218757* ⊕ *www.ristorantelaspada.it.*

★ Mangiafoco

$$ | **TUSCAN** | On a romantic medieval side street in the heart of the centro storico, this small restaurant serves Tuscan classics that reflect both the whims of the chef and what's in season. The menu features creative salads and pasta, meat, and truffle dishes, as well as *taglieri* (mixed meat and cheese plates) that are often served with jams made from Chianti, vin santo, or balsamic vinegar. **Known for:** phenomenal wines by the glass or the bottle; house-made breads and desserts; great service. $ *Average main: €20* ✉ *Borgo Santi Apostoli 26/r, Santa Maria Novella* ☎ *055/2658170* ⊕ *www.mangiafoco.com* ⊘ *Closed Wed.*

Obicà

$$ | **ITALIAN** | Mozzarella takes center stage at this sleek eatery on Florence's swankiest street. The cheese, along with its culinary cousin *burrata* (a fresh cheese filled with cream), arrives daily from southern Italy to become the centerpiece for various salads and pastas. **Known for:** mozzarella-laden menu; outstanding pizza and desserts; outdoor seating in nice weather. $ *Average main: €18* ✉ *Via Tornabuoni 16, Santa Maria Novella* ☎ *055/2773526* ⊕ *www.obica.com/restaurants/florence.*

Osteria delle Belle Donne

$$ | **TUSCAN** | Down the street from the church of Santa Maria Novella, this gaily decorated spot, always festooned with some sort of creative decoration (ropes of garlic and other vegetables have figured in the past) has an ever-changing menu and stellar service. The list of Tuscan standards is shaken up with alternatives such as *sedani con bacon, verza, e uova* (thick noodles sauced with bacon, cabbage, and egg); when avocados are ripe, they're on the menu, too, either with cold boiled shrimp or expertly grilled chicken breast. **Known for:** seasonal ingredients; many dishes not typical of Tuscany; dessert. $ *Average main: €19* ✉ *Via delle Belle Donne 16/r, Santa Maria Novella* ☎ *055/2382609* ⊕ *www.belledonneosteria.it.*

★ Procacci

$$ | **ITALIAN** | At this classy Florentine institution dating from 1885, try one of the truffle panini and swish it down with a glass of prosecco. **Known for:** pane tartufato; excellent wines by the glass; serene (but tiny) space. $ *Average main: €15* ✉ *Via Tornabuoni 64/r, Santa Maria Novella* ☎ *055/211656* ⊕ *www.procacci1885.it.*

Vincanto

$$ | **ITALIAN** | It opens at 11 am and closes at midnight: this is a rarity in Florentine dining. They do a little bit of everything here, including fine pastas, salads, pizzas, and even an American-style breakfast. **Known for:** a wide-ranging menu; kitchen stays open; outside terrace with views of a beautiful square. $ *Average main: €24* ✉ *Piazza Santa Maria Novella 23/r, Santa Maria Novella* ☎ *055/2741555* ⊕ *www.ristorantevincanto.com.*

Hotels

Gallery Hotel Art
$$$$ | **HOTEL** | High design resides at this art showcase near the Ponte Vecchio, where sleek, uncluttered rooms are dressed mostly in neutrals but have luxe touches such as leather headboards and kimono robes. **Pros:** trendy atmosphere; artistic touches; the in-house Fusion Bar serves delightful cocktails. **Cons:** some street noise; books up quickly; might be too trendy for some. $ *Rooms from: €560 ⊠ Vicolo dell'Oro 5, Santa Maria Novella ☎ 055/27263 ⊕ www.lungarnocollection.com/gallery-hotel-art ⤵ 63 rooms* ⦿ *Free Breakfast.*

Hotel L'Orologio
$$$$ | **HOTEL** | The owner of this quietly understated, elegant hotel has a real passion for watches, which is why he chose to name his hotel after them (and why you will see them throughout the property)—and the location can't be beat, as it abuts the increasingly beautiful Piazza Santa Maria Novella. **Pros:** location; great staff; stunning breakfast room. **Cons:** some folks think it's too close to the train station; gets the occasional tour group; holds conferences from time to time. $ *Rooms from: €466 ⊠ Piazza Santa Maria Novella 24, Santa Maria Novella ☎ 055/277380 ⊕ www.hotelorologioflorence.com ⤵ 60 rooms* ⦿ *Free Breakfast.*

Nuova Italia
$$ | **HOTEL** | **FAMILY** | The genial Viti family oversees this property with clean and simple rooms near the train station and well within walking distance of the sights. **Pros:** reasonable rates; close to everything; great for those on a budget. **Cons:** no elevator; the neighborhood is highly trafficked; some street noise. $ *Rooms from: €176 ⊠ Via Faenza 26, Santa Maria Novella ☎ 055/287508 ⊕ www.hotel-nuovaitalia.com ☉ Closed Dec. 20–Dec. 27 ⤵ 20 rooms* ⦿ *Free Breakfast.*

★ The Place Firenze
$$$$ | **HOTEL** | Hard to spot from the street, this sumptuous place provides all the comforts of a luxe home away from home—expect soothing earth tones in the guest rooms, free minibars, crisp linens, and room service offering organic dishes. **Pros:** private, intimate feel; stellar staff; small dogs allowed. **Cons:** breakfast at a shared table; books up quickly; might be too trendy for some. $ *Rooms from: €660 ⊠ Piazza Santa Maria Novella 7, Santa Maria Novella ☎ 055/2645181 ⊕ www.theplacefirenze.com ⤵ 20 rooms* ⦿ *Free Breakfast.*

Performing Arts

Maggio Musicale Fiorentino
MUSIC | Parco della Musica (Music Park) was designed by Paolo Desideri and associates and the landmark complex is residence for Maggio Musicale Fiorentino. The foundation also holds forth at Teatro Goldoni (⊠ *Via Santa Maria 15 ☎ 055/2776393*). Purchase tickets directly at the box office or by phone (☎ *055/2779309*). You can also buy them online. ⊠ *Piazza Vittorio Gui 1, Santa Maria Novella ☎ 055/2779309 ⊕ www.maggiofiorentino.it.*

Tuscany Hall
FESTIVALS | This large exhibition space, formerly Teatro Saschall, hosts many events throughout the year, including a large art market, visiting rock stars, and bands from all over Europe. ⊠ *Lungarno Aldo Moro 3, Lungarno North ☎ 055/6504112 ⊕ www.tuscanyhall.it.*

Shopping

Alberto Cozzi
STATIONERY | You'll find an extensive line of Florentine papers and paper products in this shop, where artisans also rebind and restore books and works on paper. Opening hours are tricky, so it's best to call before stopping by. ⊠ *Via del Parione*

35/r, Santa Maria Novella ☎ 055/294968 ⊕ www.legatoriacozzifirenze.it.

★ Angela Caputi

JEWELRY & WATCHES | Angela Caputi wows Florentine cognoscenti with her highly creative, often outsize, acrylic jewelry. A small but equally creative collection of women's clothing made of fine fabrics is also on offer. ⊠ Borgo Santi Apostoli 44/46, Santa Maria Novella ☎ 055/292993 ⊕ www.angelacaputi.com.

Antica Officina del Farmacista Dr. Vranjes

PERFUME | Dr. Vranjes elevates aromather-apy to an art form with scents for the body and home. ⊠ Via della Vigna Nuova 30/r, Santa Maria Novella ☎ 055/0945851 ⊕ www.drvranjes.it.

Brandimarte

HOUSEWARES | Most people want to buy gold (for which it is justly famous) when they come to Florence. That said, Brandimarte, which has specialized in exquisitely crafted silver objects since 1955, is well worth a visit. ⊠ Via del Moro 92/r, Santa Maria Novella ☎ 349/4220269 mobile ⊕ www.brandimarte.com.

Cellerini

LEATHER GOODS | In a city where it seems just about everybody carries an expen-sive leather bag, Cellerini is an institution. ⊠ Via del Sole 9/r, Santa Maria Novella ☎ 055/282533 ⊕ www.cellerini.it.

Emilio Pucci

MIXED CLOTHING | The aristocratic Marchese di Barsento, Emilio Pucci, became an international name in the late 1950s when the stretch ski clothes he designed for himself caught on with the dolce vita ("sweet life") crowd—his pseudopsychedelic prints and "palazzo pajamas" became all the rage. ⊠ Via Tornabuoni 20–22/r, Santa Maria Novella ☎ 055/2658082 ⊕ www.emiliopucci.com.

Ferragamo

SHOES | This classy institution, in a 13th-century palazzo, displays designer clothing and accessories, though elegant footwear still underlies the Ferragamo success. ⊠ Via Tornabuoni 14/r, Santa Maria Novella ☎ 055/292123 ⊕ store.ferragamo.com.

Gatto Bianco

JEWELRY & WATCHES | This contemporary jeweler has breathtakingly beautiful piec-es featuring semiprecious and precious stones. ⊠ Borgo Santi Apostoli 12/r, San-ta Maria Novella ☎ 055/282989 ⊕ www.gattobiancogioielli.com.

Giotti

LEATHER GOODS | You'll find multiple lines of leather bags, wallets, and other acces-sories here. ⊠ Piazza Ognissanti 3–4/r, Lungarno North ☎ 055/294265 ⊕ www.bottegagiotti.com.

★ Loretta Caponi

MIXED CLOTHING | Synonymous with Florentine embroidery, this shop sells luxury lace, linens, and lingerie that have earned the eponymous signora world-wide renown. There's also beautiful (and expensive) clothing for children. ⊠ Via delle Belle Donne 28/r, Santa Maria Novella ☎ 055/213668 ⊕ www.lorettacaponi.it/en.

★ Officina Profumo Farmaceutica di Santa Maria Novella

PERFUME | The essence of a Florentine holiday is captured in the sachets of this Art Nouveau emporium of herbal cosmet-ics and soaps that are made following centuries-old recipes created by friars. ⊠ Via della Scala 16, Santa Maria Novella ☎ 055/216276 ⊕ www.smnovella.it.

★ Pineider

STATIONERY | Although it has shops throughout the world, Pineider started out in Florence in 1774 and still does all its printing here. Stationery and business cards are the mainstay, but the stores also sell fine-leather desk accessories as well as a less stuffy, more lighthearted line of products. ⊠ Lungarno degli Acciaiuoli 72–76/r, Santa Maria Novella ☎ 055/284655 ⊕ www.pineider.com.

Principe

DEPARTMENT STORE | This Florentine institution sells casual clothes for men, women, and children at far-from-casual prices. It also has a great housewares department. ⊠ *Via del Sole 2, Santa Maria Novella* ☎ *055/292843* ⊕ *www. principedifirenze.com.*

Valli

FABRICS | Gifted seamstresses (and seamsters) should look no further than this place, which sells sumptuous silks, beaded fabrics, lace, wool, and tweeds by the meter. ⊠ *Via della Vigna Nuova 81/r, Santa Maria Novella* ☎ *055/282485* ⊕ *www.vallitessuti.com.*

Santa Croce

The Santa Croce quarter, on the southeast fringe of the historic center, was built up in the Middle Ages outside the second set of medieval city walls. The centerpiece of the neighborhood was (and is) the basilica of Santa Croce, which could hold great numbers of worshippers; the vast piazza could accommodate any overflow and also served as a fairground and, allegedly since the middle of the 16th century, as a playing field for no-holds-barred soccer games. A center of leatherworking since the Middle Ages, the neighborhood is still packed with leatherworkers and leather shops.

 Sights

Casa Buonarroti

ART MUSEUM | If you really enjoy walking in the footsteps of the great genius, you may want to complete the picture by visiting the Buonarroti family home. Michelangelo lived here from 1516 to 1525, and later gave it to his nephew, whose son, Michelangelo il Giovane (Michelangelo the Younger), turned it into a gallery dedicated to his great-uncle. The artist's descendants filled it with art treasures, some by Michelangelo

himself. Two early marble works—the *Madonna of the Stairs* and *Battle of the Centaurs*—demonstrate his genius. ⊠ *Via Ghibellina 70, Santa Croce* ☎ *055/241752* ⊕ *www.casabuonarroti.it* ⊡ *€8* ⊙ *Closed Tues.*

Piazza Santa Croce

PLAZA/SQUARE | Originally outside the city's 12th-century walls, this piazza grew with the Franciscans, who used it for public preaching. During the Renaissance, it hosted *giostre* (jousts), including one sponsored by Lorenzo de' Medici. Lined with many palazzi dating from the 15th and 16th centuries, the square remains one of Florence's loveliest and is a great place to people-watch. ⊠ *Piazza Santa Croce, Santa Croce.*

★ Santa Croce

CHURCH | The collection of art within this Gothic church is by far the most important of any church in Florence. The most famous works are the Giotto frescoes in the two chapels immediately to the right of the high altar. They illustrate scenes from the lives of St. John the Evangelist and St. John the Baptist (in the right-hand chapel), as well as those from the life of St. Francis (in the left-hand chapel). Among the church's other highlights are Donatello's *Annunciation*; 14th-century frescoes by Taddeo Gaddi (circa 1300–66) illustrating scenes from the life of the Virgin Mary; and Donatello's *Crucifix*, criticized by Brunelleschi for making Christ look like a peasant. ⊠ *Piazza Santa Croce 16, Santa Croce* ☎ *055/2466105* ⊕ *www.santacroceopera.it* ⊡ *Church and museum €8* ⊙ *Closed Tues.*

Sinagoga

SYNAGOGUE | Jews were well settled in Florence by the end of the 14th century. By 1574, however, they were required to live within the large "ghetto" at the north side of today's Piazza della Repubblica, by decree of Cosimo I. Construction of the modern Moorish-style synagogue began in 1874 as a bequest of David Levi, who wished to endow a synagogue

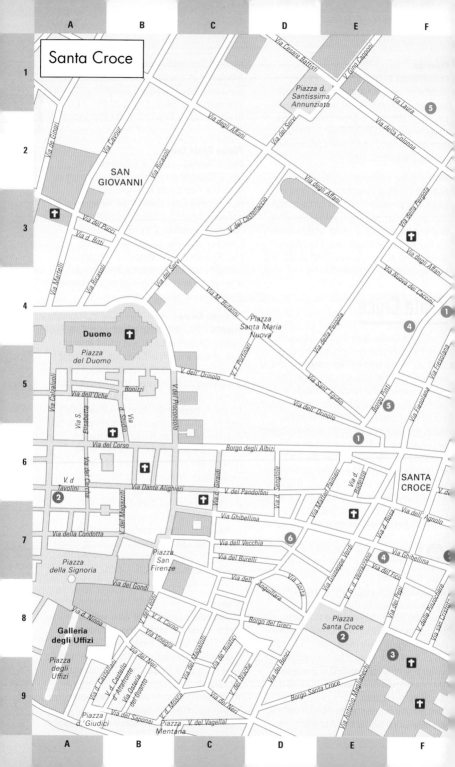

Santa Croce

SAN
GIOVANNI

Duomo ✝
Piazza
del Duomo

Piazza d.
Santissima
Annunziata

Piazza
Santa Maria
Nuova

SANTA
CROCE

Piazza
della Signoria

Piazza
San
Firenze

Galleria
degli Uffizi

Piazza
degli
Uffizi

Piazza
Santa Croce

Piazza
d. Giudici

Piazza
Mentana

6

Florence SANTA CROCE

Sights ▼
1 Casa Buonarroti **F7**
2 Piazza Santa Croce................. **E8**
3 Santa Croce **F8**
4 Sinagoga............................ **H5**

Restaurants ▼
1 Antico Noè **E6**
2 Cibrèo Ristorante **H6**
3 Cibrèo Trattoria **H6**
4 Enoteca Pinchiorri................. **F7**
5 La Giostra........................... **E5**
6 Pizzeria Caffè Italiano **D7**
7 Ruth's **H5**

Quick Bites ▼
1 da Rocco…........................... **I7**
2 Perché No!…........................ **A6**

Hotels ▼
1 Borgo Pinti.......................... **F4**
2 The Four Seasons **H1**
3 Hotel Regency **J2**
4 Monna Lisa.......................... **F4**
5 Morandi alla Crocetta............. **F1**

KEY
1 Sights
1 Restaurants
1 Quick Bites
1 Hotels

"worthy of the city." Falcini, Micheli, and Treves designed the building on a domed Greek cross plan with galleries in the transept and a roofline bearing three distinctive copper cupolas visible from all over Florence. The exterior has alternating bands of tan travertine and pink granite, reflecting an Islamic style repeated in Giovanni Panti's ornate interior. ⊠ *Via Farini 6, Santa Croce* ☎ *055/245252* ⊕ *www.firenzebraica.it/sinagoga* ⊠ *Synagogue and museum €6.50 (reservations €1)* ☾ *Closed Sat. and Jewish holidays.*

🍴 Restaurants

Antico Noè

$$ | TUSCAN | FAMILY | The short menu at the one-room eatery relies heavily on seasonal ingredients picked up daily at the market. Although the secondi are good, the antipasti and primi really shine, and the menu really comes alive during truffle and artichoke seasons (don't miss the grilled artichokes if they're available). **Known for:** attention to seasonal vegetables; artichoke dishes; porcini dishes. Ⓢ *Average main: €18* ⊠ *Volta di San Piero 6/r, Santa Croce* ☎ *055/2340838* ⊕ *www.anticonoe.com* ☾ *Closed Sun.*

★ Cibrèo Ristorante

$$$$ | TUSCAN | This upscale trattoria serves sumptuous options like the creamy crostini *di fegatini* (with a savory chicken-liver spread) and melt-in-your-mouth desserts. Many Florentines hail this as the city's best restaurant, and justifiably so—chef-owner Fabio Picchi knows Tuscan food better than anyone, and it shows. **Known for:** authentic Tuscan food; seasonal menu; multilingual staff. Ⓢ *Average main: €40* ⊠ *Via A. del Verrocchio 8/r, Santa Croce* ☎ *055/2341100* ⊕ *www.cibreo.com/en/cibreo-restaurant* ☾ *Closed Sun. and Mon.*

Cibrèo Trattoria

$$ | TUSCAN | This intimate trattoria, known to locals as Cibreino, shares its name and its kitchen with the famed Florentine restaurant but has a shorter, less-expensive menu. Save room for dessert, as the pastry chef has a deft hand with chocolate tarts. **Known for:** excellent meal at a moderate price; clever riffs on classic dishes; desserts to save room for. Ⓢ *Average main: €15* ⊠ *Via dei Macci 122/r, Santa Croce* ☎ *055/2341100* ⊕ *www.cibreo.com/en/cibreo-trattoria* ☾ *Closed Sun. and Mon.*

Enoteca Pinchiorri

$$$$ | ITALIAN | A sumptuous Renaissance palace with high, frescoed ceilings and bouquets in silver vases provides the backdrop for this restaurant, one of the most expensive in Italy. Some consider it one of the best, and others consider it inauthentic, as the cuisine extends far beyond Italian. **Known for:** creative food; wine cellar; exorbitantly high prices. Ⓢ *Average main: €90* ⊠ *Via Ghibellina 87, Santa Croce* ☎ *055/242777* ⊕ *www.enotecapinchiorri.it* ☾ *Closed Sun., Mon., and Aug. No lunch* 👔 *Jacket required, no shorts, or short-sleeved shirts.*

★ La Giostra

$$$ | ITALIAN | This clubby spot, whose name means "carousel," was created by the late Prince Dimitri Kunz d'Asburgo Lorena and is now expertly run by Soldano, one of his twin sons. The ever-changing menu generally has vegetarian and vegan options. **Known for:** sublime tiramisu and a wonderfully gooey Sacher torte; carefully curated wine list; vegetarian and vegan options. Ⓢ *Average main: €30* ⊠ *Borgo Pinti 12/r, Santa Croce* ☎ *055/241341* ⊕ *www.ristorantelagiostra.com* ☾ *No lunch weekends.*

Pizzeria Caffè Italiano

$ | PIZZA | This small pizzeria is favored by locals. Come early to grab one of the few tables in front or round the back, and

Continued on page 341

WHO'S WHO IN RENAISSANCE ART

Michelangelo. Leonardo da Vinci. Raphael. This heady triumvirate of the Italian Renaissance is synonymous with artistic genius. Yet they are only three of the remarkable cast of characters whose work defines the Renaissance, that extraordinary flourishing of art and culture in Italy, especially in Florence, as the Middle Ages drew to a close. The artists were visionaries, who redefined painting, sculpture, architecture, and even what it means to be an artist.

THE PIONEER. In the mid-14th century, a few artists began to move away the flat, two-dimensional painting of the Middle Ages. Giotto, who painted seemingly three-dimensional figures who show emotion, had a major impact on the artists of the next century.

THE GROUNDBREAKERS. The generations of Brunelleschi and Botticelli took center stage in the 15th century. Ghiberti, Masaccio, Donatello, Uccello, Fra Angelico, and Filippo Lippi were other major players. Part of the Renaissance (or "re-birth") was a renewed interest in classical sources—the texts, monuments, and sculpture of Ancient Greece and Rome. Perspective and the illusion of three-dimensional space in painting was another discovery of this era, known as the Early Renaissance. Suddenly the art appearing on the walls looked real, or more realistic than it used to.

Roman ruins were not the only thing to inspire these artists. There was an incredible exchange of ideas going on. In Santa Maria del Carmine, Filippo Lippi was inspired by the work of Masaccio, who in turn was a friend of Brunelleschi. Young artists also learned from the masters via the apprentice system. Ghiberti's workshop (bottega in Italian) included, at one time or another, Donatello, Masaccio, and Uccello. Botticelli was apprenticed to Filippo Lippi.

THE BIG THREE. The mathematical rationality and precision of 15th-century art gave way to what is known as the High Renaissance. Leonardo, Michelangelo, and Raphael were much more concerned with portraying the body in all its glory and with achieving harmony and grandeur in their work. Oil paint, used infrequently up until this time, became more widely employed: as a result, Leonardo's colors are deeper, more sensual, more alive. For one brief period, all three were in Florence at the same time. Michelangelo and Leonardo surely knew one another, as they were simultaneously working on frescoes (never completed) inside Palazzo Vecchio.

When Michelangelo left Florence for Rome in 1508, he began the slow drain of artistic exodus from Florence, which never really recovered her previous glory.

A RENAISSANCE TIMELINE

IN THE WORLD

Black Death in Europe kills one third of the population, 1347-50.

Joan of Arc burned at the stake, 1431.

IN FLORENCE

Dante, a native of Florence, writes The Divine Comedy, 1302-21.

Founding of the Medici bank, 1397.

Medici family made official papal bankers.

1434, Cosimo il Vecchio becomes de facto ruler of Florence. The Medici family will dominate the city until 1494.

1300

1400

IN ART

EARLY RENAISSANCE

Masaccio and Masolino fresco Santa Maria del Carmine, 1424-28.

GIOTTO (ca. 1267-1337)

Giotto fresoes in Santa Croce, 1320-25.

BRUNELLESCHI (1377-1446)

LORENZO GHIBERTI (ca. 1381-1455)

DONATELLO (ca. 1386-1466)

PAOLO UCCELLO (1397-1475)

FRA ANGELICO (ca. 1400-1455)

MASACCIO (1401-1428)

FILIPPO LIPPI (ca. 1406-1469)

1334, 67-year-old Giotto is appointed chief architect of Santa Maria del Fiore, Florence's Duomo (below). He begins to work on the Campanile, which will be completed in 1359, after his death.

Donatello sculpts his bronze David, ca. 144

Fra Angelico frescoes friars' cells in San Marco, c. 1438-45.

Ghiberti wins the competition for the Baptistery doors (above) in Florence, 1401.

Uccello's Sir John Hawkwood, ca. 1436.

Brunelleschi wins the competition for the Duomo's cupola, 1418.

Gutenberg Bible is printed, 1455.

Columbus discovers America, 1492.

Martin Luther posts his 95 theses on the door at Wittenberg, kicking off the Protestant Reformation, 1517.

Constantinople falls to the Turks, 1453.

Machiavelli's Prince appears, 1513.

Copernicus proves that the earth is not the center of the universe, 1530-43.

Lorenzo "il Magnifico" (right), the Medici patron of the arts, rules in Florence, 1449-92.

Two Medici popes Leo X (1513-21) and Clement VII (1523-34) in Rome.

Catherine de'Medici becomes Queen of France, 1547.

1450   **1500**   **1550**

HIGH RENAISSANCE   MANNERISM

Fra Filippo Lippi's Madonna and Child, ca. 1452.

1508, Raphael begins work on the chambers in the Vatican, Rome.

Giorgio Vasari publishes his first edition of Lives of the Artists, 1550.

1504, Michelangelo's David is put on display in Piazza della Signoria, where it remains until 1873.

Michelangelo begins to fresco the Sistine Chapel ceiling, 1508.

Botticelli paints the Birth of Venus, ca. 1482.

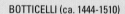

BOTTICELLI (ca. 1444-1510)

LEONARDO DA VINCI (1452-1519)

RAPHAEL (1483-1520)

MICHELANGELO (1475-1564)

Leonardo paints The Last Supper (below) in Milan, 1495-98.

Giotto's Nativity

Donatello's St. John the Baptist

Ghiberti's Gates of Paradise

GIOTTO (CA. 1267-1337)
Painter/architect from a small town north of Florence.

He unequivocally set Italian painting on the course that led to the triumphs of the Renaissance masters. Unlike the rather flat, two-dimensional forms found in then prevailing Byzantine art, Giotto's figures have a fresh, life-like quality. The people in his paintings have bulk, and they show emotion, which you can see on their faces and in their gestures. This was something new in the late Middle Ages. Without Giotto, there wouldn't have been a Raphael.

In Florence: **Santa Croce; Uffizi; Campanile; Santa Maria Novella**
Elsewhere in Italy: **Scrovegni Chapel, Padua; Vatican Museums, Rome**

FILIPPO BRUNELLESCHI (1377-1446)
Architect/engineer from Florence.

If Brunelleschi had beaten Ghiberti in the Baptistery doors competition in Florence, the city's Duomo most likely would not have the striking appearance and authority that it has today. After his loss, he sulked off to Rome, where he studied the ancient Roman structures first-hand. Brunelleschi figured out how to vault the Duomo's dome, a structure unprecedented in its colossal size and great height. His Ospedale degli Innocenti employs classical elements in the creation of a stunning, new architectural state-ment; it is the first truly Renaissance structure.

In Florence: **Duomo; Ospedale degli Innocenti; San Lorenzo; Santo Spirito; Baptistery Doors Competition Entry, Bargello; Santa Croce**

LORENZO GHIBERTI (CA. 1381-1455)
Sculptor from Florence.

Ghiberti won a competition—besting his chief rival, Brunelleschi—to cast the gilded bronze North Doors of the Baptistery in Florence. These doors, and the East Doors that he subsequently executed, took up the next 50 years of his life. He created intricately worked figures that are more true-to-life than any since antiquity, and he was one of the first Renaissance sculptors to work in bronze. Ghiberti taught the next generation of artists; Donatello, Uccello, and Masaccio all passed through his studio.

In Florence: **Door Copies, Baptistery; Original Doors, Museo dell'Opera del Duomo; Baptistry Door Competition Entry, Bargello; Orsanmichele**

DONATELLO (CA. 1386-1466)
Sculptor from Florence.

Donatello was an innovator who, like his good friend Brunelleschi, spent most of his long life in Florence. Consumed with the science of optics, he used light and shadow to create the effects of nearness and distance. He made an essentially flat slab look like a three- dimensional scene. His bronze is probably the first free-standing male nude since antiquity. Not only technically brilliant, his work is also emotionally resonant; few sculptors are as expressive.

In Florence: **David, Bargello; St. Mark, Orsanmichele; Palazzo Vecchio; Museo dell'Opera del Duomo; San Lorenzo; Santa Croce**
Elsewhere in Italy: **Padua; Prato; Venice**

Fra Angelico's Déposition de Croix

Masaccio's Trinity

Filippo Lippi's Madonna and Child with Two Angels

PAOLO UCCELLO (1397-1475)
Painter from Florence.

Renaissance chronicler Vasari once observed that had Uccello not been so obsessed with the mathematical problems posed by perspective, he would have been a very good painter. The struggle to master single-point perspective and to render motion in two dimensions is nowhere more apparent than in his battle scenes. His first major commission in Florence was the gargantuan fresco of the English mercenary Sir John Hawkwood (the Italians called him Giovanni Acuto) in Florence's Duomo.

In Florence: **Sir John Hawkwood, Duomo; Battle of San Romano, Uffizi; Santa Maria Novella**

Elsewhere in Italy: **Urbino, Prato**

FRA ANGELICO (CA. 1400-1455)
Painter from a small town north of Florence.

A Dominican friar, who eventually made his way to the convent of San Marco, Fra Angelico and his assistants painted frescoes for aid in prayer and meditation. He was known for his piety; Vasari wrote that Fra Angelico could never paint a crucifix without a tear running down his face. Perhaps no other painter so successfully translated the mysteries of faith and the sacred into painting. And yet his figures emote, his command of perspective is superb, and his use of color startles even today.

In Florence: **Museo di San Marco; Uffizi**
Elsewhere in Italy: **Vatican Museums, Rome; Fiesole; Cortona; Perugia; Orvieto**

MASACCIO (1401-1428)
Painter from San Giovanni Valdarno, southeast of Florence.

Masaccio and Masolino, a frequent collaborator, worked most famously together at Santa Maria del Carmine. Their frescoes of the life of St. Peter use light to mold figures in the painting by imitating the way light falls on figures in real life. Masaccio also pioneered the use of single-point perspective, masterfully rendered in his His friend Brunelleschi probably introduced him to the technique, yet another step forward in rendering things the way the eye sees them. Masaccio died young and under mysterious circumstances.

In Florence: **Santa Maria del Carmine; Trinity, Santa Maria Novella**

FILIPPO LIPPI (CA. 1406-1469)
Painter from Prato.

At a young age, Filippo Lippi entered the friary of Santa Maria del Carmine, where he was highly influenced by Masaccio and Masolino's frescoes. His religious vows appear to have made less of an impact; his affair with a young nun produced a son, Filippino (Little Philip, who later apprenticed with Botticelli), and a daughter. His religious paintings often have a playful, humorous note; some of his angels are downright impish and look directly out at the viewer. Lippi links the earlier painters of the 15th century with those who follow; Botticelli apprenticed with him.

In Florence: **Uffizi; Palazzo Medici Riccardi; San Lorenzo; Palazzo Pitti**
Elsewhere in Italy: **Prato**

Botticelli's Primavera

Leonardo's Portrait of a
Young Woman

Raphael's Madonna on
the Meadow

BOTTICELLI (CA. 1444-1510)
Painter from Florence.

Botticelli's work is characterized by stunning, elongated blondes, cherubic angels (something he undoubtedly learned from his time with Filippo Lippi), and tender Christs. Though he did many religious paintings, he also painted monumental, nonreligious panels—his Birth of Venus and Primavera being the two most famous of these. A brief sojourn took him to Rome, where he and a number of other artists frescoed the Sistine Chapel walls.

In Florence:
Birth of Venus, Primavera, Uffizi; Palazzo Pitti
Elsewhere in Italy:
Vatican Museums, Rome

LEONARDO DA VINCI (1452-1519)
Painter/sculptor/engineer from Anchiano, a small town outside Vinci.

Leonardo never lingered long in any place; his restless nature and his international reputation led to commissions throughout Italy, and took him to Milan, Vigevano, Pavia, Rome, and, ultimately, France. Though he is most famous for his mysterious Mona Lisa (at the Louvre in Paris), he painted other penetrating, psychological portraits in addition to his scientific experiments: his design for a flying machine (never built) predates Kitty Hawk by nearly 500 years. The greatest collection of Leonardo's work in Italy can be seen on one wall in the Uffizi.

In Florence: Adoration of the Magi, Uffizi
Elsewhere in Italy: Last Supper, Santa Maria delle Grazie, Milan

RAPHAEL (1483-1520)
Painter/architect from Urbino.

Raphael spent only four highly productive years of his short life in Florence, where he turned out made-to-order panel paintings of the Madonna and Child for a hungry public; he also executed a number of portraits of Florentine aristocrats. Perhaps no other artist had such a fine command of line and color, and could render it, seemingly effortlessly, in paint. His painting acquired new authority after he came up against Michelangelo toiling away on the Sistine ceiling. Raphael worked nearly next door in the Vatican, where his figures take on an epic, Michelangelesque scale.

In Florence: Uffizi; Palazzo Pitti
Elsewhere in Italy: Vatican Museums, Rome

MICHELANGELO (1475-1564)
Painter/sculptor/architect from Caprese.

Although Florentine and proud of it (he famously signed his St. Peter's Pietà to avoid confusion about where he was from), he spent most of his 89 years outside his native city. He painted and sculpted the male body on an epic scale and glorified it while doing so. Though he complained throughout the proceedings that he was really a sculptor, Michelangelo's Sistine Chapel ceiling is arguably the greatest fresco cycle ever painted (and the massive figures owe no small debt to Giotto).

In Florence: David, Galleria dell'Accademia; Uffizi; Casa Buonarroti; Bargello
Elsewhere in Italy: St. Peter's Basilica, Vatican Museums, and Piazza del Campidoglio in Rome

don't mind the fact that service here is intentionally rushed: turning tables is paramount. **Known for:** its limited (but very tasty) pizza offerings; limited seating; local favorite. $ *Average main: €10* ✉ *Via Isole delle Stinche 11/r, Santa Croce* ☎ *055/289080* ⊕ *www.caffeitaliano.it.*

Ruth's

$$ | TUSCAN | The only kosher–vegetarian restaurant in Tuscany is Ruth's, adjacent to Florence's synagogue. On the menu: inexpensive vegetarian and Mediterranean dishes and a large selection of kosher wines. **Known for:** harissa; nice wine list; friendly staff. $ *Average main: €20* ✉ *Via Farini 2/a, Santa Croce* ☎ *055/2480888* ⊕ *www.kosheruth.com* ☉ *No dinner Fri. No lunch Sat.*

☕ Coffee and Quick Bites

da Rocco

$ | TUSCAN | At one of Florence's biggest markets, you can grab lunch to go, or you can cram into one of the booths and pour from the straw-cloaked flask (wine here is *da consumo,* which means they charge you for how much you drink). Food is abundant, Tuscan, and fast; locals pack in. **Known for:** tasty food at rock-bottom prices; ever-changing menu; takeout. $ *Average main: €8* ✉ *Mercato Sant'Ambrogio, Piazza Ghiberti, Santa Croce* ☎ *339/8384555 mobile* ⊕ *www. daroccotrattoria.com* ☉ *Closed Sun. No dinner.*

★ Perché No!

$ | ICE CREAM | FAMILY | What many consider the best gelateria in the centro storico embodies the "practice makes perfect" adage. It's been making ice cream since 1939. **Known for:** gelati made daily; one of the oldest gelaterias in the city; unusual flavors and vegan options. $ *Average main: €3* ✉ *Via dei Tavolini 19r, Duomo* ☎ *055/2398969* ⊕ *www.facebook.com/ GelateriaPercheNo.*

Hotels

Borgo Pinti

$ | B&B/INN | Nuns of the Oblates of the Assumption run this convent holiday house, where some of the simple but spotlessly clean rooms have views of the Duomo's cupola, and others look out onto a garden where you are welcome to relax. **Pros:** great location and (mostly) quiet rooms; Mass held daily; a soothing, somewhat untended garden. **Cons:** some have observed that there's hall noise; rooms facing the street can be noisy; rooms are frugal. $ *Rooms from: €90* ✉ *Borgo Pinti 15, Santa Croce* ☎ *055/2346291* ⊕ *www.oblate.it* ⤵ *40 rooms* ⫿⊙⫿ *Free Breakfast.*

The Four Seasons

$$$$ | HOTEL | This 15th-century palazzo is perhaps the city's most luxurious hotel, where many guest rooms have original 17th-century frescoes, and an 11-acre garden is dotted with centuries-old trees. **Pros:** pool; state-of-the-art spa; Michelin-starred Il Palagio restaurant. **Cons:** ultra-pricey; splashing children in the pool can be a nuisance for some; small rooms. $ *Rooms from: €2000* ✉ *Borgo Pinti 99, Santa Croce* ☎ *055/26261* ⊕ *www.fourseasons.com/florence* ⤵ *117 rooms* ⫿⊙⫿ *No Meals.*

Hotel Regency

$$$$ | HOTEL | Though it's just 10 minutes from the Accademia and Michelangelo's *David,* this hotel—in a 19th-century mansion adorned with rich fabrics and period-appropriate furnishings—is a true retreat from the city's noise and crowds. **Pros:** faces one of the few green spaces in central Florence; quiet residential setting; lovely, on-site Relais le Jardin restaurant. **Cons:** somewhat removed from the city center; rooms facing the park can be noisy; books up quickly. $ *Rooms from: €387* ✉ *Piazza d'Azeglio 3, Santa Croce* ☎ *055/245247* ⊕ *www. regency-hotel.com* ⤵ *31 rooms* ⫿⊙⫿ *Free Breakfast.*

★ Monna Lisa

$$ | HOTEL | Although some rooms are small, all are tastefully decorated and housed in a 15th-century palazzo that retains its original staircase and some of its wood-coffered ceilings. **Pros:** lavish buffet breakfast; cheerful, multilingual staff; pretty garden. **Cons:** rooms in annex are less charming than those in palazzo; street noise in some rooms; thin walls have been noted. [$] *Rooms from: €186* ✉ *Borgo Pinti 27, Santa Croce* ☎ *055/2479751* 🌐 *www.monnalisa.it* 🛏 *48 rooms* 🍴 *Free Breakfast.*

★ Morandi alla Crocetta

$$$ | B&B/INN | You're made to feel like friends of the family at this charming and distinguished residence, furnished comfortably in the classic style of a gracious Florentine home and former convent. **Pros:** interesting, offbeat location near the sights; affable staff; historic touches like fragments of a 17th-century fresco. **Cons:** books up quickly; far from the "true" historical center; some say breakfast could be better. [$] *Rooms from: €207* ✉ *Via Laura 50, Santissima Annunziata* ☎ *055/2344747* 🌐 *www.hotelmorandi.it* 🛏 *10 rooms* 🍴 *Free Breakfast.*

Nightlife

Caffè Sant'Ambrogio

BARS | Come here when it's summer for outdoor seating with a view of an 11th-century church (Sant'Ambrogio) directly across the street. Come here at any time of the year for perfectly mixed drinks and a lively atmosphere filled with (mostly) locals. ✉ *Piazza Sant'Ambrogio 7–8/r, Santa Croce* ☎ *055/2477277* 🌐 *www.caffesantambrogio.it.*

Jazz Club

LIVE MUSIC | Enjoy live music in this small basement club. ✉ *Via Nuova de' Caccini 3, at Borgo Pinti, Santa Croce* 🌐 *www.facebook.com/jazzclubfirenze.it.*

Rex

BARS | A trendy, artsy clientele frequents this bar at aperitivo time. By 10 pm, the place is packed with mostly young folks sipping cocktails. ✉ *Via Fiesolana 23–25/r, Santa Croce* ☎ *055/2480331* 🌐 *www.rexfirenze.com.*

Shopping

★ Mercato di Sant'Ambrogio

MARKET | FAMILY | It's possible to strike gold at this lively market, where clothing stalls abut those with fruits and vegetables. ✉ *Piazza Ghiberti, off Via dei Macci, Santa Croce* ☎ *055/2480778* 🌐 *www.mercatosantambrogio.it.*

Oreria

JEWELRY & WATCHES | The two women who run Oreria create divine designs using silver and semiprecious stones. ✉ *Borgo Pinti 87/a, Santa Croce* ☎ *055/244708* 🌐 *www.oreria.net.*

★ Scuola del Cuoio

LEATHER GOODS | Leatherworkers ply their trade at Scuola del Cuoio (Leather School), a consortium in the former dormitory of the convent of Santa Croce. High-quality, fairly priced jackets, belts, and purses are sold here. ✉ *Piazza Santa Croce 16, Santa Croce* ☎ *055/244533* 🌐 *www.scuoladelcuoio.com.*

The Oltrarno

A walk through the Oltrarno (literally "the other side of the Arno") takes in two very different aspects of Florence: the splendor of the Medici, manifest in the riches of the mammoth Palazzo Pitti and the gracious Giardino di Boboli; and the charm of the Oltrarno, a gentrified former working-class neighborhood with artisans' and antiques shops.

⊙ Sights

Giardino Bardini

GARDEN | Garden lovers, those who crave a view, and those who enjoy a nice hike should visit this lovely villa, whose history spans centuries. It had a walled garden as early as the 14th century; its "Grand Stairs"—a zigzag ascent well worth scaling—have been around since the 16th. The garden is filled with irises, roses, and heirloom flowers. It also has a Japanese garden and statuary. ⊠ *Costa San Giorgio 2, San Niccolò* ☎ *055/2638599* ⊕ *www. villabardini.it* ⊡ *€6 garden only, €10 garden and exhibits* ⊗ *Closed Mon. (with occasional exceptions).*

Giardino di Boboli (*Boboli Gardens*)

GARDEN | The main entrance to these gardens is from the right side of the courtyard of Palazzo Pitti. The landscaping began to take shape in 1549, when the Pitti family sold the palazzo to Eleanor of Toledo, wife of the Medici grand duke Cosimo I. A visit here can be disappointing because the gardens are somewhat sparse, but the pleasant walk offers excellent views. ⊠ *Piazza de' Pitti, Palazzo Pitti* ☎ *055/294883* ⊕ *www.uffizi. it/giardino-boboli* ⊡ *€6* ⊗ *Closed 1st and last Mon. of month.*

Museo Bardini

ART MUSEUM | The 19th-century collector and antiquarian Stefano Bardini turned his palace into his own private museum. Upon his death, the collection was turned over to the state and includes an interesting assortment of Etruscan pieces, sculpture, paintings, and furniture that dates mostly from the Renaissance and the Baroque. ⊠ *Via dei Renai 37, Oltrarno* ☎ *055/2342427* ⊕ *cultura. comune.fi.it* ⊡ *€7* ⊗ *Closed Tues.–Thurs.*

Palazzo Pitti

ART MUSEUM | This enormous palace is one of Florence's largest architectural set pieces. The original palazzo, built for the Pitti family around 1460, consisted of the main entrance and the sections extending as far as three windows on either side. In 1549, the property was sold to the Medici, and Bartolomeo Ammannati was called in to make substantial additions. Today, the palace houses several museums. The Museo degli Argenti displays a vast collection of Medici treasures and the Galleria d'Arte Moderna holds a collection of 19th- and 20th-century paintings, mostly Tuscan. ⊠ *Piazza Pitti, Palazzo Pitti* ☎ *055/294883* ⊕ *www.uffizi.it/palazzo-pitti* ⊡ *From €10* ⊗ *Closed Mon.*

Piazzale Michelangelo

PLAZA/SQUARE | FAMILY | From this lookout you have a marvelous view of Florence and the hills around it, rivaling the vista from the Forte di Belvedere. A copy of Michelangelo's *David* overlooks outdoor cafés packed with tourists during the day and evening. In May, the Giardino dell'Iris (Iris Garden) off the piazza is abloom with more than 2,500 varieties of the flower. The Giardino delle Rose (Rose Garden) on the terraces below the piazza is also in full bloom in May and June. ⊠ *Piazzale Michelangelo, San Niccolò.*

San Miniato al Monte

CHURCH | This abbey, like the Baptistery a fine example of Romanesque architecture, is one of the oldest churches in Florence, dating from the 11th century. A 12th-century mosaic topped by a gilt bronze eagle, emblem of San Miniato's sponsors, the Calimala (cloth merchants' guild), crowns the green-and-white marble facade. Inside are a 13th-century inlaid-marble floor and apse mosaic. Artist Spinello Aretino (1350–1410) covered the walls of the Sagrestia with frescoes of scenes from the life of St. Benedict. ⊠ *Via delle Porte Sante 34, San Niccolò* ☎ *055/2342731* ⊕ *www.sanminiatoalmonte.it.*

Santa Felicita

CHURCH | This late-Baroque church (its facade was remodeled between 1736 and 1739) contains the Mannerist Jacopo Pontormo's *Deposition,* the centerpiece of the Cappella Capponi

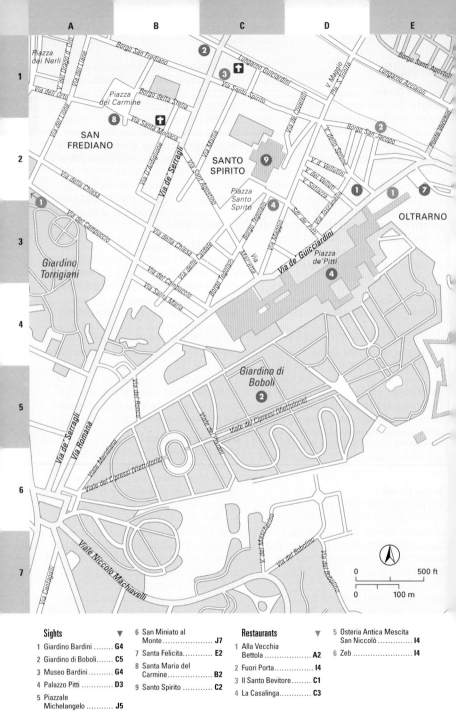

Sights ▼

1 Giardino Bardini **G4**

2 Giardino di Boboli...... **C5**

3 Museo Bardini **G4**

4 Palazzo Pitti **D3**

5 Piazzale
Michelangelo **J5**

6 San Miniato al
Monte **J7**

7 Santa Felicita............ **E2**

8 Santa Maria del
Carmine................. **B2**

9 Santo Spirito **C2**

Restaurants ▼

1 Alla Vecchia
Bettola **A2**

2 Fuori Porta................ **I4**

3 Il Santo Bevitore **C1**

4 La Casalinga............. **C3**

5 Osteria Antica Mescita
San Niccolò **I4**

6 Zeb **I4**

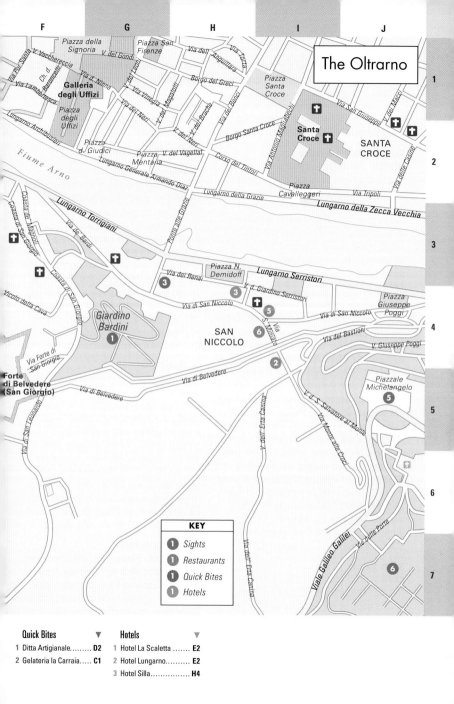

The Oltrarno

F	G	H	I	J

Piazza della Signoria
V. Vacchereccia
V. Por Santa
Ch. d. Baroncelli
Via Lambertesca
Lungarno Archibusieri
Via del Gondi
Piazza San Firenze
Via dei Leoni
Via d. Ninna
Via dei Neri
Via dei Neri
Via Vinegia
Via dei Neri
Via dell' Anguillara
Via Torta
Borgo dei Greci
Via Magazzini
V. dei Neri
V. de' Bentaccordi
V. del Bracche
Borgo Santa Croce
Via del Banco
Galleria degli Uffizi
Piazza degli Uffizi
Piazza d. Giudici
Piazza Mentana
V. del Vagellai
Corso dei Tintori
Via Antonio Magliabechi
Piazza Santa Croce
Via San Giuseppe
Via dei Macci
Santa Croce
SANTA CROCE
Via delle Casine

Fiume Arno
Lungarno Generale Armando Diaz
Lungarno della Grazie
Piazza Cavallegger
Via Tripoli
Lungarno della Zecca Vecchia

Coasta de' Magnoli
Coasta di San Giorgio
Lungarno Torrigiani
Via de' Bardi
Ponte alle Grazie
Via dei Renai
Piazza N. Demidoff
Lungarno Serristori
V. d. Giardino Serristori
Via di San Niccolo
Piazza Giuseppe Poggi
Vicolo della Cava
Giardino Bardini
Via di San Niccolo
S. Miniato
Via di San Niccolo
Via del Bastioni
Via Forte di San Giorgio
SAN NICCOLO
Via S. Mimato
V. Giuseppe Poggi
Forte di Belvedere (San Giorgio)
Via di Belvedere
Via di Belvedere
V. d. S. Salvatore al Monte
Piazzale Michelangelo
Via di San Leonardo
Via dell' Erta Canina
Via Monte alle Croci
Via dell' Erta Canina
Viale Galileo Galilei
Via delle Porte

1	2	3	4	5	6	7

KEY

- ① Sights
- ① Restaurants
- ① Quick Bites
- ① Hotels

Quick Bites ▼
1 Ditta Artigianale......... **D2**
2 Gelateria la Carraia..... **C1**

Hotels ▼
1 Hotel La Scaletta **E2**
2 Hotel Lungarno.......... **E2**
3 Hotel Silla................ **H4**

(executed 1525–28) and a masterpiece of 16th-century Florentine art. The granite column in the piazza was erected in 1381 and marks a Christian cemetery. ⊠ *Piazza Santa Felicita 3, Palazzo Pitti* ☎ *055/213018* ⊗ *Closed Sun.*

Santa Maria del Carmine

CHURCH | The Cappella Brancacci, at the end of the right transept of this church, contains a masterpiece of Renaissance painting: a fresco cycle that changed the course of Western art. It is the work of Masaccio and Masolino (1383–circa 1447), who began it around 1424, and Filippino Lippi, who finished it some 50 years later.

It was, however, Masaccio's work that opened a new frontier for painting, as he was among the first artists to employ single-point perspective. His style predominates in the *Tribute Money,* on the upper-left wall; *St. Peter Baptizing,* on the upper altar wall; the *Distribution of Goods,* on the lower altar wall; and the *Expulsion of Adam and Eve,* on the chapel's upper-left entrance pier. The figures of Adam and Eve possess a startling presence thanks to the dramatic way in which their bodies seem to reflect light. In their faces, you also see terrible shame and suffering depicted with a humanity rarely achieved in art. ⊠ *Piazza del Carmine, Santo Spirito* ☎ *055/2768224 reservations* ⊕ *bigliettimusei.comune.fi.it* ⊠ *€10* ⊗ *Closed Tues.–Thurs.* ⌂ *Reservations to visit the Cappella Brancacci are essential.*

Santo Spirito

CHURCH | The interior of this church is one of a pair designed in Florence by Filippo Brunelleschi in the early decades of the 15th century (the other is San Lorenzo). It was here that Brunelleschi supplied definitive solutions to a major problem of interior Renaissance church design: how to build a cross-shape interior using classical architectural elements borrowed from antiquity. His solution was design the church so that all its parts were proportionally related. He believed that mathematical

regularity and aesthetic beauty were flip sides of the same coin. ⊠ *Piazza Santo Spirito 30, Oltrarno* ☎ *055/210030* ⊕ *www.basilicasantospirito.it* ⌂ *Church free; tour €2* ⊗ *Closed Wed.*

Restaurants

Alla Vecchia Bettola

$$ | TUSCAN | The name doesn't exactly mean "old dive," but it comes pretty close. The recipes here come from "wise grandmothers" and celebrate Tuscan food in its glorious simplicity—prosciutto is sliced with a knife, grilled meats are tender, service is friendly, and the wine list is well priced and good. **Known for:** grilled meats; firmly Tuscan menu; just outside the centro storico but worth the taxi ride. $ *Average main: €16* ⊠ *Viale Vasco Pratolini 3/5/7, Oltrarno* ☎ *055/224158* ⊗ *Closed Sun. and Mon.*

★ Fuori Porta

$ | WINE BAR | One of Florence's oldest wine bars serves cured meats and cheeses, pastas, salads, and daily specials. Crostini and *crostoni*—grilled breads topped with a mélange of cheeses and meats—are the house specialty, but the *verdure sott'olio* (vegetables in oil) are divine, too. **Known for:** lengthy wine list; crostini and crostoni; changing daily specials. $ *Average main: €11* ⊠ *Via Monte alle Croci 10, San Niccolò* ☎ *055/2342483* ⊕ *www.fuoriporta.it.*

★ Il Santo Bevitore

$$ | TUSCAN | Florentines and other lovers of good food flock to "The Holy Drinker" for tasty Tuscan dishes. Unpretentious white walls, dark wood furniture, and paper place mats provide the simple decor; start with the exceptional verdure sott'olio or the *terrina di fegatini* (a creamy chicken-liver spread) before sampling any of the divine pastas. **Known for:** Tuscan dishes with flair; delicious potato gratin; friendly waitstaff. $ *Average main: €19* ⊠ *Via Santo Spirito 64/r–66/r, Santo Spirito* ☎ *055/211264* ⊕ *www.ilsantobevitore.com.*

★ La Casalinga

$ | **TUSCAN** | *Casalinga* means "house-wife," and this place, which has been around since 1963, has the nostalgic charm of a mid-century kitchen with Tuscan comfort food to match. If you eat ribollita anywhere in Florence, eat it here—it couldn't be more authentic. **Known for:** ribollita; liver, Venetian style; often packed. $ *Average main: €14* ⊠ *Via Michelozzi 9/r, Santo Spirito* ☎ *055/218624* ⊕ *www.trattorialacasalinga.it* ⊗ *Closed Sun.*

Osteria Antica Mescita San Niccolò

$ | **TUSCAN** | Always crowded—but always good and inexpensive—this osteria is next to San Niccolò church, and, if you sit in the lower part, you'll be in what was once a chapel dating from the 11th century. The subtle but dramatic background nicely complements the food, which is simple Tuscan at its best. **Known for:** delicious soup; great, simple salads; outdoor seating in a small, lovely square. $ *Average main: €12* ⊠ *Via San Niccolò 60/r, San Niccolò* ☎ *055/2342836* ⊕ *www.osteriasanniccolo.it.*

Zeb

$$ | **TUSCAN** | "Zeb" stands for *zuppa e bollito* (soup and boiled things), but you can't go wrong with anything at this small *alimentari* (delicatessen). It's home-style Tuscan cuisine at its very best, served in unpretentious, intimate surroundings: there's room for only about 15 guests. **Known for:** fantastic soup; terrific pasta; lovely wine list. $ *Average main: €17* ⊠ *Via San Miniato 2, Oltrarno* ☎ *055/2342864* ⊕ *www.zebgastronomia.com* ⊗ *Closed Wed. Nov.–Mar. No dinner Sun. No dinner Mon. and Tues. Apr.–Oct.*

Coffee and Quick Bites

Ditta Artigianale

$ | **CAFÉ** | Founded in 2013 as a micro coffee roaster on Via de' Neri, Ditta Artigianale now has four spots throughout Florence. Follow a side street off the Palazzo Pitti to take a coffee break with a classic espresso, drip coffee, or the inventive Coffemisu (espresso, cookies, cocoa, and mascarpone cream) in a space that's more like an airy mid-century modern living room, than a coffee shop. **Known for:** fair trade coffee; extensive brunch menu; lively atmosphere, popular with expats. $ *Average main: €10* ⊠ *Via dello Sprone 5/r, Oltrarno* ☎ *055/0457163* ⊕ *www.dittaartigianale.com.*

Gelateria la Carraia

$ | **ICE CREAM** | **FAMILY** | At the foot of Ponte Carraia, two bridges down from the Ponte Vecchio, find standard gelato flavors or creative options such as *limone con biscotti* (lemon sorbet with cookies). **Known for:** super-creamy gelato; generous €1 tasting cones; every flavor is worth a taste. $ *Average main: €3* ⊠ *Piazza Nazario Sauro 2, Santo Spirito* ☎ *055/280695* ⊕ *www.gelaterialacarraia.it/en.*

🛏 Hotels

Hotel La Scaletta

$$ | **HOTEL** | In addition to a tremendous view of the Boboli Gardens, this cozy pensione near the Ponte Vecchio and Palazzo Pitti has simply furnished but large rooms and a sunny breakfast room. **Pros:** in-house restaurant with stunning views; wonderful, multilingual staff; in a lively neighborhood. **Cons:** small elevator; many steps; books up quickly; neighborhood can be noisy. $ *Rooms from: €169* ⊠ *Via Guicciardini 13, Palazzo Pitti* ☎ *055/283028* ⊕ *www.hotellascaletta.it* ⮍ *36 rooms* ⧉ *Free Breakfast.*

Hotel Lungarno

$$$$ | **HOTEL** | Many rooms and suites here have private terraces that jut out over the Arno, granting stunning views of the Palazzo Vecchio and the Lungarno; a studio suite in a 13th-century tower preserves details like exposed stone walls and old archways, and looks over a little square with a medieval tower covered in jasmine. **Pros:** upscale without

being stuffy; lovely Arno views; Borgo San Jacopo, its attached restaurant. **Cons:** rooms without Arno views feel less special; street noise happens; walls can be thin. $ *Rooms from: €680* ⊠ *Borgo San Jacopo 14, Oltrarno* ☏ *055/27261* ⊕ *www.lungarnocollection.com* ↝ *67 rooms* |⚪| *Free Breakfast.*

Hotel Silla

$$ | HOTEL | Rooms in this 15th-century palazzo, entered via a courtyard with potted plants and sculpture-filled niches, are simply furnished; some have Arno views, others have stuccoed ceilings. **Pros:** in the middle of everything except the crowds; cordial, friendly staff; great breakfast. **Cons:** street noise; small rooms; could use an update. $ *Rooms from: €130* ⊠ *Via de' Renai 5, San Nic-colò* ☏ *055/2342888* ⊕ *www.hotelsilla.it* ↝ *36 rooms* |⚪| *Free Breakfast.*

Shopping

★ Giulio Giannini e Figlio

STATIONERY | One of Florence's oldest paper-goods stores is *the* place to buy marbleized stock, which comes in many shapes and sizes, from flat sheets to boxes and even on pencils. ⊠ *Piazza Pitti 37/r, Oltrarno* ☏ *055/212621* ⊕ *www.giuli-ogiannini.com.*

★ Il Torchio

STATIONERY | Photograph albums, frames, diaries, and other objects dressed in handmade paper are high quality, and the prices lower than usual. ⊠ *Via dei Bardi 17, San Niccolò* ☏ *055/2342862* ⊕ *www. legatoriailtorchio.com.*

★ Madova

HATS & GLOVES | Complete your winter wardrobe with a pair of high-quality leather gloves, available in a rainbow of colors and a choice of linings (silk, cashmere, and unlined), from Madova. It's been in business for more than 100 years. ⊠ *Via Guicciardini 1/r, Palazzo Pitti* ☏ *055/2396526* ⊕ *www.madova.com.*

Pitti Mosaici

HOUSEWARES | Stones are worked into exquisite tables, pictures, and jewelry at Pitti Mosaici, which continues the *pietre dure* (mosaic) tradition that was all the rage of 16th-century Florence. ⊠ *Piazza dei Pitti 23/r, Palazzo Pitti* ☏ *055/282127* ⊕ *www.pittimosaici.com.*

Santo Spirito Markets

MARKET | FAMILY | The second Sunday of every month brings the Oltrarno Arts and Crafts Market in Piazza Santo Spirito with clothing, antiques, and homewares. On the third Sunday of the month, vendors at the La Fierucola in the piazza sell such delectables as honeys, jams, spice mix-es, and fresh vegetables. ⊠ *Piazza Santo Spirito, Santo Spirito* ⊕ *en.comune.fi.it/ city/culture_and_tourism/markets.html.*

A Side Trip from Florence

Fiesole

10 km (6 miles) north of Florence.

A half-day excursion to Fiesole, in the hills above Florence, gives you a pleasant respite from museums and a wonderful view of the city. From here the view of the Duomo gives you a new appreciation for what the Renaissance accomplished. Fiesole began life as an ancient Etruscan and later Roman village that held some power until it succumbed to barbarian invasions. Eventually it gave up its inde-pendence in exchange for Florence's pro-tection. The medieval cathedral, ancient Roman amphitheater, and lovely old villas behind garden walls are clustered on a series of hilltops. A walk around Fiesole can take from one to two or three hours, depending on how far you stroll from the main piazza.

GETTING HERE AND AROUND

The trip from Florence by car takes 20–30 minutes. Drive to Piazza Liberta and cross the Ponte Rosso heading in the direction of the SS65/SR65. Turn right on to Via Salviati and continue on to Via Roccettini. Make a left turn to Via Vecchia Fiesolana, which will take you directly to the center of town. There are several possible routes for the two-hour walk from central Florence to Fiesole. One route begins in a residential area of Florence called Salviatino (Via Barbacane, near Piazza Edison, on the No. 7 bus route), and after a short time, offers peeks over garden walls of beautiful villas, as well as the view over your shoulder at the panorama of Florence in the valley. Buses also run to Fiesole from the center of Florence; check Autolinee Toscane for timetables (⊕ *www.at-bus.it*).

VISITOR INFORMATION

CONTACT Fiesole Tourism Office. ✉ *Via Portigiani 3, Fiesole* ☎ *055/5961311* ⊕ *www.fiesoleforyou.it.*

 # Sights

Anfiteatro Romano (*Roman Amphitheater*)
RUINS | The beautifully preserved, 2,000-seat Anfiteatro Romano, near the Duomo, dates from the 1st century BC and is still used for summer concerts. To the right of the amphitheater are the remains of the Terme Romani (Roman Baths), where you can see the gymnasium, hot and cold baths, and rectangular chamber where the water was heated. ✉ *Via Portigiani 1, Fiesole* ☎ *055/5961293* ⊕ *www.museidifiesole.it* 🎟 *€12, includes access to archaeological park and museums* 🕐 *Hrs change each season, check website for closure days.*

Badia Fiesolana

CHURCH | From the church of San Domenico it's a five-minute walk northwest to Fiesole's original cathedral. Dating from the 11th century, it was first the home of the Camaldolese monks. Thanks to Cosimo il Vecchio de'Medici, the complex was substantially restructured. The facade, never completed owing to Cosimo's death, contains elements of its original Romanesque decoration. ✉ *Via della Badia dei Roccettini 9, Fiesole* ☎ *055/4685399* ⊕ *www.eui.eu* 🕐 *Closed weekends.*

Duomo

CHURCH | A stark medieval interior yields many masterpieces. In the raised presbytery, the Cappella Salutati was frescoed by 15th-century artist Cosimo Rosselli, but it was his contemporary, sculptor Mino da Fiesole (1430–84), who put the town on the artistic map. The Madonna on the altarpiece and the tomb of Bishop Salutati are fine examples of the artist's work. ✉ *Piazza Mino da Fiesole, Fiesole* ☎ *055/5961311* ⊕ *www.fiesoleforyou.it/cattedrale-di-san-romolo.*

San Domenico

CHURCH | If you really want to stretch your legs, walk 4 km (2½ miles) toward the center of Florence along Via Vecchia Fiesolana, a narrow lane in use since Etruscan times, to the church of San Domenico. Sheltered in the church is the *Madonna and Child with Saints* by Fra Angelico, who was a Dominican friar here before he moved to Florence. ✉ *Piazza San Domenico, off Via Giuseppe Mantellini, Fiesole* ☎ *055/59230* 🕐 *Closed Sun.*

San Francesco

CHURCH | This lovely hilltop church has a good view of Florence and the plain below from its terrace and benches. Off the little cloister is a small, eclectic museum containing, among other things, two Egyptian mummies. Halfway up the hill you'll see sloping steps to the right; they lead to a fragrant wooded park with trails that loop out and back to the church. ✉ *Via San Francesco 13, Fiesole* ☎ *055/59175* ⊕ *www.fratifiesole.it* 🎟 *Free.*

 Restaurants

La Reggia degli Etruschi

$$$ | **ITALIAN** | Atop a steep hill, en route to the church of San Francesco, this lovely little eatery is certainly worth the trek. Indulge in inventive reworkings of Tuscan classics, like the *mezzaluna di pera a pecorino* (little half-moon pasta stuffed with pear and pecorino) sauced with Roquefort and poppy seeds. **Known for:** out-of-the-way location; good wine list and friendly service; small terrace with outdoor seating. $ *Average main: €25* ⊠ *Via San Francesco 18, Fiesole* ☎ *333/3556126 mobile* ⊕ *www.lareggia-deglietruschi.com.*

Hotels

Villa San Michele

$$$$ | **HOTEL** | The cypress-lined driveway provides an elegant preamble to this incredibly gorgeous (and very expensive) hotel nestled in the hills of Fiesole. **Pros:** exceptional convent conversion; stunning views; shuttle bus makes frequent forays to and from Florence. **Cons:** money must be no object; some rooms are small; you must either depend on the shuttle bus or have a car. $ *Rooms from: €1715* ⊠ *Via Doccia 4, Fiesole* ☎ *055/5678200* ⊕ *www.belmond.com/hotels/europe/ italy/florence/belmond-villa-san-michele* ⊗ *Closed Nov.–May* ⇴ *45 rooms* ⊙ *Free Breakfast.*

Chapter 7

TUSCANY AND UMBRIA

7

Updated by
Liz Humphreys
and Liz Shemaria

◉ Sights	🍴 Restaurants	🛏 Hotels	🛍 Shopping	🍸 Nightlife
★★★★★	★★★★★	★★★★★	★★☆☆☆	★★☆☆☆

WELCOME TO TUSCANY AND UMBRIA

TOP REASONS TO GO

★ **Leaning Tower of Pisa:** It may be touristy, but it's still a whole lot of fun to climb to the top and admire the view.

★ **Wine tasting in Chianti:** Sample the fruits of the region's gorgeous vineyards, either at the wineries themselves or in the wine bars found in the towns.

★ **Piazza del Campo, Siena:** Sip a cappuccino or enjoy some gelato as you take in this spectacular shell-shaped piazza.

★ **Assisi, shrine to St. Francis:** Recharge your soul in this rose-colored hill town with a visit to the gentle saint's majestic basilica, adorned with great frescoes.

★ **Spoleto, Umbria's musical mecca:** Crowds may descend and prices ascend here during summer's Festival dei Due Mondi, but Spoleto's hushed charm enchants year-round.

★ **Orvieto's Duomo:** Arresting visions of heaven and hell on the facade and brilliant frescoes within make this Gothic cathedral a dazzler.

A mix of forests, vineyards, olive groves, and poppy fields, the hill regions of central Italy add up to Italian countryside at its most beautiful. The hillside towns wear their history on their sleeves.

1 Lucca. Historic town with 99 churches.

2 Pisa. There's more than just its leaning tower.

3 Chianti. The heart of Italy's most famous wine region.

4 Volterra. Handicrafts made with alabaster can be purchased here.

5 San Gimignano. Hilltown with medieval "skyscrapers."

6 Siena. Charming medieval town.

7 Arezzo. Tuscany's third-largest city.

8 Cortona. This ancient stone town was made famous by the book *Under the Tuscan Sun.*

9 Perugia. Umbria's largest town.

10 Assisi. The city of St. Francis.

11 Spoleto. Come to see the Piazza del Duomo.

12 Orvieto. Carved out of volcanic rock and known today for wine and shoe shopping.

Florence

Greve

Tavarnelle

Arezzo

Sansepolcro

TUSCANY

UMBRIA

CHIANTI

3

Siena

6

326

Cortona

8

E45

298

Montalcino

9 Perugia

Assisi

10

223

Lago Di
Trasimeno

Foligno

2

78

448

3

Todi

Spoleto

11

Grossieto

12 Orvieto

A1

204

4

Orbetello

1

Lago di
Bolsena

Rieti

Tarquinia

2

LAZIO

3

Lago di
Bracciano

A24

Terni

1

ROME

Tivoli

A1

A91

Lido di Ostia

601

EATING AND DRINKING WELL IN TUSCANY

Affettati misti (Italian cured meat platter)

The influence of the ancient Etruscans—who favored the use of fresh herbs—is still felt in Tuscan cuisine three millennia later. Simple and earthy, Tuscan food celebrates the seasons with fresh vegetable dishes, wonderful bread-based soups, and meats perfumed with sage, rosemary, and thyme.

Throughout Tuscany there are excellent upscale restaurants that serve elaborate dishes, but to get a real taste of the flavors of the region, head for the family-run trattorias found in every town. The service and setting are often basic, but the food can be memorable.

Few places serve lighter fare at midday, so expect substantial meals at lunch and dinner, especially in out-of-the-way towns. Dining hours are fairly standard: lunch between 12:30 and 2, dinner between 7:30 and 10.

HOLD THE SALT

Tuscan bread is famous for what it's missing: salt. That's because it's intended to pick up seasoning from the food it accompanies, not be eaten alone. That doesn't mean Tuscans don't like to start a meal with bread, but usually it's prepared in some way. It can be grilled and drizzled with olive oil (*fettunta*), covered with chicken liver spread (*crostino con fegatini*), or toasted, rubbed with garlic, and topped with tomatoes (*bruschetta*).

AFFETTATI MISTI

The name, roughly translated, means "mixed cold cuts," and it's something Tuscans do exceptionally well. A platter of cured meats, served as an antipasto, is sure to include *prosciutto crudo* (cured pork, cut paper-thin) and *salame* (dry sausage, prepared in dozens of ways—some spicy, some sweet). The most distinctly Tuscan affettati are made from *cinta senese* (a once nearly extinct pig found only in the heart of the region) and *cinghiale* (wild boar, which roam all over Italy). You can eat these delicious slices unadorned or layered on a piece of bread.

PASTA

Restaurants throughout Tuscany serve dishes similar to those in Florence, but they also have their own local specialties. Many recipes are from the *nonna* (grandmother) of the restaurant's owner, handed down over time but never written down.

Look in particular for pasta creations made with *pici* (a long, thick, hand-rolled spaghetti). Pappardelle (a long, ribbonlike pasta noodle) is frequently paired with sauces made with game, such as *lepre* (hare) or cinghiale. In the northwest, a specialty of Lucca is *tordelli di carne al ragù* (meat-stuffed pasta with a meat sauce).

Fiorentina steak

Ribbon-like pasta with mushrooms

MEAT

Bistecca alla fiorentina (a thick T-bone steak, grilled rare) is the classic meat dish of Tuscany, but there are other specialties as well. Many menus will include *tagliata di manzo* (thinly sliced, roasted beef, drizzled with olive oil), *arista di maiale* (roast pork with sage and rosemary), and *salsiccia e fagioli* (pork sausage and beans). In the southern part of the region, don't be surprised to find *piccione* (pigeon), which can be roasted, stuffed, or baked.

WINE

Grape cultivation here also dates from Etruscan times, and vineyards are abundant, particularly in Chianti. The resulting medium-body red wine is a staple on most tables; however, you can select from a multitude of other varieties, including such reds as Brunello di Montalcino and Vino Nobile di Montepulciano and such whites as vermentino and vernaccia.

Super Tuscans (a fanciful name given to a group of wines by American journalists) now command attention as some of the best produced in Italy; they have great depth and complexity. The dessert wine vin santo is made throughout the region and is often sipped with biscotti (twice-baked almond cookies), perfect for dunking.

EATING AND DRINKING WELL IN UMBRIA AND THE MARCHES

Porchetta (roasted pork)

Central Italy is mountainous, and its food is hearty and straightforward, with a stick-to-the-ribs quality that sees hardworking farmers and artisans through a long day's work and helps them make the steep climb home at night.

In restaurants here, as in much of Italy, you're rewarded for seeking out the local cuisines, and you'll often find better and cheaper food if you're willing to stray a few hundred yards from the main sights. Spoleto is noted for its good food and service, probably a result of high expectations from the international arts crowd. For gourmet food, however, it's hard to beat Montefalco and Bevagna, which have both excellent restaurants and first-rate wine merchants.

A rule of thumb for eating well throughout Umbria is to order what's in season; stroll through local markets to see what's for sale. Also, a number of restaurants in the region offer *degustazione* (tasting) menus that give you a chance to try different local specialties without breaking the bank.

TASTY TRUFFLES

More truffles are found in Umbria than anywhere else in Italy. Spoleto and Norcia are prime territory for the *tartufo nero* (reddish-black interior and fine white veins), prized for its extravagant flavor and intense aroma.

The mild summer truffle, *scorzone estivo* (black outside and beige inside), is in season from May through December. The *scorzone autunnale* (burnt brown color and visible veins inside) is found from October through December.

OLIVE OIL

Nearly everywhere you look in Umbria, olive trees grace the hillsides. The soil of the Apennines allows the olives to ripen slowly, guaranteeing low acidity, a cardinal virtue of fine oil. Look for restaurants that proudly display their own oil, often a sign that they care about their food.

Umbria's finest oil is found in Trevi, where the local product is intensely green and fruity. You can sample it in the town's wine bars, which often offer olive-oil tastings.

Olive oil

PORK PRODUCTS

Much of traditional Umbrian cuisine revolves around pork. It can be cooked in wood-fired stoves, sometimes basted with a rich sauce made from innards and red wine. The roasted pork known as *porchetta* is grilled on a spit and flavored with fennel and herbs, leaving a crisp outer sheen.

In Norcia, the art of pork processing has been handed down through generations, so much so that charcuterie producers throughout Italy are often known as *norcini*. Don't miss *prosciutto di Norcia,* which is aged for two years.

LENTILS AND SOUPS

Throughout Umbria, look for *imbrecciata,* a soup of beans and grains,

Black truffles

delicately flavored with local herbs. The town of Castelluccio di Norcia is particularly known for its lentils and its farro (a grain used by the Romans, similar to wheat), as well as for the variety of beans used in its soups. Other ingredients that find their way into thick Umbrian soups are wild beets, sorrel, mushrooms, spelt, chickpeas, and the elusive, fragrant saffron, grown in nearby Cascia.

WINE

Sagrantino grapes are the star in Umbria's most notable red wines. For centuries they've been used in Sagrantino *passito,* a semisweet wine made by leaving the grapes to dry for a period after picking to intensify their sugar content. In recent decades, Montefalco Sagrantino *secco* (dry) has occupied the front stage. Both passito and secco have a deep, ruby-red color, with a full body and rich flavor.

The abundance of *enotecas* (wineshops and wine bars) has made it easier to arrange tastings. Many establishments also let you sample different olive oils on toasted bread, known as bruschetta. Some wine information centers, such as La Strada del Sagrantino in the town of Montefalco, will help set up appointments for tastings.

No place better epitomizes the beauty and splendor of Italy than the central regions of Tuscany and Umbria. They are both characterized by midsize cities and small hilltop towns, each with its own rich history and art treasures. Highlights include the walled city of Lucca; Pisa and its Leaning Tower; Siena, home of the Palio; and Assisi, the city of St. Francis. In between, the gorgeous countryside produces some of Italy's finest wine.

The beauty of the landscape here proves the perfect foil for the regions abundance of outstanding art and architecture. Many cities and towns in this region have retained the same fundamental character over the past 500 years. Civic rivalries that led to bloody battles centuries ago have given way to serious soccer rivalries.

MAJOR REGIONS

Tuscany. Nature outdid herself with Tuscany, the central Italian region that has Florence as its principal city. Descriptions and photographs can't do the landscape justice—the hills, draped with woods, vineyards, and olive groves are magical. Assisi is famous for its basilica, Lucca has 99 churches, Pisa's leaning tower is infamous, and the hilltop towns of Volterra, San Gimignano, Siena, Arezzo, and Cortona are magical.

Umbria. The landscape here is wilder, the valleys deeper, and the mountains higher. The trendy boutiques in Perugia are a

pleasure and the towns of Spoleto and Orvieto are good bases for exploration.

Planning

When to Go

Throughout Tuscany and Umbria, the best times to visit are spring and fall. Days are warm, nights are cool, and though there are still tourists, the crowds are smaller. In the countryside the scenery is gorgeous, with abundant greenery and flowers in spring, and burnished leaves in autumn.

July and August are the most popular times to visit. Note, though, that the heat is often oppressive and mosquitoes are prevalent. Try to start your days early and visit major sights first to beat the crowds and the midday sun. For relief from the heat, head to the mountains of the Garfagnana, where hiking is spectacular, or hit the beach at resort towns such as

Forte dei Marmi and Viareggio, along the Maremma coast, on the island of Elba, or on the long, flat stretches of sandy beach on the east coast of the Marches.

November through March you might wonder who invented the term "sunny Italy." The panoramas are still beautiful, even with overcast skies, frequent rain, and occasional snow. In winter Florence benefits from shorter museum lines and less competition for restaurant tables. Outside the cities, though, many hotels and restaurants close for the season.

Planning Your Time

Central Italy isn't the place for a jam-packed itinerary. One of the greatest pleasures here is indulging in rustic hedonism, marked by long lunches and show-stopping sunsets. Whether by car, by bike, or on foot, you'll want to get out into the glorious landscape, but it's smart to keep your plans modest. Set a church or a hill town or an out-of-the-way restaurant as your destination, know-ing that half the pleasure is in getting there—admiring as you go the stately pal-aces, the tidy geometry of row upon row of grapevines, the fields vibrant with red poppies, sunflowers, and yellow broom.

In Tuscany, you'll need to devise a strate-gy for seeing the sights. Take Siena: this beautiful, art-filled town simply can't be missed; it's compact enough that you can see the major sights on a day trip, and that's exactly what most people do. Spend the night, though, and you'll get to see the town breathe a sigh and relax on the day-trippers' departure. In Pisa, the famous tower and rest of the Camposan-to are not only worth seeing but a must-see, a highlight of any trip to Italy. But nearby Lucca must not be overlooked either. In fact, this walled town has greater charms than Pisa does, making it a better choice for an overnight, so you should come up with a plan that takes in both places.

Umbria is a nicely compact collection of character-rich hill towns; you can settle in one, then explore the others, as well as the countryside and forest in between, on day trips. Perugia, Umbria's largest and liveliest city, is a logical choice for your base, particularly if you're arriving from the north. If you want something a little quieter, virtually any other town in the region will suit your purposes; even Assisi, which overflows with bus tours during the day, is delightfully quiet in the evening and early morning. Spoleto and Orvieto are the most developed towns to the south, but they're still of modest proportions.

Getting Here and Around

Most flights to Tuscany originating in the United States stop either in Rome, Lon-don, Paris, or Frankfurt, and then connect to Florence's small Aeroporto A. Vespucci (commonly called Peretola), or to Pisa's Aeroporto Galileo Galilei. Delta currently has one seasonal direct flight from New York (JFK) to Pisa.

Alternatively, it's an hour by train or an hour and a half by car to reach the lovely town of Orvieto from Rome's Aeroporto Leonardo da Vinci (commonly called Fiumicino). Another option is to fly to Milan and pick up a connecting flight to Pisa, Florence, Perugia, or Ancona in the Marches.

Buses are a reliable but time-consum-ing means of getting around the region because they tend to stop in every town. Trains are a better option in virtually every respect when you're headed to Pisa, Lucca, Arezzo, and other cities with good rail service. But for most smaller towns, buses are the only option. Be aware that making arrangements for bus travel, particularly for a non-Italian speaker, can be a test of patience. Several direct daily trains run by the Italian state railway, FS-Trenitalia (⊕ www.trenitalia.com), link Florence and Rome with Perugia and

Assisi, and local service to the same area is available from Terontola (on the Rome–Florence line) and from Foligno (on the Rome–Ancona line). Intercity trains between Rome and Florence make stops in Orvieto, and the main Rome–Ancona line passes through Narni, Terni, Spoleto, and Foligno.

Driving is the only way (other than hiking or biking) to reach many of central Italy's small towns and vineyards.

Restaurants

A meal in central Italy traditionally consists of five courses, and every menu you encounter will be organized along this plan of antipasto, primo, secondo, contorno, and dolce. The crucial rule of restaurant dining is that you should order at least two courses. Otherwise, you'll likely end up with a lonely piece of meat and no sides.

Hotels

A visit to central Italy is a trip into the country. There are plenty of good hotels in the larger towns, but the classic experience is to stay in one of the rural accommodations—often converted private homes, sometimes working farms or vineyards (known as *agriturismi*). Virtually every older town, no matter how small, has some kind of hotel. A trend, particularly around Gubbio, Orvieto, and Todi, is to convert old villas, farms, and monasteries into first-class hotels. The natural splendor of the countryside more than compensates for the distance from town—provided you have a car. Hotels in town tend to be simpler than their country cousins, with a few notable exceptions in Spoleto, Gubbio, and Perugia.

Although it's tempting to think you can stumble upon a little out-of-the-way hotel at the end of the day, you're better off not testing your luck. Make reservations before you go. If you don't have a reservation, you may be able to get help finding a room from the local tourist office.

⇨ *Prices in the dining reviews are the average cost of a main course at dinner, or, if dinner is not served, at lunch. Prices in the reviews are the lowest cost of a standard double room in high season. Restaurant and hotel reviews have been shortened. For full information, visit Fodors.com.*

What It Costs in Euros			
$	$$	$$$	$$$$
RESTAURANTS			
under €15	€15–€24	€25–€35	over €35
HOTELS			
under €125	€125–€200	€201–€300	over €300

Lucca

90 km (56 miles) west of Florence.

Ramparts built in the 16th and 17th centuries enclose a charming fortress town filled with churches (99 of them), terra-cotta–roofed buildings, and narrow cobblestone streets, along which locals maneuver bikes to do their daily shopping. Here Caesar, Pompey, and Crassus agreed to rule Rome as a triumvirate in 56 BC; Lucca was later the first Tuscan town to accept Christianity. The town still has a mind of its own, and when most of Tuscany was voting communist as a matter of course, Lucca's citizens rarely followed suit. The famous composer Giacomo Puccini (1858–1924) was born here; he is celebrated during the summer Opera Theater and Music Festival of Lucca. The ramparts circling the centro storico are the perfect place to stroll, bicycle, or just admire the view.

GETTING HERE AND AROUND

You can reach Lucca easily by train from Florence; the centro storico is a short walk from the station. If you're driving, take the A11/E76.

VISITOR INFORMATION

CONTACT Lucca Tourism Office. ✉ Piazzale Verdi, Lucca ☎ 0583/583150 ⊕ www.luccaturismo.it.

 # Sights

Duomo

CHURCH | The blind arches on the cathedral's facade are a fine example of the rigorously ordered Pisan Romanesque style, in this case happily enlivened by an extremely varied collection of small, carved columns. Take a closer look at the decoration of the facade and that of the portico below; they make this one of the most entertaining church exteriors in Tuscany.

The Gothic interior contains a moving Byzantine crucifix—called the Volto Santo, or Holy Face—brought here, according to legend, in the 8th century (though it probably dates from between the 11th and early 13th century). The masterpiece of the Sienese sculptor Jacopo della Quercia (circa 1371–1438) is the marble Tomb of Ilaria del Carretto (1407–08). ✉ Piazza San Martino 8, Lucca ☎ 0583/490530 ⊕ www.museocattedralelucca.it ▱ €3.

Museo Nazionale di Villa Guinigi

ART MUSEUM | Although this museum presents a noteworthy overview of Lucca's artistic traditions up through the 17th century, you might find few other visitors exploring its extensive collections of local Etruscan, Roman, Romanesque, and Renaissance art. It's all housed in the 15th-century former villa of the Guinigi family, on the eastern end of the historic center. ✉ Via della Quarquonia 4, Lucca ☎ 0583/496033 ⊕ www.luccamuseinazionali.it ▱ €4 ⊗ Closed Mon. and 2nd, 4th, and 5th Sun. of month.

★ Passeggiata delle Mura

CITY PARK | FAMILY | On nice days, the citizens of Lucca cycle, jog, stroll, or kick a soccer ball in this green, beautiful, and very large circular park. It's neither inside nor outside the city but rather right atop and around the ring of ramparts that defines Lucca. Sunlight streams through two rows of tall plane trees to dapple the passeggiata delle mura (walk on the walls), which is 4 km (2½ miles) long. Ten bulwarks are topped with lawns, many with picnic tables and some with play equipment for children. Be aware at all times of where the edge is—there are no railings, and the drop to the ground outside the city is a precipitous 40 feet. ✉ Lucca.

Piazza dell'Anfiteatro

PLAZA/SQUARE | FAMILY | Here's where the ancient Roman amphitheater once stood. Some of the medieval buildings built over the amphitheater retain its original oval shape and brick arches. ✉ Piazza dell'Anfiteatro, Lucca.

San Frediano

CHURCH | A 14th-century mosaic decorates the facade of this church just steps from the anfiteatro. Inside are works by Jacopo della Quercia and Matteo Civitali (1436–1501), as well as the lace-clad mummy of St. Zita (circa 1218–78), the patron saint of household servants. ✉ Piazza San Frediano, Lucca ☎ 349/8440290 ⊕ www.sanfredianolucca.com ▱ €3.

San Michele in Foro

CHURCH | The facade here is even more fanciful than that of the Duomo. Its upper levels have nothing but air behind them (after the front of the church was built, there were no funds to raise the nave), and the winged archangel Michael, who stands at the very top, seems precariously poised for flight. The facade, heavily restored in the 19th century, displays busts of such Italian patriots as Garibaldi and Cavour. Check out the superb Filippino Lippi (1457/58–1504) panel painting of Saints Jerome, Sebastian, Rocco, and

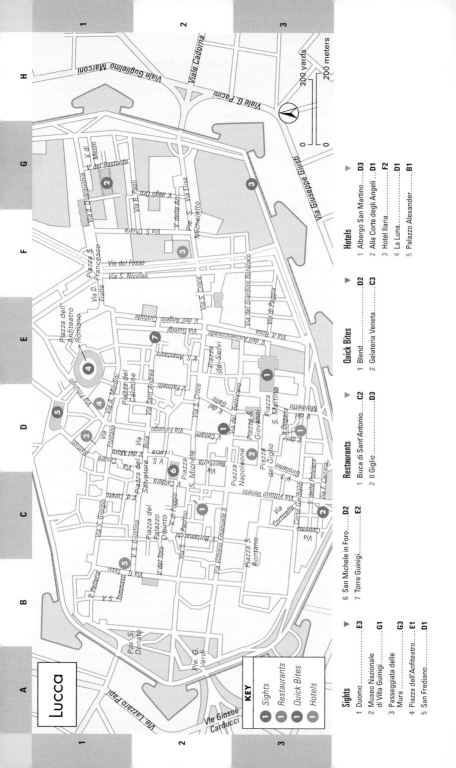

Lucca

KEY

- ① Sights
- ① Restaurants
- ① Quick Bites
- ① Hotels

Sights ▶

1 Duomo **E3**
2 Museo Nazionale di Villa Guinigi **G1**
3 Passeggiata delle Mura **G3**
4 Piazza dell'Anfiteatro **E1**
5 San Frediano **D1**
6 San Michele in Foro **D2**
7 Torre Guinigi **E2**

Restaurants ▶

1 Buca di Sant'Antonio **C2**
2 Il Giglio **D3**

Quick Bites ▶

1 Blend **D2**
2 Gelateria Veneta **C3**

Hotels ▶

1 Albergo San Martino **D3**
2 Alla Corte degli Angeli ... **D1**
3 Hotel Ilaria **F2**
4 La Luna **D1**
5 Palazzo Alexander **B1**

200 yards

200 meters

0

0

Helen in the right transept. ✉ *Piazza San Michele, Lucca* ☎ *0583/53576* 🌐 *www.luccatranoi.it.*

Torre Guinigi

NOTABLE BUILDING | FAMILY | The tower of the medieval Palazzo Guinigi contains one of the city's most curious sights: a grove of ilex trees has grown at the top of the tower, and their roots have pushed their way into the room below. From the top you have a magnificent view of the city and the surrounding countryside. (Only the tower is open to the public, not the palazzo.) ✉ *Via Sant'Andrea, Lucca* ☎ *0583/48090* 🌐 *www.comune.lucca.it* 🎫 *€5.*

🍴 Restaurants

★ Buca di Sant'Antonio

$$ | TUSCAN | The staying power of Buca di Sant'Antonio—it's been around since 1782—is the result of superlative Tuscan food brought to the table by waitstaff who don't miss a beat. The menu includes the simple but blissful *tortelli lucchesi al sugo* (meat-stuffed pasta with a tomato-and-meat sauce), as well as more daring dishes such as roast *capretto* (kid goat) with herbs. **Known for:** superlative pastas; excellent sommelier; classy, family-run ambience. [$] *Average main: €20* ✉ *Via della Cervia 3, Lucca* ☎ *0583/55881* 🌐 *www.bucadisantantonio.com* ⏲ *Closed Mon., 1 wk in Jan., and 1 wk in July. No dinner Sun.*

★ Il Giglio

$$$ | TUSCAN | Divine, cutting-edge food and Tuscan classics are served in this one-room space, where in winter, there's a roaring fireplace and, in warmer months there's outdoor seating on a pretty little piazza. If mushrooms are in season, try the *tacchoni con funghi,* a homemade pasta with mushrooms and a native herb called *nepitella.* A local favorite during winter is the *coniglio con olive* (rabbit stew with olives). **Known for:** creative menu with seasonal ingredients; fine service; the wine list, especially its selection of local wines. [$] *Average main: €35* ✉ *Piazza del Giglio 2, Lucca* ☎ *0583/494508* 🌐 *www.ristorantegiglio.com* ⏲ *Closed Tues. and Wed. and 15 days in Nov.*

☕ Coffee and Quick Bites

Blend

$ | ITALIAN | If you're looking for a lovely spot to recharge, stop by this place (just around the corner from the Duomo), and have a fantastic sandwich, or a glass of wine, or a tasty salad, a coffee, or dessert. It's open from late morning to late in the evening. **Known for:** good salads; near the Duomo; open late. [$] *Average main: €7* ✉ *Piazza S. Giusto 8, Duomo* ☎ *0583/050442.*

Gelateria Veneta

$ | ITALIAN | FAMILY | The outstanding gelato, sorbet, and ices, some of which are sugar-free, served here are prepared three times a day according to the same recipes used by the Arnoldo brothers when they opened the place in 1927. The pièces de résistance are frozen fruits stuffed with creamy filling: don't miss the apricot sorbet–filled apricot. **Known for:** longtime local favorite; sorbet-stuffed frozen fruits; delicious ices on a stick. [$] *Average main: €3* ✉ *Via V. Veneto 74, Lucca* ☎ *0583/467037* 🌐 *www.gelateria-veneta.net* ⏲ *Closed Nov.–Mar.*

🛏 Hotels

★ Albergo San Martino

$$ | HOTEL | FAMILY | The brocade bedspreads of this inn in the heart of the centro storico are fresh and crisp; the proprietor is friendly; and the breakfast, served in a cheerful apricot room, is more than ample. **Pros:** comfortable beds; tucked away on a small, sunny square; friendly staff. **Cons:** parking is difficult; pleasant and stylish but not luxurious; slightly noisy during Lucca Music Festival. [$] *Rooms from: €129* ✉ *Via*

della Dogana 9, Lucca ☎ 0583/469181 ⊕ www.albergosanmartino.it ➪ 18 rooms ⊚| No Meals.

Alla Corte degli Angeli

$$ | **B&B/INN** | This charming hotel with a friendly staff is right off the main shopping drag, Via Fillungo. **Pros:** many rooms are connecting, making them good for families; great location; fantastic on-site restaurant. **Cons:** some rooms have tubs but no showers; not all rooms are created equal; books up quickly. $ Rooms from: €196 ✉ Via degli Angeli 23, Lucca ☎ 0583/469204 ⊕ www.allacortedegli-angeli.it ➪ 21 rooms ⊚| Free Breakfast.

Hotel Ilaria

$$ | **HOTEL** | The former stables of the Villa Bottini have been transformed into a modern hotel with stylish rooms done in a warm wood veneer with blue-and-white fittings. **Pros:** modern; free bicycles; multilingual, pleasant staff. **Cons:** though in the city center, it's a little removed from main attractions; some find it overpriced; books up quickly. $ Rooms from: €168 ✉ Via del Fosso 26, Lucca ☎ 0583/47615 ⊕ www.hotelilaria.com ➪ 44 rooms ⊚| Free Breakfast.

La Luna

$$$ | **B&B/INN** | On a quiet, airy courtyard close to the Piazza del Mercato, this hotel, run by the Barbieri family for more than four decades, occupies two renovated wings of an old building. **Pros:** professional staff; the annex has wheelchair-accessible rooms; central location. **Cons:** some rooms feel dated; street noise can be a bit of a problem; may be too central for some. $ Rooms from: €202 ✉ Corte Compagni 12, at Via Fillungo, Lucca ☎ 0583/493634 ⊕ www.hotellaluna.it ⊗ Closed Jan. 7–31 ➪ 29 rooms ⊚| Free Breakfast.

Palazzo Alexander

$$ | **HOTEL** | This hotel, in a building dating from the 12th century, has public rooms with timbered ceilings, warm yellow walls, and brocaded chairs and guest rooms with high ceilings and still more of that glorious damask. **Pros:** intimate feel; gracious staff; a short walk from San Michele in Foro. **Cons:** some complain of too-thin walls; books up quickly; might be too quiet for some. $ Rooms from: €170 ✉ Via S. Giustina 48, Lucca ☎ 0583/583571 ⊕ www.hotelpalazzoalexander.it ➪ 13 rooms ⊚| Free Breakfast.

 # Shopping

★ Antica Bottega di Prospero

FOOD | Stop by this shop for top-quality local food products, including farro, dried porcini mushrooms, olive oil, and wine. ✉ Via San Lucia 13, Lucca ☎ 0583/494875.

★ Caniparoli

CHOCOLATE | **FAMILY** | Chocolate lovers will be pleased with the selection of artisanal chocolates, marzipan delights, and gorgeous cakes. Creations become even more fanciful during Christmas and Easter. ✉ Via San Paolino 44, Lucca ☎ 0583/53456 ⊕ www.caniparolicioccolateria.it.

★ Enoteca Vanni

WINE/SPIRITS | A huge selection of wines, as well as an ancient cellar, make this place worth a stop. For the cost of the wine only, tastings can be organized through the shopkeepers and are held in the cellar or outside in a lovely little piazza. All of this can be paired with affettati misti (sliced cured meats) and cheeses of the highest caliber. ✉ Piazza San Salvatore 7, Lucca ☎ 0583/491902 ⊕ www.enotecavanni.com.

★ Pasticceria Taddeucci

FOOD | **FAMILY** | A particularly delicious version of buccellato—the sweet, anise-flavored bread with raisins that is a Luccan specialty—is baked at Pasticceria Taddeucci. ✉ Piazza San Michele 34, Lucca ☎ 0583/494933 ⊕ www.buccellatotaddeucci.com.

Activities

Poli Antonio Biciclette

BIKING | FAMILY | This is one of the best options for bicycle rentals on the east side of town. ✉ *Piazza Santa Maria 42, Lucca East* ☎ *0583/493787* ⊕ *www. biciclettepoli.com.*

Pisa

19 km (11 miles) southwest of Lucca.

If you can get beyond the kitsch of the stalls hawking cheap souvenirs around the Leaning Tower, you'll find that Pisa has much to offer. Its treasures aren't as abundant as those of Florence, to which it is inevitably compared, but the cathedral-baptistery-tower complex of Piazza del Duomo, known collectively as the Campo dei Miracoli (Field of Miracles), is among the most dramatic settings in Italy.

Pisa may have been inhabited as early as the Bronze Age. It was certainly populated by the Etruscans and, in turn, became part of the Roman Empire. In the early Middle Ages this city on the Arno River flourished as an economic powerhouse—along with Amalfi, Genoa, and Venice, it was one of the four maritime republics. The city's economic and political power ebbed in the early 15th century as it fell under Florence's domination, though it enjoyed a brief resurgence under Cosimo I de' Medici in the mid-16th century. Pisa sustained heavy damage during World War II, but the Duomo and the Leaning Tower were spared, along with some other grand Romanesque structures.

GETTING HERE AND AROUND

Pisa is an easy hour's train ride from Florence. By car it's a straight shot on the Firenze–Pisa–Livorno ("Fi-Pi-Li") autostrada. The Pisa–Lucca train runs frequently and takes about 30 minutes.

VISITOR INFORMATION

CONTACT Pisa Tourism Office. ✉ *Piazza del Duomo 7, Pisa* ☎ *050/550100* ⊕ *www. turismo.pisa.it.*

Sights

Battistero

NOTABLE BUILDING | This lovely Gothic baptistery, which stands across from the Duomo's facade, is best known for the pulpit carved by Nicola Pisano (circa 1220–84; father of Giovanni Pisano) in 1260. Every half hour, an employee will dramatically close the doors, then intone, thereby demonstrating how remarkable the acoustics are in the place. ✉ *Piazza del Duomo, Pisa* ☎ *050/835011* ⊕ *www. opapisa.it* ✍ *From €7, discounts available if bought in combination with tickets for other monuments.*

Camposanto

CEMETERY | According to legend, the cemetery—a walled structure on the western side of the Piazza dei Miracoli—is filled with earth that returning Crusaders brought back from the Holy Land. Contained within are numerous frescoes, notably *The Drunkenness of Noah,* by Renaissance artist Benozzo Gozzoli (1422–97), and the disturbing *Triumph of Death* (14th century; artist uncertain), whose subject matter shows what was on people's minds in a century that saw the ravages of the Black Death. ✉ *Piazza del Duomo, Pisa* ☎ *050/835011* ⊕ *www. opapisa.it* ✍ *From €7.*

Duomo

CHURCH | Pisa's cathedral brilliantly utilizes the horizontal marble-stripe motif (borrowed from Moorish architecture) that became common on Tuscan cathedrals. It is famous for the Romanesque panels on the transept door facing the tower that depict scenes from the life of Christ. The beautifully carved 14th-century pulpit is by Giovanni Pisano. ✉ *Piazza del Duomo, Pisa* ☎ *050/835011* ⊕ *www.opapisa.it* ✍ *Free.*

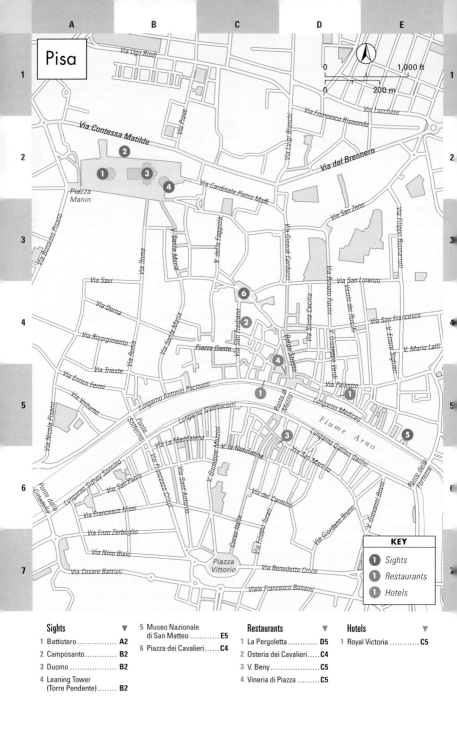

Pisa

Sights ▼

1 Battistero **A2**
2 Camposanto **B2**
3 Duomo **B2**
4 Leaning Tower
(Torre Pendente) **B2**

5 Museo Nazionale
di San Matteo **E5**
6 Piazza dei Cavalieri **C4**

Restaurants ▼

1 La Pergoletta **D5**
2 Osteria dei Cavalieri **C4**
3 V. Beny **C5**
4 Vineria di Piazza **C5**

Hotels ▼

1 Royal Victoria **C5**

★ Leaning Tower (Torre Pendente)

NOTABLE BUILDING | **FAMILY** | Legend holds that Galileo conducted an experiment on the nature of gravity by dropping metal balls from the top of the 187-foot-high Leaning Tower of Pisa (whether it's true is a matter of debate). Work on this tower, built as a campanile for the Duomo, started in 1173. The lopsided settling began when construction reached the third story. The architects attempted to compensate by making the remaining floors slightly taller on the leaning side, but the extra weight made the problem worse. By the late 20th century, many feared the tower would simply topple over. The structure has since been firmly anchored to the earth and restored to its original tilt of 300 years ago.

Reservations, which are essential, can be made online or by calling the Museo dell'Opera del Duomo. It's also possible to arrive at the ticket office and book for the same day. Note, though, that children under eight aren't allowed to climb. ✉ *Piazza del Duomo, Pisa* ☎ *050/835011* 🌐 *www.opapisa.it* 🎟 *€20.*

Museo Nazionale di San Matteo

ART MUSEUM | On the north bank of the Arno, this museum contains some beautiful examples of local Romanesque and Gothic art. Despite the fact that it has stunning works by Donatello and Benozzo Gozzoli (among others), here you'll find very few other visitors. ✉ *Piazza Matteo in Soarta 1, Pisa* ☎ *050/541865* 🌐 *www.polomusealetoscana.beniculturali.it* 🎟 *€5* 🕓 *Closed Mon.*

Piazza dei Cavalieri

PLAZA/SQUARE | The piazza, with its fine Renaissance Palazzo dei Cavalieri, Palazzo dell'Orologio, and Chiesa di Santo Stefano dei Cavalieri, was laid out by Giorgio Vasari in about 1560. The square was the seat of the *Ordine dei Cavalieri di San Stefano* (Order of the Knights of St. Stephen), a military and religious institution meant to defend the coast from possible invasion by the Turks.

Also in this square is the prestigious Scuola Normale Superiore, founded by Napoléon in 1810 on the French model. Here graduate students pursue doctorates in literature, philosophy, mathematics, and science. In front of the school is a large statue of Ferdinando I de' Medici dating from 1596. On the extreme left is the tower where the hapless Ugolino della Gherardesca (died 1289) was imprisoned with his two sons and two grandsons—legend holds that he ate them. Dante immortalized him in Canto XXXIII of his *Inferno.* Duck into the Church of Santo Stefano (if you're lucky enough to find it open) and check out Bronzino's splendid *Nativity of Christ* (1564–65). ✉ *Piazza dei Cavalieri, Pisa.*

🍴 Restaurants

La Pergoletta

$$ | **TUSCAN** | **FAMILY** | On an old town street named for its beautiful towers, this small, simple restaurant is in one such tower itself and is a place where Pisans come to celebrate. Three intimate rooms, one particularly charming with a pergola, are usually filled with locals eating dishes laced with imagination. **Known for:** inventive, seasonal menu; festive atmosphere; gracious waitstaff. [$] *Average main: €18* ✉ *Via delle Belle Torri 36, Pisa* ☎ *050/542458* 🌐 *www.ristorantelapergoletta.com* 🕓 *Closed Mon. and 1 wk in Aug. No lunch Sat.*

Osteria dei Cavalieri

$$ | **ITALIAN** | This charming, white-walled restaurant, a few steps from Piazza dei Cavalieri, is reason enough to come to Pisa. They can do it all here—serve up exquisitely grilled fish dishes, please vegetarians, and prepare tagliata for meat lovers. **Known for:** location in the centro storico; classic Tuscan dishes; catch-of-the-day fish tasting menu. [$] *Average main: €16* ✉ *Via San Frediano 16, Pisa* ☎ *050/580858* 🌐 *www.osteriacavalieri.pisa.it* 🕓 *Closed Sun., 2 wks in Aug., and Dec. 29–Jan. 7. No lunch Wed.*

⭐ **V. Beny**

$$$ | **TUSCAN** | Apricot walls hung with etchings of Pisa make this small, single-room restaurant warmly romantic. Husband and wife Damiano and Sandra Lazzerini have been running the place for two decades, and it shows in their obvious enthusiasm while talking about the menu (fish is a focus) and daily specials, which often astound. **Known for:** superb fish dishes; gracious service; terrific wine list. $ *Average main: €27* ⊠ *Piazza Gambacorti 22, Pisa* ☎ *050/25067* ⊗ *Closed Sun. and 2 wks in mid-Aug. No lunch Sat.*

⭐ **Vineria di Piazza**

$$ | **ITALIAN** | It's set in a lively, historic market square and frequented by locals. The menu adheres to Tuscan tradition, often including high-quality bistecca alla fiorentina, but also indulges in some flights of fantasy, as evidenced by a whimsical dessert that riffs on a liquid Livornese classic. **Known for:** inventive pasta dishes; baccalà (salt cod) served in inventive ways; charming, energetic staff. $ *Average main: €20* ⊠ *Piazza delle Vettovaglie 13, Pisa* ☎ *050/5207846.*

 Hotels

Royal Victoria

$ | **HOTEL** | In a pleasant palazzo facing the Arno, a 10-minute walk from the Campo dei Miracoli, this hotel has room styles that range from the 1800s, complete with frescoes, to the 1920s; the most charming are in the old tower. **Pros:** friendly staff; lovely views of the Arno from many rooms; old-world charm. **Cons:** rooms vary significantly in size; rooms a little worn; not all rooms have views of the Arno. $ *Rooms from: €95* ⊠ *Lungarno Pacinotti 12, Pisa* ☎ *050/940111* ⊕ *www.royalvictoria.it* ↵ *38 rooms* �‖ *Free Breakfast.*

 **Performing Arts**

Fondazione Teatro di Pisa

THEATER | Pisa has a lively performing-arts scene, most of which happens at the 19th-century Teatro Verdi. Music and dance performances are presented from September through May. Contact Fondazione Teatro di Pisa for schedules and information. ⊠ *Via Palestro 40, Lungarni, Pisa* ☎ *050/941111* ⊕ *www.teatrodipisa. pi.it.*

Chianti

This is the heartland: both sides of the Strada Chiantigiana (SR222) are embraced by glorious panoramic views of vineyards, olive groves, and castle towers. Traveling south from Florence, you first reach the aptly named one-street town of Strada in Chianti. Farther south, the number of vineyards on either side of the road dramatically increases—as do the signs inviting you in for a free tasting. Beyond Strada lies Greve in Chianti, completely surrounded by wineries and filled with wineshops. There's art to be had as well: Passignano, west of Greve, has an abbey that shelters a 15th-century *Last Supper* by Domenico and Davide Ghirlandaio. Farther still, along the Strada Chiantigiana, are Panzano and Castellina in Chianti, both hill towns. It's from near Panzano and Castellina that branch roads head to the other main towns of eastern Chianti: Radda in Chianti, Gaiole in Chianti, and Castelnuovo Berardenga.

The Strada Chiantigiana gets crowded during the high season, but no one is in a hurry. The slow pace gives you time to soak up the beautiful scenery.

Greve in Chianti

40 km (25 miles) north of Siena, 28 km (17½ miles) south of Florence.

If there is a capital of Chianti, it is Greve, a friendly market town with no shortage of cafés, enoteche, and crafts shops lining its streets.

GETTING HERE AND AROUND

Driving from Florence or Siena, Greve is easily reached via the Strada Chiantigiana (SR222). Autolinee Toscane buses travel frequently between Florence and Greve. The bus system also connects Siena and Greve, but a direct trip is virtually impossible. There is no train service to Greve.

VISITOR INFORMATION

CONTACT Greve in Chianti Tourism Office. ✉ *Piazza Matteotti 11, Greve in Chianti* ☎ *055/8546299* 🌐 *www.visitchianti.net.*

Sights

Montefioralle
TOWN | A tiny hilltop hamlet, about 2 km (1 mile) west of Greve in Chianti, Montefioralle is the ancestral home of Amerigo Vespucci (1454–1512), the mapmaker, navigator, and explorer who named America. (His cousin-in-law, Simonetta, may have been the inspiration for Sandro Botticelli's *Birth of Venus*, painted sometime in the 1480s.) ✉ *Greve in Chianti.*

Piazza Matteotti
PLAZA/SQUARE | Greve's gently sloping and asymmetrical central piazza is surrounded by an attractive arcade with shops of all kinds. In the center stands a statue of the discoverer of New York harbor, Giovanni da Verrazzano (circa 1480–1527). Check out the lively market held here on Saturday morning. ✉ *Piazza Matteotti, Greve in Chianti.*

Restaurants

Enoteca Fuoripiazza
$$ | **TUSCAN** | Detour off Greve's flower-strewn main square for food that relies heavily on local ingredients (like cheese and salami produced nearby). The lengthy wine list provides a bewildering array of choices to pair with affettati misti or one of the *primi* (first courses)—the *pici* (a thick, hand-rolled spaghetti) are deftly prepared here. **Known for:** alfresco dining; local cheese and salami; attentively prepared food. [$] *Average main: €19* ✉ *Via I Maggio 2, Greve in Chianti* ☎ *055/8546313* 🌐 *www.enotecaristorantefuoripiazza.it* 🕒 *Closed Mon.*

★ **Ristoro di Lamole**
$$ | **TUSCAN** | Up a winding road lined with olive trees and vineyards, this place is worth the effort it takes to find. The view from the outdoor terrace is divine, as is the simple, exquisitely prepared Tuscan cuisine—start with the bruschetta drizzled with olive oil or the sublime *verdure sott'olio* (marinated vegetables) before moving on to any of the fine secondi. **Known for:** coniglio is a specialty; sweeping view from the terrace; your hosts Paolo and Filippo. [$] *Average main: €20* ✉ *Via di Lamole 6, Località Lamole, Greve in Chianti* ☎ *055/8547050* 🌐 *www.ristorodilamole.it* 🕒 *Closed Nov.–Apr.*

Hotels

Albergo del Chianti
$$ | **B&B/INN** | **FAMILY** | Simple but pleasantly decorated bedrooms with plain modern cabinets and wardrobes and wrought-iron beds have views of the town square or out over the tile rooftops toward the surrounding hills. **Pros:** central location; best value in Greve; swimming pool. **Cons:** rooms facing the piazza can be noisy; small bathrooms; remote: a car is a necessity. [$] *Rooms from: €145* ✉ *Piazza Matteotti 86, Greve in Chianti* ☎ *055/853763* 🌐 *www.albergodelchianti.*

it ⏲ Closed Jan.–early Mar. 🛏 16 rooms 🍴 No Meals.

★ Villa Bordoni
$$ | **B&B/INN** | Scottish expats David and Catherine Gardner transformed a ramshackle, 16th-century villa into a stunning retreat where no two rooms are alike—all have stenciled walls; some have four-poster beds, others small mezzanines. **Pros:** splendidly isolated in the hills above Greve; beautiful decor; wonderful hosts. **Cons:** on a long and bumpy dirt road; need a car to get around; books up quickly. [$] *Rooms from: €175* ✉ *Via San Cresci 31/32, Greve in Chianti* ☎ *055/8546230* 🌐 *www.villabordoni.com* ⏲ *Closed Dec.–Feb.* 🛏 *12 rooms* 🍴 *Free Breakfast.*

★ Villa Il Poggiale
$$ | **B&B/INN** | **FAMILY** | Renaissance gardens, beautiful rooms with high ceilings and elegant furnishings, a panoramic pool, and expert staff are just a few of the things that make a stay at this 16th-century villa memorable. **Pros:** beautiful gardens and panoramic setting; elegant historical building; exceptionally professional staff. **Cons:** private transportation necessary; some rooms face a country road and may be noisy during the day; it may be too isolated for some. [$] *Rooms from: €179* ✉ *Via Empolese 69, San Casciano Val di Pesa* ✥ *20 km (12 miles) northwest of Greve* ☎ *055/828311* 🌐 *www.villailpoggiale.it* ⏲ *Closed Jan. and Feb.* 🛏 *26 rooms* 🍴 *Free Breakfast.*

Panzano

7 km (4½ miles) south of Greve, 36 km (22 miles) south of Florence.

The magnificent views of the valleys of the Pesa and Greve rivers easily make Panzano one of the prettiest stops in Chianti. The triangular Piazza Bucciarelli is the heart of the new town. A short stroll along Via Giovanni da Verrazzano brings you up to the old town, Panzano Alto, which is still partly surrounded by medieval walls. The town's 13th-century castle is now almost completely absorbed by later buildings (its central tower is now a private home).

GETTING HERE AND AROUND

From Florence or Siena, Panzano is easily reached by car along the Strada Chiantigiana (SR222). Autolinee Toscane buses travel frequently between Florence and Panzano and less often from Siena. There is no train service to Panzano.

Sights

San Leolino
CHURCH | Ancient even by Chianti standards, this hilltop church probably dates from the 10th century, but it was completely rebuilt in the Romanesque style sometime in the 13th century. It has a 14th-century cloister worth seeing. The 16th-century terra-cotta tabernacles are attributed to Giovanni della Robbia, and there's also a remarkable triptych (attributed to the Master of Panzano) that was executed sometime in the mid-14th century. Open days and hours are unpredictable; check with the tourist office in Greve in Chianti for the latest information. ✉ *Località San Leolino, Panzano* ✥ *3 km (2 miles) south of Panzano.*

Restaurants

★ Officina della Bistecca
$$$$ | **ITALIAN** | **FAMILY** | Local butcher and restaurateur, Dario Cecchini, has extended his empire of meat to include this space above his butcher's shop. In addition to two tasting menus—one heavily meat laden, the other with none—you'll find a homemade version of *giardiniera sott'olio* (pickled and preserved vegetables) that's second to none. **Known for:** convivial atmosphere; performing waitstaff; enormously popular, especially in summer. [$] *Average main: €50* ✉ *Via XX Luglio 11, Panzano* ☎ *055/852020* 🌐 *www.dariocecchini.com/officina.*

★ Solociccia

$$$$ | TUSCAN | FAMILY | As at his other eateries, Dario Cecchini, Panzano's local merchant of meat, offers two set menus for lunch—one where beef products dominate every course and the other vegetarian. The *musetto al limone e brodo vero* (an interesting salame served with stunning beef broth) might kick off the proceedings. **Known for:** choice of two set menus; great service; party atmosphere. $ *Average main: €40* ✉ *Via XX Luglio 11, Panzano* ☎ *055/852020* ⊕ *www.dariocecchini.com/solociccia* ☽ *No dinner.*

 Hotels

★ Villa Le Barone

$$$ | B&B/INN | Once the home of the Viviani della Robbia family, this 16th-century villa in a grove of ancient cypress trees retains many aspects of a private country dwelling, complete with homey guest quarters. **Pros:** beautiful location; wonderful restaurant; great base for exploring the region. **Cons:** some rooms are a bit small; 15-minute walk to nearest town; a car is a must. $ *Rooms from: €220* ✉ *Via San Leolino 19, Panzano* ☎ *055/852621* ⊕ *www.villalebarone. com* ☽ *Closed Oct.–Easter* ⤵ *28 rooms* ⦿ *Free Breakfast.*

Radda in Chianti

26 km (15 miles) southeast of Panzano, 55 km (34 miles) south of Florence.

Radda in Chianti sits on a ridge stretching between the Val di Pesa and Val d'Arbia. It is easily reached by following the SR429 from Castellina. It's another one of those tiny villages with steep streets for strolling; follow the signs that point you toward the *camminamento medioevale*, a covered 14th-century walkway that circles part of the city inside the walls.

GETTING HERE AND AROUND

Radda can be reached by car from either Siena or Florence along the SR222 (Strada Chiantigiana), and from the A1 autostrada. A few buses each day travel from Siena to Radda on Autolinee Toscane. There is no direct bus from Florence or train service convenient to Radda.

VISITOR INFORMATION

CONTACT Radda in Chianti Tourism Office. ✉ *Piazza Castello 6, Radda in Chianti* ☎ *0577/738494* ⊕ *www.chianti.com.*

 Sights

Badia a Coltibuono (*Abbey of the Good Harvest*)

WINERY | This Romanesque abbey has been owned by internationally acclaimed cookbook author Lorenza de' Medici's family for more than a century and a half (the family isn't related to the Florentine Medici). Wine has been produced here since the abbey was founded by Vallombrosan monks in the 11th century. Today, the family continues the tradition, making wines, cold-pressed olive oil, and various flavored vinegars. Don't miss the jasmine-draped courtyard and the inner cloister with its antique well. ✉ *Località Badia a Coltibuono, Gaiole in Chianti* ✛ *4 km (2½ miles) north of Gaiole* ☎ *0577/74481 tours* ⊕ *www.coltibuono. com* ⤓ *Abbey €10.*

★ Castello di Brolio

CASTLE/PALACE | If you have time for only one castle in Tuscany, this is it. At the end of the 12th century, when Florence conquered southern Chianti, Brolio became Florence's southernmost outpost, and it was often said, "When Brolio growls, all Siena trembles." It was built about AD 1000 and owned by the monks of the Badia Fiorentina. The "new" owners, the Ricasoli family, have been in possession since 1141. Bettino Ricasoli (1809–80), the so-called Iron Baron, was one of the founders of modern Italy and is said to have invented the original formula for Chianti wine.

Brolio, one of Chianti's best-known labels, is still justifiably famous. The grounds are worth visiting, and some of the guided tours do provide a glimpse of the castle's interior. The entrance fee includes a wine tasting in the enoteca. A small museum, where the Ricasoli Collection is housed in a 12th-century tower, displays objects that relate the long history of the family and the origins of Chianti wine. There are various options for an overnight here. ⊠ *Località Madonna a Brolio, Gaiole in Chianti* ⊹ *2 km (1 mile) southeast of Gaiole* ☎ *0577/730280* ⊕ *www.ricasoli.com* 🖃 *€7 gardens* ⊗ *Closed Jan.*

Palazzo del Podestà

GOVERNMENT BUILDING | Radda's town hall (aka Palazzo Comunale), in the middle of town, was built in the second half of the 14th century and has always served the same function. The 51 coats of arms (the largest is the Medici's) embedded in the facade represent the past governors of the town, but unless you have official business, the building is closed to the public. ⊠ *Piazza Ferrucci 1, Radda in Chianti.*

 Restaurants

Osteria Le Panzanelle

$ | **TUSCAN** | Silvia Bonechi's experience in the kitchen—with the help of a few precious recipes handed down from her grandmother—is one of the reasons for the success of this small restaurant in the tiny hamlet of Lucarelli; the other is the front-room hospitality of Nada Michelassi. These two *panzanelle* (women from Panzano) serve a short menu of tasty and authentic dishes at what the locals refer to as *il prezzo giusto* (the right price). **Known for:** fine home cooking; good wine list; unpretentious atmosphere. $ *Average main: €13* ⊠ *Località Lucarelli 29, Radda in Chianti*

⊹ *8 km (5 miles) northwest of Radda on road to Panzano* ☎ *0577/733511* ⊕ *www.lepanzanelle.it* ⊗ *Closed Mon. and Jan. and Feb.*

Hotels

La Bottega di Giovannino

$ | **B&B/INN** | This is a fantastic place for the budget-conscious traveler, as rooms are immaculate and most have a stunning view of the surrounding hills. **Pros:** great location in the center of town; close to restaurants and shops; super value. **Cons:** some rooms are small; books up quickly; basic decor. $ *Rooms from: €65* ⊠ *Via Roma 6–8, Radda in Chianti* ☎ *057/70738056* ⊕ *www.labottegadigiovannino.it* 🛏 *9 rooms* ❖ *No Meals.*

Palazzo San Niccolò

$ | **HOTEL** | The wood-beam ceilings, terra-cotta floors, and some of the original frescoes of a 19th-century town palace remain, but the marble bathrooms have all been updated, some with Jacuzzi tubs. **Pros:** central location; friendly staff; pool (though a car is necessary to get there). **Cons:** some rooms face a main street; room sizes vary; some street noise in some rooms. $ *Rooms from: €122* ⊠ *Via Roma 16, Radda in Chianti* ☎ *0577/735666* ⊕ *www.hotelsanniccolo.com* ⊗ *Closed Nov.–Mar.* 🛏 *18 rooms* ❖ *Free Breakfast.*

★ Relais Fattoria Vignale

$$ | **B&B/INN** | A refined and comfortable country house offers numerous sitting rooms with terra-cotta floors and attractive stonework, as well as wood-beamed guest rooms filled with simple wooden furnishings and handwoven rugs. **Pros:** intimate public spaces; excellent restaurant; nice grounds and pool. **Cons:** single rooms are small; annex across a busy road; a car is necessary. $ *Rooms from: €161* ⊠ *Via Pianigiani 9, Radda in Chianti* ☎ *0577/738300* ⊕ *www.vignale.it* ⊗ *Closed Nov.–Mar.* 🛏 *41 rooms* ❖ *Free Breakfast.*

Castellina in Chianti

13 km (8 miles) south of Panzano, 59 km (35 miles) south of Florence, 22 km (14 miles) north of Siena.

Castellina in Chianti—or simply Castellina—is on a ridge above three valleys: the Val di Pesa, Val d'Arbia, and Val d'Elsa. No matter what direction you turn, the panorama is bucolic. The strong 15th-century medieval walls and fortified town gate give a hint of the history of this village, which was an outpost during the continuing wars between Florence and Siena. In the main square, the Piazza del Comune, there's a 15th-century palace and a 15th-century fort constructed around a 13th-century tower. It now serves as the town hall.

GETTING HERE AND AROUND

As with all the towns along the Strada Chiantigiana (SR222), Castellina is an easy drive from either Siena or Florence. From Siena, Castellina is also well served by Autolinee Toscane. There's no direct bus from Florence. The closest train station is at Castellina Scalo, some 15 km (9 miles) away.

VISITOR INFORMATION

CONTACT Castellina in Chianti Tourism Office. ✉ *Via Ferruccio 40, Castellina in Chianti* ☎ *0577/741392* 🌐 *www.visitchianti.net.*

🍴 Restaurants

Albergaccio

$$$ | **TUSCAN** | The fact that the dining room can seat only about 35 guests makes a meal here an intimate experience, and the ever-changing menu mixes traditional and creative dishes. In late September and October, *zuppa di funghi e castagne* (mushroom and chestnut soup) is a treat; grilled meats and seafood are on offer throughout the year. **Known for:** creative menu; superb wine list; marvelous waitstaff. [$] *Average main: €28* ✉ *Via Fiorentina 63, Castellina in Chianti* ☎ *0577/741042* 🌐 *www.ristorantealbergaccio.com* 🕒 *Closed Sun.*

Ristorante Le Tre Porte

$$ | **TUSCAN** | Grilled meat dishes are the specialty at this popular restaurant, with a bistecca alla fiorentina (served very rare, as always) taking pride of place; paired with grilled fresh porcini mushrooms when in season (spring and fall), it's a heady dish. The panoramic terrace is a good choice for dining in summer. **Known for:** views from the terrace; their way with mushrooms; fine wine list with lots of local bottles. [$] *Average main: €18* ✉ *Via Trento e Trieste 4, Castellina in Chianti* ☎ *0577/741163* 🌐 *www.treporte.com* 🕒 *Closed Mon.–Wed.*

Sotto Le Volte

$$ | **TUSCAN** | As the name suggests, you'll find this small restaurant under the arches of Castellina's medieval walkway, and the eatery's vaulted ceilings make for a particularly romantic setting. The menu is short and eminently Tuscan, with typical soups and pasta dishes. **Known for:** unique setting; flair for Tuscan classics; attentive waitstaff. [$] *Average main: €17* ✉ *Via delle Volte 14–16, Castellina in Chianti* ☎ *0577/741299* 🌐 *www.sottolevolteristorante.it* 🕒 *Closed Wed. and Jan.–Mar.*

🛏 Hotels

★ **Palazzo Squarcialupi**

$$ | **B&B/INN** | In this lovely 15th-century palace, spacious rooms have high ceilings, tile floors, and 18th-century furnishings, and many have views of the valley below. **Pros:** great location in town center; elegant public spaces; nice spa, pool, and grounds. **Cons:** on a street with no car access; across from a busy restaurant; rooms facing the street can experience some noise. [$] *Rooms from: €161* ✉ *Via Ferruccio 22, Castellina in Chianti* ☎ *0577/741186* 🌐 *www.squarcialupirelaxinchianti.com* 🕒 *Closed Nov.–Mar.* 🔑 *17 rooms* 🍴 *Free Breakfast.*

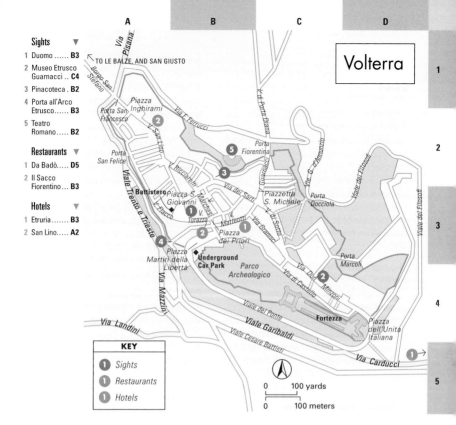

Volterra

30 km (18 miles) southwest of San Gimignano.

As you approach the town through bleak, rugged terrain, you can see that not all Tuscan hill towns rise above rolling green fields. Volterra stands mightily over Le Balze, a stunning series of gullied hills and valleys formed by erosion that has slowly eaten away at the foundation of the town—now considerably smaller than it was during its Etruscan glory days some 2,000 years ago.

GETTING HERE AND AROUND

By car, the best route from San Gimignano follows the SP1 south to Castel San Gimignano and then the SS68 west to Volterra. Coming from the west, take the SS1, a coastal road to Cecina, then follow the SS68 east to Volterra. Either way, there's a long, winding climb at the end of your trip. Traveling to Volterra by bus or train is complicated; avoid it if possible, especially if you have lots of luggage. From Florence or Siena the journey by public transit is best made by bus and involves a change in Colle di Val d'Elsa. From Rome or Pisa, it is best to take the train to Cecina and transfer to the Volterra-Saline station. The latter is 10 km (6 miles) from town.

VISITOR INFORMATION

CONTACT Volterra Tourism Office. ✉ *Piazza dei Priori 10, Volterra* ☎ *0588/86099* ⊕ *www.volterratur.it.*

Sights

Duomo

CHURCH | Behind the textbook 13th-century Pisan–Romanesque facade is proof that Volterra counted for something during the Renaissance, when many important Tuscan artists came to decorate the church. Three-dimensional stucco portraits of local saints are on the gold, red, and blue ceiling (1580) designed by Francesco Capriani, including St. Linus, the successor to St. Peter as pope and claimed by the Volterrans to have been born here.

The highlight of the Duomo is the brightly painted, 13th-century, wooden, life-size *Deposition* in the chapel of the same name. The unusual Cappella dell'Addolorata (Chapel of the Grieved) has two terra-cotta Nativity scenes; the depiction of the arrival of the Magi has a background fresco by Benozzo Gozzoli. ⊠ *Piazza San Giovanni, Volterra* ☏ *0588/86099* ⊕ *www. volterratur.it/poi/cattedrale-e-battistero.*

★ Museo Etrusco Guarnacci

HISTORY MUSEUM | An extraordinary collection of Etruscan relics is made all the more interesting by clear explanations in English. The bulk of the collection is comprised of roughly 700 carved funerary urns. The oldest, dating from the 7th century BC, were made from tufa (volcanic rock). A handful are made of terra-cotta, but most—dating from the 3rd to 1st century BC—are done in alabaster. The urns are grouped by subject, and, taken together, they form a fascinating testimony about Etruscan life and death. ⊠ *Via Don Minzoni 15, Volterra* ☏ *0586/894563* ⊕ *www.comune.volterra.pi.it/musei/ museo-etrusco-guarnacci* ☞ *From €10.*

Pinacoteca

ART MUSEUM | One of Volterra's best-looking Renaissance buildings contains an impressive collection of Tuscan paintings arranged chronologically on two floors. Head straight for Room 12, with Luca Signorelli's (circa 1445–1523) *Madonna and Child with Saints* and Rosso Fiorentino's later *Deposition.* Though painted just 30 years apart, they illustrate the shift in style from the early 16th-century Renaissance ideals to full-blown Mannerism: the balance of Signorelli's composition becomes purposefully skewed in Fiorentino's painting, where the colors go from vivid but realistic to emotively bright. Other important paintings in the small museum include Ghirlandaio's *Apotheosis of Christ with Saints* and a polyptych of the *Madonna and Saints* by Taddeo di Bartolo, which once hung in the Palazzo dei Priori. ⊠ *Via dei Sarti 1, Volterra* ☏ *0588/87580* ⊕ *www.comune.volterra. pi.it/pinacoteca_civica* ☞ *From €10.*

Porta all'Arco Etrusco

RUINS | Even if a good portion of the arch was rebuilt by the Romans, three dark, weather-beaten, 4th-century-BC heads (thought to represent Etruscan gods) still face outward to greet those who enter here. A plaque on the outer wall recalls the efforts of the locals who saved the arch from destruction by filling it with stones during the German withdrawal at the end of World War II. ⊠ *Via Porta all'Arco, Volterra* ☏ *0588/86099* ⊕ *www. volterratur.it/poi/la-porta-all-arco.*

Teatro Romano

RUINS | Just outside the walls, past Porta Fiorentina, are the ruins of the 1st-century-BC Roman theater, one of the best-preserved in Italy, with adjacent remains of the Roman *terme* (baths). You can enjoy an excellent bird's-eye view of the theater from Via Lungo le Mura. ⊠ *Viale Francesco Ferrucci, Volterra* ☏ *0588/86099* ⊕ *www.volterratur.it/poi/ il-teatro-romano* ☞ *€10.*

🍴 Restaurants

Da Badò

$ | **TUSCAN** | Family-run Da Badò—with Lucia in the kitchen and her sons, Giacomo and Michele, waiting tables—is the best place in town to eat traditional food elbow-to-elbow with locals. Lucia likes to concentrate on just a few dishes, so it won't take long to decide between the standards, all prepared with a sure hand. **Known for:** excellent traditional dishes; small menu; local favorite. $ *Average main: €14* ✉ *Borgo San Lazzaro 9, Volterra* ☎ *0588/80402* ✕ *Closed Wed.*

Il Sacco Fiorentino

$$ | **TUSCAN** | This lovely trattoria has been around for a long time, and with good reason. Here, they turn out Tuscan classics, relying heavily on the local cheese (pecorino) and local meats (especially wild boar, among others). **Known for:** well-priced menu; tranquil setting; excellent wine list. $ *Average main: €16* ✉ *Via Giusto Turazza 13, Volterra* ☎ *0588/88537* ⊕ *il-sacco-fiorentino.business.site* ✕ *Closed Wed.*

 Hotels

Etruria

$ | **B&B/INN** | The rooms are modest, and there's no elevator, but the central location, the ample buffet breakfast, and the modest rates make this a good choice for those on a budget. **Pros:** great central location; friendly staff; tranquil garden with rooftop views. **Cons:** some rooms can be noisy during the day; books up quickly as it's good value; no elevator. $ *Rooms from: €102* ✉ *Via Matteotti 32, Volterra* ☎ *0588/87377* ⊕ *www.albergoetruria.it* ✕ *Closed Jan. and Feb.* ⊷ *15 rooms* ⦿ *Free Breakfast.*

San Lino

$ | **HOTEL** | Within the town's medieval walls, this convent-turned-hotel has wood-beam ceilings, graceful archways, and terra-cotta floors, with nice contemporary furnishings and ironwork in the rooms. **Pros:** steps from center of town; friendly and helpful staff; convenient parking. **Cons:** rooms facing the street can be noisy; books up quickly; though in the center, somewhat removed from things. $ *Rooms from: €89* ✉ *Via San*

Lino 26, Volterra ☎ *0588/85250* ⊕ *www.hotelsanlino.net* ✕ *Closed Nov.–Mar.* ⊷ *43 rooms* ⦿ *No Meals.*

San Gimignano

14 km (9 miles) northwest of Colle di Val d'Elsa, 38 km (24 miles) northwest of Siena, 54 km (34 miles) southwest of Florence.

When you're on a hilltop surrounded by soaring medieval towers silhouetted against the sky, it's difficult not to fall under the spell of San Gimignano. Its tall walls and narrow streets are typical of Tuscan hill towns, but it's the medieval "skyscrapers" that set the town apart from its neighbors. Today 14 towers remain, but at the height of the Guelph–Ghibelline conflict there was a forest of more than 70, and it was possible to cross the town by rooftop rather than by road.

Today San Gimignano isn't much more than a gentrified walled city, touristy but still very much worth exploring because, despite the profusion of cheesy souvenir shops lining the main drag, there's some serious Renaissance art to be seen here.

GETTING HERE AND AROUND

You can reach San Gimignano by car from the Florence–Siena superstrada. Exit at Poggibonsi Nord and follow signs for San Gimignano. Although it involves changing buses in Poggibonsi, getting to San Gimignano by bus from Florence is a relatively straightforward affair. There's also direct bus service from Siena to San Gimignano several times daily. All the buses are operated by Autolinee Toscane. You cannot reach San Gimignano by train.

VISITOR INFORMATION

CONTACT San Gimignano Tourism Office. ✉ *Piazza Duomo 1, San Gimignano* ☎ *0577/940008* ⊕ *www.sangimignano.com.*

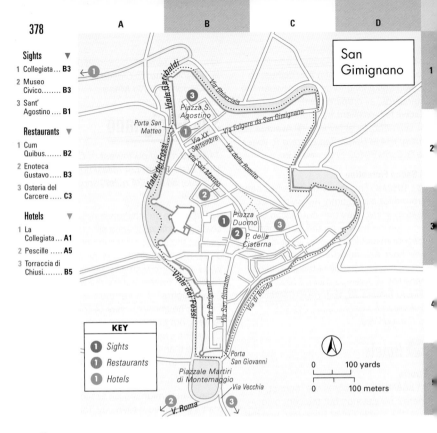

Sights ▼
1 Collegiata... **B3**
2 Museo Civico........ **B3**
3 Sant' Agostino **B1**

Restaurants ▼
1 Cum Quibus....... **B2**
2 Enoteca Gustavo **B3**
3 Osteria del Carcere **C3**

Hotels ▼
1 La Collegiata... **A1**
2 Pescille **A5**
3 Torraccia di Chiusi........ **B5**

KEY

1 *Sights*
1 *Restaurants*
1 *Hotels*

0   100 yards
0   100 meters

◉ Sights

★ Collegiata

CHURCH | The town's main church is not officially a duomo (cathedral), because San Gimignano has no bishop. But behind the simple facade of the Romanesque Collegiata lies a treasure trove of fine frescoes, covering nearly every wall. Bartolo di Fredi's 14th-century fresco cycle of Old Testament scenes extends along one wall. Their distinctly medieval feel, with misshapen bodies, buckets of spurting blood, and lack of perspective, contrasts with the much more reserved scenes from the Life of Christ (attributed to 14th-century artist Lippo Memmi) painted on the opposite wall just 14 years later. ⊠ *Piazza Pecori 1–2, entrance on left side of church, San Gimignano* ☎ *0577/286300* ⊕ *www.duomosangimignano.it* ⌨ *€5.*

Museo Civico

CASTLE/PALACE | The impressive civic museum occupies what was the "new" Palazzo del Popolo; the Torre Grossa is adjacent. Dante visited San Gimignano for only one day as a Guelph ambassador from Florence to ask the locals to join the Florentines in supporting the pope—just long enough to get the main council chamber named after him.

Upstairs, paintings by famous Renaissance artists Pinturicchio (*Madonna Enthroned*) and Benozzo Gozzoli (*Madonna and Child*), and two large *tondi* (circular paintings) by Filippino Lippi (circa 1457–1504) attest to the importance and wealth of San Gimignano. ⊠ *Piazza Duomo 2, San Gimignano* ☎ *0577/286300* ⊕ *www.sangimignanomusei.it* ⌨ *€9 cumulative ticket, €13 San Gimignano Pass (museums and duomo).*

Sant'Agostino

CHURCH | Make a beeline for Benozzo Gozzoli's superlative 15th-century fresco cycle depicting scenes from the life of St. Augustine. The saint's work was essential to the early development of church doctrine. Benozzo's 17 scenes on the choir wall depict Augustine as a man who traveled and taught extensively in the 4th and 5th centuries. The 15th-century altarpiece by Piero del Pollaiolo (1443–96) depicts *The Coronation of the Virgin* and the various protectors of the city. ⊠ *Piazza Sant'Agostino 10, San Gimignano* ☎ *0577/904313* ⊕ *www.conventosantagostino.it* ✉ *Free.*

🍴 Restaurants

★ Cum Quibus

$$$ | **ITALIAN** | This is, without a doubt, one of the region's most creative restaurants—an intimate place with a menu that's Tuscan but not (its signature egg yolk starter is done with élan). Not a step is missed, and although it's possible to order à la carte, the tasting menu is also popular. **Known for:** marvelous tasting menu; incorporation of non-Tuscan ingredients into Tuscan food; amazing wine list with prices to suit all budgets. Ⓢ *Average main: €25* ⊠ *Via San Martino 17, San Gimignano* ☎ *0577/943199* ⊕ *www.mktn. it/cumquibus* ☾ *Closed Wed. and Thurs. and Jan. and Feb.*

Enoteca Gustavo

$ | **WINE BAR** | There's no shortage of places to try Vernaccia di San Gimignano, the justifiably famous white wine with which San Gimignano is often singularly associated. At this wine bar, you can buy a glass of Vernaccia di San Gimignano and sit down with a cheese plate or one of the fine crostini. **Known for:** friendly staff; fine list of wines by the glass; quality products. Ⓢ *Average main: €15* ⊠ *Via San Matteo 29, San Gimignano* ☎ *0577/940057* ⊕ *www.facebook.com/ enotecagustavo.*

Osteria del Carcere

$ | **ITALIAN** | Although it calls itself an *osteria* (tavern), this place much more resembles a wine bar, with a bill of fare that includes several different types of pâtés and a short list of seasonal soups and salads. The sampler of goat cheeses, which can be paired with local wines, should not be missed. **Known for:** excellent chef-proprietor; inventive dishes; housed in a former jail. Ⓢ *Average main: €15* ⊠ *Via del Castello 13, San Gimignano* ☎ *0577/941905* ☾ *Closed early Jan.–Mar. No lunch Thurs.*

Hotels

La Collegiata

$$$ | **HOTEL** | After serving as a Franciscan convent and then the residence of the noble Strozzi family, the Collegiata has been converted into a fine hotel, with no expense spared in the process. **Pros:** gorgeous views from terrace; elegant rooms in main building; wonderful staff. **Cons:** long walk into town; service can be impersonal; some rooms are dimly lit. Ⓢ *Rooms from: €235* ⊠ *Località Strada 27, San Gimignano* ⊹ *1 km (½ mile) north of San Gimignano town center* ☎ *0577/943201* ⊕ *www.lacollegiata.it* ☾ *Closed Nov.–Mar.* ⊐ *20 rooms* ⦿ *Free Breakfast.*

Pescille

$$ | **B&B/INN** | A rambling farmhouse has been transformed into a handsome hotel with understated contemporary furniture in the bedrooms and country-classic motifs in the bar. **Pros:** splendid views; quiet atmosphere; 10-minute walk to town. **Cons:** furnishings a bit austere; there's an elevator for luggage but not for guests; a vehicle is a must. Ⓢ *Rooms from: €138* ⊠ *Località Pescille, San Gimignano* ⊹ *4 km (2½ miles) south of San Gimignano* ☎ *0577/940186* ⊕ *www. pescille.it* ☾ *Closed mid-Oct.–Easter* ⊐ *38 rooms* ⦿ *Free Breakfast.*

Torraccia di Chiusi

$$ | **B&B/INN** | **FAMILY** | A perfect retreat for families, this tranquil hilltop *agriturismo* (farm stay) offers simple, comfortably decorated accommodations on extensive grounds 5 km (3 miles) from the hubbub of San Gimignano. **Pros:** great walking possibilities; family-run hospitality; delightful countryside view. **Cons:** 30 minutes from the nearest town on a winding gravel road; need a car to get here; might be too remote for some. [$] *Rooms from: €180* ✉ *Località Montauto, San Gimignano* ☎ *0577/941972* 🌐 *www.torracciadichiusi.it* 🛏 *11 rooms* 🍴 *Free Breakfast.*

Siena

76 km (47 miles) south of Florence, 27km (16 miles) southeast of Colle di Val d'Elsa.

With its narrow streets and steep alleys, a Gothic Duomo, a bounty of early Renaissance art, and the glorious Palazzo Pubblico overlooking its magnificent Campo, Siena is often described as Italy's best-preserved medieval city. It is also remarkably modern: many shops sell clothes by up-and-coming designers. Make a point of catching the *passeggiata* (evening stroll), when locals throng the Via di Città, Banchi di Sopra, and Banchi di Sotto, the city's three main streets.

Victory over Florence in 1260 at Montaperti marked the beginning of Siena's golden age. Even though Florentines avenged the loss 29 years later, Siena continued to prosper. During the following decades Siena erected its greatest buildings (including the Duomo); established a model city government presided over by the Council of Nine; and became a great art, textile, and trade center. All of these achievements came together in the decoration of the Sala della Pace in Palazzo Pubblico. It makes you wonder what greatness the city might have gone on to achieve had its fortunes been different, but in 1348 the Black Death decimated the population, brought an end to the Council of Nine, and left Siena economically vulnerable. Siena succumbed to Florentine rule in the mid-16th century, when a yearlong siege virtually eliminated the native population. Ironically, it was precisely this decline that, along with Sienese pride, prevented further development, to which we owe the city's marvelous medieval condition today.

But although much looks as it did in the early 14th century, Siena is no museum. Walk through the streets and you can see that the medieval contrade—17 neighborhoods into which the city has been historically divided—are a vibrant part of modern life. You may see symbols of the *contrada* emblazoned on banners and engraved on building walls: Tartuca (turtle), Oca (goose), Istrice (porcupine), Torre (tower)—among others. The Sienese still strongly identify themselves with the contrada where they were born and raised; loyalty and rivalry run deep. At no time is this more visible than during the centuries-old Palio, a twice-yearly horse race held in the Piazza del Campo, but you need not visit then to come to know the rich culture of Siena, evident at every step.

GETTING HERE AND AROUND

From Florence, the quickest way to Siena is via the Florence–Siena superstrada. Otherwise, take the Via Cassia (SR2) for a scenic route. Coming from Rome, leave the A1 at Valdichiana, and follow the Siena–Bettole superstrada. Autolinee Toscane provides frequent bus service between Florence and Siena. Because buses are direct and speedy, they are preferable to the train, which sometimes involves a change in Empoli.

If you come by car, you're better off leaving it in one of the parking lots around the perimeter of town. Driving is difficult or impossible in most parts of the city center. Practically unchanged since medieval times, Siena is laid out in a "Y"

Siena's cathedral, with its striking campanile, is one of the most beautiful Gothic churches in Italy.

over the slopes of several hills, dividing the city into *terzi* (thirds).

TIMING

It's a joy to walk in Siena—hills notwithstanding—as it's a rare opportunity to stroll through a medieval city rather than just a town. (There is quite a lot to explore, in contrast to tiny hill towns that can be crossed in minutes.) The walk can be done in as little as a day, with minimal stops at the sights. But stay longer and take time to tour the churches and museums, and to enjoy the streetscapes themselves. Many of the sites have reduced hours Sunday afternoon and Monday.

VISITOR INFORMATION

CONTACT Siena Tourism Office. ⊠ *Piazza Gramsci, Siena* ☎ *0577/292222* ⊕ *www. terresiena.it.*

 Sights

Battistero

RELIGIOUS BUILDING | The Duomo's 14th-century Gothic Baptistery was built to prop up the apse of the cathedral. There are frescoes throughout, but the highlight is a large bronze 15th-century baptismal font designed by Jacopo della Quercia. It's adorned with bas-reliefs by various artists, including two by Renaissance masters: the *Baptism of Christ* by Lorenzo Ghiberti (1378–1455) and the *Feast of Herod* by Donatello. ⊠ *Piazza San Giovanni, Città* ☎ *0577/286300* ⊕ *www.operaduomo.siena.it* ☒ *€13 combined ticket includes the Duomo, Cripta, and Museo dell'Opera.*

★ Cripta

CEMETERY | Routine excavation work revealed this crypt, which had been hidden for centuries under the grand *pavimento* (floor) of the Duomo and was opened to the public in 2003. In the late

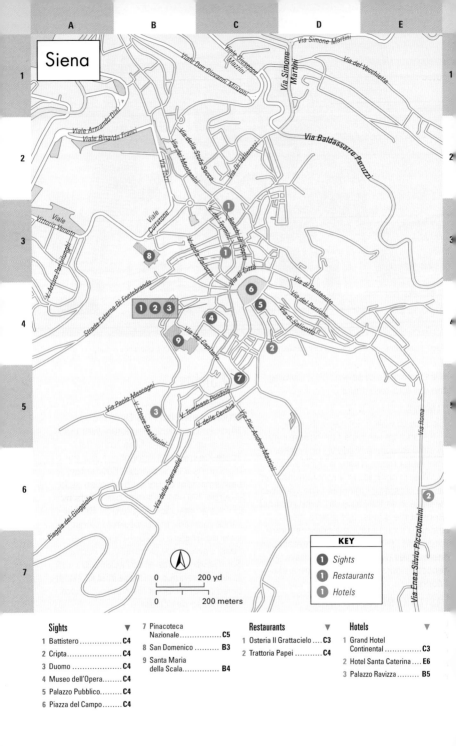

Siena

A B C D E

1 2 3 4 5 6 7

Via Simone Martini
Viale Giuseppe Mazzini
Viale Don Giovanni Minzoni
Via Simone Martini
Via del Vecchietta
Viale Armando Diaz
Viale Rinaldo Franci
Via Baldassarre Peruzzi
Viale delle Sturfa Sanza
Via Di Vallerozzi
Via Tozzi
Viale Curtatone
Viale Vittorio Veneto
Viale di Fontebranda
Via dei Montanini
Via di Terrini Di Sopra
Via della Galluzza
Via di Città
Via di Pantaneto
Via del Porrione
Via di Salicotto
Strada Esterna Di Fontebranda
Via Del Capitano
Via Paolo Mascagni
V. Ettore Bastianini
Via Tommaso Pendola
V. delle Cerchia
Via Pier Andrea Mattioli
Viale delle Sperandie
Piaggie del Giuggiolo
Via Enea Silvio Piccolomini
Via Roma

0 ——— 200 yd

0 ——— 200 meters

KEY

1 Sights

1 Restaurants

1 Hotels

Sights ▼

1 Battistero C4
2 Cripta.......................C4
3 Duomo C4
4 Museo dell'Opera........C4
5 Palazzo Pubblico.........C4
6 Piazza del Campo........C4
7 Pinacoteca
  Nazionale.................C5
8 San Domenico B3
9 Santa Maria
  della Scala...............B4

Restaurants ▼

1 Osteria Il Grattacielo C3
2 Trattoria Papei C4

Hotels ▼

1 Grand Hotel
  Continental C3
2 Hotel Santa Caterina E6
3 Palazzo Ravizza B5

13th century, an unknown master executed the crypt's breathtaking frescoes, which have sustained remarkably little damage and have retained their original colors. The *Deposition/Lamentation* proves that the Sienese school could paint emotion just as well as the Florentine school—and that it did so some 20 years before Giotto. ⊠ *Scale di San Giovanni, Città* ✛ *Down steps to right side of cathedral* ☎ *0577/286300* ⊕ *www. operaduomo.siena.it* ⊠ *€13 combined ticket includes the Duomo, Battistero, and Museo dell'Opera.*

★ **Duomo**

CHURCH | Siena's cathedral, completed in two brief phases at the end of the 13th and 14th centuries, is beyond question one of the finest Gothic churches in Italy. The multicolored marble and painted decoration are typical of the Italian approach to Gothic architecture, and the amazingly detailed facade has few rivals. Highlights of the Duomo's striking interior include dark-green-and-white striping; a coffered and gilded dome; a stained-glass window that's the oldest (circa 1288) example of such work in Italy; a carousel pulpit carved around 1265; and magnificent Renaissance frescoes in the Biblioteca Piccolomini.

The Duomo is most famous, though, for its inlaid-marble floors, which took almost 200 years to complete. More than 40 artists contributed to the magnificent work, made up of 56 separate compositions depicting biblical scenes, allegories, religious symbols, and civic emblems. The floors are covered for most of the year but are unveiled from the end of June until the end of July and from mid-August until mid-October. ⊠ *Piazza del Duomo, Città* ☎ *0577/286300* ⊕ *www.operaduomo.siena.it* ⊠ *€13 combined ticket includes Cripta, Battistero, and Museo dell'Opera.*

★ **Museo dell'Opera**

ART MUSEUM | Part of the unfinished nave of what was to have been a new cathedral, the museum contains the Duomo's treasury and some of the original decoration from its facade and interior. The first room on the ground floor displays weather-beaten 13th-century sculptures by Giovanni Pisano that were brought inside for protection and replaced by copies, as was a tondo of the *Madonna and Child* (now attributed to Donatello) that once hung on the door to the south transept. The masterpiece is unquestionably Duccio's *Maestà,* one side with 26 panels depicting episodes from the Passion, the other side with a *Madonna and Child Enthroned*. The second floor is divided between the treasury, with a crucifix by Giovanni Pisano, and *La Sala della Madonna degli Occhi Grossi* (the Room of the Madonna with the Big Eyes), named after the 13th-century painting. There is a fine view from the tower inside the museum. ⊠ *Piazza del Duomo 8, Città* ☎ *0577/286300* ⊕ *www. operaduomo.siena.it* ⊠ *€13 combined ticket includes the Duomo, Cripta, and Battistero.*

Palazzo Pubblico

GOVERNMENT BUILDING | The Gothic Palazzo Pubblico, the focal point of the Piazza del Campo, has served as Siena's town hall since the 1300s. It now also contains the Museo Civico, with walls covered in early Renaissance frescoes. The nine governors of Siena once met in the Sala della Pace, famous for Ambrogio Lorenzetti's frescoes called *Allegories of Good and Bad Government*, painted in the late 1330s to demonstrate the dangers of tyranny. The good government side depicts utopia, showing first the virtuous ruling council surrounded by angels and then scenes of a perfectly running city and countryside. Conversely, the bad government fresco tells a tale straight out of Dante. The evil ruler and his advisers have horns and fondle strange animals, and the town scene depicts the seven mortal sins in action.

The Torre del Mangia, the palazzo's famous bell tower, is named after one of its first bell ringers, Giovanni di Duccio (called Mangiaguadagni, or earnings eater). The climb up to the top is long and steep, but the view makes it worth every step. ⊠ *Piazza del Campo 1, Città* ☎ *0577/292232* ⊕ *www.comune.siena.it* ⊠ *Museum €6, tower €10, museum and tower €15.*

★ Piazza del Campo

PLAZA/SQUARE | The fan-shaped Piazza del Campo, known simply as *Il Campo* (The Field), is one of the finest squares in Italy. Constructed toward the end of the 12th century on a market area unclaimed by any contrada, it's still the heart of town. Its brickwork is patterned in nine different sections—representing each member of the medieval Council of Nine.

At the top of the Campo is a copy of the early 15th-century Fonte Gaia by Siena's greatest sculptor, Jacopo della Quercia. The 13 sculpted reliefs of biblical events and virtues that line the fountain are 19th-century copies; the originals are in the museum complex of Santa Maria della Scala. On Palio horse-race days (July 2 and August 16), the Campo and all its surrounding buildings are packed with cheering, frenzied locals and tourists craning their necks to take it all in. ⊠ *Piazza del Campo, Città.*

Pinacoteca Nazionale

ART MUSEUM | The superb collection of five centuries of local painting in Siena's national picture gallery can easily convince you that the Renaissance was by no means just a Florentine thing. Accordingly, the most interesting section of the collection, chronologically arranged, has several important firsts. Room 1 contains a painting of the *Stories of the True Cross* (1215) by the so-called Master of Tressa, the earliest identified work by a painter of the Sienese

school, and is followed in Room 2 by late-13th-century artist Guido da Siena's *Stories from the Life of Christ,* one of the first paintings ever made on canvas (earlier painters used wood panels).

Rooms 3 and 4 are dedicated to Duccio, a student of Cimabue (circa 1240–1302) and considered to be the last of the proto-Renaissance painters. Ambrogio Lorenzetti's landscapes in Room 8 are among the first truly secular paintings in Western art. Among later works in the rooms on the floor above, keep an eye out for the preparatory sketches used by Domenico Beccafumi (1486–1551) for the 35 etched marble panels he made for the floor of the Duomo. ⊠ *Via San Pietro 29, Città* ☎ *0577/281161* ⊕ *www.pinacotecanazionale.siena.it* ⊠ *€6.*

San Domenico

CHURCH | Although the Duomo is celebrated as a triumph of 13th-century Gothic architecture, this church, built at about the same time, turned out to be an oversize, hulking brick box that never merited a finishing coat in marble, let alone a graceful facade. Named for the founder of the Dominican order, the church is now more closely associated with St. Catherine of Siena. Just to the right of the entrance is the chapel in which she received the stigmata. On the wall is the only known contemporary portrait of the saint, made in the late 14th century by Andrea Vanni (circa 1332–1414). Farther down is the famous Cappella delle Santa Testa, the church's official shrine.

On either side of the chapel are well-known frescoes by Sodoma (aka Giovanni Antonio Bazzi, 1477–1549) of *St. Catherine in Ecstasy.* Don't miss the view of the Duomo and town center from the apse-side terrace. ⊠ *Piazza San Domenico, Camollìa* ☎ *0577/286848* ⊕ *www. basilicacateriniana.it.*

★ Santa Maria della Scala

ART MUSEUM | For more than 1,000 years, this complex across from the Duomo was home to Siena's hospital, but it now serves as a museum. Restored 15th-century frescoes in the Sala del Pellegrinaio tell the history of the hospital, which was created to give refuge to passing pilgrims and others in need and to distribute charity to the poor. Incorporated into the complex is the church of the Santissima Annunziata, with a celebrated *Risen Christ* by Vecchietta (also known as Lorenzo di Pietro, circa 1412–80). Down in the dark, Cappella di Santa Caterina della Notte is where St. Catherine went to pray at night. Displays in the subterranean archaeological museum are clearly marked and serve as a good introduction to the history of regional excavations. Don't miss della Quercia's stunning original sculpted reliefs from the Fonte Gaia. ✉ *Piazza del Duomo 2, Città* ☎ *0577/292615* 🌐 *www.santamariadellascala.com* 🎟 *€9* 🕓 *Closed Tues.*

🍴 Restaurants

Osteria Il Grattacielo

$ | TUSCAN | If you're wiped out from too much sightseeing, consider a meal at this hole-in-the-wall restaurant where locals congregate for a simple lunch over a glass of wine. There's a collection of verdure sott'olio, a wide selection of affettati misti, and various types of frittatas—all of which can be washed down with the cheap, yet eminently drinkable, house wines. **Known for:** simple, good-value food, earthy ambience; usually filled with local men arguing about the Palio. [$] *Average main: €10* ✉ *Via Pontani 8, Camollìa* ☎ *331/7422835* 🌐 *www.sites.google.com/view/ilgrattacielo1840* 🕓 *Closed Sun.*

Trattoria Papei

$ | TUSCAN | The menu hasn't changed for years, and why should it? This place, which has been in the Papei family for three generations, attracts both locals and visitors with basic but fine Sienese specialties and reasonable prices. **Known for:** great place to sample local specialties; lively atmosphere; outdoor seating. [$] *Average main: €13* ✉ *Piazza del Mercato 6, Città* ☎ *0577/280894* 🌐 *www.anticatrattoriapapei.com.*

🛏 Hotels

Grand Hotel Continental

$$$$ | HOTEL | Pope Alexander VII of the famed Sienese Chigi family gave this palace to his niece as a wedding present in 1600, and, through the centuries, it has been a private family home as well as a grand hotel—one that exudes elegance from its stately pillared entrance to its crisp-linen sheets. **Pros:** luxurious accommodations; great location on the main drag; first-rate concierge. **Cons:** sometimes stuffy atmosphere; lots of noise if your room is street-side; breakfast costs extra. [$] *Rooms from: €378* ✉ *Banchi di Sopra 85, Camollìa* ☎ *0577/56011* 🌐 *collezione.starhotels.com/en/our-hotels/grand-hotel-continental-siena* 🛏 *51 rooms* 🍽 *No Meals.*

Hotel Santa Caterina

$$ | B&B/INN | The atmosphere here is welcoming, hospitable, and enthusiastic, and the staff goes out of their way to ensure a fine stay; rooms in the back look out onto the lush grounds or the countryside in the distance. **Pros:** friendly staff; a short walk to center of town; breakfast in the garden. **Cons:** on a busy intersection; outside city walls; 15-minute (easy) walk into the historic center. [$] *Rooms from: €134* ✉ *Via Piccolomini 7, San Martino* ☎ *0577/221105* 🌐 *www.hotelsantacaterinasiena.com* 🛏 *22 rooms* 🍽 *Free Breakfast.*

★ Palazzo Ravizza

$$ | HOTEL | This charming palazzo exudes a sense of an age gone by; its guest rooms have high ceilings, antique furnishings, and bathrooms decorated with hand-painted tiles. **Pros:** 10-minute walk to the center of town; pleasant garden with a view beyond the city walls; professional staff. **Cons:** not all rooms have

views; some rooms are a little cramped; somewhat removed from the center of things. [$] *Rooms from: €154* ✉ *Pian dei Mantellini 34, Città* ☎ *0577/280462* 🌐 *www.palazzoravizza.it* 🛏 *41 rooms* 🍴 *Free Breakfast.*

Arezzo

63 km (39 miles) northeast of Siena, 81 km (50 miles) southeast of Florence.

Arezzo is best known for the magnificent Piero della Francesca frescoes in the church of San Francesco. It's also the birthplace of the poet Petrarch (1304–74), the Renaissance artist and art historian Giorgio Vasari, and Guido d'Arezzo (aka Guido Monaco), the inventor of contemporary musical notation. Arezzo dates from pre-Etruscan times, when around 1000 BC the first settlers erected a cluster of huts. Arezzo thrived as an Etruscan capital from the 7th to the 4th century BC, and was one of the most important cities in the Etruscans' anti-Roman 12-city federation, resisting Rome's rule to the last.

The city eventually fell and in turn flourished under the Romans. In 1248 Guglielmino degli Ubertini, a member of the powerful Ghibelline family, was elected bishop of Arezzo. This sent the city headlong into the enduring conflict between the Ghibellines (pro-emperor) and the Guelphs (pro-pope). In 1289 Florentine Guelphs defeated Arezzo in a famous battle at Campaldino. Among the Florentine soldiers was Dante Alighieri (1265–1321), who often referred to Arezzo in his *Divine Comedy.* Guelph–Ghibelline wars continued to plague Arezzo until the end of the 14th century, when Arezzo lost its independence to Florence.

GETTING HERE AND AROUND

Arezzo is easily reached by car from the A1, the main highway running between Florence and Rome. Direct trains connect Arezzo with Rome (2½ hours) and Florence (1 hour). Direct bus service is available from Florence but not from Rome.

VISITOR INFORMATION

CONTACT Arezzo Tourism Office. ✉ *Via Giorgio Vasari, 13, Arezzo* ☎ *0575/377468* 🌐 *www.discoverarezzo.com.*

Sights

★ Basilica di San Francesco

CHURCH | The famous Piero della Francesca frescoes depicting *The Legend of the True Cross* (1452–66) were executed on the three walls of the Capella Bacci, the apse of this 14th-century church. What Sir Kenneth Clark called "the most perfect morning light in all Renaissance painting" may be seen in the lowest section of the right wall, where the troops of Emperor Maxentius flee before the sign of the cross. Reservations are required and can be made online. ✉ *Piazza San Francesco 2, Arezzo* ☎ *0575/377468* 🌐 *www.discoverarezzo.com/en/ticket-office* 🎟 *€12* 🕒 *Closed Wed.*

Duomo

CHURCH | Arezzo's medieval cathedral at the top of the hill contains a fresco of a tender *Maria Maddalena* by Piero della Francesca (1420–92); look for it in the north aisle next to the large marble tomb near the organ. Construction of the Duomo began in 1278 but twice came to a halt, and the church wasn't completed until 1510. The ceiling decorations and the stained-glass windows date from the 16th century. The facade, designed by Arezzo's Dante Viviani, was added later (1901–14). ✉ *Piazza del Duomo 1, Arezzo* ☎ *0575/4027226* 🌐 *www.discoverarezzo.com/en/location/the-cathedral-of-arezzo.*

Museo Archeologico

HISTORY MUSEUM | The Archaeological Museum in the Convento di San Bernardo, just outside the Anfiteatro Romano, exhibits a fine collection of Etruscan bronzes. The ticket allows admission to the Anfiteatro Romano. ✉ *Via*

Sights

1 Basilica di San Francesco... **C3**
2 Duomo...... **C3**
3 Museo Archeologico........ **B5**
4 Piazza Grande...... **C3**
5 Santa Maria della Pieve... **C3**

Restaurants

1 Il Grottino... **C4**
2 La Lancia d'Oro........ **C3**
3 La Torre di Gnicche..... **C4**

Hotels

1 Castello di Gargonza... **B5**
2 Il Borro...... **B1**

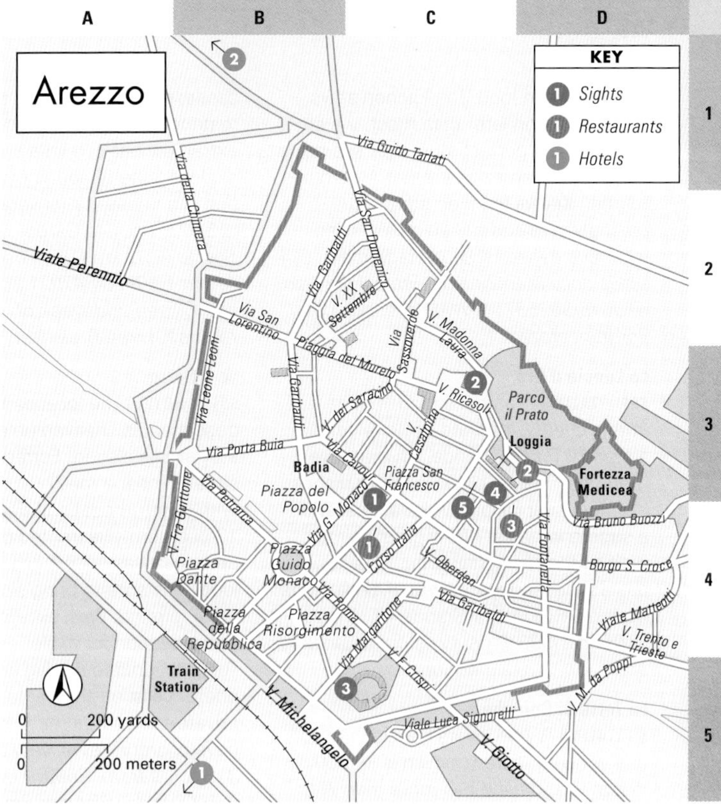

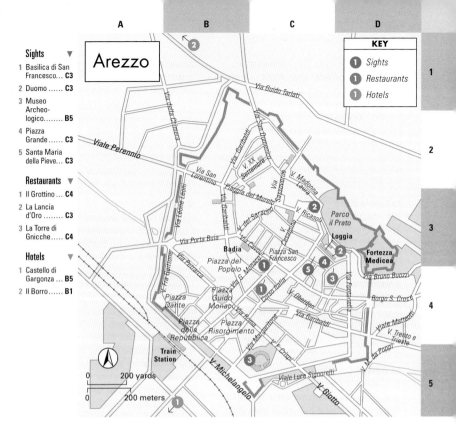

Margaritone 10, Arezzo ☎ *0575/20882* 🌐 *www.polomusealetoscana.beniculturali.it* 🎫 *€6* ⏲ *Closed Sun. except 1st Sun. of the month.*

Piazza Grande

PLAZA/SQUARE | With its irregular shape and sloping brick pavement, framed by buildings of assorted centuries, Arezzo's central piazza echoes Siena's Piazza del Campo. Though not quite so magnificent, it's lively enough during the outdoor antiques fair the first weekend of the month and when the Giostra del Saracino (Saracen Joust), featuring medieval costumes and competition, is held here on the third Saturday of June and on the first Sunday of September. ✉ *Piazza Grande, Arezzo* ☎ *0575/377468* 🌐 *www.discoverarezzo.com/en/i-am-piazza-grande-and-this-is-my-story.*

Santa Maria della Pieve (*Church of Saint Mary of the Parish*)

CHURCH | The curving, tiered apse on Piazza Grande belongs to a church that was originally an early Christian structure—itself constructed over the remains of a Roman temple. The church was rebuilt in Romanesque style in the 12th century. The splendid facade dates from the early 13th century but includes granite Roman columns. A magnificent polyptych, depicting the Madonna and Child with four saints, by Pietro Lorenzetti (circa 1290–1348), embellishes the high altar. ✉ *Corso Italia 7, Arezzo.*

Restaurants

Il Grottino

$ | **ITALIAN** | **FAMILY** | It's small, but the very cheery staff is only too happy to provide you with wonderful plates of typical Tuscan food. The kitchen stays open a little bit later than most, which makes this a perfect stop after seeing some of the amazing art that Arezzo has to offer. **Known for:** their soups; surprisingly well-composed mixed salads; inventive desserts. $ *Average main: €14* ⊠ *Via della Madonna del Prato 1, Arezzo* ☎ *0575/302537* ⊕ *www.facebook.com/ ilgrottinoarezzo.*

La Lancia d'Oro

$$$ | **ITALIAN** | Fantastic food is to be had at this cheery, intimate trattoria with a view of Piazza Grande. An inventive menu has Tuscan classics; other dishes have unusual flavor combinations, and a superb wine list offers great pairings with all the food. **Known for:** fantastic pastas; desserts; stellar staff. $ *Average main: €26* ⊠ *Piazza Grande 18, Arezzo* ☎ *0575/21033* ⊕ *www.ristorantelanci- adoro.it* ⊗ *No dinner Sun.*

La Torre di Gnicche

$ | **ITALIAN** | Wine lovers shouldn't miss this wine bar/eatery, which is just off Piazza Grande and has more than 700 labels on its list. Seasonal traditional dishes, such as *acquacotta del casenti- no* (porcini mushroom soup) or *baccalà in umido* (salt-cod stew), are served in the simply decorated, vaulted dining room. **Known for:** the extensive wine list, with many choices by the glass; an ever-changing menu; rustic setting. $ *Average main: €12* ⊠ *Piaggia San Mar- tino 8, Arezzo* ☎ *0575/352035* ⊕ *www. latorredignicche.it* ⊗ *Closed Wed. and Jan.*

 ## Hotels

★ Castello di Gargonza

$$ | **HOTEL** | **FAMILY** | Enchantment reigns at this tiny 13th-century countryside hamlet, part of the fiefdom of the aristocratic Florentine Guicciardini family and reinvented by the modern Count Roberto Guicciardini. **Pros:** romantic, one-of-a-kind accommodation in a medieval castle; peaceful, isolated setting; on-site restaurant. **Cons:** standard rooms are extremely basic; a little out of the way for exploring the region; private transportation is a necessity. $ *Rooms from: €180* ⊠ *SR73, Località Gargonza, Monte San Savino* ✛ *32 km (19 miles) southwest of Arezzo* ☎ *0575/847021* ⊕ *www.gargonza. it* ⊗ *Closed 2nd week of Jan.–Mar.* ⊅ *47 rooms* ⊙| *Free Breakfast.*

★ Il Borro

$$$$ | **HOTEL** | The location has been described as "heaven on earth," and a stay at this elegant Ferragamo estate— situated near a medieval village and with accommodations that include a 10-bedroom villa (rented out as a single unit) that was once a luxurious hunting lodge—is sure to bring similar descriptions to mind. **Pros:** exceptional service; great location for exploring eastern Tuscany; unique setting and atmosphere. **Cons:** off the beaten track, making private transport a must; not all suites have country views; very expensive. $ *Rooms from: €590* ⊠ *Località Il Borro 1* ✛ *Outside village of San Giustino Valdarno, 20 km (12 miles) northwest of Arezzo* ☎ *055/977053* ⊕ *www.ilborro.it* ⊗ *Closed Dec.–Mar.* ⊅ *61 rooms* ⊙| *Free Breakfast.*

Cortona

29 km (18 miles) south of Arezzo, 79 km (44 miles) east of Siena, 117 km (73 miles) southeast of Florence.

Brought into the limelight by Frances Mayes's book *Under the Tuscan Sun* and a subsequent movie, Cortona is no longer the destination of just a few specialist art historians and those seeking reprieve from busier tourist venues. The main street, Via Nazionale, is now lined with souvenir shops and fills with crowds during summer. Although the main sights of Cortona make braving the bustling center worthwhile, much of the town's

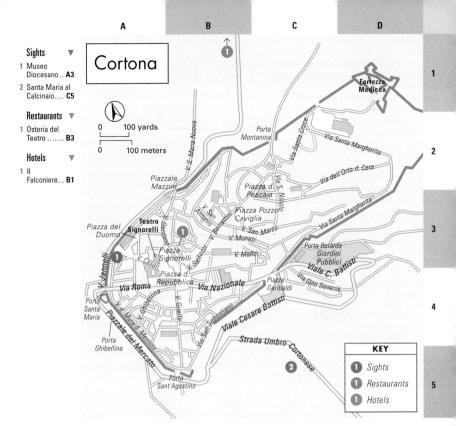

Sights ▼

1 Museo
Diocesano.. **A3**

2 Santa Maria al
Calcinaio.... **C5**

Restaurants ▼

1 Osteria del
Teatro **B3**

Hotels ▼

1 Il
Falconiere... **B1**

Cortona

0 ___ 100 yards
0 ___ 100 meters

KEY

① Sights
① Restaurants
① Hotels

charm lies in its maze of quiet backstreets. It's here that you will see laundry
hanging from windows, find children
playing, and catch the smell of simmer-
ing pasta sauce. Wander off the beaten
track and you won't be disappointed.

GETTING HERE AND AROUND

Cortona is easily reached by car from the
A1 autostrada: take the Valdichiana exit
toward Perugia, then follow signs for Cortona. Regular bus service, provided by
Autolinee Toscane, is available between
Arezzo and Cortona (one hour). Train
service to Cortona is made inconvenient
by the location of the train station, in
the valley 3 km (2 miles) steeply below
the town itself. From there, you have to
rely on bus or taxi service to get up to
Cortona.

VISITOR INFORMATION

CONTACT Cortona Tourism Office. ✉ Piazza
Signorelli 9, Cortona ☎ 0575/637269
⊕ www.comunedicortona.it.

◉ Sights

Museo Diocesano

ART MUSEUM | Housed in part of the orig-
inal cathedral structure, this nine-room
museum has an impressive number of
large, splendid paintings by native son
Luca Signorelli (1445–1523), as well as a
delightful *Annunciation* by Fra Angelico
(1387/1400–55). The church was built
between 1498 and 1505 and restruc-
tured by Giorgio Vasari in 1543. Frescoes depicting sacrifices from the Old
Testament by Doceno (1508–56), based
on designs by Vasari, line the walls. ✉ Piazza Duomo 1, Cortona ☎ 0575/286300

🌐 *www.cortonatuseibellezza.it* 🎫 *€6* ⏲ *Closed weekdays Nov.–Mar.*

Santa Maria al Calcinaio
CHURCH | Legend has it that the image of the Madonna appeared on a wall of a medieval *calcinaio* (lime pit used for curing leather), the site on which the church was then built between 1485 and 1513. The linear gray-and-white interior recalls Florence's Duomo. Sienese architect Francesco di Giorgio (1439–1502) most likely designed the sanctuary: the church is a terrific example of Renaissance architectural principles. ✉ *Località Il Calcinaio 227, Cortona* ✥ *3 km (2 miles) southeast of Cortona's center* ☎ *0575/62537* 🌐 *www.calcinaio.it.*

🍴 Restaurants

Osteria del Teatro
$$ | **TUSCAN** | Photographs from theatrical productions spanning many years line the walls of this tavern off Cortona's large Piazza del Teatro. The food is simply delicious—try the *filetto al lardo di colonnata e prugne* (beef cooked with bacon and prunes); service is warm and friendly. **Known for:** food that's in season; lively atmosphere; pretty dining room. [$] *Average main: €20* ✉ *Via Maffei 2, Cortona* ☎ *0575/630556* 🌐 *www.osteria-del-teatro.it* ⏲ *Closed Wed. and 2 wks in Nov.*

🛏 Hotels

★ Il Falconiere
$$$$ | **B&B/INN** | Accommodation options at this sumptuous property include rooms and suites in an 18th-century villa, or for more seclusion, private suites and villas at the far end of the property. **Pros:** attractive setting in the valley beneath Cortona; excellent service; elegant, but relaxed. **Cons:** a car is a must; some find rooms in main villa a little noisy; might be too isolated for some. [$] *Rooms from: €576* ✉ *Località San Martino 370, Cortona* ✥ *3 km (2 miles) north of Cortona* ☎ *0575/612679* 🌐 *www.ilfalconiere.it* ⏲ *Closed Nov.–Jan.* 🛏 *33 rooms* 🍴 *Free Breakfast.*

Perugia

157 km (98 miles) southeast of Florence, 65 km (40 miles) east of Montepulciano.

Perugia is a majestic, handsome, wealthy city, and with its trendy boutiques, refined cafés, and grandiose architecture, it doesn't try to hide its affluence. A student population of around 30,000 means that the city, with a permanent population of about 165,000, is abuzz with activity throughout the year. Umbria Jazz, one of the region's most important music festivals, attracts music lovers from around the world every July, and Eurochocolate, the international chocolate festival, is an irresistible draw each October for anyone with a sweet tooth.

GETTING HERE AND AROUND

The best approach to the city is by train. The area around the station doesn't attest to the rest of Perugia's elegance, but buses running from the station to Piazza d'Italia, the heart of the old town, are frequent. If you're in a hurry, take the *minimetro,* a one-line subway, to Stazione della Cupa.

If you're driving to Perugia and your hotel doesn't have parking facilities, leave your car in one of the lots close to the center. Electronic displays indicate the location of lots and the number of available spaces. If you park in the Piazza Partigiani, take the escalators that pass through the fascinating subterranean excavations of the city's Roman foundations and lead to the town center.

👁 Sights

Collegio del Cambio (*Bankers' Guild Hall*)
HISTORIC SIGHT | These elaborate rooms, on the ground floor of the Palazzo dei Priori, served as the meeting hall and chapel of the guild of bankers and money

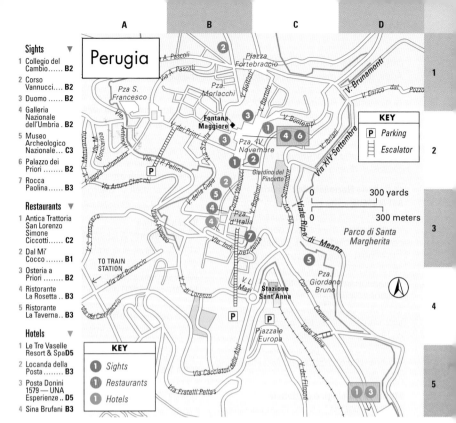

Sights ▼

1 Collegio del
   Cambio...... **B2**
2 Corso
   Vannucci.... **B2**
3 Duomo **B2**
4 Galleria
   Nazionale
   dell'Umbria . **B2**
5 Museo
   Archeologico
   Nazionale... **C3**
6 Palazzo dei
   Priori **B2**
7 Rocca
   Paolina...... **B3**

Restaurants ▼

1 Antica Trattoria
   San Lorenzo
   Simone
   Ciccotti...... **C2**
2 Dal Mi'
   Cocco **B1**
3 Osteria a
   Priori **B2**
4 Ristorante
   La Rosetta .. **B3**
5 Ristorante
   La Taverna.. **B3**

Hotels ▼

1 Le Tre Vaselle
   Resort & Spa **D5**
2 Locanda della
   Posta **B3**
3 Posta Donini
   1579 — UNA
   Esperienze .. **D5**
4 Sina Brufani **B3**

changers. Most of the frescoes were completed by the most important Perugian painter of the Renaissance, Pietro Vannucci, better known as Perugino. He included a remarkably honest self-portrait on one of the pilasters. The iconography includes common religious themes, such as the Nativity and the Transfiguration seen on the end walls. ⊠ *Corso Vannucci 25, Perugia* ☎ *075/5728599* ⊕ *www. collegiodelcambio.it* ⊠ *€6* ⊗ *Closed Sun. and Mon. afternoon.*

Corso Vannucci

STREET | A string of elegantly connected palazzi expresses the artistic nature of this city center, the heart of which is concentrated along Corso Vannucci. Stately and broad, this pedestrian-only street runs from Piazza Italia to Piazza IV Novembre. Along the way, the entrances to many of Perugia's side streets might

tempt you to wander off and explore. But don't stray too far as evening falls, when Corso Vannucci fills with Perugians out for their evening *passeggiata,* a pleasant predinner stroll that may include a pause for an aperitif at one of the many bars that line the street. ⊠ *Perugia.*

Duomo

CHURCH | Severe yet mystical, the Cathedral of San Lorenzo is most famous for being the home of the wedding ring of the Virgin Mary, stolen by the Perugians in 1488 from the nearby town of Chiusi. The ring, kept high up in a red-curtained vault in the chapel immediately to the left of the entrance, is stored under lock and key—15 locks, to be precise—most of the year. It's shown to the public on July 30 (the day it was brought to Perugia) and the second-to-last Sunday in January (Mary's wedding anniversary). The cathedral itself dates from the Middle Ages, and has many additions from the 15th and 16th centuries. ✉ *Piazza IV Novembre, Perugia* ☎ *075/5723832* 🌐 *www.cattedrale.perugia.it* 🎟 *Cathedral audio guide €3, museum €8, Underground Perugia tour €10, Cloister Pass (museum and Underground Perugia) €15* 🕒 *Closed during religious services.*

★ **Galleria Nazionale dell'Umbria**
ART MUSEUM | The region's most comprehensive art gallery is housed on the fourth floor of the Palazzo dei Priori. The collection includes work by native artists—most notably Pintoricchio (1454–1513) and Perugino (circa 1450–1523). In addition to paintings, the gallery has frescoes, sculptures, and some superb examples of crucifixes from the 13th and 14th centuries. ✉ *Corso Vannucci 19, Piazza IV Novembre, Perugia* ☎ *075/5721009* 🌐 *gallerianazionaledellumbria.it* 🎟 *€10* 🕒 *Closed Mon. morning July–Dec.*

Museo Archeologico Nazionale
HISTORY MUSEUM | An excellent collection of Etruscan artifacts from throughout the region sheds light on Perugia as a flourishing city long before it fell under Roman domination in 310 BC. Little else remains of Perugia's mysterious ancestors, although the Arco di Augusto, in Piazza Fortebraccio, the northern entrance to the city, is of Etruscan origin. ✉ *Piazza G. Bruno 10, Perugia* ☎ *075/5727141* 🌐 *www.musei.umbria.beniculturali.it* 🎟 *€5* 🕒 *Closed Mon. and 3rd Sun. of the month.*

Palazzo dei Priori (*Palace of the Priors*)
GOVERNMENT BUILDING | A series of elegant, connected buildings serves as Perugia's city hall and houses three museums. The buildings string along Corso Vannucci and wrap around the Piazza IV Novembre, where the original entrance is located. The steps here lead to the *Sala dei Notari* (Notaries' Hall). Other entrances lead to the Galleria Nazionale dell'Umbria, the Collegio del Cambio, and the Collegio della Mercanzia.

The Sala dei Notari, which dates from the 13th century and was the original meeting place of the town merchants, had become the seat of the notaries by the second half of the 15th century. Wooden beams and an array of interesting frescoes attributed to Maestro di Farneto embellish the room. ✉ *Piazza IV Novembre 25, Perugia* 🎟 *Free.*

Rocca Paolina
HISTORIC SIGHT | A labyrinth of little streets, alleys, and arches, this underground city was originally part of a fortress built at the behest of Pope Paul III between 1540 and 1543 to confirm papal dominion over the city. Parts of it were destroyed after the end of papal rule, but much still remains. Begin your visit by taking the escalators that descend through the subterranean ruins from Piazza Italia down to Via Masi. In summer, this is the coolest place in the city. ✉ *Piazza Italia, Perugia* 🎟 *Free.*

🍴 Restaurants

Antica Trattoria San Lorenzo Simone Ciccotti
$$ | **UMBRIAN** | Both the food and the service are outstanding at this popular small, brick-vaulted eatery next to the Duomo. Particular attention is paid to adapting traditional Umbrian cuisine to the modern palate, and there's also a nice variety of seafood dishes on the menu, both à la carte and in good-value tasting menus—the *pacchero* (pasta with smoked eggplant, cod, and scampi) is a real treat. **Known for:** impeccable service; modernized versions of local recipes; fish and truffle tasting menus. [$] *Average main: €24* ✉ *Piazza Danti 19/a, Perugia* ☎ *075/5721956* 🌐 *anticatrattoriasanlorenzo.business.site* 🕒 *No lunch Wed. No dinner Sun.*

Umbria Through the Ages

The earliest inhabitants of Umbria, the Umbri, were thought by the Romans to be the most ancient inhabitants of Italy. Little is known about them: with the coming of Etruscan culture, the tribe fled into the mountains in the eastern portion of the region. The Etruscans, who founded some of the great cities of Umbria, were in turn supplanted by the Romans. Unlike Tuscany and other regions of central Italy, Umbria had few powerful medieval families to exert control over the cities in the Middle Ages—its proximity to Rome ensured that it would always be more or less under papal domination.

In the center of the country, Umbria has, for much of its history, been a battlefield where armies from north and south clashed. Hannibal destroyed a Roman army on the shores of Lake Trasimeno, and the bloody course of the interminable Guelph–Ghibelline conflict of the Middle Ages

was played out here. Dante considered Umbria the most violent place in Italy. Trophies of war still decorate the Palazzo dei Priori in Perugia, and the little town of Gubbio continues a warlike rivalry begun in the Middle Ages—every year it challenges the Tuscan town of Sansepolcro to a cross-bow tournament. Today the bowmen shoot at targets, but neither side has forgotten that 500 years ago they were shooting at each other.

In spite of—or perhaps because of—this bloodshed, Umbria has produced more than its share of Christian saints. The most famous is St. Francis, the decidedly pacifist saint whose life shaped the Church of his time. His great shrine at Assisi is visited by hundreds of thousands of pilgrims each year. St. Clare, his devoted follower, was Umbria-born, as were St. Benedict, St. Rita of Cascia, and the patron saint of lovers, St. Valentine.

Dal Mi' Cocco

$$ | **UMBRIAN** | Favored by Perugia's university students, this casual spot with vaulted ceilings is fun, crowded, and inexpensive. Fixed-price meals change with the season and include starters, pasta, a main meat course, and dessert; each day of the week brings some new creation *dal cocco* (from the "coconut," or head) of the chef. **Known for:** authentically casual feel; honest prices; abundant portions. $ *Average main: €15* ✉ *Corso Garibaldi 12, Perugia* ☎ *075/5732511* ⊕ *www.facebook.com/ristorantedalmicocco* ☽ *Closed Mon. and late July–mid-Aug.*

Ristorante La Rosetta

$$$ | **ITALIAN** | The dining room of the hotel of the same name is a peaceful, elegant

spot to get away from the bustle of central Perugia; in winter you dine inside under medieval vaults, and in summer, in the cool courtyard. The food is simple but reliable, and flawlessly served. **Known for:** elegant, old-fashioned setting; refined versions of local meat dishes; professional service. $ *Average main: €25* ✉ *Piazza Italia 19, Perugia* ☎ *075/3747858* ⊕ *www.ristorantelarosettaperugia.com.*

Ristorante La Taverna

$$$ | **UMBRIAN** | Medieval steps lead to a rustic two-story space where wine bottles and artful clutter decorate the walls. The regional menu features lots of delicious homemade pastas and grilled meats prepared by chef Claudio and served up in substantial portions, plus generous shavings of truffle in season.

Known for: Umbrian specialties; swift and efficient service; welcoming ambience. $ *Average main: €25* ✉ *Via delle Streghe 8, off Corso Vannucci, Perugia* ☎ *075/5732536* ⊕ *www.ristorantelaverna.com.*

★ Osteria a Priori

$ | **MODERN ITALIAN** | This charming wine-and-olive-oil shop with a restaurant (featuring vaulted ceilings and exposed brick) tucked into the back offers up small plates using ingredients with a "zero-kilometer" philosophy: everything comes from local and artisanal Umbrian producers. Regional cheeses, homemade pastas, and slow-cooked meats steal the show, and, as might be expected, the selection of wine is top-notch. **Known for:** all Umbrian products; knowledgeable servers; local, nontouristy atmosphere. $ *Average main: €14* ✉ *Via dei Priori 39, Perugia* ☎ *075/5727098* ⊕ *www.osteriaapriori.it* ☾ *Closed Sun.*

 Hotels

Le Tre Vaselle Resort & Spa

$$ | **HOTEL** | **FAMILY** | Rooms spread throughout four stone buildings are spacious and graced with floors of typical, red-clay, Tuscan tiles; olive groves surround the outdoor pool, and the indoor spa specializes in wine treatments. **Pros:** perfect for visiting the Torgiano wine area and Deruta; friendly staff; nice pool. **Cons:** somewhat far from Perugia; amid an uninspiring village; service occasionally falters. $ *Rooms from: €169* ✉ *Via Garibaldi 48, Torgiano* ☎ *075/9880447* ⊕ *www.3vaselle.it* ⇆ *52 rooms* ⊚ *Free Breakfast.*

★ Locanda della Posta

$$ | **HOTEL** | This friendly, centrally located, converted 18th-century palazzo off the bustling pedestrian-only Corso Vannucci features spacious rooms soothingly decorated in muted colors; some include original frescoes and beamed ceilings. **Pros:** some fine views; central location;

exudes good taste and refinement. **Cons:** some street noise; no real lobby; no gym or spa. $ *Rooms from: €173* ✉ *Corso Vannucci 97, Perugia* ☎ *075/5728925* ⊕ *www.locandadellapostahotel.it* ⇆ *17 rooms* ⊚ *Free Breakfast.*

★ Posta Donini 1579 – UNA Esperienze

$$ | **HOTEL** | **FAMILY** | Beguilingly comfortable guest rooms set on lovely grounds—where gardeners go quietly about their business—along with a small but charming spa and a well-regarded restaurant make this historical hotel south of Perugia worth a stay. **Pros:** plush atmosphere; a quiet and private getaway; great restaurant. **Cons:** outside Perugia; uninteresting village; parking area can get full. $ *Rooms from: €152* ✉ *Via Deruta 43, San Martino in Campo* ⊹ *15 km (9 miles) south of Perugia* ☎ *075/609132* ⊕ *www.postadonini.it* ⇆ *48 rooms* ⊚ *Free Breakfast.*

Sina Brufani

$$ | **HOTEL** | Though a tad old-fashioned, this elegant, centrally located hotel dating from 1884 with a magnificent spa is the most upscale accommodation in town. **Pros:** wonderful location; unique spa area; excellent views from many rooms. **Cons:** could use a refresh; in-house restaurant not up to par; service can be hit-or-miss. $ *Rooms from: €195* ✉ *Piazza Italia 12, Perugia* ☎ *075/5732541* ⊕ *www.sinahotels.com* ⇆ *94 rooms* ⊚ *Free Breakfast.*

Assisi

28 km (17 miles) southeast of Perugia.

The small town of Assisi is one of the Christian world's most important pilgrimage sites and home of the Basilica di San Francesco—built to honor St. Francis (1182–1226) and erected swiftly after his death. The peace and serenity of the town are a welcome respite from the hustle and bustle of Italy's major cities.

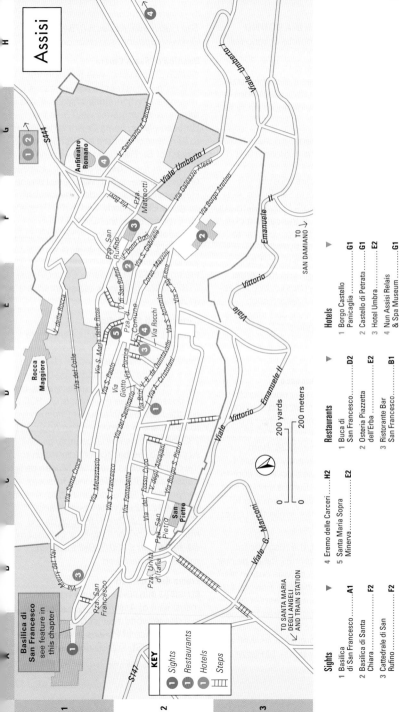

Assisi

Sights ▶

1 Basilica
di San Francesco **A1**

2 Basilica di Santa
Chiara **F2**

3 Cattedrale di San
Rufino **F2**

4 Eremo delle Carceri **H2**

5 Santa Maria Sopra
Minerva **E2**

Restaurants ▶

1 Buca di
San Francesco **D2**

2 Osteria Piazzetta
dell'Erba **E2**

3 Ristorante Bar
San Francesco **B1**

4 Trattoria
Pallotta Assisi **E2**

Hotels ▶

1 Borgo Castello
Panicaglia **G1**

2 Castello di Petrata **G1**

3 Hotel Umbra **E2**

4 Nun Assisi Relais
& Spa Museum **G1**

KEY
- ● Sights
- ● Restaurants
- ● Hotels
- Steps

Rocca
Maggiore

Anfiteatro
Romano

Basilica di
San Francesco
see feature in
this chapter

0   200 yards
0   200 meters

TO SANTA MARIA
DEGLI ANGELI
AND TRAIN STATION

TO
SAN DAMIANO →

GETTING HERE AND AROUND

Assisi lies on the Terontola–Foligno rail line, with almost hourly connections to Perugia and direct trains to Rome and Florence several times a day. The Stazione Centrale is 4 km (2½ miles) from town, with a bus service about every half hour.

Assisi is easily reached from the A1/E35 autostrada (Rome–Florence) and the SS75 highway. The walled town is closed to traffic, so cars must be left in the parking lots at Porta San Pietro, near Porta Nuova, or beneath Piazza Matteotti. Pay your parking fee at the *cassa* (ticket booth) before you return to your car to get a ticket to insert in the machine that will allow you to exit. It's a short but sometimes steep walk into the center of town; frequent minibuses (buy tickets from a newsstand or tobacco shop near where you park your car) make the rounds for weary pilgrims.

 Sights

★ Basilica di San Francesco

CHURCH | The basilica isn't one church but two: the Gothic church on the upper level, and the Romanesque church on the lower level. Work on this two-tiered monolith was begun in 1228. Both churches are magnificently decorated artistic treasure houses, covered floor to ceiling with some of Europe's finest frescoes: the Lower Basilica is dim and full of candlelight shadows, while the Upper Basilica is bright and airy.

In the Upper Church, the magnificent frescoes from 13th-century Italian painter Giotto, painted when he was only in his twenties, show that he was a pivotal artist in the development of Western painting. The Lower Church features frescoes by celebrated Sienese painters Simone Martini and Pietro Lorenzetti, as well as by Giotto (or his assistants). ⊠ *Piazza di*

San Francesco, Assisi ☎ *075/8190084* ⊕ *www.sanfrancescoassisi.org* 🖼 *Free.*

Basilica di Santa Chiara

CHURCH | The lovely, wide piazza in front of this church is reason enough to visit. The red-and-white-striped facade frames the piazza's panoramic view over the Umbrian plains. Santa Chiara is dedicated to St. Clare, one of the earliest and most fervent of St. Francis's followers and the founder of the order of the Poor Ladies—or Poor Clares—which was based on the Franciscan monastic order. The church contains Clare's body, and in the Cappella del Crocifisso (on the right) is the cross that spoke to St. Francis. A heavily veiled nun of the Poor Clares order is usually stationed before the cross in adoration of the image. ⊠ *Piazza Santa Chiara, Assisi* ☎ *075/812216* ⊕ *www.assisisantachiara.it* 🖼 *Free.*

Cattedrale di San Rufino

CHURCH | St. Francis and St. Clare were among those baptized in Assisi's Cattedrale, which was the principal church in town until the 12th century. The baptismal font has since been redecorated, but it's possible to see the crypt of St. Rufino, the bishop who brought Christianity to Assisi and was martyred on August 11, 238 (or 236 by some accounts), as well as climb to the bell tower. Admission to the crypt includes the small Museo della Cattedrale, with its detached frescoes and artifacts. ⊠ *Piazza San Rufino, Assisi* ☎ *075/812712* ⊕ *www.assisimuseo-diocesano.it* 🖼 *Church free, crypt and museum €3.50, bell tower and museum €4, bell tower €1.50* 🕑 *Bell tower and museum closed Wed.*

Eremo delle Carceri

RELIGIOUS BUILDING | About 4 km (2½ miles) east of Assisi is a monastery set in a dense wood against Monte Subasio: the Hermitage of Prisons. This was the place where St. Francis and his followers went to "imprison" themselves

Continued on page 400

ASSISI'S BASILICA DI SAN FRANCESCO

The legacy of St. Francis, founder of the Franciscan monastic order, pervades Assisi. Each year the town hosts several million pilgrims, but the steady flow of visitors does nothing to diminish the singular beauty of one of Italy's most important religious centers. The pilgrims' ultimate destination is the massive Basilica di San Francesco, which sits halfway up Assisi's hill, supported by graceful arches.

The basilica is not one church but two. The Romanesque Lower Church came first; construction began in 1228, just two years after St. Francis's death, and was completed within a few years. The low ceilings and candlelit interior make an appropriately solemn setting for St. Francis's tomb, found in the crypt below the main altar. The Gothic Upper Church, built only half a century later, sits on top of the lower one, and is strikingly different, with soaring arches and tall stained-glass windows (the first in Italy). Inside, both churches are covered floor to ceiling with some of Europe's finest frescoes: the Lower Church is dim and full of candlelit shadows, and the Upper Church is bright and airy.

VISITING THE BASILICA

THE LOWER CHURCH

The most evocative way to experience the basilica is to begin with the dark Lower Church. As you enter, give your eyes a moment to adjust. Keep in mind that the artists at work here were conscious of the shadowy environment—they knew this was how their frescoes would be seen.

In the first chapel to the left, a superb fresco cycle by Simone Martini depicts scenes from the life of St. Martin. As you approach the main altar, the vaulting above you is decorated with the *Three Virtues of St. Francis* (poverty, chastity, and obedience) and *St. Francis's Triumph*, frescoes attributed to Giotto's followers. In the transept to your left, Pietro Lorenzetti's *Madonna and Child with St. Francis and St. John* sparkles when the sun hits it. Notice Mary's thumb; legend has it Jesus is asking which saint to bless, and Mary is pointing to Francis. Across the way in the right transept, Cimabue's *Madonna Enthroned Among Angels and St. Francis* is a famous portrait of the saint. Surrounding the portrait are painted scenes from the childhood of Christ, done by the assistants of Giotto. Nearby is a painting of the crucifixion attributed to Giotto himself.

You reach the crypt via stairs midway along the nave—on the crypt's altar, a stone coffin holds the saint's body. Steps up from the transepts lead to the cloister, where there's a gift shop, and the treasury, which contains holy objects.

THE UPPER CHURCH

The St. Francis fresco cycle is the highlight of the Upper Church. (See facing page.) Also worth special note is the 16th-century choir, with its remarkably delicate inlaid wood. When a 1997 earthquake rocked the basilica, the St. Francis cycle sustained little damage, but portions of the ceiling above the entrance and altar collapsed, reducing their frescoes (attributed to Cimabue and Giotto) to rubble. The painstaking restoration is ongoing. ⚠ The dress code is strictly enforced—no bare shoulders or bare knees.

FRANCIS, ITALY'S PATRON SAINT

St. Francis was born in Assisi in 1181, the son of a noblewoman and a well-to-do merchant. His troubled youth included a year in prison. He planned a military career, but after a long illness Francis heard the voice of God, renounced his father's wealth, and began a life of austerity. His mystical embrace of poverty, asceticism, and the beauty of man and nature struck a responsive chord in the medieval mind; he quickly attracted a vast number of followers. Francis was the first saint to receive the stigmata (wounds in his hands, feet, and side corresponding to those of Christ on the cross). He died on October 4, 1226, in the Porziuncola, the secluded chapel in the woods where he had first preached the virtue of poverty to his disciples. St. Francis was declared patron saint of Italy in 1939, and today the Franciscans make up the largest of the Catholic orders.

THE UPPER CHURCH'S ST. FRANCIS FRESCO CYCLE

The 28 frescoes in the Upper Church depicting the life of St. Francis are the most admired works in the entire basilica. They're also the subject of one of art history's biggest controversies. For centuries they thought to be by Giotto (1267-1337), the great early Renaissance innovator, but inconsistencies in style, both within this series and in comparison to later Giotto works, have thrown their origin into question. Some scholars now say Giotto was the brains behind the cycle, but that assistants helped with the execution; others claim he couldn't have been involved at all.

Two things are certain. First, the style is revolutionary—which argues for

Giotto's involvement. The tangible weight of the figures, the emotion they show, and the use of perspective all look familiar to modern eyes, but in the art of the time there was nothing like it. Second, these images have played a major part in shaping how the world sees St. Francis. In that respect, who painted them hardly matters.

Starting in the transept, the frescoes circle the church, showing events in the saint's life (and afterlife). Some of the best are grouped near the church's entrance—look for the nativity at Greccio, the miracle of the spring, the death of the knight at Celano, and, most famously, the sermon to the birds.

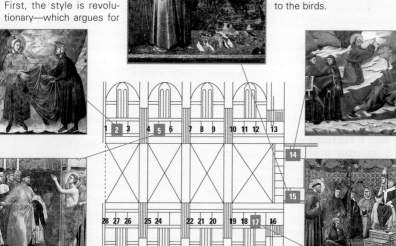

The St. Francis fresco cycle
1. Homage of a simple man
2. Giving cloak to a poor man
3. Dream of the palace
4. Hearing the voice of God
5. Rejection of worldly goods
6. Dream of Innocent III
7. Confirmation of the rules
8. Vision of flaming chariot
9. Vision of celestial thrones
10. Chasing devils from Arezzo
11. Before the sultan
12. *Ecstasy of St. Francis*
13. Nativity at Greccio
14. Miracle of the spring
15. Sermon to the birds
16. Death of knight at Celano
17. Preaching to Honorius III
18. Apparition at Arles
19. Receiving the stigmata
20. *Death of St. Francis*
21. Apparition before Bishop Guido and Fra Agostino
22. Verification of the stigmata
23. *Mourning of St. Clare*
24. Canonization
25. Apparition before Gregory IX
26. Healing of a devotee
27. Confession of a woman
28. Repentant heretic freed

in prayer. The only site in Assisi that remains essentially unchanged since St. Francis's time, the church and monastery are the kinds of tranquil places that St. Francis would have appreciated. The walk out from town is very pleasant, and many trails lead from here across the wooded hillside of Monte Subasio. ⌧ *Via Eremo delle Carceri 38, Assisi* ✛ *4 km (2½ miles) east of Assisi* ☎ *075/812301* ⊕ *www.santuarioeremodellecarceri.org* ✉ *Donations accepted.*

Santa Maria Sopra Minerva

CHURCH | Dating from the time of the Emperor Augustus (27 BC–AD 14), this structure was originally dedicated to the Roman goddess of wisdom, and in later times it was used as a monastery and prison before being converted into a church in the 16th century. The expectations raised by the perfect classical facade are not met by the interior, which was subjected to a thorough Baroque transformation in the 17th century. ⌧ *Piazza del Comune 14, Assisi* ☎ *075/812361* ✉ *Free.*

 Restaurants

Buca di San Francesco

$ | **UMBRIAN** | In summer, dine in a cool green garden; in winter, under the low brick arches of the cozy cellars. The unique settings and the first-rate (though straightforward) fare make this central restaurant one of Assisi's busiest; try the namesake homemade spaghetti *alla buca*, served with a roasted mushroom sauce. **Known for:** cozy atmosphere; historical surroundings; warm and welcoming service. ⑂ *Average main: €14* ⌧ *Via Eugenio Brizi 1, Assisi* ☎ *075/812204* ⊕ *buca-di-san-francesco.business.site* ⊗ *Closed Mon. and 10 days in late July.*

★ Osteria Piazzetta dell'Erba

$$ | **UMBRIAN** | Hip service and sophisticated presentations attract locals, who enjoy Italian cuisine with unusual twists (think porcini mushroom risotto

with blue cheese and blueberries), a nice selection of salads—unusual for an Umbrian restaurant—plus sushi options and intriguing desserts. The enthusiastic young team keep things running smoothly and the energy high. **Known for:** friendly staff; inventive dishes; intimate ambience. ⑂ *Average main: €20* ⌧ *Via San Gabriele dell'Addolorata 15/b, Assisi* ☎ *075/815352* ⊕ *www.osteriapiazzetta-dellerba.it* ⊗ *Closed Mon. and a few wks in Jan. or Feb.*

Ristorante Bar San Francesco

$$ | **UMBRIAN** | An excellent view of the Basilica di San Francesco from the covered terrace is just one reason to patronize this traditional restaurant, where Umbrian dishes are made with aromatic locally grown herbs. Menus change seasonally and include a fine selection of pastas and mains; appetizers and desserts are also especially good. **Known for:** prime Assisi location; tasty seasonal dishes; pleasant staff. ⑂ *Average main: €23* ⌧ *Via di San Francesco 52, Assisi* ☎ *075/813302* ⊕ *www.ristorante-sanfrancesco.com.*

Trattoria Pallotta Assisi

$$ | **UMBRIAN** | At this homey, family-run trattoria with a crackling fireplace and stone walls, the women do the cooking and the men serve the food; try the *strangozzi alla pallotta* (thick spaghetti with a pesto of olives and mushrooms). Connected to the restaurant is an inn whose eight rooms have firm beds and some views across the rooftops of town. **Known for:** traditional local dishes; delicious meat plates, including pigeon and rabbit; fast and courteous service. ⑂ *Average main: €18* ⌧ *Vicolo della Volta Pinta 3, Assisi* ☎ *075/8155273* ⊕ *www.trattoriapallotta.it* ⊗ *Closed Tues.*

 Hotels

★ Borgo Castello Panicaglia

$$$ | **HOTEL** | **FAMILY** | This rustic-chic, 17-room hotel between Assisi and

Gubbio, dating from 1266 but thoroughly modernized inside, is a relaxing base for exploring the pretty Umbrian countryside. **Pros:** modern amenities in a historical building; extremely family-friendly atmosphere; tasty and inventive meals. **Cons:** location is quite rural; no spa; need a car to get around the area. [$] *Rooms from: €205* ⊠ *Località Panicaglia, Nocera* ✣ *24 km (15 miles) northeast of Assisi* ☎ *0742/81663* ⊕ *www.borgocastello-panicaglia.com* ⥅ *17 rooms* |◎| *Free Breakfast.*

★ Castello di Petrata

$$ | **HOTEL** | Wood beams and sections of exposed medieval stonework add a lot of character to this 14th-century fortress, while creature comforts make each individually decorated room a delightful retreat. **Pros:** great views of town and country; medieval character; peaceful pool. **Cons:** slightly isolated; far from Assisi town center; limited choices in restaurant. [$] *Rooms from: €142* ⊠ *Via Petrata 25, Località Petrata, Assisi* ☎ *075/815451* ⊕ *www.castellopetrata.it* ⊗ *Closed Sun.–Thurs. Jan. and Feb.* ⥅ *20 rooms* |◎| *Free Breakfast.*

Hotel Umbra

$ | **HOTEL** | Rooms on the upper floors of this charming 16th-century town house near Piazza del Comune look out over the Assisi rooftops to the valley below, as does the sunny, vine-covered terrace. **Pros:** very central; pleasant small garden; excellent valley views from some rooms. **Cons:** difficult parking; some small rooms; uninspiring breakfasts. [$] *Rooms from: €110* ⊠ *Via degli Archi 6, Assisi* ☎ *075/812240* ⊕ *www.hotelumbra.it* ⊗ *Closed Nov.–late Mar.* ⥅ *24 rooms* |◎| *Free Breakfast.*

★ Nun Assisi Relais & Spa Museum

$$$$ | **HOTEL** | Within walking distance of Assisi's restaurants and shops, this monastery built in 1275 has been converted into a thoroughly contemporary, high-end place to stay with a fabulous spa carved out of 2,000-year-old Roman baths. **Pros:**

fantastic blend of the historical and modern; excellent restaurant; wonderful place to relax. **Cons:** on the expensive side; on-site parking costs extra; split-level rooms with stairs difficult for those with mobility issues. [$] *Rooms from: €590* ⊠ *Via Eremo delle Carceri 1A, Assisi* ☎ *075/8155150* ⊕ *www.nunassisi.com* ⥅ *18 rooms* |◎| *Free Breakfast.*

Spoleto

24 km (15 miles) southeast of Montefalco, 46 km (29 miles) south of Assisi, 63 km (39 miles) southeast of Perugia, 80 km (50 miles) east of Orvieto.

For most of the year, Spoleto is one more in a pleasant succession of sleepy hill towns, resting regally atop a mountain. But for more than two weeks every summer the town shifts into high gear for a turn in the international spotlight during the *Festival dei Due Mondi* (Festival of Two Worlds), an extravaganza of theater, opera, music, painting, and sculpture.

As the world's top artists vie for honors, throngs of art aficionados vie for hotel rooms. If you plan to spend the night in Spoleto during the festival, make sure you have confirmed reservations, or you may find yourself scrambling at sunset.

GETTING HERE AND AROUND

Spoleto is an hour's drive from Perugia. From the E45 highway, take the exit toward Assisi and Foligno, then merge onto the SS75 until you reach the Foligno Est exit. Merge onto the SS3, which leads to Spoleto. There are regular trains on the Perugia–Foligno line. From the train station it's a 15-minute uphill walk to the center, so you may want to take a local bus or a taxi.

VISITOR INFORMATION

CONTACT Spoleto Tourism Office. ⊠ *Largo Ferrer 6, off Corso Mazzini, Spoleto* ☎ *0743/218620* ⊕ *www.comune.spoleto.pg.it.*

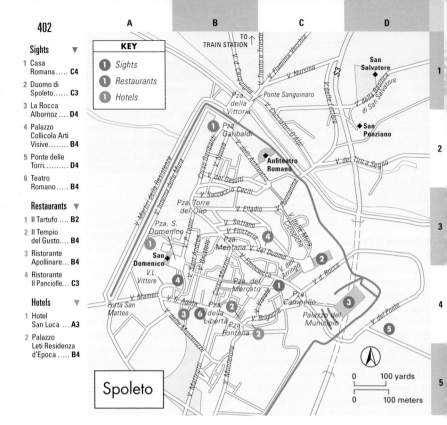

Sights ▼

1 Casa Romana..... **C4**

2 Duomo di Spoleto...... **C3**

3 La Rocca Albornoz **D4**

4 Palazzo Collicola Arti Visive........ **B4**

5 Ponte delle Torri.......... **D4**

6 Teatro Romano **B4**

Restaurants ▼

1 Il Tartufo **B2**

2 Il Tempio del Gusto.... **B4**

3 Ristorante Apollinare... **B4**

4 Ristorante Il Panciolle... **C3**

Hotels ▼

1 Hotel San Luca ... **A3**

2 Palazzo Leti Residenza d'Epoca **B4**

◉ Sights

Casa Romana (*Roman House*)

RUINS | Spoleto became a Roman colony in the 3rd century BC, but the best excavated remains date from the 1st century AD. Best preserved among them is the Casa Romana. According to an inscription, it belonged to Vespasia Polla, the mother of Emperor Vespasian (one of the builders of the Colosseum and perhaps better known by the Romans for taxing them to install public toilets, later called "Vespasians"). The rooms, arranged around a large central atrium built over an *impluvium* (rain cistern), are decorated with black-and-white geometric mosaics. ✉ *Palazzo del Municipio, Via di Visiale 9, Spoleto* ☎ *0743/40255* 🎟 *€3; included with Spoleto Card* ⏱ *Closed Tues.*

★ **Duomo di Spoleto** (*Spoleto Cathedral*)
CHURCH | One of the finest cathedrals in the region is lit by eight rose windows that are especially dazzling in the late afternoon sun. Above the church's entrance is Bernini's bust of Pope Urban VIII (1568–1644), who had the church redecorated in 17th-century Baroque; fortunately he didn't touch the 15th-century frescoes painted in the apse by Fra Filippo Lippi (circa 1406–69) between 1466 and 1469. These immaculately restored masterpieces—the *Annunciation, Nativity,* and *Dormition*—tell the story of the life of the Virgin. The *Coronation of the Virgin,* adorning the half dome, is the literal and figurative high point. Portraits of Lippi and his assistants are on the right side of the central panel. ✉ *Piazza del Duomo 2, Spoleto* ☎ *0577/286300* ⊕ *www.duomospoleto.it* 🎟 *Cathedral is free, €5 for audio guide, €9 for a tour*

including the upper part of the Cathedral, Bell Tower, Sala della Grande Bellezza, Diocesan Museum, and Church of Sant'Eufemia.

La Rocca Albornoz

CASTLE/PALACE | Built in the mid-14th century for Cardinal Egidio Albornoz, this massive fortress served as a seat for the local pontifical governors, a tangible sign of the restoration of the Church's power in the area when the pope was ruling from Avignon. Several popes spent time here, and, in 1499, one of them, Alexander VI, sent his capable teenage daughter, Lucrezia Borgia (1480–1519), to serve as governor for three months. The Gubbio-born architect Gattapone (14th century) used the ruins of a Roman acropolis as a foundation and took materials from many Roman-era sites, including the Teatro Romano.

La Rocca's plan is long and rectangular, with six towers and two grand courtyards, an upper loggia, and grand interior reception rooms. In the largest tower, Torre Maestà, you can visit an apartment with some interesting frescoes. ⊠ *Piazza Campello, Spoleto* ☎ *0743/224952* ⊠ *€7.50, including the Museo Nazionale del Ducato; free with Spoleto Card.*

★ Palazzo Collicola Arti Visive

ART MUSEUM | Spoleto's compact but delightful modern art museum, housed in an 18th-century palace, features a fine collection of works from Italian contemporary artists, including renowned Spoleto sculptor Leoncillo and Umbria-based American sculptor Barbara Pepper. International artists such as Alexander Calder and Richard Serra, are also represented, and an entire room is devoted to a large-scale wall drawing by Sol Lewitt. The Appartamento Nobile is a reproduction of an 18th-century nobleman's house, and the Pictures Gallery has paintings from the 16th to 19th centuries. ⊠ *Piazza Collicola 1, Spoleto* ☎ *0743/46434* ⊕ *www. palazzocollicola.it* ⊠ *€9; included with Spoleto Card* ⊘ *Closed Tues.*

★ Ponte delle Torri (*Bridge of the Towers*)

BRIDGE | Standing massive and graceful through the deep gorge that separates Spoleto from Monteluco, this 14th-century bridge is one of Umbria's most photographed monuments, and justifiably so. Built over the foundations of a Roman-era aqueduct, it soars 262 feet above the forested gorge—higher than the dome of St. Peter's in Rome. A must-see sight, the bridge offers spectacular views of Monteluco, and is particularly impressive on a starry night. ⊠ *Via del Ponte, Spoleto* ⊠ *Free.*

Teatro Romano

RUINS | **FAMILY** | The Romans who colonized the city in 241 BC constructed this small theater in the 1st century AD; for centuries afterward it was used as a quarry for building materials. The most intact portion is the hallway that passes under the *cavea* (stands). The rest was heavily restored in the early 1950s and serves as a venue for Spoleto's Festival dei Due Mondi. The theater was the site of a gruesome episode in Spoleto's history: during the medieval struggle between Guelph (papal) and Ghibelline (imperial) forces, Spoleto took the side of the Holy Roman Emperor. Afterward, 400 Guelph supporters were massacred in the theater, their bodies burned in an enormous pyre. In the end, the Guelphs were triumphant, and Spoleto was incorporated into the states of the Church in 1354. ⊠ *Piazza della Libertà, Spoleto* ☎ *0743/223277* ⊠ *€4, free with Spoleto Card* ⊘ *Closed Mon.–Wed.*

🍴 Restaurants

Il Tartufo

$$ | **UMBRIAN** | As the name indicates, dishes prepared with truffles are the specialty here—don't miss the risotto al tartufo. Incorporating the ruins of a Roman villa, the surroundings are rustic on the ground floor and more modern upstairs; in summer, tables appear outdoors, and the traditional fare is spiced up to appeal to the cosmopolitan crowd attending (or performing in) the Festival dei Due Mondi. **Known for:** recipes incorporating truffles; charming staff; abundant portions, well presented. [$] *Average main: €20* ✉ *Piazza Garibaldi 24, Spoleto* ☎ *0743/40236* 🌐 *www.ristoranteiltartufo.it* 🕒 *Closed Mon. and early Jan.–early Feb. No dinner Sun.*

Il Tempio del Gusto

$$ | UMBRIAN | In charming shabby-chic environs, this welcoming eatery near the Arco di Druso (ancient Roman arch) serves up Italian with a subtle twist. Along with an extensive selection of thoughtfully chosen Umbrian wines, you'll find lots of veggie options, mounds of truffles in season, and, to finish things off, a superlative version of Spoleto sponge cake. **Known for:** flavorful Umbrian cuisine; friendly atmosphere; quaint setting. [$] *Average main: €18* ✉ *Via Arco di Druso 11, Spoleto* ☎ *0743/47121* 🌐 *www.iltempiodelgusto.com* 🕒 *Closed Thurs.*

★ Ristorante Apollinare

$$ | UMBRIAN | Low wooden ceilings and flickering candlelight make this monastery from the 10th and 11th centuries Spoleto's most romantic spot; in warm weather, you can dine under a canopy on the piazza. The kitchen serves sophisticated, innovative variations on local dishes, including long, slender strengozzi pasta with such toppings as cherry tomatoes, mint, and a touch of red pepper or (in season) porcini mushrooms or truffles. **Known for:** modern versions of traditional Umbrian dishes; intimate and elegant setting; impeccable service. [$] *Average main: €22* ✉ *Via Sant'Agata 14, Spoleto* ☎ *0743/223256* 🌐 *www.ristoranteapollinare.it* 🕒 *Closed Tues.*

Ristorante Il Panciolle

$ | UMBRIAN | A small garden filled with lemon trees in the heart of Spoleto's medieval quarter provides one of the most appealing settings you could wish for. Dishes, which change throughout the year, might include pastas served with asparagus or mushrooms, as well as grilled meats; more expensive dishes prepared with fresh truffles are also available in season. **Known for:** authentic local cuisine; affable staff; panoramic terrace. [$] *Average main: €14* ✉ *Via del Duomo 3/5, Spoleto* ☎ *0743/45677* 🌐 *www.ilpanciolle.it* 🕒 *Closed Wed. Sept.–Mar.*

Hotels

★ Hotel San Luca

$ | HOTEL | Hand-painted friezes decorate the walls of the spacious guest rooms, and elegant comfort is the grace note throughout—you can sip afternoon tea in oversize armchairs by the fireplace or take a walk in the sweet-smelling rose garden. **Pros:** very helpful staff; spacious rooms; close to escalators for exploring city. **Cons:** outside the town center; restaurant only open for groups; can feel soulless in winter. [$] *Rooms from: €104* ✉ *Via Interna delle Mura 21, Spoleto* ☎ *0743/223399* 🌐 *www.hotelsanluca.com* 🛏 *35 rooms* 🍴 *Free Breakfast.*

★ Palazzo Leti Residenza d'Epoca

$ | HOTEL | Fabulously landscaped gardens, complete with fountains and sculptures, along with panoramic views provide a grand entrance to this late-13th-century residence turned charming hotel high up in Spoleto's old town. **Pros:** feels like a private hideaway; unbeatable views; friendly owners happy to help. **Cons:** reaching on-site parking can be tricky; often booked far in advance; few amenities (no restaurant, gym, or spa). [$] *Rooms from: €120* ✉ *Via degli Eremiti 10, Spoleto* ☎ *0743/224930* 🌐 *www.palazzoleti.com* 🛏 *12 rooms* 🍴 *Free Breakfast.*

Orvieto

30 km (19 miles) southwest of Todi, 78 km (48 miles) southwest of Perugia, 81 km (51 miles) west of Spoleto.

Carved from an enormous plateau of volcanic rock high above a green valley, Orvieto has natural defenses that made the high walls seen in many Umbrian towns unnecessary. The Etruscans were the first to settle here, digging a honeycombed network of more than 1,200 wells and storage caves out of the soft stone.

The Romans attacked, sacked, and destroyed the city in 283 BC. Since then, it has grown up out of the rock into an enchanting maze of alleys and squares. Orvieto was solidly Guelph in the Middle Ages, and, for several hundred years, popes sought refuge in the city, at times needing protection from their enemies, at times seeking respite from the summer heat in Rome.

GETTING HERE AND AROUND

Orvieto is well connected by train to Rome, Florence, and Perugia. It's also adjacent to the A1 autostrada that runs between Florence and Rome. Parking areas in the upper town tend to be crowded. A better idea is to follow the signs for the Campo Della Fiera parking lot, then take the escalators or elevator that carry people up the hill.

VISITOR INFORMATION

The Carta Orvieto Unica (single ticket) is expensive but a great deal if you want to visit everything. For €25 you get admission to nine museums and monuments, including the three major sights in town—Cappella di San Brizio (at the Duomo), Museo Etrusco Claudio Faina, and Orvieto Underground—along with entry to the Torre del Moro, with views of Orvieto, plus a bus and funicular pass. You can buy the card online or at any of the included museums.

CONTACT Orvieto Tourism Office. ⊠ *Piazza del Duomo 24, Orvieto* ☎ *0763/341772* ⊕ *www.liveorvieto.com.*

Sights

★ **Duomo di Orvieto** (*Orvieto Cathedral*)
CHURCH | Orvieto's stunning cathedral was built to commemorate the Miracle at Bolsena. In 1263, a young priest who questioned the miracle of transubstantiation (in which the Communion bread and wine become the flesh and blood of Christ) was saying Mass at nearby Lago di Bolsena. A wafer he had just blessed suddenly started to drip blood, staining the linen covering the altar. Thirty years later, construction began on a duomo in Orvieto to celebrate the miracle and house the stained altar cloth.

The cathedral's interior is rather vast and empty; the major works are in the transepts. To the left is the Cappella del Corporale, where the square linen cloth (*corporale*) is kept in a golden reliquary that's modeled on the cathedral and inlaid with enamel scenes of the miracle. In the right transept is the Cappella di San Brizio, which holds one of Italy's greatest fresco cycles, notable for its influence on Michelangelo's *Last Judgment*, as well as for the extraordinary beauty of the figuration. In these works, a few by Fra Angelico and most by Luca Signorelli, the damned fall to hell, demons breathe fire and blood, and Christians are martyred. The Museo dell'Opera dell Duomo next to the cathedral is worth a short visit to see its small collection of historical paintings and sculptures. ⊠ *Piazza del Duomo, Orvieto* ☎ *0763/342477* ⊕ *www. opsm.it* ⊠ *€5, including Cappella di San Brizio and Museo dell'Opera dell Duomo; included with Carta Unica.*

Museo Etrusco Claudio Faina
HISTORY MUSEUM | This superb private collection, beautifully arranged and presented, goes far beyond the usual smattering of local remains displayed at many

Hiking the Umbrian Hills

Magnificent scenery makes the heart of Italy excellent walking, hiking, and mountaineering country. In Umbria, the area around Spoleto is particularly good; several pleasant, easy, and well-signed trails begin at the far end of the Ponte alle Torri bridge over Monteluco. From Cannara, an easy half-hour walk leads to the fields of Pian d'Arca, the site of St. Francis's sermon to the birds.

For slightly more arduous walks, follow the saint's path uphill from Assisi to the Eremo delle Carceri, and then continue along the trails that crisscross Monte Subasio. At 4,250 feet, the treeless summit affords views of Assisi, Perugia, far-off Gubbio, and the distant mountain ranges of Abruzzo. For even more challenging hiking, the northern reaches of the Valnerina are exceptional; the mountains around Norcia should not be missed.

Throughout Umbria and the Marches, most recognized trails are marked with the distinctive red-and-white blazes of the Club Alpino Italiano. Tourist offices are a good source for walking and climbing itineraries to suit all ages and levels of ability, and bookstores, *tabacchi* (tobacconists), and *edicole* (newsstands) often have maps and guides that detail the best area routes. Wear comfortable walking shoes or hiking boots, depending on your route, and bring plenty of water.

museums. The collection is particularly rich in Greek- and Etruscan-era pottery, from large Attic amphorae (6th–4th century BC) to Attic black- and red-figure pieces to Etruscan *bucchero* (dark-reddish clay) vases. Other interesting items include a 6th-century sarcophagus and a substantial display of Roman-era coins. ✉ *Piazza del Duomo 29, Orvieto* ☎ *0763/341216* 🌐 *museofaina.it* 🎟 *€6* ⏲ *Closed Tues.*

Orvieto Underground

RUINS | FAMILY | More than just about any other town, Orvieto has grown from its own foundations. The Etruscans, the Romans, and those who followed dug into the tufa (the same soft volcanic rock from which catacombs were made) to create more than 1,000 separate cisterns, caves, passages, storage areas, and production areas for wine and olive oil. Much of the tufa removed was used as building blocks for the city that exists today, and some was partly ground into pozzolana, which was made into mortar. You can see the labyrinth of dugout chambers beneath the city on the Orvieto Underground tour, which runs daily at 11, 12:15, 4, and 5:15 (reservations recommended), departing from Piazza del Duomo 23. ✉ *Piazza del Duomo 23, Orvieto* ☎ *0763/340688* 🌐 *www.orvietounderground.it* 🎟 *Tours €7; included with Carta Unica.*

Pozzo della Cava

RUINS | If you're short on time but want a quick look at the cisterns and caves beneath the city, head for the Pozzo della Cava, an Etruscan well for spring water. On a walk through nine excavated caves you can see the fascinating ruins of medieval houses and unearthed archaeological artifacts. ✉ *Via della Cava 28, Orvieto* ☎ *0763/342373* 🌐 *www.pozzodellacava.it* 🎟 *€4; included with Carta Unica* ⏲ *Closed mid- to late Jan.*

🍴 Restaurants

Le Grotte del Funaro

$$ | UMBRIAN | Dine inside tufa caves under central Orvieto, where the two windows afford splendid views of the hilly countryside. The traditional Umbrian food is reliably good, with simple grilled meats and vegetables and pizzas—oddly, though, the food is outclassed by an extensive wine list, with top local and Italian labels and quite a few rare vintages. **Known for:** unusual setting; crusty pizzas; good choice of wines. $ *Average main: €16* ✉ *Via Ripa Serancia 41, Orvieto* ☎ *0763/343276* ⊕ *www. grottedelfunaro.com* ⊘ *Closed Mon. and 10 days in July.*

Ristorante Maurizio

$$ | UMBRIAN | Off a busy pedestrian street near the Duomo, this welcoming, family-owned restaurant has an ultra contemporary look but is actually housed in a 14th-century medieval building with arched ceilings. The Martinelli family's own products, including balsamic vinegar, olive oil, and pasta, are used in their robustly flavored dishes, and you can also sample their well-regarded Montefalco wines. **Known for:** complimentary balsamic vinegar tasting to start; traditional Umbrian dishes; local wines. $ *Average main: €16* ✉ *Via del Duomo 78, Orvieto* ☎ *0763/343212* ⊕ *www.ristorante-maurizio.com.*

Trattoria La Grotta

$ | UMBRIAN | The vaulted, plant-filled dining area—where white walls are adorned with paintings, antique vases, and other knickknacks—makes a congenial setting for this small, rustic-style trattoria, which is lauded for its homemade pasta, perhaps with an artichoke, duck, or wild-boar sauce. Roast lamb, veal, and pork are all also good, and the desserts are supplied by Orvieto's most eminent *pasticceria* (pastry shop). **Known for:** tasty homemade pastas; fresh, local ingredients; warm and welcoming service. $ *Average main: €14* ✉ *Via Luca Signorelli 5, Orvieto* ☎ *0763/341348* ⊕ *www.trattorialagrottaorvieto.com* ⊘ *Closed Tues.*

Hotels

Hotel Palazzo Piccolomini

$$ | HOTEL | This 16th-century family palazzo has been beautifully restored, with inviting public spaces and handsome guest quarters where contemporary surroundings are accented with old beams, vaulted ceilings, and other distinctive touches. **Pros:** private parking; efficient staff; good location. **Cons:** underwhelming breakfasts; four-star category not completely justified; some rooms and bathrooms are small. $ *Rooms from: €150* ✉ *Piazza Ranieri 36, Orvieto* ☎ *0763/341743* ⊕ *www.palazzopiccolomini.it* ⊘ *Closed Jan. and Feb.* ⇥ *33 rooms* ⦿ *Free Breakfast.*

★ Locanda Palazzone

$$$ | HOTEL | Spending the night in this 13th-century building just 5 km (3 miles) northwest of Orvieto is like staying in a sophisticated country home, albeit one with vineyard views, a private chef, and two-level rooms with modern furnishings. **Pros:** tranquil surroundings; extremely friendly owners and staff; tasty meals served nightly. **Cons:** no à la carte menus; limited public spaces to lounge in; split-level rooms can be difficult for those with mobility issues or young children. $ *Rooms from: €252* ✉ *Località Rocca Ripesena 68, Orvieto* ☎ *0763/393614* ⊕ *www.locandapalazzone.it* ⇥ *7 rooms* ⦿ *Free Breakfast.*

Index

A

Abano Terme, *219*
Acquario Civico di Milano, *247*
ADI Design Museum Compasso d'Oro, *256*
Aethos Milan ⊠ , *265–266*
Ai Tre Scalini (wine bar), *68*
Air travel, *34, 48*
Florence, *299*
Venice, *147*
Al Duca d'Aosta (shop), *167*
Al Paradiso ✕ , *182*
Al Ponte Antico ⊠ , *191*
Albergo San Martino ⊠ , *363–364*
Algiubagiò ✕ , *187*
Alle Testiere ✕ , *195*
Altare della Patria, *102*
Ancient Rome, *18–19, 58–69*
Anfiteatro Romano (Arezzo), *386–387*
Anfiteatro Romano (Fiesole), *349*
Angela Caputi (shop), *330*
Antica Bottega di Prospero (shop), *364*
Antica Dimora Johlea ⊠ , *322*
Antica Osteria al Duomo ✕ , *230*
Antiche Carampane ✕ , *182*
Antico Arco ✕ , *130*
Aquariums, *247*
Ara Pacis Augustae, *19, 101*
Arche Scaligere, *226*
Architecture, *22–23, 157, 236–237*
Arco dei Gavi, *226*
Arco di Costantino, *59*
Arena di Verona, *226*
Arena di Verona Opera Festival, *44*
Arezzo, *386–388*
Armando al Pantheon ✕ , *92*
Armani Hotel Milano ⊠ , *253*
Armani/Silos, *267*
Arsenale, *22, 194*
Art galleries and museums
Florence, *24–25, 302–303, 306, 317, 318, 319, 323–324, 331, 343*
Northern Italy, *222, 229, 239, 242, 247–248, 252, 256, 259, 261, 262, 263, 265, 267, 279, 281, 287–288, 293*
Rome, *20–21, 63, 72, 73, 85–86, 101, 114–115, 121, 127, 133*
Tuscany and Umbria, *361, 367, 376, 378, 383, 384–385, 389–390, 392, 403*
Venice, *160, 161, 170–171, 178, 179, 182*
Art Hotel Orologio ⊠ , *284*
Atelier Segalin di Daniela Ghezzo (shop), *167*
Assisi, *394–401*
Auditorium Parco della Musica, *126*
Aventino, *132–138*

B

Ba' Ghetto ✕ , *93*
Badia a Coltibuono, *372*
Badia Fiesolana, *349*
Banco Lotto No. 10 (shop), *201*
Bar Longhi, *167*
Bargello, *24, 302–303*
Baroni Alimentari (shop), *323*
Basilica di San Francesco (Arezzo), *386*
Basilica di San Francesco (Assisi), *396, 397–399*
Basilica di San Lorenzo, *317*
Basilica di San Marco, *152*
Basilica di San Petronio, *278–279*
Basilica di San Pietro, *69, 72*
Basilica di San Vitale, *291*
Basilica di Santa Chiara, *396*
Basilica di Sant'Ambrogio, *249–250*
Basilica di Sant'Antonio, *219*
Battistero (Florence), *303*
Battistero (Pisa), *365*
Battistero (Siena), *381*
Battistero Neoniano, *291*
Battistero Paleocristiano/Baptistry of San Giovanni ale Fonti, *238–239*
Beaches, *206*
Belmond Hotel Cipriani ⊠ , *203–304*
Bernardo (shop), *315*
Biblioteca Medicea Laurenziana, *317*
Bicocca (Milan), *263*
Bicycling and bike travel
Florence, *299*
Lucca, *365*
Milan, *238*
Biennale di Venezia, *44*
Blue Note (nightclub), *257*
Bocca della Verità, *18*
Bologna, *278–286*
Bonci Pizzarium ✕ , *82–83*
Borgo, *69–83*
Borgo Castello Panicaglia ⊠ , *400–401*
Braccialini (shop), *113*
Brera (Milan), *247–249*
Bridges, *164, 313, 403*
Brioni (shop), *110*
Brunelleschi, Filippo, *312*
Buca di Sant'Antonio ✕ , *363*
Buenos Aires (Milan), *262*
[Bu:r] di Eugenio Boer ✕ , *265*
Burchiello Excursion, Brenta Canal, *219, 221*
Bus travel, *34, 48*
Florence, *299*
Rome, *55*
Venice, *147*
Business hours, *57, 300–301*

C

Ca' da Mosto, *23*
Ca' dei Dogi ⊠ , *199*
Ca' d'Oro, *186*
Ca Maria Adele ⊠ , *175*
Ca' Pesaro, *178*
Ca' Rezzonico, *168–169*
Caffè Borsari ✕ , *230*
Caffè Florian ✕ , *165–166*
Caffè Pedrocchi ✕ , *225*
Campanile (Florence), *303*
Campanile di San Marco, *152, 160*
Campidoglio, The, *59–60*
Campo de' Fiori, *84–101*
Campo San Polo, *178*
Campo Santa Margherita, *169*
Camposanto, *365*
Caniparoli (shop), *364*
Cannaregio (Venice), *185–193*
Cantine del Vino già Schiavi ✕ , *174–175*
Cappella degli Scrovegni, *221–222*
Cappella Sistina, *72, 74–81*
Cappelle Medicee, *317*
Capuchin Museum, *114*
Car travel, *35*
Florence, *299*
Venice, *147*
Carnevale, *44, 150*
Cartoleria Pantheon dal 1910 (shop), *100*
Casa Buonarroti, *331*
Casa-Museo Boschi di Stefano, *262*
Casa Romana, *402*
Casa Romei, *286–287*
Casinos, *187*
Castel Sant'Angelo, *72–73*
Castellina in Chianti, *374*
Castello (Milan), *245*
Castello (Venice), *193–201*
Castello di Brolio, *372–373*
Castello di Gargonza ⊠ , *388*
Castello di Petrata ⊠ , *401*
Castello Estense, *287*
Castello Sforzesco, *245*
Castelvecchio, *228*
Castles, palaces, and fortresses
Florence, *313, 318–319, 324–325, 343*
Northern Italy, *222–223, 228–229, 232–233, 245, 281, 286–287, 288*
Rome, *72–73, 86–87, 103, 130*
Tuscany and Umbria, *372–373, 378, 392, 403*
Venice, *161*
Castroni (shop), *83*
Catacombe di San Callisto, *138*
Catacombe di San Sebastiano, *138–139*
Cattedrale di San Rufino, *396*
Celio, *58–69*
Cemeteries, crypts, and tombs
Florence, *311*
Northern Italy, *226, 291, 293*
Rome, *73, 85, 102, 114, 138–139*
Tuscany and Umbria, *365, 381, 383*
Venice, *205*
Centrale Montemartini, *21, 133*
Ceresio 7 Pools & Restaurant ✕ , *257*
Chez Dede (shop), *100*
Chianti, *368–374*
Chiesa degli Eremitani, *222*
Chiesa del Gesù, *84–85*

Chiesa di San Maurizio al Monastero Maggiore, 250
Church of St. John the Baptist, 269
Churches
Fiesole, 349
Florence, 303, 306, 317, 319, 325, 331, 343, 346
Northern Italy, 219, 221–222, 228, 229–230, 233, 238–239, 242, 249–250, 265, 269, 275, 278–279, 281, 287, 291, 293
Rome, 59, 66–67, 69, 72, 74–81, 84–85, 90–91, 103, 106, 118–119, 121, 124, 127, 130, 133, 136
Tuscany and Umbria, 361, 363, 365, 376, 378, 379, 381, 383, 384, 386, 387, 390, 391–392, 396, 397–399, 400, 402–403, 405
Venice, 152, 170, 171, 179, 186–187, 194–195, 203
Cibrèo Ristorante ✕ , 334
Cimitero di San Michele, 205
Cinque Giornate (Milan), 259
Cinque Terre, 270–274
Circo Massimo (Circus Maximus), 18, 60
Cittamani ✕ , 248
Classis Ravenna – Museo della Città el del Territorio, 291
Collegiata (San Gimignano), 378
Collegio del Cambio, 390–391
Colosseum, 18, 60
Consulates, 40
Contacts, 48
Corniglia, 275
Corso Vannucci, 391
Corte Sconta ✕ , 195, 198
Cortona, 388–390
Court, The (bar), 68
Cripta, 381, 383
Cruising, 153–159
Crypta Balbi, 85
Crypts. ➪ See Cemeteries, crypts, and tombs
Cul de Sac ✕ , 93
Cum Quibus ✕ , 379

Da Cesari ✕ , 282
Da Enzo ✕ , 130
Da Nerbone ✕ , 322
Dalla Marisa ✕ , 190
Dance, 294
Dance clubs, 315
Dante's tomb, 293
Davide Penso (shop), 208
Dining, 30, 38. ➪ See also under specific cities, towns, and regions
Emilian cuisine, 214–215
Northern Italian cuisine, 212–215
prices, 57, 149, 218, 302, 360
Roman cuisine, 52–53
tipping, 40
Tuscan cuisine, 354–355
Umbrian cuisine, 356–357
Venetian Arc cuisine, 212–213
Venetian cuisine, 144–145

Dittura Massimo (shop), 167–168
DMAG Outlet (shop), 255
Dolce & Gabbana (shop), 255
Domus Aurea, 60–61
Domus dei Tappeti di Pietra, 291
Dorsoduro (Venice), 168–177
Duomo (Arezzo), 386
Duomo (Ferrara), 287
Duomo (Fiesole), 349
Duomo (Florence), 302–316
Duomo (Lucca), 361
Duomo (Milan), 238–245
Duomo (Perugia), 391–392
Duomo (Pisa), 365
Duomo (Siena), 383
Duomo (Verona), 228
Duomo (Volterra), 376
Duomo di Orvieto, 405
Duomo di Spoleto, 402–403

E

Embassies and consulates, 40
Emergencies, 38
Emilia Burano (shop), 208
Emma ✕ , 93–94
Enoteca al Brindisi ✕ , 288–289
Enoteca dei Tadi ✕ , 223
Enoteca Internazionale ✕ , 277
Enoteca Vanni (shop), 364
Eremo delle Carceri, 396, 400
Esquilino, 138–140
Estro Vino e Cucina ✕ , 171
Etiquette and behavior, 56
Eurochocolate Festival, 45

F

Fatamorgana Monti ✕ , 67–68
Ferrara, 286–290
Festa del Redentore, 45
Festa di San Giovanni (Feast of St. John the Baptist), 45
Festival dei Due Mondi, 45
Festivals and seasonal events, 44–45
Florence, 329
Venice, 149–150
Fiera and San Siro (Milan), 251
Fiesole, 348–350
Flavio al Velavevodetto ✕ , 136
Florence, 15, 296–350
business hours, 300–301
dining, 301, 313–314, 319, 322, 325, 328, 334, 341, 346–347, 350
Duomo and environs, 302–316
festivals and seasonal events, 329
history of, 307, 312, 318, 324
lodging, 301–302, 304–315, 322–323, 329, 341–342, 347–348, 350
nightlife, 315, 342
Oltrarno, The, 342–348
performing arts, 315, 329
prices, 302
reservations, 301
San Lorenzo, 316–323
Santa Croce, 331–334, 341–342

Santa Maria Novella, 323–331
shopping, 302, 306, 315–316, 317–318, 323, 329–331, 342, 348
side trips, 348–350
timing the visit, 300–301
top reasons to go, 296
transportation, 299–300
visitor information, 302
Fondazione Giorgio Cini, 201
Fondazione Luigi Rovati, 261
Fondazione Prada (Milan), 263
Fontana delle Api, 114
Fontana del Nettuno, 279
Fontana delle Tartarughe, 85
Fontana di Trevi, 106
Fori Imperiali, 61
Formula 1 racing, 262
Foro di Traiano, 18, 61, 63
Fortresses. ➪ See Castles, palaces, and fortresses
Fountains
Bologna, 279
Rome, 85, 106, 114
Francis, Saint, 398
Freni e Frizioni (bar), 132
Funicular of Castel San Pietro, 228
Fuori Porta ✕ , 346

G

Galleria Borghese, 20, 121
Galleria d'Arte Moderna (Milan), 259
Galleria d'Arte Moderna (Rome), 101
Galleria degli Uffizi, 24, 306
Galleria dell'Accademia, 24, 317
Galleria Nazionale d'Arte Antica, 115
Galleria Nazionale d'Arte Moderna e Contemporanea, 20
Galleria Nazionale dell'Umbria, 392
Galleria Spada, 85–86
Galleria Vittorio Emanuele II, 239
Gallerie dell'Accademia, 170
GAM: Galleria d'Arte Moderna/Villa Reale, 259
Gardens
Florence, 343
Milan, 261
Padua, 222
Gesuati (Dorsoduro), 170
Gesuiti (Cannaregio), 186
Ghiberti, Lorenzo, 312
Gianni Basso Stampatore (shop), 193
Giardini Pubblici Indro Montanelli, 261
Giardino Bardini, 343
Giardino di Boboli, 343
Giolitti ✕ , 96
Giudecca (Venice), 201–204
Giuliana Longo (shop), 168
Giulio Giannini e Figlio (shop), 348
Gondolas, 164
Gran Caffè Quadri ✕ , 166
Gran Priorato di Roma dell'Ordine di Malta, 133
Grand Canal, 153–159
Greve in Chianti, 369, 371

Gritti Palace, The ⛨ , *166*
Gucci Osteria ✕ , *314*

H

Harry's Bar ✕ , *165*
Hassler, The ⛨ , *108*
Health and safety, *38–39*
Hiking, *270–274, 365, 406*
Hotel al Ponte Mocenigo ⛨ , *184*
Hotel Campo Marzio ⛨ , *235*
Hotel Danieli ⛨ , *199–200*
Hotel de la Ville ⛨ , *108*
Hotel de Russie ⛨ , *125*
Hotel Eden ⛨ , *109*
Hotel San Luca ⛨ , *404*
Hotel Vilòn ⛨ , *109*
Hotels. ⇨ See Lodging
Houses of historic interest
  Florence, *318*
  Milan, *252, 259, 261, 262*
  Rome, *102*
  Venice, *195*
  Vicenza, *233–234*
  Hyatt Centric Murano Venice ⛨ , *207–208*

I

Il Borro ⛨ , *388*
Il Caffè Rosso, *177*
Il Cenacolo, *250*
Il Convivio Troiani ✕ , *94*
Il Desco ✕ , *230*
Il Falconiere ⛨ , *390*
Il Giardino Incantato ⛨ , *278*
Il Giglio ✕ , *363*
Il Marchese ✕ , *106*
Il Marmoraro (shop), *126*
Il Mercante (bar), *184*
Il Ridotto ✕ , *198*
Il Santo Bevitore ✕ , *346*
Il Tabarro San Marco di Monica
  Daniele (shop), *185*
Il Torchio (shop), *348*
Imperial Forums, *61*
In Piazza della Signoria ⛨ , *315*
'Ino ✕ , *314*
INOR dal 1952 (shop), *99*
Islands of the Lagoon, *204–208*
Isola Tiberina, *127*
Italian Grand Prix, *262*
Italian vocabulary, *46–47*
Itineraries, *41–43*

J

Jesurum Venezia 1870 (shop), *168*
Jewish ghettos
  Ferrara, *288*
  Rome, *84–101*
  Venice, *22, 186*
JW Marriott Venice Resort & Spa
  ⛨ , *208*

K

Keats-Shelley Memorial House, *102*

L

La Bitta ✕ , *174*
La Casalinga ✕ , *347*
La Giostra ✕ , *334*
La Pergola ✕ , *124–125*
La Rinacente (shop), *112*
La Rocca Albornoz, *403*
La Sostanza ✕ , *325, 328*
La Torretta ✕ , *275*
Language, *46–47*
L'Archivio di Monserrato (shop), *99*
Last Supper/Il Cenacolo/Santa Maria
  delle Grazie, *250*
Le Due Torri, *279*
Leaning Tower, *367*
Libraries, *317*
Lido di Venezia Beaches, *206*
L'Oca Giuliva ✕ , *289*
Local ✕ , *198*
Locanda Borgonuovo ⛨ , *290*
Locanda della Posta ⛨ , *394*
Locanda Palazzone ⛨ , *407*
Lodging, *30, 39*. ⇨ *See also under
  specific cities, towns, and regions*
  prices, *57, 149, 218, 302, 360*
  tipping, *40*
Loggia del Consiglio, *228*
Loreto (Milan), *262–263*
Loretta Caponi (shop), *330*
Lucca, *360–365*
Luminaria, *45*

M

MACRO, *20, 114–115*
Madonna dell'Orto, *23, 186–187*
Madova (shop), *348*
Maison Halaby (shop), *100*
MaMa Salvadore Murano (shop), *208*
MAMbo and Museo Morandi, *279*
Manarola, *269, 274–275*
Mandarin Oriental, Milan ⛨ , *253,
  255*
Mangiafoco ✕ , *328*
MAR-Museo Nazionale di Ravenna,
  293
Marghe ✕ , *262*
Marigold ✕ , *137*
Mario ✕ , *319*
Mausoleo di Augusto, *102*
Mausoleo di Cecilia Metella, *139*
Mausoleo di Galla Placidia, *291, 293*
MAXXI–Museo Nazionale delle Arti
  del XXI Secolo, *21, 121*
Medici family, *324*
Mercato Centrale (Florence), *317–318*
Mercato di Sant'Ambrogio, *342*
Mercato Nuovo, *306*
Mercato Sotto il Salone, *225*
Metro travel, *54–55*

Metropole ⛨ , *200*
Michelangelo, works by, *72, 74–81*
Milan, *235, 238–267*
Milan Design Week, *44*
Milano Osservatorio–Fondazione
  Prada, *239*
Milky ✕ , *277*
Molino Stucky, *22*
Moma ✕ , *107*
Money matters, *30, 39*
Monna Lisa ⛨ , *342*
Montefioralle, *369*
Montegrotto Terme, *222*
Monterosso al Mare, *277–278*
Monti, *58–69*
Monumento a Vittorio Emanuele
  II, *102*
Mopeds, *299*
Morandi alla Crocetta ⛨ , *342*
MUDEC (Museo delle Culture), *265*
Murano, *169*
MuranoVitrum (shop), *168*
Musei Capitolini, *20, 63*
Musei Civici degli Eremitani, *222*
Musei Vaticani, *21, 73*
Museo Archeologico (Arezzo), *386–387*
Museo Archeologico and Teatro
  Romano (Verona), *228*
Museo Archeologico Nazionale
  (Perugia), *392*
Museo Bagatti Valsecchi, *252*
Museo Bardini, *343*
Museo Civico (San Gimignano), *378*
Museo Civico Archeologico (Milan),
  250
Museo Correr, *160*
Museo del Vetro (Glass Museum),
  206
Museo della Cattedrale, *287–288*
Museo del Merletto (Lace Museum),
  205–206
Museo del Novecento, *239*
Museo dell'Opera, *383*
Museo dell'Opera del Duomo, *24, 306*
Museo di Casa Martelli, *318*
Museo di San Marco, *318*
Museo Diocesano, *389–390*
Museo Etrusco Claudio Faina,
  405–406
Museo Etrusco Guarnacci, *376*
Museo Internazionale e Biblioteca
  della Musica di Bologna, *279*
Museo Morandi, *279*
Museo Nazionale della Scienza e
  Tecnologia Leonardo da Vinci, *251*
Museo Nazionale dell'Ebraismo
  Italiano e della Shoah, *288*
Museo Nazionale di San Matteo, *367*
Museo Nazionale di Villa Guinigi,
  361
Museo Nazionale Etrusco di Villa
  Giulia, *20*
Museo Novecento, *323*
Museo Poldi-Pezzoli, *252*
Museo Salvatore Ferragamo, *25, 324*

Museo Stibbert, *324*
Museums. ⇨ **See also Art galleries and museums**
  antiquities, 63, 121, 228, 250, 293
  Capuchin order, 114
  clothing, 267
  Dante, 252
  design, 247, 256
  ethnography, 265
  Etruscan artifacts, 261, 343, 376, 386–387, 392, 405–406
  in Florence, 24–25, 302–303, 306, 317, 318, 319, 323–324, 331, 343
  glass, 206
  history, 160, 168–169, 186, 228, 250, 261, 291, 376, 386–387, 392, 405–406
  Jewish culture, 91–92, 288
  Keats, 102
  lace, 205–206
  Medici, 343
  music, 279
  in Northern Italy, 222, 228, 229, 232, 239, 242, 247–248, 250, 251, 252, 256, 259, 261, 762, 263, 265, 267, 279, 281, 287–288, 291, 293
  Palladio, 232
  in Rome, 20–21, 63, 72, 73, 85–86, 101–102, 114–115, 121, 127, 133
  science, 251, 282
  science and technology of Leonardo da Vinci, 251
  Shelley, 102
  Shoah, 288
  shoes, 324
  in Tuscany and Umbria, 361, 367, 376, 378, 383, 384–385, 386–387, 389–391, 392, 403, 405–406
  Vatican, 21, 73
  in Venice, 160, 161, 168–169, 170–171, 178, 179, 182, 186, 201, 205–206
Music
  festivals, 45
  Florence, 315, 329, 342
  Northern Italy, 244, 245, 266, 284–285, 294
  Rome, 126

N

Navigli (Milan), *266–267*
Necropoli Vaticana, *73*
Nightlife. ⇨ **See under specific cities, towns, and regions**
Northern Italy, *14–15, 210–294*
  Bologna, 278–286
  Cinque Terre, 270–274
  Corniglia, 275
  cuisine, 212–215
  dining, 217–218, 223–224, 230, 234, 242–243, 248–249, 251, 252–253, 257, 258, 259, 261–262, 263, 265, 266, 276, 277, 282–284, 288–289, 292–294
  Ferrara, 286–290
  history of, 221
  lodging, 218, 224–225, 230–231, 235, 243–244, 249, 251, 253, 255, 257, 258–259, 265–266, 267, 275, 276–278, 284, 289–290, 294
  Manarola, 269, 274–275
  Milan, 235, 238–267
  Monterosso al Mare, 277–278
  nightlife, 223, 225, 244, 249, 255, 257, 259, 266, 284–285
  Padua, 218–225
  performing arts, 244–245, 266, 285, 294
  prices, 218
  Ravenna, 290–294
  Riomaggiore, 267, 269
  shopping, 225, 239, 245, 249, 255–256, 258, 267, 285–286
  sports and the outdoors, 251, 262, 270–274
  timing the visit, 216–217
  top reasons to go, 210
  tours, 238
  transportation, 217
  Vernazza, 275–277
  Verona, 225–231
  Vicenza, 231–235
  weather, 216–217
Novecento 📷 , *166*
Nun Assisi Relais & Spa Museum 📷 , *401*

O

Officina della Bistecca ✕ , *371*
Officina Profumo Farmaceutica di Santa Maria Novella (shop), *330*
Oltrarno, The, *342–348*
Oltre il Giardino 📷 , *184*
Opera
  festivals, 44
  Northern Italy, 244–245, 285, 294
  Rome, 120
Orsanmichele, *306*
Orto Botanico, *222*
Orvieto, *405–407*
Orvieto Underground, *406*
Osteria a Priori ✕ , *394*
Osteria alla Bifora ✕ , *174*
Osteria del Sole (wine bar), *284*
Osteria del Tempo Perso ✕ , *294*
Osteria di Santa Marina ✕ , *198*
Osteria Enoteca ai Artisti ✕ , *174*
Osteria Il Cursore ✕ , *234*
Osteria Piazzetta dell'Erba ✕ , *400*

P

Padua, *218–225*
Palaces. ⇨ **See Castles, palaces, and fortresses**
Palatine Hill, *63*
Palazzo Abadessa 📷 , *192*
Palazzo Altemps, *86*
Palazzo Barbaran da Porto (Palladio Museum), *232*
Palazzo Barberini/Galleria Nazionale d'Arte Antica, *115*
Palazzo Chiericati, *232–233*
Palazzo Collicola Arti Visive, *403*
Palazzo Colonna, *103*
Palazzo Comunale, *279, 281*
Palazzo Corsini, *127*
Palazzo Davanzati, *313*
Palazzo degli Scaligeri, *228–229*
Palazzo dei Cavalieri, *367*
Palazzo dei Diamanti, *288*
Palazzo dei Priori, *392*
Palazzo del Bo, *222*
Palazzo del Podestà (Bologna), *281*
Palazzo del Podestà (Radda in Chianti), *373*
Palazzo della Ragione (Padua), *222–223*
Palazzo della Ragione (Verona), *229*
Palazzo Doria Pamphilj, *20, 103*
Palazzo Ducale, *23, 161*
Palazzo Farnese, *86–87*
Palazzo Grassi, *161*
Palazzo Leti Residenza d'Epoca 📷 , *404*
Palazzo Massimo alle Terme, *115*
Palazzo Medici-Riccardi, *318–319*
Palazzo Pitti, *24, 343*
Palazzo Pubblico, *383–384*
Palazzo Ravizza 📷 , *385–386*
Palazzo Re Enzo, *281*
Palazzo Reale, *239, 242*
Palazzo Schifanoia, *288*
Palazzo Squarcialupi 📷 , *374*
Palazzo Stern 📷 , *176*
Palazzo Strozzi, *25, 324–325*
Palazzo Vecchio, *25, 313*
Palazzo Vendramin-Calergi, *187*
Palestro (Milan), *259, 261*
Palladian architecture, *236–237*
Pantheon, *18, 87*
Panzano, *371–372*
Papier Mache—Laboratorio di Artigianato Artistico (shop), *201*
Parco degli Acquedotti, *139–140*
Parco di Monza, *262*
Parco Sempione, *247*
Park Hyatt Milan 📷 , *244*
Passeggiata delle Mura, *361*
Passports, *40*
Pasticceria Taddeucci (shop), *364*
Patrizia Pepe (shop), *111*
Pavè ✕ , *258*
Peggy Guggenheim Collection, *170*
Pegna (shop), *316*
Penko (shop), *316*
Perché No! ✕ , *341*
Performing arts. ⇨ **See under specific cities, towns, and regions**
Perugia, *390–394*
Pianostrada ✕ , *95*
Piazza Campo de' Fiori, *87, 90*
Piazza dei Signori (Padua), *223*
Piazza dei Signori (Vicenza), *233*
Piazza del Campo, *384*
Piazza del Popolo, *121*
Piazza del Quirinale, *115, 118*
Piazza della Repubblica (Florence), *313*
Piazza della Repubblica (Rome), *118*
Piazza della Signoria, *313*
Piazza dell'Anfiteatro, *361*
Piazza delle Erbe, *229*
Piazza di Spagna, *101–113*
Piazza Gae Aulenti, *256*
Piazza Grande, *387*
Piazza Navona, *84–101*

412

Piazza San Marco, *161, 164*
Piazza San Pietro, *73, 82*
Piazza Santa Croce, *331*
Piazza Matteotti, *369*
Piazzale Michelangelo, *343*
Pierluigi ✕ , *95*
Pinacoteca (Volterra), *376*
Pinacoteca Ambrosiana, *242*
Pinacoteca di Brera, *247–248*
Pinacoteca Nazionale (Bologna), *281*
Pinacoteca Nazionale (Siena), *384*
Pineider (shop), *330*
Pirelli Hangar/Bicocca, *263*
Pisa, *365–368*
Piz ✕ , *242*
Place Firenze, The 🖫 , *329*
Ponte delle Torri, *403*
Ponte di Rialto, *22, 164*
Ponte Vecchio, *313*
Porta all'Arco Etrusco, *376*
Porta dei Borsari, *229*
Porta Garibaldi (Milan), *256–258*
Porta Leoni, *229*
Porta Maggiore, *140*
Porta Romana (Milan), *263–264*
Porta Venezia (Milan), *261–262*
Portico d'Ottavia, *90*
Posta Donini 1579 – UNA Esperienze 🖫 , *394*
Pozzo della Cava, *406*
Prati, *69–83*
Prices
dining and lodging, *57, 149, 218, 302, 360*
Florence, *302*
Northern Italy, *218*
Rome, *57*
Tuscany and Umbria, *360*
Venice, *149*
Procacci ✕ , *328*
Public transportation, *147, 238–239*
Punta della Dogana, *22, 170–171*

Q

Quadrilatero (Milan), *252–256*
Quel Fantastico Giovedi ✕ , *289*
Quirinale, The, *113–120*

R

Radda in Chianti, *372–373*
Ravenna, *290–294*
Ravenna Festival, *45*
Relais Fattoria Vignale 🖫 , *373*
Renaissance art, *335–340*
Repubblica (Milan), *258–259*
Repubblica (Rome), *113–120*
Riomaggiore, *267, 269*
Ristorante Apollinare ✕ , *404*
Ristorante Belforte ✕ , *276*
Ristorante Osteria Da Fiore ✕ , *183*
Ristorante Quadri ✕ , *165*
Ristoro di Lamole ✕ , *369*
Rivoire ✕ , *314*
Rocca Paolina, *392*

Roccati (shop), *286*
Roma Pass, *58*
Roman Forum, *18, 66*
Roman ruins
Fiesole, *349*
Northern Italy, *226, 228, 229, 291*
Rome, *18–19, 58–61, 63, 66, 85, 87, 90, 102, 136, 140*
Tuscany and Umbria, *361, 376, 386–387, 402, 403, 406*
Rome, *14, 50–140*
addresses, *56*
Ancient Rome, Monti, and Celio, *18–19, 58–69*
Aventino and Testaccio, *132–138*
business hours, *57*
cuisine, *52–53*
dining, *56–57, 67–68, 82–83, 92–96, 106–107, 119, 124–125, 130–131, 136–137, 140*
Esquilino and Via Appia Antica, *138–140*
etiquette, *56*
lodging, *57, 68, 83, 96–98, 107–110, 120, 125–126, 131–132, 137*
nightlife, *68, 83, 98, 110, 126, 132, 137–138*
performing arts, *98, 120, 126*
Piazza di Spagna, *101–113*
Piazza Navona, Campo de' Fiori, and the Jewish Ghetto, *84–101*
prices, *57*
Repubblica and the Quirinale, *113–120*
Roma Pass, *58*
shopping, *69, 83, 99–101, 110–113, 126, 132, 138*
timing the visit, *55*
top reasons to go, *50*
tours, *58*
transportation, *54–55*
Trastevere, *126–132*
Vatican, Borgo, and Prati, *69–83*
Villa Borghese and environs, *120–126*
visitor information, *58*
Room Mate Giulia 🖫 , *244*
Roscioli Sallumerio con Cucina ✕ , *95–96*

S

Sacripante (shop), *69*
Safety, *38–39*
Sagra Musicale Umbria, *45*
St. Regis Venice, The 🖫 , *167*
Salviati (shop), *208*
San Carlo alle Quattro Fontane, *118*
San Clemente, *66–67*
San Domenico (Bologna), *281*
San Domenico (Fiesole), *349*
San Domenico (Siena), *384*
San Francesco, *349*
San Francesco della Vigna, *22, 194*
San Frediano, *361*
San Giacomo dell'Orio, *179*
San Gimignano, *377–380*
San Giorgio Maggiore (Venice), *201–204*
San Giovanni Elemosinario, *179*
San Leolino, *371*
San Lorenzo (district; Florence), *316–323*

San Lorenzo Maggiore alle Colonne, *265*
San Luigi dei Francesi, *90*
San Marco (Venice), *151–152, 160–168*
San Michele in Foro, *361, 363*
San Miniato al Monte, *343*
San Pietro, *275*
San Polo (Venice), *178–185*
San Sebastiano, *171*
San Siro (Milan), *251*
San Stae, *179*
San Zaccaria, *194*
San Zeno Maggiore, *229*
Santa Cecilia in Trastevere, *127*
Santa Corona, *233*
Santa Croce (Florence), *331–334, 341–342*
Santa Croce (Venice), *25, 178–185*
Santa Felicita, *343, 346*
Santa Maria al Calcinaio, *390*
Santa Maria dei Miracoli, *187*
Santa Maria del Carmine, *346*
Santa Maria del Popolo, *121, 124*
Santa Maria della Pieve, *387*
Santa Maria della Salute, *22, 171*
Santa Maria della Scala, *384–385*
Santa Maria della Vittoria, *118*
Santa Maria delle Grazie, *250*
Santa Maria di Aracoeli, *59*
Santa Maria Gloriosa dei Frari, *179*
Santa Maria in Cosmedin, *133, 136*
Santa Maria in Trastevere, *130*
Santa Maria Maggiore, *67*
Santa Maria Novella (Florence), *25, 323–331*
Santa Maria Presso San Satiro, *242*
Santa Maria Sopra Minerva (Assisi), *400*
Santa Maria sopra Minerva (Rome), *91*
Santa Trinita, *325*
Sant'Agostino, *379*
Sant'Ambrogio (Milan), *249–251*
Sant'Anastasia, *229–230*
Sant'Andrea al Quirinale, *118–119*
Sant'Andrea della Valle, *91*
Sant'Apollinare in Classe, *293*
Sant'Apollinare Nuovo, *293*
Santi Giovanni e Paolo, *194–195*
Sant'Ignazio, *103, 106*
Santissima Annunziata, *319*
Santissimo Redentore, *203*
Sant'Ivo alla Sapienza, *91*
Santo Spirito, *346*
Santo Stefano, *281*
Savonarola, Girolamo, *318*
Scoppio del Carro (Explosion of the Cart), *44*
Scuola del Cuoio (shop), *342*
Scuola di San Giorgio degli Schiavoni, *195*
Scuola Grande dei Carmini, *171*
Scuola Grande di San Rocco, *179, 182*
Sempione (Milan), *245–247*
Seta ✕ , *252*

Shopping. ⇨ **See under specific cities, towns, and regions**
Siena, 380–386
Simone Cenedese (shop), 208
Sinagoga (Florence), 331, 334
Sinagoga (Rome), 91–92
Sistine Chapel, 72, 74–81
Skyline Rooftop Bar, 204
Soccer, 251
Solociccia ✕, 372
Spanish Steps, 106
Spedale degli Innocenti, 319
Spoleto, 401–404
Sports and the outdoors. ⇨ **See under specific cities, towns, and regions**
Stravinskij Bar at the Hotel de Russie, 126
Synagogues, 91–92, 331, 334

T

Tamburini ✕, 283–284
Taxis
Florence, 299–300
Milan, 238
tipping, 40
Venice, 147
Teatro alla Scala, 244–245
Teatro Argentina, 98
Teatro dell'Opera, 120
Teatro Marcello, 19
Teatro Olimpico, 233
Teatro Romano (Spoleto), 403
Teatro Romano (Verona), 228
Teatro Romano (Volterra), 376
10 Corso Como (shop), 268
Terme di Caracalla, 19, 136
Tessitura Luigi Bevilacqua (shop), 185
Testaccio, 132–138
Theater
Bologna, 294
Pisa, 368
Rome, 98, 126
Vicenza, 233
Ticinese (Milan), 265–266
Timing the visit, 40. ⇨ See also under specific cities, towns, and regions
Tipping, 40
Tod's (shop), 113
Tomba di Dante, 293
Tombs. ⇨ **See Cemeteries, crypts, and tombs**
Torre Branca, 247
Torre dei Lamberti, 229
Torre dell'Orologio (Clock Tower), 281–282
Torre Guinigi, 363
Torre Pendente, 367
Tortona (Milan), 267
Tours
Northern Italy, 238
Rome, 58
tipping, 40
Venice, 151, 164
Towers

Florence, 303
Northern Italy, 229, 247, 279, 281–282
Tuscany and Umbria, 363, 367
Venice, 152, 160
Train travel, 35, 48
Florence, 300
Venice, 147
Tram Depot ✕, 137–138
Tram travel, 55
Transportation, 30, 34–35, 48. ⇨ See also under specific cities, towns, and regions
Trastevere, 126–132
Trattoria di Via Serra ✕, 283
Trattoria Gianni a la Vecia Bulagna ✕, 283
Trattoria Sergio Gozzi ✕, 322
Trevi Fountain, 106
Triennale Design Museum, 247
Tuscany and Umbria, 15, 26–27, 352–407
Arezzo, 386–388
Assisi, 394–401
Chianti, 368–374
Cortona, 388–390
cuisine, 354–357
dining, 360, 363, 367–368, 369, 371–372, 373, 374, 375–377, 379, 385, 387–388, 390, 392–394, 400, 403–404, 407
history, 393
lodging, 360, 363–364, 368, 369, 371, 372, 373, 374, 377, 379–380, 385–386, 388, 390, 394, 400–401, 404, 407
Lucca, 360–365
Orvieto, 405–407
performing arts, 368
Perugia, 390–394
Pisa, 365–368
prices, 360
San Gimignano, 377–380
shopping, 364
Siena, 380–386
Spoleto, 401–404
sports and the outdoors, 365, 406
timing the visit, 358–259
top reasons to go, 352
transportation, 359–360
Volterra, 375–377
weather, 358–259

U

U.S. embassies and consulates, 40
Ugo Bar, 266
Umbria. ⇨ **See Tuscany and Umbria**
Umbria Jazz Festival, 45
Università di Bologna, 282

V

V. Beny ✕, 368
Vatican, 69–83
Vatican Museums, 21, 73
Vatican Necropolis, 73
Venetian art glass, 169
Venice, 14, 142–208
architecture, 22–23, 157
beaches, 206
Cannaregio, 185–193
Castello, 193–201

cuisine, 144–145
dining, 148, 165–166, 171, 174–175, 182–184, 187, 190–191, 195, 198–199, 203, 206–207
Dorsoduro, 168–177
festivals and seasonal events, 149–150
getting oriented, 146, 160
Grand Canal, 153–159
Islands of the Lagoon, 204–208
Jewish Ghetto, 22, 186
lodging, 148–149, 166–167, 175–176, 184, 191–192, 199–200, 203–204, 207–208
nightlife, 149, 167, 176, 184–185, 192, 200, 204
passes and discounts, 149
performing arts, 149–150
prices, 149
San Giorgio Maggiore and the Giudecca, 201–204
San Marco, 151–152, 160–168
San Polo and Santa Croce, 178–185
shopping, 150, 167–168, 176, 185, 192, 201, 204, 208
timing the visit, 148
top reasons to go, 142
tours, 151, 164
transportation, 147, 164
visitor information, 151
Venissa ✕, 207
Vernazza, 275–277
Verona, 225–231
Via Appia Antica, 19, 138–140
Via delle Volte, 288
Via Giulia, 92
Vicenza, 231–235
Villa Bordoni ⛺, 371
Villa Borghese and environs, 120–126
Villa della Rotonda (Villa Almerico Capra), 233
Villa Farnesina, 130
Villa Il Poggiale ⛺, 371
Villa Le Barone ⛺, 372
Villa Necchi Campiglio, 259, 261
Villa Pisani, 223
Villa Valmarana ai Nani, 234
Vineria di Piazza ✕, 368
Vini da Gigio ✕, 191
Vinitaly, 44
Vino Vero ✕, 191
Visas, 40
Visitor information
Florence, 302
Rome, 58
Venice, 151
Vocabulary, 46–47
Volpetti (shop), 138
Volterra, 375–377

W

Water taxis and buses, 147
Weather, 40, 216–217, 358–259
Wineries, 372

Z

Zanarini (café), 284

Photo Credits

Front Cover: Zoonar GmbH/Alamy Stock Photo [Descr.:Basilica of San Vitale, Ravenna,nItaly]. **Back cover, from left to right:** Muratart/ Shutterstock. MZeta/Shutterstock. Maudanros/Shutterstock. **Spine:** Waku/Shutterstock. **Interior, from left to right:** Freesurf69/ Dreamstime (1). Shaiith/Dreamstime (2-3). SerrNovik/iStockphoto (5). **Chapter 1: Experience the Best of Italy:** Minnystock/Dream- stime (6-7). Mapics/Dreamstime (8-9). Carso80/Shutterstock (9). Pcruciatti/Shutterstock (9). Vladimir Korostyshevskiy/Shutterstock (10). Inguaribile Vlaggiatore/Shutterstock (10). Renata Sedmakova/Shutterstock (10). Chen Min Chun/Shutterstock (10). Anibal Trejo/shutterstock (11). Jaroslaw Pawlak/Shutterstock (11). Muharremz/Shutterstock (12). Pixel creator/Shutterstock (12). Tombor Szabina/Shutterstock (12). Xbrchx/Dreamstime (12). Omas Photo/Shutterstock (13). Phant/Shutterstock (18). Boris Stroujko/Shutterstock (18). R.nagy/Shutterstock (18). Nattee Chalermtiragool/Shutterstock (19). Vasilii L/Shutterstock (19). DFLC Prints/Shutterstock (20). Wjarek/Shutterstock (20). Valery Rokhin/ Shutterstock (20). Isogood_patrick/Shutterstock (20). Viacheslav Lopatin/Shutterstock (21). Andrew Soundarajan/iStockphoto (22). Andrea Astes/iStockphoto (22). Robert Zehetmayer/Dreamstime (22). Liz Coughlan/Shutterstock (22). Venezia, Palazzo Ducale (23). Leonid Andronov/ Dreamstime (24). Luciano Mortula/Dreamstime (25). Kavalenkava/Shutterstock (26). StevanZZ/Shutterstock (27). **Chapter 3: Rome:** AngeloCampus (49). Erica Duecy (52). AngeloCampus (53). Lisay/iStockphoto (53). Gush Photography/Shutterstock (74-75). TTaylor/Wikime- dia Commons (74). RPBaiao/Shutterstock (76). Imaengine/Dreamstime (78-79). Imaengine/Dreamstime (80-81). **Chapter 4: Venice:** Paul D'Innocenzo (141). Paul D'Innocenzo (144). Jess_h/Shutterstock (145). Lz89/Shutterstock (145). Mapics/Dreamstime (153). Alexey Arkhipov/ Shutterstock (154). Agiampiccolo/Dreamstime(155). Paul D'Innocenzo (155). Minnystock/Dreamstime (156) Steve Allen/Brand X Pictures (157). Jaru68/Shutterstock (157). EtJRoy/Shutterstock (158). Corbis RF (159). Walencienne/Shutterstock (159). Minnystock/Dreamstime (202). **Chapter 5: Northern Italy:** Cristiano Palazzini/Shutterstock (209). Giovanni1232/iStockphoto (212). From_my_point_of_view/iStockphoto (213). ChiccoDodiFC/iStockphoto (213). Fabiomax/iStockphoto (214). Dietmarrauscher/Dreamstime (215). Alemasche72/Dreamstime (215). Jan Cattaneo/Shutterstock (248). Oana Dragan/iStockphoto (271). Whatafoto/Shutterstock (272). Borut Trdina/Shutterstock (272). Elephotos/ Shutterstock (272). Nightcap/Shutterstock (272). Sanga Park/iStockphoto (273). Aliaksandr Antanovich/Shutterstock (273). Viviane Teles (273). Only Fabrizio/Shutterstock (287). **Chapter 6: Florence:** Alysta/Shutterstock (295). SerrNovik/iStockphoto (308-309). Web Gallery of Art/ Wikimedia Commons (310). Sailko/Wikimedia Commons (310). Sailko/Wikimedia Commons (310). Pocholo Calapre/Shutterstock (311). AlfioGiannotti/Viesti Associates, Inc. (311). Escudeirof /Dreamstime (311). Wjarek/iStockphoto (312). Everett Collection/Shutterstock (335). Everett Collection/Shutterstock (335). Marzolino/Shutterstock (335). Romas_Photo/Shutterstock (336). Steve Allen/Shutterstock (336). Karl Allen Lugmayer/Shutterstock (337). Giannit/Dreamstime (337). MisterStock/Shutterstock (337). Yuri Turkov/Shutterstock (337). Web Gallery of Art/ Wikimedia Commons (338). Virtusincertus/Flickr (338). Cysun/Shutterstock (338). Jean Louis Mazieres/Flickr (339). Bill Perry/ Shutterstock (339). Deb Nystrom/Flickr (339). Web Gallery of Art/ Wikimedia Commons (340). Ambrosiana.it/Wikimedia Commons (340). Dgu- endel/Wikimedia Commons (340). **Chapter 7: Tuscany and Umbria:** Christopher Salerno/Shutterstock (351). Kuvona/Dreamstime (354). Kwasny221/iStockphoto (355). Ylenia Cancelli/Shutterstock (355). B&Y Photography/Alamy (356). Dusanzidar/Dreamstime (357). Brizius/ iStockphoto (357). Rasto SK/Shutterstock (381). StevanZZ/Shutterstock (397). Threerivers1/Dreamstime (398). Fototeca ENIT (399). Fototeca ENIT (399). Fototeca ENIT (399). Fototeca ENIT (399). Fototeca ENIT (399). **About Our Writers:** All photos are courtesy of the writers except for the following: Nick Bruno, courtesy of Graeme Ogston; Liz Shemaria, courtesy of Ian Tuttle.

Every effort has been made to trace the copyright holders, and we apologize in advance for any accidental errors. We would be happy to apply the corrections in the following edition of this publication.

Fodor's THE BEST OF ITALY

Publisher: Stephen Horowitz, *General Manager*

Editorial: Douglas Stallings, *Editorial Director;* Jill Fergus, Amanda Sadlowski, *Senior Editors;* Brian Eschrich, Alexis Kelly, *Editors;* Angelique Kennedy-Chavannes, *Assistant Editor;* Yoojin Shin, *Associate Editor*

Design: Tina Malaney, *Director of Design and Production;* Jessica Gonzalez, *Senior Designer;* Jaimee Shaye, *Graphic Design Associate*

Production: Jennifer DePrima, *Editorial Production Manager;* Elyse Rozelle, *Senior Production Editor;* Monica White, *Production Editor*

Maps: Rebecca Baer, *Senior Map Editor;* David Lindroth, Mark Stroud (Moon Street Cartography), *Cartographers*

Photography: Viviane Teles, *Director of Photography;* Namrata Aggarwal, Neha Gupta, Payal Gupta, Ashok Kumar, *Photo Editors;* Jade Rodgers, *Photo Production Intern*

Business and Operations: Chuck Hoover, *Chief Marketing Officer;* Robert Ames, *Group General Manager*

Public Relations and Marketing: Joe Ewaskiw, *Senior Director of Communications and Public Relations*

Fodors.com: Jeremy Tarr, *Editorial Director;* Rachael Levitt, *Managing Editor*

Technology: Jon Atkinson, *Executive Director of Technology;* Rudresh Teotia, *Associate Director of Technology;* Alison Lieu, *Project Manager*

Writers: Robert Andrews, Nick Bruno, Liz Humphreys, Laura Itzkowitz, Natalie Kennedy, Liz Shemaria

Editor: Jill Fergus

Production Editor: Elyse Rozelle

4th Edition

ISBN 978-1-64097-666-5

ISSN 2476-0951

SPECIAL SALES
This book is available at special discounts for bulk purchases for sales promotions or premiums. For more information, e-mail SpecialMarkets@fodors.com.

PRINTED IN CHINA

10 9 8 7 6 5 4 3 2 1

About Our Writers

 Born of Sicilian stock, **Robert Andrews** has been living and working in various parts of Italy for most of his adult life. He has written articles and guidebooks on this multifaceted peninsula, and provides travel consultancy services as well as leading individual and small-group tours in Sicily and Sardinia. For this edition, Robert updated the Northern Italy chapter.

 Nick Bruno is an Italy specialist and frequent Fodor's contributor. As well as authoring and updating books and features, he makes radio packages for the BBC. A lifelong interest in history and Italian language has led to a project researching his paternal Italian family during the Il Ventennio Fascista period. Nick updated the Experience, Travel Smart, and Northern Italy chapters. Follow him on Instagram and Twitter @nickjgbruno and ⊕ *barbruno.com*.

 Liz Humphreys is a transplant to Europe from New York City, where she edited for media companies including Condé Nast and Time Inc. Since then she's written for publications including *Condé Nast Traveler*, *Michelin Green Guides*, and *Forbes Travel Guide*. Liz has an advanced certificate in wine studies from WSET (Wine & Spirit Education Trust), which comes in handy when exploring her beloved Italian wine regions. Liz updated the Venice and Tuscany and Umbria chapters. Follow Liz on Instagram @winederlust_wanderings.

 Laura Itzkowitz is a freelance writer and editor based in Rome with an MFA in creative writing and a passion for covering travel, arts and culture, lifestyle, design, food and wine. Her writing has appeared in *Travel + Leisure*, *Architectural Digest*, *Vogue*, *GQ*, *Departures*, *AFAR*, and others. Laura updated the Rome chapter. Follow her on Instagram and Twitter @lauraitzkowitz.

 Originally from California, **Natalie Kennedy** moved to Rome planning to stay for only a year, but has now called the Eternal City home for nearly a decade and runs a popular blog about Roman life (⊕ *anamericaninrome.com*). For this edition, she updated Rome.

 Liz Shemaria is an award-winning journalist and third-generation Northern Californian who has trekked solo in Himalaya and interviewed artists in military-ruled Burma. Liz is a founding editor at Hidden Compass and has contributed to more than a dozen publications and organizations including Human Rights Watch, BBC Travel, *AFAR*, and Roads & Kingdoms. Liz lives in Italy and updated the Florence, Tuscany and Umbria, and Northern Italy chapters. Follow her on Instagram @lizshemaria.